THIRD EDITION

The Norton Field Guide to Writing
with handbook

THIRD EDITION

The Norton
Field Guide
to Writing

with handbook

Richard Bullock
WRIGHT STATE UNIVERSITY

Francine Weinberg

W. W. NORTON & COMPANY

New York • London

W. W. Norton & Company has been independent since its founding in 1923, when William Warder Norton and Mary D. Herter Norton first published lectures delivered at the People's Institute, the adult education division of New York City's Cooper Union. The firm soon expanded its program beyond the Institute, publishing books by celebrated academics from America and abroad. By mid-century, the two major pillars of Norton's publishing program—trade books and college texts—were firmly established. In the 1950s, the Norton family transferred control of the company to its employees, and today—with a staff of four hundred and a comparable number of trade, college, and professional titles published each year—W. W. Norton & Company stands as the largest and oldest publishing house owned wholly by its employees.

Editor: Marilyn Moller
Developmental editor: John Elliott
Project editor: Rebecca Homiski
Editorial assistants: Tenyia Lee, Erica Wnek
Production manager: Andrew Ensor
Emedia editor: Cliff Landesman
Marketing Manager: Lib Triplett
Text Design: Anna Palchik
Composition: Cenveo Publisher Services
Manufacturing: R. R. Donnelley—Crawfordsville

Cataloging-in-Publication information is on file with the Library of Congress.

ISBN: 978-0-393-91958-5

W. W. Norton & Company, Inc., 500 Fifth Avenue, New York, NY 10110-0017
wwnorton.com

W. W. Norton & Company Ltd., Castle House, 75/76 Wells Street, London W1T 3QT

1 2 3 4 5 6 7 8 9 0

Preface

The Norton Field Guide to Writing began as an attempt to offer the kind of writing guides found in the best rhetorics in a format as user-friendly as the best handbooks, and on top of that, to be as brief as could be. We wanted to create a handy guide to help college students with all their written work. Just as there are field guides for bird watchers, for gardeners, and for accountants, this would be one for writers. In its first two editions, the book obviously touched a chord with many writing instructors, and it became the best-selling college rhetoric — a success that leaves us humbled and grateful. Those teachers, though, have often asked for a little more coverage here and there, especially on choosing genres and the distinctive challenges of writing online, creating multimodal texts, and writing in academic contexts. So we're happy now to offer a third edition that answers those requests.

The Norton Field Guide still aims to offer both the guidance new teachers and first-year writers need and the flexibility many experienced teachers want. From our own experiences as teachers and WPAs, we've seen how well explicit guides to writing work for students and novice teachers. But too often, writing textbooks provide far more information than students need or instructors can assign and as a result are bigger and more expensive than they should be. So we've tried to provide enough structure without too much detail—to give the information college writers need to know while resisting the temptation to tell them everything there is to know.

Most of all, we've tried to make the book easy to use. To that end, it includes menus, directories, a glossary/index, and color-coded links to make it simple for students to find what they're looking for and navigate the parts. The links are also the key to keeping the book brief: chapters are short, but the links send students to pages elsewhere in the book *if* they need more detail.

What's in the Book

The Norton Field Guide covers 14 genres often assigned in college. Much of the book is in the form of guidelines, designed to help students consider the choices they have as writers. The book is organized into seven parts:

1. **RHETORICAL SITUATIONS.** Chapters 1–6 focus on purpose, audience, genre, stance, media and design, and writing in academic contexts. In addition, almost every chapter includes a short list of tips to help students focus on their particular rhetorical situation.

2. **GENRES.** Chapters 7–21 cover 14 genres, 4 of them — literacy narrative, textual analysis, report, and argument — treated in greater detail. Chapter 21 helps students choose genres when they need to.

3. **PROCESSES.** Chapters 22–29 offer advice for generating ideas and text, drafting, revising and rewriting, editing, proofreading, compiling a portfolio, collaborating with others, and writing as inquiry.

4. **STRATEGIES.** Chapters 30–42 cover familiar ways of developing and organizing text — writing effective beginnings and endings, coming up with good titles and developing effective thesis statements, comparing, describing, and using dialogue. Chapters 41 and 42 offer strategies for reading and taking essay exams.

5. **RESEARCH/DOCUMENTATION.** Chapters 43–51 offer advice on how to do academic research; work with sources; quote, paraphrase, and summarize source materials; and document sources using MLA and APA styles.

6. **MEDIA/DESIGN.** Chapters 52–56 give guidance on choosing the appropriate print, electronic, or spoken medium; designing text; using images and sound; giving spoken presentations; and writing online.

7. **HANDBOOK.** At the end of the book is a handbook to help students edit what they write. We've organized the handbook around the intuitive categories of sentences, language, and punctuation to make it easy to use.

What's Online

The Norton Field Guide to Go. A brief, quick-reference version will be available in a digital format for smartphones and other handheld devices. Portable, searchable, and interactive, it will be free with the purchase of the book — and $10 net otherwise.

Ebooks. All versions of *The Norton Field Guide* are available as ebooks and include all the readings and images found in the print books. Offered at less than half the price of the print books, the ebooks are completely searchable and allow readers to highlight and attach sticky notes.

A companion website includes model papers, exercises and quizzes, and more. Access the site at wwnorton.com/write/fieldguide.

norton/write. A free and open site with author bios, plagiarism tutorials, exercises — and more. Access the site at wwnorton.com/write.

What's Available for Instructors

A Guide to Teaching with **The Norton Field Guides.** Written by Richard Bullock and several other teachers, this is a comprehensive guide to teaching first-year writing, from developing a syllabus to facilitating group work, teaching multimodal writing to assessing student writing. Free of charge.

Coursepacks are available absolutely free and in a variety of formats, including *Blackboard, Desire2Learn, Moodle, Canvas,* and *Angel.* The *Field Guide* Coursepack includes model papers, quizzes and exercises, video tutorials, documentation guidelines, and more — all of it fully customizable. You can choose the content you want to use, rearrange it, add to it, edit it as you wish to suit your course — and your students. Access the Coursepack at wwnorton.com/instructors.

FRED. An online commenting system that allows you to respond to drafts in writing — and with audio or video. Created by CritiqueIt and customized for college writing classes.

Highlights

It's easy to use. Menus, directories, and a glossary/index make it easy for students to find what they're looking for. Color-coded templates and documentation maps even make MLA and APA documentation easy.

It has just enough detail, with short chapters that include color-coded links sending students to more detail *if* they need more.

It's uniquely flexible for teachers. Short chapters can be assigned in any order — and color-coded links help draw from other chapters as need be.

A user-friendly handbook, with an intuitive organization around sentences, language, and punctuation to make it easy for students to find what they need. And we go easy on the grammatical terminology, with links to the glossary for students who need detailed definitions.

What's New

A new chapter on writing in academic contexts, helping students understand what's expected of their writing in college. (Chapter 6)

A new chapter on choosing genres. (Chapter 21)

11 new readings, including 4 multimodal readings.

New reading strategies helping students assess their knowledge of a topic, deal with difficult texts, and use a coding system for responding to a text. (Chapter 41)

A new chapter on choosing media, helping students decide which media (print, electronic, or spoken) and which modes (words, images, video, audio, hyperlinks) best suit their needs. (Chapter 52)

A new chapter on designing text. (Chapter 53)

A new chapter on incorporating images and sound — photographs, graphs, charts, videos, sound effects, and more. (Chapter 54)

A new chapter on writing online, with advice on managing files; LMS's; and using email, blogs, and social media in academic contexts. (Chapter 55)

Ways of Teaching with *The Norton Field Guide to Writing*

The Norton Field Guide is designed to give you both support and flexibility. It has clear assignment sequences if you want them, or you can create your own. If, for example, you assign a position paper, there's a full chapter. If you want students to use sources, add the appropriate research chapters. If you want them to submit a topic proposal, add that chapter.

If you're a new teacher, the genre chapters offer explicit assignment sequences — and the color-coded links will remind you of other detail that you may want to bring in. The instructor's manual is designed for new teachers, with advice on creating a syllabus, responding to writing, and more.

If you focus on genres, there are complete chapters on all the genres college students are often assigned. Color-coded links will help you bring in details about research or other writing strategies as you wish.

If you organize your course thematically, Chapter 24 on generating ideas can help get students thinking about a theme. You can also assign them to do research on the theme, starting with Chapter 44 on finding sources, or perhaps with Chapter 22 on writing as inquiry. If they then write in a particular genre, there will be a chapter to guide them.

If you want students to do research, there are 9 chapters on the research process, including guidelines and sample papers demonstrating MLA and APA documentation.

If you focus on modes, you'll find chapters on narration, description, and so on. The chapters assume these to be strategies that a writer might use for many writing purposes, and also include links that lead students through the process of writing an essay organized around a particular mode.

If you teach online, the book is available as an ebook — and in a quick-reference version for use on mobile devices. In addition, a companion Coursepack includes exercises, quizzes, video tutorials, and more.

Acknowledgments

As we've traveled around the country and met many of the students, teachers, and WPAs who are using *The Norton Field Guide*, we've been gratified to hear that so many find it helpful, to the point that some students tell us that they aren't going to sell it back to the bookstore when the term ends — the highest form of praise. As much as we like the positive response, though, we are especially grateful when we receive suggestions for ways the book might be improved. In this third edition, as we did in the second edition, we have tried to respond to the many good suggestions we've gotten from students, colleagues, reviewers, and editors. Thank you all, both for your kind words and for your good suggestions.

Some people need to be singled out for thanks, especially Marilyn Moller, the guiding editorial spirit of the *Field Guide* through all three editions. When we presented Marilyn with the idea for this book, she encouraged us and helped us conceptualize it — and then taught us how to write a textbook. The quality of the *Field Guide* is due in large part to her knowledge of the field of composition, her formidable editing and writing skills, her sometimes uncanny ability to see the future of the teaching of writing — and her equally formidable, if not uncanny, stamina.

Development editor John Elliott has shepherded the third edition through its revisions and additions with a careful hand and a clear eye for appropriate content and language. His painstaking editing of every chapter shows throughout the book, and we're grateful for his ability to make us appear to be better writers than we are.

Many others have contributed, too. Thanks to project editor Rebecca Homiski for her energy, patience, and great skill in coordinating the tightly scheduled production process for the book and her wonderful talent for researching and handling the new images. Erica Wnek helped find readings, managed the reviewing process, and contributed to the planning of the new edition; Tenyia Lee helped find photos, check pageproofs, and more. Anna Palchik designed the award-winning, user-friendly, and attractive interior, and Kimberly Glyder created the beautiful new cover design. Francine Weinberg wrote the ingenious documentation chapters and the glossary, and did heavy lifting on much of the first edition. Jane Searle and Andy Ensor transformed a scribbled-over manuscript into a finished product with admirable speed and precision, while Jude Grant copyedited and

Mark Gallaher proofread. Megan Jackson and Bethany Salminen cleared text permissions, coping efficiently with ongoing changes, and Michael Fodera cleared permission for the images. Juliana Fidler, our excellent intern, located author images and updated manuscript files. Cliff Landesman planned, designed, and produced the sensational website with help from Stefani Wallace. Steve Dunn and especially Lib Triplett helped us all keep our eyes on the market. Thanks to all, and to Roby Harrington, Drake McFeely, and Julia Reidhead for supporting this project in the first place.

Rich has many, many people at Wright State University to thank for their support and assistance. Jane Blakelock has taught Rich most of what he knows about electronic text and writing on and for the web and has assembled an impressive list of useful links for the book's website. Adrienne Cassel, now at Sinclair Community College, and Catherine Crowley read and commented on many drafts. Peggy Lindsey shared her students' work and the idea of using charts to show how various genres might be organized. Brady Allen, Debbie Bertsch (now at Columbus State Community College), Vicki Burke, Melissa Carrion, Jimmy Chesire, Carol Cornett, Byron Crews, Deborah Crusan, Sally DeThomas, Stephanie Dickey, Scott Geisel, Karen Hayes, Chuck Holmes, Beth Klaisner, Nancy Mack, Marty Maner, Cynthia Marshall, Sarah McGinley, Kristie McKiernan, Michelle Metzner, Kristie Rowe, Bobby Rubin, Cathy Sayer, David Seitz, Caroline Simmons, Tracy Smith, Rick Strader, Mary Van Loveren, and A. J. Williams responded to drafts, submitted good models of student writing, contributed to the instructor's manual, tested the *Field Guide* in their classes, provided support, and shared some of their best teaching ideas. Henry Limouze and then Carol Loranger, chairs of the English Department, gave him room to work on this project with patience and good humor. Sandy Trimboli, Becky Traxler, and Lynn Morgan, the secretaries to the writing programs, kept him anchored. And he thanks especially the more than 300 graduate teaching assistants and 10,000 first-year students who class-tested various editions of the *Field Guide* and whose experiences helped — and continue to help — to shape it.

Thanks to the teachers across the country who reviewed the second edition of the *Field Guide* and helped shape this third edition: Brock Adams, University of South Carolina Upstate; Jill Adams, University of South Carolina Upstate; Steven Adkison, Wallace Community College; Stevens Russell Amidon, Indiana University–Purdue University Fort Wayne; Irene Anders, Indiana University–Purdue University Fort Wayne; Susan Barkley, Dallas County

Community College District; Scott Bayer, Purdue University North Central; James Beitler, Roger Williams University; Kay Berg, Sinclair Community College; Scott Berzon, St. Louis School; Jacqueline Blackwell, Thomas Nelson Community College; Sheena D. Boran, University of Mississippi; Ehel Bowden, Central Maine Community College; Kimberly Britt, Horry Georgetown Technical College; Adrienne Cassel, Sinclair Community College; Jill Channing, Mitchell Community College; Benjamin Child, University of Mississippi; Angie Cook, Cisco College; Robert E. Cummings, University of Mississippi; Judy Deisler, Pasco-Hernando Community College; Alexandra DeSiato, Alamance Community College; Gordon H. Dunkin III, University of Mississippi; Gloria Dyc, University of New Mexico; Jeremiah Dyehouse, University of Rhode Island; Sean Ennis, University of Mississippi; Jason Faulkner, East Carolina University; Shanna Flaschka, University of Mississippi; Shawnda Floyd, Brookdale Community College; Catherine Fox, St. Cloud State University; Robert B. Galin, University of New Mexico–Gallup; Anne Gray, Ivy Tech Community College, Bloomington; Jennifer Gray, College of Coastal Georgia; Wendy Howard Gray, J. Sargeant Reynolds Community College; Shauna Gobble, Northampton Community College; Esther Godfrey, University of Southern California Upstate; Deborah Goodwyn, Virginia State University; Timothy Hackett, East Carolina University; Audley Hall, Northwest Arkansas Community College; Anne Helms, Alamance Community College; Furaha Henry-Jones, Sinclair Community College; Mildred Ann Henson, Moraine Valley Community College; Mark Horstmeyer, Moraine Valley Community College; Susan E. Howard, Ivy Tech Community College; Yi-Wen Huang, University of New Mexico–Gallup; Jo Johnson, Ivy Tech Community College; Amy Jorgensen, North Carolina State University; Sara Kaplan, Del Mar College; Bridget R. Kozlow, North Carolina State University; Celena Kusch, University of South Carolina Upstate; Sharon Gavin Levy, Northampton Community College; Chantelle MacPhee, Elizabeth City State University; Sarah K. McKinney Maddalena, North Carolina State University; Terri Mann, El Paso Community College; Stephen March, Elizabeth City State University; Stephen L. Mathewson, Central New Mexico Community College; Jeanne McDonald, Waubonsee Community College; Tom McLaren, University of New Mexico at Gallup; Tara L. McLellan, University of Mississippi; Mary Pat McQueeney, Johnson County Community College; Robert Mellin, Purdue University North Central; Dodie M. Miller, Ivy Tech Community College; Don Miller, Alamance Community

College; Moraine Valley Community College Foundation; Roxanne Munch, Joliet Junior College; Denise Nemec, Northwest Arkansas Community College; James O'Brien, University of Mississippi; Kristina Onder, Sinclair Community College; Michael Pennell, University of Rhode Island; Brietta Perez, Alvin Community College; Staci Perryman-Clark, Western Michigan University; Daniel Portincaso, Waubonsee Community College; Nancy Riecken, Ivy Tech Community College; Mauricio Rodriguez, El Paso Community College; DaRelle M. Rollins, Hampton University; Theodore (Ted) Rollins, Johnson County Community College; Brian Royse, Ivy Tech Community College; Matthew W. Schmeer, Johnson County Community College; Danielle Sellers, University of Mississippi; Marilyn M. Senter, Johnson County Community College; Brandi Smith Wallace, Wallace Community College; Jennifer Stewart, Indiana University–Purdue University Fort Wayne; Danielle Sullivan, San Juan College; Martha Tolleson, Collin County College; Sara Webb-Sunderhaus, Indiana University–Purdue University Fort Wayne; George H. Williams, University of South Carolina Upstate; Leah Williams, University of New Hampshire; Glenda O. Yount, Alamance Community College.

Thanks also to the many teachers across the country who have reviewed various previous versions and offered valuable input and encouragement: Alan Ainsworth, Houston Community College; Jonathan Alexander, University of California at Irvine; Althea Allard, Community College of Rhode Island; James Allen, College of DuPage; Cathryn Amdahl, Harrisburg Area Community College; Jeff Andelora, Mesa Community College; Anne Beaufort, University of Washington, Tacoma; Sue Beebe, Texas State University; Patrick Bizzaro, East Carolina University; Kevin Brooks, North Dakota State University; Ron Brooks, Oklahoma State University; Cheryl Brown, Towson University; Gina Caison, University of Alabama, Birmingham; Jill Channing, Mitchell Community College; Ron Christiansen, Salt Lake Community College; Susan Cochran-Miller, North Carolina State University at Raleigh Durham; Billye Currie, Samford University; Paul C. Davis, Northland Community and Technical College; Pat Densby, San Jacinto College Central; Marvin Diogenes, Stanford University; Sarah Duerdan, Arizona State University; Russel Durst, University of Cincinnati; Sylvia Edwards, Longview Community College; Karen Fitts, West Chester University; Paul Formisano, University of New Mexico; Lloren A. Foster, Hampton University; Ivonne M. Garcia, Ohio State University; Anne Gervasi, DeVry University; Gregory Glau,

Arizona State University; Emily Golson, University of Northern Colorado; Richard Hansen, California State Fresno; Susanmarie Harrington, University of Vermont; Lory Hawkes, DeVry Institute of Technology; Gary Hawkins, Warren Wilson College; Paul Heilker, Virginia Polytechnic Institute and State University; Hal Hellwig, Idaho State University; Michael Hennessy, Texas State University; Cheryl Huff, Germanna Community College; Maurice Hunt, Baylor University; Teresa James, South Florida Community College; Kim Jameson, Oklahoma City Community College; Peggy Jolly, University of Alabama, Birmingham; Mitzi Walker Jones, University of Arkansas, Fort Smith; Jeanne Kelly, Holmes Community College; Rhonda Kyncl, University of Oklahoma; Sally Lahmon, Sinclair Community College; Erin Lebacqz, University of New Mexico; Paul Lynch, Purdue University; T. Michael Mackey, Community College of Denver; Magdalena Maczynska, Marymount Manhattan College; Leigh A. Martin, Community College of Rhode Island; Deborah McCollister, Dallas Baptist University; Miles McCrimmon, J. Sargeant Reynolds Community College; Jeanne McDonald, Waubonsee Community College; Jacqueline McGrath, College of DuPage; Pat McQueeny, Johnson County Community College; Shellie Michael, Volunteer State Community College; Thomas Miller, University of Arizona; Bryan Moore, Arkansas State University; Mary Ellen Muesing, University of North Carolina, Charlotte; Roxanne Munch, Joliet Junior College; Terry Novak, Johnson & Wales University; Peggy Oliver, San Jacinto College; Amy Patrick, Western Illinois University; Ann Pearson, San Jacinto College; Irv Peckham, Louisiana State University; K. J. Peters, Loyola Marymount University; Deirdre Pettipiece, University of the Sciences; Donna Qualley, Western Washington University; Daniela Ragusa, Southern Connecticut State University; Dana Resente, Montgomery County Community College; Nedra Reynolds, University of Rhode Island; Althea Rhodes, University of Arkansas, Fort Smith; Mauricio Rodriguez, El Paso Community College; Gardner Rogers, University of Illinois at Urbana-Champaign; Tony Russell, Purdue University; Matthew Samra, Kellogg Community College; Lisa L. Sandoval, Joliet Junior College; Lisa M. Schwerdt, California University of Pennsylvania; Michelle Sidler, Auburn University; William H. Smith, Weatherford College; Leah Sneider, University of New Mexico; Jeffrey Larsen Snodgrass, Prince George's Community College; Jean Sorensen, Grayson County College; Brady J. Spangenberg, Purdue University; Candace Stewart, Ohio University; Jennifer Stewart,

Indiana University–Purdue University, Fort Wayne; Amy Ferdinandt Stolley, Purdue University; Mary Stripling, Dallas Baptist University; Martha Swearingen, University of District Columbia; Elyssa Tardiff, Purdue University; Linda Tetzlaff, Normandale Community College; John M. Thomson, Johnson County Community College; Monica Parrish Trent, Montgomery College, Rockville Campus; Griselda Valerio, University of Texas at Brownsville; Jarica Watts, University of Utah; Scott Weeden, Indiana University–Purdue University Fort Wayne; Candice Welhausen, University of New Mexico; Carol Westcamp, University of Arkansas, Fort Smith; Barbara Whitehead, Hampton University; Melissa E. Whiting, University of Arkansas, Fort Smith; and Anne-Marie Yerks, University of Michigan. Thanks especially to Avon Crismore's students at Indiana University–Purdue University Fort Wayne for their thoughtful (and well-written) evaluations.

The Norton Field Guide has also benefited from the good advice and conversations we've had with writing teachers across the country, including (among many others) Maureen Mathison, Susan Miller, Tom Huckin, Gae Lyn Henderson, and Sundy Watanabe at the University of Utah; Christa Albrecht-Crane, Doug Downs, and Brian Whaley at Utah Valley State College; Anne Dvorak and Anya Morrissey at Longview Community University; Jeff Andelora at Mesa Community College; Robin Calitri at Merced College; Lori Gallinger, Rose Hawkins, Jennifer Nelson, Georgia Standish, and John Ziebell at the Community College of Southern Nevada; Stuart Blythe at Indiana University–Purdue University Fort Wayne; Janice Kelly at Arizona State University; Jeanne McDonald at Waubonsee Community College; Web Newbold, Mary Clark-Upchurch, Megan Auffart, Matt Balk, Edward James Chambers, Sarah Chavez, Desiree Dighton, Ashley Ellison, Theresa Evans, Keith Heller, Ellie Isenhart, Angela Jackson-Brown, Naoko Kato, Yuanyuan Liao, Claire Lutkewitte, Yeno Matuki, Casey McArdle, Tibor Munkacsi, Dani Nier-Weber, Karen Neubauer, Craig O'Hara, Martha Payne, Sarah Sandman, and Kellie Weiss at Ball State University; Patrick Tompkins at Tyler Community College; George Kanieski and Pamela Hardman at Cuyahoga Community College; Daniela Regusa, Jeff Partridge, and Lydia Vine at Capital Community College; Elizabeth Woodworth, Auburn University–Montgomery; Stephanie Eason at Enterprise Community College; and Kate Geiselman at Sinclair Community College.

We wouldn't have met most of these people without the help of the Norton travelers, the representatives who spend their days visiting faculty, showing and discussing the *Field Guide* and Norton's many other fine textbooks. Thanks especially to Kathy Church, Scott Cook, John Darger, Peter Wentz, Mary Helen Willett, Lauren Winkler, and all the other Norton travelers. And we'd especially like to thank Mike Wright, Lib Triplett, Ashley Cain, and Doug Day for promoting this book so enthusiastically and professionally.

It's customary to conclude by expressing gratitude to one's spouse and family, and for good reason. Writing and revising *The Norton Field Guide* over the past several years, we have enjoyed the loving and unconditional support of our spouses, Barb and Larry, who provide the foundation for all we do. Thank you. We couldn't have done it without you.

How to Use This Book

There's no one way to do anything, and writing is no exception. Some people need to do a lot of planning on paper; others write entire drafts in their heads. Some writers compose quickly and loosely, going back later to revise; others work on one sentence until they're satisfied with it, then move on to the next. And writers' needs vary from task to task, too: sometimes you know what you're going to write about and why, but need to figure out how to do it; other times your first job is to come up with a topic. *The Norton Field Guide* is designed to allow you to chart your own course as a writer, offering guidelines that suit your writing needs. It is organized in seven parts:

1. **RHETORICAL SITUATIONS**: No matter what you're writing, it will always have some purpose, audience, genre, stance, and medium and design. This part will help you consider each of these elements, as well as the particular kinds of rhetorical situations created by academic assignments.

2. **GENRES**: Use these chapters for help with specific kinds of writing, from abstracts to lab reports to memoirs and more. You'll find more detailed guidance for four especially common assignments: literacy narratives, textual analyses, reports, and arguments. There's also help with choosing which genre to use when an assignment doesn't specify one.

3. **PROCESSES**: These chapters offer general advice for all writing situations — from generating ideas and text to drafting, revising and rewriting, compiling a portfolio — and more.

4. **STRATEGIES**: Use the advice in this part to develop and organize your writing — to write effective beginnings and endings, to guide readers through your text, and to use comparison, description, dialogue, and other strategies as appropriate.

5. **RESEARCH / DOCUMENTATION**: Use this section for advice on how to do research, work with sources, and compose and document research-based texts using MLA and APA styles.

6. **MEDIA / DESIGN**: This section offers guidance in designing your work and using visuals and sound, and in deciding whether and how to deliver what you write on paper, on screen, or in person.

7. **HANDBOOK**: Look here for help with sentence-level editing.

Ways into the Book

The Norton Field Guide gives you the writing advice you need, along with the flexibility to write in the way that works best for you. Here are some of the ways you can find what you need in the book.

Brief menus.   Inside the front cover you'll find a list of all the chapters; start here if you are looking for a chapter on a certain kind of writing or a general writing issue. Inside the back cover is a menu of all the topics covered in the **HANDBOOK**.

Complete contents.   Pages xxi–xxxviii contain a detailed table of contents. Look here if you need to find a reading or a specific section in a chapter.

Guides to writing.   If you know the kind of writing you need to do, you'll find guides to writing 14 common genres in Part 2. These guides are designed to help you through all the decisions you have to make — from coming up with a topic to editing and proofreading your final draft.

Color-coding.   The parts of this book are color-coded for easy reference: red for **RHETORICAL SITUATIONS**, green for **GENRES**, lavender for **PROCESSES**, orange for **STRATEGIES**, blue for **RESEARCH / DOCUMENTATION**, gold for **MEDIA / DESIGN**, and yellow for the **HANDBOOK**. You'll find a key to the colors on the front cover flap and also at the foot of each left-hand page. When you see a word highlighted in a color, that tells you where you can find additional detail on the topic.

Glossary / index.   At the back of the book is a combined glossary and index, where you'll find full definitions of key terms and topics, along with a list of the pages where everything is covered in detail.

Directories to MLA and APA documentation.   A brief directory at the back of the book will lead you to guidelines on citing sources and composing a list of references or works cited. The documentation models are color-coded so you can easily see the key details.

The website.   You can also start at wwnorton.com/write/fieldguide. There you'll find model essays; worksheets; MLA and APA guidelines; more than 1,000 exercises focused on sentences, language, and punctuation; an online handbook; and more.

Ways of Getting Started

If you know your genre, simply turn to the appropriate genre chapter. There you'll find model readings, a description of the genre's Key Features, and a Guide to Writing that will help you come up with a topic, generate text, organize and write a draft, get response, revise, edit, and proofread. The genre chapters also point out places where you might need to do research, use certain writing strategies, design your text a certain way — and direct you to the exact pages in the book where you can find help doing so.

If you know your topic, you might start with some of the activities in Chapter 24, Generating Ideas and Text. From there, you might turn to Chapter 44, for help Finding Sources on the topic. When it comes time to narrow your topic and come up with a thesis statement, Chapter 31 can help. If you get stuck at any point, you might turn to Chapter 22, Writing as Inquiry; it provides tips that can get you beyond what you already know about your topic. If your assignment or your thesis defines your genre, turn to that chapter; if not, consult Chapter 21 for help determining the appropriate genre, and then turn to that genre chapter. The genre chapters point out places where you might need to do more research, use certain writing strategies, design your text a certain way — and direct you to the exact pages in the book where you can find help doing so.

Contents

Part 3 Processes *249*

Part 6   Media / Design   *575*

Part 7   Handbook   *HB-1*

Sentences   *HB-3*

Language   *HB-38*

Punctuation / Mechanics   *HB-60*

THIRD EDITION

The Norton Field Guide to Writing
with handbook

part 1

Rhetorical Situations

Whenever we write, whether it's a text to a friend or a toast for a wedding, an English essay or a résumé, we face some kind of rhetorical situation. We have a PURPOSE, a certain AUDIENCE, a particular STANCE, a GENRE, and a MEDIUM to consider — and often as not a DESIGN. All are important elements that we need to think about carefully. The following chapters offer brief discussions of those elements of the rhetorical situation, along with questions that can help you make the choices you need to as you write. A chapter on WRITING IN ACADEMIC CONTEXTS offers help with the demands of college writing. See also the fourteen GENRES chapters for guidelines for considering your rhetorical situation in each of these specific kinds of writing.

Rhetorical Situations

All writing has a purpose. We write to explore our thoughts and emotions, to express ourselves, to entertain; we write to record words and events, to communicate with others, to try to persuade others to believe as we do or to behave in certain ways. In fact, we often have several purposes at the same time. We may write an essay in which we try to explain something to an audience, but at the same time we may be trying to persuade that audience of something. Look, for example, at this passage from a 2012 *New York Times* op-ed essay by economist and editorial columnist Paul Krugman about social and economic trends among "the traditional working-class family" — declining rates of marriage and of male participation in the labor force and increasing numbers of out-of-wedlock births. Krugman asserts that the primary reason for those statistics is a "drastic reduction in the work opportunities available to less-educated men":

> Most of the numbers you see about income trends in America focus on households rather than individuals, which makes sense for some purposes. But when you see a modest rise in incomes for the lower tiers of the income distribution, you have to realize that all — yes, all — of this rise comes from the women, both because more women are in the paid labor force and because women's wages aren't as much below male wages as they used to be.
>
> For lower-education working men, however, it has been all negative. Adjusted for inflation, entry-level wages of male high school graduates have fallen 23 percent since 1973. Meanwhile, employment benefits have collapsed. In 1980, 65 percent of recent high-school graduates working in the private sector had health benefits, but, by 2009, that was down to 29 percent.
>
> So we have become a society in which less-educated men have great difficulty finding jobs with decent wages and good benefits.
>
> —Paul Krugman, "Money and Morals"

Krugman is reporting information here, outlining how the earnings and benefits of less-educated men have dropped over the last forty years. He is also making an argument, that these economic setbacks are the cause of the social ills among working-class Americans and not, as some would have it, the result of them. (Krugman, writing for a newspaper, is also using a style — including dashes, contractions, and other informal elements — that strives to be engaging while it informs and argues.)

Even though our purposes may be many, knowing our primary reason for writing can help us shape that writing and understand how to proceed with it. Our purpose can determine the genre we choose, our audience, even the way we design what we write.

Identify your purpose. While a piece of writing often has many purposes, a writer usually focuses on one. When you get an assignment or see a need to write, ask yourself what the primary purpose of the writing task is: to entertain? to inform? to persuade? to demonstrate your knowledge or your writing ability? What are your own goals? What are your audience's expectations, and do they affect the way you define your purpose?

Thinking about Purpose

- **What do you want your audience to do, think, or feel?** How will they use what you tell them?

- **What does this writing task call on you to do?** Do you need to show that you have mastered certain content or skills? Do you have an assignment that specifies a particular **STRATEGY** or **GENRE** — to compare two things, perhaps, or to argue a position?

- **What are the best ways to achieve your purpose?** What kind of **STANCE** should you take? Should you write in a particular genre? Do you have a choice of **MEDIUM,** and does your text require any special format or **DESIGN** elements?

297 ◆

25 ▲

12–15 ■

575 ☐

Audience 2

Who will read (or hear) what you are writing? A seemingly obvious but crucially important question. Your audience affects your writing in various ways. Consider a piece of writing as simple as a text from a mother to her son:

> *Pls. take chicken out to thaw and feed Annye. Remember Dr. Wong at 4.*

On the surface, this brief note is a straightforward reminder to do three things. But in fact it is a complex message filled with compressed information for a specific audience. The writer (the mother) counts on the reader (her son) to know a lot that can be left unsaid. She expects that he knows that the chicken is in the freezer and needs to thaw in time to be cooked for dinner; she knows that he knows who Annye is (a pet?), what he or she is fed, and how much; she assumes that he knows who (and where) Dr. Wong is. She doesn't need to spell any of that out because she knows what her son knows and what he needs to know—and in her text she can be brief. She understands her audience. Think how different such a reminder would be were it written to another audience—a babysitter, perhaps, or a friend helping out while Mom is out of town.

What you write, how much you write, how you phrase it, even your choice of **GENRE** (memo, essay, email, note, speech)—all are influenced by the audience you envision. And your audience will interpret your writing according to their own expectations and experiences, not yours.

9–11

When you are a student, your audience is most often your teachers, so you need to be aware of their expectations and know the conventions (rules, often unstated) for writing in specific academic fields. You may make statements that seem obvious to you, not realizing that your instructors may consider them assertions that must be proved with evidence of one sort or another. Or you may write more or less formally than teachers expect. Understanding your audience's expectations — by asking outright, by reading materials in your field of study, by trial and error — is important to your success as a college writer.

This point is worth dwelling on. You are probably reading this textbook for a writing course. As a student, you will be expected to produce essays with few or no errors. If as part of your job or among friends and family you correspond using email and texts you may question such standards; after all, many of the messages you get in these contexts are not grammatically perfect. But in a writing class, the instructor needs to see your best work. Whatever the rhetorical situation, your writing must meet the expectations of your audience.

Identify your audience.   Audiences may be defined as *known, multiple,* or *unknown. Known audiences* can include people with whom you're familiar as well as people you don't know personally but whose needs and expectations you do know. You yourself are a known, familiar audience, and you write to and for yourself often. Class notes, to-do lists, reminders, and journals are all written primarily for an audience of one: you. For that reason, they are often in shorthand, full of references and code that you alone understand.

Other known, familiar audiences include anyone you actually know — friends, relatives, teachers, classmates — and whose needs and expectations you understand. You can also know what certain readers want and need, even if you've never met them personally, if you write for them within a specific shared context. Such a known audience might include PC gamers who read cheat codes that you have posted on the Internet for beating a game; you don't know those people, but you know roughly what they know about the game and what they need to know, and you know how to write about it in ways they will understand.

You often have to write for *multiple audiences.* Business memos or reports may be written initially for a supervisor, but he or she may pass them along to others. Grant proposals may be reviewed by four to six levels of readers — each, of course, with its own expectations and perspectives.

■ rhetorical situations
▲ genres
○ processes
◆ strategies
● research MLA / APA
▢ media / design
◹ handbook

Even writing for a class might involve multiple audiences: your instructor and your classmates.

Unknown audiences can be the most difficult to address since you can't be sure what they know, what they need to know, how they'll react. Such an audience could be your downstairs neighbor, with whom you're chatted occasionally in the laundry room. How will she respond to your letter asking her to sponsor you in an upcoming charity walk? Another unknown audience — perhaps surprisingly — might be many of your instructors, who want — and expect! — you to write in ways that are new to you. While you can benefit from analyzing any audience, you need to think most carefully about those you don't know.

Thinking about Audience

- *Whom do you want to reach?* To whom are you writing (or speaking)?
- *What is your audience's background — their education and life experiences?* It may be important for you to know, for example, whether your readers attended college, fought in a war, or have young children.
- *What are their interests?* What do they like? What motivates them? What do they care about?
- *Is there any demographic information that you should keep in mind?* Consider whether race, gender, sexual orientation, disabilities, occupations, religious beliefs, economic status, and so on should affect what or how you write. For example, writers for *Men's Health*, *InStyle*, and *Out* must consider the particular interests of each magazine's readers.
- *What political circumstances may affect their reading?* What attitudes — opinions, special interests, biases — may affect the way your audience reads your piece? Are your readers conservative, liberal, or middle of the road? Politics may take many other forms as well — retirees on a fixed income may object to increased school taxes, so a letter arguing for such an increase would need to appeal to them differently than would a similar letter sent to parents of young children.

- *What does your audience already know—or believe—about your topic? What do you need to tell them? What is the best way to do so?* Those retirees who oppose school taxes already know that taxes are a burden for them; they may need to know why schools are justified in asking for more money every few years. A good way to explain this may be with a bar graph showing how property values benefit from good schools with adequate funding. Consider which **STRATEGIES** will be effective—narrative, comparison, something else?

297 ◆

- *What's your relationship with your audience, and how should it affect your language and tone?* Do you know them, or not? Are they friends? Colleagues? Mentors? Adversaries? Strangers? Will they likely share your **STANCE?** In general, you need to write more formally when you're addressing readers you don't know, and you may address friends and colleagues more informally than you would a boss.

12–15 ■

- *What does your audience need and expect from you?* Your history professor, for example, may need to know how well you can discuss the economy of the late Middle Ages in order to assess your learning; he may expect you to write a carefully reasoned argument, drawing conclusions from various sources, with a readily identifiable thesis in the first paragraph. Your boss, on the other hand, may need an informal email that briefly lists your sales contacts for the day; she may expect that you list the contacts in the order in which you saw them, that you clearly identify each one, and that you briefly say how well each contact went. What **GENRE** is most appropriate?

25 ▲

- *What kind of response do you want?* Do you want readers to believe or do something? To accept as valid your information on a topic? To understand why an experience you once had matters to you?

575 ☐

- *How can you best appeal to your audience?* Is there a particular **MEDIUM** that will best reach them? Are there any **DESIGN** requirements? (Elderly readers may need larger type, for instance.)

Genre   3

Genres are kinds of writing. Letters, profiles, reports, position papers, poems, blog posts, instructions, parodies—even jokes—are genres. For example, here is the beginning of a **PROFILE** of a mechanic who repairs a specific kind of automobile:

191–204

> Her business card reads Shirley Barnes, M.D., and she's a doctor, all right—a Metropolitan Doctor. Her passion is the Nash Metropolitan, the little car produced by Austin of England for American Motors between 1954 and 1962. Barnes is a legend among southern California Met lovers—an icon, a beacon, and a font of useful knowledge and freely offered opinions.

A profile offers a written portrait of someone or something that informs and sometimes entertains, often examining its subject from a particular angle—in this case, as a female mechanic who fixes Nash Metropolitans. While the language in this example is informal and lively ("she's a doctor, all right"), the focus is on the subject, Shirley Barnes, "M.D." If this same excerpt were presented as a poem, however, the new genre would change our reading:

> Her business card reads
> Shirley Barnes, M.D.,
> and she's a doctor, all right
> —a Metropolitan Doctor.
> Her passion is the Nash Metropolitan,
> the little car produced by Austin of England
> for American Motors between 1954 and 1962.
> Barnes is a legend
> among southern California Met lovers
> — an icon,

9

a beacon,
and a font of useful knowledge and
freely offered opinions.

The content hasn't changed, but the different presentation invites us to read not only to learn about Shirley Barnes but also to explore the significance of the words and phrases on each line, to read for deeper meaning and greater appreciation of language. The genre thus determines how we read and how we interpret what we read.

Genres help us write by establishing features for conveying certain kinds of content. They give readers clues about what sort of information they're likely to find and so help them figure out how to read ("This article begins with an abstract, so it's probably a scholarly source" or "Thank goodness! I found the instructions for editing videos on my phone"). At the same time, writers sometimes challenge genre conventions, reshaping them as communicative needs and technologies change. For example, computers have enabled us to add audio and video content to texts that once could appear only on paper.

25 ▲
Identify your genre. Does your writing situation call for a certain **GENRE?** A memo? A report? A proposal? A letter? Academic assignments generally specify the genre ("take a position," "analyze the text"), but if not, see
243–48 ▲
Chapter 21 for help **CHOOSING GENRES** — or ask your instructor.

Thinking about Genre

- *What is your genre, and how does it affect what content you can or should include?* Objective information? Researched source material? Your own opinions? Personal experience?

297 ◆
173–82 ▲
- *Does your genre call for any specific* **STRATEGIES?** Profiles, for example, usually include some narration; **LAB REPORTS** often explain a process.

205–13 ▲
- *Does your genre require a certain organization?* Most **PROPOSALS**, for instance, first identify a problem and then offer a solution. Some genres leave room for choice. Business letters delivering good news might be organized differently than those making sales pitches.

- *Does your genre affect your tone?* An abstract of a scholarly paper calls for a different **TONE** than a memoir. Should your words sound serious and scholarly? Brisk and to the point? Objective? Opinionated? Sometimes your genre affects the way you communicate your **STANCE.**

■ 13

■ 12–15

- *Does the genre require formal (or informal) language?* A letter to the mother of a friend asking for a summer job in her bookstore calls for more formal language than does an email to the friend thanking him for the lead.

- *Do you have a choice of medium?* Some genres call for print; others for an electronic medium. Sometimes you have a choice: a résumé, for instance, can be printed to bring to an interview, or it may be emailed. Some teachers want reports turned in on paper; others prefer that they be emailed or posted in the class course management system. If you're not sure what **MEDIUM** you can use, ask.

☐ 575

- *Does your genre have any design requirements?* Some genres call for paragraphs; others require lists. Some require certain kinds of fonts — you wouldn't use **Impact** for a personal narrative, nor would you likely use Chiller for an invitation to Grandma's sixty-fifth birthday party. Different genres call for different **DESIGN** elements.

☐ 575

4 Stance

Whenever you write, you have a certain stance, an attitude toward your topic. The way you express that stance affects the way you come across to your audience as a writer and a person. This email from a college student to his father, for example, shows a thoughtful, reasonable stance for a carefully researched argument:

> Hi Dad,
> I'll get right to the point: I'd like to buy a car. I saved over $3500 from working this summer, and I've found three different cars that I can get for under $3000. That'll leave me $400 to cover the insurance. I can park in Lot J, over behind Monte Hall, for $75 for both semesters. And I can earn gas and repair money by upping my hours at the cafeteria. It won't cost you any more, and if I have a car, you won't have to come and pick me up when I want to come home. May I buy it?
> Love,
> Michael

While such a stance can't guarantee that Dad will give permission, it's more likely to produce results than this version:

> Hi Dad,
> I'm buying a car. A guy in my Western Civ course has a cool Chevy he wants to get rid of. I've got $3500 saved from working this summer, it's mine, and I'm going to use it to get some wheels. Mom said you'd blow your top if I did, but I want this car. OK?
> Michael

The writer of the first email respects his reader and offers reasoned arguments and evidence of research to convince him that buying a car is an action that will benefit them both. The writer of the second, by contrast, seems impulsive, ready to buy the first car that comes along, and

rhetorical situations

genres

processes

strategies

research
MLA / APA

media / design

handbook

defiant — he's picking a fight. Each email reflects a certain stance that shows the writer as a certain kind of person dealing with a topic in a certain way and establishing a certain relationship with his audience.

Identify your stance. What is your attitude toward your topic? Objective? Critical? Curious? Opinionated? Passionate? Indifferent? Your stance may be affected by your relationship to your AUDIENCE. How do you want them to see you? As a colleague sharing information? As a good student showing what you can do? As an advocate for a position? Often your stance is affected by your GENRE: for example, lab reports require an objective, unemotional stance that emphasizes the content and minimizes the writer's own attitudes. Memoir, by comparison, allows you to reveal your feelings about your topic. Your stance is also affected by your PURPOSE, as the two emails about cars show. Your stance in a piece written to entertain will likely differ from the stance you'd adopt to persuade.

■ 5–8

▲ 25

■ 3–4

You communicate (or downplay) your stance through your tone — through the words you use and other ways your text expresses an attitude toward your subject and audience. For example, in an academic essay you would state your position directly — "the *Real Housewives* series reflects the values of American society today" — a confident, assertive tone. In contrast, using qualifiers like "might" or "I think" can give your writing a wishy-washy, uncertain tone: "I think the *Real Housewives* series might reflect some of the values of American society today." The following paragraph, from an essay analyzing a text, has a sarcastic tone that might be appropriate for a comment on a blog post, but that isn't right for an academic essay:

> In "Just Be Nice," Stephen M. Carter complains about a boy who wore his pants too low, showing his underwear. Is that really something people should worry about? We have wars raging and terrorism happening every day, and he wants to talk about how inconsiderate it is for someone to wear his pants too low? If by that boy pulling his pants up, the world would be a better place and peace would break out in the Middle East, I'm sure everyone would buy a belt.

This writer clearly thinks Carter's complaint is trivial in comparison with the larger issues of the day, but her sarcastic tone belittles Carter's argument instead of answering it with a serious counterargument. Like every other element of writing, your tone must be appropriate for your rhetorical situation.

Just as you likely alter what you say depending on whether you're speaking to a boss, an instructor, a parent, or a good friend, so you need to make similar adjustments as a writer. It's a question of appropriateness: we behave in certain ways in various social situations, and writing is a social situation. You might sign an email to a friend with an x and an o, but in an email to your supervisor you'll likely sign off with a "Many thanks" or "Sincerely." To write well, you need to write with integrity, to say as much as possible what you wish to say; yet you also must understand that in writing, as in speaking, your stance and tone need to suit your purpose, your relationship to your audience, the way in which you wish your audience to perceive you, and your medium. In writing as in other aspects of life, the Golden Rule applies: "Do unto audiences as you would have them do unto you." Address readers respectfully if you want them to respond to your words with respect.

Thinking about Stance

- *What is your stance, and how does it relate to your purpose for writing?* If you feel strongly about your topic and are writing an argument that tries to persuade your audience to feel the same way, your stance and your **PURPOSE** fit naturally together. But suppose you are writing about the same topic with a different purpose — to demonstrate the depth of your knowledge about the topic, for example, or your ability to consider it in a detached, objective way. You will need to adjust your stance to meet the demands of this different purpose.

- *How should your stance be reflected in your tone?* Can your tone grow directly out of your stance, or do you need to "tone down" your attitude toward the topic or take a different tone altogether? Do you want to be seen as reasonable? Angry? Thoughtful? Gentle? Funny? Ironic? If you're writing about something you want to be seen as taking very

3–4 ▪

seriously, be sure that your language and even your font reflect that seriousness. Check your writing for words that reflect the tone you want to convey — and for ones that do not (and revise as necessary).

- *How is your stance likely to be received by your audience?* Your tone and especially the attitude it projects toward your **AUDIENCE** will affect how they react to the content of what you say.

5–8

- *Should you openly reveal your stance?* Do you want or need to announce your own perspective on your topic? Will doing so help you reach your audience, or would it be better not to say directly where you're coming from?

5 Media / Design

In its broadest sense, a medium is a go-between: a way for information to be conveyed from one person to another. We communicate through many media, verbal and nonverbal: our bodies (we catch someone's eye, wave, nod); our voices (we whisper, talk, shout, groan); and various technologies, including handwriting, print, telephone, radio, CD, film, and computer.

Each medium has unique characteristics that influence both what and how we communicate. As an example, consider this message: "I haven't told you this before, but I love you." Most of the time, we communicate such a message in person, using the medium of voice (with, presumably, help from eye contact and touch). A phone call will do, though most of us would think it a poor second choice, and a handwritten letter or note would be acceptable, if necessary. Few of us would break such news on a website, with a tweet, or during a radio call-in program.

By contrast, imagine whispering the following sentence in a darkened room: "By the last decades of the nineteenth century, the territorial expansion of the United States had left almost all Indians confined to reservations." That sentence starts a chapter in a history textbook, and it would be strange indeed to whisper it into someone's ear. It is appropriate, however, in the textbook, in print or in an e-book, or on a *PowerPoint* slide accompanying an oral presentation.

As you can see, we can often choose among various media depending on our purpose and audience. In addition, we can often combine media to create **MULTIMEDIA** texts. And different media allow us to use different ways or modes of expressing meaning, from words to images to sound to hyperlinks, that can be combined into **MULTIMODAL** formats.

No matter the medium or media, a text's design affects the way it is received and understood. A typed letter on official letterhead sends a different message than the same words handwritten on pastel stationery.

579

rhetorical situations

genres

processes

strategies

research MLA / APA

media / design

handbook

Classic type sends a different message than *flowery italics*. Some genres and media (and audiences) demand **PHOTOS, DIAGRAMS,** or color. Some information is easier to explain—and read—in the form of a **PIE CHART** or a **BAR GRAPH** than in the form of a paragraph. Some reports and documents are so long and complex that they need to be divided into sections, which are then best labeled with **HEADINGS.** These are some of the elements to consider when you are thinking about how to design what you write.

593–95

588–89

Identify your media and design needs.   Does your writing situation call for a certain medium and design? A printed essay? An oral report with visual aids? A blog? A podcast? Academic assignments often assume a particular medium and design, but if you're unsure about your options or the degree of flexibility you have, check with your instructor.

Thinking about Media

- *What medium are you using*—print? spoken? electronic? a combination? —and how does it affect the way you will create your text? A printed résumé is usually no more than one page long; a scannable résumé sent via email has no length limits. An oral presentation should contain detailed information; accompanying slides should provide only an outline.

- *How does your medium affect your organization and* **STRATEGIES?** Long paragraphs are fine on paper but don't work well on the web. On presentation slides, phrases or key words work better than sentences. In print, you need to define unfamiliar terms; on the Web, you can sometimes just add a link to a definition found elsewhere.

297

- *How does your medium affect your language?* Some print documents require a more formal voice than spoken media; email and texting often invite greater informality.

- *How does your medium affect what elements besides words you include?* Should your text include photos, graphics, audio or video files, or links? Do you need slides, handouts, or other visuals to accompany an oral presentation?

Thinking about Design

1

- *What's the appropriate look for your* RHETORICAL SITUATION? Should your text look serious? Whimsical? Personal? Something else? What design elements will suit your audience, purpose, genre, and medium?

- *What elements need to be designed?* Is there any information you would like to highlight by putting it in a box? Are there any key terms that should be boldfaced? Do you need navigation buttons? How should you indicate links?

- *What font(s) are appropriate* to your audience, purpose, genre, and medium?

591–99
5–8

- *Are you including any* VISUALS? Should you? Will your AUDIENCE expect or need any? Is there any information in your text that would be easier to understand as a chart or graph? If you need to include video or audio clips, how should the links be presented?

9–11
17

- *Should you include headings?* Would they help you organize your materials and help readers follow the text? Does your GENRE or MEDIUM require them?

Writing in Academic Contexts 6

In an introductory psychology course, you're assigned to write an essay taking a position on whether genes or environment do more to determine people's intelligence. Your environmental science instructor asks you to research and write a report on the environmental effects of electricity-generating windmills. Your marketing professor requires you to write a proposal, including a multimedia presentation, for a sales campaign. Academic writing serves many purposes: you may write to explore a topic, to explain what's known about it, to outline what others have said about it, to say what you think about it and why — or for various other purposes. Whatever your topic or purpose, academic writing is a way of adding your voice to some larger conversation. This chapter will help you think about some of the key features expected in academic contexts.

Key Features of Academic Writing

Evidence that you've carefully considered the subject. Whether you're writing a personal narrative, a report, or an argument, you need to demonstrate that you've thought seriously about the topic and done any necessary research. You can use a variety of ways to show that you've considered the subject thoughtfully, from citing authoritative sources to incorporating information you learned in class to pointing out connections among ideas.

A clear, appropriately qualified THESIS. When you write in an academic context, you're expected to state your main point explicitly, often in a thesis statement. MIT student Joanna MacKay states her thesis clearly in her

313–15

314–15

essay "Organ Sales Will Save Lives": "Governments should not ban the sale of human organs; they should regulate it." Often, you'll need to **QUALIFY** your thesis statement to acknowledge that the subject is complicated and there may be more than one way of seeing it, or exceptions to the generalization you're making about it. Here, for example, is a qualified thesis, from an essay about whether texting affects writing by Michaela Cullington, a student at Marywood University: "Although some believe that texting has either a positive or negative effect on writing, it in fact seems likely that texting has no significant effect on student writing." The beginning of the sentence acknowledges other views, and the use of words like *seems likely* and *significant* indicates that Cullington is not making an absolute, unqualified claim that texting has no effect at all.

A response to what others have said. Whatever your topic, it is unlikely that you'll be the first one to write about it. And if, as this chapter assumes, all academic writing is part of a larger conversation, you are in a way adding your own voice to that conversation. One good way of doing that is to present your ideas as a response to what others have said about your topic — to begin by quoting, paraphrasing, or summarizing what others have said and then to agree, disagree, or both.

For example, in an essay arguing that the American Dream is alive and well, Brandon King presents the views of two economists who say that because wealth is concentrated in the hands "of a rich minority . . . the American Dream is no longer possible for most Americans." He then responds by disagreeing, arguing that "the American Dream . . . is based on perception, on the way someone *imagines* how to be successful."

326–35

Good reasons supported by evidence. You need to provide good **REASONS** for your thesis and **EVIDENCE** to support those reasons. For example, MacKay offers several reasons why sales of human kidneys should be legalized: there is a surplus of kidneys, the risk to the donor is not great, and legalization would allow the trade in kidneys to be regulated. Evidence to support your reasons sometimes comes from your own experience, but more often from published research and scholarship, research you do yourself, or first-hand accounts by others.

Compared with other kinds of writing, academic writing is generally expected to be more detached and objective and less personal and emotional. You may find *Romeo and Juliet* deeply moving or cry when you watch *Titanic* — but when you write about the play or the film for a class, you must do so using evidence from the text to support your thesis. Similarly, you may find someone's ideas deeply offensive, but you should respond to them primarily with reason, rather than with emotional appeals or personal attacks.

Acknowledgment of multiple perspectives. Debates and arguments in popular media are often framed in "pro/con" terms, a view in which there are only two sides to an issue. Once you begin seriously studying a topic, though, you're likely to find that there are several sides, and that each of them deserves serious consideration. In your academic writing, you need to represent fairly the range of perspectives on your topic — to explore three, four, or more positions on it as you research and write. King, for instance, looks at the American Dream from several angles: the ways it is defined, the effects of taxes and other government policies on the ability of people to achieve the Dream, the role of education, and more.

Carefully documented sources. Clearly acknowledging sources and DOCUMENTING them carefully and correctly is a basic requirement of academic writing. When you use the words or ideas of others — including visuals, video, or audio — those sources must be documented both in the text and in a works cited or references list at the end. (If you're writing something that will appear online, you may also refer readers to your sources by using hyperlinks in the text; check with your instructor first, and ask if you need to include a list of references or works cited.)

480–83

A confident, authoritative STANCE. Since one of the goals of academic writing is to contribute to a larger conversation, your tone should convey confidence and establish your authority to write about your subject. Ways to achieve such a tone include using active verbs ("X claims" rather than "it seems"), avoiding such phrases as "in my opinion" and "I think," and

12–15

writing in a straightforward, direct style. For example, here is the final paragraph of Cullington's essay on texting and writing:

> On the basis of my own research, expert research, and personal observations, I can confidently state that texting is not interfering with students' use of standard written English and has no effect on their writing abilities in general. It is interesting to look at the dynamics of the arguments over these issues. Teachers and parents who claim that they are seeing a decline in the writing abilities of their students and children mainly support the negative-impact argument. Other teachers and researchers suggest that texting provides a way for teens to practice writing in a casual setting and thus helps prepare them to write formally. Experts and students themselves, however, report that they see no effect, positive or negative. Anecdotal experiences should not overshadow the actual evidence.

Cullington's use of simple, declarative sentences ("Other teachers and researchers suggest . . . ," "Anecdotal experiences should not overshadow . . .") and her straightforward summary of the arguments surrounding texting, along with her strong, unequivocal ending ("texting is not interfering with students' use of standard written English") lend her writing a confident tone. Her stance sends the message that she's done the research and knows what she's talking about.

An indication of why your topic matters. You need to help your readers understand why your topic is worth exploring and why your writing is worth reading. Even if you are writing in response to an assigned topic, you can better make your point and achieve your purpose by showing your readers why your topic is important and why they should care about it. For example, in "Throwing Like a Girl," James Fallows explains why his topic, the differences between the ways men and women throw a baseball, is worth writing about:

> The phrase "throwing like a girl" has become an embattled and offensive one. Feminists smart at its implication that to do something "like a girl" is to do it the wrong way. Recently, on the heels of the O. J. Simpson case, a book appeared in which the phrase was used to help explain why male athletes, especially football players, were involved in

rhetorical situations
genres
processes
strategies
research MLA / APA
media / design
handbook

so many assaults against women. Having been trained (like most American boys) to dread the accusation of doing anything "like a girl," athletes were said to grow into the assumption that women were valueless, and natural prey.

By explaining that the topic matters because it reflects attitudes about gender that have potentially serious consequences, he gives readers reason to read on about the mechanics of "throwing like a girl."

Careful attention to correctness. Whether you're writing something formal or informal, in an essay or an email, you should almost always write in complete sentences, use appropriate capitalization and punctuation, and check that your spelling is correct. In general, academic writing is no place for or texting abbreviations. If you're quoting someone, you can reproduce that person's language exactly, but in your own writing you should try hard to be correct — and always proofread carefully.

Thinking about an Academic Rhetorical Situation

- *What* GENRE *does the assignment require?* An essay? If so, is it a narrative, a report, a reflection, an analysis, an argument, or something else? Does the assignment specify the genre, or if not, can you figure out what's required from the verb or other key terms in the assignment wording? If not, do you get to CHOOSE YOUR GENRE?   ■ 9–11   ▲ 243–48

- *What do you see as your instructor's purpose for this assignment?* To have you demonstrate learning of some kind? Show your understanding of course material? Discuss ideas, concepts, or facts? Explore ideas and look for connections among them? Have you been given a description of what your writing should include?

- *What is your* PURPOSE *as the writer, apart from fulfilling your instructor's expectations?* To persuade your audience to do or believe something? To inform them about something and help them understand it? To play with ideas and see where they lead?   ■ 3–4

5–8
- *Who is your* **AUDIENCE?** Your instructor? your classmates? others? How much does the audience know about the topic? Are they in an academic field with particular conventions you need to follow?

12–15
- *How can you convey a confident, authoritative* **STANCE?** By showing that you understand the larger context of your topic? By showing confidence in what you say? By stating your claims forthrightly and clearly? By adopting a tone appropriate for your genre?

16–18
- *What* **MEDIA** *are available, permitted, and appropriate? Are any required?* Will you present your work as a paper document? As a digital text? As an oral presentation? Can you — and should you — use photos, drawings, charts, graphs, or slides or embed audio or video files?

16–18
- *What* **DESIGN** *issues need to be considered?* Should you assume that your written text should follow MLA or APA formatting guidelines? Do you need to include any visual or audio elements? How much freedom do you have to design your work?

part 2

Genres

When we make a shopping list, we automatically write each item we need in a single column. When we email a friend, we begin with a salutation: "Hi, Brian." Whether we are writing a letter, a résumé, a lab report, or a proposal, we know generally what it should contain and what it should look like because we are familiar with each of those genres. Genres are kinds of writing, and texts in any given genre share goals and features—a proposal, for instance, generally starts out by identifying a problem and then suggests a certain solution. The chapters in this part provide guidelines for writing in thirteen common academic genres. First come detailed chapters on four genres often assigned in writing classes: LITERACY NARRATIVES, essays ANALYZING TEXTS, REPORTS, and ARGUMENTS, followed by brief chapters on NINE OTHER GENRES and two on MIXING and CHOOSING GENRES.

25

Genres

Writing a Literacy Narrative **7**

Narratives are stories, and we read and tell them for many different purposes. Parents read their children bedtime stories as an evening ritual. Preachers base their Sunday sermons on Bible stories to teach lessons about moral behavior. Grandparents tell how things used to be (sometimes the same stories year after year). Schoolchildren tell teachers that their dog ate their homework. College applicants write about significant moments in their lives. Writing students are often called upon to compose literacy narratives to explore their experiences with reading and writing. This chapter provides detailed guidelines for writing a literacy narrative. We'll begin with four good examples, the first annotated to point out the key features found in most literacy narratives.

EMILY VALLOWE

Write or Wrong Identity

Emily Vallowe wrote this literacy narrative for a writing class at the University of Mary Washington in Virginia. In it, she explores her lifelong identity as a writer — and her doubts about that identity.

I'm sitting in the woods with a bunch of Catholic people I just met yesterday. Suddenly, they ask me to name one of the talents God has given me. I panic for a split second and then breathe an internal sigh of relief. I tell them I'm a writer. As the group leaders move on to question someone else, I sit trying to mentally catch my breath. It will take a moment before the terror leaves my forearms, chest, and stomach,

Attention-getting opening.

27

but I tell myself that I have nothing to fear. I am a writer. Yes, I most definitely am a writer. *Now breathe*, I tell myself . . . *and suppress that horrifying suspicion that you are actually not a writer at all.*

The retreat that prepared me for my eighth-grade confirmation was not the first time I found myself pulling out the old "I'm a writer" card and wondering whether I was worthy enough to carry this sacred card in the wallet of my identity. Such things happen to people with identity crises.

Clearly described details.

In kindergarten I wrote about thirty books. They were each about five pages long, with one sentence and a picture on each page. They were held together with three staples on the left side or top and had construction paper covers with the book's title and the phrase "By Emily Vallowe" written out in neat kindergarten-teacher handwriting. My mom still has all of these books in a box at the bottom of her closet.

One day at the very end of the school year, my kindergarten teacher took me to meet my future first-grade teacher, Mrs. Meadows. I got to make a special trip to meet her because I had been absent on the day the rest of the kindergarteners had gone to meet their future teachers. Mrs. Meadows's classroom was big and blue and different from the kindergarten class, complete with bigger, different kids (I think Mrs. Meadows had been teaching third or fourth graders that year, so her students were much older than I was). During this visit, Mrs. Meadows showed me a special writing desk, complete with a small, old-fashioned desk lamp (with a lamp shade and everything). I'm not sure if I understood why she was showing me this writing area. She may have said that she'd heard good things about me.

Vallowe traces her identity as a writer through her life.

This handful of images is all I can remember about the most sig- 5
nificant event in my writing life. I'm not sure why I connect the memory of my kindergarten books with the image of me sitting in Mrs. Meadows's old classroom (for by the time I had her she was in a room on the opposite side of the school). I guess I don't even know exactly when this major event happened. Was it kindergarten? First grade? Somewhere in between? All I know is that some event occurred in early elementary school that made me want to be a writer. I don't even clearly remember what this event was, but it is something that has actively affected me for the fourteen years since then.

I have wanted to be a writer my entire life — or at least that's what I tell people. Looking back, I don't know if I ever *wanted* to be a writer. The idea might never have even occurred to me. Yet somehow I was marked as a writer. My teachers must have seen something in my writing that impressed them and clued me in on it. Teachers like to recognize kids for their strengths, and at the age of five, I probably started to notice that different kids were good at different things: Bobby was good at t-ball; Sally was good at drawing; Jenny could run really fast. I was probably starting to panic at the thought that I might not be good at anything — and then a teacher came along and told me I was good at writing. Someone gave me a compliment, and I ran with it. I declared myself to be a writer and have clung to this writer identity ever since.

There are certain drawbacks to clinging to one unchanging identity since the age of five. Constant panic is one of these drawbacks. It is a strange feeling to grow up defining yourself as something when you don't know if that something is actually true. By the time I got to middle school, I could no longer remember having become a writer; I had just always been one — and had been one without any proof that I deserved to be called one. By the age of ten, I was facing a seasoned writer's terror of "am I any good?!" and this terror has followed me throughout my entire life since then. Every writing assignment I ever had was a test — a test to see if I was a real writer, to prove myself to teachers, to classmates, to myself. I approached every writing assignment thinking, "I am supposed to be good at this," not "I am going to try to make this good," and such an attitude is not a healthy way to approach anything.

It doesn't help that, if I am a writer, I am a very slow one. I can't sit down and instantly write something beautiful like some people I know can. I have been fortunate to go to school with some very smart classmates, some of whom can whip out a great piece of writing in minutes. I still find these people threatening. If they are faster than I am, does that make them better writers than I am? *I thought I was supposed to be "the writer"!*

My obsession with being "the" writer stems from my understanding of what it means to be "the" anything. My childhood was marked by a belief in many abstract absolutes that I am only now allowing to crumble. I was born in Chicago (and was thus the fourth

Ongoing discussion of the central issue: is she a writer or not?

generation of my family to live there), but I grew up in northern Virginia. I came to look down on my Virginia surroundings because I had been taught to view Chicago as this great Mecca — the world's most amazing city to which I must someday return, and to which all other places on earth pale in comparison. Throughout my childhood, I gathered that Chicago is a real city in which average people live and which has an economy historically based in shipping and manufacturing; Washington, D.C., on the other hand, where my dad works, has a population that includes a bizarre mix of impoverished people and the most influential leaders and diplomats in the world — and so manufactures nothing but political power. People in Chicago know how to deal with snow; Virginians panic at the *possibility* of snow. Chicago rests on soil that is so fertile it's *black*; Virginia does not even have soil — it has reddish clay suitable for growing nothing except tobacco. Even Chicago's tap water tastes amazing; D.C.'s tap water is poisoned with lead. I grew up thinking that every aspect of Chicago was perfect — so perfect that Chicago became glorious to the point of abstraction. No other city could compare, and after a while I forgot *why* no other city could compare. I just knew that Chicago was "the" city . . . and that if "the" city exists, there must also be an abstract "the" everything.

Vallowe examines the roots of her identity as a writer — and why she questions that identity.

I grew up with this and many other abstract ideals that I would 10 defend against my friends' attacks . . . until I learned that they were just abstractions — and so was I. My writing identity was just another ideal, an absolute that I clung to without any basis in fact. I used to use writing as an easy way to define myself on those over-simplistic surveys teachers always asked us to fill out in elementary and middle school — the surveys that assumed that someone could know all about me simply by finding out my favorite color, my favorite TV show, or my hobbies. I used to casually throw out the "I'm a writer" card just to get these silly surveys over with. "I'm a writer" was just an easy answer to the complicated question, "Who are you?" I always thought the surveys avoided asking this question, but maybe I was the one avoiding it. For years, I had been defining myself as "the writer" without really pondering what this writer identity meant. Is a writer simply someone who writes all the time? Well, I often went through long stretches in which I did not write anything, so this definition did not seem to suit me. Is a writer someone who is good at writing? Well, I've already mentioned that I've been having "am I any good?!" thoughts since elementary school, so this definition didn't seem to fit me, either. I was identifying myself as "the writer" as an abstraction, without any just cause to do so.

The funny thing is that I recognized my writing identity as an abstract ideal before I recognized any of the other ideals I was clinging to, but that didn't make the situation any better. It is one thing to learn that dead people have been voting in Chicago elections for decades, and so perhaps Chicago isn't the perfect city, but what happens when the absolute ideal is you? More important, what would happen if *this* absolute were to crumble? It was terrifying to think that I might discover that I was not a writer because to not be a writer was to suddenly be nothing. If a writer was the only thing that I had ever been, what would happen if writing was a lie? I would vanish. Looking back, the logical part of my brain tells me that, if I am not a writer, I am still plenty of other things: I am a Catholic; I am a Vallowe; people tell me that I have other good qualities. But when facing these horrifying spells of writer's doubt, my brain doesn't see these other things. I am driven only by the fear of nothingness and the thought that I have to be a writer because I'm not good at anything else.

Am I really not good at anything else? I used to blame this entire writer's complex on whoever it was that told me I was a writer. If that person hadn't channeled this burdensome identity into me, I might never have expected great literary things from myself, and life would have been easier. I had these thoughts until one day in high school I mentioned something to my mom about the fact that I'd been writing since I was five years old. My mom corrected me by saying that I'd been writing since I was three years old. At the age of three I couldn't even physically form letters, but apparently I would dictate stories to my mom on a regular basis. My mom explained to me how I would run to her and say, "Mommy, Mommy, write my story for me!"

This new information was both comforting and unsettling. On one hand, it was a great relief to know that I had been a writer all along— that I would have been a writer even if no one had told me that I was one. On the other hand, the knowledge that I had been a writer all along drove me into an entirely new realm of panic.

I've been a writer my entire life?
WHAT?!

She continues to explore her identity as a writer.

15

I've been a writer since I was three? Three? *Three* years old: How is that even possible? I didn't know it was possible to be anything at age three, let alone the thing that might define me for my entire life.

I have been taught that each person has a vocation — a calling that he or she must use to spread God's love to others. Yet I've also assumed that one must go on some sort of journey to figure out what this vocation is. If I found my vocation at the age of three, have I skipped this journey? And if I've skipped the journey, does that mean that the vocation isn't real? Or am I just really lucky for having found my vocation so early? Was I really born a writer? Was I born to do one thing and will I do that one thing for my entire life? Can anything be that consistent? That simple? And if I am living out some divine vocation, is that any comfort at all? If I am channeling some divine being in my writing, and everything I write comes from some outside source, where does that leave me? Am I nothing even if I am a writer?

This questioning has not led me to any comforting conclusions. I still wonder if my writer identity has been thrust upon me, and what it means to have someone else determine who I am. If I am a writer, then I am someone who passionately seeks originality — someone who gets pleasure from inventing entire fictional worlds. Yet if someone — either a teacher or a divine being — is channeling an identity into me, then I am no more original than the characters that I create in my fiction. If my identity is not original, then this identity is not real, and if I am not real . . . I can't even finish this sentence.

I don't know if I really wrote thirty books in kindergarten. It might have been twenty — or fifteen — or ten — or five. I might have made up that part about the special writing desk in Mrs. Meadows's old classroom. I don't know if God predestined me to write masterpieces or if a teacher just casually mentioned that I wrote well and I completely overreacted to the compliment. Questioning my identity as "the writer" has led me to new levels of fear and uncertainty, but this questioning is not going to stop. Even if I one day sit, withered and gray, with a Nobel Prize for Literature proudly displayed on my desk as I try to crank out one last novel at the age of ninety-two, my thoughts will probably drift back to Mrs. Meadows and those books I wrote in kindergarten. In my old age, I still might not understand my writer identity,

Ending refers back to the opening anecdote.

Conclusion is tentative (since the end of the story is decades in the future).

but maybe by that point, I will have written a novel about a character with an identity crisis — and maybe the character will have come through all right.

In this literacy narrative, Vallowe reflects on the origins of her identity as a writer: her early teachers, her parents, God, herself. The significance of her story lies in her inability to settle on any one of these possibilities.

MARJORIE AGOSÍN

Always Living in Spanish: Recovering the Familiar, through Language

Marjorie Agosín, a Spanish professor at Wellesley College, wrote this literacy narrative for Poets & Writers *magazine in 1999. Originally written in Spanish, it tells of Agosín's Chilean childhood and her continuing connection to the Spanish language.*

In the evenings in the northern hemisphere, I repeat the ancient ritual that I observed as a child in the southern hemisphere: going out while the night is still warm and trying to recognize the stars as it begins to grow dark silently. In the sky of my country, Chile, that long and wide stretch of land that the poets blessed and dictators abused, I could easily name the stars: the three Marias, the Southern Cross, and the three Lilies, names of beloved and courageous women.

But here in the United States, where I have lived since I was a young girl, the solitude of exile makes me feel that so little is mine, that not even the sky has the same constellations, the trees and the fauna the same names or sounds, or the rubbish the same smell. How does one recover the familiar? How does one name the unfamiliar? How can one be another or live in a foreign language? These are the dilemmas of one who writes in Spanish and lives in translation.

Since my earliest childhood in Chile I lived with the tempos and the melodies of a multiplicity of tongues: German, Yiddish, Russian, Turkish, and many Latin songs. Because everyone was from somewhere else, my relatives laughed, sang, and fought in a Babylon of languages. Spanish was reserved for matters of extreme seriousness, for commercial transactions, or for illnesses, but everyone's mother tongue was always associated with the memory of spaces inhabited in the past: the shtetl, the flowering and vast Vienna avenues, the minarets of Turkey, and the Ladino whispers of Toledo. When my paternal grandmother sang old songs in Turkish, her voice and body assumed the passion of one who was there in the city of Istanbul, gazing by turns toward the west and the east.

Destiny and the always ambiguous nature of history continued my family's enforced migration, and because of it I, too, became one who had to live and speak in translation. The disappearances, torture, and clandestine deaths in my country in the early seventies drove us to the United States, that other America that looked with suspicion at those who did not speak English and especially those who came from the supposedly uncivilized regions of Latin America. I had left a dangerous place that was my home, only to arrive in a dangerous place that was not: a high school in the small town of Athens, Georgia, where my poor English and my accent were the cause of ridicule and insult. The only way I could recover my usurped country and my Chilean childhood was by continuing to write in Spanish, the same way my grandparents had sung in their own tongues in diasporic sites.

The new and learned English language did not fit with the visceral 5 emotions and themes that my poetry contained, but by writing in Spanish I could recover fragrances, spoken rhythms, and the passion of my own identity. Daily I felt the need to translate myself for the strangers living all around me, to tell them why we were in Georgia, why we are different, why we had fled, why my accent was so thick, and why I did not look Hispanic. Only at night, writing poems in Spanish, could I return to my senses, and soothe my own sorrow over what I had left behind.

This is how I became a Chilean poet who wrote in Spanish and lived in the southern United States. And then, one day, a poem of mine was translated and published in the English language. Finally, for the first time since I had left Chile, I felt I didn't have to explain myself. My poem, expressed in another language, spoke for itself . . . and for me.

Sometimes the austere sounds of English help me bear the solitude of knowing that I am foreign and so far away from those about whom

rhetorical situations

genres

processes

strategies

research MLA / APA

media / design

handbook

I write. I must admit I would like more opportunities to read in Spanish to people whose language and culture is also mine, to join in our common heritage and in the feast of our sounds. I would also like readers of English to understand the beauty of the spoken word in Spanish, that constant flow of oxytonic and paraoxytonic syllables (*Vérde qué té quiéro vérde*),* the joy of writing — of dancing — in another language. I believe that many exiles share the unresolvable torment of not being able to live in the language of their childhood.

I miss that undulating and sensuous language of mine, those baroque descriptions, the sense of being and feeling that Spanish gives me. It is perhaps for this reason that I have chosen and will always choose to write in Spanish. Nothing else from my childhood world remains. My country seems to be frozen in gestures of silence and oblivion. My relatives have died, and I have grown up not knowing a young generation of cousins and nieces and nephews. Many of my friends were disappeared, others were tortured, and the most fortunate, like me, became guardians of memory. For us, to write in Spanish is to always be in active pursuit of memory. I seek to recapture a world lost to me on that sorrowful afternoon when the blue electric sky and the Andean cordillera bade me farewell. On that, my last Chilean day, I carried under my arm my innocence recorded in a little blue notebook I kept even then. Gradually that diary filled with memoranda, poems written in free verse, descriptions of dreams and of the thresholds of my house surrounded by cherry trees and gardenias. To write in Spanish is for me a gesture of survival. And because of translation, my memory has now become a part of the memory of many others.

Translators are not traitors, as the proverb says, but rather splendid friends in this great human community of language.

Agosín's narrative uses vivid detail to bring her childhood in Chile to life for her readers. Her love for her homeland and its people is clear, as is the significance of her narrative — with her childhood home gone, to write in Spanish is a "gesture of survival."

---

*"*Vérde qué té quiéro vérde*" ("Green, how I want you, green") is the opening line of a famous Spanish poem that demonstrates the interplay of words with the main stress on the final syllable (oxytonic) and those with the main stress on the next-to-last syllable (paroxytonic) in Spanish. [Editor's note]

SHANNON NICHOLS

"Proficiency"

In the following literacy narrative, Shannon Nichols, a student at Wright State University, describes her experience taking the standardized writing proficiency test that high school students in Ohio must pass to graduate. She wrote this essay for a college writing course, where her audience included her classmates and instructor.

The first time I took the ninth-grade proficiency test was in March of eighth grade. The test ultimately determines whether students may receive a high school diploma. After months of preparation and anxiety, the pressure was on. Throughout my elementary and middle school years, I was a strong student, always on the honor roll. I never had a GPA below 3.0. I was smart, and I knew it. That is, until I got the results of the proficiency test.

Although the test was challenging, covering reading, writing, math, and citizenship, I was sure I had passed every part. To my surprise, I did pass every part — except writing. "Writing! Yeah right! How did I manage to fail writing, and by half a point, no less?" I thought to myself in disbelief. Seeing my test results brought tears to my eyes. I honestly could not believe it. To make matters worse, most of my classmates, including some who were barely passing eighth-grade English, passed that part.

Until that time, I loved writing just as much as I loved math. It was one of my strengths. I was good at it, and I enjoyed it. If anything, I thought I might fail citizenship. How could I have screwed up writing? I surely spelled every word correctly, used good grammar, and even used big words in the proper context. How could I have failed?

Finally I got over it and decided it was no big deal. Surely I would pass the next time. In my honors English class I worked diligently, passing with an A. By October I'd be ready to conquer that writing test. Well, guess what? I failed the test again, again with only 4.5 of the 5 points needed to pass. That time I did cry, and even went to my English teacher, Mrs. Brown, and asked, "How can I get A's in all my English classes but fail the writing part of the proficiency test twice?" She couldn't answer my question. Even my friends and classmates were confused. I felt like a failure. I had disappointed my family and seriously let myself down. Worst of all, I still couldn't figure out what I was doing wrong.

I decided to quit trying so hard. Apparently—I told myself—the people grading the tests didn't have the slightest clue about what constituted good writing. I continued to excel in class and passed the test on the third try. But I never again felt the same love of reading and writing.

This experience showed me just how differently my writing could be judged by various readers. Obviously all my English teachers and many others enjoyed or at least appreciated my writing. A poem I wrote was put on television once. I must have been a pretty good writer. Unfortunately the graders of the ninth-grade proficiency test didn't feel the same, and when students fail the test, the state of Ohio doesn't offer any explanation.

After I failed the test the first time, I began to hate writing, and I started to doubt myself. I doubted my ability and the ideas I wrote about. Failing the second time made things worse, so perhaps to protect myself from my doubts, I stopped taking English seriously. Perhaps because of that lack of seriousness, I earned a 2 on the Advanced Placement English Exam, barely passed the twelfth-grade proficiency test, and was placed in developmental writing in college. I wish I knew why I failed that test because then I might have written what was expected on the second try, maintained my enthusiasm for writing, and continued to do well.

Nichols's narrative focuses on her emotional reaction to failing a test that she should have passed easily. The contrast between her demonstrated writing ability and her repeated failures creates a tension that captures readers' attention. We want to know what will happen to her.

SOFIA GOMEZ
Mother Goose in Monterrey

In this literacy narrative from Ohio State's Digital Archive of Literacy Narratives, Sofia Gomez describes how she learned English, both at home and at school, in her native Mexico. In the online version, available via wwnorton.com/write/ fieldguidelinks, she also includes the video of herself and her brother and sister that she describes in the text.

I wish that I could memorize my class curriculum as easily as I memorized Timon and Pumba's arguments, or Iago's witty complaints, or Pocahontas's explanation of her strange dream. I know these things (by heart) now because as a little girl, I used to watch Disney movies over and over. At the time it seemed like a great pastime, but looking back, I'm grateful to see that these movies did way more than just entertain me: they helped me learn English.

When you're a child, everything around you is a learning experience. So when you're exposed to foreign things, like a new language, they are assimilated as much as any other lesson like learning manners or learning to count. I think that introducing a second language for children is an advantage, since their minds are much more receptive to new things than when they're adults.

My English education started mainly at home. I grew up in a small town called Montemorelos, an hour away from Monterrey, Mexico's second-largest industrial city. Being so close to the American border, my family made very frequent shopping trips to Texas. Every so often, we would go to McAllen, Texas, to buy some clothes, household items, and if we were lucky, a new movie. At home we didn't have cable, so if we watched anything on TV it would be a movie, probably a Disney classic or a *Sesame Street* video. If I look them up now, we're probably missing only a couple of movies from the entire classics collection.

We children loved watching movies in English so much that we would hate it when we got a translated version of an American movie. As we grew older (before DVD was invented), we would avoid buying movies in Mexico because the dialogue wasn't the same for us if it wasn't in the original language: English. In fact, we only had two movies in Spanish — *Pocahontas* and *The Aristocats* — and eventually we were insistent enough that we got a second copy of them in English.

We also read a lot in English. One of my aunts was the head of the English department of a school in Monterrey, so every time she ordered English textbooks, my mom would ask her to order a few extra ones for me and my siblings. Every night we read an English book and a Spanish book, to the point of memorizing them. So I knew all the traditional Mexican nursery rhymes, like Cri Cri and others, but I also learned about Mother Goose and other classic English children's

5

stories like "Five Little Monkeys," "The Wheels on the Bus," "Three Little Kittens," and "The Little Red Hen." We also had Disney books about the movies we watched and about other stories as well. (I dare anyone to challenge me on Disney trivia, because I'll probably kick their butts.)

We read like crazy. At some point, my mom would take her jumbo clear Scotch tape and reinforce the bindings on each page because some books were falling apart from so much use. We even had several copies of the same book, either by chance or because my mom thought that four children in the same household might need a bigger library. There's a very funny home video in which my younger brother and sister are arguing about holding a book, and I randomly cross the frame, storm away frustrated from hearing them bicker, come back with the second copy of the book, give it to them so they would stop arguing, and then without a word walk away to return to whatever I was doing.

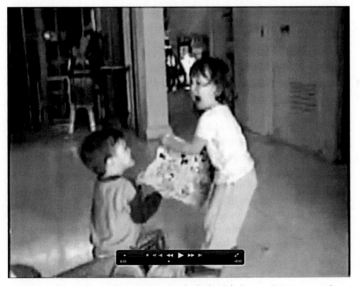

A scene from the video Gomez included with her written narrative.

I attended a very small and conservative Catholic school, in Montemorelos, where I received very basic English lessons for only a couple of hours a week. My parents wanted us to learn more English, so we took private afternoon lessons with a good teacher from Canada. We also traveled twice to Canada to attend YMCA summer camps, and where my brothers and I got the opportunity of being immersed into an English-speaking environment. The first time, I remember being struck by the fact that everyone around me was speaking English and that I had no choice but to make an effort and do so myself. The second time, however, I found myself much more comfortable being around children who didn't speak my first language, and even though I wasn't as fluent as I am now, I managed to make lots of friends in spite of my limited English.

All this experience came in handy when my family decided to move to the big city and pursue a better grade school education for us. Private schools in Monterrey are very expensive, competitive, and selective. My parents worked hard to find the right one for us, and more important, to get us accepted into it. After an arduous search, they narrowed the choice down to two schools. One of them, very highly regarded, rejected us out of hand. The people in charge of admissions said we did not have the necessary bilingual education to catch up with the rest of the students, although they didn't bother to test us on our English or on other subjects, for that matter. All they saw was the name of our small Catholic school, and they turned us down. The other school, however, the American Institute of Monterrey (AIM), opened its doors to us, assisting us in the transition from a monolingual to a bilingual school. I was very nervous about being a new student, not only because I had to meet new people and try to fit in but also because the AIM was bigger, bolder, and quite frankly, so foreign compared to our little small-town Catholic school.

The summer we moved to Monterrey, we were assigned teachers by the AIM to prepare us to enter a bilingual school. I was assigned to Miss Ale, who taught in her house, in a ranch a few minutes outside the city. She instructed me in some math and spelling but mostly in English grammar. What I remember the most about her lessons were her two black Doberman dogs, which were always around and scared the English out of me. At times, she would let me work by myself on short assignments and would leave the room. The dogs would watch me work, sometimes circle the table a few times, and every once in a while growl to each other. I felt like they were judging me, and their presence would force me to concentrate on my work. I remember trying to finish faster and accurately so as to get Miss Ale to come back and spare me the guard dogs. It wasn't until five weeks later, when Miss Ale talked to my mother about my progress and how well I worked by myself, that I realized I had greatly improved my English skills. The day of our last lesson, my older brother came along. While Miss Ale and I wrapped up our remedial course, he played outside with the dogs. When my lesson was over, I found myself going out and joining them. The dogs weren't so scary anymore, and neither was entering a new bilingual school.

Literacy transitions are always complicated. As Mike Rose points 10 out in *Lives on the Boundary*, struggling with writing or reading does not mark a person as "illiterate." In his book, he discusses some students in remedial classes he observed who participated very effectively in the classroom, contributing valuable points to the lesson. "These are [supposedly] the truly illiterate among us," Rose remarks. His story resonates with mine and helped me understand that aptitude is not always measured by grades but by life experiences and the education one receives at home when growing up. Just because I needed help adapting to a new environment, especially one involving a second language, doesn't mean I was poorly educated.

I started my AIM life in August 1998, as I entered the fifth grade. Four years later, the Monterrey Institute of Technology and Superior Studies (ITESM), the largest combined high school and university in all of Mexico, granted me an Excellence Scholarship for high school, an honor given to the graduating secondary (middle-school) student of each private school in Monterrey with the highest grade in his or her class. After secondary school, most students in Monterrey who go on to high school attend the same one: ITESM. I was surprised to find out that Lili Tello, the student in the ITESM class with the Excellence Scholarship from that school that had rejected us four years ago, had a lower grade than I. My mother likes to brag about this, but I like to think of it as a way of showing how things are not always what they seem, and that education, especially early education, comes from many places (mostly home) and not just from school.

Today, Lili and I are great friends. We developed a strong partnership in high school, working together on projects and such since we have similar temperaments regarding school. It's a shame I didn't get to meet her sooner (in her school) when we first moved to Monterrey, but I wouldn't trade my AIM experience, or any other English preparation I had, for the world.

Gomez's narrative tells of her parents' efforts to give their children a good education and strong grounding in English. Vivid details, from the tape holding the family's books together to a teacher's Dobermans, bring her narrative to life — as does the video of her brother and sister fighting over a book.

Key Features / Literacy Narratives

A well-told story.   As with most narratives, those about literacy often set up some sort of situation that needs to be resolved. That need for resolution makes readers want to keep reading. We want to know whether Nichols ultimately will pass the proficiency test. Some literacy narratives simply explore the role that reading or writing played at some time in someone's life — assuming, perhaps, that learning to read or write is a challenge to be met.

Vivid detail.   Details can bring a narrative to life for readers by giving them vivid mental sensations of the sights, sounds, smells, tastes, and textures of the world in which your story takes place. The details you use when describing something can help readers picture places, people, and events; dialogue can help them hear what is being said. We get a picture of Agosín's Chilean childhood when she writes of the "blue electric sky" and her "little blue notebook" in which she described her "house surrounded by cherry trees and gardenias." We can see the tutor's dogs circling the table where Gomez was trying to work and hear them "growl to each other." Similarly, we can picture and hear Vallowe as a little girl running to her mother and saying, "Mommy, Mommy, write my story for me!"

Sometimes you can provide detail through visuals or audio, as Gomez does with her home video.

Some indication of the narrative's significance. By definition, a literacy narrative tells something the writer remembers about learning to read or write. In addition, the writer needs to make clear why the incident matters to him or her. You may reveal its significance in various ways. Nichols does it when she says she no longer loves to read or write. Agosín points out that she writes in Spanish because "nothing else from my childhood world remains. . . . To write in Spanish is for me a gesture of survival." The trick is to avoid tacking a brief statement about your narrative's significance onto the end as if it were a kind of moral of the story. Vallowe's narrative would be less effective if, instead of questioning her identity as a writer from several perspectives, she had simply said, "I became a writer at the age of three."

A GUIDE TO WRITING LITERACY NARRATIVES

Choosing a Topic

In general, it's a good idea to focus on a single event that took place during a relatively brief period of time. For example:

- any early memory about writing or reading that you recall vividly
- someone who taught you to read or write
- a book or other text that has been significant for you in some way
- an event at school that was related to reading or writing and that you found interesting, humorous, or embarrassing
- a writing or reading task that you found (or still find) especially difficult or challenging
- a memento that represents an important moment in your literacy development (perhaps the start of a **LITERACY PORTFOLIO**)   295–96
- the origins of your current attitudes about writing or reading

- learning to text, learning to write email appropriately, creating and maintaining a *Facebook* page or blog

Make a list of possible topics, and then choose one that you think will be interesting to you and to others — and that you're willing to share with others. If several seem promising, try them out on a friend or classmate. Or just choose one and see where it leads; you can switch to another if need be. If you have trouble coming up with a topic, try **FREEWRITING, LISTING, CLUSTERING,** or **LOOPING.**

259–62

Considering the Rhetorical Situation

3–4

PURPOSE Why do you want to tell this story? To share a memory with others? To fulfill an assignment? To teach a lesson? To explore your past learning? Think about the reasons for your choice and how they will shape what you write.

5–8

AUDIENCE Are your readers likely to have had similar experiences? Would they tell similar stories? How much explaining will you have to do to help them understand your narrative? Can you assume that they will share your attitudes toward your story, or will you have to work at making them see your perspective? How much about your life are you willing to share with this audience?

12–15

STANCE What attitude do you want to project? Affectionate? Neutral? Critical? Do you wish to be sincere? serious? humorously detached? self-critical? self-effacing? something else? How do you want your readers to see you?

16–18

MEDIA / DESIGN Will your narrative be in print? presented orally? online? Should you use photos, tables, graphs, or video or audio clips? Is there a font that conveys the right tone? Do you need headings?

Generating Ideas and Text

Good literacy narratives share certain elements that make them interesting and compelling for readers. Remember that your goals are to tell the story as clearly and vividly as you can and to convey the meaning the incident has for you today. Start by writing out what you remember about the setting and those involved, perhaps trying out some of the methods in the chapter on GENERATING IDEAS AND TEXT. You may also want to INTERVIEW a teacher or parent who figures in your narrative.

259–65
448–49

Describe the setting.   Where does your narrative take place? List the places where your story unfolds. For each place, write informally for a few minutes, DESCRIBING what you remember:

367–75

- *What do you see?* If you're inside, what color are the walls? What's hanging on them? What can you see out any windows? What else do you see? Books? Lined paper? Red ink? Are there people? places to sit? a desk or a table?
- *What do you hear?* A radiator hissing? Leaves rustling? The wind howling? Rain? Someone reading aloud? Shouts? Cheers? Children playing? Music? The zing of an instant message arriving?
- *What do you smell?* Sweat? Perfume? Incense? Food cooking?
- *How and what do you feel?* Nervous? Happy? Cold? Hot? A scratchy wool sweater? Tight shoes? Rough wood on a bench?
- *What do you taste?* Gum? Mints? Graham crackers? Juice? Coffee?

Think about the key people.   Narratives include people whose actions play an important role in the story. In your literacy narrative, you are probably one of those people. A good way to develop your understanding of the people in your narrative is to write about them:

- *Describe each person in a paragraph or so.* What do the people look like? How do they dress? How do they speak? Quickly? Slowly? With an accent? Do they speak clearly, or do they mumble? Do they use any distinctive words or phrases? You might begin by describing their movements, their posture, their bearing, their facial expressions. Do they have a distinctive scent?

- *Recall (or imagine) some characteristic dialogue.* A good way to bring people to life and move a story along is with **DIALOGUE,** to let readers hear them rather than just hearing about them. Try writing six to ten lines of dialogue between two people in your narrative. If you can't remember an actual conversation, make up one that could have happened. (After all, you are telling the story, and you get to decide how it is to be told.) Try to remember (and write down) some of the characteristic words or phrases that the people in your narrative used.

376–81

Write about "what happened."   At the heart of every good **NARRATIVE** is the answer to the question "What happened?" The action in a literacy narrative may be as dramatic as winning a spelling bee or as subtle as a conversation between two friends; both contain action, movement, or change that the narrative tries to capture for readers. A good story dramatizes the action. Try **SUMMARIZING** the action in your narrative in a paragraph — try to capture what happened. Use active and specific verbs (*pondered*, *shouted*, *laughed*) to describe the action as vividly as possible.

387–95
407–8

Consider the significance of the narrative.   You need to make clear the ways in which any event you are writing about is significant for you now. Write a page or so about the meaning it has for you. How did it change or otherwise affect you? What aspects of your life now can you trace to that event? How might your life have been different if this event had not happened or had turned out differently? Why does this story matter to you?

Ways of Organizing a Literacy Narrative

Start by **OUTLINING** the main events in your narrative. Then think about how you want to tell the story. Don't assume that the only way to tell your story is just as it happened. That's one way — starting at the beginning of the action and continuing to the end. But you could also start in the middle — or even at the end. Shannon Nichols, for example, could have begun her narrative by telling how she finally passed the proficiency test

263–64

and then gone back to tell about the times she tried to pass it, even as she was an A student in an honors English class. Several ways of organizing a narrative follow.

[Chronologically, from beginning to end]

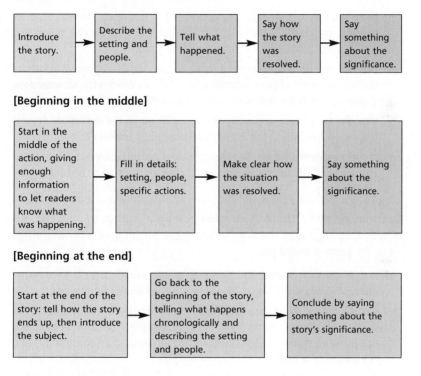

| Introduce the story. | Describe the setting and people. | Tell what happened. | Say how the story was resolved. | Say something about the significance. |

[Beginning in the middle]

| Start in the middle of the action, giving enough information to let readers know what was happening. | Fill in details: setting, people, specific actions. | Make clear how the situation was resolved. | Say something about the significance. |

[Beginning at the end]

| Start at the end of the story: tell how the story ends up, then introduce the subject. | Go back to the beginning of the story, telling what happens chronologically and describing the setting and people. | Conclude by saying something about the story's significance. |

Writing Out a Draft

Once you have generated ideas and thought about how you want to organize your narrative, it's time to begin **DRAFTING.** Do this quickly—try to write a complete draft in one sitting, concentrating on getting the story on paper or screen and on putting in as much detail as you can. Some writers find

266–68

it helpful to work on the beginning or ending first. Others write out the main event first and then draft the beginning and ending.

299–306 **Draft a BEGINNING.**   A good narrative grabs readers' attention right from the start. Here are some ways of beginning:

- *Jump right in.* Sometimes you may want to get to the main action as quickly as possible. Nichols, for example, begins as she takes the ninth-grade proficiency test for the first time.

- *Describe the context.* You may want to provide background information at the start of your narrative, as Vallowe does with an anecdote exposing her fears that she may not be who she thinks she is.

- *Describe the setting, especially if it's important to the narrative.* Agosín begins by describing the constellations in her native Chile.

- *Provoke readers' interest.* Gomez opens her narrative by describing how she watched Disney movies over and over, memorizing the main characters' lines.

306–10 **Draft an ENDING.**   Think about what you want readers to read last. An effective ending helps them understand the meaning of your narrative. Here are some possibilities:

- *End where your story ends.* It's up to you to decide where a narrative ends. Vallowe ends far in the future, in her imagined old age.

- *Say something about the significance of your narrative.* Nichols observes that she no longer loves to write, for example. The trick is to touch upon the narrative's significance without stating it too directly, like the moral of a fable.

- *Refer back to the beginning.* Vallowe refers back to her kindergarten writing; Nichols ends by contemplating the negative effects of failing the proficiency test.

- *End on a surprising note.* Agosín catches our attention when she tells us of the deaths and disappearances of her friends and relatives.

rhetorical
situations

genres

processes

strategies

research
MLA / APA

media /
design

handbook

Come up with a title.   A good **TITLE** indicates something about the sub- 312–13 ject of your narrative—and makes readers want to take a look. Nichols's title, " 'Proficiency,' " is also her subject; her use of quote marks around this word calls its meaning into question in a way that might make read- ers wonder — and read on. Vallowe focuses on the significance of her nar- rative: "Write or Wrong Identity." Agosín makes her title an expression of her sense of identity: "Always Living in Spanish."

Considering Matters of Design

You'll probably write your narrative in paragraph form, but think about the information you're presenting and how you can design it to enhance your story and appeal to your audience.

- What would be an appropriate **FONT?** Something serious, like Times 585–86 Roman? Something whimsical, like *Comic Sans*? Something else?

- Would it help your readers if you added **HEADINGS** in order to divide 588–89 your narrative into shorter sections?

- Would photographs or other **VISUALS** show details better than you can 591–99 describe them with words alone? If you're writing about learning to read, for example, you might scan in an image of one of the first books you read. Or if your topic is learning to write, you could include some- thing you wrote. You could even include a family video, as Gomez does. Would your narrative best be conveyed as a multimodal com- position that combines written text, images, and video or audio?

Getting Response and Revising

The following questions can help you study your draft with a critical eye. **GETTING RESPONSE** from others is always good, and these questions can 275–76 guide their reading, too. Make sure they know your purpose and audience.

- Do the title and first few sentences make readers want to read on? If not, how else might you begin?

- Is the sequence of events in the narrative clear? Does it flow, and are there effective transitions? Does the narrative get sidetracked at any point?

- Is anything confusing?

- Is there enough detail, and is it interesting? Will readers be able to imagine the setting? Can they picture the characters and sense what they're like? Would it help to add some dialogue, so that readers can "hear" them?

- Are visuals used effectively and integrated smoothly with the written text? If there are no visuals, would using some strengthen the narrative?

- Have you made the narrative meaningful enough for readers so that they wonder and care about what will happen?

- Do you narrate any actions clearly? vividly? Does the action keep readers engaged?

- Is the significance of the narrative clear?

- Is the ending satisfying? What are readers left thinking?

276–79 ◯ The preceding questions should identify aspects of your narrative you need to work on. When it's time to **REVISE,** make sure your text appeals to your audience and achieves your purpose as successfully as possible.

Editing and Proofreading

Readers equate correctness with competence. Once you've revised your draft, follow these guidelines for **EDITING** a narrative:

282–85 ◯

387–95 ◆
317

- Make sure events are **NARRATED** in a clear order and include appropriate time markers, **TRANSITIONS,** and summary phrases to link the parts and show the passing of time.

HB-36 ⋏

- Be careful that **VERB TENSES ARE CONSISTENT** throughout. If you start your narrative in the past tense ("he *taught* me how to use a computer"), be careful not to switch to the present ("So I *look* at him and *say* . . . ") along the way.

- Check to see that **VERB TENSES** correctly indicate when an action took place. If one action took place before another action in the past, for example, you should use the past perfect tense: "I forgot to dot my i's, a mistake I *had made* many times before."

  HB-11–14

- Punctuate **DIALOGUE** correctly. Whenever someone speaks, surround the speech with quotation marks ("No way," I said). Periods and commas go inside quotation marks; exclamation points and question marks go inside if they're part of the quotation, outside if they're part of the whole sentence:

  376–81

INSIDE	Opening the door, Ms. Cordell announced, "Pop quiz!"
OUTSIDE	It wasn't my intention to announce "I hate to read"!

- **PROOFREAD** your finished narrative carefully before turning it in.

  285–86

Taking Stock of Your Work

- How well do you think you told the story?
- What did you do especially well?
- What could still be improved?
- How did you go about coming up with ideas and generating text?
- How did you go about drafting your narrative?
- Did you use photographs or any other visual or audio elements? What did they add? Can you think of such elements you might have used?
- How did others' responses influence your writing?
- What would you do differently next time?

> **IF YOU NEED MORE HELP**
>
> See also **MEMOIRS** (Chapter 15), a kind of narrative that focuses more generally on a significant event from your past, and **REFLECTIONS** (Chapter 18), a kind of essay for thinking about a topic in writing. See Chapter 29 if you are required to submit your literacy narrative as part of a writing **PORTFOLIO.**

183–90
214–21

287–98

8 Analyzing Texts

Both the *Huffington Post* and *National Review Online* cover the same events, but each one interprets them differently. All toothpaste ads claim to make teeth "the whitest." The Environmental Protection Agency is a guardian of America's air, water, and soil — or an unconstitutional impediment to economic growth, depending on which politician is speaking. Those are but three examples that demonstrate why we need to be careful, analytical readers of magazines, newspapers, blogs, websites, ads, political documents, even textbooks. Not only does text convey information, but it also influences how and what we think. We need to read, then, to understand not only what texts say but also how they say it and how they try to persuade or influence us.

Because understanding how texts say what they say and achieve their effects is so crucial, assignments in many disciplines ask you to analyze texts. You may be asked to analyze candidates' speeches in a political science course or to analyze imagery in James Joyce's story "Araby" for a literature class. In a statistics course, you might analyze a set of data — a numerical text — to find the standard deviation from the mean. This chapter offers detailed guidelines for writing an essay that closely examines a text both for what it says and for how it does so, with the goal of demonstrating for readers how — and how well — the text achieves its effects. We'll begin with four good examples, the first annotated to point out the key features found in most textual analyses.

HANNAH BERRY

The Fashion Industry: Free to Be an Individual

Hannah Berry wrote this analysis of two shoe ads for a first-year writing course at Wright State University.

As young women, we have always been told through the medium of advertisement that we must use certain products to make ourselves beautiful. For decades, ads for things like soap, makeup, and mouthwash have established a sort of misplaced control over our lives, telling us what will make us attractive and what will not. Recently, however, a new generation of advertisement has emerged in the fashion industry, one that cleverly equates the products shown in the ads with the quest for confident individuality. Ads such as the two for Clarks and Sorel discussed below encourage us to break free from the standard beauty mold and be ourselves; using mostly imagery, they remind us that being unique is the true origin of beauty.

Attention to the context of the ads Berry will analyze.

Clear thesis.

The first ad promotes Clarks fashion as band geek chic, quite literally raising a unique personality onto a pedestal, with the subject poised on a decorative stone platform as shown in fig. 1. Photographed in standing profile, this quirky-looking young woman is doing what she loves — playing some kind of trumpet — and looks great doing it. She is wearing her hair in a French twist with a strand tucked behind her ear, as if she recently moved it out of her face to play the music she loves without distraction. The downturn of her nose points to the short gray-black dress that stops several inches above her knees but covers her chest and shoulders modestly, with a collar situated at the base of her neck and sleeves that reach for her elbows. The dress is plain, but it is a perfect fit for the personality implied in the photo. Set against the background of a light-tan wall, the model leans back slightly as if supporting the weight of her instrument. Her right knee is bent while her left knee remains straight. The positioning of her legs not only accentuates her unbalanced posture but also points out the pair of simple brown pumps that complete the look. She wears the shoes with a pair of socks in a much darker shade of brown pulled up around her shins. Around her ankles are sandy-colored rings of shaggy fabric that are most likely attached to the socks, giving the whole outfit a sense of nerdy flair. Her expression is a simple mix of calm and concentration. It's as if the photographer happened to take the picture while she was practicing for a school recital.

Description of the first text.

Clarks has taken what looks like your average high school student and dressed her in an outfit that speaks to her own distinctive character and talents. The image sparks the idea that her beauty comes from an internal base of secure self-confidence and moves outward to infuse her physical appearance and sense of style. This ad urges us to celebrate individuality with the right look. Using an image alone, Clarks advertises

Analysis of the first text.

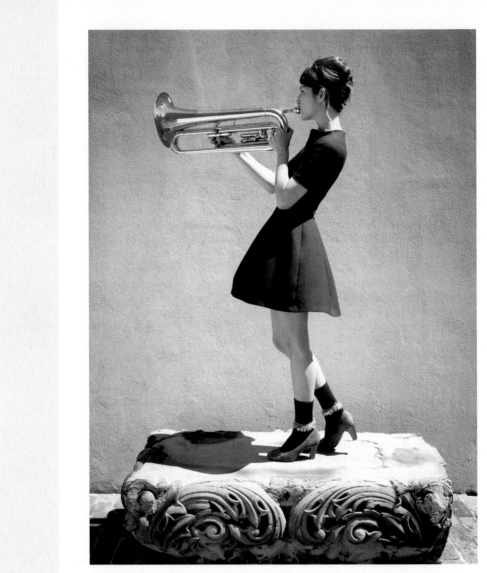

Fig. 1. Clarks ad shows a band geek doing what she loves (Clarks).

rhetorical situations

genres

processes

strategies

research
MLA / APA

media / design

handbook

its products with the simple promise that they will support you in doing what you love and keep you original.

Taking a narrower perspective on originality, the ad for Sorel boots shown in fig. 2 dramatizes the idea that spontaneity is key to a distinctive personal identity. This abstract idea is depicted in a vividly concrete way, using the featured fur-topped boots as a base for encouraging a bold sense of self. The ad dares us to break free from the mold of society and do something "fearless" (Sorel). It shows us a dark-haired, red-lipped woman sitting in a formal French upholstered chair in a dark-blue, elaborately paneled parlor. An expression of triumph and mischief adorns her sultry visage. She's wearing a revealing short white dress that overlaps slightly around her chest and falls strategically over her hips so that large portions of her upper thighs are visible. Feathers in autumn colors cover her shoulders, and a gold belt accentuates her waist. Next to her is a polished wood table supporting a lighted candle, a small glass vase of pink and white flowers, and a black-and-white-patterned orb. There is a dormant, ornate fireplace to her left. But what makes this scene extraordinary is what seems to have taken place moments before the picture was taken. One of the young woman's feet, clad in the devil-red black-laced boots being advertised, rests defiantly on top of the shattered remains of a crystal chandelier. In her right hand, the woman holds an old-looking shotgun with her forefinger still resting on the trigger.

Description of the second text.

In Sorel's explosive ad, it is apparent that the woman not only shot down the ceiling fixture but also has no regrets about doing so. Her white dress represents a sort of purity and innocence that is completely contradicted by the way she wears it — and by the boots. They gave her the power to shoot down the chandelier, the push she needed to give in to a long-held desire that perhaps she couldn't have indulged in without the extra help. They symbolize her liberty to decide to be herself and do what she wants. Along with the white dress, the formal decor represents the bounds that society tells her she must fit into — but that she decides to take a potshot at instead. Focusing on the beauty of inner power, not just the power of outer beauty, this Sorel ad punctuates its bold visual statement with a single verbal phrase: "Après anything" (Sorel). In the French language, the word *après* means "after." So, the ad suggests, no matter what outrageous or outlandish deed you do, the Sorel boots will be there for you, suitable for slipping into afterward like a negligee.

Analysis of the second text.

See the full story at sorel.com/fearless

Après anything. **SOREL**

Fig. 2. Sorel ad flaunts devil-red boots worn by a fearless woman with a shotgun (Sorel).

With these pioneering fashion ads that celebrate blowing your own horn or shooting up fancy French lighting fixtures for fun, young women are told to accessorize their inner beauty with articles of clothing geared toward their distinctive individual desires. "You don't have to just try to be beautiful in the ways other women do," they say; "you can strike out on your own, and our products will help you do it." The extent to which women will respond to these messages remains to be seen, but certainly the ads themselves achieve a strikingly different look. Whether celebrating individual talents or random acts of defiance in our everyday lives, they dare us to accessorize our personalities.

Conclusion ties together the strands of her analysis.

Works Cited

Clarks. Advertisement. *Lucky*. Sept. 2011: 55. Print.
Sorel. Advertisement. *Lucky*. Sept. 2011: 65. Print.

Berry summarizes each ad clearly and focuses her analysis on a theme running through both ads: that clothing is an expression of one's individuality. She describes patterns of images in both ads as evidence.

EMILY NUSSBAUM

In Defense of Liz Lemon

Emily Nussbaum explores the evolution of Liz Lemon, 30 Rock's *main character, in this analysis from the* New Yorker.

Judging from my Twitter feed, there's been a backlash to *30 Rock* this season, particularly the character of Liz Lemon, played by Tina Fey. . . . The argument in all these pieces (many by writers I respect) is pretty much the same: *30 Rock* used to be funny, but now it's sour and negative. Liz Lemon was once our heroine — a sassy, confident, if somewhat neurotic single career lady. Now she's become infantilized and dumb. She behaves as if Jack Donaghy (Alec Baldwin) is her daddy. She doesn't trust her own judgment, she's bad at her job, and there's something awfully misogynist about all this! Liz Lemon is pathetic.

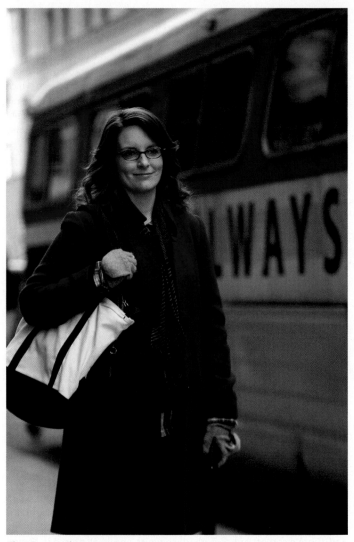

Tina Fey as Liz Lemon.

■ rhetorical situations

▲ genres

○ processes

◆ strategies

● research MLA / APA

□ media / design

▨ handbook

Well, I can't get on board the hate train, especially after last week's tour-de-force episode, in which Liz morphed from a crazy old subway lady (every New Yorker's dream: she gets her way at every turn) into Heath Ledger's Joker. Someone needs to speak up for the Lemon, and for the Fey. Because from the beginning Liz Lemon was pathetic. That was what was enthralling, and even revolutionary, about the character. Unlike some other adorable or slutty-fabulous characters I could name, Liz only superficially resembled the protagonist of a romantic comedy, ready to remove her glasses and be loved. Beneath that, she was something way more interesting: a strange, specific, workaholic, NPR-worshipping, white-guilt-infected, sardonic, curmudgeonly, hyper-nerdy New Yorker. In the first episode, Jack nails her on sight as "a New York third-wave feminist, college-educated, single-and-pretending-to-be-happy-about-it, over-scheduled, undersexed, you buy any magazine that says 'healthy body image' on the cover and every two years you take up knitting for . . . a week." Even Liz had to admit he scored a point.

That was why the show worked: it rarely made Liz an empowering role model, although many women certainly identified with her. The show let her be the George Costanza, not the Mary Richards. And, refreshingly, this appeal had little to do with sex or relationships: a lot of it was about her job. Liz was professionally successful, but she was a sellout. The lady-centric pitch for her show — it was supposed to be *The Girlie Show*, a showcase for her best friend, Jenna — had been commercialized into TGS, a mediocre SNL ripoff, with low ratings and fart gags. Liz needed Jack because her life was a mess, but their rapport wasn't primarily based around gender: it was about the cocky powerful suits versus the smug weakling creatives, although this satire was done (for once) with a woman at the center. In its apocalyptic view of the TV industry, *30 Rock* famously faced off against another show that premiered in the fall of 2006, Aaron Sorkin's accidentally hilarious *Studio 60 on the Sunset Strip*. Sorkin's show was a drama (or really, a temper tantrum) about two male comedy writers portrayed as heroic geniuses. In contrast, *30 Rock* was a brilliant comedy about a stupid comedy, a feminist sitcom about a woman whose feminism was endlessly lampooned.

Sure, Liz had tiny moments of triumph — as when she showed Jack how hard it was to be an actor — but she lost most battles from the start, because that's the nature of network TV: compromise, compromise, compromise. (She didn't win that "Followship" award for nothing.) Also, Liz's nerdliness was not cute, and, over time, it was often quite disgusting: she wore Duane Reade bags for underwear, she binged on cheese, she was pathologically prudish. In the first season, she lived with a beeper sales-man, Dennis, whose nickname for her was "Dummy." After finally get-ting the guts to end it with Dennis, Liz had several promising relationships, including one great one, when she dated an ex-alcoholic named Floyd. But he moved away to Cleveland and got engaged to someone else, which I thought was fantastic: sometimes, that's what happens. In her late thir-ties, Liz dated a white British guy named Wesley Snipes, who was end-lessly thrown at her in classic rom-com soulmate style. She refused to settle. And she got her dream: airline pilot Carol Burnett, who was too similar to Liz in the end, since he shared her cranky, unforgiving bent. The relationship climaxed with one of the best scenes on the show, a crazy screaming match down the aisle of Carol's airplane in which Liz nearly killed an elderly hostage in order to win an argument.

That has always been one of the most radical things about *30 Rock*, 5 the way it has continually punctured Liz's image of herself as a spunky brunette underdog. Early on, she went to her high-school reunion and discovered that she had not in fact been the overlooked nerd — she had been the sarcastic bully, throwing zingers at women she envied (an insight Tina Fey has regularly expressed about herself). When her old boyfriend Floyd came back to town, he got drunk and blurted out the truth about why he prefers his young aerobics-instructor fiancée: "She's alive! Like a deer who runs and sniffs and jumps and stares. Not like the badger, with her glasses and her rules about weekday sex."

All that stuff was true about Liz, and I thought it was great when, last season, in the "Reaganing" episode, Liz finally confronted her own anxieties about sex, a hallmark of the character from the beginning. (The episode featured a montage of every prudish remark Liz has made.) In the midst of a massive run in which he fixes the problems of everyone around him, Jack helps Liz flash back to a childhood masturbation trauma, which, with typical wackiness, involved roller skates and posters of Griz-zly Adams and Tug McGraw. The anti-Lemon squad might not like that Jack was the one who guided Liz to that insight, but after all, his life has changed too: yes, he's married and a father, but from the perspective of Jack's future self, he's a pathetic failure, currently running a worthless network bought by the lame Philadelphia conglomerate Kabletown.

And the thing is, Liz's confrontations with her worst qualities have actually strengthened her. That's what so odd about the backlash. This season, Liz is happier than ever — and for once, she's *rejecting* Jack's influence, finding her own bliss, embracing her oddball nature, going on the Oprah-style vacations she feels like taking. Unbeknownst to Jack, she began dating a cute younger guy who made no money, had a stupid career path, but treated her well. Of course, when Jack found out, he judged her for this, got inside her head, and made fun of her boyfriend's name (which is, to be fair, Criss Chros). But then Liz realized that she actually likes Criss and was an idiot to dump him for shallow reasons; i.e., Jack's reasons. She goes back to him, against Jack's advice.

On Valentine's Day, she and Criss have a fight at IKEA and she assumes they've broken up. Instead, when she goes home, he's made dinner. "You wanted a table, I wasn't super-helpful, who cares?" he says. "I tend to care," she admits. "I let little things ruin stuff. I stopped shopping at Kmart because I found out Kathy Ireland didn't design any of her signature socks." Liz tells him that, at forty-one, she can finally change, but Criss thinks that's ridiculous. "Eh, why bother. You can get mad at dumb stuff, that's your thing. I'll get over it, that's my thing. It's kind of perfect." And he gives her a table he made from a Herman Cain poster and fallen branches from Riverside Park.

As for her career, while Liz was once a people-pleasing, prickly, masochistic workaholic, she's gotten awfully laissez-faire. This is not a bad thing. She's in her forties now and she's stopped obsessing about whether she'll have a baby or whether her job is ideal. She took a fun hobby that Jack would never approve of, shaking her butt as a middle-aged cheerleader for the Liberty. She used Jack's negotiating tricks against him, getting him so exasperated that he negotiated against himself on her behalf. She's now paid well (while Liz used to be bad with money, she's now outright rich) and she's more chill and she's getting laid with a handsome, nice guy. I'm not seeing what's so pathetic. In fact, the show seems to recognize how good her life has become, because they brought in the excellent Kristen Schaal as a female intern who is so impressed by Liz she wishes she could wear her lips as a mask. In *30 Rock* terms, that's a huge compliment.

Still, maybe the best thing about Liz Lemon is that all her idiosyn- 10 crasies—her sourness, her prudishness, her love of *The Real Housewives*—don't have to mean as much, anyway. When the show started, every bespectacled, slovenly, overworked media chick was delighted to finally have a character who reflected her. (I should know.) But we're living in a golden age for female comedy, post-*Bridesmaids* and post–*Young Adult* (a movie I loved, but we can argue about that later). On TV in particular, this season has been a fat sweep of sitcoms starring or made by women, some of which I deeply enjoy, some of which I hate: *New Girl,*

Suburgatory, Whitney, Up All Night, Two Broke Girls, that Chelsea Handler disaster, and the upcoming *Don't Trust the B— in Apt 23.* There are amazing female characters on *Raising Hope, Cougar Town, Community, Happy Endings, The Middle, The Office,* and *It's Always Sunny in Philadelphia.* Actually, Jenna Maroney of *30 Rock* has also had a solid recent plot arc, one of the kinkiest and most sex-positive I've ever seen on TV. Plus, Lena Dunham's terrific new series *Girls* launches on HBO in April.

And then there is Leslie Knope, of *Parks and Recreation,* a very different character from Liz Lemon — sunny and positive and eyes-on-the-prize and currently juggling more than one man. I love them both. We all know this has always been the goal: enough female funny out there that each one doesn't have to hold the banner quite so high. As for me, I'm still on Team Lemon. Or, to quote the woman herself, "Man, do my feet hurt in heels sometimes . . . and other things women talk about."

Nussbaum analyzes the success of 30 Rock *in terms of its refusal to portray Liz Lemon as a stereotypical career woman — "A spunky brunette underdog" — instead showing her as a deeply flawed person, just like her viewers.*

WILLIAM SAFIRE

A Spirit Reborn

Just before the first anniversary of September 11, 2001, New York Times columnist William Safire analyzed the Gettysburg Address for what it meant to Americans after 9/11.

Abraham Lincoln's words at the dedication of the Gettysburg cemetery will be the speech repeated at the commemoration of September 11 by the governor of New York and by countless other speakers across the nation.

The lips of many listeners will silently form many of the famous phrases. "Four score and seven years ago" — a sonorous way of recalling the founding of the nation eighty-seven years before he spoke — is a phrase many now recite by rote, as is "the last full measure of devotion."

But the selection of this poetic political sermon as the oratorical centerpiece of our observance need not be only an exercise in historical evocation, nonpolitical correctness, and patriotic solemnity. What makes this particular speech so relevant for repetition on this first anniversary of the worst bloodbath on our territory since Antietam Creek's waters ran red is this: now, as then, a national spirit rose from the ashes of destruction.

Here is how to listen to Lincoln's all-too-familiar speech with new ears.

In those 236 words, you will hear the word *dedicate* five times. The ⁵ first two times refer to the nation's dedication to two ideals mentioned in the Declaration of Independence, the original ideal of "liberty" and the ideal that became central to the Civil War: "that all men are created equal."

The third, or middle, *dedication* is directed to the specific conse-cration of the site of the battle of Gettysburg: "to dedicate a portion of that field as a final resting place." The fourth and fifth times Lincoln repeated *dedicate* reaffirmed those dual ideals for which the dead being honored fought: "to the unfinished work" and then "to the great task remaining before us" of securing freedom and equality.

Those five pillars of dedication rested on a fundament of religious metaphor. From a president not known for his piety — indeed, often criticized for his supposed lack of faith — came a speech rooted in the theme of national resurrection. The speech is grounded in conception, birth, death, and rebirth.

Consider the barrage of images of birth in the opening sentence. The nation was "conceived in liberty" and "brought forth" — that is, delivered into life — by "our fathers" with all "created" equal. (In the nineteenth century, both "men" and "fathers" were taken to embrace women and mothers.) The nation was born.

Then, in the middle dedication, to those who sacrificed themselves, ¹⁰ come images of death: "final resting place" and "brave men, living and dead."

Finally, the nation's spirit rises from this scene of death: "that this nation, under God, shall have a new birth of freedom." Conception, birth, death, rebirth. The nation, purified in this fiery trial of war, is resurrected. Through the sacrifice of its sons, the sundered nation would be reborn as one.

An irreverent aside: All speechwriters stand on the shoulders of ora-tors past. Lincoln's memorable conclusion was taken from a fine oration by the Reverend Theodore Parker at an 1850 Boston antislavery convention. That social reformer defined the transcendental "idea of freedom" to be "a government of all the people, by all the people, for all the people."

Lincoln, thirteen years later, dropped the "alls" and made the phrase his own. (A little judicious borrowing by presidents from previous orators shall not perish from the earth.) In delivering that final note, the Union's defender is said to have thrice stressed the noun "people" rather than the prepositions "of," "by," and "for." What is to be emphasized is not rhetorical rhythm but the reminder that our government's legitimacy springs from America's citizens; the people, not the rulers, are sovereign. Not all nations have yet grasped that.

Do not listen on September 11 only to Lincoln's famous words and comforting cadences. Think about how Lincoln's message encompasses but goes beyond paying "fitting and proper" respect to the dead and the bereaved. His sermon at Gettysburg reminds "us the living" of our "unfinished work" and "the great task remaining before us"—to resolve that this generation's response to the deaths of thousands of our people leads to "a new birth of freedom."

Safire's analysis focuses on patterns of specific words and images—he identifies dedicate *as a key term and analyzes how its meaning changes and develops each time it is used. He shows how Lincoln shaped his text around images of birth, death, and resurrection to assert that although a nation's soldiers die, their deaths permit the rebirth of the nation. In doing so, Safire builds an argument linking Lincoln's words to current circumstances.*

SAM ANDERSON

Just One More Game . . . : Angry Birds, Farmville, and Other Hyperaddictive Stupid Games

Journalist and critic Sam Anderson analyzes the lure of video games in this essay, which appeared in print in the New York Times Sunday Magazine *and simultaneously online at NYTimes.com. In addition to the text reproduced here, the online version, available via* wwnorton.com/write/fieldguidelinks, *includes illustrations, a simulation of the online game* Kick Ass, *and personal narratives of Anderson's video gaming experiences.*

In 1989, as communism was beginning to crumble across Eastern Europe, just a few months before protesters started pecking away at the Berlin Wall, the Japanese game-making giant Nintendo reached across the world to unleash upon America its own version of freedom. The new product was the Game Boy — a hand-held, battery-powered plastic slab that promised to set gamers loose, after all those decades of sweaty bondage, from the tyranny of rec rooms and pizza parlors and arcades.

The unit came bundled with a single cartridge: Tetris, a simple but addictive puzzle game whose goal was to rotate falling blocks — over and over and over and over and over and over and over — in order to build the most efficient possible walls. (Well, it was complicated. You were both building walls and not building walls; if you built them right, the walls disappeared, thereby ceasing to be walls.) This turned out to be a perfect symbiosis of game and platform. Tetris's graphics were simple enough to work on the Game Boy's small gray-scale screen; its motion was slow enough not to blur; its action was a repetitive, storyless puzzle that could be picked up, with no loss of potency, at any moment, in any situation. The pairing went on to sell more than 70 million copies, spreading the freedom of compulsive wall-building into every breakfast nook and bank line in the country.

And so a tradition was born: a tradition I am going to call (half descriptively, half out of revenge for all the hours I've lost to them) "stupid games." In the nearly 30 years since Tetris's invention — and especially over the last five, with the rise of smartphones — Tetris and its offspring (Angry Birds, Bejeweled, Fruit Ninja, etc.) have colonized our pockets and our brains and shifted the entire economic model of the video-game industry. Today we are living, for better and worse, in a world of stupid games.

Game-studies scholars (there are such things) like to point out that games tend to reflect the societies in which they are created and played. Monopoly, for instance, makes perfect sense as a product of the 1930s — it allowed anyone, in the middle of the Depression, to play at being a tycoon. Risk, released in the 1950s, is a stunningly literal expression of cold-war realpolitik. Twister is the translation, onto a game board, of the mid-1960s sexual revolution. One critic called it "sex in a box."

Tetris was invented exactly when and where you would expect — in a Soviet computer lab in 1984 — and its game play reflects this origin. The enemy in Tetris is not some identifiable villain (Donkey Kong, Mike Tyson, Carmen Sandiego) but a faceless, ceaseless, reasonless force that threatens constantly to overwhelm you, a churning production of blocks against which your only defense is a repetitive, meaningless sorting. It is bureaucracy in pure form, busywork with no aim or end, impossible to avoid or escape. And the game's final insult is that it annihilates free will. Despite its obvious futility, somehow we can't make ourselves stop rotating blocks. Tetris, like all the stupid games it spawned, forces us to choose to punish ourselves.

In 2009, 25 years after the invention of Tetris, a nearly bankrupt Finnish company called Rovio hit upon a similarly perfect fusion of game and device: Angry Birds. The game involves launching peevish birds at green pigs hiding inside flimsy structures. Its basic mechanism — using your index finger to pull back a slingshot, over and over and over and over and over and over and over — was the perfect use of the new technology of the touch screen: simple enough to lure a suddenly immense new market of casual gamers, satisfying enough to hook them.

Within months, Angry Birds became the most popular game on the iPhone, then spread across every other available platform. Today it has been downloaded, in its various forms, more than 700 million times. It has also inspired a disturbingly robust merchandising empire: films, T-shirts, novelty slippers, even plans for Angry Birds "activity parks" featuring play equipment for kids. For months, a sign outside my local auto-repair shop promised, "Free Angry Birds pen with service." The game's latest iteration, Angry Birds Space, appeared a couple weeks ago with a promotional push from Wal-Mart, T-Mobile, National Geographic Books, MTV and NASA. (There was an announcement on the International Space Station.) Angry Birds, it seems, is our Tetris: the string of digital prayer beads that our entire culture can twiddle in moments of rapture or anxiety — economic, political or existential. . . .

Humans have always played stupid games. Dice are older than recorded history. Ancient Egyptians played a board game called Senet, which archaeologists believe was something like sacred backgammon. We have rock-paper-scissors, tick-tack-toe, checkers, dominoes and solitaire — small, abstract games in which sets of simple rules play out in increasingly complex scenarios. (Chess, you might say, is the king of stupid games: the tide line where stupid games meet genius.)

But pre-Tetris games were different in a primal way. They required human opponents or at least equipment — the manipulation of three-dimensional objects in space. When you sat down to play them, chances were you meant to sit down and play them.

Stupid games, on the other hand, are rarely occasions in themselves. They are   10
designed to push their way through the cracks of other occasions. We play them incidentally, ambivalently, compulsively, almost accidentally. They're less an activity in our day than a blank space in our day; less a pursuit than a distraction from other pursuits. You glance down to check your calendar and suddenly it's 40 minutes later and there's only one level left before you jump to the next stage, so you might as well just launch another bird. . . .

Then, in 2007, the iPhone appeared. Games were much easier to develop and easier to distribute through Apple's app store. Instead of just passing their work around to one another on blogs, independent game designers suddenly had a way to reach everyone — not just hard-core gamers, but their mothers, their mail-men and their college professors. Consumers who never would have put a quarter into an arcade or even set eyes on an Xbox 360 were now carrying a sophisticated game console with them, all the time, in their pockets or their purses.

This had a profound impact on game design. In the era of consoles, most games were designed to come to life on a stationary piece of furniture — a television or a desktop computer. The games were built accordingly, around long narratives (quests, wars, the rise and fall of civilizations) that could be explored comfortably while sitting cross-legged on a living-room carpet.

Smartphone games are built on a very different model. The iPhone's screen is roughly the size of a playing card; it responds not to the fast-twitch button combos of a controller but to more intuitive and intimate motions: poking, pinching, tapping, tickling. This has encouraged a very different kind of game: Tetris-like little puzzles, broken into discrete bits, designed to be played anywhere, in any context, without a manual, by any level of player. (Charles Pratt, a researcher in New York University's Game Center, refers to such games as "knitting games.") You could argue that these are *pure* games: perfectly designed minisystems engineered to take us directly to the core of gaming pleasure without the distraction of narrative. The Angry Birds creators like to compare their game with Super Mario Brothers. But the first and simplest level of Super Mario Brothers takes about a minute and a half to finish. The first level of Angry Birds takes around 10 seconds. . . .

There are people who see the proliferation of stupid games as a good thing. In fact, they believe that games may be the answer to all of humanity's problems. In her book "Reality Is Broken," Jane McGonigal argues that play is possibly the best, healthiest, most productive activity a human can undertake — a gateway to our ideal psychological state. Games aren't an escape from reality, McGonigal contends, they are an optimal form of engaging it. In fact, if we could just find a way to impose game mechanics on top of everyday life, humans would be infinitely better off. We might even use these approaches to help solve real-world problems like obesity, education and government abuse. Some proponents point to successful examples of games applied to everyday life: Weight Watchers and frequent-flier miles, for example.

Corporations, of course, have been using similar strategies for decades, hooking consumers on products by giving them constant small victories for spending money (think of the old Monopoly game promotion at McDonald's). The buzzword for this is "gamification" and the ubiquity of computers and smartphones has only supercharged these tendencies. Gartner, a technology research firm, 15 predicted last year that, in the near future, "a gamified service for consumer-goods marketing and customer retention will become as important as Facebook, eBay or Amazon." Companies have already used online games to sneakily advertise sugary cereals directly to children.

Although there is a certain utopian appeal to McGonigal's "games for change" model, I worry about the dystopic potential of gamification. Instead of just bombarding us with jingles, corporations will be able to inject their messages directly into our minds with ads disguised as games. Gamification seeks to turn the world into one giant chore chart covered with achievement stickers — the kind of thing parents design for their children — though it raises the potentially terrifying question of who the parents are. This, I fear, is the dystopian future of stupid games: amoral corporations hiring teams of behavioral psychologists to laser-target our addiction cycles for profit. . . .

[Game designer Frank] Lantz seemed undisturbed by the dark side of stupid games, like addiction or cynical corporate hijacking. He said that real games are far too fragile and complex to be engineered by corporations and that their appeal goes much deeper than reward schedules. "It's as hard to make a really good game as it is to make a really good movie or opera or hat," he told me. "Sure, there's mathematics to it, but it's also a piece of culture. The type of game you play is also a part of how you think about yourself as a person. There's no formula that's going to solve that equation. It's impossible, because it's infinitely deep and wonderful."

As for my nightmare vision of a world splintered by addiction to stupid games, Lantz had a different perspective. He said that he liked to think Drop7 [a game Lantz designed that combines elements of Tetris and Sudoku] was not only addictive but also, on some level, about addiction. Games, he told me, are like "home-brew neuroscience" — "a little digital drug you can use to run experiments on your own brain." Part of the point of letting them seduce you, as Lantz sees it, is to come out the other side a more interesting and self-aware person; more conscious of your habits, weaknesses, desires and strengths. "It's like heroin that is abstracted or compressed or stylized," he said. "It gives you a window into your brain that doesn't crush your brain."

I tried to think about what — if anything — I had learned from this window into my brain. Like their spiritual forefather, Tetris, most stupid games are about walls: building them, scaling them, knocking them down. Walls made of numbers, walls made of digital bricks, walls with green pigs hiding behind them. They're like miniature boot camps of containment. Ultimately, I realized, these games are also about a more subtle and mysterious form of wall-building: the internal walls we build to compartmentalize our time, our attention, our lives. The legendary game designer Sid Meier once defined a game as, simply, "a series of interesting choices." Maybe that's the secret genius of stupid games: they force us to make a series of interesting choices about what matters, moment to moment, in our lives. . . .

Anderson describes Tetris *and other games clearly and outlines their relationship to older "stupid games." He interprets the "gamification" of American culture positively and provides evidence from experts as well as the games themselves, including the playable online* Kick Ass *game, to support his interpretation.*

Key Features / Textual Analysis

A summary of the text.   Your readers may not know the text you are analyzing, so you need to include it or tell them about it before you can analyze it. Because Safire's text is so well known, he describes it only briefly as "Abraham Lincoln's words at the dedication of the Gettysburg cemetery." Texts that are not so well known require a more detailed summary. Berry includes the ads she analyzes and also describes them in detail.

Attention to the context.   Texts don't exist in isolation: they are influenced by and contribute to ongoing conversations, controversies, or debates, so to understand a particular text, you need to understand its larger context. Nussbaum opens by describing fans' critical response to the evolution of *30 Rock's* main character. Safire notes the source of the phrase "of the people, by the people, for the people" and is clearly writing in the context of the United States after 9/11.

A clear interpretation or judgment.   Your goal in analyzing a text is to lead readers through careful examination of the text to some kind of interpretation or reasoned judgment, sometimes announced clearly in a thesis statement. When you interpret something, you explain what you think it means, as Berry does when she argues that the two ads suggest that our clothing choices enhance our individuality. She might instead have chosen to judge the effectiveness of the ads, perhaps noting that they promise the impossible: uniqueness through mass-produced clothing. Anderson judges "stupid games" to be positive, as "they force us to make a series of interesting choices about what matters, moment to moment, in our lives."

Reasonable support for your conclusions. Written analysis of a text is generally supported by evidence from the text itself and sometimes from other sources. The writer might support his or her interpretation by quoting words or passages from a written text or referring to images in a visual text. Safire, for example, looks at Lincoln's repetition of the word "dedicate" in the Gettysburg Address as a way of arguing that the speech was still relevant in 2002, on the anniversary of the 9/11 attacks. Berry examines patterns of both language and images in her analysis of the two ads. Nussbaum describes several scenes and plotlines from *30 Rock*. Note that the support you offer for your interpretation need only be "reasonable" — there is never any one way to interpret something.

A GUIDE TO WRITING TEXTUAL ANALYSES

Choosing a Text to Analyze

Most of the time, you will be assigned a text or a type of text to analyze: a poem in a literature class, the work of a political philosopher in a political science class, a speech in a history or communications course, a painting or sculpture in an art class, a piece of music in a music theory course. If you must choose a text to analyze, look for one that suits the demands of the assignment—one that is neither too large or complex to analyze thoroughly (a Dickens novel or a Beethoven symphony is probably too big) nor too brief or limited to generate sufficient material (a ten-second TV news brief or a paragraph from *Moneyball* would probably be too small). You might also choose to analyze three or four texts by examining elements common to all. Be sure you understand what the assignment asks you to do, and ask your instructor for clarification if you're not sure.

Considering the Rhetorical Situation

3–4 ■ **PURPOSE** Why are you analyzing this text? To demonstrate that you understand it? To show how its argument works — or doesn't? Or are you using the text as a way to make some other point?

rhetorical situations
△ genres
○ processes
◆ strategies
● research MLA / APA
□ media / design
▧ handbook

AUDIENCE   Are your readers likely to know your text? How much detail will you need to supply?

5–8

STANCE   What interests you (or not) about your text? Why? What do you know or believe about it, and how will your own beliefs affect your analysis?

12–15

MEDIA / DESIGN   Will your analysis appear in print? on the web? How will your medium affect your analysis? If you are analyzing a visual text, you will probably need to include an image of it.

16–18

Generating Ideas and Text

In analyzing a text, your goal is to understand what it says, how it works, and what it means. To do so, you may find it helpful to follow a certain sequence: read, respond, summarize, analyze, and draw conclusions from your analysis.

Read to see what the text says.   Start by reading carefully, to get a sense of what it says. This means first skimming to **PREVIEW THE TEXT**, rereading for the main ideas, then questioning and **ANNOTATING**.

399
400–401
400

Consider your **INITIAL RESPONSE.** Once you have a sense of what the text says, what do you think? What's your reaction to the argument, the tone, the language, the images? Do you find the text difficult? puzzling? Do you agree with what the writer says? disagree? agree *and* disagree? Your reaction to a text can color your analysis, so start by thinking about how you react—and why. Consider both your intellectual and any emotional reactions. Identify places in the text that trigger or account for those reactions. If you think that you have no particular reaction or response, try to articulate why. Whatever your response, think about what accounts for it.

Next, consolidate your understanding of the text by **SUMMARIZING** (or, if it's a visual text, **DESCRIBING**) what it says in your own words. You may find it helpful to **OUTLINE** its main ideas. See, for instance, how Hannah Berry carefully described what the shoe ads she was analyzing show and say. Some of this analysis ended up in her essay.

470–71
367–75
263–64

Photographed in standing profile, this quirky-looking young woman is doing what she loves — playing some kind of trumpet — and looks great doing it. She is wearing her hair in a French twist with a strand tucked behind her ear, as if she recently moved it out of her face to play the music she loves without distraction. The downturn of her nose points to the short gray-black dress that stops several inches above her knees but covers her chest and shoulders modestly, with a collar situated at the base of her neck and sleeves that reach for her elbows. The dress is plain, but it is a perfect fit for the personality implied in the photo. Set against the background of a light-tan wall, the model leans back slightly as if supporting the weight of her instrument. Her right knee is bent while her left knee remains straight. The positioning of her legs not only accentuates her unbalanced posture but also points out the pair of simple brown pumps that complete the look. She wears the shoes with a pair of socks in a much darker shade of brown pulled up around her shins. Around her ankles are sandy-colored rings of shaggy fabric that are most likely attached to the socks, giving the whole outfit a sense of nerdy flair. Her expression is a simple mix of calm and concentration. It's as if the photographer happened to take the picture while she was practicing for a school recital.

Decide what you want to analyze.   Having read the text carefully, think about what you find most interesting or intriguing and why. Does the argument interest you? its logic? its attempt to create an emotional response? its reliance on the writer's credibility or reputation? its use of design to achieve its aims? its context? Does the text's language, imagery, or structure intrigue you? something else? You might begin your analysis by exploring what attracted your notice.

Think about the larger context.   All texts are part of larger conversations with other texts that have dealt with the same topic. An essay arguing for handgun trigger locks is part of an ongoing conversation about gun control, which is itself part of a conversation on individual rights and responsibilities. Academic texts include documentation in part to weave in voices from the conversation. And, in fact, any time you're reading to learn, you're probably reading for some larger context. Whatever your reading goals, being aware of that larger context can help you better understand what you're reading. Here are some specific aspects of the text to pay attention to:

- **Who else cares about this topic?** Especially when you're reading in order to learn about a topic, the texts you read will often reveal which people or groups are part of the conversation — and might be sources of further reading. For example, an essay describing the formation of Mammoth Cave could be of interest to geologists, spelunkers, travel writers, or tourists. If you're reading such an essay while doing research on the cave, you should consider how the audience addressed determines the nature of the information provided — and its suitability as a source for your research.

- **Ideas.** Does the text refer to any concepts or ideas that give you some sense that it's part of a larger conversation? An argument on airport security measures, for example, is part of larger conversations about government response to terrorism, the limits of freedom in a democracy, and the possibilities of using technology to detect weapons and explosives, among others.

- **Terms.** Is there any terminology or specialized language that reflects the writer's allegiance to a particular group or academic discipline? If you run across words like *false consciousness*, *ideology*, and *hegemony*, for example, you might guess the text was written by a Marxist scholar.

- **Citations.** Whom does the writer cite? Do the other writers have a particular academic specialty, belong to an identifiable intellectual school, share similar political leanings? If an article on politics cites Michael Moore and Barbara Ehrenreich in support of its argument, you might assume the writer holds liberal opinions; if it cites Rush Limbaugh and Sean Hannity, the writer is likely a conservative.

Write a brief paragraph describing the larger context surrounding the text and how that context affects your understanding of the text.

Consider what you know about the writer or artist. What you know about the person who created a text can influence your understanding of it. His or her CREDENTIALS, other work, reputation, stance, and beliefs are all useful windows into understanding a text.

454

Then write a sentence or two summarizing what you know about the writer and how that information affects your understanding of the text.

Study how the text works.   Written texts are made up of various components, including words, sentences, paragraphs, headings, lists, punctuation — and sometimes images as well. Visual texts might be made up of images, lines, angles, color, light and shadow, and sometimes words. To analyze these elements, look for patterns in the way they're used and try to decide what those patterns reveal about the text. How do they affect its message? See the sections on **THINKING ABOUT HOW THE TEXT WORKS** and **IDENTIFYING PATTERNS** for specific guidelines on examining patterns this way. Then write a sentence or two describing the patterns you've discovered and how they contribute to what the text says.

405–7
408–11

Analyze the argument.   Every text makes an argument. Both verbal and visual texts make certain assertions and provide some kind of support for those claims. An important part of understanding any text is to recognize its argument—what the writer or artist wants the audience to believe, feel, or do. Here are some questions you'll want to consider when you analyze an argument:

- *What is the claim?*   What is the main point the writer is trying to make? Is there a clearly stated **THESIS,** or is the thesis merely implied? Is it appropriately qualified?

313–15

- *What support does the writer offer for the claim?*   What **REASONS** are given to support the claim? What **EVIDENCE** backs up those reasons? Facts? Statistics? Examples? Testimonials by authorities? Appropriate anecdotes or stories? Are the reasons and evidence appropriate, plausible, and sufficient? Are you convinced by them? If not, why not?

326–35

- *How does the writer appeal to readers?*   Does he or she appeal to your **EMOTIONS?** rely on **LOGIC?** try to establish **COMMON GROUND?** demonstrate **CREDIBILITY?**

338
324–34
334–35
334–37

- *How evenhandedly does the writer present the argument?* Is there any mention of **COUNTERARGUMENTS?** If so, how does the writer deal with them? By refuting them? By acknowledging them and responding to them reasonably? Does the writer treat other arguments respectfully? dismissively?

  336–37

- *Does the writer use any logical* **FALLACIES?** Are the arguments or beliefs of others distorted or exaggerated? Is the logic faulty?

  338–40

- *What authorities or other sources of outside information does the writer use?* How are they used? How credible are they? Are they in any way biased or otherwise unreliable? Are they current?

- *How does the writer address you as the reader?* Does the writer assume that readers know something about what is being discussed? Does his or her language include you or exclude you? (Hint: If you see the word *we*, do you feel included?) Do you sense that you and the writer share any beliefs or attitudes? If the writer is not writing to you, what audience is the target? How do you know?

Then write a brief paragraph summarizing the argument the text makes and the main way the writer argues it, along with your reactions to or questions about that argument.

Come up with a thesis. When you analyze a text, you are basically **ARGUING** that the text should be read in a certain way. Once you've studied the text thoroughly, you need to identify your analytical goal: do you want to show that the text has a certain meaning? uses certain techniques to achieve its purposes? tries to influence its audience in particular ways? relates to some larger context in some significant manner? should be taken seriously—or not? something else? Come up with a tentative **THESIS** to guide your thinking and analyzing—but be aware that your thesis may change as you continue to work.

323–41

313–15

Ways of Organizing a Textual Analysis

263–64 ○

Examine the information you have to see how it supports or complicates your thesis. Look for clusters of related information that you can use to structure an **OUTLINE**. Your analysis might be structured in at least two ways. You might, as Safire does, discuss patterns or themes that run through the text. Alternatively, you might analyze each text or section of text separately, as Berry does. Following are graphic representations of some ways of organizing a textual analysis.

[Thematically]

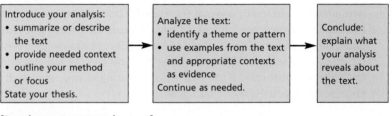

[Part by part, or text by text]

Writing Out a Draft

In drafting your analysis, your goal should be to integrate the various parts into a smoothly flowing, logically organized essay. However, it's easy to get bogged down in the details. Consider writing one section of the analysis first, then another and another until you've drafted the entire middle; then draft your beginning and ending. Alternatively, start by summarizing the text and moving from there to your analysis and then to your ending. However you do it, you need to support your analysis with evidence: from the text itself (as Berry's analysis of advertisements and Nussbaum's analysis of *30 Rock* do), or from **RESEARCH** on the larger context of the text (as Safire does), or by incorporating various experts' views of your subject (as Anderson does).

419

Draft a BEGINNING. The beginning of an essay that analyzes a text generally has several tasks: to introduce or summarize the text for your readers, to offer any necessary information on the larger context, and to present your thesis.

299–306

- *Summarize the text.* If the text is one your readers don't know, you need to give a brief **SUMMARY** early on that introduces it to them and shows that you understand it fully. For example, Berry begins each analysis of a shoe advertisement with a brief summary of its content.

470–71

- *Show the text.* If you're analyzing a visual text or any text that is available online, consider starting off with an image, a video, or a link to it or something similar, as Anderson does by illustrating his essay with a playable video game.

- *Provide a context for your analysis.* If there is a larger context that is significant for your analysis, you might mention it in your introduction. Safire does this when he frames his analysis of the Gettysburg Address as a "centerpiece" of 9/11 commemorations.

- *State your thesis.* Berry ends her first paragraph by stating the **THESIS** of her analysis: These ads for Clarks and Sorel encourage us to break free from the standard beauty mold and be ourselves; "using mostly imagery, they remind us that being unique is the true origin of beauty."

313–15

306–10 **Draft an ENDING.** Think about what you want your readers to take away from your analysis, and end by getting them to focus on those thoughts.

- *Restate your thesis — and say why it matters.* Berry, for example, ends by asserting that the ads she examines invite women to "be ourselves" by "accessoriz[ing] our personalities."

- *Explain what your analysis reveals.* Your analysis should tell your readers something about the way the text works or about the meaning of the text. Safire, for example, states that "[Lincoln's] sermon at Gettysburg reminds 'us the living' of our 'unfinished work' and 'the great task remaining before us' — to resolve that this generation's response to the deaths of thousands of our people leads to 'a new birth of freedom.'"

312–13 **Come up with a TITLE.** A good title indicates something about the subject of your analysis — and makes readers want to see what you have to say about it. Nussbaum's title forthrightly declares her topic. And Berry's title provides a preview of her thesis that the ads she is analyzing are selling a vision of clothing as a vehicle for being unique.

Considering Matters of Design

- If you cite written text as evidence, be sure to set long quotations and 480–83 **DOCUMENTATION** according to the style you're using.
- If your essay is lengthy, consider whether **HEADINGS** would make your 588–89 analysis easier for readers to follow.
- If you're analyzing a visual text, include a copy of the image and a caption identifying it.
- If you're submitting your essay electronically, provide links to the text, image, webpage, or other material you are analyzing.
- If you're analyzing an image or a screen shot, consider annotating elements of it, as is done in the following editorial cartoon about the September 11, 2012, attack on the U.S. Consulate in Benghazi, Lybia.

In 2011, a wave of protest demonstrations led to the overthrow of several governments in the Arab world. This movement was called the "Arab Spring" and a common cartoonist's symbol for it was a flower growing in the desert.

Frost kills flowers, and the cartoonist is suggesting that not only are the U.S. officials to be mourned, but that the attack signals the end of the Arab Spring itself.

Ambassador Christopher Stevens, Sean Smith, Glen Doherty, and Tyrone Woods (the unnamed "Diplomat") were killed during the attack on the U.S. Consulate in Benghazi, Libya.

The attack was carried out by armed terrorists, which the cartoonist labels "Extremists."

— Jeff Darcy *The Plain Dealer*

Getting Response and Revising

The following questions can help you and others study your draft with a
critical eye. Make sure that anyone you ask to read and **RESPOND** to your
text knows your purpose and audience.

275–76 ◌

- Is the beginning effective? Does it make a reader want to continue?
- Does the introduction provide an overview of your analysis and con-
  clusions? Is your thesis clear?
- Is the text described or summarized clearly and sufficiently?
- Is the analysis well organized and easy to follow? Do the parts fit
  together coherently? Does it read like an essay rather than a collec-
  tion of separate bits of analysis?
- Does each part of the analysis relate to the thesis?
- Is anything confusing or in need of more explanation?
- Are all quotations accurate and correctly documented?
- Is it clear how the analysis leads to the interpretation? Is there ade-
  quate evidence to support the interpretation?
- Does the ending make clear what your findings mean?

276–00 ◌

Then it's time to **REVISE**. Make sure your text appeals to your audience and
achieves your purpose as successfully as possible.

Editing and Proofreading

Readers equate correctness with competence. Once you've revised your
draft, edit carefully:

313–15 ◆

- Is your **THESIS** clearly stated?

462–74 ●
480–83

- Check all **QUOTATIONS**, **PARAPHRASES**, and **SUMMARIES** for accuracy and
  form. Be sure that each has the required **DOCUMENTATION**.

- Make sure that your analysis flows clearly from one point to the next and that you use TRANSITIONS to help readers move through your text.

◆ 317

- PROOFREAD your finished analysis carefully before turning it in.

◉ 285–86

Taking Stock of Your Work

Take stock of what you've written and learned by writing out answers to these questions:

- How did you go about analyzing the text? What methods did you use — and which ones were most helpful?
- How did you go about drafting your essay?
- How well did you organize your written analysis? What, if anything, could you do to make it easier to read?
- Did you provide sufficient evidence to support your analysis?
- What did you do especially well?
- What could still be improved?
- Did you use any visuals, and if so, what did they add? Could you have shown the same thing with words?
- How did other readers' responses influence your writing?
- What would you do differently next time?
- Are you pleased with your analysis? What did it teach you about the text you analyzed? Did it make you want to study more works by the same writer or artist?

LITERARY ANALYSES

Literary analyses are essays in which we examine literary texts closely to understand their messages, interpret their meanings, and appreciate their writers' techniques. You might read *Macbeth* and notice that Shakespeare's play contains a pattern of images of blood. You could explore the distinctive point of view in Ambrose Bierce's story "An Occurrence at Owl Creek Bridge." Or you could point out the differences between Stephen King's *The Shining* and Stanley Kubrick's screenplay based on that novel. In all these cases, you use specific analytical tools to go below the surface of the work to deepen your understanding of how it works and what it means. Here is a sonnet by the nineteenth-century English Romantic poet Percy Bysshe Shelley, followed by one student's analysis of it written for a literature course at Wright State University.

PERCY BYSSHE SHELLEY

Sonnet: "Lift not the painted veil which those who live"

Lift not the painted veil which those who live
Call Life: though unreal shapes be pictured there,
And it but mimic all we would believe
With colours idly spread,—behind, lurk Fear
And Hope, twin Destinies; who ever weave   5
Their shadows, o'er the chasm, sightless and drear.
I knew one who had lifted it—he sought,
For his lost heart was tender, things to love,
But found them not, alas! nor was there aught
The world contains, the which he could approve.   10
Through the unheeding many he did move,
A splendour among shadows, a bright blot
Upon this gloomy scene, a Spirit that strove
For truth, and like the Preacher found it not.

STEPHANIE HUFF

Metaphor and Society in Shelley's "Sonnet"

In his sonnet "Lift not the painted veil which those who live," Percy Bysshe Shelley introduces us to a bleak world that exists behind veils and shadows. We see that although fear and hope both exist, truth is dishearteningly absent. This absence of truth is exactly what Shelley chooses to address as he uses metaphors of grim distortion and radiant incandescence to expose the counterfeit nature of our world.

The speaker of Shelley's poem presents bold assertions about the nature of our society. In the opening lines of the poem, he warns the reader, "Lift not the painted veil which those who live / Call Life" (lines 1–2). Here, the "painted veil" serves as a grim metaphor for life. More specifically, the speaker equates the veil with what people like to *call* life. In this sense, the speaker asserts that what we believe to be pure reality is actually nothing more than a covering that masks what really lies beneath. Truth is covered by a veil of falsehood and is made opaque with the paint of people's lies.

This painted veil does not completely obstruct our view but rather distorts what we can see. All that can be viewed through it are "unreal shapes" (2) that metaphorically represent the people that make up this counterfeit society. These shapes are not to be taken for truth. They are unreal, twisted, deformed figures of humanity, people full of falsities and misrepresentations.

Most people, however, do not realize that the shapes and images seen through the veil are distorted because all they know of life is the veil — this life we see as reality only "mimic[s] all we would believe" (3), using "colours idly spread" (4) to create pictures that bear little resemblance to that which they claim to portray. All pure truths are covered up and painted over until they are mere mockeries. The lies that cloak the truth are not even carefully constructed, but are created idly, with little attention to detail. The paint is not applied carefully but merely spread across the top. This idea of spreading brings to mind images of paint slopped on so heavily that the truth beneath becomes nearly impossible to find. Even the metaphor of color suggests only superficial beauty — "idly spread" (4) — rather than any sort of pure beauty that could penetrate the surface of appearances.

What really lies behind this facade are fear and hope, both of which 5 "weave / Their shadows, o'er the chasm, sightless and drear" (5–6). These two realities are never truly seen or experienced, though. They exist only as shadows. Just as shadows appear only at certain times of day, cast only sham images of what they reflect, and are paid little attention, so too do these emotions of hope and fear appear only as brief, ignored imitations of themselves when they enter the artificiality of this chasmlike world. Peering into a chasm, one cannot hope to make out what lies at the bottom. At best one could perhaps make out shadows and even that cannot be done with any certainty as to true appearance. The world is so large, so caught up in itself and its counterfeit ways, that it can no longer see even the simple truths of hope and fear. Individuals and civilizations have become sightless, dreary, and as enormously empty as a chasm.

This chasm does not include *all* people, however, as we are introduced to one individual, in line 7, who is trying to bring to light whatever truth may yet remain. This one person, who defies the rest of the world, is portrayed with metaphors of light, clearly standing out among the dark representations of the rest of mankind. He is first presented to us as possessing a "lost heart" (8) and seeking things to love. It is important that the first metaphor applied to him be a heart because this is the organ with which we associate love, passion, and purity. We associate it with brightness of the soul, making it the most radiant spot of the body. He is then described as a "splendour among shadows" (12), his purity and truth brilliantly shining through the darkness of the majority's falsehood. Finally, he is equated with "a bright blot / Upon this gloomy scene" (12–13), his own bright blaze of authenticity burning in stark contrast to the murky phoniness of the rest of the world.

These metaphors of light are few, however, in comparison to those of grim distortion. So, too, are this one individual's radiance and zeal too little to alter the warped darkness they temporarily pierce. This one person, though bright, is not bright enough to light up the rest of civilization and create real change. The light simply confirms the dark falsity that comprises the rest of the world. Shelley gives us one flame of hope, only to reveal to us what little chance it has under the suffocating veil. Both the metaphors of grim distortion and those of radiant incandescence work together in this poem to highlight the world's counterfeit nature.

Huff focuses her analysis on patterns in Shelley's imagery. In addition, she pays careful attention to individual words and to how, as the poem unfolds, they create a certain meaning. That meaning is her interpretation.

Key Features / Literary Analyses

An arguable thesis.   A literary analysis is a form of argument; you are arguing that your analysis of a literary work is valid. Your thesis, then, should be arguable, as Huff's is: "[Shelley] uses metaphors of grim distortion and radiant incandescence to expose the counterfeit nature of our world." A mere summary — "Shelley writes about a person who sees reality and seeks love but never finds it" — would not be arguable and therefore is not a good thesis.

Careful attention to the language of the text.   The key to analyzing a text is looking carefully at the language, which is the foundation of its meaning. Specific words, images, metaphors — these are where analysis begins. You may also bring in contextual information, such as cultural, historical, or biographical facts, or you may refer to similar texts. But the words, phrases, and sentences that make up the text you are analyzing are your primary source when dealing with texts. That's what literature teachers mean by "close reading": reading with the assumption that every word of a text is meaningful.

Attention to patterns or themes.   Literary analyses are usually built on evidence of meaningful patterns or themes within a text or among several texts. These patterns and themes reveal meaning. In Shelley's poem, images of light and shadow and artifice and reality create patterns of meaning, while the poem's many half rhymes (*live/believe, love/approve*) create patterns of sound that may contribute to the overall meaning.

A clear interpretation.   A literary analysis demonstrates the plausibility of its thesis by using evidence from the text and, sometimes, relevant contextual evidence to explain how the language and patterns found there support a particular interpretation. When you write a literary analysis, you show readers one way the text may be read and understood; that is your interpretation.

MLA style. Literary analyses usually follow MLA style. Even though Huff's essay has no works-cited list, it refers to line numbers using MLA style.

Considering the Rhetorical Situation

3–4 **PURPOSE** What do you need to do? Show that you have examined the text carefully? Offer your own interpretation? Demonstrate a particular analytical technique? Or some combination? If you're responding to an assignment, does it specify what you need to do?

5–8 **AUDIENCE** What do you need to do to convince your readers that your interpretation is plausible and based on sound analysis? Can you assume that readers are already familiar with the text you are analyzing, or do you need to tell them about it?

12–15 **STANCE** How can you see your subject through interested, curious eyes — and then step back in order to see what your observations might *mean*?

16–18 **MEDIA / DESIGN** Will your analysis focus on an essentially verbal text or one that has significant visual content, such as a graphic novel? Will you need to show visual elements in your analysis? Will it be delivered in a print, spoken, or electronic medium? Are you required to follow MLA or some other style?

IF YOU NEED MORE HELP

266–68
269–74
275–81
282–86
287–98

See Chapter 25 for guidelines on **DRAFTING**, Chapter 26 on **ASSESSING YOUR OWN WRITING**, Chapter 27 on **GETTING RESPONSE AND REVISING**, and Chapter 28 on **EDITING AND PROOFREADING**. See Chapter 29 if you are required to submit your analysis in a writing **PORTFOLIO**.

---

rhetorical situations   genres   processes   strategies   research MLA / APA   media / design   handbook

Reporting Information   **9**

Many kinds of writing report information. Newspapers report on local and world events; textbooks give information about biology, history, writing; websites provide information about products (*jcrew.com*), people (*justinbiebermusic.com*), institutions (*smithsonian.org*). We write out a lot of information ourselves, from a note we post on our door saying we've gone to choir practice to an essay we're assigned to write for a history class, reporting what we've learned about the state of U.S. diplomacy in the days before the bombing of Pearl Harbor. This chapter focuses on reports that are written to inform readers about a particular topic. Very often this kind of writing calls for some kind of research: you need to know your subject in order to report on it! When you write to report information, you are the expert. This chapter offers guidelines for writing essays that inform. We'll begin with four good examples, the first annotated to show the key features found in most reports.

MICHAELA CULLINGTON

Does Texting Affect Writing?

This essay by a student at Marywood University was published in Young Scholars in Writing, *a journal of undergraduate writing published by the University of Missouri–Kansas City.*

> It's taking over our lives. We can do it almost anywhere — walking to class, waiting in line at the grocery store, or hanging out at home. It's

quick, easy, and convenient. It has become a concern of doctors, parents, and teachers alike. What is it? It's texting!

Text messaging — or texting, as it's more commonly called — is the process of sending and receiving typed messages via a cellular phone. It is a common means of communication among teenagers and is even becoming popular in the business world because it allows quick messages to be sent without people having to commit to a telephone conversation. A person is able to say what is needed, and the other person will receive the information and respond when it's convenient to do so.

Definitions of key terms.

In order to more quickly type what they are trying to say, many people use abbreviations instead of words. The language created by these abbreviations is called textspeak. Some people believe that using these abbreviations is hindering the writing abilities of students, and others argue that texting is actually having a positive effect on writing. In fact, it seems likely that texting has no significant effect on student writing.

Here's the thesis.

Concerns about Textspeak

A September 2008 article in *USA Today* entitled "Texting, Testing Destroys Kids' Writing Style" summarizes many of the most common complaints about the effect of texting. It states that according to the National Center for Education Statistics, only 25% of high school seniors are "proficient" writers. The article quotes Jacquie Ream, a former teacher and author of *K.I.S.S .— Keep It Short and Simple*, a guide for writing more effectively. Ream states, "[W]e have a whole generation being raised without communication skills." She blames the use of acronyms and shorthand in text messages for students' inability to spell and ultimately to write well. Ream also points out that students struggle to convey emotion in their writing because, as she states, in text messages "emotions are always sideways smiley faces."

Analysis of causes and effects.

This debate became prominent after some teachers began to 5 believe they were seeing a decline in the writing abilities of their students. Many attributed this perceived decline to the increasing popularity of text messaging and its use of abbreviations. Naomi Baron, a linguistics professor at American University, blames texting for what she sees as the fact that "so much of American society has become sloppy and laissez faire about the mechanics of writing" ("Should We Worry or LOL?"). Teachers report finding "2" for "to," "gr8" for "great," "dat" for "that," and "wut" for "what," among other examples of textspeak, in their students' writing. A Minnesota teacher of the seventh and ninth grades says that she has to spend extra time in class editing papers and must "explicitly" remind her students that it is not acceptable to use text slang and abbreviations in writing (Walsh). Another English teacher believes that text language has become "second nature" to her students (Carey); they are so used to it that they do not even catch themselves doing it.

Many also complain that because texting does not stress the importance of punctuation, students are neglecting it in their formal writing. Teachers say that their students are forgetting commas, apostrophes, and even capital letters to begin sentences. Another complaint is that text messages lack emotion. Many argue that texts lack feeling because of their tendency to be short, brief, and to the point. Because students are not able to communicate emotion effectively through texts, some teachers worry, they may lose the ability to do so in writing.

To get a more personal perspective on the question of how teachers perceive texting to be influencing student writing, I interviewed two of my former high school teachers — my junior-year English teacher and my senior-year theology teacher. Both teachers stress the importance of writing in their courses. They maintain that they notice text abbreviations in their students' writing often. To correct this problem, they point it out when it occurs and take points off for its use. They also remind their students to use proper sentence structure and complete sentences. The English teacher says that she believes texting inhibits good writing — it reinforces simplistic writing that may be acceptable for conversation but is "not so good for critical thinking or analysis." She suggests that texting tends to generate topic sentences without emphasizing the following explanation. According to these teachers, then, texting is inhibiting good writing. However, their evidence is limited, based on just a few personal experiences rather than on a significant amount of research.

Responses to Concerns about Textspeak

In response to these complaints that texting is having a negative impact on student writing, others insist that texting should be viewed as beneficial because it provides students with motivation to write, practice in specific writing skills, and an opportunity to gain confidence in their writing. For example, Sternberg, Kaplan, and Borck argue that texting is a good way to motivate students: teens enjoy texting, and if they frequently write through texts, they will be more motivated to write formally. Texting also helps to spark students' creativity, these authors argue, because they are always coming up with new ways to express their ideas (417).

In addition, because they are engaging in written communication rather than oral speech, texting teens learn how to convey their message to a reader in as few words as possible. In his book *Txtng: The Gr8 Db8*, David Crystal discusses a study that concludes that texting actually helps foster "the ability to summarize and express oneself concisely" in writing (168). Furthermore, Crystal explains that texting actually helps people to "sharpen their diplomatic skills . . . [because] it allows more time to formulate their thoughts and express them carefully" (168). One language arts teacher from Minnesota believes that texting helps students develop their own "individual voice" (qtd. in Walsh). Perfecting such a voice allows the writer to offer personal insights and express feelings that will interest and engage readers.

Synthesis of various sources of information.

Supporters of texting also argue that it not only teaches elements 10 of writing but provides extra practice to those who struggle with the conventions of writing. As Crystal points out, children who struggle with literacy will not choose to use a technology that requires them to do something that is difficult for them. However, if they do choose to text, the experience will help them "overcome their awkwardness and develop their social and communication skills" (*Txtng* 171). Shirley Holm, a junior high school teacher, describes texting as a "comfortable form of communication" (qtd. in Walsh). Teenagers are used to texting, enjoy doing so, and as a result are always writing. Through this experience of writing in ways they enjoy, they can learn to take pleasure in writing formally. If students are continually writing in some form, they will eventually develop better skills.

Furthermore, those who favor texting explain that with practice comes the confidence and courage to try new things, which some observers believe they are seeing happen with writing as a result of texting. Teenagers have, for example, created an entirely new language — one that uses abbreviations and symbols instead of words, does not require punctuation, and uses short, incomplete phrases throughout the entire conversation. It's a way of speaking that is a language in and of itself. Crystal, among others, sees this "language evolution" as a positive effect of texting; he seems, in fact, fascinated that teenagers are capable of creating such a phenomenon, which he describes as the "latest manifestation of the human ability" (*Txtng* 175). David Warlick, a teacher and author of books about technology in the classroom, would agree with Crystal. He believes students should be given credit for "inventing a new language ideal for communicating in a high-tech world" (qtd. in Carey). •········

Methods

I decided to conduct my own research into this controversy. I wanted •········ to get different, more personal, perspectives on the issue. First, I surveyed seven students on their opinions about the impact of texting on writing. Second, I questioned two high school teachers, as noted above. Finally, in an effort to compare what students are actually doing to people's perceptions of what they are doing, I analyzed student writing samples for instances of textspeak.[1]

To let students speak for themselves, I created a list of questions for seven high school and college students, some of my closest and most reliable friends. Although the number of respondents was small, I could trust my knowledge of them to help me interpret their responses. In addition, these students are very different from one another, and I believed their differences would allow for a wide array of thoughts and opinions on the issue. I was thus confident in the reliability and diversity of their answers but was cautious not to make too many assumptions because of the small sample size.

I asked the students how long they had been texting; how often they texted; what types of abbreviations they used most and how often they used them; and whether they noticed themselves using any type of textspeak in their formal writing. In analyzing their responses, I looked for commonalities to help me draw conclusions about the students' texting habits and if/how they believed their writing was affected.

I created a list of questions for teachers similar to the one for the students and asked two of my high school teachers to provide their input. I asked if they had noticed their students using textspeak in their writing assignments and, if so, how they dealt with it. I also asked if they believed texting had a positive or negative effect on writing. Next, I asked if they were texters themselves. And, finally, I solicited their

Firsthand research: interviews and survey.

15

opinions on what they believed should be done to prevent teens from using text abbreviations and other textspeak in their writing.

I was surprised at how different the students' replies and opinions were from the teachers'. I decided to find out for myself whose impressions were more accurate by comparing some students' actual writing with students' and teachers' perceptions of that writing. To do this I looked at twenty samples of student writing — end-of-semester research arguments written in two first-year college writing courses with different instructors. The topics varied from increased airport security after September 11 to the weapons of the Vietnam War to autism, and lengths ranged from eight to ten pages. To analyze the papers for the presence of textspeak, I looked closely for use of abbreviations and other common slang terms, especially those usages which the students had stated in their surveys were most common. These included "hbu" ("How about you?"); "gtg" ("Got to go"); and "cuz" ("because"). I also looked for the numbers 2 and 4 used instead of the words "to" and "for."

Comparison and contrast.

Discussion of Findings

My research suggests that texting actually has a minimal effect on student writing. It showed that students do not believe textspeak is appropriate in formal writing assignments. They recognize the difference between texting friends and writing formally and know what is appropriate in each situation. This was proven true in the student samples, in which no examples of textspeak were used. Many experts would agree that there is no harm in textspeak, as long as students continue to be taught and reminded that occasions where formal language is expected are not the place for it. As Crystal explains, the purpose of the abbreviations used in text messages is not to replace language but rather to make quick communications shorter and easier, since in a standard text message, the texter is allowed only 160 characters for a communication ("Texting" 81).

Dennis Baron, an English and linguistics professor at the University of Illinois, has done much research on the effect of technology on writing, and his findings are aligned with those of my own study. In his book *A Better Pencil: Readers, Writers, and the Digital Revolution,* he concludes that students do not use textspeak in their writing. In fact, he suggests students do not even use abbreviations in their text messages very often. Baron says that college students have "put away such

Summary and quotations of sources.

rhetorical situations · genres · processes · strategies · research MLA / APA · media / design · handbook

childish things, and many of them had already abandoned such signs of middle-school immaturity in high school" (qtd. in "A Better Pencil").

In surveying the high school and college students, I found that most have been texting for a few years, usually starting around ninth grade. The students said they generally text between thirty and a hundred messages every day but use abbreviations only occasionally, with the most common being "lol" ("Laugh out loud"), "gtg" ("Got to go"), "hbu" ("How about you?"), "cuz" ("because"), and "jk" ("Just kidding"). None of them believed texting abbreviations were acceptable in formal writing. In fact, research has found that most students, report that they do not use textspeak in formal writing. As one Minnesota high school student says, "[T]here is a time and a place for everything," and formal writing is not the place for communicating the way she would if she were texting her friends (qtd. in Walsh). Another student admits that in writing for school she sometimes finds herself using these abbreviations. However, she notices and corrects them before handing in her final paper (Carey). One teacher reports that, despite texting, her students' "formal writing remains solid." She occasionally sees an abbreviation; however, it is in informal, "warm-up" writing. She believes that what students choose to use in everyday types of writing is up to them as long as they use standard English in formal writing (qtd. in Walsh).

Summary of survey results with quotations.

Also supporting my own research findings are those from a study which took place at a midwestern research university. This study involved eighty-six students who were taking an Introduction to Education course at the university. The participants were asked to complete a questionnaire that included questions about their texting habits, the spelling instruction they had received, and their proficiency at spelling. They also took a standardized spelling test. Before starting the study, the researchers had hypothesized that texting and the use of abbreviations would have a negative impact on the spelling abilities of the students. However, they found that the results did not support their hypothesis. The researchers did note that text messaging is continuing to increase in popularity; therefore, this issue should continue to be examined (Shaw, Carlson, and Waxman).

20

Summary of research that supports her own.

I myself am a frequent texter. I chat with my friends from home every day through texting. I also use texting to communicate with my school friends, perhaps to discuss what time we are going to meet for dinner or

Pertinent personal experience.

to ask quick questions about homework. According to my cell phone bill, I send and receive around 6,400 texts a month. In the messages I send, I rarely notice myself using abbreviations. The only time I use them is if I do not have time to write out the complete phrase. However, sometimes I find it more time-consuming to try to figure out how to abbreviate something so that my message will still be comprehensible.

Since I rarely use abbreviations in my texting, I never use them in my formal writing. I know that they are unacceptable and that it would make me look unintelligent if I included acronyms and symbols instead of proper and formal language. I also have not noticed an effect on my spelling as a result of texting. I am confident in my spelling abilities, and even when I use an abbreviation, I know how to spell the word(s) it stands for.

Conclusion: summary of research and restatement of claim.

On the basis of my own research, expert research, and personal observations, I can confidently state that texting is not interfering with students' use of standard written English and has no effect on their writing abilities in general. It is interesting to look at the dynamics of the arguments over these issues. Teachers and parents who claim that they are seeing a decline in the writing abilities of their students and children mainly support the negative-impact argument. Other teachers and researchers suggest that texting provides a way for teens to practice writing in a casual setting and thus helps prepare them to write formally. Experts and students themselves, however, report that they see no effect, positive or negative. Anecdotal experiences should not overshadow the actual evidence.

Note
1. All participants in the study have given permission for their responses to be published.

Works Cited
Baron, Dennis. *A Better Pencil: Readers, Writers, and the Digital Revolution.* Oxford: Oxford UP, 2009. Print.
"A Better Pencil." *Inside Higher Ed.*, 18 Sept. 2009: n. pag. Web. 9 Nov. 2009.
Carey, Bridget. "The Rise of Text, Instant Messaging Vernacular Slips into Schoolwork." *Miami Herald* 6 Mar. 2007: n. pag. *Academic Search Elite.* Web. 27 Oct. 2009.

Crystal, David. "Texting." *ELT Journal* 62.1 (2008): 77–83. *WilsonWeb*. Web. 8 Nov. 2009.

———. *Txtng: The Gr8 Db8*. Oxford: Oxford UP, 2008. Print.

Shaw, Donita M., Carolyn Carlson, and Mickey Waxman. "An Exploratory Investigation into the Relationship between Text Messaging and Spelling." *New England Reading Association Journal* 43 (2007): 57–62. *WilsonWeb*. Web. 8 Nov. 2009.

"Should We Worry or LOL?" *NEA Today* Mar. 2004: 12. *Academic Search Elite*. Web. 27 Oct. 2009.

Sternberg, Betty, Karen A. Kaplan, and Jennifer E. Borck. "Enhancing Adolescent Literacy Achievement through Integration of Technology in the Classroom." *Reading Research Quarterly* 42 (2007): 416–20. *WilsonWeb*. Web. 8 Nov. 2009.

"Texting, Testing Destroys Kids' Writing Style." *USA Today* 137.2760 (2008): 8. *Academic Search Elite*. Web. 9 Nov. 2009.

Walsh, James. "Txt Msgs Creep in2 class; Some Say That's gr8." *Star Tribune* 23 Oct. 2007: n. pag. *Academic Search Elite*. *Web*. 27 Oct. 2009.

Cullington's essay examines whether or not texting affects students' writing. Her information is based on both published scholarship and a small survey of students and teachers.

NICHOLAS CARR

Rural > City > Cyberspace: The Biggest Migration in Human History

In this essay, from The Shallows: What the Internet Is Doing to Our Brains, *cultural critic Nicholas Carr explains how our wired environment is shaping our thinking.*

It was a warm summer morning in Concord, Massachusetts. The year was 1844. An aspiring novelist named Nathaniel Hawthorne was sitting in a small clearing in the woods, a particularly peaceful spot known around town as Sleepy Hollow. Deep in concentration, he was attending to every passing impression, turning himself into what Emerson, the leader of Concord's Transcendentalist movement, had eight years earlier termed a "transparent eyeball." Hawthorne saw, as he would record in his notebook later that day, how "sunshine glimmers through shadow, and shadow effaces sunshine, imaging that pleasant mood of mind where gayety and pensiveness intermingle." He felt a slight breeze, "the gentlest sigh imaginable, yet with a spiritual potency, insomuch that it seems to penetrate, with its mild, ethereal coolness, through the outward clay, and breathe upon the spirit itself, which shivers with gentle delight." He smelled on the breeze a hint of "the fragrance of the white pines." He heard "the striking of the village clock" and "at a distance mowers whetting their scythes," though "these sounds of labor, when at a proper remoteness, do but increase the quiet of one who lies at his ease, all in a mist of his own musings."

Abruptly, his reverie was broken:

> But, hark! there is the whistle of the locomotive, — the long shriek, harsh above all other harshness, for the space of a mile cannot mollify it into harmony. It tells a story of busy men, citizens from the hot street, who have come to spend a day in a country village, — men of business, — in short, of all unquietness; and no wonder that it gives such a startling shriek, since it brings the noisy world into the midst of our slumbrous peace. (qtd. in Hawthorne 503)

. . .

What exactly was going on in Hawthorne's head as he sat in the green seclusion of Sleepy Hollow and lost himself in contemplation? And how was it different from what was going through the minds of the city dwellers on that crowded, noisy train? A series of psychological studies over the past twenty years has revealed that after spending time in a quiet rural setting, close to nature, people exhibit greater attentiveness, stronger memory, and generally improved cognition. Their brains become both calmer and sharper. The reason, according to attention restoration theory, or ART, is that when people aren't being bombarded by external stimuli, their brains can, in effect, relax. They no longer have to tax their working memories by processing a stream of bottom-up distractions. The resulting state of contemplativeness strengthens their ability to control their mind.

rhetorical situations

genres

processes

strategies

research MLA / APA

media / design

handbook

The results of the most recent such study were published in *Psychological Science* at the end of 2008. A team of University of Michigan researchers, led by psychologist Marc Berman, recruited some three dozen people and subjected them to a rigorous, and mentally fatiguing, series of tests designed to measure the capacity of their working memory and their ability to exert top-down control over their attention. The subjects were then divided into two groups. Half of them spent about an hour walking through a secluded woodland park, and the other half spent an equal amount of time walking along busy downtown streets. Both groups then took the tests a second time. Spending time in the park, the researchers found, "significantly improved" people's performance on the cognitive tests, indicating a substantial increase in attentiveness. Walking in the city, by contrast, led to no improvement in test results.

The researchers then conducted a similar experiment with another 5 set of people. Rather than taking walks between the rounds of testing, these subjects simply looked at photographs of either calm rural scenes or busy urban ones. The results were the same. The people who looked at pictures of nature scenes were able to exert substantially stronger control over their attention, while those who looked at city scenes showed no improvement in their attentiveness. "In sum," concluded the researchers, "simple and brief interactions with nature can produce marked increases in cognitive control." Spending time in the natural world seems to be of "vital importance" to "effective cognitive functioning" (1212).

There is no Sleepy Hollow on the Internet, no peaceful spot where contemplativeness can work its restorative magic. There is only the endless, mesmerizing buzz of the urban street. The stimulations of the Net, like those of the city, can be invigorating and inspiring. We wouldn't want to give them up. But they are, as well, exhausting and distracting. They can easily, as Hawthorne understood, overwhelm all quieter modes of thought. One of the greatest dangers we face as we automate the work of our minds, as we cede control over the flow of our thoughts and memories to a powerful electronic system, is the one that informs the fears of both the scientist Joseph Weizenbaum and the artist Richard Foreman: a slow erosion of our humanness and our humanity.

It's not only deep thinking that requires a calm, attentive mind. It's also empathy and compassion. Psychologists have long studied how people experience fear and react to physical threats, but it's only recently that they've begun researching the sources of our nobler instincts. What they're finding is that, as Antonio Damasio, the director of USC's Brain and Creativity Institute, explains, the higher emotions emerge from neural processes that "are inherently slow" (qtd. in Marzali). In one recent experiment, Damasio and his colleagues had subjects listen to stories describing people experiencing physical or psychological pain. The subjects were then put into a magnetic resonance imaging machine and their brains were scanned as they were asked to remember the stories. The experiment revealed that while the human brain reacts very quickly to demonstrations of physical pain — when you see someone injured, the primitive pain centers in your own brain activate almost instantaneously — the more sophisticated mental process of empathizing with psychological suffering unfolds much more slowly. It takes time, the researchers discovered, for the brain "to transcend immediate involvement of the body" and begin to understand and to feel "the psychological and moral dimensions of a situation" (Immordino-Yang, McColl, Damasio, and Damasio 8025).

The experiment, say the scholars, indicates that the more distracted we become, the less able we are to experience the subtlest, most distinctively human forms of empathy, compassion, and other emotions. "For some kinds of thoughts, especially moral decision-making about other people's social and psychological situations, we need to allow for adequate time and reflection," cautions Mary Helen Immordino-Yang, a member of the research team. "If things are happening too fast, you may not ever fully experience emotions about other people's psychological states" (qtd. in Marzali). It would be rash to jump to the conclusion that the Internet is undermining our moral sense. It would not be rash to suggest that as the Net reroutes our vital paths and diminishes our capacity for contemplation, it is altering the depth of our emotions as well as our thoughts.

There are those who are heartened by the ease with which our minds are adapting to the Web's intellectual ethic. "Technological progress does not reverse," writes a *Wall Street Journal* columnist, "so the trend toward multitasking and consuming many different types of information will only continue." We need not worry, though, because our "human software" will in time "catch up to the machine technology that made the information abundance possible." We'll "evolve" to become more agile consumers of data (Crovitz A11). The writer of a cover story in *New York* magazine says that as we become used to "the 21st-century task" of "flitting" among bits of online information, "the wiring of the brain will inevitably change to deal more efficiently with more information." We may lose our capacity "to concentrate on a complex task from beginning to end," but in recompense we'll gain new skills, such as the ability to "conduct 34 conversations simultaneously across six different media" (Anderson). A prominent economist writes, cheerily, that "the web allows us to borrow cognitive strengths from autism and to be better infovores" (Cowen 10). An *Atlantic* author suggests that our "technology-induced ADD" may be "a short-term problem," stemming from our reliance on "cognitive habits evolved and perfected in an era of limited information flow." Developing new cognitive habits is "the only viable approach to navigating the age of constant connectivity" (Cascio).

These writers are certainly correct in arguing that we're being molded by our new information environment. Our mental adaptability, built into the deepest workings of our brains, is a keynote of intellectual history. But if there's comfort in their reassurances, it's of a very cold sort. Adaptation leaves us better suited to our circumstances, but qualitatively it's a neutral process. What matters in the end is not our becoming but what we become. In the 1950s, Martin Heidegger observed that the looming "tide of technological revolution" could "so captivate, bewitch, dazzle, and beguile man that calculative thinking may someday come to be accepted and practiced *as the only* way of thinking." Our ability to engage in "meditative thinking," which he saw as the very essence of our humanity, might become a victim of headlong progress (*Discourse* 56). The tumultuous advance of technology could, like the arrival of the locomotive at the Concord station, drown out the refined perceptions, thoughts, and emotions that arise only through contemplation and reflection. The "frenziedness of technology," Heidegger wrote, threatens to "entrench itself everywhere" (*The Question* 35).

It may be that we are now entering the final stage of that entrenchment. We are welcoming the frenziedness into our souls.

Works Cited

Anderson, Sam. "In Defense of Distraction." *New York*. New York Magazine, 25 May 2009. Web. 11 Feb. 2012.

Berman, Marc G., John Jonides, and Stephen Kaplan. "The Cognitive Benefits of Interacting with Nature." *Psychological Science* 19.12 (2008): 1207–12. Print.

Cascio, Jamais. "Get Smarter." *TheAtlantic.com*. Atlantic Monthly Group, July/Aug. 2009. Web. 11 Feb. 2012.

Cowen, Tyler. *Create Your Own Economy*. New York: Dutton, 2009. Print.

Crovitz, L. Gordon. "Information Overload? Relax." *Wall Street Journal*, 6 July 2009: A11. Print.

Hawthorne, Julian. *Nathaniel Hawthorne and His Wife: A Biography*. Vol. 1. Boston: Osgood, 1885. Print.

Heidegger, Martin. *Discourse on Thinking*. New York: Harper, 1966. Print.

———. *The Question concerning Technology and Other Essays*. New York: Harper, 1977. Print.

Immordino-Yang, Mary Helen, Andrea McColl, Hanna Damasio, and Antonio Damasio. "Neural Correlates of Admiration and Compassion." *Proceedings of the National Academy of Sciences* 106.19 (2009): 8021–26. Print.

Marziali, Carl. "Nobler Instincts Take Time." *USC Dornsife*. U of Southern California, 14 Apr. 2009. Web. 11 Feb. 2012.

This report explores the effects of distraction and the way we interact with the internet on our abilities to think and even feel. Carr relies primarily on the results of two research studies to establish the basis for his assertions and then offers several perspectives, positive and negative, on our increasing loss of the ability to contemplate.

JAMES FALLOWS

Throwing Like a Girl

In the following report for the Atlantic, national correspondent James Fallows explores the art of throwing a baseball and the misconceptions that lead to the phrase "throwing like a girl."

rhetorical situations ▲ genres ○ processes ◆ strategies ● research MLA / APA ▢ media / design ▨ handbook

Most people remember the 1994 baseball season for the way it ended — with a strike rather than a World Series. I keep thinking about the way it began. On opening day, April 4, Bill Clinton went to Cleveland and, like many Presidents before him, threw out a ceremonial first pitch. That same day Hillary Rodham Clinton went to Chicago and, like no First Lady before her, also threw out a first ball, at a Cubs game in Wrigley Field.

The next day photos of the Clintons in action appeared in newspapers around the country. Many papers, including the *New York Times* and the *Washington Post*, chose the same two photos to run. The one of Bill Clinton showed him wearing an Indians cap and warm-up jacket. The President, throwing lefty, had turned his shoulders sideways to the plate in preparation for delivery. He was bringing the ball forward from behind his head in a clean-looking throwing action as the photo was snapped. Hillary Clinton was pictured wearing a dark jacket, a scarf, and an oversized Cubs hat. In preparation for her throw she was standing directly facing the plate. A right-hander, she had the elbow of her throwing arm pointed out in front of her. Her forearm was tilted back, toward her shoulder. The ball rested on her upturned palm. As the picture was taken, she was in the middle of an action that can only be described as throwing like a girl.

Hillary and Bill Clinton throw the first ball of the season at two games in 1994.

The phrase "throwing like a girl" has become an embattled and offensive one. Feminists smart at its implication that to do something "like a girl" is to do it the wrong way. Recently, on the heels of the O. J. Simpson case, a book appeared in which the phrase was used to help explain why male athletes, especially football players, were involved in so many assaults against women. Having been trained (like most American boys) to dread the accusation of doing anything "like a girl," athletes were said to grow into the assumption that women were valueless, and natural prey.

I grant the justice of such complaints. I am attuned to the hurt caused by similar broad-brush stereotypes when they apply to groups I belong to — "dancing like a white man," for instance, or "speaking foreign languages like an American," or "thinking like a Washingtonian."

Still, whatever we want to call it, the difference between the two   5 Clintons in what they were doing that day is real, and it is instantly recognizable. And since seeing those photos I have been wondering, Why, exactly, do so many women throw "like a girl"? If the motion were easy to change, presumably a woman as motivated and self-possessed as Hillary Clinton would have changed it. (According to her press secretary, Lisa Caputo, Mrs. Clinton spent the weekend before opening day tossing a ball in the Rose Garden with her husband, for practice.) Presumably, too, the answer to the question cannot be anything quite as simple as, Because they *are* girls.

A surprising number of people think that there is a structural difference between male and female arms or shoulders — in the famous "rotator cuff," perhaps — that dictates different throwing motions. "It's in the shoulder joint," a well-educated woman told me recently. "They're hinged differently." Someday researchers may find evidence to support a biological theory of throwing actions. For now, what you'll hear if you ask an orthopedist, an anatomist, or (especially) the coach of a women's softball team is that there is no structural reason why men and women should throw in different ways. This point will be obvious to any male who grew up around girls who liked to play baseball and became good at it. It should be obvious on a larger scale this summer, in broadcasts of the Olympic Games. This year [1996], for the first time, women's fast-pitch softball teams will compete in the Olympics. Although the pitchers in these games will deliver the ball underhand, viewers will see female shortstops, center fielders, catchers, and so on pegging the ball to one another at speeds few male viewers could match.

Even women's tennis is a constant if indirect reminder that men's and women's shoulders are "hinged" the same way. The serving motion in tennis is like a throw—but more difficult, because it must be coordinated with the toss of the tennis ball. The men in professional tennis serve harder than the women, because they are bigger and stronger. But women pros serve harder than most male amateurs have ever done, and the service motion for good players is the same for men and women alike. There is no expectation in college or pro tennis that because of their anatomy female players must "serve like a girl." "I know many women who can throw a lot harder and better than the normal male," says Linda Wells, the coach of the highly successful women's softball team at Arizona State University. "It's not gender that makes the difference in how they throw."

At a superficial level it's easy to tick off the traits of an awkward-looking throw. The fundamental mistake is the one Mrs. Clinton appeared to be making in the photo: trying to throw a ball with your body facing the target, rather than rotating your shoulders and hips ninety degrees away from the target and then swinging them around in order to accelerate the ball. A throw looks bad if your elbow is lower than your shoulder as your arm comes forward (unless you're throwing sidearm). A throw looks really bad if, as the ball leaves your hand, your wrist is "inside your elbow"—that is, your elbow joint is bent in such a way that your forearm angles back toward your body and your wrist is closer to your head than your elbow is. Slow-motion film of big-league pitchers shows that when they release the ball, the throwing arm is fully extended and straight from shoulder to wrist. The combination of these three elements—head-on stance, dropped elbow, and wrist inside the elbow—mechanically dictates a pushing rather than a hurling motion, creating the familiar pattern of "throwing like a girl."

It is surprisingly hard to find in the literature of baseball a deeper explanation of the mechanics of good and bad throws. Tom Seaver's pitching for the Mets and the White Sox got him into the Hall of Fame, but his book *The Art of Pitching* is full of bromides that hardly clarify the process of throwing, even if they might mean something to accomplished pitchers. His chapter "The Absolutes of Pitching Mechanics," for instance, lays out these four unhelpful principles: "Keep the Front Leg Flexible!" "Rub Up the Baseball!" "Hide the Baseball!" "Get It Out, Get It Up!" (The fourth refers to the need to get the ball out of the glove and into the throwing hand in a quick motion.)

A variety of other instructional documents, from *Little League's Official How-to-Play Baseball Book* to *Softball for Girls & Women*, mainly reveal the difficulty of finding words to describe a simple motor activity that everyone can recognize. The challenge, I suppose, is like that of writing a manual on how to ride a bike, or how to kiss. Indeed, the most useful description I've found of the mechanics of throwing comes from a man whose specialty is another sport: Vic Braden made his name as a tennis coach, but he has attempted to analyze the physics of a wide variety of sports so that they all will be easier to teach.

Braden says that an effective throw involves connecting a series of links in a "kinetic chain." The kinetic chain, which is Braden's tool for analyzing most sporting activity, operates on a principle like that of crack-the-whip. Momentum builds up in one part of the body. When that part is suddenly stopped, as the end of the "whip" is stopped in crack-the-whip, the momentum is transferred to and concentrated in the next link in the chain. A good throw uses six links of chain, Braden says. The first two links involve the lower body, from feet to waist. The first motion of a throw (after the body has been rotated away from the target) is to rotate the legs and hips back in the direction of the throw, building up momentum as large muscles move body mass. Then those links stop—a pitcher stops turning his hips once they face the plate—and the momentum is transferred to the next link. This is the torso, from waist to shoulders, and since its mass is less than that of the legs, momentum makes it rotate faster than the hips and legs did. The torso stops when it is facing the plate, and the momentum is transferred to the next link—the upper arm. As the upper arm comes past the head, it stops moving forward, and the momentum goes into the final links—the forearm and wrist, which snap forward at tremendous speed.

This may sound arcane and jerkily mechanical, but it makes perfect sense when one sees Braden's slow-mo movies of pitchers in action. And it explains why people do, or don't, learn how to throw. The implication of Braden's analysis is that throwing is a perfectly natural action (millions and millions of people can do it), but not at all innate. A

10

successful throw involves an intricate series of actions coordinated among muscle groups, as each link of the chain is timed to interact with the next. Like bike riding or skating, it can be learned by any-one — male or female. No one starts out knowing how to ride a bike or throw a ball. Everyone has to learn.

Fallows describes in detail what distinguishes a successful baseball throw from an awkward-looking one, concluding with the point that throwing a baseball effectively is a learned activity. He draws on various sources — including a women's softball coach, a tennis coach, and his own observations — to support his claim. Notice how he establishes the context for his essay by focusing on the differences between the stances of the Clintons when photographed throwing a baseball.

MATTHEW O'BRIEN

The Strange Economics of Engagement Rings

Writing in his blog on TheAtlantic.com, Matthew O'Brien looks at the economic reasons behind the tradition of giving diamond engagement rings. The words and phrases underlined here represent links to other websites from the online version of the essay, which is available via wwnorton.com/write/ fieldguidelinks.

Why do men buy diamond rings for our fiancées? There's the emotional story. We enjoy making grand gestures of commitment to the people we love. Behind that, there's the marketing story. DeBeers' historic ad campaign, crafted by the real-life mad men at N. W. Ayers, convinced generations of lovers that diamond bands were synonymous with eternal devotion. But behind that, there is economic story that is just as important and fascinating.

Once upon a time, diamond rings weren't just gifts. They were, frankly, virginity insurance.

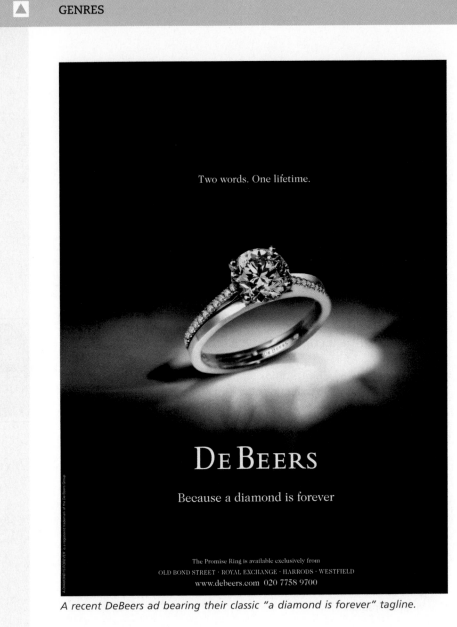

A recent DeBeers ad bearing their classic "a diamond is forever" tagline.

A now-obsolete law called the "Breach of Promise to Marry" once allowed women to sue men for breaking off an engagement. Back then, there was a high premium on women being virgins when they married — or at least when they got engaged. Surveys from the 1940s show that roughly half of engaged couples reported being intimate before the big day. If the groom-to-be walked out after he and the bride-to-be had sex, that left her in a precarious position. From a social angle, she had been permanently "damaged." From an economic angle, she had lost her market value. So Breach of Promise to Marry was born.

But in the 1930s, states began striking down the "Breach of Promise to Marry" law. By 1945, 16 states representing nearly half of the nation's population had made Breach of Promise a historical relic. At the same time, the diamond engagement ring began its transformation from decorative to de rigueur. Legal scholar Margaret Brinig doesn't think that's a coincidence, and she has the math to prove it. Regressing the percent of people living in states without Breach of Promise against a handful of other variables — including advertising, per capita income and the price of diamonds — Brinig found that this legal change was actually the *most* significant factor in the rise of the diamond engagement ring. It's historically plausible. The initial mini-surge in

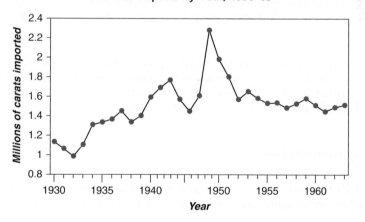

Diamond Imports by Year, 1930–63

diamond imports came in 1935, four years before DeBeers launched its celebrated advertising campaign. What's going on here?

Let's think like an economist. An engaged couple aren't all that different from a borrower and a lender. The woman is lending her hand in marriage to the man, who promises to tie the knot at a later date. In the days of Breach of Promise, the woman would do this on an unsecured basis — that is, the man didn't have to pledge any collateral — because the law provided her something akin to bankruptcy protection. Put simply, if the man didn't fulfill his obligation to marry, the woman had legal recourse. This calculus changed once the law changed. Suddenly, women wanted an upfront financial assurance from their men. Basically, collateral. That way, if the couple never made it down the aisle, she'd at least be left with *something*. And that something was almost always small and shiny. The diamond ring was insurance.

So, should a jilted bride give back the engagement ring? Today, the answer is often yes. But back when rings first came into vogue, part of the point was that she wouldn't. It was a security against a default on the engagement. The good news is that this seems so alien to us today. Women have their own careers. They earn more degrees. And, for the younger generation, they out-earn men. More importantly, the stigma against premarital sex has disappeared. A broken engagement isn't a lasting financial disaster for a woman like it was before. The diamond engagement ring has itself undergone a transformation. It's no longer a security. It's just about signaling nowadays. It's anachronistic. But don't try telling your girlfriend that.

O'Brien explains the evolution of the symbolism of engagement rings by presenting a narrative of their history over the last century, coupled with an image of a ring, a chart showing diamond imports by year, and several links to websites that define important terms or offer additional information.

Key Features / Reports

A tightly focused topic. The goal of this kind of writing is to inform readers about something without digressing—and without, in general, bringing in the writer's own opinions. All four examples focus on a particular topic—texting, the mental effects of the internet, throwing a baseball, and diamond engagement rings — and present information about the topics evenhandedly.

Accurate, well-researched information.   Reports usually require some research. The kind of research depends on the topic. Library research to locate scholarly sources may be necessary for some topics—Cullington, for example, uses various sources available through her library's database. Other topics may require field research—interviews, observations, and so on. Fallows interviewed two coaches in addition to reading several books on pitching baseballs.

Various writing strategies.   Presenting information usually requires various organizing patterns—defining, comparing, classifying, explaining processes, analyzing causes and effects, and so on. Fallows explains the process governing throwing a baseball and classifies different ways of throwing. Carr describes several psychological experiments, and Cullington analyzes the effects (or lack of effects) of texting on students' writing ability.

Clear definitions.   Reports need to provide clear definitions of any key terms that their audience may not know. Cullington defines both *texting* and *textspeak*. Fallows defines several pitching terms, such as *inside your elbow*. And O'Brien defines *collateral* as it applies to wedding rings.

Appropriate design.   Reports often combine paragraphs with information presented in lists, tables, diagrams, and other illustrations. When you're presenting information, you need to think carefully about how to design it—numerical data, for instance, can be easier to understand and remember in a table than in a paragraph. Often a photograph can bring a subject to life, as do the photos on page 101, which accompany "Throwing Like a Girl." The caption provides important information that is explained more fully in the essay itself. Online reports offer the possibility of video and audio clips as well as links to source materials and more detailed information.

A GUIDE TO WRITING REPORTS

Choosing a Topic

Whether you get to choose your topic or are working with an assigned one, see if you can approach the topic from an angle that interests you.

If you get to choose. What interests you? What do you wish you knew more about? The possible topics for informational reports are limitless, but the topics that you're most likely to write well on are those that engage you. They may be academic in nature or reflect your personal interests or both. If you're not sure where to begin, here are some places to start:

- an intriguing technology: hybrid cars, smartphones, roller coasters
- sports: soccer, snowboarding, ultimate Frisbee, basketball
- an important world event: the Arab Spring, the fall of Rome, the Black Death
- a historical period: the African diaspora, the Middle Ages, the Ming dynasty, the Great Depression
- a common object: hoodies, gel pens, mascara, Post-it notes
- a significant environmental issue: Arctic oil drilling, deer overpopulation, mercury and the fish supply
- the arts: hip-hop, outsider art, the Crystal Bridges Museum of American Art, Savion Glover, Mary Cassatt

260–61 ◐ **LIST** a few possibilities, and then choose one that you'd like to know more about — and that your audience might find interesting, too. You might start out by phrasing your topic as a question that your research will attempt to answer. For example:

> How is Google different from Yahoo!?
> How was the Great Pyramid constructed?
> What kind of training do football referees receive?

rhetorical situations genres processes strategies research MLA / APA media / design handbook

If your topic is assigned. If your assignment is broad — "Explain some aspect of the U.S. government" — try focusing on a more limited topic within the larger topic: federalism, majority rule, political parties, states' rights. Even if an assignment seems to offer little flexibility — "Explain the physics of roller coasters" — your task is to decide how to research the topic — and sometimes even narrow topics can be shaped to fit your own interests and those of your audience.

Considering the Rhetorical Situation

PURPOSE	Why are you presenting this information? To teach readers about the subject? To demonstrate your research and writing skills? For some other reason?	3–4
AUDIENCE	Who will read this report? What do they already know about the topic? What background information do they need in order to understand it? Will you need to define any terms? What do they want or need to know about the topic? Why should they care about it? How can you attract their interest?	5–8
STANCE	What is your own attitude toward your subject? What interests you most about it? What about it seems important?	12–15
MEDIA / DESIGN	What medium are you using? What is the best way to present the information? Will it all be in paragraph form, or is there information that is best presented as a chart or a table? Do you need headings? Would diagrams, photographs, or other illustrations help you explain the information?	16–18

Generating Ideas and Text

Good reports share certain features that make them useful and interesting to readers. Remember that your goal is to present information clearly and accurately. Start by exploring your topic.

Explore what you already know about your topic.   Write out whatever you know or want to know about your topic, perhaps by **FREEWRITING,**
LISTING, or **CLUSTERING.** Why are you interested in this topic? What questions do you have about it? Such questions can help you decide what you'd
like to focus on and how you need to direct your research efforts.

259–62 ◯

Narrow your topic.   To write a good report, you need to narrow your
focus — and to narrow your focus, you need to know a fair amount about
your subject. If you are assigned to write on a subject like biodiversity, for
example, you need to know what it is, what the key issues are, and so on.
If you do, you can simply list or brainstorm possibilities, choose one, and
start your research. If you don't know much about the subject, though,
you need to do some research to discover focused, workable topics. This
research may shape your thinking and change your focus. Start with
SOURCES that can give you a general sense of the subject, such as an encyclopedia entry, a magazine article, a website, perhaps an interview with
an expert. Your goal at this point is simply to find out what issues your
topic might include and then to focus your efforts on an aspect of the topic
you will be able to cover.

432–52 ●

Come up with a tentative thesis.   Once you narrow your topic, write out
a statement that explains what you plan to report or explain. A good
THESIS is potentially interesting (to you and your readers) and limits your
topic enough to make it manageable. Fallows phrases his thesis as a question: "Why, exactly, do so many women throw 'like a girl'?" Cullington
frames her thesis in relation to the context surrounding her topic: "Some
people believe that using these abbreviations is hindering the writing abilities of students, and others argue that texting is actually having a positive effect on writing. In fact, it seems likely that texting has no significant
effect on student writing." At this point, however, you need only a tentative thesis that will help focus any research you do.

313–15 ◆

Do any necessary research, and revise your thesis.   To focus your
research efforts, **OUTLINE** the aspects of your topic that you expect to discuss. Identify any aspects that require additional research and **DEVELOP**
A RESEARCH PLAN. Expect to revise your outline as you do your research,

263–64 ◯
421–31 ●

■ rhetorical situations   ▲ genres   ◯ processes   ◆ strategies   ● research MLA / APA   ☐ media / design   ⬠ handbook since more information will be available for some aspects of your topic than others, some may prove irrelevant to your topic, and some may turn out to be more than you need. You'll need to revisit your tentative thesis once you've done any research, to finalize your statement.

Ways of Organizing a Report

Reports can be organized in various ways. Here are three common ones:

[Reports on topics that are unfamiliar to readers]

[Reports on an event]

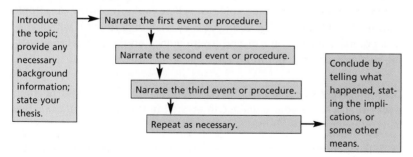

[Reports that compare and contrast]

Many reports use a combination of organizational structures; don't be afraid to use whatever method of organization best suits your material and your purpose.

Writing Out a Draft

266–68 ○

Once you have generated ideas and thought about how you want to organize your report, it's time to start **DRAFTING.** Do this quickly — try to write a complete draft in one sitting, concentrating on getting the report on paper or screen and on putting in as much detail as you can.

382–86 ◆
318–22
348–55

Writing that reports information often calls for certain writing strategies. The report on throwing a baseball, for example, **EXPLAINS THE PROCESS** of throwing, whereas the report on cyberspace **ANALYZES THE EFFECTS** of multitasking on our thinking abilities. When you're reporting on a topic your readers aren't familiar with, you may wish to **COMPARE** it with something more familiar; you can find useful advice on these and other writing strategies in Part 4 of this book.

299–306 ◆

Draft a **BEGINNING.** Essays that report information often need to begin in a way that will get your audience interested in the topic. Here are a few ways of beginning:

- *Simply state your thesis.* Cullington states her thesis about texting after only a brief introduction. Opening with a thesis works well when you can assume your readers have enough familiarity with your topic that you don't need to give much detailed background information.

- *Start with something that will provoke readers' interest.* O'Brien's report begins by provocatively describing diamond rings as more than "just gifts. They were, frankly, virginity insurance." Such a surprising characterization of a common symbol of being engaged to be married is likely to make readers curious to read further.

- *Begin with an illustrative example.* Fallows uses the contrasting photographs of the Clintons throwing baseballs as a way of defining "throwing like a girl."

Draft an ENDING.   Think about what you want your readers to read last. An effective ending leaves them thinking about your topic.

306–10

- *Summarize your main points.* This is a good way to end when you've presented several key points you want readers to remember. Cullington ends this way, summarizing the debate about texting's effects and the results of her research.

- *Point out the implications of your report.* Carr ends with the gloomy suggestion that the "technological revolution" of computers and the internet has already made contemplation and deep thinking obsolete.

- *Frame your report by referring to its introduction.* Cullington begins and ends her report by referring to the positive or negative effects of texting on student writing.

- *Tell what happened.* If you are reporting on an event, you could conclude by telling how it turns out.

Come up with a title.   You'll want a title that tells readers something about your subject—and makes them want to know more. Cullington's title, "Does Texting Affect Writing?," is a straightforward description of what's to come. O'Brien's title, "The Strange Economics of Engagement Rings," gets our interest by its intriguing wording (What's strange about it?) and by its relevance to anyone who is or might become engaged. See the

312–17 chapter on **GUIDING YOUR READER** for tips on coming up with titles that are informative and enticing enough to make readers wish to read on.

Considering Matters of Design

You'll probably write the main text of your report in paragraph form, but think about what kind of information you're presenting and how you can design and format it to make it as easy as possible for your readers to understand. You might ask yourself these questions:

585–86
- What is an appropriate **FONT?** Something serious like Times Roman, something traditional like Courier, something else?

588–89
- Would it help your readers if you divided your report into shorter sections and added **HEADINGS?**

587
- Is there any information that would be easier to follow in a **LIST?**

593–95
- Could any of your information be summarized in a **TABLE** or **FIGURE?**

593–95
- Do you have any data that readers would more easily understand in the form of a bar **GRAPH,** line graph, or pie chart?

591–99
- Would **ILLUSTRATIONS** (diagrams, photos, drawings, and so on), video or audio clips, or links help you explain anything in your report?

Getting Response and Revising

The following questions can help you study your draft with a critical eye. 275–76 **GETTING RESPONSE** from others is always good, and these questions can guide their reading, too. Make sure they know your purpose and audience.

- Do the title and opening sentences get readers' interest? If not, how might they do so?

- What information does this text provide, and for what purpose?

- Does the introduction explain why this information is being presented? Does it place the topic in a larger context?

- Are all key terms defined that need to be?

rhetorical situations

genres

processes

strategies

research MLA / APA

media / design

handbook

- Do you have any questions? Where might more explanation or an example help you understand something better?

- Is any information presented visually, with a chart, graph, table, drawing, or photograph? If so, is it clear how the illustration relates to the written text? Is there any text that would be more easily understood if it were presented visually?

- Is any information presented through digital media, such as hyperlinks, video clips, or audio files? If so, is the relation of these elements to the written text made clear? Would any aspect of the report be clearer if presented using such elements?

- Does the organization help make sense of the information? Does the text include description, comparison, or any other writing strategies? Does the topic or rhetorical situation call for any particular strategies that should be added?

- If the report cites any sources, are they quoted, paraphrased, or summarized effectively (and with appropriate documentation)?

- Does the report end in a satisfying way? What are readers left thinking?

These questions should identify aspects of your report you need to work on. When it's time to **REVISE,** make sure your report appeals to your audience and achieves your purpose as successfully as possible.

276–79

Editing and Proofreading

Readers equate correctness with the writer's competence. Once you've revised your draft, follow these guidelines for **EDITING** a report:

282–85

- Check your use of key terms. Repeating key words is acceptable in reports; using synonyms for unfamiliar words may confuse readers, while the repetition of key words or the use of clearly identified **PRONOUNS** for them can be genuinely helpful.

HB-25–31

- Check to be sure you have **TRANSITIONS** where you need them.

317

- If you have included **HEADINGS,** make sure they're parallel in structure and consistent in design.

588–89

591–99 • Make sure that any photos or other **ILLUSTRATIONS** have captions, that charts and graphs have headings—and that all are referred to in the main text. Use white space as necessary to separate sections of your report and to highlight graphic elements.

480–83 • Check any **DOCUMENTATION** to see that it follows the appropriate style without mistakes.

285–86 • **PROOFREAD** and spell-check your report carefully.

Taking Stock of Your Work

• How well did you convey the information? Is it complete enough for your audience's needs?

• What strategies did you rely on, and how did they help you achieve your purpose?

• How well did you organize the report?

• How did you go about researching the information for this piece?

• How did you go about drafting this piece?

• Did you use any tables, graphs, diagrams, photographs, illustrations, or other graphics effectively?

• How did others' responses influence your writing?

• What did you do especially well?

• What could still be improved?

• What would you do differently next time?

IF YOU NEED MORE HELP

287–96
150–54
173–82
191–204

See Chapter 29 if you are required to submit your report in a writing **PORTFOLIO.** See also Chapter 11 on **ABSTRACTS** if your report requires one; Chapter 14 on **LAB REPORTS,** a kind of report written in the sciences; and Chapter 16 on **PROFILES,** a report based on firsthand research.

Arguing a Position   **10**

Everything we say or do presents some kind of argument, takes some kind of position. Often we take overt positions: "Everyone in the United States is entitled to affordable health care." "The university needs to offer more language courses." "Photoshopped images should carry disclosure notices." But arguments can be less direct and specific as well, from yellow ribbons that honor U.S. troops to a yellow smiley face, which might be said to argue for a good day. In college course work, you are constantly called on to argue positions: in an English class, you may argue for a certain interpretation of a poem; in a business course, you may argue for the merits of a flat tax; in a linguistics class, you may argue that English is now a global language. All of those positions are arguable—people of goodwill can agree or disagree with them and present reasons and evidence to support their positions. This chapter provides guidelines for writing an essay that argues a position. We'll begin with four good examples, the first one annotated to point out key features of this kind of writing.

JOANNA MACKAY

Organ Sales Will Save Lives

In this essay, written for a class on ethics and politics in science, MIT student Joanna MacKay argues that the sale of human organs should be legal.

There are thousands of people dying to buy a kidney and thousands of people dying to sell a kidney. It seems a match made in heaven. So why are we standing in the way? Governments should not ban the sale of human organs; they should regulate it. Lives should not be wasted; they should be saved.

Clear and arguable position.

119

About 350,000 Americans suffer from end-stage renal disease, a state of kidney disorder so advanced that the organ stops functioning altogether. There are no miracle drugs that can revive a failed kidney, leaving dialysis and kidney transplantation as the only possible treatments (McDonnell and Mallon, Pars. 2 and 3).

Dialysis is harsh, expensive, and, worst of all, only temporary. Acting as an artificial kidney, dialysis mechanically filters the blood of a patient. It works, but not well. With treatment sessions lasting three hours, several times a week, those dependent on dialysis are, in a sense, shackled to a machine for the rest of their lives. Adding excessive stress to the body, dialysis causes patients to feel increasingly faint and tired, usually keeping them from work and other normal activities.

Kidney transplantation, on the other hand, is the closest thing to a cure that anyone could hope for. Today the procedure is both safe and reliable, causing few complications. With better technology for confirming tissue matches and new anti-rejection drugs, the surgery is relatively simple.

But those hoping for a new kidney have high hopes indeed. In the year 2000 alone, 2,583 Americans died while waiting for a kidney transplant; worldwide the number of deaths is around 50,000 (Finkel 27). With the sale of organs outlawed in almost every country, the number of living donors willing to part with a kidney for free is small. When no family member is a suitable candidate for donation, the patient is placed on a deceased donors list, relying on the organs from people dying of old age or accidents. The list is long. With over 60,000 people in line in the United States alone, the average wait for a cadaverous kidney is ten long years.

Daunted by the low odds, some have turned to an alternative solution: purchasing kidneys on the black market. For about $150,000, they can buy a fresh kidney from a healthy, living donor. There are no lines, no waits. Arranged through a broker, the entire procedure is carefully planned out. The buyer, seller, surgeons, and nurses are flown to a predetermined hospital in a foreign country. The operations are performed, and then all are flown back to their respective homes. There is no follow-up, no paperwork to sign (Finkel 27).

The illegal kidney trade is attractive not only because of the promptness but also because of the chance at a living donor. An organ from a cadaver will most likely be old or damaged, estimated to function for about ten years at most. A kidney from a living donor can last

Necessary background information.

over twice as long. Once a person's transplanted cadaverous kidney stops functioning, he or she must get back on the donors list, this time probably at the end of the line. A transplanted living kidney, however, could last a person a lifetime.

While there may seem to be a shortage of kidneys, in reality there is a surplus. In third world countries, there are people willing to do anything for money. In such extreme poverty these people barely have enough to eat, living in shacks and sleeping on dirt floors. Eager to pay off debts, they line up at hospitals, willing to sell a kidney for about $1,000. The money will go towards food and clothing, or perhaps to pay for a family member's medical operation (Goyal et al. 1590–1). Whatever the case, these people need the money.

Reason (donors need the money) supported by evidence.

There is certainly a risk in donating a kidney, but this risk is not great enough to be outlawed. Millions of people take risks to their health every day for money, or simply for enjoyment. As explained in *The Lancet*, "If the rich are free to engage in dangerous sports for pleasure, or dangerous jobs for high pay, it is difficult to see why the poor who take the lesser risk of kidney selling for greater rewards . . . should be thought so misguided as to need saving from themselves" (Radcliffe-Richards et al. 1951). Studies have shown that a person can live a healthy life with only one kidney. While these studies might not apply to the poor living under strenuous conditions in unsanitary environments, the risk is still theirs to take. These people have decided that their best hope for money is to sell a kidney. How can we deny them the best opportunity they have?

Counterargument (donating a kidney is risky) acknowledged.

Some agree with Pope John Paul II that the selling of organs is morally wrong and violates "the dignity of the human person" (qtd. in Finkel 26), but this is a belief professed by healthy and affluent individuals. Are we sure that the peasants of third world countries agree? The morals we hold are not absolute truths. We have the responsibility to protect and help those less fortunate, but we cannot let our own ideals cloud the issues at hand.

Counterargument (selling organs is wrong) acknowledged.

In a legal kidney transplant, everybody gains except the donor. The doctors and nurses are paid for the operation, the patient receives a new kidney, but the donor receives nothing. Sure, the donor will have the warm, uplifting feeling associated with helping a fellow human being, but this is not enough reward for most people to part with a piece of themselves. In an ideal world, the average person would be altruistic

Reason (altruism is not enough) supported by evidence.

10

enough to donate a kidney with nothing expected in return. The real world, however, is run by money. We pay men for donating sperm, and we pay women for donating ova, yet we expect others to give away an entire organ for no compensation. If the sale of organs were allowed, people would have a greater incentive to help save the life of a stranger.

While many argue that legalizing the sale of organs will exploit the poorer people of third world countries, the truth of the matter is that this is already the case. Even with the threat of a $50,000 fine and five years in prison (Finkel 26), the current ban has not been successful in preventing illegal kidney transplants. The kidneys of the poor are still benefiting only the rich. While the sellers do receive most of the money promised, the sum is too small to have any real impact on their financial situation. A study in India discovered that in the long run, organ sellers suffer. In the illegal kidney trade, nobody has the interests of the seller at heart. After selling a kidney, their state of living actually worsens. While the $1,000 pays off one debt, it is not enough to relieve the donor of the extreme poverty that placed him in debt in the first place (Goyal et al. 1591).

These impoverished people do not need stricter and harsher penalties against organ selling to protect them, but quite the opposite. If the sale of organs were made legal, it could be regulated and closely monitored by the government and other responsible organizations. Under a regulated system, education would be incorporated into the application process. Before deciding to donate a kidney, the seller should know the details of the operation and any hazards involved. Only with an understanding of the long-term physical health risks can a person make an informed decision (Radcliffe-Richards et al. 1951).

Regulation would ensure that the seller is fairly compensated. In the illegal kidney trade, surgeons collect most of the buyer's money in return for putting their careers on the line. The brokers arranging the procedure also receive a modest cut, typically around ten percent. If the entire practice were legalized, more of the money could be directed towards the person who needs it most, the seller. By eliminating the middleman and allowing the doctors to settle for lower prices, a regulated system would benefit all those in need of a kidney, both rich and poor. According to Finkel, the money that would otherwise be spent on dialysis treatment could not only cover the charge of a kidney

Counterargument (poor people are exploited) acknowledged.

Reason (regulating organ sales would lead to better decisions).

Reason (fairness to sellers) followed by evidence.

transplant at no cost to the recipient, but also reward the donor with as much as $25,000 (32). This money could go a long way for people living in the poverty of third world countries.

Critics fear that controlling the lawful sale of organs would be too difficult, but could it be any more difficult than controlling the unlawful sale of organs? Governments have tried to eradicate the kidney market for decades to no avail. Maybe it is time to try something else. When "desperately wanted goods" are made illegal, history has shown that there is more opportunity for corruption and exploitation than if those goods were allowed (Radcliffe-Richards et al. 1951). (Just look at the effects of the prohibition of alcohol, for example.) Legalization of organ sales would give governments the authority and the opportunity to closely monitor these live kidney operations.

Regulation would also protect the buyers. Because of the need for secrecy, the current illegal method of obtaining a kidney has no contracts and, therefore, no guarantees. Since what they are doing is illegal, the buyers have nobody to turn to if something goes wrong. There is nobody to point the finger at, nobody to sue. While those participating in the kidney market are breaking the law, they have no other choice. Without a new kidney, end-stage renal disease will soon kill them. Desperate to survive, they are forced to take the only offer available. It seems immoral to first deny them the opportunity of a new kidney and then to leave them stranded at the mercy of the black market. Without laws regulating live kidney transplants, these people are subject to possibly hazardous procedures. Instead of turning our backs, we have the power to ensure that these operations are done safely and efficiently for both the recipient and the donor.

Those suffering from end-stage renal disease would do anything for the chance at a new kidney, take any risk or pay any price. There are other people so poor that the sale of a kidney is worth the profit. Try to tell someone that he has to die from kidney failure because selling a kidney is morally wrong. Then turn around and try to tell another person that he has to remain in poverty for that same reason. In matters of life and death, our stances on moral issues must be reevaluated. If legalized and regulated, the sale of human organs would save lives. Is it moral to sentence thousands to unnecessary deaths?

15

Counterargument (controlling organ sales would be difficult) acknowledged.

Reason (fairness to buyers) supported by examples.

Concludes by asking a question for readers to consider.

Works Cited

Finkel, Michael. "This Little Kidney Went to Market." *New York Times Magazine* 27 May 2001: 26–33, 40, 52, 59. Print.

Goyal, Madhav, et al. "Economic and Health Consequences of Selling a Kidney in India." *Journal of the American Medical Association* 288 (2002): 1589–92. Print.

McDonnell, Michael B., and William K. Mallon. "Kidney Transplant." *eMedicine Health*. WebMD, 18 Aug. 2008. Web. 30 Nov. 2008.

Radcliffe-Richards, J., et al. "The Case for Allowing Kidney Sales." *Lancet* 351.9120 (1998): 1950–52. Print.

MacKay clearly states her position at the beginning of her text: "Governments should not ban the sale of human organs; they should regulate it." Her argument appeals to her readers' sense of fairness; when kidney sales are legalized and regulated, both sellers and buyers will benefit from the transaction. She uses MLA style to document her sources.

HEATHER E. DOUGLAS

The Dark Side of Science

In this text, philosopher of science Heather E. Douglas argues that scientists are responsible for the effects of their research. It first appeared in November 2011 in The Scientist, a magazine dedicated to "exploring life, inspiring innovation."

Within the burgeoning field of synthetic biology, teams of biologists and engineers are making great strides in understanding the cell and its functioning. . . . However, there is more that should be discussed than the triumphs. There are also the dark purposes to which science (and synthetic biology in particular) can be put. Worries range from the development of pathogenic bioweapons to the potential contamination of native gene pools in our environment. The question is, are scientists responsible for the potentially negative impacts of their work?

Some have argued that the answer to this question is no — that it is not researchers' responsibility how science gets used in society. But that is sophistry. Scientists are responsible for both the impacts they

Albert Einstein sits with J. Robert Oppenheimer, who went on to develop the atomic bomb.

intend and some of the impacts they do not intend, if they are readily foreseeable in specific detail. These are the standards to which we are all held as moral agents. If I were to negligently throw a used match into a dry field (merely because I wanted to dispose of it), for example, I would be responsible for the resulting wild fire. In contrast, Einstein was not responsible for the use of his $E=mc^2$ equation to build an atomic bomb and its use in wartime, though the scientists at Los Alamos were.

Of course, impacts (whether harmful or beneficial) are not solely scientists' responsibility — others involved will also bear responsibility for their actions. If scientific knowledge is used in a biological attack, the terrorists are first and foremost responsible for their heinous act. But the researchers who generated the knowledge may be also partly responsible. Consider, for example, the knowledge of how to build a virus like smallpox from the ground up or how to create other pathogenic, tailored organisms — targeted either to humans or the foods on which we depend. If it is readily foreseeable that such knowledge could be used for nefarious purposes, the scientists who introduce such new technological capacities are partially responsible for an attack that could ultimately cause millions of deaths.

Scientists can no longer hope naively that people will only use science for the public good. The world will always have the mentally unbalanced, the delusional, the vicious, and the sociopathic members of society, some of whom will also be intelligent enough to use the results of science. Recognizing this should be part of the everyday backdrop of science, the assessment of its potential, and the desirability of the pursuit of a particular project.

As scientists plumb the depths of the cell, they must be particularly cognizant of the potentially harmful uses of their work, in addition to all its intended benefits. For example, knowledge of how to generate specific strings of nucleotides with high precision greatly aids research by providing particular and accurate DNA sequences with which scientists can assess cell functioning and design new living systems. But such knowledge can also produce the raw materials for building known pathogens from scratch, as has already been done (for research purposes) with the polio virus and the Spanish flu virus. As scientists develop ways to generate sequences of base-pairs ever more cheaply and efficiently, the opportunity for the malicious or the simply unreflective to play with pathogens to see what kind of traits arise looms larger. And it is not just technological know-how that can be problematic. The detailed knowledge of cellular or genetic functioning can have worrisome implications as well. Knowledge of what makes a virus more transmissible can assist us in detecting when a virus might be more prone to producing an epidemic, but it could also be used to make viruses more virulent.

In sum, scientists are responsible for both what they intend to achieve and that which is readily foreseeable, as we all are. There is nothing inherent in becoming a scientist that removes this burden of responsibility. The burden can be shared — scientists can come together to decide how to proceed, or ask for input from ethicists, social scientists, even the broader public. Alternatively, scientists could decide (and it has been proposed) that some forms of regulation — either in the selection of projects or in the control and dissemination of results — be imposed on the field of synthetic biology, to reduce the risks. The more oversight scientists submit to, the less responsibility they bear, but it comes at the cost of the freedom to choose the type of work they can do and how they do it. This is the essential tension: as long as there is freedom of research, there is the responsibility that comes with it.

As a philosopher, Douglas supports her claim primarily with logical arguments, but her choice of examples also appeals to readers' emotions.

LAWRENCE LESSIG

Some Like It Hot
OK, P2P Is "Piracy." But So Was the Birth of Hollywood, Radio, Cable TV, and (Yes) the Music Industry.

This essay on electronic piracy appeared in Wired *magazine in March 2004. Lawrence Lessig is an authority on copyright law. He is a professor at Harvard Law School.*

If piracy means using the creative property of others without their permission, then the history of the content industry is a history of piracy. Every important sector of big media today — film, music, radio, and cable TV — was born of a kind of piracy. The consistent story is how each generation welcomes the pirates from the last. Each generation — until now.

The Hollywood film industry was built by fleeing pirates. Creators and directors migrated from the East Coast to California in the early twentieth century in part to escape controls that film patents granted the inventor Thomas Edison. These controls were exercised through the Motion Pictures Patents Company, a monopoly "trust" based on Edison's creative property and formed to vigorously protect his patent rights.

California was remote enough from Edison's reach that filmmakers like Fox and Paramount could move there and, without fear of the law, pirate his inventions. Hollywood grew quickly, and enforcement of federal law eventually spread west. But because patents granted their holders a truly "limited" monopoly of just seventeen years (at that time), the patents had expired by the time enough federal marshals appeared. A new industry had been founded, in part from the piracy of Edison's creative property.

Meanwhile, the record industry grew out of another kind of piracy. At the time that Edison and Henri Fourneaux invented machines for reproducing music (Edison the phonograph; Fourneaux the player piano), the law gave composers the exclusive right to control copies and public performances of their music. Thus, in 1900, if I wanted a copy of Phil Russel's 1899 hit, "Happy Mose," the law said I would have to pay for the right to get a copy of the score, and I would also have to pay for the right to perform it publicly.

But what if I wanted to record "Happy Mose" using Edison's phono- 5 graph or Fourneaux's player piano? Here the law stumbled. If I simply sang the piece into a recording device in my home, it wasn't clear that I owed the composer anything. And more important, it wasn't clear whether I owed the composer anything if I then made copies of those recordings. Because of this gap in the law, I could effectively use someone else's song without paying the composer anything. The composers (and publishers) were none too happy about this capacity to pirate.

In 1909, Congress closed the gap in favor of the composer and the recording artist, amending copyright law to make sure that composers would be paid for "mechanical reproductions" of their music. But rather than simply granting the composer complete control over the right to make such reproductions, Congress gave recording artists a right to record the music, at a price set by Congress, after the composer allowed it to be recorded once. This is the part of copyright law that makes cover songs possible. Once a composer authorizes a recording of his song, others are free to record the same song, so long as they pay the original composer a fee set by the law. So, by limiting musicians' rights—by partially pirating their creative work—record producers and the public benefit.

A similar story can be told about radio. When a station plays a composer's work on the air, that constitutes a "public performance." Copyright law gives the composer (or copyright holder) an exclusive right to public performances of his work. The radio station thus owes the composer money.

But when the station plays a record, it is not only performing a copy of the *composer's* work. The station is also performing a copy of the *recording artist's* work. It's one thing to air a recording of "Happy Birthday" by the local children's choir; it's quite another to air a recording of it by the Rolling Stones or Lyle Lovett. The recording artist is adding to the value of the composition played on the radio station. And if the law were perfectly consistent, the station would have to pay the artist for his work, just as it pays the composer.

But it doesn't. This difference can be huge. Imagine you compose a piece of music. You own the exclusive right to authorize public

A "pirated" image combines photographs of Marilyn Monroe and Cyril Ritchard (as Captain Hook) to poke fun at overly controlling copyright laws.

performances of that music. So if Madonna wants to sing your song in public, she has to get your permission.

Imagine she does sing your song, and imagine she likes it a lot. She then decides to make a recording of your song, and it becomes a top hit. Under today's law, every time a radio station plays your song, you get some money. But Madonna gets nothing, save the indirect effect on the sale of her CDs. The public performance of her recording is not a "protected" right. The radio station thus gets to pirate the value of Madonna's work without paying her a dime.

No doubt, one might argue, the promotion artists get is worth more than the performance rights they give up. Maybe. But even if that's the case, this is a choice that the law ordinarily gives to the creator. Instead, the law gives the radio station the right to take something for nothing.

Cable TV, too: When entrepreneurs first started installing cable in 1948, most refused to pay the networks for the content that they hijacked and delivered to their customers—even though they were basically selling access to otherwise free television broadcasts. Cable companies were thus Napsterizing broadcasters' content, but more egregiously than anything Napster ever did—Napster never charged for the content it enabled others to give away.

Broadcasters and copyright owners were quick to attack this theft. As then Screen Actors Guild president Charlton Heston put it, the cable outfits were "free riders" who were "depriving actors of compensation."

Copyright owners took the cable companies to court. Twice the Supreme Court held that the cable companies owed the copyright owners nothing. The debate shifted to Congress, where almost thirty years later it resolved the question in the same way it had dealt with phonographs and player pianos. Yes, cable companies would have to pay for the content that they broadcast, but the price they would have to pay was not set by the copyright owner. Instead, lawmakers set the price so that the broadcasters couldn't veto the emerging technologies of cable. The companies thus built their empire in part upon a piracy of the value created by broadcasters' content.

As the history of film, music, radio, and cable TV suggest, even if 15 some piracy is plainly wrong, not all piracy is. Or at least not in the sense that the term is increasingly being used today. Many kinds of piracy are useful and productive, either to create new content or foster new ways of doing business. Neither our tradition, nor any tradition, has ever banned all piracy.

This doesn't mean that there are no questions raised by the latest piracy concern—peer-to-peer file sharing. But it does mean that we need to understand the harm in P2P sharing a bit more before we condemn it to the gallows.

Like the original Hollywood, P2P sharing seeks to escape an overly controlling industry. And like the original recording and radio industries, it is simply exploiting a new way of distributing content. But unlike cable TV, no one is selling the content that gets shared on P2P services. This difference distinguishes P2P sharing. We should find a way to protect artists while permitting this sharing to survive.

Much of the "piracy" that file sharing enables is plainly legal and good. It provides access to content that is technically still under copyright but that is no longer commercially available—in the case of music, some four million tracks. More important, P2P networks enable sharing of content that copyright owners want shared, as well as work already in the public domain. This clearly benefits authors and society.

Moreover, much of the sharing—which is referred to by many as piracy—is motivated by a new way of spreading content made possible by changes in the technology of distribution. Thus, consistent with the tradition that gave us Hollywood, radio, the music industry, and cable TV, the question we should be asking about file sharing is how best to preserve its benefits while minimizing (to the extent possible) the wrongful harm it causes artists.

The question is one of balance, weighing the protection of the law 20 against the strong public interest in continued innovation. The law should seek that balance, and that balance will be found only with time.

Lessig argues that the "piracy" that Napster and other peer-to-peer music-sharing services are accused of is similar to that practiced by every other electronic medium in the last one hundred years. He offers a clear definition of piracy and carefully supports his assertions with historical evidence for each one.

ANDREW LEONARD

Black Friday: Consumerism Minus Civilization

This essay arguing that advertising for day-after-Thanksgiving sales has gone too far first appeared on Salon, where it includes several videos and links to other websites, which are underlined in this text. The online version may be accessed via wwnorton.com/write/fieldguidelinks.

Here's a Thanksgiving recipe guaranteed to deliver a nervous breakdown impervious to even the most bleeding-edge psychopharmaceutical wonder drug. Go to YouTube, search for "Black Friday commercials," start watching, and then, once you've sated yourself on grown men screaming at Justin Bieber, remakes of Rebecca Black's "Friday," and, most distressingly, the continuing adventures of the Crazy Target Lady, ask yourself this question:

What does it all mean?

I stared into this heart of retail panic darkness, and the more I clicked and pondered, the more confused — (mind-boggled? fascinated? flabbergasted?) — I became. The Crazy Target Lady, so proud of her OCD — obsessive Christmas disorder — is not funny. She's scary. She's why people trample each other to death. She is wrong.

Grown men scream at Justin Bieber in the Macy's Black Friday ad.

There is a point in our culture beyond which camp and kitsch no longer make the least ironic sense, where consumerism loses its last mooring to civilization, where even seemingly legitimate protest devolves into farce. That point is Black Friday.

Let me be clear. I am not opposed to vigorous sprees of retail spending. For the sake of the U.S. economy, I would love to see a robust Christmas shopping season and I plan to do my part. I find the notion that we should "occupy Black Friday" and withhold our consumer dollars as a way of hitting back at the 1 percent just nutty. Voluntarily subtracting demand from the economy hurts *us*. A general consumer strike would result in more layoffs and pay cuts and bankruptcies and foreclosures. Sure, Wal-Mart would take a hit, but so would Wal-Mart employees.

But there's also a point where healthy consumerism becomes out-of-control marketing-driven commodity fetishism, and when we find ourselves checking our smartphones for last minute online deals while standing in line for a chain store opening at midnight on Thanksgiving, we are clearly too far gone. That's insanity.

And corporate America knows this. The retail moguls are counting on it. They are outright encouraging it — and role-modeling the appropriate behavior for us. The Crazy Target Lady is not a joke. Watch her cannibalize her gingerbread man, or strategize her reverse psychology shopping techniques, or show off her shopping utility belt: You cannot avoid the dual conclusion that a) she is not a healthy woman, and b) she is *America*. She might be a lunatic, but it's a culturally approved lunacy — the kind that keeps the American engine of capitalism all stoked up. The message that keeps getting blasted across my TV is that we should all be more like her — doing our patriotic duty to boost fourth-quarter retail sales. Sure, you can laugh at her. But then get in line and keep your credit card handy.

But, of course, the big story of this year's Black Friday has been the welcome news that at least some subsection of the population of the United States has come to the realization that it's time to step back from the brink. The budding protests against the decision by some of the country's biggest retailers — Target, Macy's, Best Buy, Kohl's — to move the start of their Black Friday sales to midnight Thanksgiving, or even earlier, is laudable.

The Crazy Target Lady models her shopping utility belt.

The nearly 200,000 signatures on part-time Target employee Anthony Hardwick's petition to "Save Thanksgiving" is proof that both employees and customers of Target are beginning to see this endless race by retailers to one-up each other as dehumanizing and ridiculous. What does a Target employee forced to go to work at 11 p.m. on Thanksgiving have to give thanks for?

(Although, even here, in the protest arena, it's hard to know what 10 to make of the "Respect the Bird" campaign hosted at AllRecipes.com that mixes pledges to "take back Thanksgiving" with KitchenAid mixer promotions and ads for pop-up turkey timers. Even the *protests* are inseparable from consumerist mania.)

The chains are lamely defending their move as a response to forces beyond their control:

"As that is the busiest shopping day of the year, it is imperative that we be competitive," said Anahita Cameron, a Target human resources director, in a statement quoted by the *L.A. Times*. "Our guests have expressed that they would prefer to kick off their holiday shopping by heading out after their holiday celebrations rather than getting up in the middle of the night."

The "Friday" parody used in the Kohl's campaign.

rhetorical situations

genres

processes

strategies

research MLA / APA

media / design

handbook

Guests? Pre-programmed automatons would be more accurate. I am undoubtedly reading too much into the "Black Friday" parody of Rebecca Black's "Friday" currently touting the midnight Thanksgiving sale at Kohl's, but there is an awfully revealing moment at the very end of the ad.

After the perky Stepford-wife shopper sings joyfully about how she's "been in line since yesterday" and how everybody's going to Kohl's at "midnight, midnight" the ad ends with her observing, with a mild air of perturbance, that she "can't get this darn song out of my head."

Ladies and gentlemen, there's your winner of the 2011 award for 15 honesty in advertising. A commercial attempting to brainwash consumers into lining up for a midnight sale manages also to explicitly reference the difficulty of shaking free from mindless jingles.

That's kind of brilliant. But also very wrong. Which makes it the perfect commercial for summing up the culture-wide psychotic spasm that is Black Friday. Stay home Thanksgiving night. Go shopping after getting a full night's rest. Sure, you might miss a sale or two. But you'll be a better human being.

Leonard's claim, that Black Friday represents "out-of-control marketing-driven commodity fetishism" or, more concisely, "insanity," is vividly illustrated by several videos of commercials that provide both background information and evidence for his argument. He acknowledges the need for "vigorous sprees of retail spending" while decrying the "psychotic spasm that is Black Friday."

Key Features / Arguments

A clear and arguable position. At the heart of every argument is a claim with which people may reasonably disagree. Some claims are not arguable because they're completely subjective, matters of taste or opinion ("I hate sauerkraut"), because they are a matter of fact ("The first *Star Wars* movie came out in 1977"), or because they are based on belief or faith ("There is life after death"). To be arguable, a position must reflect one of at least two points of view, making reasoned argument necessary: Internet file sharing should (or should not) be considered fair use; selling human organs should be legal (or illegal). In college writing, you will often argue not that a position is correct but that it is plausible — that it is reasonable, supportable, and worthy of being taken seriously.

Necessary background information.   Sometimes we need to provide some background on a topic we are arguing so that readers can understand what is being argued. MacKay establishes the need for kidney donors before launching her argument for legalizing the selling of organs; Douglas describes scientific progress in synthetic biology.

Good reasons.   By itself, a position does not make an argument; the argument comes when a writer offers reasons to back the position up. There are many kinds of good reasons. Lessig makes his argument by comparing, showing many examples of so-called piracy in other media. Douglas reasons that scientists must recognize that their research may be used for destructive purposes. MacKay bases her argument in favor of legalizing the sale of human organs on the grounds that doing so would save more lives, that impoverished people should be able to make risky choices, and that regulation would protect such people who currently sell their organs on the black market as well as desperate buyers.

Convincing evidence.   Once you're given reasons for your position, you then need to offer evidence for your reasons: facts, statistics, expert testimony, anecdotal evidence, case studies, textual evidence. All four arguments use a mix of these types of evidence. MacKay cites statistics about Americans who die from renal failure to support her argument for legalizing organ sales; Lessig offers facts from the history of the broadcast media to support his argument for file sharing. Douglas outlines the positive and negative uses to which cell research has been put. Leonard

rhetorical situations

genres

processes

strategies

research MLA / APA

media / design

handbook

presents several videos to demonstrate how excessive Black Friday advertising has become.

Appeals to readers' values. Effective arguers try to appeal to readers' values and emotions. Both MacKay and Lessig appeal to basic values—MacKay to the value of compassion, both writers to the value of fairness. These are deeply held values that we may not think about very much and as a result may see as common ground we share with the writers. And some of MacKay's evidence appeals to emotion—her descriptions of people dying from kidney disease and of poor people selling their organs are likely to evoke an emotional response in many readers.

A trustworthy tone. Arguments can stand or fall on the way readers perceive the writer. Very simply, readers need to trust the person who's making the argument. One way of winning this trust is by demonstrating that you know what you're talking about. Lessig offers plenty of facts to show his knowledge of copyright history—and he does so in a self-assured tone. There are many other ways of establishing yourself (and your argument) as trustworthy—by showing that you have some experience with your subject, that you're fair, and of course that you're honest. Occasionally, an outraged tone such as Leonard's is appropriate, especially when it is tempered by good reasons and qualified as he does in noting that he is "undoubtedly reading too much into the Kohl's . . . parody."

Careful consideration of other positions. No matter how reasonable and careful we are in arguing our positions, others may disagree or offer counterarguments. We need to consider those other views and to acknowledge and, if possible, refute them in our written arguments. MacKay, for example, acknowledges that some believe that selling organs is unethical, but she counters that it's usually healthy, affluent people who say this — not people who need either an organ or the money they could get by selling one.

A GUIDE TO WRITING ARGUMENTS

Choosing a Topic

A fully developed argument requires significant work and time, so choosing a topic in which you're interested is very important. Students often find that widely debated topics such as "animal rights" or "gun control" can be difficult to write on because they don't feel any personal connection to them. Better topics include those that

- interest you right now
- are focused but not too narrowly
- have some personal connection to your life

259–65 ◯

One good way to **GENERATE IDEAS** for a topic that meets those three criteria is to explore your own roles in life.

260–61 ◯

Start with your roles in life. Make four columns with the headings "Personal," "Family," "Public," and "School." Then **LIST** the roles you play that relate to it. Here is a list one student wrote:

Personal	Family	Public	School
gamer	son	voter	college student
dog owner	younger	homeless-shelter	work-study
old-car owner	brother	volunteer	employee
male	grandson	American	dorm resident
white		resident	primary-education
middle class		of Ohio	major

Identify issues that interest you. Think, then, about issues or controversies that may concern you as a member of one or more of those groups. For instance, as a primary-education major, this student cares about the controversy over whether teachers' jobs should be focused on preparing kids for high-stakes standardized tests. As a college student, he cares about the costs of a college education. Issues that stem from these subjects could include the following: Should student progress be measured by standardized tests? Should college cost less than it does?

Pick four or five of the roles you list. In five or ten minutes, identify issues that concern or affect you as a member of each of those roles. It might help to word each issue as a question starting with *Should*.

Frame your topic as a problem. Most position papers address issues that are subjects of ongoing debate — their solutions aren't easy, and people disagree on which ones are best. Posing your topic as a problem can help you think about the topic, find an issue that's suitable to write about, and find a clear focus for your essay.

For example, if you wanted to write an argument on the lack of student parking at your school, you could frame your topic as one of several problems: What causes the parking shortage? Why are the university's parking garages and lots limited in their capacity? What might alleviate the shortage?

Choose one issue to write about. Remember that the issue should be interesting to you and have some connection to your life. It is a tentative choice; if you find later that you have trouble writing about it, simply go back to your list of roles or issues and choose another.

Considering the Rhetorical Situation

PURPOSE	Do you want to persuade your audience to do something? Change their minds? Consider alternative views? Accept your position as plausible — see that you have thought carefully about an issue and researched it appropriately?
AUDIENCE	Who is your intended audience? What do they likely know and believe about this issue? How personal is it for them? To what extent are they likely to agree or disagree with you? Why? What common ground can you find with them?

3–4

5–8

12–15 ■ **STANCE** What's your attitude toward your topic, and why? How do you want your audience to perceive your attitude? How do you want your audience to perceive you? As an authority on your topic? As someone much like them? As calm? reasonable? impassioned or angry? something else?

16–18 ■ **MEDIA / DESIGN** What media will you use, and how do your media affect your argument? Does your print or online argument call for photos or charts? If you're giving an oral presentation, should you put your reasons and support on slides? If you're writing online, should you include audio or video evidence or links to counterarguments?

Generating Ideas and Text

Most essays that successfully argue a position share certain features that make them interesting and persuasive. Remember that your goal is to stake out a position and convince your readers that it is plausible.

Explore what you already know about the issue. Write out whatever you know about the issue by **FREEWRITING** or as a **LIST** or **OUTLINE.** Why are
259–61 ○
263–64
you interested in this topic? What is your position on it at this point, and why? What aspect do you think you'd like to focus on? Where do you need to focus your research efforts? This activity can help you discover what more you need to learn. Chances are you'll need to learn a lot more about the issue before you even decide what position to take.

Do some research. At this point, try to get an overview. Start with one
439–40 ●
GENERAL SOURCE of information that will give you a sense of the ins and outs of your issue, one that isn't overtly biased. *The Daily Beast, Time,* and other online newsmagazines can be good starting points on current issues.
448–49 ●
For some issues, you may need to **INTERVIEW** an expert. For example, one

student who wanted to write about chemical abuse of animals at 4H competitions interviewed an experienced show competitor. Use your overview source to find out the main questions raised about your issue and to get some idea about the various ways in which you might argue it.

Explore the issue strategically.   Most issues may be argued from many different perspectives. You'll probably have some sense of the different views that exist on your issue, but you should explore multiple perspectives before deciding on your position. The following methods are good ways of exploring issues:

- As a matter of **DEFINITION.** What is it? How should it be defined? How can *organic* or *genetically modified food* be defined? How do proponents of *organic food* define it—and how do they define *genetically modified food*? How do advocates of *genetically modified food* define it—and how do they define *organic food*? Considering such definitions is one way to identify different perspectives on the topic.

  356–66

- As a matter of **CLASSIFICATION.** Can the issue be divided into categories? Are there different kinds of, or different ways of, producing organic foods and genetically modified foods? Do different categories suggest particular positions or perhaps a way of supporting a certain position? Are there other ways of categorizing foods?

  342–47

- As a matter of **COMPARISON.** Is one subject being considered better than another? Is organic food healthier or safer than genetically modified food? Is genetically modified food healthier or safer than organic? Is the answer somewhere in the middle?

  348–55

- As a matter of **PROCESS.** Should somebody do something? What? Should people buy and eat more organic food? More genetically modified food? Should they buy and eat some of each?

  382–86

Reconsider whether the issue can be argued.   Is this issue worth discussing? Why is it important to you and to others? What difference will it make if one position or another prevails? Is it **ARGUABLE?** At this point, you want to be sure that your topic is worth arguing about.

323–41

Draft a thesis. Having explored the possibilities, decide your position, and write it out as a complete sentence. For example:

> Barry Bonds should not be eligible for the Hall of Fame.
>
> Reading should be taught using a mix of whole language and phonics.
>
> Genetically modified foods should be permitted in the United States.

Qualify your thesis. Rather than taking a strict pro or con position, in most cases you'll want to QUALIFY YOUR POSITION—in certain circumstances, with certain conditions, with these limitations, and so on. This is not to say that we should settle, give in, sell out; rather, it is to say that our position may not be the only "correct" one and that other positions may be valid as well. QUALIFYING YOUR THESIS also makes your topic manageable by limiting it. For example:

325
314–15

> Barry Bonds should not be eligible for the Hall of Fame, though he should be permitted to contribute to major league baseball in other ways.
>
> Reading should be taught using a mix of phonics and whole language, but the needs of individual students, not a philosophy, should be the primary focus.
>
> Genetically modified foods should be permitted in the United States if they are clearly labeled as such.

Come up with good reasons. Once you have a thesis, you need to come up with good REASONS to convince your readers that it's plausible. Write out your position, and then list several reasons. For instance, if your thesis is that Barry Bonds should not be eligible for the Hall of Fame, two of your reasons might be:

326–27

> He almost certainly used steroids in the later part of his career.
>
> Using steroids gives athletes unfair advantages and must be considered cheating.

Think about which reasons are best for your purposes: Which seem the most persuasive? Which are most likely to be accepted by your audience? Which seem to matter the most now? If your list of reasons is short or you think you'll have trouble developing them enough to write an appropriate essay, this is a good time to rethink your topic — before you've invested too much time in it.

Develop support for your reasons. Next, you have to come up with *327–35* EVIDENCE to support your reasons: facts, statistics, examples, testimony by authorities and experts, anecdotal evidence, scenarios, case studies and observation, and textual evidence. For some topics, you may want or need to use evidence in visual form like photos, graphs, and charts; online, you could also use video or audio evidence and links to evidence in other websites.

What counts as evidence varies across audiences. Statistical evidence may be required in certain disciplines but not in others; anecdotes may be accepted as evidence in some courses but not in engineering. Some audiences will be persuaded by emotional appeals while others will not. For example, if you argue that Barry Bonds should be eligible for the National Baseball Hall of Fame because he's one of the greatest baseball players of all time, you could support that reason with *facts*: he was named Major League Player of the Year three times. Or you could support it with *statistics*: Bonds holds Major League records for the most career home runs, walks, and intentional walks. *Expert testimony* might include *Sports Illustrated* columnist Jon Heyman, who writes, "A baseball Hall of Fame would be empty without Bonds."

Identify other positions. Now, think about positions that differ from yours and about the reasons people are likely to give for those positions. Be careful to represent their points of view as accurately and fairly as you can. Then decide whether you need to acknowledge or to refute each position.

Acknowledging other positions. Some positions can't be refuted but are too important to ignore, so you need to ACKNOWLEDGE concerns and objec- *336* tions they raise to show that you've considered other perspectives. For example, in an essay arguing that vacations are necessary to maintain good health, medical writer Alina Tugend acknowledges that "in some cases, these trips — particularly with entire families in tow — can be stressful in their own way. The joys of a holiday can also include lugging around a ridiculous amount of paraphernalia, jet-lagged children sobbing on airplanes, hotels that looked wonderful on the Web but are in reality next to a construction site." Tugend's acknowledgment moderates her position and makes her argument appear more reasonable.

Refuting other positions. State the position as clearly and as fairly as you can, and then **REFUTE** it by showing why you believe it is wrong. Perhaps the reasoning is faulty or the supporting evidence inadequate. Acknowledge the merits of the position, if any, but emphasize its short-comings. Avoid the **FALLACY** of attacking the person holding the position or bringing up a competing position that no one seriously entertains.

337

338–40

Ways of Organizing an Argument

Readers need to be able to follow the reasoning of your argument from beginning to end; your task is to lead them from point to point as you build your case. Sometimes you'll want to give all the reasons for your argument first, followed by discussion of any other positions. Alternatively, you might discuss each reason and any opposing arguments together.

[Reasons to support your argument, followed by opposing arguments]

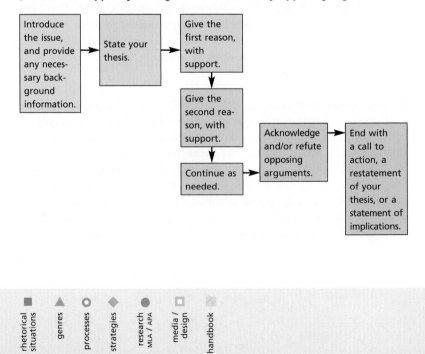

[Reason / opposing argument, reason/opposing argument]

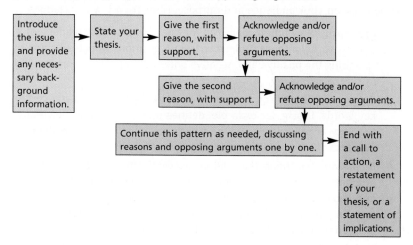

Consider carefully the order in which you discuss your reasons. Usually what comes last makes the strongest impression on readers and what comes in the middle the least impression, so you might want to put your most important or strongest reasons first and last.

Writing Out a Draft

Once you have generated ideas, done some research, and thought about how you want to organize your argument, it's time to start **DRAFTING.** Your goal in the initial draft is to develop your argument—you can fill in support and transitions as you revise. You may want to write your first draft in one sitting, so that you can develop your reasoning from beginning to end. Or you may write the main argument first and the introduction and conclusion after you've drafted the body of the essay; many writers find that beginning and ending an essay are the hardest tasks they face. Here is some advice on how you might **BEGIN AND END** your argument:

○ 266–68

◆ 299–311

Draft a beginning.   There are various ways to begin an argument essay, depending on your audience and purpose. Here are a few suggestions.

- *Offer background information.* You may need to give your readers information to help them understand your position. Douglas begins by sketching the positive and negative potential impacts of current work in synthetic biology.

- *Define a key term.* You may need to show how you're using certain key words. Lessig, for example, defines piracy as "using the creative property of others without their permission" in his first sentence, a **DEFINITION** that is central to his argument.

356–66

- *Begin with something that will get readers' attention.* MacKay begins emphatically: "There are thousands of people dying to buy a kidney and thousands of people dying to sell a kidney . . . So why are we standing in the way?" Leonard offers still photos from two commercials and links to two more available online.

- *Explain the context for your position.* All arguments are part of a larger, ongoing conversation, so you might begin by showing how your position fits into the arguments others have made. Lessig provides a history of piracy in four different electronic media.

Draft an ending.   Your conclusion is the chance to wrap up your argument in such a way that readers will remember what you've said. Here are a few ways of concluding an argument essay.

- *Summarize your main points.* Especially when you've presented a complex argument, it can help readers to **SUMMARIZE** your main point. MacKay sums up her argument with the sentence "If legalized and regulated, the sale of human organs would save lives."

470–71

- *Call for action.* Lessig does this when he concludes by saying the law should seek a balance between copyright law and the need for continued innovation. Leonard presents an alternative to Black Friday's excesses: "Stay home Thanksgiving night. Go shopping after getting a full night's rest."

- *Frame your argument by referring to the introduction.* MacKay does this when she ends by reiterating that selling organs benefits both seller and buyer.

Come up with a title. Most often you'll want your title to tell readers something about your topic—and to make them want to read on. MacKay's "Organ Sales Will Save Lives" tells us both her topic and position. Douglas's title, "The Dark Side of Science," entices us with melodrama. See the chapter on GUIDING YOUR READER for more advice on composing a good title.

◆ 312–17

Considering Matters of Design

You'll probably write the main text of your argument in paragraph form, but think about what kind of information you're presenting and how you can design it to make your argument as easy as possible for your readers to understand. Think also about whether any visual or audio elements would be more persuasive than written words.

- What would be an appropriate FONT? Something serious like Times Roman? Something traditional like Courier? Something else?

□ 585–86

- Would it help your readers if you divided your argument into shorter sections and added HEADINGS?

□ 588–89

- If you're making several points, would they be easier to follow if you set them off in a LIST?

□ 587

- Do you have any supporting evidence that would be easier to understand in the form of a bar GRAPH, line graph, or pie chart?

□ 593–95

- Would ILLUSTRATIONS—photos, diagrams, or drawings—add support for your argument? Online, would video, audio, or links help?

□ 591–99

Getting Response and Revising

At this point you need to look at your draft closely, and if possible GET RESPONSE from others as well. Following are some questions for looking at an argument with a critical eye.

◉ 275–76

- Is there sufficient background or context?
- Is the thesis clear and appropriately qualified?
- Are the reasons plausible?
- Is there enough evidence to support these reasons? Is that evidence appropriate?
- Can readers follow the steps in your reasoning?
- Have you considered potential objections or other positions? Are there any others that should be addressed?
- Have you cited enough sources, and are these sources credible?
- Are source materials documented carefully and completely, with in-text citations and a works cited or references section?
- Are any visuals or links that are included used effectively and integrated smoothly with the rest of the text? If there are no visuals or links, would using some strengthen the argument?

276–79 Next it's time to **REVISE,** to make sure your argument offers convincing evidence, appeals to readers' values, and achieves your purpose.

Editing and Proofreading

Readers equate correctness with competence. Once you've revised your 283–85 draft, follow these guidelines for **EDITING** an argument:

- Check to see that your tone is appropriate and consistent throughout, 12–15 reflects your **STANCE** accurately, and enhances the argument you're making.
- Be sure readers will be able to follow the argument; check to see you've 317 provided **TRANSITIONS** and summary statements where necessary.
- 462–74 Make sure you've smoothly integrated **QUOTATIONS**, **PARAPHRASES**, and 480–83 **SUMMARIES** from source material into your writing and **DOCUMENTED** them accurately.
- Look for phrases such as "I think" or "I feel" and delete them; your essay itself expresses your opinion.

- Make sure that **ILLUSTRATIONS** have captions and that charts and graphs have headings — and that all are referred to in the main text.
- **PROOFREAD** and spell-check your essay carefully.

591–99

285–86

Taking Stock of Your Work

Take stock of what you've written by writing out answers to these questions:

- What did you do well in this piece?
- What could still be improved?
- How did you go about researching your topic?
- How did others' responses influence your writing?
- How did you go about drafting this piece?
- Did you use visual elements (tables, graphs, diagrams, photographs), audio elements, or links effectively? If not, would they have helped?
- What would you do differently next time?
- What have you learned about your writing ability from writing this piece? What do you need to work on in the future?

IF YOU NEED MORE HELP

See Chapter 29 if you are required to submit your argument as part of a writing **PORTFOLIO.** See also Chapter 8 on **ANALYZING A TEXT,** Chapter 13 on **EVALUA-TIONS,** and Chapter 17 on **PROPOSALS** for advice on writing those specific types of arguments.

287–96
52–86
164–72
205–13

11 Abstracts

Abstracts are summaries written to give readers the gist of a report or presentation. Sometimes they are published in conference proceedings or databases. In some academic fields, you may be required to include an abstract in a **REPORT** or as a preview of a presentation you plan to give at an academic or professional conference. Abstracts are brief, typically 100–200 words, sometimes even shorter. Three common kinds are *informative abstracts*, *descriptive abstracts*, and *proposal abstracts*.

87–118 ▲

INFORMATIVE ABSTRACTS

Informative abstracts state in one paragraph the essence of a whole paper about a study or a research project. That one paragraph must mention all the main points or parts of the paper: a description of the study or project, its methods, the results, and the conclusions. Here is an example of the abstract accompanying a seven-page essay that appeared in the *Journal of Clinical Psychology*:

> The relationship between boredom proneness and health-symptom reporting was examined. Undergraduate students ($N = 200$) completed the Boredom Proneness Scale and the Hopkins Symptom Checklist. A multiple analysis of covariance indicated that individuals with high boredom-proneness total scores reported significantly higher ratings on all five subscales of the Hopkins Symptom Checklist (Obsessive–Compulsive, Somatization, Anxiety, Interpersonal Sensitivity, and Depression). The results suggest that boredom proneness may be an important element to consider when assessing symptom reporting. Implications for determining the effects of boredom proneness on psychological- and physical-health symptoms, as well as the application in clinical settings, are discussed.
>
> —Jennifer Sommers and Stephen J. Vodanovich,
> "Boredom Proneness"

rhetorical situations · genres · processes · strategies · research MLA / APA · media / design · handbook

The first sentence states the nature of the study being reported. The next summarizes the method used to investigate the problem, and the following one gives the results: students who, according to specific tests, are more likely to be bored are also more likely to have certain medical or psychological symptoms. The last two sentences indicate that the paper discusses those results and examines the conclusion and its implications.

DESCRIPTIVE ABSTRACTS

Descriptive abstracts are usually much briefer than informative abstracts and provide much less information. Rather than summarizing the entire paper, a descriptive abstract functions more as a teaser, providing a quick overview that invites the reader to read the whole. Descriptive abstracts usually do not give or discuss results or set out the conclusion or its implications. A descriptive abstract of the boredom-proneness essay might simply include the first sentence from the informative abstract plus a final sentence of its own:

> The relationship between boredom proneness and health-symptom reporting was examined. The findings and their application in clinical settings are discussed.

PROPOSAL ABSTRACTS

Proposal abstracts contain the same basic information as informative abstracts, but their purpose is very different. You prepare proposal abstracts to persuade someone to let you write on a topic, pursue a project, conduct an experiment, or present a paper at a scholarly conference. This kind of abstract is not written to introduce a longer piece but rather to stand alone, and often the abstract is written before the paper itself. Titles and other aspects of the proposal deliberately reflect the theme of the proposed work, and you may use the future tense, rather than the past, to describe work not yet completed. Here is a possible proposal for doing research on boredom:

Undergraduate students will complete the Boredom Proneness Scale and the Hopkins Symptom Checklist. A multiple analysis of covariance will be performed to determine the relationship between boredom-proneness total scores and ratings on the five subscales of the Hopkins Symptom Checklist (Obsessive–Compulsive, Somatization, Anxiety, Interpersonal Sensitivity, and Depression).

Key Features / Abstracts

A summary of basic information. An informative abstract includes enough information to substitute for the report itself, a descriptive abstract offers only enough information to let the audience decide whether to read further, and a proposal abstract gives an overview of the planned work.

Objective description. Abstracts present information on the contents of a report or a proposed study; they do not present arguments about or personal perspectives on those contents. The informative abstract on boredom proneness, for example, offers only a tentative conclusion: "The results *suggest* that boredom proneness *may* be an important element to consider."

Brevity. Although the length of abstracts may vary, journals and organizations often restrict them to 120–200 words — meaning you must carefully select and edit your words.

A BRIEF GUIDE TO WRITING ABSTRACTS

Considering the Rhetorical Situation

3–4 ■	**PURPOSE**	Are you giving a brief but thorough overview of a completed study? Only enough information to create interest? Or a proposal for a planned study or presentation?
5–8 ■	**AUDIENCE**	For whom are you writing this abstract? What information about your project will your readers need?

STANCE   Whatever your stance in the longer work, your abstract must be objective.

12–15

MEDIA / DESIGN   How will you set your abstract off from the rest of the text? If you are publishing it online, should it be on a separate page? What format do your readers expect?

16–18

Generating Ideas and Text

Write the paper first, the abstract last.   You can then use the finished work as the guide for the abstract, which should follow the same basic structure. *Exception:* You may need to write a proposal abstract months before the work it describes will be complete.

Copy and paste key statements.   If you've already written the work, highlight your **THESIS,** objective, or purpose; basic information on your methods; your results; and your conclusion. Copy and paste those sentences into a new document to create a rough version of your abstract.

313–15

Pare down the rough abstract.   **SUMMARIZE** the key ideas in the document, editing out any nonessential words and details. In your first sentence, introduce the overall scope of your study. Also include any other information that seems crucial to understanding your paper. Avoid phrases that add unnecessary words, such as "It is concluded that." In general, you probably won't want to use "I"; an abstract should cover ideas, not say what you think or will do.

470–71

Conform to any requirements.   In general, an informative abstract should be at most 10 percent as long as the original and no longer than the maximum length allowed. Descriptive abstracts should be shorter still, and proposal abstracts should conform to the requirements of the organization calling for the proposal.

Ways of Organizing an Abstract

[An informative abstract]

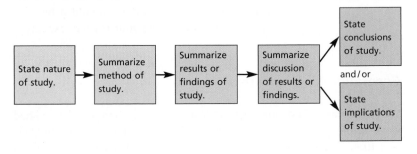

State nature of study. → Summarize method of study. → Summarize results or findings of study. → Summarize discussion of results or findings. → State conclusions of study. and/or State implications of study.

[A descriptive abstract]

Announce subject of study. → Give brief overview of full paper.

[A proposal abstract]

Announce subject of study. → Summarize method to be used.

266–68
269–74
282–86

> **IF YOU NEED MORE HELP**
>
> See Chapter 25 for guidelines on **DRAFTING,** Chapter 26 on **ASSESSING YOUR OWN WRITING,** Chapter 27 on **GETTING RESPONSE AND REVISING,** and Chapter 28 on **EDITING AND PROOFREADING.**

rhetorical situations ■ genres ▲ processes ○ strategies ◆ research MLA / APA ● media / design □ handbook ⌃

Annotated Bibliographies **12**

Annotated bibliographies describe, give publication information for, and sometimes evaluate each work on a list of sources. When we do research, we may consult annotated bibliographies to evaluate potential sources. You may also be assigned to create annotated bibliographies to weigh the potential usefulness of sources and to document your search efforts so that teachers can assess your ability to find, describe, and evaluate sources. There are two kinds of annotations, *descriptive* and *evaluative*; both may be brief, consisting only of phrases, or more formal, consisting of sentences and paragraphs. Sometimes an annotated bibliography is introduced by a short statement explaining its scope.

Descriptive annotations simply summarize the contents of each work, without comment or evaluation. They may be very short, just long enough to capture the flavor of the work, like the examples in the following excerpt from a bibliography of books and articles on teen films, published in the *Journal of Popular Film and Television*.

MICHAEL BENTON, MARK DOLAN, AND REBECCA ZISCH

Teen Film$

In the introduction to his book *The Road to Romance and Ruin*, Jon Lewis points out that over half of the world's population is currently under the age of twenty. This rather startling fact should be enough to make most Hollywood producers drool when they think of the potential profits from a target movie audience. Attracting the largest demographic group is, after all, the quickest way to box-office success.

In fact, almost from its beginning, the film industry has recognized the importance of the teenaged audience, with characters such as Andy Hardy and locales such as Ridgemont High and the 'hood.

Beyond the assumption that teen films are geared exclusively toward teenagers, however, film researchers should keep in mind that people of all ages have attended and still attend teen films. Popular films about adolescents are also expressions of larger cultural currents. Studying the films is important for understanding an era's common beliefs about its teenaged population within a broader pattern of general cultural preoccupations.

This selected bibliography is intended both to serve and to stimulate interest in the teen film genre. It provides a research tool for those who are studying teen films and their cultural implications. Unfortunately, however, in the process of compiling this list we quickly realized that it was impossible to be genuinely comprehensive or to satisfy every interest.

Doherty, Thomas. *Teenagers and Teenpics: The Juvenilization of American Movies in the 1950s*. Boston: Unwin Hyman, 1988. Print.
Historical discussion of the identification of teenagers as a targeted film market.

Foster, Harold M. "Film in the Classroom: Coping with Teen Pics." *English Journal* 76.3 (1987): 86–88. Print.
Evaluation of the potential of using teen films such as *Sixteen Candles*, *The Karate Kid*, *Risky Business*, *The Flamingo Kid*, and *The Breakfast Club* to instruct adolescents on the difference between film as communication and film as exploitation.

Washington, Michael, and Marvin J. Berlowitz. "Blaxploitation Films and High School Youth: Swat Superfly." *Jump Cut* 9 (1975): 23–24. Print.
Marxist reaction to the trend of youth-oriented black action films. Article seeks to illuminate the negative influences the films have on high school students by pointing out the false ideas about education, morality, and the black family espoused by the heroes in the films.

These annotations are purely descriptive; the authors express none of their own opinions. They describe works as "historical" or "Marxist" but do not indicate whether they're "good." The bibliography entries are documented in MLA style.

Evaluative annotations offer opinions on a source as well as describe it. They are often helpful in assessing how useful a source will be for your own writing. The following evaluative annotations are from a bibliography by Jessica Ann Olson, a student at Wright State University.

JESSICA ANN OLSON

Global Warming

Gore, Al. *An Inconvenient Truth: The Planetary Emergency of Global Warming and What We Can Do about It*. New York: Rodale, 2006. Print.

This publication, which is based on Gore's slide show on global warming, stresses the urgency of the global warming crisis. It centers on how the atmosphere is very thin and how greenhouse gases such as carbon dioxide are making it thicker. The thicker atmosphere traps more infrared radiation, causing warming of the Earth. Gore argues that carbon dioxide, which is created by burning fossil fuels, cutting down forests, and producing cement, accounts for eighty percent of greenhouse gas emissions. He includes several examples of problems caused by global warming. Penguins and polar bears are at risk because the glaciers they call home are quickly melting. Coral reefs are being bleached and destroyed when their inhabitants overheat and leave. Global warming is now affecting people's lives as well. For example, the highways in Alaska are only frozen enough to be driven on fewer than eighty days of the year. In China and elsewhere, record-setting floods and droughts are taking place. Hurricanes are on the rise. This source's goal is to inform its audience about the ongoing global warming crisis and to inspire change across the world. It is useful because it relies on scientific data that can be referred to easily and it provides a solid foundation for me to build on. For example, it explains how carbon dioxide is produced and how it is currently affecting plants and animals. This evidence could potentially help my research on how humans are biologically affected by global warming. It will also help me structure my essay, using its general information to lead into the specifics of my topic. For example, I could introduce the issue by explaining the thinness of the atmosphere and the effect of greenhouse gases, then focus on carbon dioxide and its effects on organisms.

Parmesan, Camille, and Hector Galbraith. "Executive Summary." *Observed Impacts of Global Climate Change in the U.S.* Pew Center on Global Climate Change, Nov. 2004. Web. 17 Jan. 2007.

This report summarizes recent scientific findings that document the impact changes in the climate have had on the distribution of plants and animals in the United States and on how they interact within their communities. For example, it explains how a shift has taken place in the blooming period for plants and the breeding period for animals caused by global warming. Because of changes in their geographic range, species may interact differently, possibly resulting in population declines. For example, the red fox is now found in areas dominated by the arctic fox and is threatening its survival. The report stresses that such shifts can harm the world's biodiversity. Plants and animals that are rare now face extinction. The annual cycle of carbon dioxide levels in the atmosphere has also changed, largely due to the lengthening of the growing season, affecting basic ecosystem processes. I did not find this report as helpful as other sources because its information is based only on observations made in the United States. The information appears reliable, though, because it is based on scientific evidence. This essay will be helpful to my essay because it focuses on how plants and animals are currently affected, such as their shifting communities and how they are clashing. I could use this to explain human changes by providing evidence of what is happening to other species. This source will not be as helpful in explaining the climate's effects on human biological function in particular, but it will provide some framework. For example, I could explain how the plants that help convert carbon dioxide into oxygen are being harmed and relate that to how the humans will suffer the consequences.

These annotations not only describe the sources in detail, but also evaluate their usefulness for the writer's own project. They show that the writer understands the content of the sources and can relate it to her own anticipated needs as a researcher and writer.

Key Features / Annotated Bibliographies

A statement of scope.   Sometimes you need or are asked to provide a brief introductory statement to explain what you're covering. The authors of the bibliography on teen films introduce their bibliography with three paragraphs establishing a context for the bibliography and announcing their purpose for compiling it.

Complete bibliographic information.   Provide all the information about each source using one documentation system (MLA, APA, or another one) so that your readers or other researchers will be able to find the source easily.

A concise description of the work.   A good annotation describes each item as carefully and objectively as possible, giving accurate information and showing that you understand the source. These qualities will help to build authority—for you as a writer and for your annotations.

Relevant commentary.   If you write an evaluative bibliography, your comments should be relevant to your purpose and audience. The best way to achieve relevance is to consider what questions a potential reader might have about the sources. Your evaluation might also focus on the text's suitability as a source for your writing, as Olson's evaluative annotations do.

Consistent presentation.   All annotations should follow a consistent pattern: if one is written in complete sentences, they should all be. Each annotation in the teen films bibliography, for example, begins with a phrase (not a complete sentence) characterizing the work.

A BRIEF GUIDE TO WRITING ANNOTATED BIBLIOGRAPHIES

Considering the Rhetorical Situation

| PURPOSE | Will your bibliography need to demonstrate the depth or breadth of your research? Will your readers actually track down and use your sources? Do you need or want to convince readers that your sources are good? | 3–4 |

5–8 **AUDIENCE** For whom are you compiling this bibliography? What does your audience need to know about each source?

12–15 **STANCE** Are you presenting yourself as an objective describer or evaluator? Or are you expressing a particular point of view toward the sources you evaluate?

16–18 **MEDIA / DESIGN** If you are publishing the bibliography online, will you provide links from each annotation to the source itself? Online or off, do you need to distinguish the bibliographic information from the annotation by using a different font?

Generating Ideas and Text

Decide what sources to include. You may be tempted to include in a bibliography every source you find or look at. A better strategy is to include only those sources that you or your readers may find potentially useful in researching your topic. For an academic bibliography, you need to consider the qualities in the list below. Some of these questions are not ones whose answers should rule a source in or out; they simply raise issues you need to think about.

- *Appropriateness.* Is this source relevant to your topic? Is it a primary source or a secondary source? Is it aimed at an appropriate audience? General or specialized? Elementary, advanced, or somewhere in between?

- *Credibility.* Is the author reputable? Is the publication, publishing company, or sponsor of the site reputable? Do the ideas more or less agree with those in other sources you've read?

- *Balance.* Does the source present enough evidence for its assertions? Does it show any particular bias? Does it present countering arguments fairly?

- *Timeliness.* Is the source recent enough? Does it reflect current thinking or research about the subject?

432–52 If you need help **FINDING SOURCES,** see Chapter 45.

rhetorical situations genres processes strategies research MLA / APA media / design handbook

Compile a list of works to annotate. Give the sources themselves in whatever documentation style is required; see the guidelines for **MLA** and **APA** styles in Chapters 51 and 52.

MLA 484–532
APA 533–74

Determine what kind of bibliography you need to write. Descriptive or evaluative? Will your annotations be in the form of phrases? Complete sentences? Paragraphs? The form will shape your reading and note taking. If you're writing a descriptive bibliography, your reading goal will be just to understand and capture the writer's message as clearly as possible. If you're writing an evaluative bibliography, you will also need to assess the source as you read in order to include your own opinions of it.

Read carefully. To write an annotation, you must understand the source's argument, but when you are writing an annotated bibliography as part of a **PROPOSAL,** you may have neither the time nor the need to read the whole text. Here's a way of quickly determining whether a source is likely to serve your needs:

▲ 205–13

- Check the publisher or sponsor (university press? scholarly journal? popular magazine? website sponsored by a reputable organization?).

- Read the preface (of a book), abstract (of a scholarly article), introduction (of an article in a nonscholarly magazine or a website).

- Skim the table of contents or the headings.

- Read the parts that relate specifically to your topic.

Research the writer, if necessary. If you are required to indicate the writer's credentials, you may need to do additional research. You may find information by typing the writer's name into a search engine or looking up the writer in *Contemporary Authors*. In any case, information about the writer should take up no more than one sentence in your annotation.

Summarize the work in a sentence or two. **DESCRIBE** it as objectively as possible: even if you are writing an evaluative annotation, you can evaluate the central point of a work better by stating it clearly first. *If you're writing a descriptive annotation, you're done.*

◆ 367–75

164–72 ▲
Establish criteria for evaluating sources. If you're **EVALUATING** sources for a project, you'll need to evaluate them in terms of their usefulness for your project, their **STANCE,** and their overall credibility.

12–15 ■

Write a brief evaluation of the source. If you can generalize about the worth of the entire work, fine. You may find, however, that some parts are useful while others are not, and what you write should reflect that mix.

Be consistent—in content, sentence structure, and format.

- *Content.* Try to provide about the same amount of information for each entry. If you're evaluating, don't evaluate some sources and just describe others.

HB-4–7
- *Sentence structure.* Use the same style throughout—**COMPLETE SEN-TENCES,** brief phrases, or a mix.

585–86 □
- *Format.* Use one documentation style throughout; use a consistent **FONT** for each element in each entry—for example, italicize or underline all book titles.

Ways of Organizing an Annotated Bibliography

Depending on their purpose, annotated bibliographies may or may not include an introduction. Most annotated bibliographies cover a single topic and so are organized alphabetically by author's or editor's last name. When a work lacks a named author, alphabetize it by the first important word in its title. Consult the documentation system you're using for additional details about alphabetizing works appropriately.

Sometimes an annotated bibliography needs to be organized into several subject areas (or genres, periods, or some other category); if so, the entries are listed alphabetically within each category. For example, a bibliography about terrorism breaks down into subjects such as "Global Terrorism" and "Weapons of Mass Destruction."

[Multicategory bibliography]

IF YOU NEED MORE HELP

See Chapter 25 for guidelines on **DRAFTING**, Chapter 26 on **ASSESSING YOUR OWN WRITING**, Chapter 27 on **GETTING RESPONSE AND REVISING**, and Chapter 28 on **EDITING AND PROOFREADING**. See Chapter 29 if you are required to submit your bibliography in a writing **PORTFOLIO**.

○ 266–68
269–74
275–81
282–86
287–98

13 Evaluations

a standard on which a judgment or decision may be based on

ConsumerReports.org evaluates cars and laundry detergents. The *Princeton Review* and *U.S. News & World Report* evaluate colleges and universities. You probably consult such sources to make decisions, and you probably evaluate things all the time — when you recommend a film (or not) or a teacher (ditto). An evaluation is at bottom a judgment; you judge something according to certain criteria, supporting your judgment with reasons and evidence. You need to give your reasons for evaluating it as you do because often your evaluation will affect your audience's actions: they must see this movie, needn't bother with this book, should be sure to have the Caesar salad at this restaurant, and so on. In a review on the following page, written for a first-year writing class at Wright State University, Ali Heinekamp offers her evaluation of the film *Juno*.

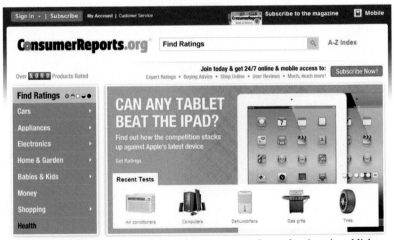

ConsumerReports.org uses lab testing to support the evaluations it publishes.

rhetorical situations · genres · processes · strategies · research MLA / APA · media / design · handbook

ALI HEINEKAMP

Juno: *Not Just Another Teen Movie*

It all starts with a chair, where Juno (Ellen Page) has unprotected sex with her best friend Bleeker (Michael Cera). Several weeks later, she's at a convenience store, buying a pregnancy test. Only sixteen, Juno faces the terrifying task of telling her parents that she is pregnant. With their support, Juno moves forward in her decision to give birth and give the child to Mark (Jason Bateman) and Vanessa (Jennifer Garner), a wealthy and seemingly perfect married couple looking to adopt. Although the situations *Juno*'s characters find themselves in and their dialogue may be criticized as unrealistic, the film, written by Diablo Cody and directed by Jason Reitman, successfully portrays the emotions of a teen being shoved into maturity way too fast.

Much of the time, *Juno* seems unrealistic because it seems to treat the impact of teen pregnancy so lightly. The consequences of Juno's pregnancy are sugar-coated to such an extent that in many cases, they are barely apparent. The film downplays the emotional struggle that a pregnant woman would feel in deciding to give birth and then put that child up for adoption, and it ignores the discomforts of pregnancy, such as mood swings and nausea.

Likewise, *Juno*'s dialogue is too good to be true—funny and clever, but unrealistic. For example, Juno tells Mark and Vanessa "If I could just have the thing and give it to you now, I totally would. But I'm guessing it looks probably like a sea monkey right now, and we should let it get a little cuter." At another point, talking about her absent mother, Juno says, "Oh, and she inexplicably mails me a cactus every Valentine's Day. And I'm like, 'Thanks a heap, coyote ugly. This cactus-gram stings even worse than your abandonment.'" As funny as they are, the creatively quirky one-liners often go a bit too far, detracting from both the gravity of Juno's situation and the film's believability.

But although the situations and dialogue are unrealistic, the emotional heart of the movie is believable—and moving. Despite the movie's lack of realism in portraying her pregnancy, Juno's vulnerability transforms her character and situation into something much more believable. Juno mentions at various times that her classmates stare at her stomach and talk about her behind her back, but initially she seems

Ellen Page as Juno.

unconcerned with the negative attention. This façade falls apart, however, when Juno accuses Bleeker, the baby's father, of being ashamed of the fact that he and Juno have had sex. The strong front she is putting up drops when she bursts out, "At least you don't have to have the evidence under your sweater." This break in Juno's strength reveals her vulnerability and makes her character relatable and believable.

The juxtaposition of Juno's teenage quirks and the adult situation   5
she's in also reminds us of her youth and vulnerability. As a result of the adult situation Juno finds herself in and her generally stoic demeanor, it's easy to see her as a young adult. But the film fills each scene with visual reminders that Juno is just a kid being forced into situations beyond her maturity level. At a convenience store, Juno buys a pregnancy test along with a licorice rope. She calls Women Now, an abortion clinic, on a phone that looks like a hamburger. And while she is giving birth, she wears long, brightly striped socks. These subtle visual cues help us remember the reality of Juno's position as both physically an adult and emotionally an adolescent.

While the dialogue is too clever to be realistic, in the end it's carried by the movie's heart. Scott Tobias from the entertainment website

rhetorical situations

genres

processes

strategies

research MLA / APA

media / design

handbook

The A.V. Club says it best when he writes that the colorful dialogue is often "too ostentatious for its own good, but the film's sincerity is what ultimately carries it across." In fact, intensely emotional scenes are marked by their *lack* of witty dialogue. For example, when Juno runs into Vanessa at the mall, Vanessa, reluctantly at first, kneels down to talk to the baby through Juno's stomach. Vanessa's diction while talking to the baby is so simple, so expected. She simply starts with, "Hi baby, it's me. It's Vanessa," and then continues, "I can't wait to meet you." This simple, everyday statement stands out in comparison to the rest of the well-crafted, humorous script. For her part, Juno simply stares admiringly at Vanessa. She doesn't have to say anything to transform the scene into a powerful one. Another scene in which the dialogue stops being clever is the one in which Juno and Bleeker lie side by side in a hospital bed after Juno has given birth, Juno in tears and Bleeker lost in thought. They don't need to say anything for us to feel their pain at the realization that although the pregnancy is over, it will never truly be in the past. The absence of dialogue in scenes such as these actually contributes to their power. We finally see more than stoicism and sarcasm from Juno: we see caring and fear, which are feelings most would expect of a pregnant teen.

There has been much concern among critics that as a pregnant teenager, Juno doesn't present a good role model for teen girls. Worrying that teens may look up to Juno so much that being pregnant becomes "cool," Dana Stevens writes in *Slate*, "Let's hope that the teenage girls of America don't cast their condoms to the wind in hopes of becoming as cool as 16-year-old Juno MacGuff." But it is not Juno's pregnancy that makes her cool: it is her ability to overcome the difficult obstacles thrown at her, and that strength does make her a good role model. Another critic, Lisa Schwarzbaum from *Entertainment Weekly*, feels that the movie might have been more realistic had Juno chosen to go through with an abortion. It's true that Juno may have chosen the more difficult answer to a teen pregnancy, but she is far from alone in her decision. Perhaps Schwarzbaum underestimates teens in thinking that they would not be able to cope with the emotionally difficult situation Juno chooses. Again, in her strength, Juno is a role model for young women.

Although *Juno* is a comedy filled with improbable situations, exaggerations, and wit, its genuine emotion allows us to connect with and relate to the film. The reality of the characters' emotions in controversial and serious situations allows *Juno* to transcend its own genre. It reaches depths of emotion that are unusual for teenage comedies, proving that *Juno* is not just another teen movie.

Works Cited

Cody, Diablo, scr. *Juno.* Dir. Jason Reitman. Perf. Ellen Page, Michael Cera, Jennifer Garner, Jason Bateman. Fox Searchlight, 2007. Film.

Schwarzbaum, Lisa. Rev. of *Juno,* dir. Jason Reitman. *EW.com.* Entertainment Weekly, 28 Nov. 2007. Web. 14 Apr. 2008.

Stevens, Dana. "Superpregnant: How *Juno* Is *Knocked Up* from the Girl's Point of View." Rev. of *Juno,* dir. Jason Reitman. *Slate.com.* Slate, 5 Dec. 2007. Web. 12 Apr. 2008.

Tobias, Scott. Rev. of *Juno,* dir. Jason Reitman. *The A.V. Club.* The Onion, 6 Dec. 2007. Web. 13 Apr. 2008.

Heinekamp quickly summarizes Juno's *plot and then evaluates the film according to clearly stated criteria. In the process, she responds to several reviewers' comments, joining the critical conversation about the film. She documents her sources according to MLA style.*

Key Features / Evaluations

A concise description of the subject.　You should include just enough information to let readers who may not be familiar with your subject understand what it is; the goal is to evaluate, not summarize. Depending on your topic and medium, some of this information may be in visual or audio form. Heinekamp briefly describes *Juno's* main plot points in her first paragraph, only providing what readers need to understand the context of her evaluation.

Clearly defined criteria.　You need to determine clear criteria as the basis for your judgment. In reviews or other evaluations written for a broad audience, you can integrate the criteria into the discussion as reasons for your assessment, as Heinekamp does in her evaluation of *Juno*. In more formal evaluations, you may need to announce your criteria explicitly. Heinekamp evaluates the film based on the power of its emotion and the realism of its situations, characters, and dialogue.

A knowledgeable discussion of the subject.   To evaluate something credibly, you need to show that you know it yourself and that you've researched what other authoritative sources say. Heinekamp cites many examples from *Juno*, showing her knowledge of the film. She also cites reviews from three internet sources, showing that she's researched others' views as well.

A balanced and fair assessment.   An evaluation is centered on a judgment. Heinekamp concedes that *Juno*'s situations and dialogue are unrealistic, but she says it nevertheless "reaches depths of emotion that are unusual for teenage comedies." It is important that any judgment be balanced and fair. Seldom is something all good or all bad. A fair evaluation need not be all positive or all negative; it may acknowledge both strengths and weaknesses. For example, a movie's soundtrack may be wonderful while the plot is not. Heinekamp criticizes *Juno*'s too-witty dialogue and unrealistic situations, even as she appreciates its heart.

Well-supported reasons.   You need to argue for your judgment, providing reasons and evidence that might include visual and audio as well as verbal material. Heinekamp gives several reasons for her positive assessment of *Juno*—the believability of its characters, the intensely emotional scenes, the strength of the main character as a role model—and she supports these reasons with many quotations and examples from the film.

A BRIEF GUIDE TO WRITING EVALUATIONS

Choosing Something to Evaluate

You can more effectively evaluate a limited subject than a broad one: review certain dishes at a local restaurant rather than the entire menu; review one film or episode rather than all the films by Alfred Hitchcock or all eighty *Star Trek* episodes. The more specific and focused your subject, the better you can write about it.

Considering the Rhetorical Situation

3–4

PURPOSE Are you writing to affect your audience's opinion of a subject? to help others decide what to see, do, or buy? to demonstrate your expertise in a field?

5–8

AUDIENCE To whom are you writing? What will your audience already know about the subject? What will they expect to learn from your evaluation of it? Are they likely to agree with you or not?

12–15

STANCE What is your attitude toward the subject, and how will you show that you have evaluated it fairly and appropriately? Think about the tone you want to use: should it be reasonable? Passionate? Critical?

16–18

MEDIA / DESIGN How will you deliver your evaluation? In print? Online? As a speech? Can you show images or audio or video clips? If you're submitting your text for publication, are there any format requirements?

Generating Ideas and Text

259–60

Explore what you already know. **FREEWRITE** to answer the following questions: What do you know about this subject or subjects like it? What are your initial or gut feelings, and why do you feel as you do? How does this subject reflect or affect your basic values or beliefs? How have others evaluated subjects like this?

Identify criteria. Make a list of criteria you think should be used to evaluate your subject. Think about which criteria will likely be important to your **AUDIENCE.** You might find **CUBING** and **QUESTIONING** to be useful processes for thinking about your criteria.

5–8
262–63

Evaluate your subject.   Study your subject closely to determine to what extent it meets each of your criteria. You may want to list your criteria and take notes related to each one, or you may develop a rating scale for each criterion to help stay focused on it. Come up with a tentative judgment.

Compare your subject with others.   Often, evaluating something involves COMPARING AND CONTRASTING it with similar things. We judge movies in comparison with the other movies we've seen and french fries with the other fries we've tasted. Sometimes those comparisons can be made informally. For other evaluations, you may have to do research — to try on several pairs of jeans before buying any, for example — to see how your subject compares.

348–55

State your judgment as a tentative thesis statement.   Your THESIS STATEMENT should be one that addresses both pros and cons. "*Covert Affairs* is fun to watch despite its stilted dialogue." "Of the five sport-utility vehicles tested, the Toyota 4Runner emerged as the best in comfort, power, and durability, though not in styling or cargo capacity." Both of these examples offer a judgment but qualify it according to the writer's criteria.

313–15

Anticipate other opinions.   I think Will Ferrell is a comic genius whose movies are first-rate. You think Will Ferrell is a terrible actor who makes awful movies. How can I write a review of his latest film that you will at least consider? One way is by ACKNOWLEDGING other opinions — and REFUTING those opinions as best I can. I may not persuade you to see Ferrell's next film, but I can at least demonstrate that by certain criteria he should be appreciated. You may need to RESEARCH how others have evaluated your subject.

336
337
419

Identify and support your reasons.   Write out all the REASONS you can think of that will convince your audience to accept your judgment. Review your list to identify the most convincing or important reasons. Then review how well your subject meets your criteria and decide how best to SUPPORT your reasons: through examples, authoritative opinions, statistics, visual or audio evidence, or something else.

326–27
327–35

Ways of Organizing an Evaluation

Evaluations are usually organized in one of two ways. One way is to introduce what's being evaluated, followed by your judgment, discussing your criteria along the way. This is a useful strategy if your audience may not be familiar with your subject.

[Start with your subject]

Describe what you're evaluating. → State your judgment. → Provide reasons and evidence, discussing criteria as you apply them. → Acknowledge objections or other opinions. → Restate your overall judgment.

You might also start by identifying your criteria and then follow with a discussion of how well your subject meets those criteria. This strategy foregrounds the process by which you reached your conclusions.

[Start with your criteria]

Identify criteria for evaluation. → Describe what you're evaluating. → Evaluate it against each of your criteria, one at a time, adding potential objections or other opinions in relation to each criterion. → State your overall judgment.

266–68
269–74
275–81
282–86
287–98

> **IF YOU NEED MORE HELP**
>
> See Chapter 25 for guidelines on **DRAFTING**, Chapter 26 on **ASSESSING YOUR DRAFT**, Chapter 27 on **GETTING RESPONSE AND REVISING**, and Chapter 28 on **EDITING AND PROOFREADING**. See Chapter 29 if you are required to submit your report in a writing **PORTFOLIO**.

■ rhetorical situations ▲ genres ○ processes ◆ strategies ● research MLA / APA □ media / design ▨ handbook

Lab Reports 14

Lab reports describe the procedures and results of experiments in the natural sciences, the social sciences, and engineering. We write reports of lab work in school to show instructors that we have followed certain procedures, achieved appropriate results, and drawn accurate conclusions. On the job, lab reports not only describe what we did and what we learned; they may also present data and interpretations to attempt to persuade others to accept our hypotheses, and they become a record that others may refer to in the future. As an example, here is a lab report written by a student for a psychology class at Wittenberg University.

SARAH THOMAS

The Effect of Biofeedback Training on Muscle Tension and Skin Temperature

Purpose

The purpose of this lab was for subjects to train themselves to increase their skin temperature, measured on the index finger of their non-dominant hand, and to decrease their muscle tension, measured over the frontalis muscle, by using biofeedback training. This study is based on the research of Miller and Brucker (1979), which demonstrated that smooth muscles could experience operant conditioning.

Methods

Subjects

Seven subjects were used in this study: five female and two male. The subjects were the undergraduate students of Dr. Jo Wilson in her honors psychophysiology class at Wittenberg University in Springfield, Ohio. All subjects were in their early 20s.

Apparatus

Equipment used in this lab included an Apple Microlab system configured to measure (a) skin temperature through a thermode taped with paper surgical tape onto the index finger of the subjects' nondominant hand and (b) frontalis muscle tension via three electrodes placed over the frontalis. When subjects' skin temperatures were more than the means for the previous 90-second intervals, the computer emitted a tone. It also emitted a tone when muscle tension in the frontalis was less than the mean of the previous interval. See the Procedure section for exact electrode placement specifications.

Materials

Materials used in this lab included paper surgical tape, alcohol to clean off the forehead, conducting gel, wire, electrode collars, and a chair.

Procedure

Upon arriving at the lab, the researchers turned on the Apple Micro- 5
lab computer. With the aid of Dr. Wilson, subjects had either electrodes attached to their forehead or a thermode attached to the nondominant hand's index finger. The treatment order was random for each subject, and it was reversed for his or her second biofeedback session. The forehead was swiped with alcohol to clean the skin. Electrodes with conducting gel were placed over the frontalis muscle by putting the ground electrode in the center of the forehead and the white electrodes two inches on either side of the center of the forehead. Premeasured electrode collars allowed the researchers to place the conducting gel on the electrodes, peel off the backing on the collar, and place it on the subjects' forehead. The researchers still made sure the electrodes were placed properly. The wire running from the electrodes to the computer was then taped to the subjects' back so it would be out of the way. Subjects were then seated in a comfortable chair with their back to the computer.

Depending on the experimental condition, subjects were told to reduce their frontalis muscle tension by relaxing and even thinking of holding something warm in their hands. They were told that they would know they were meeting the goal when they heard a tone emitted by the computer.

Each session began with a 90-second baseline period, followed by fifteen 90-second trial periods. During each trial period, a tone was emitted by the computer each time the subjects' frontalis muscle tension was below their mean tension for the previous trial; the tone served as the rewarding stimulus in the operant conditioning paradigm.

When skin temperature was to be measured, a thermode was attached to the index finger of the subjects' nondominant hand with surgical tape. The wire running from the thermode to the computer was taped to the back of their hand so it would be out of their way. Then a 90-second baseline period occurred, followed by fifteen 90-second trial periods. During each trial period, a tone was emitted by the computer each time the subjects' skin temperature was above their mean temperature for the previous trial; once again, the tone served as the rewarding stimulus in the operant conditioning paradigm.

Results

The results of this lab were generally similar (Tables 1 and 2). All subjects demonstrated the ability to increase their skin temperature and decrease the tension in their frontalis muscle in at least one of their sessions. Five subjects were able to increase their skin temperature in both sessions; the same number decreased their muscle tension in both trials.

The majority of subjects (five) were able to both increase the skin   10 temperature of the index finger of their nondominant hand and decrease the tension of their frontalis muscle more during the second trial than the first.

Specifically, Subject 7 had atypical results. This subject's overall average skin temperature was less than the baseline value; the subject's overall average muscle tension was more than the baseline value.

Discussion

The bulk of the data collected in this study validated the research of Neal Miller; the subjects appeared to undergo operant conditioning of their smooth muscles in order to relax their frontalis muscles and increase their skin temperatures. Subjects 3 and 6 each failed to do this in one session; Subject 7 failed to do this several times. This finding is difficult to explain precisely. It is possible that for Subjects 3 and 6, this

Table 1

Skin Temperature in Degrees Fahrenheit During Sessions 1 and 2

	Subject 1	Subject 2	Subject 3	Subject 4	Subject 5	Subject 6	Subject 7
Baseline, Session 1	75.2	77.3	78.5	74.3	78.0	67.7	75.1
Mean skin temp, Session 1	79.3	85.6	78.5	74.4	83.2	73.5	72.6
Mean minus baseline, Session 1	4.1	8.3	0.0	0.1	5.2	5.8	−2.5
Baseline, Session 2	77.9	80.1	69.5	80.9	67.2	73.7	88.0
Mean skin temp, Session 2	79.9	86.3	70.7	84.6	76.8	79.7	88.8
Mean minus baseline, Session 2	2.0	6.2	1.2	3.7	9.6	6.0	0.8
Overall average of mean skin temp minus baseline	3.1	7.3	0.6	1.9	7.4	5.9	−0.85

data was a fluke. For Subject 7, it is likely that the subject was simply stressed due to outside factors before arriving for the first trials of EMG and skin temperature, and this stress skewed the data.

The effect of biofeedback training was generally greater as the operant conditioning became better learned. Learning was indicated by the finding that the majority of the subjects performed better on the second trials than on the first trials. This finding shows the effectiveness of

Table 2

EMG of the Frontalis Muscle in Microvolts for Sessions 1 and 2

	Subject 1	Subject 2	Subject 3	Subject 4	Subject 5	Subject 6	Subject 7
Baseline, Session 1	4.4	4.5	2.8	3.8	7.9	3.1	2.4
Mean EMG, Session 1	2.1	1.4	1.7	3.2	2.0	3.7	3.2
Baseline minus mean, Session 1	2.3	3.1	1.1	0.6	5.9	−0.6	−0.8
Baseline, Session 2	4.1	2.3	3.0	2.9	11.1	6.5	1.9
Mean EMG, Session 2	1.3	1.3	1.4	2.3	2.5	3.2	1.4
Baseline minus mean, Session 2	2.8	1.0	1.6	0.6	8.6	3.3	0.5
Overall average of mean EMG minus baseline	2.6	2.1	1.4	0.6	7.3	1.4	−0.15

biofeedback on reducing factors associated with stress, like muscle tension and low skin temperature; biofeedback's impact is even greater when it is administered over time. The implications of this information are without limits, especially for the treatment of a variety of medical disorders.

There were a few problems with this lab. The subjects all were at different levels of relaxation to begin with. It is impossible to determine the effects of outside events, like exams or other stresses, on their EMG and skin temperature levels. Skin temperature itself could have been altered by cold outside temperatures. Being in a lab may have altered the stress level of some subjects, and noises from outside the lab may have had an effect as well.

If this study were repeated, it would be a good idea to let sub-   15 jects simply be in the lab for a period of time before measures are taken. This would allow the effect of outside temperature to be minimized. It would also reduce the effect of getting used to the lab, decreasing the orienting response. Finally, it would also be good to do the experiment in a soundproof room.

Reference

Miller, N. E., & Brucker, B. S. (1979). A learned visceral response apparently independent of skeletal ones in patients paralyzed by spinal lesions. In N. Birnbaumer & H. D. Kimmel (Eds.), *Biofeedback and self-regulation* (pp. 287–304). Hillsdale, NJ: Erlbaum.

This report includes sections commonly part of lab reports in the natural and social sciences: purpose, method, results, discussion, and references. Some reports keep results and discussion in one section; some reports include an abstract; and some reports include one or more appendices containing tables, calculations, and other supplemental material, depending on the audience and publication. In this example, the author assumes that her audience understands basic terms used in the report, such as frontalis muscle and biofeedback. The report is formatted and documented according to APA style.

Key Features / Lab Reports

An explicit title.   Lab report titles should describe the report factually and explicitly to let readers know exactly what the report is about and to provide keywords for indexes and search engines. Avoid phrases like "an Investigation into" or "a Study of" and titles that are clever or cute. Thomas's title, "The Effect of Biofeedback Training on Muscle Tension and Skin Temperature," clearly describes the report's subject and includes the keywords needed for indexing (*biofeedback training, muscle tension, skin temperature*).

Abstract.   Some lab reports include a one-paragraph, 100–200-word abstract, a summary of the report's purpose, method, and discussion.

Purpose.   Sometimes called an "Introduction," this section describes the reason for conducting the study: Why is this research important, and why are you doing it? What has been done by others, and how does your work relate to previous work? What will your research tell your audience?

Methods.   Here you describe how you conducted the study, including the materials and equipment you used and the procedures you followed. This section is usually written as a narrative, explaining the process you followed in order to allow others to repeat your study, step-by-step. Your explanation should thoroughly describe the following:

- subjects studied and any necessary contextual information
- apparatus — equipment used, by brand and model number
- materials used
- procedures — including reference to the published work that describes any procedures you used that someone else had already followed; the techniques you used and any modifications you made to them; any statistical methods you used

Results and discussion.   Here you analyze the results and present their implications, explain your logic in accepting or rejecting your initial hypotheses, relate your work to previous work in the field, and discuss the experiment's design and techniques and how they may have affected the results: what did you find out, and what does it mean? In longer reports, you may have two separate sections. "Results" should focus on the factual data you collected by doing the study; "Discussion" should speculate about what the study means: why the results turned out as they did, and what the implications for future studies may be.

References. List works cited in your report, alphabetized by author's last name and using the appropriate documentation style.

Appendices. Appendices are optional, presenting information that is too detailed for the body of the report.

Appropriate format. The design conventions for lab reports vary from discipline to discipline, so you'll need to check to see that yours meets the appropriate requirements. Find out whether any sections need to start their own page, whether you need to include a list of figures, whether you need to include a separate title page — and whether there are any other conventions you need to follow.

A BRIEF GUIDE TO WRITING LAB REPORTS

Considering the Rhetorical Situation

3–4	**PURPOSE**	Why are you writing? To demonstrate your ability to follow the appropriate methods and make logical inferences? To persuade others that your hypotheses are sound and your conclusions believable? To provide a record of the experiment for others?
5–8	**AUDIENCE**	Can you assume that your audience is familiar with the field's basic procedures? How routine were your procedures? Which procedures need to be explained in greater detail so your audience can repeat them?
12–15	**STANCE**	Whatever your attitude toward the topic, lab reports need to have an impersonal, analytical tone. Take care not to be too informal, and don't try to be cute.
16–18	**MEDIA / DESIGN**	Are you planning to deliver your report in print or online? All lab reports have headings; choose a typeface that includes bold or italics so your headings will show clearly.

Generating Ideas and Text

Research your subject.   Researchers do not work in isolation; rather, each study contributes to an ever-growing body of information, and you need to situate your work in that context. RESEARCH what studies others have done on the same subject and what procedures they followed.

419

Take careful notes as you perform your study.   A lab report must be repeatable. Another researcher should be able to duplicate your study exactly, using only your report as a guide, so you must document every method, material, apparatus, and procedure carefully. Break down procedures and activities into discrete parts, and record them in the order in which they occurred. ANALYZE CAUSES AND EFFECTS; think about whether you should COMPARE your findings with other studies. Take careful notes so that you'll be able to EXPLAIN PROCESSES you followed.

318–22
348–55
382–86

Draft the report a section at a time.   You may find it easiest to start with the "Methods" or "Results" section first, then DRAFT the "Discussion," followed by the "Purpose." Do the "Abstract" last.

266–68

- Write in COMPLETE SENTENCES and paragraphs.

HB-4–7

- Avoid using the first person *I* or *we*; keep the focus on the study and the actions taken.

- Use the ACTIVE VOICE as much as possible ("the rats pushed the lever" rather than "the lever was pushed by the rats").

HB-18–19

- Use the PAST TENSE throughout the report.

HB-12

- Place subjects and verbs close together to make your sentences easy to follow.

- Use PRECISE TERMS consistently throughout the report; don't alternate among synonyms.

HB-41–44

- Be sure that each PRONOUN refers clearly to one noun.

HB-25–31

Organizing a Lab Report

Lab reports vary in their details but generally include these sections:

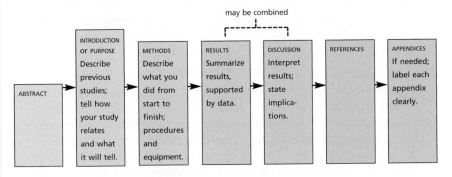

269–74 ◓
275–81
282–86
287–98

IF YOU NEED MORE HELP

See Chapter 26 on ASSESSING YOUR OWN WRITING, Chapter 27 on GETTING RESPONSE AND REVISING, and Chapter 28 on EDITING AND PROOFREADING. See Chapter 29 if you are required to submit your report in a writing PORTFOLIO.

rhetorical situations   genres   processes   strategies   research MLA / APA   media / design   handbook

We write memoirs to explore our past—about shopping for a party dress with Grandma, or driving a car for the first time, or breaking up with our first love. Memoirs focus on events and people and places that are important to us. We usually have two goals when we write a memoir: to capture an important moment and to convey something about its significance for us. The following example is from Pulitzer Prize–winning journalist Rick Bragg's autobiography, *All Over but the Shoutin'*. Bragg grew up in Alabama, and in this memoir he recalls when, as a teenager, he paid a final visit to his dying father.

RICK BRAGG

All Over but the Shoutin'

He was living in a little house in Jacksonville, Alabama, a college and mill town that was the closest urban center—with its stoplights and a high school and two supermarkets—to the country roads we roamed in our raggedy cars. He lived in the mill village, in one of those houses the mills subsidized for their workers, back when companies still did things like that. It was not much of a place, but better than anything we had ever lived in as a family. I knocked and a voice like an old woman's, punctuated with a cough that sounded like it came from deep in the guts, told me to come on in, it ain't locked.

It was dark inside, but light enough to see what looked like a bundle of quilts on the corner of a sofa. Deep inside them was a ghost of a man, his hair and beard long and going dirty gray, his face pale and cut with deep grooves. I knew I was in the right house because my daddy's only real possessions, a velvet-covered board pinned with medals, sat inside a glass cabinet on a table. But this couldn't be him.

He coughed again, spit into a can and struggled to his feet, but stopped somewhere short of standing straight up, as if a stoop was all he could manage. "Hey, Cotton Top," he said, and then I knew. My daddy, who was supposed to be a still-young man, looked like the walking dead, not just old but damaged, poisoned, used up, crumpled up and thrown in a corner to die. I thought that the man I would see would be the trim, swaggering, high-toned little rooster of a man who stared back at me from the pages of my mother's photo album, the young soldier clowning around in Korea, the arrow-straight, good-looking boy who posed beside my mother back before the fields and mop handle and the rest of it took her looks. The man I remembered had always dressed nice even when there was no cornmeal left, whose black hair always shone with oil, whose chin, even when it wobbled from the beer, was always angled up, high.

I thought he would greet me with that strong voice that sounded so fine when he laughed and so evil when, slurred by a quart of corn likker, he whirled through the house and cried and shrieked, tormented by things we could not see or even imagine. I thought he would be the man and monster of my childhood. But that man was as dead as a man could be, and this was what remained, like when a snake sheds its skin and leaves a dry and brittle husk of itself hanging in the Johnson grass.

"It's all over but the shoutin' now, ain't it, boy," he said, and when he let the quilt slide from his shoulders I saw how he had wasted away, how the bones seemed to poke out of his clothes, and I could see how it killed his pride to look this way, unclean, and he looked away from me for a moment, ashamed. 5

He made a halfhearted try to shake my hand but had a coughing fit again that lasted a minute, coughing up his life, his lungs, and after that I did not want to touch him. I stared at the tops of my sneakers, ashamed to look at his face. He had a dark streak in his beard below his lip, and I wondered why, because he had never liked snuff. Now I know it was blood.

I remember much of what he had to say that day. When you don't see someone for eight, nine years, when you see that person's life red on their lips and know that you will never see them beyond this day, you listen close, even if what you want most of all is to run away.

"Your momma, she alright?" he said.

I said I reckon so.

"The other boys? They alright?"   10
I said I reckon so.
Then he was quiet for a minute, as if trying to find the words to a question to which he did not really want an answer.
"They ain't never come to see me. How come?"
I remember thinking, fool, why do you think? But I just choked down my words, and in doing so I gave up the only real chance I would ever have to accuse him, to attack him with the facts of his own sorry nature and the price it had cost us all. The opportunity hung perfectly still in the air in front of my face and fists, and I held my temper and let it float on by. I could have no more challenged him, berated him, hurt him, than I could have kicked some three-legged dog. Life had kicked his ass pretty good.
"How come?"   15
I just shrugged.
For the next few hours—unless I was mistaken, having never had one before—he tried to be my father. Between coughing and long pauses when he fought for air to generate his words, he asked me if I liked school, if I had ever gotten any better at math, the one thing that just flat evaded me. He asked me if I ever got even with the boy who blacked my eye ten years ago, and nodded his head, approvingly, as I described how I followed him into the boys' bathroom and knocked his dick string up to his watch pocket, and would have dunked his head in the urinal if the aging principal, Mr. Hand, had not had to pee and caught me dragging him across the concrete floor.
He asked me about basketball and baseball, said he had heard I had a good game against Cedar Springs, and I said pretty good, but it was two years ago, anyway. He asked if I had a girlfriend and I said, "One," and he said, "Just one?" For the slimmest of seconds he almost grinned and the young, swaggering man peeked through, but disappeared again in the disease that cloaked him. He talked and talked and never said a word, at least not the words I wanted.
He never said he was sorry.
He never said he wished things had turned out different.   20
He never acted like he did anything wrong.
Part of it, I know, was culture. Men did not talk about their feelings in his hard world. I did not expect, even for a second, that he would bare his soul. All I wanted was a simple acknowledgment that

he was wrong, or at least too drunk to notice that he left his pretty wife and sons alone again and again, with no food, no money, no way to get any, short of begging, because when she tried to find work he yelled, screamed, refused. No, I didn't expect much.

After a while he motioned for me to follow him into a back room where he had my present, and I planned to take it and run. He handed me a long, thin box, and inside was a brand-new, well-oiled Remington .22 rifle. He said he had bought it some time back, just kept forgetting to give it to me. It was a fine gun, and for a moment we were just like anybody else in the culture of that place, where a father's gift of a gun to his son is a rite. He said, with absolute seriousness, not to shoot my brothers.

I thanked him and made to leave, but he stopped me with a hand on my arm and said wait, that ain't all, that he had some other things for me. He motioned to three big cardboard egg cartons stacked against one wall.

Inside was the only treasure I truly have ever known.   25

I had grown up in a house in which there were only two books, the King James Bible and the spring seed catalog. But here, in these boxes, were dozens of hardback copies of everything from Mark Twain to Sir Arthur Conan Doyle. There was a water-damaged Faulkner, and the nearly complete set of Edgar Rice Burroughs's *Tarzan*. There was poetry and trash, Zane Grey's *Riders of the Purple Sage,* and a paperback with two naked women on the cover. There was a tiny, old copy of *Arabian Nights,* threadbare Hardy Boys, and one Hemingway. He had bought most of them at a yard sale, by the box or pound, and some at a flea market. He did not even know what he was giving me, did not recognize most of the writers. "Your momma said you still liked to read," he said.

There was Shakespeare. My father did not know who he was, exactly, but he had heard the name. He wanted them because they were pretty, because they were wrapped in fake leather, because they looked like rich folks' books. I do not love Shakespeare, but I still have those books. I would not trade them for a gold monkey.

"They's maybe some dirty books in there, by mistake, but I know you ain't interested in them, so just throw 'em away," he said. "Or at least, throw 'em away before your momma sees 'em." And then I swear to God he winked.

I guess my heart should have broken then, and maybe it did, a little. I guess I should have done something, anything, besides mumble

rhetorical situations

genres

processes

strategies

research MLA / APA

media / design

handbook

"Thank you, Daddy." I guess that would have been fine, would not have betrayed in some way my mother, my brothers, myself. But I just stood there, trapped somewhere between my long-standing, comfortable hatred, and what might have been forgiveness. I am trapped there still.

Bragg's memoir illustrates all the features that make a memoir good: how the son and father react to each other creates the kind of suspense that keeps us reading; vivid details and rich dialogue bring the scene to life. His later reflections make the significance of that final meeting very clear.

Key Features / Memoirs

A good story. Your memoir should be interesting, to yourself and others. It need not be about a world-shaking event, but your topic — and how you write about it — should interest your readers. At the center of most good stories stands a conflict or question to be resolved. The most compelling memoirs feature some sort of situation or problem that needs resolution. That need for resolution is another name for suspense. It's what makes us want to keep reading.

Vivid details. Details bring a memoir to life by giving readers mental images of the sights, sounds, smells, tastes, and textures of the world in which your story takes place. The goal is to show as well as tell, to take readers there. When Bragg describes a "voice like an old woman's, punctuated with a cough that sounded like it came from deep in the guts," we can hear his dying father ourselves. A memoir is more than simply a report of what happened; it uses vivid details and dialogue to bring the events of the past to life, much as good fiction brings to life events that the writer makes up or embellishes. Depending on your topic and medium, you may want to provide some of the details in audio or visual form.

Clear significance. Memories of the past are filtered through our view from the present: we pick out some moments in our lives as significant, some as more important or vivid than others. Over time, our interpretations change, and our memories themselves change.

A good memoir conveys something about the significance of its subject. As a writer, you need to reveal something about what the incident means to you. You don't, however, want to simply announce the significance as if you're tacking on the moral of the story. Bragg tells us that he's "trapped between [his] long-standing, comfortable hatred, and what might have been forgiveness," but he doesn't come right out and say that's why the incident is so important to him.

A BRIEF GUIDE TO WRITING MEMOIRS

Choosing an Event to Write About

LIST several events or incidents from your past that you consider significant in some way. They do not have to be earthshaking; indeed, they may involve a quiet moment that only you see as important — a brief encounter with a remarkable person, a visit to a special place, a memorable achievement (or failure), something that makes you laugh whenever you think about it. Writing about events that happened at least a few years ago is often easier than writing about recent events because you can more easily step back and see those events with a clear perspective. To choose the event that you will write about, consider how well you can recall what happened, how interesting it will be to readers, and whether you want to share it with an audience.

260–61

Considering the Rhetorical Situation

3–4

PURPOSE What is the importance of the memory you are trying to convey? How will this story help your readers (and you yourself) understand you, as you were then and as you are now?

5–8

AUDIENCE Who are your readers? What do you want them to think of you after reading your memoir? How can you help them understand your experience?

STANCE   What impression do you want to give, and how can your
words contribute to that impression? What tone do you
want to project? Sincere? Serious? Humorous? Detached?
Self-critical?
■ 12–15

MEDIA / DESIGN   Will your memoir be a print document? A speech? Will it
be posted on a website? Can you include photographs,
audio or video clips, or other visual texts?
■ 16–18

Generating Ideas and Text

Think about what happened.   Take a few minutes to write out an
account of the incident: **WHAT** happened, **WHERE** it took place, **WHO** else
was involved, what was said, how you feel about it, and so on. Can you
identify any tension or conflict that will make for a compelling story? If
not, you might want to rethink your topic.
● 262–63

Consider its significance.   Why do you still remember this event? What
effect has it had on your life? What makes you want to tell someone else
about it? Does it say anything about you? What about it might interest
someone else? If you have trouble answering these questions, you should
probably find another topic. But in general, once you have defined the significance of the incident, you can be sure you have a story to tell — and a
reason for telling it.

Think about the details.   The best memoirs connect with readers by giving them a sense of what it was like to be there, leading them to experience in words and images what the writer experienced in life. Spend some
time **DESCRIBING** the incident, writing what you see, hear, smell, touch, and
taste when you envision it. Do you have any photos or memorabilia or
other **VISUAL** materials you might include in your memoir? Try writing out
DIALOGUE, things that were said (or, if you can't recall exactly, things that
might have been said). Look at what you come up with — is there detail
enough to bring the scene to life? Anything that might be called vivid? If
you don't have enough detail, you might reconsider whether you recall
◆ 367–75

□ 591–99
◆ 376–81

enough about the incident to write about it. If you have trouble coming up with plenty of detail, try **FREEWRITING, LISTING,** or **LOOPING.**

259–61

Ways of Organizing Memoirs

[Tell about the event from beginning to end]

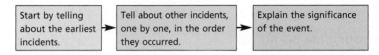

| Start by telling about the earliest incidents. | → | Tell about other incidents, one by one, in the order they occurred. | → | Explain the significance of the event. |

[Start at the end and tell how the event came about]

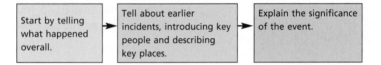

| Start by telling what happened overall. | → | Tell about earlier incidents, introducing key people and describing key places. | → | Explain the significance of the event. |

IF YOU NEED MORE HELP

See Chapter 25 for guidelines on **DRAFTING,** Chapter 26 on **ASSESSING YOUR OWN WRITING,** Chapter 27 on **GETTING RESPONSE AND REVISING,** and Chapter 28 on **EDITING AND PROOFREADING.** See Chapter 29 if you are required to submit your memoir in a writing **PORTFOLIO.**

266–68
269–74
275–81
282–86
287–98

Profiles are written portraits—of people, places, events, or other things. We find profiles of celebrities, travel destinations, and offbeat festivals in magazines and newspapers, on radio and TV. A profile presents a subject in an entertaining way that conveys its significance, showing us something or someone that we may not have known existed or that we see every day but don't know much about. Here, for example, is a profile of one student's quest to break a Guinness world record. It originally appeared in *Prized Writing*, an anthology of writing done by students at the University of California at Davis.

CHRISTIAN DANIELSEN

Paperclip Man

Radhakant Bajpai of India currently has the longest bunch of ear hair in the world, measuring just over 5 inches. In 1997, Davis Huxly of Australia pulled a Boeing 747 weighing 184 tons a distance of 91 meters. And In 1993, the Italian clothing firm Benetton constructed what is still the largest condom ever made: a 72-foot monster that covered an obelisk in Paris to mark World AIDS Day. Such is the world of world records, where the physically amazing, the painfully stupid, and the laughably bizarre are meticulously recorded in *Guinness World Records*, the ultimate authority on superlative feats.

Some records are truly pointless. Enter Daniel Meyer, a 22-year-old student at the University of California at Davis. Dan has wanted a world record since high school, but always knew that his title would have to be something, well, obscure. And after a lot of consideration, Dan decided to challenge the world record for the longest chain of paper-clips put together in a 24-hour period. This is the story of Dan. The Paper-clip Man.

A week before his attempt took place on May 23, Dan spoke to me about his world-record dream. Dan is basketball-player tall and thin with short brown hair. He laughed frequently and answered my questions with a dry and slightly self-mocking sense of humor. "I've always wanted a record. The ones requiring strength and agility, anything studly really, were immediately out," he said. "It was really a process of elimination, going through the book and crossing out records that definitely weren't me. And when I came across the paperclip record, I thought, 'Yes. I can do this.'" The current record was set in 2000 and stands at 895 yards, or just shy of nine football fields. That chain contained 22,025 paperclips.

Ms. Jeanine Van der Meiren of Belgium is the owner of that record. Dan didn't try to contact Meiren about his attempt to dethrone her and said he would have no remorse about claiming the title for himself: "At first, I was very concerned about breaking her record. Very concerned. But then I found out that she actually has more than one record. So I'm not taking this little old lady's reason for living away from her." He also deadpanned, "I do harvest a secret paranoia that she's going to find out where I'm doing this and she'll come and try to disrupt it, but I probably give myself too much credit."

Setting a world record is a complex process. Dan was required to videotape the entire 24-hour period. He had to have some kind of local media coverage. He also had to furnish color photographs and have two witnesses with "some standing in the community" watch the entire event. Finding two people to watch him assemble paperclips for 24 hours was a challenge. Dan offered perks to anyone willing to help him out, including an Internet connection, food, and a television with DVD and video hookups, but even so, the response was underwhelming.

By May 17, only one week before his attempt, Dan had only secured the help of his friend Troy Sammons, a vet student and a friend of Dan's through their church. Troy wasn't terribly excited about his assignment, but was glad he could help out his friend: "It's kind of humorous, and I really admire Dan for setting a goal and going for it." With only a week to go before "D-Day," as Dan called it, he was getting a little nervous about finding another witness. His publicity effort included an open call for witnesses on his website at www.paperclipchallenge.com and

5

This image of Daniel Meyer by John Burgess won first prize in the 31st annual San Francisco Bay Area Press Photographers Association contest.

conducting an interview for the UC Davis newspaper, the *California Aggie*, in the hopes of catching someone's attention. "People seem to be very attracted to the weirdness of it, so I'm hoping that will help," he said. The website also has a message board. Various notes offer Dan encouragement, sarcastic advice, and one marriage proposal. Dan's website even reached one fan in Leipzig, Germany, who invited him to join the International Record Breakers' Club (www.recordholders.org) if he were to succeed.

Dan is a mathematics major and hopes to teach eventually. As he described his vision for how the 24 hours would play out, he spoke logically, with attention to every detail. He spent months preparing. Along with accounting for Guinness requirements, Dan had to find a corporate sponsor willing to donate 50,000 paperclips (about $200 worth), more than enough to break the record. He clearly wanted to make sure his effort would remain standing for a while, "I definitely want to smash the old record," he said. "I've done practice rounds with a spreadsheet that makes projections; and right now I would probably go about 1,000 feet (about 12,000 clips) over." Dan sent out four letters to various office supply companies. He got two polite declines and one no-answer. But then, Dan said, "Office Depot called and wanted to know if it was legit. At first their representative was suspicious that it was some kind of prank. I was so happy that someone had replied. Eventually I convinced him and they sent me 50,000 paperclips and some t-shirts."

That brought up another problem. What does one do with a chain of paperclips that would stretch out almost a mile long? Borrowing an idea from Jeanine van der Meiren's strategy, Dan constructed a giant wooden spool that an assistant would use to wind up the chain as Dan would work through the night. Unfortunately, according to Guinness rules, Dan was required to verify the chain's length by stretching it out fully when finished, all within the 24-hour period. Dan didn't work out all the details of this annoying requirement before the attempt, but he imagined going out to one of Davis's many country roads and unraveling it, praying for no tangles. As for what he wanted to do with the chain when everything was done? "I have no idea."

I showed up at Dan's apartment on May 23 at 2:50 p.m., ten minutes early. A van from the local NBC news affiliate was parked outside. Apparently Dan had gotten his media coverage. A typed sign on his front door was the only other indication that a world record attempt was being made here. It read, "Record Breaking in Progress. Come in!" I walked in out of the heat to see an elaborate setup. The couches had been moved into an arc facing the giant spool and a small card table with several chairs. A television displayed the video feed of the room and a digital clock of the current time. The little dining room had an iMac set up with Dan's spreadsheet and AOL's instant messenger, allowing Dan to get detailed statistics on his pace as he worked and also the ability to give dictated updates to friends online. In one corner were two giant stacks of small boxes, each containing exactly 100 paperclips. Each stack had a sign above it reading "For the Tie" and "For the Win," respectively. Dan greeted me as I walked in the door and then quickly went back to checking last-minute details, nervously giving orders to his support staff of friends while the clock clicked ahead to 3:00:00 p.m. He was wearing his bright red Office Depot t-shirt.

Standing next to the card table were a cameraman and Sacramento   10
reporter John Alston. John was testing his microphone. The expression on his face alternated between amusement and the look of a reporter who was seeing a slow news day. Troy Sammons was sitting on one of the couches, along with Dan's second witness, David Fillingame. Another student and friend from Dan's church, David had known about the project for a long time and was holding out as a possible emergency witness. "There are worse things you could do with your day," he laughed. "Like going to class."

Other friends scurried into position as the final seconds approached. Dan had a total of four assistants: one spooler, two people to unload and untangle paperclips from boxes and finally, one person to pass Dan paperclips in the right orientation to allow for maximum speed. All legal under Guinness rules.

3:00 p.m. Everyone let out a cheer as Dan began to clip away. His technique was flawless, fingers racing like an intricate machine while he talked and made jokes, only rarely taking his eyes off of his hands. At one point he had to ask his assistants to speed up. The spool was being held in place by a stack of books on either side, specifically, Dan's math textbooks. "The irony is not lost on me," he quipped cheerfully.

Most of Dan's friends were excited about the prospect of being on TV as Alston prepared to broadcast a teaser segment for the six o'clock news. "I need some Vaseline for my teeth!" cracked Dan, clipping furiously. All of a sudden, Alston went into broadcast mode, locked onto the camera and speaking with the anchors back in the studio in a pro-nounced and practiced voice. "Dave and Lois, I'm standing here with UC Davis student Dan Meyer who is attempting to break the world record for longest paperclip chain. It's not as dull as watching paint dry . . . but it's close. How are you feeling, champ?"

Dan's reply, "I'm great, John. No cramping here!" Laughter broke out behind the camera.

12:31 a.m. A small crisis broke out at around midnight. With the spool containing three tightly wound layers of almost 10,000 clips, David asked the uncomfortable question of whether they would really come off of the spool like that without tangling. Realizing the terrible possibility that nine hours of work might have gone to waste, Dan took only his sec-ond break to come up with a plan. Several of Dan's engineering friends were present, and they eagerly threw out suggestions. Eventually, some-one came up with the clever idea of separating each layer with Saran Wrap and duct tape. Immediately Dan went back to work. He was clearly annoyed, furious with himself that he could have overlooked such an important detail, and frightened by the thought that now he would now have to race just to break the old record, instead of obliterating it. 15

4:15 a.m. A small cheer went up as the latest spreadsheet numbers informed Dan that he had broken the old record, as far as total num-ber of clips put together. His pace had slowed a little, but he was deter-mined to make his margin of victory as large as possible. He also wanted to account for the possibility that the first 10,000 clips would be essen-tially useless. His friends, meanwhile, had succumbed to fatigue. Dave and Troy slouched on the sofa, eyes drooping as they watched a movie to fight off sleep and boredom. "Watching Dan is kind of hypnotizing," Dave yawned. "Otherwise I'm sure I would have dropped off a long time ago."

Sleep deprivation also produced some strange commentary. Dan's friend Miranda asked him, "You know what you should do with all these paperclips Dan, when this is all done?"

"What?"

"You should . . . you should fill up a swimming pool and jump in!"

"What a weird, non sequitur thing to say, Miranda," Dan replied, laughing. 20

1:30 p.m. A small army of friends came out to a remote farming road to help Dan stretch the chain out to full length. A KCRA cameraman was present for a follow-up, and Dan's parents had also come out to help. Dan's mom walked next to the crew, looking proud and amused at the same time. "Dan's always had a lot of initiative and leadership skills, and he's wanted to do something like this for a long time," she said. "Of all the things he could be doing in college, this is OK by me."

The unspooling process was slow, frustrating work. Dan soon discovered how flimsy paperclips are as they broke under the slightest tug from the spool. As the crew walked slowly down the road, Dan had to continually order halts to fix broken links as well as tangles and snags, all eating up precious time. The Saran Wrap turned out to have worked reasonably well, but the duct tape was a mistake. It tore the wrap as Dan yanked it off, exposing underlying layers and causing more tangles. At this point, Dan hadn't slept for close to 36 hours, and the frustration of this rather banal detail derailing all his work was starting to take its toll. His friends offered well-intentioned advice and tried to take charge, but this usually made matters worse. Dan's mom wanted him to drink more water. The cameraman asked him distracting interview questions. As a particularly bad tangle halted them, with only about a quarter of the spool unrolled, Dan let out a yell of frustration. With less than an hour to go, he could only unroll as much as possible and hope the people at Guinness would understand.

One week after Dan's attempt at immortality, his website posts the disappointing news: despite having put together almost 40,000 paperclips, he was unable to measure out enough of them in a straight line to officially break the record. Dan is pinning his hopes on the video that he will send to Guinness, over twenty hours of paperclip assembly footage. He is not optimistic: "The rules are fairly strict, so I would say there's probably only a twenty percent chance they'll accept it." But despite what would seem like a total failure, he speaks cheerfully about his favorite moments of the experience. What started out as one small dream to be the best in the world at something snowballed into a massive undertaking. It came to involve Dan's friends, his family, his school and the local community, and thanks to the Internet, randomly interested people around the globe. A note on his website claims even people in Hawaii saw him on the news. "I think my favorite part was at around 11 p.m. on Friday," he says. "There were almost twenty-five people crammed in my living room and the lights from the news camera were on me. I just never expected it to get that big. I had a lot of fun."

But of course, the million-dollar question is, after losing on a technicality, will he try it again some day? "Well," he laughs, "this paperclip thing is my Mt. Everest. And you don't quit climbing Mt Everest because one of your sherpas dies. But it won't be for a while."

This profile focuses on Daniel Meyer and his quest for a world record. The writer engages our interest first by admitting the pointlessness of Meyer's attempt and then by meticulously chronicling his preparation and eventual failure.

Key Features / Profiles

An interesting subject. The subject may be something unusual, or it may be something ordinary shown in an intriguing way. You might profile an interesting person (like Daniel Meyer), a place (like the site of a world record attempt), or an event (like the attempt to break a record).

Any necessary background. A profile usually includes just enough information to let readers know something about the subject's larger context. Danielson lets us know that Meyer is a mathematics major at UC Davis and wants to teach but focuses on his activities involving paperclips.

An interesting angle. A good profile captures its subject from a particular angle. Sometimes finding an angle will be fairly easy because your topic — like trying to build a record-breaking paperclip chain — is offbeat enough to be interesting in and of itself. Other topics, though, may require you to find a particular aspect that you can focus on. For example, a profile of a person might focus on the important work the person does or a challenging hobby he or she pursues; it would likely ignore aspects of the person's life that don't relate to that angle.

A firsthand account.   Whether you are writing about a person, place, or event, you need to spend time observing and interacting with your subject. With a person, interacting means watching and conversing. Journalists tell us that "following the guy around," getting your subject to do something and talk about it at the same time, yields excellent material for a profile. When one writer met Theodor Geisel (Dr. Seuss) before profiling him, she asked him not only to talk about his characters but also to draw one — resulting in an illustration for her profile. With a place or event, interacting may mean visiting and participating, although sometimes you may gather even more information by playing the role of the silent observer.

Engaging details.   You need to include details that bring your subject to life. These may include *specific information* ("The current record was set in 2000 and stands at 895 yards, or just shy of nine football fields"); *sensory images* ("As the crew walked slowly down the road, Dan had to continually order halts to fix broken links as well as tangles and snags"); *figurative language* (Meyer's fingers were "racing like an intricate machine"); *dialogue* (" 'I need some Vaseline for my teeth!' cracked Dan"); and *anecdotes* ("All of a sudden, Alston went into broadcast mode . . ."). Choose details that show rather than tell — that let your audience see and hear your subject rather than merely read an abstract description of it. Sometimes you may let them see and hear it literally, by including *photographs* or *video and audio clips*. And be sure all the details create some *dominant impression* of your subject: the impression that we get out of this profile, for example, is of a good-natured, bright, and energetic young man willing to go all out for an ultimately meaningless goal.

A BRIEF GUIDE TO WRITING PROFILES

Choosing a Suitable Subject

A person, a place, an event — whatever you choose, make sure it's something that arouses your curiosity and that you're not too familiar with. Knowing your subject too well can blind you to interesting details. **LIST**

260–61

five to ten interesting subjects that you can experience firsthand. Obviously, you can't profile a person who won't be interviewed or a place or activity that can't be observed. So before you commit to a topic, make sure you'll be able to carry out firsthand research and not find out too late that the people you need to interview aren't willing or that places you need to visit are off-limits.

Considering the Rhetorical Situation

3–4　■　**PURPOSE**　Why are you writing the profile? What angle will best achieve your purpose? How can you inform *and engage* your audience?

5–8　■　**AUDIENCE**　Who is your audience? How familiar are they with your subject? What expectations of your profile might they have? What background information or definitions do you need to provide? How interested will they be—and how can you get their interest?

12–15　■　**STANCE**　What view of your subject do you expect to present? Sympathetic? Critical? Sarcastic? Will you strive for a carefully balanced perspective?

16–18　■　**MEDIA / DESIGN**　Will your profile be a print document? Will it be published on the web? Will it be an oral presentation? Can (and should) you include images or any other visuals? Will it be recorded as an audio file or multimodal text?

Generating Ideas and Text

Explore what you already know about your subject.　Why do you find this subject interesting? What do you know about it now? What do you expect to find out about it from your research? What preconceived ideas about or emotional reactions to this subject do you have? Why do you have them? It may be helpful to try some of the activities in the chapter on **GENERATING IDEAS AND TEXT**.

259–65

Visit your subject.   If you're writing about an amusement park, go there; if you're profiling the man who runs the carousel, make an appointment to meet and interview him. Get to know your subject — if you profile Ben and Jerry, sample the ice cream! Take along a camera if there's anything you might want to show visually in your profile. Find helpful hints for **OBSERVING** and **INTERVIEWING** in the chapter on finding sources.

448–50

If you're planning to interview someone, prepare questions. Danielsen likely asked Daniel Meyer questions like, "What made you want to break the record? Why *this* record? What are the rules for Guinness record attempts?"

Do additional research.   You may be able to write a profile based entirely on your field research. You may, though, need to do some library or web **RESEARCH** as well, to deepen your understanding, get a different perspective, or fill in gaps. Often the people you interview can help you find sources of additional information; so can the sponsors of events and those in charge of places. To learn more about a city park, for instance, contact the government office that maintains it. Download any good photos of your subject that you find online (such as the one of Daniel Meyer on the following page), both to refer to as you write and to illustrate your profile.

419

Analyze your findings.   Look for patterns, images, recurring ideas or phrases, and engaging details. Look for contrasts or discrepancies: between a subject's words and actions, between the appearance of a place and what goes on there, between your expectations and your research findings. Danielsen may have expected Meyer to take his attempt seriously — but may not have been prepared to see him stay awake for thirty-six hours

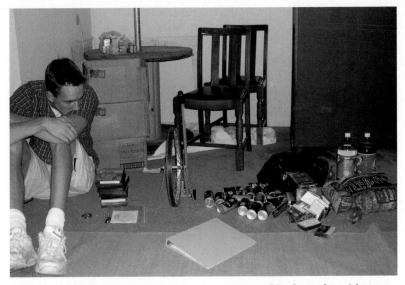

Research can lead you to more than just text sources. This photo of Daniel Meyer and the supplies he used in his attempt to break the record was found with a Google search that used his name and "paper clip" as keywords.

352–66 ◆ straight. You may find the advice in the **READING STRATEGIES** chapter helpful here.

Come up with an angle. What's most memorable about your subject? What most interests you? What will interest your audience? Danielsen focuses on a college student who, in a unique quest to be the best at something, chooses to try to break a silly world record. Sometimes you'll know your angle from the start; other times you'll need to look further 259–62 ○ into your topic. You might try **CLUSTERING, CUBING, FREEWRITING,** and **LOOPING,** activities that will help you look at your topic from many different angles.

■ rhetorical situations
▲ genres
○ processes
◆ strategies
● research MLA / APA
□ media / design
▨ handbook

Note details that support your angle.   Use your angle to focus your research and generate text. Try **DESCRIBING** your subject as clearly as you can, **COMPARING** your subject with other subjects of its sort, writing **DIALOGUE** that captures your subject. Danielsen, for instance, offers details, like Daniel Meyer's "bright red Office Depot t-shirt," that help us see his subject, and he quotes Meyer to give a sense of his attitude toward his attempt: "You don't quit climbing Mt. Everest because one of your sherpas dies." Engaging details will bring your subject to life for your audience. Together, these details should create a dominant impression of your subject.

367–75
348–55
376–81

Ways of Organizing a Profile

[As a narrative]

One common way to organize a profile is by **NARRATING.** For example, if you are profiling a chess championship, you may write about it chronologically, creating suspense as you move from start to finish. The profile of Daniel Meyer's record attempt is organized this way.

387–95

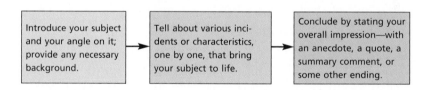

| Introduce your subject and your angle on it; provide any necessary background. | → | Tell about various incidents or characteristics, one by one, that bring your subject to life. | → | Conclude by stating your overall impression—with an anecdote, a quote, a summary comment, or some other ending. |

[As a description]

Sometimes you may organize a profile by **DESCRIBING**—a person or a place, for instance.

367–75

| Introduce your subject and your angle on it, providing any necessary background. | Present details that create some dominant impression of your subject:
• sensory details
• examples
• dialogue
• anecdotes
• *and so on* | State your overall impression, offering a final anecdote or quote or finishing a description begun earlier. |

IF YOU NEED MORE HELP

See Chapter 25 for guidelines on **DRAFTING,** Chapter 26 on **ASSESSING YOUR OWN WRITING,** Chapter 27 on **GETTING RESPONSE AND REVISING,** and Chapter 28 on **EDITING AND PROOFREADING.** See Chapter 29 if you are required to submit your analysis in a writing **PORTFOLIO.**

rhetorical situations
genres
processes
strategies
research MLA / APA
media / design
handbook

Proposals **17**

Contractors bid on building projects. Musicians and educators apply for grants. Researchers seek funding. Student leaders call for lights on bike paths. You offer to pay half the cost of a car and insurance if your parents will pay the other half. Lovers propose marriage; friends propose sharing dinner and a movie. These are all examples of proposals: ideas put forward for consideration that say, "Here is a solution to a problem" or "This is what ought to be done." All proposals are arguments: when you propose something, you are trying to persuade others to see a problem in a particular way and to accept your solution to the problem. For example, here is a proposal for reducing the costs of college textbooks, written by an accounting professor at the University of Texas who is chairman of the university's Co-op Bookstore and himself a textbook author.

MICHAEL GRANOF

Course Requirement: Extortion

By now, entering college students and their parents have been warned: textbooks are outrageously expensive. Few textbooks for semester-long courses retail for less than $120, and those for science and math courses typically approach $180. Contrast this with the $20 to $30 cost of most hardcover best sellers and other trade books.

Perhaps these students and their parents can take comfort in knowing that the federal government empathizes with them, and in an attempt to ease their pain Congress asked its Advisory Committee on Student Financial Assistance to suggest a cure for the problem. Unfortunately, though, the committee has proposed a remedy that would only worsen the problem.

The committee's report, released in May, mainly proposes strengthening the market for used textbooks—by encouraging college bookstores to guarantee that they will buy back textbooks, establishing online book swaps among students, and urging faculty to avoid switching textbooks from one semester to the next. The fatal flaw in that proposal (and similar ones made by many state legislatures) is that used books are the cause of, not the cure for, high textbook prices.

Yet there is a way to lighten the load for students in their budgets, if not their backpacks. With small modifications to the institutional arrangements between universities, publishers, and students, textbook costs could be reduced—and these changes could be made without government intervention.

Today the used-book market is exceedingly well organized and efficient. Campus bookstores buy back not only the books that will be used at their university the next semester but also those that will not. Those that are no longer on their lists of required books they resell to national wholesalers, which in turn sell them to college bookstores on campuses where they will be required. This means that even if a text is being adopted for the first time at a particular college, there is almost certain to be an ample supply of used copies.

As a result, publishers have the chance to sell a book to only one of the multiple students who eventually use it. Hence, publishers must cover their costs and make their profit in the first semester their books are sold— before used copies swamp the market. That's why the prices are so high.

As might be expected, publishers do what they can to undermine the used-book market, principally by coming out with new editions every three or four years. To be sure, in rapidly changing fields like biology and physics, the new editions may be academically defensible. But in areas like algebra and calculus, they are nothing more than a transparent attempt to ensure premature textbook obsolescence. Publishers also try to discourage students from buying used books by bundling the text with extra materials like workbooks and CDs that are not reusable and therefore cannot be passed from one student to another.

The system could be much improved if, first of all, colleges and publishers would acknowledge that textbooks are more akin to computer software than to trade books. A textbook's value, like that of a software program, is not in its physical form, but rather in its intellectual content. Therefore, just as software companies typically "site license" to colleges, so should textbook publishers.

5

Here's how it would work: A teacher would pick a textbook, and the college would pay a negotiated fee to the publisher based on the number of students enrolled in the class. If there were 50 students in the class, for example, the fee might be $15 per student, or $750 for the semester. If the text were used for ten semesters, the publisher would ultimately receive a total of $150 ($15 × 10) for each student enrolled in the course, or as much as $7,500.

In other words, the publisher would have a stream of revenue for as long as the text was in use. Presumably, the university would pass on this fee to the students, just as it does the cost of laboratory supplies and computer software. But the students would pay much less than the $900 a semester they now typically pay for textbooks. 10

Once the university had paid the license fee, each student would have the option of using the text in electronic format or paying more to purchase a hard copy through the usual channels. The publisher could set the price of hard copies low enough to cover only its production and distribution costs plus a small profit, because it would be covering most of its costs and making most of its profit by way of the license fees. The hard copies could then be resold to other students or back to the bookstore, but that would be of little concern to the publisher.

A further benefit of this approach is that it would not affect the way courses are taught. The same cannot be said for other recommendations from the Congressional committee and from state legislatures, like placing teaching materials on electronic reserve, urging faculty to adopt cheaper "no frills" textbooks, and assigning mainly electronic textbooks. While each of these suggestions may have merit, they force faculty to weigh students' academic interests against their fiscal concerns and encourage them to rely less on new textbooks.

Neither colleges nor publishers are known for their cutting-edge innovations. But if they could slightly change the way they do business, they would make a substantial dent in the cost of higher education and provide a real benefit to students and their parents.

This proposal clearly defines the problem—some textbooks cost a lot—and explains why. It proposes a solution to the problem of high textbook prices and offers reasons why this solution will work better than others. Its tone is reasonable and measured, yet decisive.

Key Features / Proposals

A well-defined problem.   Some problems are self-evident and relatively simple, and you would not need much persuasive power to make people act — as with the problem "This university discards too much paper." While some people might see nothing wrong with throwing paper away, most are likely to agree that recycling is a good thing. Other issues are controversial: some people see them as problems while others do not, such as this one: "Motorcycle riders who do not wear helmets risk serious injury and raise health-care costs for everyone." Some motorcyclists believe that wearing or not wearing a helmet should be a personal choice; you would have to present arguments to convince your readers that not wearing a helmet is indeed a problem needing a solution. Any written proposal must establish at the outset that there is a problem — and that it's serious enough to require a solution. For some topics, visual or audio evidence of the problem may be helpful.

A recommended solution.   Once you have defined the problem, you need to describe the solution you are suggesting and to explain it in enough detail for readers to understand what you are proposing. Again, photographs, diagrams, or other visuals may help. Sometimes you might suggest several solutions, weigh their merits, and choose the best one.

A convincing argument for your proposed solution.   You need to convince readers that your solution is feasible — and that it is the best way to solve the problem. Sometimes you'll want to explain in detail how your proposed solution would work. See, for example, how the textbook proposal details the way a licensing system would operate. Visuals may strengthen this part of your argument as well.

A response to anticipated questions.   You may need to consider any questions readers may have about your proposal — and to show how its advantages outweigh any disadvantages. Had the textbook proposal been written for college budget officers, it would have needed to anticipate and answer questions about the costs of implementing the proposed solution.

A call to action.   The goal of a proposal is to persuade readers to accept your proposed solution. This solution may include asking readers to take action.

Granof's proposal for reducing textbook prices via licensing fees might benefit from a photograph like this one, which provides a comparison of other approaches to the problem.

An appropriate tone.   Since you're trying to persuade readers to act, your tone is important—readers will always react better to a reasonable, respectful presentation than to anger or self-righteousness.

A BRIEF GUIDE TO WRITING PROPOSALS

Deciding on a Topic

Choose a problem that can be solved. Complex, large problems, such as poverty, hunger, or terrorism, usually require complex, large solutions. Most of the time, focusing on a smaller problem or a limited aspect of a large problem will yield a more manageable proposal. Rather than tackling the problem of world poverty, for example, think about the problem faced by people in your community who have lost jobs and need help until they find employment.

Considering the Rhetorical Situation

3–4 **PURPOSE**   Do you have a vested interest in a particular solution, or do you simply want to eliminate the problem by whatever solution might be adopted?

5–8 **AUDIENCE**   Do you know if readers share your view of the problem or how receptive or resistant to trying to solve it they are likely to be? Do they have the authority to carry out a proposed solution?

12–15 **STANCE**   How can you show your audience that your proposal is reasonable and should be taken seriously? How can you demonstrate your own authority and credibility?

16–18 **MEDIA / DESIGN**   How will you deliver your proposal? In print? Online? As a speech? Would visuals, or video or audio clips help support your proposal?

Generating Ideas and Text

Explore potential solutions to the problem. Many problems can be solved in more than one way, and you need to show your readers that you've examined several potential solutions. You may develop solutions on your own; more often, though, you'll need to do **RESEARCH** to see how 419 others have solved—or tried to solve—similar problems. Don't settle on a single solution too quickly—you'll need to **COMPARE** the advantages and 348–55 disadvantages of several solutions in order to argue convincingly for one.

Decide on the most desirable solution(s). One solution may be head and shoulders above others—but be open to rejecting all the possible solutions on your list and starting over if you need to, or to combining two or more potential solutions in order to come up with an acceptable fix.

Think about why your solution is the best one.   Why did you choose your solution? Why will it work better than others? What has to be done to enact it? What will it cost? What makes you think it can be done? Writing out answers to these questions will help you argue for your solution: to show that you have carefully and objectively outlined a problem, analyzed the potential solutions, weighed their merits, and determined the reasons the solution you propose is the best.

Ways of Organizing a Proposal

You can organize a proposal in various ways, but always you will begin by establishing that there is a problem. You may then identify several possible solutions before recommending one of them or a combination of several. Sometimes, however, you might discuss only a single solution.

[Several possible solutions]

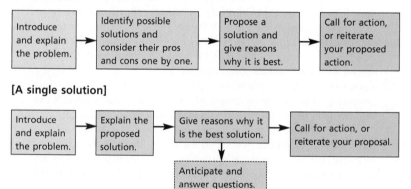

[A single solution]

TOPIC PROPOSALS

Instructors often ask students to write topic proposals to ensure that their topics are appropriate or manageable. Some instructors may also ask for an **ANNOTATED BIBLIOGRAPHY** showing that appropriate sources of information are available—more evidence that the project can be carried out. Here a

▲ 155–63

first-year student proposes a topic for an assignment in a writing course in which she has been asked to take a position on a global issue.

JENNIFER CHURCH

Biodiversity Loss and Its Effect on Medicine

The loss of biodiversity—the variety of organisms found in the world—is affecting the world every day. Some scientists estimate that we are losing approximately one hundred species per day and that more than a quarter of all species may vanish within fifty years. I recently had the issue of biodiversity loss brought to my attention in a biological sciences course that I am taking this quarter. I have found myself interested in and intrigued by the subject and have found an abundance of information both in books and on the Internet.

In this paper, I will argue that it is crucial for people to stop this rapid loss of our world's biodiversity. Humans are the number-one cause of biodiversity loss in the world. Whether through pollution or toxins, we play a crucial role in the extinction of many different species. For example, 80 percent of the world's medicine comes from biological species and their habitats. One medicine vanishing due to biodiversity loss is TAXOL. Found in the Wollemi pine tree, TAXOL is one of the most promising drugs for the treatment of ovarian and breast cancer. If the Wollemi pine tree becomes extinct, we will lose this potential cure.

I will concentrate primarily on biodiversity and its effects on the medical field. If we keep destroying the earth's biodiversity at the current rate, we may lose many opportunities to develop medicines we need to survive. The majority of my information will be found on the Internet, because there are many reliable Web sites from all around the world that address the issue of biodiversity loss and medicine.

Church defines and narrows her topic (from biodiversity loss to the impact of that loss on medicine), discusses her interest, outlines her argument, and discusses her research strategy. Her goal is to convince her instructor that she has a realistic writing project and a clear plan.

Key Features / Topic Proposals

You'll need to explain what you want to write about, why you want to explore it, and what you'll do with your topic. Unless your instructor has additional requirements, here are the features to include:

A concise discussion of the subject.   Topic proposals generally open with a brief discussion of the subject, outlining any important areas of controversy or debate associated with it and clarifying the extent of the writer's current knowledge of it. In its first two paragraphs, Church's proposal includes a concise statement of the topic she wishes to address.

A clear statement of your intended focus.   State what aspect of the topic you intend to write on as clearly as you can, narrowing your focus appropriately. Church does so by stating her intended topic — loss of biodiversity — and then showing how she will focus on the importance of biodiversity to the medical field.

A rationale for choosing the topic.   Tell your instructor why this topic interests you and why you want to write about it. Church both states what made her interested in her topic and hints at a practical reason for choosing it: plenty of information is available.

Mention of resources.   To show your instructor that you can achieve your goal, you need to identify the available research materials.

IF YOU NEED MORE HELP

See Chapter 25 for guidelines on **DRAFTING,** Chapter 26 on **ASSESSING YOUR OWN WRITING,** Chapter 27 on **GETTING RESPONSE AND REVISING,** and Chapter 28 on **EDITING AND PROOFREADING.** See Chapter 29 if you are required to submit your proposal in a writing **PORTFOLIO.**

266–68
269–74
275–81
282–86
287–98

18 Reflections

Sometimes we write essays just to think about something—to speculate, ponder, probe; to play with an idea, develop a thought; or simply to share something. Reflective essays are our attempt to think something through by writing about it and to share our thinking with others. If such essays make an argument, it is about things we care or think about more than about what we believe to be "true." Have a look at one example by Jonathan Safran Foer, a novelist who lives in Brooklyn. This essay originally appeared on the Op-Ed page of the *New York Times* in 2006.

JONATHAN SAFRAN FOER

My Life as a Dog

For the last twenty years, New York City parks without designated dog runs have permitted dogs to be off-leash from 9 p.m. to 9 a.m. Because of recent complaints from the Juniper Park Civic Association in Queens, the issue has been revisited. On December 5, the Board of Health will vote on the future of off-leash hours.

Retrievers in elevators, Pomeranians on No. 6 trains, bull mastiffs crossing the Brooklyn Bridge . . . it is easy to forget just how strange it is that dogs live in New York in the first place. It is about as unlikely a place for dogs as one could imagine, and yet 1.4 million of them are among us. Why do we keep them in our apartments and houses, always at some expense and inconvenience? Is it even possible, in a city, to provide a good life for a dog, and what is a "good life"? Does the health board's vote matter in ways other than the most obvious?

I adopted George (a Great Dane/Lab/pit/greyhound/ridgeback/whatever mix—a.k.a. Brooklyn shorthair) because I thought it would be fun. As it turns out, she is a major pain an awful lot of the time.

rhetorical situations · genres · processes · strategies · research MLA / APA · media / design · handbook

She mounts guests, eats my son's toys (and occasionally tries to eat my son), is obsessed with squirrels, lunges at skateboarders and Hasids,* has the savant-like ability to find her way between the camera lens and subject of every photo taken in her vicinity, backs her tush into the least interested person in the room, digs up the freshly planted, scratches the newly bought, licks the about-to-be-served, and occasionally relieves herself on the wrong side of the front door. Her head is resting on my foot as I type this. I love her.

Our various struggles — to communicate, to recognize and accommodate each other's desires, simply to coexist — force me to interact with something, or rather someone, entirely "other." George can respond to a handful of words, but our relationship takes place almost entirely outside of language. She seems to have thoughts and emotions, desires and fears. Sometimes I think I understand them; often I don't. She is a mystery to me. And I must be one to her.

Of course our relationship is not always a struggle. My morning walk with George is very often the highlight of my day — when I have my best thoughts, when I most appreciate both nature and the city, and in a deeper sense, life itself. Our hour together is a bit of compensation for the burdens of civilization: business attire, email, money, etiquette, walls, and artificial lighting. It is even a kind of compensation for language. Why does watching a dog be a dog fill one with happiness? And why does it make one feel, in the best sense of the word, human?

It is children, very often, who want dogs. In a recent study, when asked to name the ten most important "individuals" in their lives, 7- and 10-year-olds included two pets on average. In another study, 42 percent of 5-year-olds spontaneously mentioned their pets when asked, "Whom do you turn to when you are feeling, sad, angry, happy, or wanting to share a secret?" Just about every children's book in my local bookstore has an animal for its hero. But then, only a few feet away in the cookbook section, just about every cookbook includes recipes for cooking animals. Is there a more illuminating illustration of our paradoxical relationship with the nonhuman world?

In the course of our lives, we move from a warm and benevolent relationship with animals (learning responsibility through caring for

*Hasids: a Jewish sect whose members dress distinctively. [Editor's note]

our pets, stroking and confiding in them) to a cruel one (virtually all animals raised for meat in this country are factory farmed — they spend their lives in confinement, dosed with antibiotics and other drugs).

How do you explain this? Is our kindness replaced with cruelty? I don't think so. I think in part it's because the older we get, the less exposure we have to animals. And nothing facilitates indifference or forgetfulness so much as distance. In this sense, dogs and cats have been very lucky: they are the only animals we are intimately exposed to daily.

Folk parental wisdom and behavioral studies alike generally view 10 the relationships children have with companion animals as beneficial. But one does not have to be a child to learn from a pet. It is precisely my frustrations with George, and the inconveniences she creates, that reinforce in me how much compromise is necessary to share space with other beings.

The practical arguments against off-leash hours are easily refuted. One doesn't have to be an animal scientist to know that the more a dog is able to exercise its "dogness" — to run and play, to socialize with other dogs — the happier it will be. Happy dogs, like happy people, tend not to be aggressive. In the years that dogs have been allowed to run free in city parks, dog bites have decreased 90 percent. But there is another argument that is not so easy to respond to: some people just don't want to be inconvenienced by dogs. Giving dogs space necessarily takes away space from humans.

We have been having this latter debate, in different forms, for ages. Again and again we are confronted with the reality — some might say the problem — of sharing our space with other living things, be they dogs, trees, fish, or penguins. Dogs in the park are a present example of something that is often too abstracted or far away to gain our consideration.

The very existence of parks is a response to this debate: earlier New Yorkers had the foresight to recognize that if we did not carve out places for nature in our cities, there would be no nature. It was recently estimated that Central Park's real estate would be worth more than $500 billion. Which is to say we are half a trillion dollars inconvenienced by trees and grass. But we do not think of it as an inconvenience. We think of it as balance.

Living on a planet of fixed size requires compromise, and while we are the only party capable of negotiating, we are not the only party at the table. We've never claimed more, and we've never had less. There has never been less clean air or water, fewer fish or mature trees. If we are not simply ignoring the situation, we keep hoping for (and expecting) a technological solution that will erase our destruction, while allowing us to continue to live without compromise. Maybe zoos will be an adequate replacement for wild animals in natural habitats. Maybe we will be able to recreate the Amazon somewhere else. Maybe one day we will be able to genetically engineer dogs that do not wish to run free. Maybe. But will those futures make us feel, in the best sense of the word, human?

I have been taking George to Prospect Park twice a day for more 15 than three years, but her running is still a revelation to me. Effortlessly, joyfully, she runs quite a bit faster than the fastest human on the planet. And faster, I've come to realize, than the other dogs in the park. George might well be the fastest land animal in Brooklyn. Once or twice every morning, for no obvious reason, she'll tear into a full sprint. Other dog owners can't help but watch her. Every now and then someone will cheer her on. It is something to behold.

A vote regarding off-leash hours for dogs sparks Foer's reflection on the relationship between dogs and humans. He begins by thinking about his relationship with his own dog, then goes on to consider the paradoxical nature of our treatment of animals in general. From there, he moves into a larger discussion of the compromises we make to "share space with other beings." Finally, he brings his reflection back to the personal, describing the joy of watching his dog be herself, off-leash.

Key Features / Reflections

A topic that intrigues you.   A reflective essay has a dual purpose: to ponder something you find interesting or puzzling and to share your thoughts with an audience. Your topic may be anything that interests you.

You might write about someone you have never met and are curious about, an object or occurrence that makes you think, a place where you feel comfortable or safe. Your goal is to explore the meaning that the person, object, event, or place has for you in a way that will interest others. One way to do that is by making connections between your personal experience and more general ones that readers may share. Foer writes about his experience with his dog, but in so doing he raises questions and offers insights about the way everyone relates to others, human and nonhuman alike.

Some kind of structure.   A reflective essay can be structured in many ways, but it needs to *be* structured. It may seem to wander, but all its paths and ideas should relate, one way or another. The challenge is to keep your readers' interest as you explore your topic and to leave readers satisfied that the journey was pleasurable, interesting, and profitable. Foer brings his essay full-circle, introducing the vote on the off-leash law in his opening, then considering our complex relationship with dogs, and, after suggesting some of the compromises we make to share our world with other nonhuman living things, closing with an indelible image of the joy that freedom from a leash brings.

Specific details.   You'll need to provide specific details to help readers understand and connect with your subject, especially if it's an abstract or unfamiliar one. Foer offers a wealth of details about his dog: "She mounts guests, eats my son's toys (and occasionally tries to eat my son), is obsessed by squirrels, lunges at skateboarders and Hasids." Anecdotes can bring your subject to life: "Once or twice every morning, for no obvious reason, she'll tear into a full sprint. Other dog owners can't help but watch her. Every now and then someone will cheer her on." Reflections may be about causes, such as why dogs make us feel more human; comparisons, such as when Foer compares animals as pets and as food; and examples: "virtually all animals raised for meat in this country are factory farmed." Photographs or other visuals may help provide details as well as set a certain tone for a reflection, as discussed below.

A questioning, speculative tone.   In a reflective essay, you are working toward answers, not providing them neatly organized and ready for consumption. So your tone is usually tentative and open, demonstrating a willingness to entertain, accept, and reject various ideas as your essay progresses from beginning to end. Foer achieves this tone by looking at people's relationships with dogs from several different perspectives as well as by asking questions for which he provides no direct answers.

A BRIEF GUIDE TO WRITING REFLECTIONS

Deciding on a Topic

Choose a subject you want to explore. Write a list of things that you think about, wonder about, find puzzling or annoying. They may be big things—life, relationships—or little things—quirks of certain people's behavior, curious objects, everyday events. Try **CLUSTERING** one or more of those things, or begin by **FREEWRITING** to see what comes to mind as you write.

261–62
259–60

Considering the Rhetorical Situation

PURPOSE   What's your goal in writing this essay? To introduce a topic that interests you? Entertain? Provoke readers to think about something? What aspects of your subject do you want to ponder and reflect on?

3–4

AUDIENCE   Who is the audience? How familiar are they with your subject? How will you introduce it in a way that will interest them?

5–8

STANCE   What is your attitude toward the topic you plan to explore? Questioning? Playful? Critical? Curious? Something else?

12–15

MEDIA / DESIGN   Will your essay be a print document? An oral presentation? Will it be posted on a website? Would it help to include any visuals or video or audio files?

16–18

Generating Ideas and Text

Explore your subject in detail.   Reflections often include descriptive details. Foer, for example, **DESCRIBES** the many ways he encounters dogs in New York: "Retrievers in elevators, Pomeranians on No. 6 trains, bull mastiffs crossing the Brooklyn Bridge." Those details provide a base for the speculations to come. You may also make your point by **DEFINING, COMPARING,** even **CLASSIFYING.** Virtually any organizing pattern will help you explore your subject.

Back away.   Ask yourself why your subject matters: why is it important or intriguing or significant? You may try **LISTING** or **OUTLINING** possibilities, or you may want to start **DRAFTING** to see where the writing takes your thinking. Your goal is to think on screen (or paper) about your subject, to play with its possibilities.

Think about how to keep readers with you.   Reflections may seem loose or unstructured, but they must be carefully crafted so that readers can follow your train of thought. It's a good idea to sketch out a rough **THESIS** to help focus your thoughts. You may not include the thesis in the essay itself, but every part of the essay should in some way relate to it.

Ways of Organizing a Reflective Essay

Reflective essays may be organized in many ways because they mimic the way we think, associating one idea with another in ways that make sense but do not necessarily form a "logical" progression. In general, you might consider organizing a reflection using this overall strategy:

| Begin by defining or describing your subject or perhaps with an anecdote or observation. | → | Explore your topic with
• anecdotes
• observations
• definitions
• speculations | → | End with
• a telling image
• material for further thought
• a statement about the implications of your topic |

367–75
356–66
348–55
342–47
260–61
263–64
266–68
313–15

Another way to organize this type of essay is as a series of brief reflections that together create an overall impression:

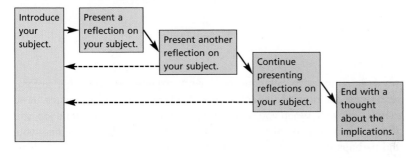

IF YOU NEED MORE HELP

See Chapter 25 for guidelines on **DRAFTING**, Chapter 26 on **ASSESSING YOUR OWN WRITING**, Chapter 27 on **GETTING RESPONSE AND REVISING**, and Chapter 28 on **EDITING AND PROOFREADING**. See Chapter 29 if you are required to submit your reflection in a writing **PORTFOLIO**.

266–68
269–74
275–81
282–86
287–98

19 Résumés and Job Letters

Résumés summarize our education, work experience, and other accomplishments for prospective employers. Application letters introduce us to those employers. When you send a letter and résumé applying for a job, you are making an argument for why that employer should want to meet you, and perhaps hire you. In a way, the two texts together serve as an advertisement selling your talents and abilities to someone who likely has to sift through many applications to decide whom to invite for an interview. That's why résumés and application letters require a level of care that few other documents do. In the same way, sending a thank-you letter following an interview completes your presentation of yourself to potential employers. Résumés, application letters, and thank-you letters are obviously very different genres—yet they share one common purpose and are done for the same audience. Thus, they are presented together in this chapter.

RÉSUMÉS

This chapter covers two kinds of résumés, print ones and scannable ones. *Print résumés* are presented on paper to be read by people. You usually design a print résumé to highlight key information typographically, using italic or bold type for headings, for instance. *Scannable résumés* can be delivered on paper or via email, but they are formatted to be read by a computer. Therefore, you need to use a single sans serif font without any bold or italics or even indents, and you need to write the résumé using keywords that you hope will match words found in the computer's job description database.

Following are two résumés—the first one print and the second one scannable—both written by a college student applying for an internship before his senior year.

Print Résumé

Samuel Praeger •······························· *name in boldface*
28 Murphy Lane
Springfield, OH 45399
937-555-2640
spraeger22@webmail.com

OBJECTIVE   To obtain an internship with a public relations firm •············· *objective*
                                                                                       tailored to
                                                                                       specific job
                                                                                       sought

EDUCATION   Wittenberg University, Springfield, OH
Fall 2009–present • B.A. in Psychology expected in May 2013
                   • Minor in East Asian Studies

EXPERIENCE
2011–present   Department of Psychology, Wittenberg University •········· *work experience*
                   Research Assistant   *in reverse*
                   • Collect and analyze data   *chronological*
                   • Interview research participants   *order*

Summer   Landis and Landis Public Relations, Springfield, OH
2011   *Events Coordinator*
                   • Organized local charity events
                   • Coordinated database of potential donors
                   • Produced two radio spots for event promotion

Summers   Springfield Aquatic Club, Springfield, OH
2009, 2010   *Assistant Swim Coach*
                   • Instructed children ages 5–18 in competitive swimming

HONORS
2012   Psi Chi National Honor Society in Psychology

2010–2012   Community Service Scholarship, Wittenberg University

ACTIVITIES   Varsity Swim Team; Ronald McDonald House Fund-raiser

SKILLS   Microsoft Office; SPSS for Windows; Prezi; fluent in Japanese

REFERENCES   Available upon request   •········· *format to fill*
                                                                              entire page

Scannable Résumé

Samuel Praeger

Key words: public relations; event coordination; event promotion; sales; independent worker; responsible; collegiate athletics; Japanese language fluency

Address
28 Murphy Lane
Springfield, OH 45399
Phone: 937-555-2640
E-mail: spraeger22@webmail.com

Education
B.A. in Psychology, Minor in East Asian Studies, Wittenberg University, expected May 2013

Experience
Research Assistant, 2011–present
Wittenberg University, Springfield, OH
Data collection from research participants through interviews. Data entry and analysis, using SPSS statistical software.

Events Coordinator, summer 2011
Landis and Landis Public Relations, Springfield, OH
Organizer of charity events. Coordinator of database. Producer of two radio spots.

Assistant Swim Coach, summers 2009 and 2010
Springfield Aquatic Club, Springfield, OH
Instructor of children ages 5–18 in competitive swimming techniques and rules.

Honors
Psi Chi National Honor Society in Psychology, 2012
Community Service Scholarship, Wittenberg University, 2010–2012

Activities
Varsity Swim Team
Ronald McDonald House Fund-raiser

Skills
Microsoft Office; SPSS for Windows; Prezi; fluent in Japanese

References on request

all information in a single sans serif font, aligned on left margin

key words to aid computer searching

no underlining, bold, or italics

printed on white paper; not folded or stapled

rhetorical situations

genres

processes

strategies

research MLA / APA

media / design

handbook

Samuel Praeger's résumé is arranged chronologically, and because he was look-ing for work in a certain field, the résumé is targeted, focusing on his related work and skills and leaving out any references to high school (that he is in college allows readers to assume graduation from high school) or his past job as a house painter, which is not relevant. The print version describes his work responsibilities using action verbs to highlight what he actually did—produced, instructed, and so on—whereas the scannable version converts the verbs to nouns—producer, instructor. The scannable version is format-ted in a single standard font, with no italics, boldfacing, or other typographic variation.

Key Features / Résumés

An organization that suits your goals and experience. There are con-ventional ways of organizing a résumé but no one right way. You can organize a résumé chronologically or functionally, and it can be targeted or not. A *chronological résumé* is the most general, listing pretty much all your academic and work experience from the most recent to the earliest. A *targeted résumé* will generally announce the specific goal up top, just beneath your name, and will offer information selectively, showing only the experience and skills relevant to your goal. A *functional résumé* is organized around various kinds of experience and is not chronological. You might write a functional résumé if you wish to demonstrate a lot of experience in more than one area and perhaps if you wish to downplay dates.

Succinct. A résumé should almost always be short—one page if at all possible. Entries should be parallel but do not need to be written in com-plete sentences—"Produced two radio spots," for instance, rather than "I produced two radio spots." *Print résumés* often use action verbs ("instructed," "produced") to emphasize what you accomplished; *scannable résumés* use nouns instead ("instructor," "producer").

A design that highlights key information. It's important for a résumé to look good and to be easy to scan. *On a print résumé,* typography, white space, and alignment matter. Your name should be bold at the top. Major sections should be labeled with headings, all of which should be in one slightly larger or bolder font. And you need to surround each section and the text as a whole with adequate white space to make the parts easy to read — and to make the entire document look professional. *On a scannable résumé,* you should use one standard font throughout and *not* use any italics, boldface, bullets, or indents.

A BRIEF GUIDE TO WRITING RÉSUMÉS

Considering the Rhetorical Situation

<table>
<tr>
<td>3–4</td>
<td>PURPOSE</td>
<td>Are you seeking a job? An internship? Some other position? How will the position for which you're applying affect what you include on your résumé?</td>
</tr>
<tr>
<td>5–8</td>
<td>AUDIENCE</td>
<td>What sort of employee is the company or organization seeking? What experience and qualities will the person doing the hiring be looking for?</td>
</tr>
<tr>
<td>12–15</td>
<td>STANCE</td>
<td>What personal and professional qualities do you want to convey? Think about how you want to come across — as eager? polite? serious? ambitious? — and choose your words accordingly.</td>
</tr>
<tr>
<td>16–18</td>
<td>MEDIA / DESIGN</td>
<td>Are you planning to send your résumé and letter on paper? As an email attachment? In a scannable format? Whatever your medium, be sure both documents are formatted appropriately and proofread carefully.</td>
</tr>
</table>

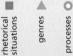

rhetorical situations · genres · processes · strategies · research MLA / APA · media / design · handbook

Generating Ideas and Text for a Résumé

Define your objective.   Are you looking for a particular job for which you should create a targeted résumé? Are you preparing a generic chronological résumé to use in a search for work of any kind? Defining your objective as specifically as possible helps you decide on the form the résumé will take and the information it will include.

Consider how you want to present yourself.   Begin by gathering the information you will need to include. As you work through the steps of putting your résumé together, think about the method of organization that works best for your purpose — chronological, targeted, or functional.

- *Contact information.* At the top of your résumé, list your full name, a permanent address (rather than your school address), a permanent telephone number with area code, and your email address (which should sound professional; addresses like hotbabe334@gmail.com do not make a good first impression on potential employers).

- *Your education.* Start with the most recent: degree, major, college attended, and minor (if any). You may want to list your GPA (if it's over 3.0) and any academic honors you've received. If you don't have much work experience, list education first.

- *Your work experience.* As with education, list your most recent job first and work backward. Include job title, organization name, city and state, start and end dates, and responsibilities. Describe them in terms of your duties and accomplishments. If you have extensive work experience in the area in which you're applying, list that first.

- *Community service, volunteer, and charitable activities.* Many high school students are required to perform community service, and many students participate in various volunteer activities that benefit others. List what you've done, and think about the skills and aptitudes that participation helped you develop or demonstrate.

- *Other activities, interests, and abilities.* What do you do for fun? What skills do your leisure activities require? (For example, if you play a sport, you probably have a good grasp of the value of teamwork. You should describe your skills in a way that an employer might find useful.)

Choose references. Whether you list references on your résumé or offer to provide them on request, ask people to serve as references for you before you send out a résumé. It's a good idea to provide each reference with a one-page summary of relevant information about you (for example, give professors a list of courses you took with them, including the grades you earned and the titles of papers you wrote).

Choose your words carefully. Remember, your résumé is a sales document—you're trying to present yourself as someone worth a second look. Focus on your achievements, using action verbs that say what you've done. If, however, you're composing a scannable résumé, use nouns rather than verbs, and use terms that will function as keywords. Keywords help the computer match your qualifications to the organization's needs. People in charge of hiring search the database of résumés by entering keywords relating to the job for which they are seeking applicants. Keywords for a lab technician, for example, might include *laboratory, technician, procedures, subjects, experiment*—among many others. To determine what key words to list on your résumé, read job ads carefully, and use the same words the ads do—as long as they accurately reflect your experience. Be honest—employers expect truthfulness, and embellishing the truth can cause you to lose a job later.

Consider key design elements. Make sure your résumé is centered on the page and that it looks clean and clear. It's usually best to use a single, simple **FONT** (serif for print, sans serif for scannable) throughout and to print on white or off-white paper. Limit paper résumés to no more—and no less—than one full page. If you plan to send a scannable résumé or post one on a website, it should *not* contain bullets, boldface, indents, italics, or underlining.

585–86 □

rhetorical situations
genres
processes
strategies
research MLA / APA
media / design
handbook

Edit and proofread carefully.   Your résumé must be perfect. Show it to others, and proofread again. You don't want even one typo.

Ways of Organizing a Résumé

If you don't have much work experience or if you've just gone back to school to train for a new career, put education before work experience; if you have extensive work experience in the area in which you're applying, list work before education.

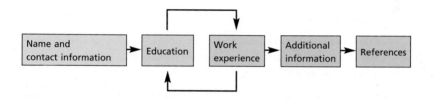

APPLICATION AND THANK YOU LETTERS

The application letter argues that the writer should be taken seriously as a candidate for a job or some other opportunity. Generally, it is sent together with a résumé, so it doesn't need to give that much information. It does, however, have to make a favorable impression: the way it's written and presented can get you in for an interview—or not. On the following page is an application letter that Samuel Praeger wrote seeking a position at the end of his junior year. Praeger tailored his letter to one specific reader at a specific organization. The letter cites details, showing that it is not a generic application letter being sent to many possible employers. Rather, it identifies a particular position—the public relations internship—and stresses the fit between Praeger's credentials and the position. Praeger also states his availability.

Application Letter

equal space at top and bottom of page, all text aligning at left margin

street address city, state ZIP date

28 Murphy Lane
Springfield, OH 45399
May 19, 2011

line space

recipient's name and title, organization, address

Barbara Jeremiah, President
Jeremiah Enterprises
44322 Commerce Way
Worthington, OH 45322

salutation, with a colon

line space

Dear Ms. Jeremiah:

position identified

I am writing to apply for the public relations internship advertised in the Sunday, May 15, *Columbus Dispatch.* The success of your company makes me eager to work with you and learn from you.

match between experience and job description

My grasp of public relations goes beyond the theories I have learned in the classroom. I worked last summer at Landis and Landis, the Springfield public relations firm, where I was responsible for organizing two charity events that drew over two hundred potential donors each. Since your internship focuses on public relations, my experience in the field should allow me to make a contribution to your company.

line space between paragraphs

availability

I will be available to begin any time after May 23, when the spring term at Wittenberg ends. I enclose my résumé, which provides detailed information about my background. I will phone this week to see if I might arrange an interview.

line space

closing

Sincerely,

4 lines space for signature

Samuel Praeger

sender's name, typed

Samuel Praeger

Thank You Letter

equal space at top and bottom of page, all text aligning at left margin

28 Murphy Lane • .... *street address*
Springfield, OH 45399 *city, state ZIP*
June 1, 2011 *date*

line space

Barbara Jeremiah, President • .... *recipient's name and title, organization, address*
Jeremiah Enterprises
44322 Commerce Way
Worthington, OH 45322

line space

Dear Ms. Jeremiah: • .... *salutation, with a colon*

Thank you for the opportunity to meet with you yesterday. I enjoyed talking • .... *thanks and confirmation of interest*
with you and meeting the people who work with you, and I continue to be very
interested in becoming an intern with Jeremiah Enterprises.

line space between paragraphs

As we discussed, I worked with a public relations firm last summer, and since • .... *brief review of qualifications*
then I have completed three courses in marketing and public relations that relate
directly to the work I would be doing as an intern.

I enclose a list of references, as you requested. • .... *enclosures*

Thank you again for your time. I hope to hear from you soon. • .... *repeat thanks*

line space

Sincerely, • .... *closing*

Samuel Praeger • .... *4 lines space for signature*

Samuel Praeger • .... *sender's name, typed*

Sending a thank you letter within a day or two of your interview is a way of showing appreciation for the interview and restating your interest in the position. It also shows that you have good manners and understand proper business etiquette. On the previous page is a letter Samuel Praeger sent to the person who interviewed him for an internship, thanking the interviewer for her time and the opportunity to meet her, indicating his interest in the position, and reiterating his qualifications.

Key Features / Application and Thank You Letters

A succinct indication of your qualifications.   In an application letter, you need to make clear why you're interested in the position or the organization—and at the same time give some sense of why the person you're writing to should at least want to meet you. In a thank you letter, you should remind the interviewer of your qualifications.

A reasonable and pleasing tone.   When writing application and thank you letters, you need to go beyond simply stating your accomplishments or saying thank you. Through your words, you need to demonstrate that you will be the kind of employee the organization wants. Presentation is also important—your letter should be neat and error-free.

A conventional, businesslike format.   Application and thank you letters typically follow a prescribed format. The most common is the block format shown in the examples. It includes the writer's address, the date, the recipient's name and address, a salutation, the message, a closing, and a signature.

A BRIEF GUIDE TO WRITING JOB LETTERS

Generating Ideas and Text for Application and Thank You Letters

Focus.   Application and thank-you letters are not personal and should not be chatty. Keep them focused: when you're applying for a position, include only information relevant to the position. Don't make your audience wade through irrelevant side issues. Stay on topic.

State the reason for the letter.   Unlike essays, which develop a thesis over several paragraphs, or emails, which announce their topic in a subject line, letters need to explicitly introduce their reason for being written, usually in the first paragraph. When you're applying for something or thanking someone, say so in the first sentence: "I am writing to apply for the Margaret Branscomb Peabody Scholarship for students majoring in veterinary science." "Thank you for meeting with me."

Think of your letter as an argument.   When you're asking for a job, you're making an ARGUMENT. You're making a claim — that you're qualified for a certain position — and you need to support your claim with reasons and evidence. Praeger, for example, cites his education and his work experience — and he offers to supply references who will support his application.

323–41

Choose an appropriate salutation.   If you know the person's name and title, use it: "Dear Professor Turnigan." If you don't know the person's title, one good solution is to address him or her by first and last name: "Dear Julia Turnigan." If, as sometimes happens, you must write to an unknown reader, your options include "To Whom It May Concern" and the more old fashioned "Dear Sir or Madam." Another option in such situations might be to omit the salutation completely and instead use a subject line, for example: "Subject: Public Relations Internship Application." Whenever possible, though, write to a specific person; call the organization and ask whom to write to. Once you've had an interview, write to your interviewer.

Proofread.   Few writing situations demand greater perfection than professional letters — especially job letters. Employers receive dozens, sometimes hundreds, of applications, and often can't look at them all. Typos, grammar errors, and other forms of sloppiness prejudice readers against applicants: they're likely to think that if this applicant can't take the time and care to PROOFREAD, how badly does he or she want this position? To compete, strive for perfection.

285–86

Ways of Organizing an Application or Thank You Letter

Application and thank you letters should both follow a conventional organization, though you might vary the details somewhat. Here are two standard organizations.

[Application letter]

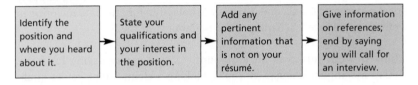

| Identify the position and where you heard about it. | → | State your qualifications and your interest in the position. | → | Add any pertinent information that is not on your résumé. | → | Give information on references; end by saying you will call for an interview. |

[Thank you letter]

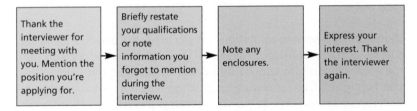

| Thank the interviewer for meeting with you. Mention the position you're applying for. | → | Briefly restate your qualifications or note information you forgot to mention during the interview. | → | Note any enclosures. | → | Express your interest. Thank the interviewer again. |

IF YOU NEED MORE HELP

266–68
269–74
275–81
282–86

See Chapter 25 for guidelines on **DRAFTING**, Chapter 26 on **ASSESSING YOUR OWN WRITING**, Chapter 27 on **GETTING RESPONSE AND REVISING**, and Chapter 28 on **EDITING AND PROOFREADING**.

rhetorical situations   genres   processes   strategies   research MLA / APA   media / design   handbook

Mixing Genres 20

Musicians regularly mix genres, blending, for instance, reggae, hip-hop, and jazz to create a unique sound. Like musicians, writers often combine different genres in a single text. An **EVALUATION** of mining practices might include a **PROFILE** of a coal company CEO. A **PROPOSAL** to start a neighborhood watch might begin with a **REPORT** on crime in the area. Here's a column that mixes genres written by Anna Quindlen for *Newsweek* magazine in 2007.

▲ 164–72
191–204
205–13
87–118

ANNA QUINDLEN
Write for Your Life

The new movie *Freedom Writers* isn't entirely about the themes the trailers suggest. It isn't only about gang warfare and racial tensions and tolerance. It isn't only about the difference one good teacher can make in the life of one messed-up kid. *Freedom Writers* is about the power of writing in the lives of ordinary people. That's a lesson everyone needs. The movie, and the book from which it was taken, track the education of a young teacher named Erin Gruwell, who shows up shiny-new to face a class of what are called, in pedagogical jargon, "at risk" students. It's a mixed bag of Latino, Asian, and black teenagers with one feckless white kid thrown in. They ignore, belittle, and dismiss her as she proffers lesson plans and reading materials seriously out of step with the homelessness, drug use, and violence that are the stuff of their precarious existences.

Textual analysis

And then one day, she gives them all marbled composition books and the assignment to write their lives, ungraded, unjudged, and the world breaks open.

"My probation officer thinks he's slick; he swears he's an expert on gangs."

"Sorry, diary, I was going to try not to do it tonight, but the little baggy of white powder is calling my name."

"If you pull up my shirtsleeves and look at my arms, you will see ⁵ black and blue marks."

"The words 'Eviction Notice' stopped me dead in my tracks."

"When I was younger, they would lock me up in the closet because they wanted to get high and beat up on each other."

Ms. G, as the kids called her, embraced a concept that has been lost in modern life: writing can make pain tolerable, confusion clearer and the self stronger.

How is it, at a time when clarity and strength go begging, that we have moved so far from everyday prose? Social critics might trace this back to the demise of letter writing. The details of housekeeping and child rearing, the rigors of war and work, advice to friends and family: none was slated for publication. They were communications that gave shape to life by describing it for others.

Report

But as the letter fell out of favor and education became profes- ¹⁰ sionalized, with its goal less the expansion of the mind than the acquisition of a job, writing began to be seen largely as the purview of writers. Writing at work also became so stylistically removed from the story of our lives that the two seemed to have nothing in common. Corporate prose conformed to an equation: information × polysyllabic words + tortured syntax = aren't you impressed?

Reflection

And in the age of the telephone most communication became evanescent, gone into thin air no matter how important or heartfelt. Think of all those people inside the World Trade Center saying goodbye by phone. If only, in the blizzard of paper that followed the collapse of the buildings, a letter had fallen from the sky for every family member and friend, something to hold on to, something to read and reread. Something real. Words on paper confer a kind of immortality. Wouldn't all of us love to have a journal, a memoir, a letter, from those we have loved and lost? Shouldn't all of us leave a bit of that behind?

The age of technology has both revived the use of writing and provided ever more reasons for its spiritual solace. Emails are letters, after all, more lasting than phone calls, even if many of them r 2 cursory 4 u. And the physical isolation they and other arms-length cyber-advances create makes talking to yourself more important than ever. That's also what writing is: not just a legacy, but therapy. As the novelist Don DeLillo once said, "Writing is a form of personal freedom. It frees us from the mass identity we see in the making all around us. In the end, writers will write not to be outlaw heroes of some under-culture but mainly to save themselves, to survive as individuals."

That's exactly what Gruwell was after when she got the kids in her class writing, in a program that's since been duplicated at other schools. Salvation and survival for teenagers whose chances of either seemed negligible. "Growing up, I always assumed I would either drop out of school or get pregnant," one student wrote. "So when Ms. G started talking about college, it was like a foreign language to me." Maybe that's the moment when that Latina girl began to speak that foreign language, when she wrote those words down. Today she has a college degree.

Argument

One of the texts Erin Gruwell assigned was *The Diary of a Young Girl* by Anne Frank. A student who balked at reading a book about someone so different, so remote, went on to write: "At the end of the book, I was so mad that Anne died, because as she was dying, a part of me was dying with her." Of course Anne never dreamed her diary would be published, much less read by millions of people after her death at the hands of the Nazis. She wrote it for the same reason the kids who called themselves Freedom Writers wrote in those composition books: to make sense of themselves. That's not just for writers. That's for people.

Quindlen argues that writing helps us understand ourselves and our world. She uses several genres to help advance her argument — textual analysis of the film Freedom Writers, *a brief report on the decline of letter writing, and a reflection on the technologies we use to write. Together, these genres help her develop her argument that writing helps us "make sense of [our]selves."*

Key Features / Texts That Mix Genres

One primary genre.   Your writing situation will often call for a certain genre that is appropriate for your purpose — an argument, a proposal, a report, a textual analysis, and so forth. Additional genres then play supporting roles. Quindlen's essay, for example, primarily argues a position and mixes in other genres, including report and reflection, to elaborate her argument and bring it to life.

A clear focus. A text that mixes genres approaches the topic several different ways, but each genre must contribute to your main point. One genre may serve as the introduction, and others may be woven throughout the text in other ways, but all must address some aspect of the topic and support the central claim. Quindlen's analysis of the film *Freedom Writers*, for example, supports her claim that writing is one way we learn about ourselves.

Careful organization. A text that combines several genres requires careful organization — the various genres must fit together neatly and clearly. Quindlen opens by analyzing the theme of *Freedom Writers*, noting that it's about "the power of writing in the lives of ordinary people." She then switches genres, reporting on how "we have moved so far from everyday prose" and then reflecting on the consequences of that move.

Clear transitions. When a text includes several genres, those genres need to be connected in some way. Transitions do that, and in so doing, they help readers make their way through the text. Transitions may include words such as "in addition" and "however," and they may also consist of phrases that sum up an idea and move it forward. See, for example, how Quindlen ends one paragraph by quoting Don DeLillo as saying that writers write "to save themselves, to survive as individuals" and then begins the next paragraph by referring to DeLillo's words, saying "That's exactly what Gruwell was after."

Some Typical Ways of Mixing Genres

It's possible to mix almost any genres together. Following are some of the most commonly mixed genres and how they combine with other genres.

Memoirs.   Sometimes a personal anecdote can help support an **ARGUMENT** or enhance a **REPORT**. Stories from your personal experience can help readers understand your motivations for arguing a certain position and can enhance your credibility as a writer.

▲ 119–49
87–118

Profiles.   One way to bring a **REPORT** on an abstract topic to life is to include a profile of a person, place, or event. For example, if you were writing a report for your boss on the need to hire more sales representatives, including a profile of one salesperson's typical day might drive home the point that your sales force is stretched too thin.

▲ 87–118

Textual analyses.   You might need to analyze a speech or other document as part of an **ARGUMENT,** especially on a historical or political topic. For instance, you might analyze speeches by Abraham Lincoln and Jefferson Davis if you're writing about the causes of the Civil War, or an advertisement for cigarettes if you're making an argument about teen smoking.

▲ 119–49

Evaluations.   You might include an evaluation of something when you write a **PROPOSAL** about it. For example, if you were writing a proposal for additional student parking on your campus, you would need to evaluate the current parking facilities to discuss their inadequacy.

▲ 205–13

A BRIEF GUIDE TO WRITING TEXTS THAT MIX GENRES

Considering the Rhetorical Situation

PURPOSE   Why are you writing this text? To inform? persuade? entertain? explore an idea? something else? What genres will help you achieve your purpose?

■ 3–4

AUDIENCE   Who are your readers? Which genres will help these readers understand your point? Will starting with a memoir or profile draw them in? Will some analysis help them

■ 5–8

understand the topic? Will a profile make the topic less abstract or make them more sympathetic to your claim?

9–11 **GENRE** What is your primary genre? What other genres might support that primary genre?

12–15 **STANCE** What is your stance on your topic—objective? opinionated? something else? Will including a textual analysis or report help you establish an objective or analytical tone? Will some reflection or a brief memoir show your personal connection to your topic?

16–18 **MEDIA / DESIGN** Will your text be a print document? An oral presentation? Will it be published on the web? Should you include illustrations? Audio or video clips? Do you need to present any information that would be best shown in a chart or graph?

Generating Ideas and Text

Identify your primary genre. If you're writing in response to an assignment, does it specify a particular genre? Look for key verbs that name specific genres — for example, *analyze, argue, evaluate,* and so on. Be aware that other verbs imply certain genres: *explain, summarize, review,* and *describe* ask for a report; *argue, prove,* and *justify* signal that you need to argue a position; and *evaluate* and *propose* specify evaluations and proposals.

3–4
5–8

If the choice of genre is up to you, consider your **PURPOSE** and **AUDIENCE** carefully to determine what genre is most appropriate. Consult the appropriate genre chapter to identify the key features of your primary genre and to generate ideas and text.

Determine if other genres would be helpful. As you write a draft, you may identify a need — for a beginning that grabs readers' attention, for a satisfying ending, for ways to make an abstract concept more concrete or to help in analyzing something. At this point, you may want to try mixing

rhetorical situations
genres
processes
strategies
research MLA / APA
media / design
handbook

one or more genres within your draft. Determine what genre will help you achieve your purpose and consult the appropriate genre chapter for advice on writing in that genre. Remember, however, that you're mixing genres into your draft to support and enhance it—so your supporting genres may not be as developed as complete texts in that genre would be and may not include all the key features. For example, if you include a brief memoir as part of an argument, it should include a good story and vivid details—but its significance may well be stated as part of the argument rather than revealed through the storytelling itself.

Integrate the genres.   Your goal is to create a focused, unified, coherent text. So you need to make sure that your genres work together to achieve that goal. Make sure that each genre fulfills a purpose within the text—for example, that a textual analysis within an argument provides evidence to support your claim, or that the profile you include in a report provides a clear illustration of the larger subject. Also, use **TRANSITIONS** to help readers move from section to section in your text.

◆ 317

Multigenre Projects

Sometimes a collection of texts can together represent an experience or advance an argument. For example, you might document a trip to the Grand Canyon in an album that contains journal entries written during the trip, photographs, a map of northern Arizona showing the canyon, postcards, an essay on the geology of the canyon, and a souvenir coin stamped with an image of the canyon. Each represents a different way of experiencing the Grand Canyon, and together they offer a multifaceted way to understand your trip.

You might also write in several different genres on the same topic. If you begin by **ARGUING** that the government should provide universal health care, for example, writing a **MEMOIR** about a time you were ill could help you explore a personal connection to the topic. Composing a **PROFILE** of a doctor might give you new insights into the issue, and writing a **PROPOSAL** for how universal health care could work might direct you to potential

◆ 323–41
▲ 183–90
191–204
205–13

solutions. You could assemble all these texts in a folder, with a title page and table of contents so that readers can see how it all fits together — or you could create an online multimodal text, combining text, images, video, sound, and links to other sites.

266–68
269–74
299–311
312–17

> **IF YOU NEED MORE HELP**
>
> See Chapter 25 for guidelines on DRAFTING, Chapter 26 on ASSESSING YOUR OWN WRITING, Chapter 31 on BEGINNING AND ENDING, and Chapter 32 on GUIDING YOUR READER.

rhetorical situations

genres

processes

strategies

research MLA / APA

media / design

handbook

Choosing Genres **21**

Write an essay responding to one of the course readings. Show how James Joyce uses financial and economic imagery in "Araby." Explore the various policies adopted toward the use of marijuana. Much of the time, your college writing assignments will specify a particular genre, but sometimes — as these examples suggest — they won't. Vague verbs like *discuss* or *explore* may leave you wondering exactly what your instructor expects. This chapter will help you decide what genre(s) to use when an assignment doesn't tell you what to do.

Recognizing Which Genres Are Required

LITERACY NARRATIVE   A personal account of how you learned to read or write or to make meaning through words, pictures, music, or other means. If you're assigned to explore your development as a writer or reader or to describe how you came to be interested in a particular subject or career, you'll likely need to write a literacy narrative. Some terms that might signal a literacy narrative: *describe a learning experience, tell how you learned, trace your development, write a story.*

▲ 27–51

TEXTUAL ANALYSIS   A careful examination of a text both for what it says and for how it says it, with the goal of demonstrating the ways the text achieves certain effects. If your assignment calls on you to look at a text to see not only what it says but how it works, you likely need to write a textual analysis. Some terms that might signal that a textual analysis is being asked for: *analyze, examine, explicate, read closely, interpret.*

▲ 52–86

87–118 ▲ **REPORT**   A presentation of information as objectively as possible to inform readers about a subject. If your task is to research a topic and then tell your audience in a balanced, neutral way what you know about it, your goal is probably to write a report. Some terms that might signal that a report is being asked for: *define, describe, explain, inform, observe, record, report, show*.

119–49 ▲ **POSITION PAPER** or **ARGUMENT**   Writing that asserts a belief or claim about an issue — usually stated as a thesis — and supports it with reasons and various kinds of evidence. Some terms that might signal that your instructor wants you to take a position or argue for or against something: *agree or disagree, argue, claim, criticize, defend, justify, position paper, prove*.

150–54 ▲
470–71 ● **ABSTRACT** or **SUMMARY**   A condensation of a text into a briefer version that conveys the main points of the original. If your assignment is to reduce a text, either someone else's or your own, into a single paragraph or so, one of these genres is called for. A summary usually either stands on its own or is inserted within a larger text you're writing; an abstract is a condensation of a text you've written yourself, and you write it either to submit the text for publication or to serve as an introduction to the text. Some terms that might signal that an abstract or summary is expected: *abridge, boil down, compress, condense, recap, summarize*.

155–63 ▲ **ANNOTATED BIBLIOGRAPHY**   A genre that includes an overview of published research and scholarship on a topic. Assignments asking you to list potential sources on a topic with complete publication information for and descriptions or evaluations of each one are likely asking for annotated bibliographies. Some terms that might signal that an annotated bibliography is expected: *an annotated list, list and comment on, list and describe, list and evaluate, list sources*.

164–72 ▲ **EVALUATION**   Writing that makes a judgment about something — a source, poem, film, restaurant, whatever — based on certain criteria. If your instructor asks you to say whether or not you like something or whether it's a good or bad example of a category or better or worse than something else, an evaluation is likely being called for. Some terms that might signal that an evaluation is expected: *assess, critique, evaluate, judge, recommend, review.*

LAB REPORT   Writing that covers the process of conducting an experiment in a controlled setting. Lab reports commonly include specific information presented in a particular order, but they vary from discipline to discipline: those in some disciplines include Materials and Data sections, while others may require sections on Participants or Procedures. Some terms that might signal that a lab report is wanted: *describe, discuss, present results might, write up.*

▲ 173–82

MEMOIR   A genre of writing that focuses on something significant in your past. If you're asked to explore an important moment or event in your life, you're probably being asked to write a memoir. Some terms that likely signal that a memoir is desired: *autobiography, chronicle, narrate, a significant personal memory, a story drawn from your experience.*

▲ 183–90

PROFILE   A type of writing that presents a person, place, or event from an interesting angle in an engaging way and is based on first-hand field research. If your instructor assigns you the task of portraying a subject in a way that is both informative and entertaining, you're likely being asked to write a profile. Some terms that might indicate that a profile is being asked for: *angle, describe, dominant impression, interview, observe, report on.*

▲ 191–204

PROPOSAL   Writing that argues for a particular solution to a problem or suggests some action — or that makes a case for pursuing a certain project. Some terms that might indicate a proposal: *argue for [a solution or action], propose, put forward, recommend.*

▲ 205–13

REFLECTION   A genre of writing that presents a writer's thoughtful, personal exploration of a subject. If your assignment calls on you to think in writing about something or to play with ideas, you are likely being asked to write a reflection. Some terms that may mean that a reflection is called for: *consider, explore, ponder, probe, reflect, speculate.*

▲ 214–21

Dealing with Ambiguous Assignments

Sometimes even the key term in an assignment doesn't indicate clearly which genre is wanted, so you need to read such an assignment especially carefully. A first step might be to consider whether it's asking for a report or an argument. For example, here are two sample assignments:

> Discuss ways in which the invention of gas and incandescent lighting significantly changed people's daily lives in the nineteenth century.
>
> Discuss why Willy Loman in *Death of a Salesman* is, or is not, a tragic hero.

Both assignments use the word *discuss*, but in very different ways. The first may be simply be requesting an informative, researched report: the thesis — new forms of lighting significantly changed people's daily lives in various ways — is already given, and you may be simply expected to research and explain what some of these changes were. It's also possible, though, that this assignment is asking you to make an argument about which of these changes were the most significant ones.

In contrast, *discuss* in the second assignment is much more open-ended. It does not lead to a particular thesis but is more clearly asking you to present an argument: to choose a position (Willy Loman is a tragic hero; Willy Loman is *not* a tragic hero; even, possibly, Willy Loman both is *and is not* a tragic hero) and to marshall reasons and evidence from the play to support your position. A clue that an argument is being asked for lies in the way the assignment offers a choice of paths.

Other potentially ambiguous words in assignments are *show* and *explore*, both of which could lead in many directions. If after a careful reading of the entire assignment you still aren't sure what it's asking for, ask your instructor to clarify the appropriate genre or genres.

Mixing Genres

Genres are seldom "pure" — a pure argument, a pure memoir, a pure literary analysis. Most of the writing we read and produce mixes genres to

rhetorical situations

genres

processes

strategies

research MLA / APA

media / design

handbook

meet the needs of the writer's purpose and audience. For example, writing that **TAKES A POSITION** rarely jumps into the argument immediately. Instead, it may include several paragraphs in which the context for the disputed position is explained or information crucial to the audience's understanding is reported. Sometimes that **REPORT** will be introduced by a brief **MEMOIR** that makes the topic personal to the writer and so less abstract. And the argument itself may well do much more than simply take a position — it may **EVALUATE** alternatives and end with a **PROPOSAL,** and even include genres in other media, such as a video clip **PROFILING** the subject of the argument.

▲ 119–49

▲ 87–118
183–90
164–72
205–13
191–204

A decision about whether to mix genres or not should depend primarily on your purpose and audience. If doing so would help you achieve your goal, and you are not restricted to a particular genre, then combining genres is appropriate. Be creative — but not to the extent that you confuse or annoy readers who expect, say, a straightforward academic report. And if you are required to write using a single genre, then you must find ways of making it suit your purpose.

Considering the Rhetorical Situation

If you're still unsure which genre or combination of genres you should use, try exploring your rhetorical situation by answering some or all of the following questions:

PURPOSE   Why are you writing? What do you hope to achieve? What genre(s) do writers typically use to achieve this purpose? Where might you find examples of these genres? What alternatives to these genres are available?

■ 3–4

AUDIENCE   To whom are you writing? How do members of this audience typically communicate with one another? What information do they typically include, and what do they omit? How much information or explanation will they need? Will they expect you to cite the work of others?

■ 5–8

9–11 **GENRE**   What will your audience expect? Which ones do they use themselves in similar situations?

12–15 **STANCE**   What stance do you wish to project — and what stances are acceptable for your audience and purpose? What is your relationship with your audience? Are you writing as an equal, a student, an interested or concerned outsider, something else? What tone is appropriate — objective, impassioned, respectful, informal, something else? What genre(s) will allow you to express that tone?

16–18 **MEDIA / DESIGN**   What media are typically used to communicate in this situation, and do these media suggest or encourage a particular genre? If so, does the genre require a particular design or format? Are charts, graphs, photos, or other visual elements typically included?

part 3

Processes

To create anything, we generally break the work down into a series of steps. We follow a recipe (or the directions on a box) to bake a cake; we break a song down into different parts and the music into various chords to arrange a piece of music. So it is when we write. We rely on various processes to get from a blank screen or page to a finished product. The chapters that follow offer advice on some of these processes—from WRITING AS INQUIRY and GENERATING IDEAS to DRAFTING to GETTING RESPONSE to EDITING to COMPILING A PORTFOLIO, and more.

Processes

Writing as Inquiry **22**

Sometimes we write to say what we think. Other times, however, we write in order to figure out what we think. Much of the writing you do in college will be the latter. Even as you learn to write, you will be writing to learn. This chapter is about writing with a spirit of inquiry—approaching writing projects with curiosity, moving beyond the familiar, keeping your eyes open, tackling issues that don't have easy answers. It's about starting with questions and going from there—and taking risks. As Mark Twain once said, "Sail away from the safe harbor. . . . Explore. Dream. Discover." This chapter offers strategies for doing just that with your writing.

Starting with Questions

The most important thing is to start with questions—with what you don't know rather than with what you do know. Your goal is to learn about your subject and then to learn more. If you're writing about a topic you know well, you want to expand on what you already know. In academic writing, good topics arise from important questions, issues, and problems that are already being discussed. As a writer, you need to find out what's being said about your topic and then see your writing as a way of entering that larger conversation.

So start with questions, and don't expect to find easy answers. If there were easy answers, there would be no reason for discussion—or for you to write. For purposes of inquiry, the best questions can't be answered by looking in a reference book. Instead, they are ones that help you explore what you think—and why. As it happens, many of the strategies in this book can help you ask questions of this kind. Following are some questions to get you started.

356–66

How can it be DEFINED? What is it, and what does it do? Look it up in a dictionary; check *Wikipedia*. Remember, though, that these are only starting points. How *else* can it be defined? What more is there to know about it? If your topic is being debated, chances are that its very definition is subject to debate. If, for instance, you're writing about gay marriage, how you define marriage will affect how you approach the topic.

367–75

How can it be DESCRIBED? What details should you include? From what vantage point should you describe your topic? If, for example, your topic were the physiological effects of running a marathon, what would those effects be—on the lungs, heart muscles, nerves, brain, and so on? How would you describe the physical experience of running over twenty-six miles from the runner's point of view?

382–86

How can it be EXPLAINED? What does it do? How does it work? If you were investigating the use of performance-enhancing drugs by athletes, for example, what exactly is the effect of these drugs? What makes them dangerous—and are they always dangerous or only in certain conditions? Why are they illegal—and should they be illegal?

348–55

What can it be COMPARED with? Again with the use of performance-enhancing drugs by athletes as an example, how does taking such supplements compare with wearing high-tech footwear or uniforms? Does such a comparison make you see taking steroids or other performance-enhancing drugs in a new light?

318–22

What may have CAUSED it? What might be its EFFECTS? Who or what does it affect? What causes cerebral palsy in children, for example? What are its symptoms? If children with cerebral palsy are not treated, what might be the consequences?

342–47

How can it be CLASSIFIED? Is it a topic or issue that can be placed into categories of similar topics or issues? What categories can it be placed into? Are there legal and illegal performance-enhancing supplements (human growth hormone and steroids, for instance), and what's the difference? Are some safe and others less safe? Classifying your topic in this way can help you consider its complexities.

How can it be ANALYZED? What parts can the topic be divided into? For example, if you were exploring the health effects of cell phone use, you might ask what evidence suggests that cell phone radiation causes cancer? What cancers are associated with cell phone use? What do medical experts and phone manufacturers say? How can cell phone users reduce their risk?

◆ 412

How can it be INTERPRETED? What does it really mean? How do you interpret it, and how does your interpretation differ from others? What evidence supports your interpretation, and what argues against it? Imagine you were exploring the topic of sports injuries among young women. Do these injuries reflect a larger cultural preoccupation with competition? a desire to win college scholarships? something else?

▲ 52–86

What expectations does it raise? What will happen next? What makes you think so? If this happens, how will it affect those involved? For instance, will the governing bodies of professional sports require more testing of athletes' blood, urine, and hair than they do now? Will such tests be unfair to athletes taking drugs for legitimate medical needs?

What are the different POSITIONS on it? What controversies or disagreements exist, and what evidence is offered for the various positions? What else might be said? Are there any groups or individuals who seem especially authoritative? If so, you might want to explore what they have said.

▲ 119–49

What are your own feelings about it? What interests you about the topic? How much do you already know about it? For example, if you're an athlete, how do you feel about competing against others who may have taken supplements? If a friend has problems with drugs, do those problems affect your thinking about drugs in sports? How do you react to what others say about the topic? What else do you want to find out?

Are there other ways to think about it? Is what seems true in this case also true in others? How can you apply this subject in another situation? Will what works in another situation also work here? What do you have to do to adapt it? Imagine you were writing about traffic fatalities. If replacing stop signs with roundabouts or traffic circles reduced traffic fatalities in England, could doing so also reduce accidents in the United States?

262–63 ◉ You can also start with the journalist's **QUESTIONS:** *Who? What? When? Where? Why? How?* Asking questions from these various perspectives can help you deepen your understanding of your topic by leading you to see it from many angles.

Keeping a Journal

One way to get into the habit of using writing as a tool for inquiry is to keep a journal. You can use a journal to record your observations, reactions, whatever you wish. Some writers find journals especially useful places to articulate questions or speculations. You may be assigned by teachers to do certain work in a journal, but in general, you can use a journal to write for yourself. Note your ideas, speculate, digress — go wherever your thoughts lead you.

Keeping a Blog

602–3 ▢ You may also wish to explore issues or other ideas online in the form of a **BLOG**. Most blogs have a comments section that allows others to read and respond to what you write, leading to potentially fruitful discussions. You can also include links to other websites, helping you connect various strands of thought and research. The blogs of others, along with online discussion forums and groups, may also be useful sources of opinion on your topic, but keep in mind that they probably aren't authoritative research sources. There are a number of search engines that can help you find blog posts related to specific topics, including *Google Blog Search*, *Ask*, and *IceRocket*. You can create your own blog on sites such as *Blogger*, *Tumblr*, or *WordPress*.

■ ▲ ○ ◆ ● ▢ ⬈

rhetorical situations

genres

processes

strategies

research MLA / APA

media / design

handbook

Collaborating **23**

Whether you're working in a face-to-face group, posting on an online discussion board or wiki, or exchanging drafts with a classmate for peer review, you likely spend a lot of time collaborating with others on writing tasks. Even if you do much of your writing sitting alone at a computer, you probably get help from others at various stages in the writing process—and provide help as well. The fact is that two heads can be better than one—and learning to work well with a team is as important as anything else you'll learn in college. This chapter offers some guidelines for collaborating successfully with other writers.

Some Ground Rules for Face-to-Face Group Work

- Make sure everyone is facing everyone else and is physically part of the group. Doing that makes a real difference in the quality of the interactions—think how much better conversation works when you're sitting around a table than it does when you're sitting in a row.

- Thoughtfulness, respect, and tact are key, since most writers (as you know) are sensitive and need to be able to trust those commenting on their work. Respond to the contributions of others as you would like others to respond to yours.

- Each meeting needs an agenda—and careful attention paid to time. Appoint one person as timekeeper to make sure all necessary work gets done in the available time.

- Appoint another person to be group leader or facilitator. That person needs to make sure everyone gets a chance to speak, no one dominates the discussion, and the group stays on task.

- Appoint a third member of the group to keep a record of the group's discussion. He or she should jot down the major points as they come up and afterward write a **SUMMARY** of the discussion that the group members approve.

470–71

Online Collaboration

Sometimes you'll need or want to work with one or more people online. Working together online offers many advantages, including the ability to collaborate without being in the same place at the same time. Nonetheless, it also presents some challenges that differ from those of face-to-face group work. When sharing writing or collaborating with others online in other ways, consider the following suggestions:

- As with all online communication, remember that you need to choose your words carefully to avoid inadvertently hurting someone's feelings. Without facial expressions, gestures, and other forms of body language and without tone of voice, your words carry all the weight.

5–8

- Remember that the **AUDIENCE** for what you write may well extend beyond your group—your work might be forwarded to others, so there is no telling who else might read it.
- Decide as a group how best to deal with the logistics of exchanging drafts and comments. You can cut and paste text directly into email, send it as an attachment to a message, or post it to your class course management system site. You may need to use a combination of methods, depending on each group member's access to equipment and software. In any case, name your files carefully so that everyone knows which version to use.

Group Writing Projects

Creating a document with a team is common in business and professional work and in some academic fields as well. Here are some tips for making collaboration of this kind work well:

rhetorical situations　genres　processes　strategies　research MLA / APA　media / design　handbook

- *Define the task as clearly as possible,* and make sure everyone understands and agrees with the stated goals.
- *Divide the task into parts.* Decide which parts can be done by individuals, which can be done by a subgroup, and which need to be done by everyone together.
- *Assign each group member certain tasks.* Try to match tasks to each person's skills and interests and to divide the work equally.
- *Establish a deadline for each task.* Allow time for unforeseen problems before the project deadline.
- *Try to accommodate everyone's style of working.* Some people value discussion; others want to get right down to the writing. There's no best way to get work done; everyone needs to be conscious that his or her way is not the only way.
- *Work for consensus — not necessarily total agreement.* Everyone needs to agree that the plan to get the writing accomplished is doable and appropriate — if not exactly the way you would do the project if you were working alone.
- *Make sure everyone performs.* In some situations, your instructor may help, but in others the group itself may have to develop a way to make sure that the work gets done well and fairly. During the course of the project, it's sometimes helpful for each group member to write an assessment both of the group's work and of individual members' contributions.

Writing Conferences

Conferences with instructors or writing tutors can be an especially helpful kind of collaboration. These one-on-one sessions often offer the most strongly focused assistance you can get — and truly valuable instruction. Here are some tips for making the most of conference time:

- *Come prepared.* Bring all necessary materials, including the draft you'll be discussing, your notes, any outlines — and, of course, any questions.

- *Be prompt.* Your instructor or tutor has set aside a block of time for you, and once that time is up, there's likely to be another student writer waiting.

- *Listen carefully, discuss your work seriously, and try not to be defensive.* Your instructor or tutor is only trying to help you produce the best piece possible. If you sense that your work is being misunderstood, explain what you're trying to say. Don't get angry! If a sympathetic reader who's trying to help can't understand what you mean, maybe you haven't conveyed your meaning well enough.

- *Take notes.* During the conference, jot down key words and suggestions. Immediately afterward, flesh out your notes so you'll have a complete record of what was said.

- *Reflect on the conference.* Afterward, think about what you learned. What do you have to do now? Create a plan for revising or doing further work, and write out questions you will ask at your next conference.

rhetorical situations

genres

processes

strategies

research MLA / APA

media / design

handbook

Generating Ideas and Text

All good writing revolves around ideas. Whether you're writing a job-application letter, a sonnet, or an essay, you'll always spend time and effort generating ideas. Some writers can come up with a topic, put their thoughts in order, and flesh out their arguments in their heads; but most of us need to write out our ideas, play with them, tease them out, and examine them from some distance and from multiple perspectives. This chapter offers activities that can help you do just that. *Freewriting, looping, listing,* and *clustering* can help you explore what you know about a subject; *cubing* and *questioning* nudge you to consider a subject in new ways; and *outlining, letter writing, journal keeping,* and *discovery drafting* offer ways to generate a text.

Freewriting

An informal method of exploring a subject by writing about it, freewriting ("writing freely") can help you generate ideas and come up with materials for your draft. Here's how to do it:

1. Write as quickly as you can without stopping for 5 to 10 minutes (or until you fill a screen or page).
2. If you have a subject to explore, write it at the top and then start writing about it, but if you stray, don't worry—just keep writing. If you don't have a subject yet, just start writing and don't stop until the time is up. If you can't think of anything to say, write that ("I can't think of anything to say") again and again until you do—and you will!
3. Once the time is up, read over what you've written, and underline or highlight passages that interest you.

4. Then write some more, starting with one of those underlined or high-lighted passages as your new topic. Repeat the process until you've come up with a usable topic.

Looping

Looping is a more focused version of freewriting; it can help you explore what you know about a subject. You stop, reflect on what you've written, and then write again, developing your understanding in the process. It's good for clarifying your knowledge and understanding of a subject and finding a focus. Here's what you do:

1. Write for 5 to 10 minutes on whatever you know about your subject. This is your first loop.

2. Read over what you wrote, and then write a single sentence summarizing the most important or interesting idea. You might try completing one of these sentences: "I guess what I was trying to say was . . . " or "What surprises me most in reading what I wrote is . . . ." This will be the start of another loop.

3. Write again for 5 to 10 minutes, using your summary sentence as your beginning and your focus. Again, read what you've written, and then write a sentence capturing the most important idea — in a third loop.

Keep going until you have enough understanding of your topic to be able to decide on a tentative focus — something you can write about.

Listing

Some writers find it useful to keep lists of ideas that occur to them while they are thinking about a topic. Follow these steps:

1. Write a list of potential ideas about a topic. Don't try to limit your list — include anything that interests you.

2. Look for relationships among the items on your list: what patterns do you see? If other ideas occur to you, add them to the list.

3. Finally, arrange the items in an order that makes sense for your purpose and can serve as the beginning of an outline for your writing.

Clustering

Clustering is a way of generating and connecting ideas visually. It's useful for seeing how various ideas relate to one another and for developing subtopics. The technique is simple:

1. Write your topic in the middle of a sheet of paper and circle it.

2. Write ideas relating to that topic around it, circle them, and connect them to the central circle.

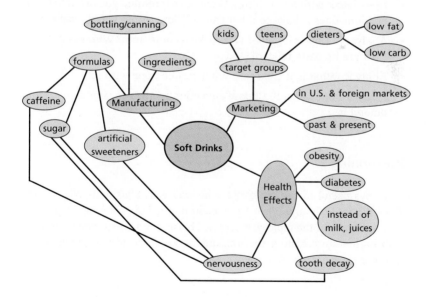

3. Write down examples, facts, or other details relating to each idea, and join them to the appropriate circles.

4. Keep going until you can't think of anything else relating to your topic.

You should end up with various ideas about your topic, and the clusters will allow you to see how they relate to one another. In the example cluster on the topic of "soft drinks" from page 261, note how some ideas link not only to the main topic or related topics but also to other ideas.

Cubing

A cube has six sides. You can examine a topic as you might a cube, looking at it in these six ways:

367–75
- **DESCRIBE** it. What's its color? shape? age? size? What's it made of?

348–55
- **COMPARE** it to something else. What is it similar to or different from?

342–47
- Associate it with other things. What does it remind you of? What connections does it have to other things? How would you **CLASSIFY** it?

- Analyze it. How is it made? Where did it come from? Where is it going? How are its parts related?

- Apply it. What is it used for? What can be done with it?

119–49
- **ARGUE** for or against it. Choose a position relating to your subject, and defend it.

Questioning

251–54
It's always useful to ask **QUESTIONS.** One way is to start with *What? Who? When? Where? How?* and *Why?* A particular method of exploring a topic is to ask questions as if the topic were a play. This method is especially useful for exploring literature, history, the arts, and the social sciences. Start with these questions:

rhetorical situations   genres   processes   strategies   research MLA / APA   media / design   handbook

- *What?* What happens? How is it similar to or different from other actions?

- *Who?* Who are the actors? Who are the participants, and who are the spectators? How do the actors affect the action, and how are they affected by it?

- *When?* When does the action take place? How often does it happen? What happens before, after, or at the same time? Would it be different at another time? Does the time have historical significance?

- *Where?* What is the setting? What is the situation, and what makes it significant?

- *How?* How does the action occur? What are the steps in the process? What techniques are required? What equipment is needed?

- *Why?* Why did this happen? What are the actors' motives? What end does the action serve?

Outlining

You may create an *informal outline* by simply listing your ideas and numbering them in the order in which you want to write about them. You might prefer to make a *working outline*, to show the hierarchy of relationships among your ideas. While still informal, a working outline distinguishes your main ideas and your support, often through simple indentation:

First main idea
    Supporting evidence or detail
    Supporting evidence or detail
Second main idea
    Supporting evidence or detail
    Supporting evidence or detail

A *formal outline* shows the hierarchy of your ideas through a system of indenting, numbering, and lettering. Remember that when you divide a point into more specific subpoints, you should have at least two of them—you can't divide something into only one part. Also, try to keep items at each level parallel in structure. Formal outlines work this way:

Thesis statement

    I. First reason
       A. Supporting evidence
          1. Detail of evidence
          2. Detail of evidence
       B. Supporting evidence
    II. Another reason

Writing out a formal outline can be helpful when you're dealing with a complex subject; as you revise your drafts, though, be flexible and ready to change your outline as your understanding of your topic develops.

Letter Writing

Sometimes the prospect of writing a report or essay can be intimidating. You may find that simply explaining your topic to someone will help you get started. In that case, write a letter to someone you know—your best friend, a parent or grandparent, a sibling—in which you discuss your subject. Explain it in terms that your reader can understand. Use the unsent letter to rehearse your topic; make it a kind of rough draft that you can then revise and develop to suit your actual audience.

Keeping a Journal

Some writers find that writing in a journal helps them generate ideas. Making note of your ideas, thoughts, feelings, or the events of your day can provide a wealth of topics, and a journal can also be a good place to explore what you think and why you think as you do.

Discovery Drafting

Some writers do best by jumping in and writing. Here are the steps to take if you're ready to write a preliminary **DRAFT:**

266–68

1. Write your draft quickly, in one sitting if possible.

2. Assume that you are writing to discover what you want to say and how you need to say it—and that you will make substantial revisions in a later part of the process.

3. Don't worry about grammatical or factual correctness—if you can't think of a word, leave a blank space to fill in later. If you're unsure of a date or spelling, put a question mark in parentheses as a reminder to check it later. Just write.

IF YOU NEED MORE HELP

See each of the **GENRE** chapters for specific strategies for generating text in each genre.

25

25 Drafting

At some point, you need to write out a draft. By the time you begin drafting, you've probably written quite a bit—in the form of notes, lists, outlines, and other kinds of informal writing. This chapter offers some hints on how to write a draft—and reminds you that as you draft, you may well need to get more information, rethink some aspect of your work, or follow new ideas that occur to you as you write.

Establishing a Schedule with Deadlines

Don't wait until the last minute to write. Computers crash, printers jam. Life intervenes in unpredictable ways. You increase your chances of success immensely by setting and meeting **DEADLINES**: Research done by ___; rough draft done by ___; revisions done by ___; final draft edited, proofread, and submitted by ___. How much time you need varies with each writing task—but trying to compress everything into twenty-four or forty-eight hours before the deadline is asking for trouble.

421–22

Getting Comfortable

When are you at your best? When do you have your best ideas? For major writing projects, consider establishing a schedule that lets you write when you stand the best chance of doing good work. Schedule breaks for exercise and snacks. Find a good place to write, a place where you've got a good surface on which to spread out your materials, good lighting, a comfortable chair, and the right tools (computer, pen, paper) for the job. Often, however, we must make do: you may have to do your drafting in a busy computer lab or classroom. The trick is to make yourself as comfortable as you can manage. Sort out what you *need* from what you *prefer*.

rhetorical situations · genres · processes · strategies · research MLA / APA · media / design · handbook

Starting to Write

All of the above advice notwithstanding, don't worry so much about the trappings of your writing situation that you don't get around to writing. Write. Start by FREEWRITING, start with a first sentence, start with awful writing that you know you'll discard later—but write. That's what gets you warmed up and going.

259–60

Write quickly in spurts.   Write quickly with the goal of writing a complete draft, or a complete section of a longer draft, in one sitting. If you need to stop in the middle, make some notes about where you were headed when you stopped so that you can easily pick up your train of thought when you begin again.

Break down your writing task into small segments.   Big projects can be intimidating. But you can always write one section or, if need be, one paragraph or even a single sentence—and then another and another. It's a little like dieting. If I think I need to lose twenty pounds, I get discouraged and head for the doughnuts; but if I decide that I'll lose one pound and I lose it, well, I'll lose another—*that* I can do.

Expect surprises.   Writing is a form of thinking; the words you write lead you down certain roads and away from others. You may end up somewhere you didn't anticipate. Sometimes that can be a good thing—but sometimes you can write yourself into a dead end or out onto a tangent. Just know that this is natural, part of every writer's experience, and it's okay to double back or follow a new path that opens up before you.

Expect to write more than one draft.   A first sentence, first page, or first draft represents your attempt to organize into words your thoughts, ideas, feelings, research findings, and more. It's likely that some of that first try will not achieve your goals. That's okay—having writing on screen or on paper that you can change, add to, and cut means you're part of the way there. As you revise, you can fill in gaps and improve your writing and thinking.

Dealing with Writer's Block

You may sit down to write but find that you can't—nothing occurs to you; your mind is blank. Don't panic; here are some ways to get started writing again:

- Think of the assignment as a problem to be solved. Try to capture that problem in a single sentence: "How do I explain the context for my topic?" "What is the best way to organize my argument?" "What am I trying to do in the conclusion?" Think of a solution to the problem, and then stop thinking about it. If you can't solve it, do something else; give yourself time. Many of us find the solution in the shower, after a good night's sleep.

- Stop trying: take a walk, take a shower, do something else. Come back in a half hour, refreshed.

259–61
- Open a new document on your computer or get a fresh piece of paper and **FREEWRITE,** or try **LOOPING** or **LISTING.** What are you trying to say? Just let whatever comes come—you may write yourself out of your box.

- If you usually write on your computer, turn it off, get out paper and pencil, and write by hand.

262–63
- Try a graphic approach: try **CLUSTERING,** or draw a chart of what you want to say; draw a picture; doodle.

419
- Do some **RESEARCH** on your topic to see what others have said about it.

275–76
- Talk to someone about what you are trying to do. If there's a writing center at your school, talk to a tutor: **GET RESPONSE.** If there's no one to talk to, talk to yourself. It's the act of talking—using your mouth instead of your hands—that can free you up.

> **IF YOU NEED MORE HELP**
>
> See the chapter on **GENERATING IDEAS AND TEXT** if you find you need more material. And once you have a draft, see the chapters on **ASSESSING YOUR OWN WRITING** and **GETTING RESPONSE AND REVISING** for help evaluating your draft.

259–65
269–74
275–81

Assessing Your Own Writing

In school and out, our work is continually assessed by others. Teachers determine whether our writing is strong or weak; supervisors decide whether we merit raises or promotions; even friends and relatives size up in various ways the things we do. As writers, we need to assess our own work—to step back and see it with a critical eye. By developing standards of our own and being conscious of the standards others use, we can assess—and shape—our writing, making sure it does what we want it to do. This chapter will help you assess your own written work.

Assessing the Writing You Do for Yourself

We sometimes write not for an audience but for ourselves—to generate ideas, reflect, make sense of things. The best advice on assessing such writing is *don't*. If you're writing to explore your thoughts, understand a subject, record the events of your day, or just for the pleasure of expressing yourself in words, shut off your internal evaluator. Let the words flow without worrying about them. Let yourself wander without censoring yourself or fretting that what you're writing is incorrect or incomplete or incoherent. That's okay.

One measure of the success of personal writing is its length. FREEWRITING, LISTING, CUBING, JOURNAL KEEPING, and other types of informal writing are like warm-up exercises to limber you up and get you thinking. If you don't give those writing exercises enough time and space, they may not do what you want them to. Often, students' best insights appear at the end of their journal entries. Had they stopped before that point, they never would have had those good ideas.

259–65

A way to study the ideas in your personal writing is to highlight useful patterns in different colors. For example, journal entries usually involve some questioning and speculating, as well as summarizing and paraphrasing. Try color coding each of these, sentence by sentence, phrase by phrase: yellow for summaries or paraphrases, green for questions, blue for speculations. Do any colors dominate? If, for example, your text is mostly yellow, you may be restating the course content too much and perhaps need to ask more questions. If you're generating ideas for an essay, you might assign colors to ideas or themes to see which ones are most promising.

Assessing the Writing You Do for Others

What we write for others must stand on its own because we usually aren't present when it is read—we rarely get to explain to readers why we did what we did and what it means. So we need to make our writing as clear as we can before we submit, post, display, or publish it. It's a good idea to assess your writing in two stages, first considering how well it meets the needs of your particular rhetorical situation, then studying the text itself to check its focus, argument, and organization. Sometimes some simple questions can get you started:

> What works?
> What still needs work?
> Where do I need to say more (or less)?

Considering the Rhetorical Situation

3–4 ■ **PURPOSE** What is your purpose for writing? If you have multiple purposes, list them, and then note which ones are the most important. How well does your draft achieve your purpose(s)? If you're writing for an assignment, what are the requirements of the assignment, and does your draft meet those requirements?

AUDIENCE   To whom are you writing? What do those readers need and expect, as far as you can tell? Does your draft answer their needs? Do you define any terms and explain any concepts they won't know?   5–8

GENRE   What is the genre, and what are the key features of that genre? Does your draft include each of those features?   9–11

STANCE   Is it clear where you stand on your topic? Does your writing project the personality, voice, and tone that you want? Look at the words you use—how do they represent you as a person?   12–15

MEDIA / DESIGN   What medium (print? spoken? electronic?) or combination of media is your text intended for, and how well does your writing suit it? How well does the design of the text suit your purpose and audience? Does it meet any requirements of the genre or of the assignment, if you're writing for one?   16–18

Examining the Text Itself

Look carefully at your text to see how well it says what you want it to say. Start with its focus, and then examine its reasons and evidence, organization, and clarity, in that order. If your writing lacks focus, the revising you'll do to sharpen the focus is likely to change everything else; if it needs more reasons and evidence, the organization may well change.

Consider your focus.   Your writing should have a clear point, and every part of the writing should support that point. Here are some questions that can help you see if your draft is adequately focused:

- What is your **THESIS?** Even if it is not stated directly, you should be able to summarize it for yourself in a single sentence.   313–15

- Is your thesis narrow or broad enough to suit the needs and expectations of your audience?

- How does the **BEGINNING** focus attention on your thesis or main point?   299–306

- Does each paragraph support or develop that point? Do any paragraphs or sentences stray from your focus?

306–10
- Does the **ENDING** leave readers thinking about your main point? Is there another way of concluding the essay that would sharpen your focus?

Consider the support you provide for your argument. Your writing needs to give readers enough information to understand your points, follow your argument, and see the logic of your thinking. How much information is enough will vary according to your audience. If they already know a lot about your subject or are likely to agree with your point of view, you may need to give less detail. If, however, they are unfamiliar with your topic or are skeptical about your views, you will probably need to provide much more.

326–34
- What **REASONS** and **EVIDENCE** do you give to support your thesis? Where might more information be helpful? If you're writing online, could you provide links to it?

356–66
- What key terms and concepts do you **DEFINE?** Are there any other terms your readers might need to have explained? Could you do so by providing links?

367–75
- Where might you include more **DESCRIPTION** or other detail?

348–55
- Do you make any **COMPARISONS?** Especially if your readers will not be familiar with your topic, it can help to compare it with something more familiar.

387–95
- If you include **NARRATIVE,** how is it relevant to your point?

297
- See Part 4 for other useful **STRATEGIES.**

Consider the organization. As a writer, you need to lead readers through your text, carefully structuring your material so that they will be able to follow your argument.

263–64 ⭕
- Analyze the structure by **OUTLINING** it. An informal outline will do since you mainly need to see the parts, not the details.

rhetorical situations

genres

processes

strategies

research MLA / APA

media / design

handbook

- Is your text complete? Does your genre require an abstract, a works-cited list, or any other elements?
- What **TRANSITIONS** help readers move from idea to idea and paragraph to paragraph? Do you need more?

  317
- If there are no **HEADINGS,** would adding them help orient readers?

  588–89

Check for clarity. Nothing else matters if readers can't understand what you write. Following are some questions that can help you see whether your meaning is clear and your text is easy to read:

- Does your **TITLE** announce the subject of your text and give some sense of what you have to say? If not, would a more direct title strengthen your argument?

  312–13
- Do you state your **THESIS** directly? If not, will readers easily understand what your main point is? Try stating your thesis outright, and see if it makes your argument easier to follow.

  313–15
- Does your **BEGINNING** tell readers what they need to understand your text, and does your **ENDING** help them make sense of what they've just read?

  299–311
- How does each paragraph relate to the ones before and after? Are those relationships clear—or do you need to add **TRANSITIONS?**

  317
- Do you vary your sentences? If all the sentences are roughly the same length or follow the same subject-verb-object pattern, your text probably lacks any clear emphasis and might even be difficult to read.
- Are **VISUALS** clearly labeled, positioned near the text they relate to, and referred to clearly in the text?

  591–99
- If you introduce materials from other sources, have you clearly distinguished **QUOTED, PARAPHRASED,** or **SUMMARIZED** ideas from your own?

  462–74
- Do you **DEFINE** all the words that your readers may not know?

  356–66
- Does your punctuation make your writing more clear or less? Incorrect punctuation can make writing difficult to follow or, worse, change the meaning from what you intended. As a best-selling punctuation manual

reminds us, there's a considerable difference between "eats, shoots, and leaves" and "eats shoots and leaves."

Thinking about Your Process

Your growth as a writer depends on how well you understand what you do when you write, so that you can build on good habits. After you finish a writing project, considering the following questions can help you see the process that led to its creation — and find ways to improve the process next time.

- How would you tell the story of your thinking? Try writing these sentences: "When I first began with my topic, I thought _____. But as I did some thinking, writing, and research about the topic, my ideas changed and I thought _____."

- At some point in your writing, did you have to choose between two or more alternatives? What were they, and how did you choose?

- What was the most difficult problem you faced while writing? How did you go about trying to solve it?

- Whose advice did you seek while researching, organizing, drafting, revising, and editing? What advice did you take, and what did you ignore? Why?

rhetorical situations

genres

processes

strategies

research
MLA / APA

media / design

handbook

Getting Response and Revising

If we want to learn to play a song on the guitar, we play it over and over again until we get it right. If we play basketball or baseball, we likely spend hours shooting foul shots or practicing a swing. Writing works the same way. Making our meaning clear can be tricky, and you should plan on revising and, if need be, rewriting in order to get it right. When we speak with someone face-to-face or on the phone or text a friend, we can get immediate response and restate or adjust our message if we've been misunderstood. In most other situations when we write, that immediate response is missing, so we need to seek out responses from readers to help us revise. This chapter includes a list of things for those readers to consider, along with various strategies for subsequent revising and rewriting.

Getting Response

Sometimes the most helpful eyes belong to others: readers you trust, including trained writing-center tutors. They can often point out problems (and strengths) that you simply cannot see in your own work. Ask your readers to consider the specific elements in the list below, but don't restrict them to those elements. Caution: If a reader says nothing about any of these elements, don't be too quick to assume that you needn't think about them yourself.

- What did you think when you first saw the **TITLE?** Is it interesting? informative? appropriate? Will it attract other readers' attention?

  312–13

- Does the **BEGINNING** grab your attention? If so, how does it do so? Does it give enough information about the topic? offer necessary background information? How else might the piece begin?

  299–306

- Is there a clear **THESIS?** What is it?

  313–15

324–34
480–83
- Is there sufficient **SUPPORT** for the thesis? Is there anywhere you'd like to have more detail? Is the supporting material sufficiently **DOCUMENTED?**

- Does the text have a clear pattern of organization? Does each part relate to the thesis? Does each part follow from the one preceding it? Was the text easy to follow? How might the organization be improved?

306–10
- Is the **ENDING** satisfying? What did it leave you thinking? How else might the piece end?

- Can you tell the writer's attitude toward the subject and audience? What words convey that attitude? Is it consistent throughout?

5–8
3–4
9–11
- How well does the text meet the needs and expectations of its **AUDIENCE?** Where might readers need more information, guidance, or clarification? How well does it achieve its **PURPOSE?** Does every part of the text help achieve the purpose? Could anything be cut? Should anything be added? Does the text meet the requirements of its **GENRE?** Should anything be added, deleted, or changed to meet those requirements?

Revising

Once you have studied your draft with a critical eye and, if possible, gotten responses from other readers, it's time to revise. Major changes may be necessary, and you may need to generate new material or do some rewriting. But assume that your draft is good raw material that you can revise to achieve your purposes. Revision should take place on several levels, from global (whole-text issues) to particular (the details). Work on your draft in that order, starting with the elements that are global in nature and gradually moving to smaller, more particular aspects. This allows you to use your time most efficiently and take care of bigger issues first. In fact, as you deal with the larger aspects of your writing, many of the smaller ones will be taken care of along the way.

Give yourself time to revise. When you have a due date, set deadlines for yourself that will give you time — preferably several days but as much as your schedule permits — to work on the text before it has to be delivered.

Also, get some distance. Often when you're immersed in a project, you can't see the big picture because you're so busy creating it. If you can, get away from your writing for a while and think about something else. When you return to it, you're more likely to see it freshly. If there's not time to put a draft away for several days or more, even letting it sit overnight or for a few hours can help.

As you revise, assume that nothing is sacred. Bring a critical eye to all parts of a draft, not only to those parts pointed out by your reviewers. Content, organization, sentence patterns, individual words — all are subject to improvement. Be aware that a change in one part of the text may require changes in other parts.

At the same time, don't waste energy struggling with writing that simply doesn't work; you can always discard it. Look for the parts of your draft that do work — the parts that match your purpose and say what you want to say. Focus your efforts on those bright spots, expanding and developing them.

Revise to sharpen your focus.   Examine your **THESIS** to make sure it matches your **PURPOSE** as you now understand it. Read each paragraph to ensure that it contributes to your main point; you may find it helpful to **OUTLINE** your draft to help you see all the parts. One way to do this is to highlight one sentence in each paragraph that expresses the paragraph's main idea. Then, copy and paste the highlighted sentences into a new document. Does one state the thesis of the entire essay? Do the rest relate to the thesis? Are they in the best order? If not, you need to either modify the parts of the draft that don't advance your thesis or revise your thesis to reflect your draft's focus and to rearrange your points so they advance your discussion more effectively.

313–15
3–4
263–64

Read your **BEGINNING AND ENDING** carefully; make sure that the first paragraphs introduce your topic and provide any needed contextual information and that the final paragraphs provide a satisfying conclusion.

299–311

Revise to strengthen the argument.   If readers find some of your claims unconvincing, you need to provide more information or more support. You may need to define terms you've assumed they will understand, offer additional examples, or provide more detail by describing, explaining

297

259–65
419

processes, adding dialogue, or using some other **STRATEGIES**. Make sure you show as well as tell — and don't forget that you might need to do so literally, with visuals like photos, graphs, or charts. You might try freewriting, clustering, or other ways of **GENERATING IDEAS AND TEXT**. If you need to provide additional evidence, you might need to do additional **RESEARCH**.

317
588–89
9–11

Revise to improve the organization.   If you've outlined your draft, number each paragraph, and make sure each one follows from the one before. If anything seems out of place, move it, or if necessary, cut it completely. Check to see if you've included appropriate **TRANSITIONS** or **HEADINGS** to help readers move through the text, and add them as needed. Check to make sure your text meets the requirements of the **GENRE** you're writing in.

312–13
313–15

356–66
462–74

593–95

Revise for clarity.   Be sure readers will be able to understand what you're saying. Look closely at your **TITLE** to be sure it gives a sense of what the text is about and at your **THESIS** to be sure readers will recognize your main point. If you don't state a thesis directly, consider whether you should. Be sure you provide any necessary background information and **DEFINE** any key terms. Make sure you've integrated any **QUOTATIONS**, **PARAPHRASES**, or **SUMMARIES** into your text smoothly. Be sure all paragraphs are focused around one main point and that the sentences in each paragraph contribute to that point. Finally, consider whether there are any data that would be more clearly presented in a **CHART**, **TABLE**, or **GRAPH**.

One way to test whether your text is clear is to switch audiences: write what you're trying to express as if you were talking to an eight-year-old. Your final draft probably won't be written that way, but the act of explaining your ideas to a young audience or readers who know nothing about your topic can help you discover any points that may be unclear.

Read and reread — and reread.   Take some advice from writing theorist Donald Murray:

> Nonwriters confront a writing problem and look away from the text to rules and principles and textbooks and handbooks and models. Writers look at the text, knowing that the text itself will reveal what needs to be done and what should not yet be done or may never be done.

The writer reads and rereads and rereads, standing far back and reading quickly from a distance, moving in close and reading slowly line by
line, reading again and again, knowing that the answers to all writing
problems lie within the evolving text.

—Donald Murray, *A Writer Teaches Writing*

Rewriting

Some writers find it useful to try rewriting a draft in various ways or from
various perspectives just to explore possibilities. Try it! If you find that
your original plan works best for your purpose, fine. But you may find that
another way will work better. Especially if you're not completely satisfied
with your draft, consider the following ways of rewriting. Experiment with
your rhetorical situation:

- Rewrite your draft from different points of view, through the eyes of
  different people perhaps or through the eyes of an animal or even
  from the perspective of an object. See how the text changes (in the
  information it presents, its perspective, its voice).

- Rewrite for a different **AUDIENCE**. How might an email detailing a   5–8
  recent car accident be written to a friend, an insurance agent, a
  parent?

- Rewrite in a different **TONE**. If the first draft was temperate and judi-   12–15
  cious, be extreme; if it was polite, be more direct. If the first draft was
  in standard English, rewrite it more informally.

- Rewrite the draft in a different **GENRE** or **MEDIUM**. Rewrite an essay as   9–11
  a letter, story, poem, speech. Which genre and medium work best to   16–18
  reach your intended audience and achieve your purpose?

Ways of rewriting a narrative

- Rewrite one scene completely in **DIALOGUE**.   376–81
- Start at the end of the story and work back to the beginning, or start
  in the middle and fill in the beginning as you work toward the end.

Ways of rewriting a textual analysis

348–55
- **COMPARE** the text you're analyzing with another text (which may be in a completely different genre—film, TV, song lyrics, computer games, poetry, fiction, whatever).
- Write a parody of the text you're analyzing. Be as silly and as funny as you can while maintaining the structure of the original text. Alternatively, write a parody of your analysis, using evidence from the text to support an outrageous analysis.

Ways of rewriting a report

5–8
- Rewrite for a different **AUDIENCE.** For example, explain a concept to your grandparents; describe the subject of a profile to a visitor from another planet.
- Be silly. Rewrite the draft as if for *The Daily Show* or the *Onion*, or rewrite it as if it were written by Bart Simpson.

Ways of rewriting an argument

119–49
- Rewrite taking another **POSITION.** Argue as forcefully for that position as you did for your actual one, acknowledging and refuting your original position. Alternatively, write a rebuttal to your first draft from the perspective of someone with different beliefs.

387–95
- Rewrite your draft as a **STORY**—make it real in the lives of specific individuals. (For example, if you were writing about abortion rights, you could write a story about a young pregnant woman trying to decide what she believes and what to do.) Or rewrite the argument as a fable or parable.
- Rewrite the draft as a letter responding to a hostile reader, trying at least to make him or her understand what you have to say.
- Rewrite the draft as an angry letter to someone, or as a table-thumping dinner-with-the-relatives discussion. Write from the most extreme position possible.

- Write an **ANALYSIS** of the topic of your argument in which you identify, as carefully and as neutrally as you can, the various positions
people hold on the issue.

▲ 74–75

Once you've rewritten a draft in any of these ways, see whether there's
anything you can use. Read each draft, considering how it might help you
achieve your purpose, reach your audience, convey your stance. Revise
your actual draft to incorporate anything you think will make your text
more effective, whether it's other genres or a different perspective.

28 Editing and Proofreading

Your ability to produce clear, error-free writing shows something about your ability as a writer and also leads readers to make assumptions about your intellect, your work habits, even your character. Readers of job-application letters and résumés, for example, may reject applications if they contain a single error, for no other reason than it's an easy way to narrow the field of potential candidates. In addition, they may well assume that applicants who present themselves sloppily in an application will do sloppy work on the job. This is all to say that you should edit and proofread your work carefully.

Editing

Editing is the stage when you work on the details of your paragraphs, sentences, words, and punctuation to make your writing as clear, precise, correct—and effective—as possible. Your goal is not to achieve "perfection" (whatever that may be) so much as to make your writing as effective as possible for your particular purpose and audience. Check a good writing handbook for detailed advice, but the following guidelines can help you check your drafts systematically for some common errors with paragraphs, sentences, and words.

Editing paragraphs

315–16 • Does each paragraph focus on one point? Does it have a **TOPIC SENTENCE** that announces that point, and if so, where is it located? If it's not the first sentence, should it be? If there's no clear topic sentence, should there be one?

rhetorical situations   genres   processes   strategies   research MLA / APA   media / design   handbook

- Does every sentence relate to the main point of the paragraph? If any sentences do not, should they be deleted, moved, or revised?

- Is there enough detail to develop the paragraph's main point? How is the point developed — with narrative? definition? some other **STRATEGY**? ◆ 297

- Where have you placed the most important information — at the beginning? the end? in the middle? The most emphatic spot is at the end, so in general that's where to put information you want readers to remember. The second most emphatic spot is at the beginning.

- Are any paragraphs especially long or short? Consider breaking long paragraphs if there's a logical place to do so — maybe an extended example should be in its own paragraph, for instance. If you have paragraphs of only a sentence or two, see if you can add to them or combine them with another paragraph.

- Check the way your paragraphs fit together. Does each one follow smoothly from the one before? Do you need to add any **TRANSITIONS?** ◆ 317

- Does the **BEGINNING** paragraph catch readers' attention? In what other ways might you begin your text? ◆ 299–306

- Does the final paragraph provide a satisfactory **ENDING?** How else might you conclude your text? ◆ 306–10

Editing sentences

- Is each sentence **COMPLETE?** Does it have someone or something (the subject) performing some sort of action or expressing a state of being (the verb)? Does each sentence begin with a capital letter and **END** with a period, question mark, or exclamation point? ◇ HB-4 ◇ HB-69

- Check your use of the **PASSIVE VOICE.** Although there are some rhetorical situations in which the passive voice ("The emperor was assassinated by an anarchist") is more appropriate than the active voice ("An anarchist assassinated the emperor") because you want to emphasize an action rather than who performed it, you'll do well to edit it out unless you have a good reason for using it. ◇ HB-18–19

- Check for **PARALLELISM.** Items in a list or series should be parallel in form—all nouns (lions, tigers, bears), all verbs (hopped, skipped, jumped), all clauses (he came, he saw, he conquered), and so on.

  HB-31

- Do many of your sentences begin with **IT** or **THERE?** Too often these words make your writing wordy and vague or even conceal needed information. Why write "There are reasons we voted for him" when you can say "We had reasons to vote for him"?

  HB-50

- Are your sentences varied? If they all start with the subject or are the same length, your writing might be dull and maybe even hard to read. Try varying your sentence openings by adding **TRANSITIONS,** introductory phrases or clauses. Vary sentence lengths by adding detail to some or combining some sentences.

  317

- Make sure you've used **COMMAS** correctly. Is there a comma after each introductory element? ("After the lead singer quit, the group nearly disbanded. However, they then produced a string of hits.") Do commas set off nonrestrictive elements—parts that aren't needed to understand the sentence? ("The books I read in middle school, like the Harry Potter series, became longer and more challenging.") Are compound sentences connected with a comma? ("I'll eat broccoli steamed, but I prefer it roasted.")

  HB-61

Editing words

- Are you sure of the meaning of every word? Use a dictionary; be sure to look up words whose meanings you're not sure about. And remember your audience—do you use any terms they'll need to have defined?

- Is any of your language too **GENERAL** or vague? Why write that you competed in a race, for example, if you could say you ran the 4 × 200 relay?

  HB-42

- What about the **TONE?** If your stance is serious (or humorous or critical or something else), make sure that your words all convey that attitude.

  13

- Do any pronouns have vague or unclear **ANTECEDENTS?** If you use "he" or "they" or "it" or "these," will readers know whom or what the words refer to?

  HB-26

- Have you used any **CLICHÉS**—expressions that are used so frequently that they are no longer fresh? "Live and let live," avoiding something

  HB-41

"like the plague," and similar expressions are so predictable that your writing will almost always be better off without them.

- Be careful with **LANGUAGE THAT REFERS TO OTHERS.** Make sure that your words do not stereotype any individual or group. Mention age, gender, race, religion, sexual orientation, and so on only if they are relevant to your subject. When referring to an ethnic group, make every effort to use the terms members of the group prefer.

  HB-56–59

- Edit out language that might be considered sexist. Do you say "he" when you mean **"HE AND SHE"**? Have you used words like *manpower* or *policeman* to refer to people who may be female? If so, substitute less gendered words such as *personnel* or *police officer*. Do your words reflect any gender stereotypes—for example, that all engineers are male, or all nurses female? If you mention someone's gender, is it even necessary? If not, eliminate the unneeded words.

  HB-58

- How many of your verbs are forms of **BE** and **DO?** If you rely too much on these words, try replacing them with more specific verbs. Why write "She did a proposal for" when you could say "She proposed"?

  HB-41

- Do you ever confuse **ITS** and **IT'S?** Use *it's* when you mean *it is* or *it has*. Use *its* when you mean *belonging to it*.

  HB-46

Proofreading

Proofreading is the final stage of the writing process, the point where you clean up your work to present it to your readers. Proofreading is like checking your appearance in a mirror before going into a job interview: being neat and well groomed looms large in creating a good first impression, and the same principle applies to writing. Misspelled words, missing pages, mixed-up fonts, and other lapses send a negative message about your work—and about you. Most readers excuse an occasional error, but by and large readers are an intolerant bunch: too many errors will lead them to declare your writing—and maybe your thinking—flawed. There goes your credibility. So proofread your final draft with care to ensure that your message is taken as seriously as you want it to be.

Up to this point, you've been told *not* to read individual words on the page and instead to read for meaning. Proofreading demands the opposite: you must slow down your reading so that you can see every word, every punctuation mark.

- Use your computer's grammar checker and spelling checker, but only as a first step, and know that they're not very reliable. Computer programs don't read writing; instead, they rely on formulas and banks of words, so what they flag (or don't flag) as mistakes may or may not be accurate. If you were to write, "I hope to sea you soon," *sea* would not be flagged as misspelled because it is a word, even though it's the wrong word in that sentence.

- To keep your eyes from jumping ahead, place a ruler or piece of paper under each line as you read. Use your finger or a pencil as a pointer.

- Some writers find it helpful to read the text one sentence at a time, beginning with the last sentence and working backward.

- Read your text out loud to yourself—or better, to others, who may *hear* problems you can't see. Alternatively, have someone else read your text aloud to you while you follow along on the screen or page.

- Ask someone else to read your text. The more important the writing is, the more important this step.

- If you find a mistake after you've printed out your text and are unable to print out a corrected version, make the change as neatly as possible in pencil or pen.

rhetorical situations

genres

processes

strategies

research MLA / APA

media / design

handbook

Compiling a Portfolio 29

Artists maintain portfolios of their work to show gallery owners, collectors, and other potential buyers. Money managers work with investment portfolios of stocks, bonds, and various mutual funds. And often as part of a writing class, student writers compile portfolios of their work. As with a portfolio of paintings or drawings, a portfolio of writing includes a writer's best work and, sometimes, preliminary and revised drafts of that work, along with a statement by the writer articulating why he or she considers it good. The *why* is as important as the work, for it provides you with an occasion for assessing your overall strengths and weaknesses as a writer. This chapter offers guidelines to help you compile both a *writing portfolio* and a *literacy portfolio*, a project that writing students are sometimes asked to complete as part of a literacy narrative.

Considering the Rhetorical Situation

As with the writing you put in a portfolio, the portfolio itself is generally intended for a particular audience but could serve a number of different purposes. It's a good idea, then, to consider these and the other elements of your rhetorical situation when you begin to compile a portfolio.

PURPOSE Why are you creating this portfolio? To create a record of your writing? As the basis for a grade in a course? To organize your research? To explore your literacy? For something else? **3–4**

AUDIENCE Who will read your portfolio? What will your readers expect it to contain? How can you help them understand the context or occasion for each piece of writing you include? **5–8**

9–11 **GENRE** What genres of writing should the portfolio contain? Do you want to demonstrate your ability to write one particular type of writing or in a variety of genres? Will your statement about the portfolio be in the form of a letter or an essay?

12–15 **STANCE** How do you want to portray yourself in this portfolio? What items should you include to create this impression? What stance do you want to take in your written assessment of its contents? Thoughtful? Enthusiastic? Something else?

16–18 **MEDIA / DESIGN** Will your portfolio be in print? Or will it be electronic? Whichever medium you use, how can you help readers navigate its contents? What design elements will be most appropriate to your purpose and medium?

A WRITING PORTFOLIO

What to Include in a Writing Portfolio

A portfolio developed for a writing course typically contains examples of your best work in that course, including any notes, outlines, preliminary drafts, and so on, along with your own assessment of your performance in the course. You might include any of the following items:

- freewriting, outlines, and other work you did to generate ideas
- drafts, rough and revised
- in-class writing assignments
- source material—copies of articles and online sources, observation notes, interview transcripts, and other evidence of your research
- tests and quizzes

- responses to your drafts
- conference notes, error logs, lecture notes, other course materials
- reflections on your work

What you include will vary depending on what your instructor asks for. You may be asked to include three or four of your best papers or everything you've written. You may also be asked to show work in several different genres. In any case, you will usually need to choose, and to do that you will need to have criteria for making your choices. Don't base your decision solely on grades (unless grades are one criterion); your portfolio should reflect *your* assessment of your work, not your instructor's. What do you think is your best work? your most interesting work? your most ambitious work? Whatever criteria you use, you are the judge.

Organizing a Portfolio

Your instructor may provide explicit guidelines for organizing your portfolio. If not, here are some guidelines. If you set up a way to organize your writing at the start of the course, you'll be able to keep track of it throughout the course, making your job at term's end much easier. Remember that your portfolio presents you as a writer, presumably at your best. It should be neat, well organized, and easy to navigate.

Paper portfolios. Choose something in which to gather your work. You might use a two-pocket folder, a three-ring binder, or a file folder, or you may need a box, basket, or some other container to accommodate bulky or odd-shaped items.

Label everything. Label each piece at the top of the first page, specifying the assignment, the draft, and the date: "Proposal, Draft 1, 9/12/12"; "Text Analysis, Final Draft, 10/10/12"; "Portfolio Self-Assessment, Final Draft, 12/11/12"—and so on. Write this information neatly on the page, or put it on a Post-it note. For each assignment, arrange your materials chronologically, with your earliest material (freewriting, for example) on the bottom, and each successive item (source materials, say, then your outline, then your first draft, and so on) on top of the last, ending with your final draft on top. That way readers can see how your writing changed from draft to draft.

Electronic portfolios. You might also create an electronic portfolio, or e-portfolio, that includes a homepage with links to your portfolio's contents. There are several tools that can help you create an e-portfolio:

- *Online tools.* Several websites offer free tools to help you create a pre-formatted e-portfolio. For example, *GoogleSites* provides templates you can use to build an e-portfolio, uploading documents, images, and videos from your computer.

- *Blogging tools.* You can create an e-portfolio using a blogging platform, like *Tumblr, WordPress* or *Weebly*, which allows you to upload files and create a network of linked pages. Readers can then comment on your e-portfolio, just as they might on your blog entries.

- *Wikis.* Wiki-based e-portfolios differ from blog-based ones in the level of interactivity they allow. In addition to commenting, readers may — if you allow them — make changes and add information. *PBworks* is one free provider, as is *WikiSpaces*.

- *Courseware.* Your school may use a learning platform, such as *Blackboard* or *Moodle*, that allows you to create a portfolio of your work.

It's also possible to create an electronic portfolio using word processing, spreadsheet, or presentation software. The programs available for your use and the requirements for publishing your portfolio vary from school to school and instructor to instructor; ask your instructor or your school's help desk for assistance (and see Chapter 55 on **WRITING ONLINE** for general guidance).

600–608

rhetorical situations

genres

processes

strategies

research MLA / APA

media / design

handbook

Reflecting on Your Writing Portfolio

The most important part of your portfolio is your written statement reflecting on your work. This is an opportunity to assess your work with a critical eye and to think about what you're most proud of, what you most enjoyed doing, what you want to improve. It's your chance to think about and say what you've learned. Some instructors may ask you to write out your assessment in essay form; others will want you to put it in letter form, which usually allows for a more relaxed and personal tone. Whatever form it takes, your statement should cover the following ground:

- *An evaluation of each piece of writing in the portfolio.* Consider both strengths and weaknesses, and give examples from your writing to support what you say. What would you change if you had more time? Which is your favorite piece, and why? your least favorite?

- *An assessment of your overall writing performance.* What do you do well? What still needs improvement? What do you *want* your work to say about you? What *does* your work say about you?

- *A discussion of how the writing you did in this course has affected your development as a writer.* How does the writing in your portfolio compare with writing you did in the past? What do you know now that you didn't know before? What can you do that you couldn't do before?

- *A description of your writing habits and process.* What do you usually do? How well does it work? What techniques seem to help you most, and why? Which seem less helpful? Cite passages from your drafts that support your conclusions.

- *An analysis of your performance in the course.* How did you spend your time? Did you collaborate with others? Did you have any conferences with your instructor? Did you visit the writing center? Consider how these or any other activities contributed to your success.

A Sample Self-Assessment

Here is a letter written by Nathaniel Cooney as part of his portfolio for his first-year writing class at Wright State University.

2 June 2013

Dear Reader,

It is my hope that in reading this letter, you will gain an understanding of the projects contained in this portfolio. I enclose three works that I have submitted for an introductory writing class at Wright State University, English 102, Writing in Academic Discourse: an informative report, an argument paper, and a genre project based largely on the content of the argument paper. I selected the topics of these works for two reasons: First, they address issues that I believe to be relevant in terms of both the intended audience (peers and instructors of the course) and the times when they were published. Second, they speak to issues that are important to me personally. Below I present general descriptions of the works, along with my review of their strengths and weaknesses.

My purpose in writing the informative report "Higher Standards in Education Are Taking Their Toll on Students" was to present a subject in a factual manner and to support it with well-documented research. My intent was not to argue a point. However, because I chose a narrowly focused topic and chose information to support a thesis, the report tends to favor one side of the issue over the other. Because as a student I have a personal stake in the changing standards in the formal education system, I chose to research recent changes in higher education and their effects on students. Specifically, I examine students' struggles to reach a standard that seems to be moving further and further beyond their grasp.

I believe that this paper could be improved in two areas. The first is a bias that I think exists because I am a student presenting information from the point of view of a student. It is my hope, however, that my inclusion of unbiased sources lessens this problem somewhat and, furthermore, that it presents the reader with a fair and accurate collection of facts and examples that supports the thesis. My second area of concern is the overall balance in the paper between outside sources supporting my own thoughts and outside sources supporting opposing points of view. Rereading the paper, I notice many places where I may have worked too hard to include sources that support my ideas.

The second paper, "Protecting Animals That Serve," is an argument intended not only to take a clear position on an issue but also to argue for that position and convince the reader that it is a valid one. That issue is the need for legislation guaranteeing that certain rights of service animals be protected. I am blind and use a guide dog. Thus, this issue is especially important to me. During the few months that I have had him, my guide dog has already encountered a number of situations where intentional or negligent treatment by others has put him in danger. At the time I was writing the paper, a bill was being written in the Ohio House of Representatives that, if passed, would protect service animals and establish consequences for those who violated the law. The purpose of the paper, therefore, was to present the reader with information about service animals, establish the need for the legislation in Ohio and nationwide, and argue for passage of such legislation.

I think that the best parts of my argument are the introduction and the conclusion. In particular, I think that the conclusion does a good job of not only bringing together the various points but also conveying the significance of the issue for me and for others. In contrast, I think that the area most in need of further attention is the body of the paper. While I think the content is strong, I believe the overall organization could be improved. The connections between ideas are unclear in places, particularly in the section that acknowledges opposing viewpoints. This may be due in part to the fact that I had difficulty understanding the reasoning behind the opposing argument.

The argument paper served as a starting point for the genre project, for which the assignment was to revise one paper written for this class in a different genre. My genre project consists of a poster and a brochure. As it was for the argument paper, my primary goal was to convince my audience of the importance of a particular issue and viewpoint—specifically, to convince my audience to support House Bill 369, the bill being introduced in the Ohio legislature that would create laws to protect the rights of service animals in the state.

Perhaps both the greatest strength and the greatest weakness of the genre project is my use of graphics. Because of my blindness, I was limited in my use of some graphics. Nevertheless, the pictures were carefully selected to capture the attention of readers and, in part, to appeal to their emotions as they viewed and reflected on the material.

I put a great deal of time, effort, and personal reflection into each project. While I am hesitant to say that they are finished and while I am dissatisfied with some of the finer points, I am satisfied with the overall outcome of this collection of works. Viewing it as a collection, I am also reminded that writing is an evolving process and that even if these works never become exactly what I envisioned them to be, they stand as reflections of my thoughts at a particular time in my life. In that respect, they need not be anything but what they already are, because what they are is a product of who I was when I wrote them. I hope that you find the papers interesting and informative and that as you read them, you, too, may realize their significance.

Respectfully,

Nathaniel J. Cooney

Enclosures (3)

Cooney describes each of the works he includes and considers their strengths and weaknesses, citing examples from his texts to support his assessment.

A LITERACY PORTFOLIO

As a writing student, you may be asked to think back to the time when you first learned to read and write or to remember significant books or other texts you've read and perhaps to put together a portfolio that chronicles your development as a reader and writer. You may also be asked to put together a literacy portfolio as part of a written narrative assignment.

What you include in such a portfolio will vary depending on what you've kept over the years and what your family has kept. You may have all of your favorite books, stories you dictated to a preschool teacher, notebooks in which you practiced writing the alphabet. Or you may have almost nothing. What you have or don't have is unimportant in the end: what's important is that you gather what you can and arrange it in a way that shows how you think about your development and growth as a literate person. What has been your experience with reading and writing? What's your earliest memory of learning to write? If you love to read, what led you to love it? Who was most responsible for shaping your writing ability? Those are some of the questions you'll ask if you write a **LITERACY NARRATIVE.** You might also compile a literacy portfolio as a good way to generate ideas and text for that assignment.

▲ 27–51

What to Include in a Literacy Portfolio

- school papers
- drawings and doodles from preschool
- favorite books
- photographs you've taken
- drawings
- poems
- letters
- journals and diaries
- lists
- reading records or logs

- marriage vows
- speeches you've given
- awards you've received

Organizing a Literacy Portfolio

You may wish to organize your material chronologically, but there are other methods of organization to consider as well. For example, you might group items according to where they were written (at home, at school, at work), by genre (stories, poems, essays, letters, notes), or even by purpose (pleasure, school, work, church, and so on). Arrange your portfolio in the way that best conveys who you are as a literate person. Label each item you include, perhaps with a Post-it note, to identify what it is, when it was written or read, and why you've included it in your portfolio.

Reflecting on Your Literacy Portfolio

- Why did you choose each item?
- Is anything missing? Are there any other important materials that should be here?
- Why is the portfolio organized as it is?
- What does the portfolio show about your development as a reader and writer?
- What patterns do you see? Are there any common themes you've read or written about? Any techniques you rely on? Any notable changes over time?
- What are the most significant items, and why?

rhetorical situations

genres

processes

strategies

research MLA / APA

media / design

handbook

part 4

Strategies

Whenever we write, we draw on many different strategies to articulate what we have to say. We may DEFINE
key terms, DESCRIBE people or places, and EXPLAIN how
something is done. We may COMPARE one thing
to another. Sometimes we may choose a pertinent story
to NARRATE, and we may even want to include some
DIALOGUE. The chapters that follow offer advice on how
to use these AND OTHER BASIC STRATEGIES for developing
and organizing the texts you write.

Strategies

Beginning and Ending 30

Whenever we pick up something to read, we generally start by looking at the first few words or sentences to see if they grab our attention, and based on them we decide whether to keep reading. Beginnings, then, are important, both attracting readers and giving them some information about what's to come. When we get to the end of a text, we expect to be left with a sense of closure, of satisfaction — that the story is complete, our questions have been answered, the argument has been made. So endings are important, too. This chapter offers advice on how to write beginnings and endings.

Beginning

How you begin depends on your **RHETORICAL SITUATION,** especially your purpose and audience. Academic audiences generally expect your introduction to establish context, explaining how the text fits into some larger conversation, addresses certain questions, or explores an aspect of the subject. Most introductions also offer a brief description of the text's content, often in the form of a thesis statement. The following opening of an essay on the effect of texting on student writing does all of this:

> It's taking over our lives. We can do it almost anywhere — walking to class, waiting in line at the grocery store, or hanging out at home. It's quick, easy, and convenient. It has become a concern of doctors, parents, and teachers alike. What it is? It's texting!
>
> Text messaging — or texting, as it's more commonly called — is the process of sending and receiving typed messages via a cellular phone. It is a common means of communication among teenagers and is even becoming popular in the business world because it allows quick messages

rhetorical situations

genres

processes

strategies

research MLA / APA

media / design

handbook

to be sent without people having to commit to a telephone conversation. A person is able to say what is needed, and the other person will receive the information and respond when it's convenient to do so.

In order to more quickly type what they are trying to say, many people use abbreviations instead of words. The language created by these abbreviations is called textspeak. Some people believe that using these abbreviations is hindering the writing abilities of students, and others argue that texting is actually having a positive effect on writing. In fact, it seems likely that texting has no significant effect on student writing.

—Michaela Cullington, "Does Texting Affect Writing?"

If you're writing for a nonacademic audience or genre—for a newspaper or a website, for example—your introduction may need to entice your readers to read on by connecting your text to their interests through shared experiences, anecdotes, or some other attention-getting device. Cynthia Bass, writing a newspaper article about the Gettysburg Address on its 135th anniversary, connects that date—the day her audience would read it—to Lincoln's address. She then develops the rationale for thinking about the speech and introduces her specific topic: debates about the writing and delivery of the Gettysburg Address:

November 19 is the 135th anniversary of the Gettysburg Address. On that day in 1863, with the Civil War only half over and the worst yet to come, Abraham Lincoln delivered a speech now universally regarded as both the most important oration in U.S. history and the best explanation—"government of the people, by the people, for the people"—of why this nation exists.

We would expect the history of an event so monumental as the Gettysburg Address to be well established. The truth is just the opposite. The only thing scholars agree on is that the speech is short—only ten sentences—and that it took Lincoln under five minutes to stand up, deliver it, and sit back down.

Everything else—when Lincoln wrote it, where he wrote it, how quickly he wrote it, how he was invited, how the audience reacted—has been open to debate since the moment the words left his mouth.

—Cynthia Bass, "Gettysburg Address: Two Versions"

rhetorical situations

genres

processes

strategies

research MLA / APA

media / design

handbook

Ways of Beginning

Explain the larger context of your topic.   Most essays are part of an ongoing conversation, so you might begin by outlining the context of the subject
to which your writing responds. An essay exploring the "emotional climate"
of the United States after Barack Obama became president begins by describing the national moods during some of his predecessors' administrations:

> Every president plays a symbolic, almost mythological role that's hard
> to talk about, much less quantify — it's like trying to grab a ball of
> mercury. I'm not referring to using the bully pulpit to shape the
> national agenda but to the way that the president, as America's most
> inescapably powerful figure, colors the emotional climate of the coun-
> try. John Kennedy and Ronald Reagan did this affirmatively, express-
> ing ideals that shaped the whole culture. Setting a buoyant tone, they
> didn't just change movies, music, and television; they changed atti-
> tudes. Other presidents did the same, only unpleasantly. Richard Nixon
> created a mood of angry paranoia, Jimmy Carter one of dreary
> defeatism, and George W. Bush, especially in that seemingly endless
> second term, managed to do both at once.
>
> —John Powers, "Dreams from My President"

State your thesis.   Sometimes the best beginning is a clear **THESIS** stat-   313–15
ing your position, like the following statement in an essay arguing that
fairy tales and nursery rhymes introduce us to "the rudiments and the
humanness of engineering":

> We are all engineers of sorts, for we all have the principles of machines
> and structures in our bones. We have learned to hold our bodies against
> the forces of nature as surely as we have learned to walk. We calculate
> the paths of our arms and legs with the computer of our brain, and we
> catch baseballs and footballs with more dependability than the most
> advanced weapons systems intercept missiles. We may wonder if human
> evolution may not have been the greatest engineering feat of all time.
> And though many of us forget how much we once knew about the
> principles and practices of engineering, the nursery rhymes and fairy
> tales of our youth preserve the evidence that we did know quite a bit.
>
> —Henry Petroski, "Falling Down Is Part of Growing Up"

Forecast your organization.   You might begin by briefly outlining the way in which you will organize your text. The following example from a scholarly paper on the role of immigrants in the U.S. labor market offers background on the subject and describes the points that the writer's analysis will discuss:

> Debates about illegal immigration, border security, skill levels of workers, unemployment, job growth and competition, and entrepreneurship all rely, to some extent, on perceptions of immigrants' role in the U.S. labor market. These views are often shaped as much by politics and emotion as by facts.
>
> To better frame these debates, this short analysis provides data on immigrants in the labor force at the current time of slowed immigration, high unemployment, and low job growth and highlights eight industries where immigrants are especially vital. How large a share of the labor force are they and how does that vary by particular industry? How do immigrants compare to native-born workers in their educational attainment and occupational profiles?
>
> The answers matter because our economy is dependent on immigrant labor now and for the future. The U.S. population is aging rapidly as the baby boom cohort enters old age and retirement. As a result, the labor force will increasingly depend upon immigrants and their children to replace current workers and fill new jobs. This analysis puts a spotlight on immigrant workers to examine their basic trends in the labor force and how these workers fit into specific industries and occupations of interest.
>
> —Audrey Singer, "Immigrant Workers in the U.S. Labor Force"

Offer background information.   If your readers may not know as much as you do about your topic, giving them information to help them understand your position can be important, as David Guterson does in an essay on the Mall of America:

> Last April, on a visit to the new Mall of America near Minneapolis, I carried with me the public-relations press kit provided for the benefit of reporters. It included an assortment of "fun facts" about the mall: 140,000 hot dogs sold each week, 10,000 permanent jobs, 44 escalators and 17 elevators, 12,750 parking places, 13,300 short tons of steel, $1 million in cash disbursed weekly from 8 automatic-teller machines.

The rotunda of the Mall of America.

Opened in the summer of 1992, the mall was built on the 78-acre site of the former Metropolitan Stadium, a five-minute drive from the Minneapolis–St. Paul International Airport. With 4.2 million square feet of floor space—including twenty-two times the retail footage of the average American shopping center—the Mall of America was "the largest fully enclosed combination retail and family entertainment complex in the United States."

—David Guterson, "Enclosed. Encyclopedic. Endured.
One Week at the Mall of America"

Visuals can also help provide context. For example, this essay on the Mall of America might have included a photo like the one on the preceding page to convey the size of the structure.

Define key terms or concepts. The success of an argument often hinges on how key terms are **DEFINED**. You may wish to provide definitions up front, as an advocacy website, *Health Care without Harm*, does in a report on the hazards of fragrances in health-care facilities:

356–66

To many people, the word "fragrance" means something that smells nice, such as perfume. We don't often stop to think that scents are chemicals. Fragrance chemicals are organic compounds that volatilize, or vaporize into the air—that's why we can smell them. They are added to products to give them a scent or to mask the odor of other ingredients. The volatile organic chemicals (VOCs) emitted by fragrance products can contribute to poor indoor air quality (IAQ) and are associated with a variety of adverse health effects.

— "Fragrances," *Health Care without Harm*

Connect your subject to your readers' interests or values. You'll always want to establish common ground with your readers, and sometimes you may wish to do so immediately, in your introduction, as in this example:

We all want to feel safe. Most Americans lock their doors at night, lock their cars in parking lots, try to park near buildings or under lights, and wear seat belts. Many invest in expensive security systems, carry pepper spray or a stun gun, keep guns in their homes, or take self-defense classes. Obviously, safety and security are important issues in American life.

—Andy McDonie, "Airport Security: What Price Safety?"

Start with something that will provoke readers' interest.   Anna Quindlen opens an essay on feminism with the following eye-opening assertion:

> Let's use the F word here. People say it's inappropriate, offensive, that it puts people off. But it seems to me it's the best way to begin, when it's simultaneously devalued and invaluable.
>
>   Feminist. Feminist, feminist, feminist.
>
> —Anna Quindlen, "Still Needing the F Word"

Start with an anecdote.   Sometimes a brief NARRATIVE helps bring a topic to life for readers. See, for example, how an essay on the dozens, a type of verbal contest played by some African Americans, begins:

387–95

> Alfred Wright, a nineteen-year-old whose manhood was at stake on Longwood Avenue in the South Bronx, looked fairly calm as another teenager called him Chicken Head and compared his mother to Shamu the whale.
>
>   He fingered the gold chain around his thin neck while listening to a detailed complaint about his sister's sexual abilities. Then he slowly took the toothpick out of his mouth; the jeering crowd of young men quieted as he pointed at his accuser.
>
>   "He was so ugly when he was born," Wright said, "the doctor smacked his mom instead of him."
>
> —John Tierney, "Playing the Dozens"

Ask a question.   Instead of a thesis statement, you might open with a question about the topic your text will explore, as this study of the status of women in science does:

> Are women's minds different from men's minds? In spite of the women's movement, the age-old debate centering around this question continues. We are surrounded by evidence of de facto differences between men's and women's intellects — in the problems that interest them, in the ways they try to solve those problems, and in the professions they choose. Even though it has become fashionable to view such differences as environmental in origin, the temptation to seek an explanation in terms of innate differences remains a powerful one.
>
> —Evelyn Fox Keller, "Women in Science: A Social Analysis"

Jump right in.   Occasionally you may wish to start as close to the key action as possible. See how one writer jumps right into his profile of a blues concert:

> Long Tongue, the Blues Merchant, strolls onstage. His guitar rides side-saddle against his hip. The drummer slides onto the tripod seat behind the drums, adjusts the high-hat cymbal, and runs a quick, off-beat tat-too on the tom-tom, then relaxes. The bass player plugs into the amplifier, checks the settings on the control panel, and nods his okay. Three horn players stand off to one side, clustered, lurking like brilliant sorcerer-wizards waiting to do magic with their musical instruments.
>
> —Jerome Washington, "The Blues Merchant"

Ending

Endings are important because they're the last words readers read. How you end a text will depend in part on your **RHETORICAL SITUATION.** You may end by wrapping up loose ends, or you may wish to give readers something to think about. Some endings do both, as Cynthia Bass does in a report on the debate over the Gettysburg Address. In her two final paragraphs, she first summarizes the debate and then shows its implications:

> What's most interesting about the Lincoln-as-loser and Lincoln-as-winner versions is how they marshal the same facts to prove different points. The invitation asks Lincoln to deliver "a few appropriate remarks." Whether this is a putdown or a reflection of the protocol of the time depends on the "spin"—an expression the highly politicized Lincoln would have readily understood—which the scholar places on it.
>
> These diverse histories should not in any way diminish the power or beauty of Lincoln's words. However, they should remind us that history, even the history of something as deeply respected as the Gettysburg Address, is seldom simple or clear. This reminder is especially useful today as we watch expert witnesses, in an effort to divine what the founders meant by "high crimes and misdemeanors," club one another with conflicting interpretations of the same events, the same words, the same precedents, and the same laws.
>
> —Cynthia Bass, "Gettysburg Address: Two Versions"

rhetorical situations

genres

processes

strategies

research MLA / APA

media / design

handbook

Bass summarizes the dispute about Lincoln's Address and then moves on to discuss the role of scholars in interpreting historical events. Writing during the Clinton impeachment hearings, she concludes by pointing out the way in which expert government witnesses often offer conflicting interpretations of events to suit their own needs. The ending combines several strategies to bring various strands of her essay together, leaving readers to interpret her final words themselves.

Ways of Ending

Restate your main point.   Sometimes you'll simply **SUMMARIZE** your central idea, as in this example from an essay arguing that we have no "inner" self and that we should be judged by our actions alone:

470–71

> The inner man is a fantasy. If it helps you to identify with one, by all means, do so; preserve it, cherish it, embrace it, but do not present it to others for evaluation or consideration, for excuse or exculpation, or, for that matter, for punishment or disapproval.
>
> Like any fantasy, it serves your purposes alone. It has no standing in the real world which we share with each other. Those character traits, those attitudes, that behavior — that strange and alien stuff sticking out all over you — *that's the real you!*
>
> — Willard Gaylin, "What You See Is the Real You"

Discuss the implications of your argument.   The following conclusion of an essay on the development of Post-it notes leads readers to consider how failure sometimes leads to innovation:

> Post-it notes provide but one example of a technological artifact that has evolved from a perceived failure of existing artifacts to function without frustrating. Again, it is not that form follows function but, rather, that the form of one thing follows from the failure of another thing to function as we would like. Whether it be bookmarks that fail to stay in place or taped-on notes that fail to leave a once-nice surface clean and intact, their failure and perceived failure is what leads to the true evolution of artifacts. That the perception of failure may take

centuries to develop, as in the case of loose bookmarks, does not reduce the importance of the principle in shaping our world.

—Henry Petroski, "Little Things Can Mean a Lot"

387–95 ◆
End with an anecdote, maybe finishing a **NARRATIVE** that was begun earlier in your text or adding one that illustrates the point you are making. See how Sarah Vowell uses a story to end an essay on students' need to examine news reporting critically:

> I looked at Joanne McGlynn's syllabus for her media studies course, the one she handed out at the beginning of the year, stating the goals of the class. By the end of the year, she hoped her students would be better able to challenge everything from novels to newscasts, that they would come to identify just who is telling a story and how that person's point of view affects the story being told. I'm going to go out on a limb here and say that this lesson has been learned. In fact, just recently, a student came up to McGlynn and told her something all teachers dream of hearing. The girl told the teacher that she was listening to the radio, singing along with her favorite song, and halfway through the sing-along she stopped and asked herself, "What am I singing? What do these words mean? What are they trying to tell me?" And then, this young citizen of the republic jokingly complained, "I can't even turn on the radio without thinking anymore."

> —Sarah Vowell, "Democracy and Things Like That"

Refer to the beginning. One way to bring closure to a text is to bring up something discussed in the beginning; often the reference adds to or even changes the original meaning. For example, Amy Tan opens an essay on her Chinese mother's English by establishing herself as a writer and lover of language who uses many versions of English in her writing:

> I am not a scholar of English or literature. I cannot give you much more than personal opinions on the English language and its variations in this country or others.
>
> I am a writer. And by that definition, I am someone who has always loved language. I am fascinated by language in daily life. I spend a

great deal of my time thinking about the power of language — the way it can evoke an emotion, a visual image, a complex idea, or a simple truth. Language is the tool of my trade. And I use them all — all the Englishes I grew up with.

At the end of her essay, Tan repeats this phrase, but now she describes language not in terms of its power to evoke emotions, images, and ideas, but in its power to evoke "the essence" of her mother. When she began to write fiction, she says,

> [I] decided I should envision a reader for the stories I would write. And the reader I decided upon was my mother, because these were stories about mothers. So with this reader in mind — and in fact she did read my early drafts — I began to write stories using all the Englishes I grew up with: the English I spoke to my mother, which for lack of a better term might be described as "simple"; the English she used with me, which for lack of a better term might be described as "broken"; my translation of her Chinese, which could certainly be described as "watered down"; and what I imagined to be her translation of her Chinese if she could speak in perfect English, her internal language, and for that I sought to preserve the essence, but neither an English nor a Chinese structure. I wanted to capture what language ability tests can never reveal: her intent, her passion, her imagery, the rhythms of her speech and the nature of her thoughts.
>
> —Amy Tan, "Mother Tongue"

Note how Tan not only repeats "all the Englishes I grew up with," but also provides parallel lists of what those Englishes can do for her: "evoke an emotion, a visual image, a complex idea, or a simple truth," on the one hand, and, on the other, capture her mother's "intent, her passion, her imagery, the rhythms of her speech and the nature of her thoughts."

Propose some action, as in the following conclusion of a report on the consequences of binge drinking among college students:

> The scope of the problem makes immediate results of any interventions highly unlikely. Colleges need to be committed to large-scale and long-term behavior-change strategies, including referral of alcohol abusers to

appropriate treatment. Frequent binge drinkers on college campuses are similar to other alcohol abusers elsewhere in their tendency to deny that they have a problem. Indeed, their youth, the visibility of others who drink the same way, and the shelter of the college community may make them less likely to recognize the problem. In addition to addressing the health problems of alcohol abusers, a major effort should address the large group of students who are not binge drinkers on campus who are adversely affected by the alcohol-related behavior of binge drinkers.

—Henry Wechsler et al., "Health and Behavioral
Consequences of Binge Drinking in College:
A National Survey of Students at 140 Campuses"

Considering the Rhetorical Situation

As a writer or speaker, think about the message that you want to articulate, the audience you want to reach, and the larger context you are writing in.

3–4 **PURPOSE** Your purpose will affect the way you begin and end. If you're trying to persuade readers to do something, you may want to open by clearly stating your thesis and end by calling for a specific action.

5–8 **AUDIENCE** Who do you want to reach, and how does that affect the way you begin and end? You may want to open with an intriguing fact or anecdote to entice your audience to read a profile, for instance, whereas readers of a report may expect it to conclude with a summary of your findings.

9–11 **GENRE** Does your genre require a certain type of beginning or ending? Arguments, for example, often provide a statement of the thesis near the beginning; proposals typically end with a call for some solution.

12–15 **STANCE** What is your stance, and can your beginning and ending help you convey that stance? For example, beginning an argument on the distribution of AIDS medications to underdeveloped countries with an anecdote may demonstrate concern for the human costs of the disease, whereas starting with a statistical analysis may suggest the stance of a careful researcher. Ending a proposal by weighing the advantages and disadvantages of the solution you propose may make you seem reasonable.

MEDIA / DESIGN   Your medium may affect the way you begin and end. A web text, for instance, may open with a home page listing a menu of the site—and giving readers a choice of where they will begin. With a print text, you get to decide how it will begin and end.

16–18

IF YOU NEED MORE HELP

See also the guides to writing in Chapters 7–10 for ways of beginning and ending a **LITERACY NARRATIVE,** an essay **ANALYZING TEXT,** a **REPORT,** or an **ARGUMENT.**

48
77–78
114–15
146

31 Guiding Your Reader

Traffic lights, street signs, and lines on the road help drivers find their way. Readers need similar guidance—to know, for example, whether they're reading a report or an argument, an evaluation or a proposal. They also need to know what to expect: What will the report be about? What perspective will it offer? What will this paragraph cover? What about the next one? How do the two paragraphs relate to each other?

When you write, then, you need to provide cues to help your readers navigate your text and understand the points you're trying to make. This chapter offers advice on guiding your reader and, specifically, on using *titles*, *thesis statements*, *topic sentences*, and *transitions*.

Titles

A title serves various purposes, naming a text and providing clues to the content. It also helps readers decide whether they want to read further, so it's worth your while to come up with a title that attracts interest. Some titles include subtitles. You generally have considerable freedom in choosing a title, but always you'll want to consider the RHETORICAL SITUATION to be sure your title serves your purpose and appeals to the audience you want to reach.

Some titles simply announce the subject of the text:

"Black Men and Public Space"
The Pencil
"Why Colleges Shower Their Students with A's"
"Does Texting Affect Writing?"

Some titles provoke readers or otherwise entice them to read:

"Kill 'Em! Crush 'Em! Eat 'Em Raw!"
"Thank God for the Atom Bomb"
"What Are Homosexuals For?"

Sometimes writers add a subtitle to explain or illuminate the title:

Aria: Memoir of a Bilingual Childhood
"It's in Our Genes: The Biological Basis of Human Mating Behavior"
"From Realism to Virtual Reality: Images of America's Wars"

Sometimes when you're starting to write, you'll think of a title that helps you generate ideas and write. More often, though, a title is one of the last things you'll write, when you know what you've written and can craft a suitable name for your text.

Thesis Statements

A thesis identifies the topic of your text along with the claim you are making about it. A good thesis helps readers understand an essay. Working to create a sharp thesis can help you focus both your thinking and your writing. Here are three steps for moving from a topic to a thesis statement:

1. State your topic as a question.   You may have an idea for a topic, such as "gasoline prices," "analysis of 'real women' ad campaigns," or "famine." Those may be good topics, but they're not thesis statements, primarily because none of them actually makes a statement. A good way to begin moving from topic to thesis statement is to turn your topic into a question:

What causes fluctuations in gasoline prices?

Are ads picturing "real women" who aren't models effective?

What can be done to prevent famine in Africa?

2. Then turn your question into a position.   A thesis statement is an assertion—it takes a stand or makes a claim. Whether you're writing a report or an argument, you are saying, "This is the way I see . . ." "My research shows . . . ," or "This is what I believe about . . ." Your thesis statement announces your position on the question you are raising about your topic, so a relatively easy way of establishing a thesis is to answer your own question:

> Gasoline prices fluctuate for several reasons.
>
> Ads picturing "real women" instead of models are effective because women can easily identify with them.
>
> The most recent famine in Somalia could have been avoided if certain measures had been taken.

3. Narrow your thesis.   A good thesis is specific, guiding you as you write and showing your audience exactly what your essay will cover. The preceding thesis statements need to be qualified and focused—they need to be made more specific. For example:

> Gasoline prices fluctuate because of production procedures, consumer demand, international politics, and oil companies' policies.
>
> Dove's "Campaign for Self-Esteem" and Cover Girl's ads featuring Queen Latifah work because consumers can identify with the women's bodies and admire their confidence in displaying them.
>
> The 2012 famine in Somalia could have been avoided if farmers had received training in more effective methods and had had access to certain technology and if other nations had provided more aid more quickly.

251–54   A good way to narrow a thesis is to ask **QUESTIONS** about it: *Why* do gasoline prices fluctuate? *How* could the Somalia famine have been avoided? The answers will help you craft a narrow, focused thesis.

4. Qualify your thesis.   Sometimes you want to make a strong argument and to state your thesis bluntly. Often, however, you need to acknowledge that your assertions may be challenged or may not be unconditionally true. In those cases, consider limiting the scope of your thesis by adding to it such terms as *may, probably, apparently, very likely, sometimes,* and *often.*

Gasoline prices *very likely* fluctuate because of production procedures, consumer demand, international politics, and oil companies' policies.

Dove's and Cover Girl's ad campaigns featuring "real women" *may* work because consumers can identify with the women's bodies and admire their confidence in displaying them.

The 2012 famine in Somalia could *probably* have been avoided if farmers had received training in more effective methods and had had access to certain technology and if other nations had provided more aid more quickly.

Thesis statements are typically positioned at or near the end of a text's introduction, to let readers know at the outset what is being claimed and what the text will be aiming to prove. A thesis doesn't necessarily forecast your organization, which may be more complex than the thesis itself. For example, Carolyn Stonehill's research paper, "It's in Our Genes: The Biological Basis of Human Mating Behavior," contains this thesis statement:

> While cultural values and messages clearly play a part in the process of mate selection, the genetic and psychological predispositions developed by our ancestors play the biggest role in determining to whom we are attracted.

However, the paper that follows includes sections on "Women's Need to Find a Capable Mate" and "Men's Need to Find a Healthy Mate," in which the "genetic and psychological predispositions" are discussed, followed by sections titled "The Influence of the Media on Mate Selection" and "If Not Media, Then What?" discussing "cultural values and messages." The paper delivers what the thesis includes without following the order in which the thesis presents the topics.

Topic Sentences

Just as a thesis statement announces the topic and position of an essay, a topic sentence states the subject and focus of a paragraph. Good paragraphs focus on a single point, which is summarized in a topic sentence. Usually, but not always, the topic sentence begins the paragraph:

Graduating from high school or college is an exciting, occasionally even traumatic event. Your identity changes as you move from being a high school teenager to a university student or a worker; your connection to home loosens as you attend school elsewhere, move to a place of your own, or simply exercise your right to stay out later. You suddenly find yourself doing different things, thinking different thoughts, fretting about different matters. As recent high school graduate T. J. Devoe puts it, "I wasn't really scared, but having this vast range of opportunity made me uneasy. I didn't know *what* was gonna happen." Jenny Petrow, in describing her first year out of college, observes, "It's a tough year. It was for all my friends."

—Sydney Lewis, *Help Wanted: Tales from the First Job Front*

Sometimes the topic sentence may come at the end of the paragraph or even at the end of the preceding paragraph, depending on the way the paragraphs relate to one another. Other times a topic sentence will summarize or restate a point made in the previous paragraph, helping readers understand what they've just read as they move on to the next point. See how the linguist Deborah Tannen does this in the first paragraphs of an article on differences in men's and women's conversational styles:

I was addressing a small gathering in a suburban Virginia living room— a women's group that had invited men to join them. Throughout the evening, one man had been particularly talkative, frequently offering ideas and anecdotes, while his wife sat silently beside him on the couch. Toward the end of the evening, I commented that women frequently complain that their husbands don't talk to them. This man quickly concurred. He gestured toward his wife and said, "She's the talker in our family." The room burst into laughter; the man looked puzzled and hurt. "It's true," he explained. "When I come home from work I have nothing to say. If she didn't keep the conversation going, we'd spend the whole evening in silence."

This episode crystallizes the irony that although American men tend to talk more than women in public situations, they often talk less at home. And this pattern is wreaking havoc with marriage.

—Deborah Tannen, "Sex, Lies, and Conversation:
Why Is It So Hard for Men and Women to Talk to Each Other?"

Transitions

Transitions help readers move from thought to thought — from sentence to sentence, paragraph to paragraph. You are likely to use a number of transitions as you draft; when you're **EDITING,** you should make a point of checking transitions. Here are some common ones:

282–85

- *To signal causes and effects:* accordingly, as a result, because, consequently, hence, so, then, therefore, thus
- *To signal comparisons:* also, in the same way, like, likewise, similarly
- *To signal changes in direction or exceptions:* although, but, even though, however, in contrast, instead, nevertheless, nonetheless, on the contrary, on the one hand . . . on the other hand, still, yet
- *To signal examples:* for example, for instance, indeed, in fact, such as
- *To signal sequences or similarities:* again, also, and, and then, besides, finally, furthermore, last, moreover, next, too
- *To signal time relations:* after, as soon as, at first, at the same time, before, eventually, finally, immediately, later, meanwhile, next, simultaneously, so far, soon, then, thereafter
- *To signal a summary or conclusion:* as a result, as we have seen, finally, in a word, in any event, in brief, in conclusion, in other words, in short, in the end, in the final analysis, on the whole, therefore, thus, to summarize

---

IF YOU NEED MORE HELP

See also Chapter 54 on **USING VISUALS, INCORPORATING SOUND** for ways of creating visual signals for your readers.

591–99

32 Analyzing Causes and Effects

Analyzing causes helps us think about why something happened, whereas thinking about effects helps us consider what might happen. When we hear a noise in the night, we want to know what caused it. Children poke sticks into holes to see what will happen. Researchers try to understand the causes of diseases. Writers often have occasion to consider causes or effects as part of a larger topic or sometimes as a main focus: in a 205–13 **PROPOSAL,** we might consider the effects of reducing tuition or the causes 183–90 of recent tuition increases; in a **MEMOIR,** we might explore why the person we had a date with failed to show up.

323–41 Usually we can only speculate about *probable* causes or *likely* effects. In writing about causes and effects, then, we are generally **ARGUING** for those we consider plausible, not proven. This chapter will help you analyze causes and effects in writing—and to do so in a way that suits your rhetorical situation.

Determining Plausible Causes and Effects

What causes ozone depletion? Sleeplessness? Obesity? And what are their effects? Those are of course large, complex topics, but whenever you have reason to ask why something happened or what could happen, there will likely be several possible causes and just as many predictable effects. There may be obvious causes, though often they will be less important than others that are harder to recognize. (Eating too much may be an obvious cause of being overweight, but *why* people eat too much has several less obvious causes: portion size, advertising, lifestyle, and physiological disorders are only a few possibilities.) Similarly, short-term effects are often less important than long-term ones. (A stomachache may be an

rhetorical situations

genres

processes

strategies

research
MLA / APA

media /
design

handbook

effect of eating too much candy, but the chemical imbalance that can result from consuming too much sugar is a much more serious effect.)

LISTING, CLUSTERING, and **OUTLINING** are useful processes for analyzing causes. And at times you might need to do some **RESEARCH** to identify possible causes or effects and to find evidence to support your analysis. When you've identified potential causes and effects, you need to analyze them. Which causes and effects are primary? Which seem to be secondary? Which are most relevant to your **PURPOSE** and are likely to convince your **AUDIENCE?** You will probably have to choose from several possible causes and effects for your analysis because you won't want or need to include all of them.

260–64
419

3–4
5–8

Arguing for Causes or Effects

Once you've identified several possible causes or predictable effects, you need to **ARGUE** that some are more plausible than others. You must provide convincing support for your argument because you usually cannot *prove* that x causes y or that y will be caused by z; you can show only, with good reasons and appropriate evidence, that x is *likely* to cause y or that y will *likely* follow from z. See, for example, how an essay on the psychological basis for risk taking speculates about two potential causes for the popularity of extreme sports:

323–41

> Studies now indicate that the inclination to take high risks may be hardwired into the brain, intimately linked to arousal and pleasure mechanisms, and may offer such a thrill that it functions like an addiction. The tendency probably affects one in five people, mostly young males, and declines with age. It may ensure our survival, even spur our evolution as individuals and as a species. Risk taking probably bestowed a crucial evolutionary advantage, inciting the fighting and foraging of the hunter-gatherer. . . .
>
> As psychologist Salvadore Maddi, PhD, of the University of California at Davis warns, "High-risk takers may have a hard time deriving meaning and purpose from everyday life." Indeed, this peculiar form of dissatisfaction could help explain the explosion of high-risk sports in America and other postindustrial Western nations. In unstable cultures, such as those at war or suffering poverty, people rarely seek

out additional thrills. But in a rich and safety-obsessed country like America, land of guardrails, seat belts, and personal-injury lawsuits, everyday life may have become too safe, predictable, and boring for those programmed for risk taking.　　　　　—Paul Roberts, "Risk"

Roberts suggests that genetics is one likely cause of extreme sports and that an American obsession with safety is perhaps a cause of their growing popularity. Notice, however, that he presents these as likely or possible, not certain, by choosing his words carefully: "studies now *indicate*"; "the inclination to take high risks *may* be hardwired"; "[r]isk taking *probably* bestowed a crucial evolutionary advantage"; "this . . . dissatisfaction *could help* explain." Like Roberts, you will almost always need to qualify what you say about causes and effects—to say that something *could explain* (rather than saying it "explains") or that it *suggests* (rather than "shows"). Causes and effects can seldom be proved definitively, so you need to acknowledge that your argument is not the last word on the subject.

Ways of Organizing an Analysis of Causes and Effects

Your analysis of causes and effects may be part of a proposal or some other genre of writing, or you may write a text whose central purpose is to analyze causes or speculate about effects. While there are many ways to organize an analysis of causes and effects, three common ways are to state a cause and then discuss its effects, to state an effect and then discuss its causes, and to identify a chain of causes and effects.

Identify a cause and then discuss its effects. If you were writing about global warming, you might first show that many scientists fear it will have several effects, including drastic climate changes, the extinction of various kinds of plants, and elevated sea levels.

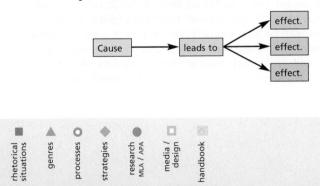

Identify an effect and then trace its causes. If you were writing about school violence, for example, you might argue that it is a result of sloppy dress, informal teacher-student relationships, low academic standards, and disregard for rules.

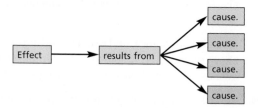

Identify a chain of causes and effects. You may sometimes discuss a chain of causes and effects. If you were writing about the right to privacy, for example, you might consider the case of Megan's law. A convicted child molester raped and murdered a girl named Megan; the crime caused New Jersey legislators to pass the so-called Megan's law (an effect), which requires that convicted sex offenders be publicly identified. As more states enact versions of Megan's law, concern for the rights of those who are identified is developing—the effect is becoming a cause of further effects.

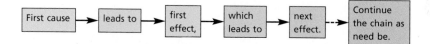

Considering the Rhetorical Situation

As a writer or speaker, you need to think about the message that you want to articulate, the audience you want to reach, and the larger context you are writing in.

PURPOSE   Your main purpose may be to analyze the causes and effects of something. But sometimes you'll have another goal that calls for such analysis—a business report, for example, might need to explain what caused a decline in sales.

3–4

AUDIENCE Who is your intended audience, and how will analyzing causes help you reach them? Do you need to tell them why some event happened or what effects resulted?

GENRE Does your genre require you to analyze causes? Proposals, for example, often need to consider the effects of a proposed solution.

STANCE What is your stance, and could analyzing causes or effects show that stance? Could it help demonstrate your seriousness or show that your conclusions are reasonable?

MEDIA / DESIGN You can rely on words to analyze causes, but sometimes a drawing will help readers *see* how causes lead to effects.

IF YOU NEED MORE HELP

See also the **PROCESSES** chapters for help generating ideas, drafting, and so on if you need to write an entire text whose purpose is to analyze causes or speculate about effects.

▪ rhetorical situations

▲ genres

○ processes

◆ strategies

● research MLA / APA

▢ media / design

▨ handbook

Arguing 33

Football fans argue about who's better, Eli or Peyton Manning. Political candidates argue that they have the most experience or best judgment. A toilet paper ad argues that "you deserve a little luxury in your life, and so does your bottom." As you likely realize, we are surrounded by arguments, and much of the work you do as a college student requires you to read and write arguments. When you write a **LITERARY ANALYSIS**, for instance, you argue for a particular interpretation. In a **PROPOSAL**, you argue for a particular solution to a problem. Even a **PROFILE** argues that a subject should be seen in a certain way. This chapter offers advice on some of the key elements of making an argument, from developing an arguable thesis and identifying good reasons and evidence that supports those reasons to building common ground and dealing with viewpoints other than your own.

81–86

205–13

191–204

Reasons for Arguing

We argue for many reasons, and they often overlap: to convince others that our position on a subject is reasonable, to influence the way they think about a subject, to persuade them to change their point of view or to take some sort of action. In fact, many composition scholars and teachers believe that all writing makes an argument.

As a student, you'll be called upon to make arguments continually: when you participate in class discussions, when you take an essay exam, when you post a comment to an online discussion or a blog. In all these instances, you are adding your opinions to some larger conversation, arguing for what you believe—and why.

Arguing Logically: Claims, Reasons, and Evidence

The basic building blocks of argument are claims, reasons, and evidence that supports those reasons. Using these building blocks, we can construct a strong logical argument.

Claims.   Good arguments are based on arguable claims—statements that reasonable people may disagree about. Certain kinds of statements cannot be argued:

- *Verifiable statements of fact.* Most of the time, there's no point in arguing about facts like "The earth is round" or "George H. W. Bush was America's forty-first president." Such statements contain no controversy, no potential opposition—and so no interest for an audience. However, you might argue about the basis of a fact. For example, until recently it was a fact that our solar system had nine planets, but when further discoveries led to a change in the definition of *planet*, Pluto no longer qualified.

- *Issues of faith or belief.* By definition, matters of faith cannot be proven or refuted. If you believe in reincarnation or don't believe there is an afterlife, there's no way I can convince you otherwise. However, in a philosophy or religion course you may be asked to argue, for example, whether or not the universe must have a cause.

- *Matters of simple opinion or personal taste.* If you think cargo pants are ugly, no amount of arguing will convince you to think otherwise. If you own every Pink CD and think she's the greatest singer ever, you won't convince your Beatles-loving parents to like her, too. If matters of taste are based on identifiable criteria, though, they may be argued in an **EVALUATION**, where "Tom Cruise is a terrible actor" is more than just your opinion—it's an assertion you can support with evidence.

164–72

You may begin with an opinion: "I think wearing a helmet makes riding a bike more dangerous, not less." As it stands, that statement can't be considered a claim—it needs to be made more reasonable and informed. To do that, you might reframe it as a question—"Do bike riders who wear helmets get injured more often than those who don't?"—that may be answered as you do research and start to write. Your opinion or question should lead you to an arguable claim, however, one that could be challenged by another thoughtful person. In this case, for example, your research might lead you to a focused, qualified claim: *Contrary to common sense, wearing a helmet while riding a bicycle increases the chances of injury, at least to adult riders.*

Qualifying a claim.   According to an old saying, there are two sides to every story. Much of the time, though, arguments don't sort themselves neatly into two sides, pro and con. No matter what your topic, your argument will rarely be a simple matter of being for or against; in most cases, you'll want to qualify your claim—that it is true in certain circumstances, with certain conditions, with these limitations, and so on. Qualifying your claim shows that you're reasonable and also makes your topic more manageable by limiting it. The following questions can help you qualify your claim.

- *Can it be true in some circumstances or at some times but not others?* For example, freedom of speech should generally be unrestricted, but individuals can sue for slander or libel.

- *Can it be true only with certain conditions?* For instance, cell phones and computer monitors should be recycled, but only by licensed, domestic recyclers.

- *Can it be true for some groups or individuals but not others?* For example, nearly everyone should follow a low-carb diet, but some people, such as diabetics, should avoid it.

SOME WORDS FOR QUALIFYING A CLAIM

sometimes	nearly	it seems/seemingly
rarely	usually	some
in some cases	more or less	perhaps
often	for the most part	possibly
routinely	in many cases	in most cases

Drafting a thesis statement.   Once your claim is focused and appropriately qualified, it can form the core of your essay's **THESIS STATEMENT**, which announces your position and forecasts the path your argument will

◆ 313–15

follow. For example, here is the opening paragraph of an essay by the executive director of the National Congress of American Indians arguing that the remains of Native Americans should be treated with the same respect given to others. The author outlines the context of her argument and then presents her thesis (here, in italics):

> What if museums, universities and government agencies could put your dead relatives on display or keep them in boxes to be cut up and otherwise studied? What if you believed that the spirits of the dead could not rest until their human remains were placed in a sacred area? The ordinary American would say there ought to be a law — and there is, for ordinary Americans. *The problem for American Indians is that there are too many laws of the kind that make us the archeological property of the United States and too few of the kind that protect us from such insults.* —Susan Shown Harjo, "Last Rites for Indian Dead: Treating Remains Like Artifacts Is Intolerable"

Reasons. Your claim must be supported by reasons that your audience will accept. A reason can usually be linked to a claim with the word *because*:

CLAIM	+	*BECAUSE*	+	REASON
iPods and other MP3 players harm society		*because*		they isolate users from other people.

Keep in mind that you likely have a further reason, a rule or principle that underlies the reason you link directly to your claim. In this argument, the underlying reason is that isolation from other people is bad. If your audience doesn't accept that principle, you may have to back it up with further reasons or evidence.

To come up with good reasons, start by stating your position and then answering the question *why?*

CLAIM: iPods and other MP3 players harm society. *Why?*

REASON: (Because) They isolate users from other people. *Why?*

UNDERLYING REASON: Isolation from other people is bad.

As you can see, this exercise can continue indefinitely as the underlying reasons grow more and more general and abstract. You can do the same with other positions:

> **CLAIM:** Smoking should be banned. *Why?*
>
> **REASON:** (Because) It is harmful to smokers and also to nonsmokers.
>
> **UNDERLYING REASON:** People should be protected from harmful substances.

Evidence. Evidence to support your reasons can come from various sources. In fact, you may need to use several kinds of evidence to persuade your audience that your claim is true. Some of the most common types of evidence include facts, statistics, examples, authorities, anecdotes, scenarios, case studies, textual evidence, and visuals.

Facts are ideas that are proven to be true. Facts can include observations or scholarly research (your own or someone else's), but they need to be accepted as true. If your audience accepts the facts you present, they can be powerful means of persuasion. For example, an essay on junk email offers these facts to demonstrate the seasonal nature of spam:

> The flow of spam is often seasonal. It slows in the spring, and then, in the month that technology specialists call "black September"—when hundreds of thousands of students return to college, many armed with new computers and access to fast Internet connections—the levels rise sharply.
>
> —Michael Specter, "Damn Spam"

Specter offers this fact with only a general reference to its origin ("technology specialists"), but given what most people know—or think they know—about college students, it rings true. A citation from a study published by a "technology specialist" would offer even greater credibility.

Statistics are numerical data, usually produced through research, surveys, or polls. Statistics should be relevant to your argument, as current as possible, accurate, and from a reliable source. An argument advocating that Americans should eat less meat presents these data to support the writer's contention that we eat far too much of it:

Americans are downing close to 200 pounds of meat, poultry, and fish per capita per year (dairy and eggs are separate, and hardly insignificant), an increase of 50 pounds per person from 50 years ago. We each consume something like 110 grams of protein a day, about twice the federal government's recommended allowance; of that, about 75 grams come from animal protein. (The recommended level is itself considered by many dietary experts to be higher than it needs to be.) It's likely that most of us would do just fine on around 30 grams of protein a day, virtually all of it from plant sources.

—Mark Bittman, "Rethinking the Meat-Guzzler"

Bittman's statistics demonstrate the extent to which Americans have increased their meat consumption over the last half century, the proportion of our diets that comes from meat, and, by comparison, how much protein our bodies require—and summarize the heart of his argument in stark numeric terms.

Examples are specific instances that illustrate general statements. In a book on life after dark in Europe, a historian offers several examples to demonstrate his point that three hundred years ago, night—without artificial lighting—was treacherous:

Even sure-footed natives on a dark night could misjudge the lay of the land, stumbling into a ditch or off a precipice. In Aberdeenshire, a fifteen-year-old girl died in 1739 after straying from her customary path through a churchyard and tumbling into a newly dug grave. The Yorkshireman Arthur Jessop, returning from a neighbor's home on a cold December evening, fell into a stone pit after losing his bearings.

—A. Roger Ekirch, *At Day's Close: Night in Times Past*

Ekirch illustrates his point and makes it come alive for readers by citing two specific individuals' fates.

Authorities are experts on your subject. To be useful, authorities must be reputable, trustworthy, and qualified to address the subject. You should EVALUATE any authorities you consult carefully to be sure they have the credentials necessary for readers to take them seriously. When you cite

453–56

experts, you should clearly identify them and the origins of their authority in a **SIGNAL PHRASE,** as does the author of an argument that deforested land can be reclaimed:

471–74

> Reed Funk, professor of plant biology at Rutgers University, believes that the vast areas of deforested land can be used to grow millions of genetically improved trees for food, mostly nuts, and for fuel. Funk sees nuts used to supplement meat as a source of high-quality protein in developing-country diets.
>
> — Lester R. Brown, *Plan B 2.0: Rescuing a Planet under Stress and a Civilization in Trouble*

Brown cites Funk, an expert on plant biology, to support his argument that humans need to rethink the global economy in order to create a sustainable world. Without the information on Funk's credentials, though, readers would have no reason to take his proposal seriously.

Anecdotes are brief **NARRATIVES** that your audience will find believable and that contribute directly to your argument. Anecdotes may come from your personal experience or the experiences of others. In an essay arguing that it's understandable when athletes give in to the temptation to use performance-enhancing drugs, sports blogger William Moller uses an anecdote to show that the need to perform can outweigh the potential negative consequences of using drugs:

387–95

> I spent my high school years at a boarding school hidden among the apple orchards of Massachusetts. Known for a spartan philosophy regarding the adolescent need for sleep, the school worked us to the bone, regularly slamming us with six hours of homework. I pulled a lot more all-nighters (of the scholastic sort) in my years there than I ever did in college. When we weren't in class, the library, study hall, or formal sit-down meals, we were likely found on a sports field. We also had school on Saturday, beginning at 8 a.m. just like every other non-Sunday morning.
>
> Adding kindling to the fire, the students were not your laid-back types; everyone wanted that spot at the top of the class, and social life was rife with competition. The type A's that fill the investment banking,

legal, and political worlds — those are the kids I spent my high school years with.

And so it was that midway through my sophomore year, I found myself on my third all-nighter in a row, attempting to memorize historically significant pieces of art out of E. H. Gombrich's *The Story of Art*. I had finished a calculus exam the day before, and the day before that had been devoted to world history. And on that one cold night in February, I had had enough. I had hit that point where you've had so little sleep over such a long time that you start seeing spots, as if you'd been staring at a bright light for too long. The grade I would compete for the next day suddenly slipped in importance, and I began daydreaming about how easy the real world would be compared to the hell I was going through.

But there was hope. A friend who I was taking occasional study breaks with read the story in the bags beneath my eyes, in the slump of my shoulders, the nervous drumming of my fingers on the chair as we sipped flat, warm Coke in the common room. My personal *deus ex machina*,* he handed me a small white pill.

I was very innocent. I matured way after most of my peers, and was probably best known for being the kid who took all the soprano solos away from the girls in the choir as a first-year student. I don't think I had ever been buzzed, much less drunk. I'd certainly never smoked a cigarette. And knowing full well that what I was doing could be nothing better than against the rules (and less importantly, illegal) I did what I felt I needed to do, to accomplish what was demanded of me. And it worked. I woke up and regained focus like nothing I'd ever experienced. Unfortunately, it also came with serious side effects: I was a hypersensitized, stuffed-up, sweaty, wide-eyed mess, but I studied until the birds started chirping. And I aced my test.

Later I found out the pill was Ritalin, and it was classified as a class 3 drug.[†] I did it again, too — only a handful of times, as the side effects were so awful. But every time it was still illegal, still against the rules.

Deus ex machina: In ancient Greek and Roman drama, a god introduced to resolve plot difficulties.

[†]*Class 3 drug:* Drug that is illegal to possess without a prescription.

■ rhetorical situations
▲ genres
○ processes
◆ strategies
● research MLA / APA
□ media / design
⬩ handbook

And as emphasized above, I was much more worried about the scholastic consequences if I were discovered abusing a prescription drug than the fact that I was breaking the law. Though I was using it in a far different manner than the baseball players who would later get caught with it in their systems, it was still very clearly a "performance-enhancing drug."

Just like every other person on this planet, I was giving in to the incentive scheme that was presented to me. The negative of doing poorly on the test was far greater than the negative of getting caught, discounted by the anesthetic of low probability.

—William Moller, "We, the Public, Place the Best Athletes on Pedestals"

Moller uses this anecdote to demonstrate the truth of his argument, that given the choice between "breaking the rules and breaking my grades" or "getting an edge" in professional sports, just about everyone will choose to break the rules.

Scenarios are hypothetical situations. Like anecdotes, "what if" scenarios can help you describe the possible effects of particular actions or offer new ways of looking at a particular state of affairs. For example, a mathematician presents this lighthearted scenario about Santa Claus in a tongue-in-cheek argument that Christmas is (almost) pure magic:

Let's assume that Santa only visits those who are children in the eyes of the law, that is, those under the age of 18. There are roughly 2 billion such individuals in the world. However, Santa started his annual activities long before diversity and equal opportunity became issues, and as a result he doesn't handle Muslim, Hindu, Jewish and Buddhist children. That reduces his workload significantly to a mere 15% of the total, namely 378 million. However, the crucial figure is not the number of children but the number of homes Santa has to visit. According to the most recent census data, the average size of a family in the world is 3.5 children per household. Thus, Santa has to visit 108,000,000 individual homes. (Of course, as everyone knows,

Santa only visits good children, but we can surely assume that, on an average, at least one child of the 3.5 in each home meets that criterion.)

—Keith Devlin, "The Mathematics of Christmas"

Devlin uses this scenario, as part of his mathematical analysis of Santa's yearly task, to help demonstrate that Christmas is indeed magical — because if you do the math, it's clear that Santa's task is physically impossible.

Case studies and observations feature detailed reporting about a subject. Case studies are in-depth, systematic examinations of an occasion, a person, or a group. For example, in arguing that class differences exist in the United States, sociologist Gregory Mantsios presents studies of three "typical" Americans to show "enormous class differences" in their lifestyles.

Observations offer detailed descriptions of a subject. Here's an observation of the emergence of a desert stream that flows only at night:

At about 5:30 water came out of the ground. It did not spew up, but slowly escaped into the surrounding sand and small rocks. The wet circle grew until water became visible. Then it bubbled out like a small fountain and the creek began.

—Craig Childs, *The Secret Knowledge of Water*

Childs presents this and other observations in a book that argues (among other things) that even in harsh, arid deserts, water exists, and knowing where to find it can mean the difference between life and death.

462–74   **Textual evidence** includes QUOTATIONS, PARAPHRASES, and SUMMARIES. Usually, the relevance of textual evidence must be stated directly, as excerpts from a text may carry several potential meanings. For example, here is an excerpt from a student essay analyzing the function of the raft in *Huckleberry Finn* as "a platform on which the resolution of conflicts is made possible":

[T]he scenes where Jim and Huck are in consensus on the raft contain the moments in which they are most relaxed. For instance, in chapter twelve of the novel, Huck, after escaping capture from Jackson's Island, calls the rafting life "solemn" and articulates their experience as living "pretty high" (Twain 75–76). Likewise, subsequent to escaping the unresolved feud between the Grangerfords and Shepherdsons in chapter eighteen, Huck is unquestionably at ease on the raft: "I was powerful glad to get away from the feuds. . . . We said there warn't no home like a raft, after all. Other places do seem so cramped up and smothery, but a raft don't. You feel mighty free and easy and comfortable on a raft" (Twain 134).

> —Dave Nichols, "'Less All Be Friends': Rafts as Negotiating Platforms in Twain's *Huckleberry Finn*"

Huck's own words support Nichols's claim that he can relax on a raft. Nichols strengthens his claim by quoting evidence from two separate pages, suggesting that Huck's opinion of rafts pervades the novel.

Visuals can be a useful way of presenting evidence. Remember, though, that charts, graphs, photos, drawings, and other **VISUAL TEXTS** seldom speak for themselves and thus must be explained in your text. Below, for example, is a photograph of a poster carried by demonstrators at the 2008 Beijing Summer Olympics, protesting China's treatment of Tibetans. If you

591–99

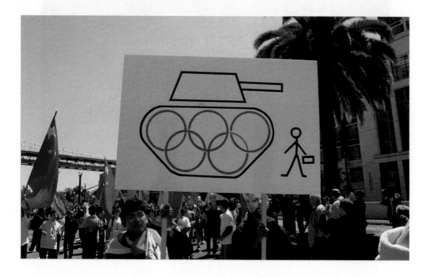

were to use this photo in an essay, you would need to explain that the poster combines the image of a protester standing before a tank during the 1989 Tiananmen Square uprising with the Olympic logo, making clear to your readers that the protesters are likening China's treatment of Tibetans to its brutal actions in the past. Similarly, the poster for a recycling campaign below uses an American flag made from household waste to argue that recycling is patriotic.

Oh say, can you recycle

Join students all across the US and Canada competing in RecycleMania, the eight-week recycling competition.

For more information please visit: www.recyclemaniacs.org

rhetorical situations

genres

processes

strategies

research MLA / APA

media / design

handbook

Choosing appropriate evidence. The kinds of evidence you provide to support your argument depends on your RHETORICAL SITUATION. If your purpose is, for example, to convince readers to accept the need for a proposed solution, you'd be likely to include facts, statistics, and anecdotes. If you're writing for an academic audience, you'd be less likely to rely on anecdotes, preferring authorities, textual evidence, statistics, and case studies instead. And even within academic communities different disciplines and genres may focus primarily on different kinds of evidence. If you're not sure what counts as appropriate evidence, ask your instructor for guidance.

1

Convincing Readers You're Trustworthy

For your argument to be convincing, you need to establish your own credibility with readers — to demonstrate your knowledge about your topic, to show that you and your readers share some common ground, and to show yourself to be evenhanded in the way you present your argument.

Building common ground.   One important element of gaining readers' trust is to identify some common ground, some values you and your audience share. For example, to introduce a book arguing for the compatibility of science and religion, author Chet Raymo offers some common memories:

> Like most children, I was raised on miracles. Cows that jump over the moon; a jolly fat man that visits every house in the world in a single night; mice and ducks that talk; little engines that huff and puff and say, "I think I can"; geese that lay golden eggs. This lively exercise of credulity on the part of children is good practice for what follows — for believing in the miracle stories of traditional religion, yes, but also for the practice of poetry or science.
>
> — Chet Raymo, *Skeptics and True Believers: The Exhilarating Connection between Science and Religion*

Raymo presents childhood stories and myths that are part of many people's shared experiences to help readers find a connection between two realms that are often seen as opposed.

Incorporating other viewpoints. To show that you have carefully considered the viewpoints of others, including those who may agree or disagree with you, you should incorporate those viewpoints into your argument by acknowledging, accommodating, or refuting them.

Acknowledging other viewpoints. One essential part of establishing your credibility is to acknowledge that there are viewpoints different from yours and to represent them fairly and accurately. Rather than weakening your argument, acknowledging possible objections to your position shows that you've thought about and researched your topic thoroughly. For example, in an essay about his experience growing up homosexual, writer Andrew Sullivan admits that not every young gay man or woman has the same experience:

> I should add that many young lesbians and homosexuals seem to have had a much easier time of it. For many, the question of sexual identity was not a critical factor in their life choices or vocation, or even a factor at all.   —Andrew Sullivan, "What Is a Homosexual?"

In response to a reasonable objection, Sullivan qualifies his assertions, making his own stance appear to be reasonable.

Accommodating other viewpoints. You may be tempted to ignore views you don't agree with, but in fact it's important to demonstrate that you are aware of them and have considered them carefully. You may find yourself conceding that opposing views have some merit and qualifying your claim or even making them part of your own argument. See, for example, how a philosopher arguing that torture is sometimes "not merely permissible but morally mandatory" addresses a major objection to his position:

> The most powerful argument against using torture as a punishment or to secure confessions is that such practices disregard the rights of the individual. Well, if the individual is all that important—and he is— it is correspondingly important to protect the rights of individuals threatened by terrorists. If life is so valuable that it must never be taken,

the lives of the innocents must be saved even at the price of hurting the one who endangers them.

—Michael Levin, "The Case for Torture"

Levin acknowledges his critics' argument that the individual is indeed important but then asserts that if the life of one person is important, the lives of many people must be even more important. In effect, he uses an opposing argument to advance his own.

Refuting other viewpoints.   Often you may need to refute other arguments and make a case for why you believe they are wrong. Are the values underlying the argument questionable? Is the reasoning flawed? Is the evidence inadequate or faulty? For example, an essay arguing for the elimination of college athletics scholarships includes this refutation:

> Some argue that eliminating athletics scholarships would deny opportunity and limit access for many students, most notably black athletes. The question is, access to what? The fields of competition or an opportunity to earn a meaningful degree? With the six-year graduation rates of black basketball players hovering in the high 30-percent range, and black football players in the high 40-percent range, despite years of "academic reform," earning an athletics scholarship under the current system is little more than a chance to play sports.
>
> —John R. Gerdy, "For True Reform, Athletics Scholarships Must Go"

Gerdy bases his refutation on statistics showing that for more than half of African American college athletes, the opportunity to earn a degree by playing a sport is an illusion.

When you incorporate differing viewpoints, be careful to avoid the **FALLACIES** of attacking the person making the argument or refuting a competing position that no one seriously entertains. It is also important that you not distort or exaggerate opposing viewpoints. If *your* argument is to be persuasive, other arguments should be represented fairly.

338–40

Appealing to Readers' Emotions

Logic and facts, even when presented by someone who seems reasonable and trustworthy, may not be enough to persuade readers. Many successful arguments include an emotional component that appeals to readers' hearts as well as to their minds. Advertising often works by appealing to its audience's emotions, as in this paragraph from a Volvo ad:

> Choosing a car is about the comfort and safety of your passengers, most especially your children. That's why we ensure Volvo's safety research examines how we can make our cars safer for everyone who travels in them—from adults to teenagers, children to babies. Even those who aren't even born yet.   —*Volvo.com*

This ad plays on the fear that children—or a pregnant mother—may be injured or killed in an automobile accident.

Keep in mind that emotional appeals can make readers feel as though they are being manipulated and, consequently, less likely to accept an argument. For most kinds of academic writing, use emotional appeals sparingly.

Checking for Fallacies

Fallacies are arguments that involve faulty reasoning. It's important to avoid fallacies in your writing because they often seem plausible but are usually unfair or inaccurate and make reasonable discussion difficult. Here are some of the most common fallacies:

- **Ad hominem** arguments attack someone's character rather than address the issues. (*Ad hominem* is Latin for "to the man.") It is an especially common fallacy in political discourse and elsewhere: "Jack Turner has no business talking about the way we run things in this city. He's just another flaky liberal." Whether or not Turner is a "flaky liberal" has no bearing on the worth of his argument about "the way we run things in this city"; insulting one's opponents isn't an argument against their positions.

- *Bandwagon appeals* argue that because others think or do something, we should, too. For example, an advertisement for a rifle association suggests that "67 percent of voters support laws permitting concealed weapons. You should, too." It assumes that readers want to be part of the group and implies that an opinion that is popular must be correct.

- *Begging the question* is a circular argument. It assumes as a given what is trying to be proved, essentially supporting an assertion with the assertion itself. Consider this statement: "Affirmative action can never be fair or just because you cannot remedy one injustice by committing another." This statement begs the question because to prove that affirmative action is unjust, it assumes that it is an injustice.

- *Either-or* arguments, also called *false dilemmas*, are oversimplifications that assert there can be only two possible positions on a complex issue. For example, "Those who oppose our actions in this war are enemies of freedom" inaccurately assumes that if someone opposes the war in question, he or she opposes freedom. In fact, people might have many other reasons for opposing the war.

- *False analogies* compare things that resemble each other in some ways but not in the most important respects — for example, "Trees pollute the air just as much as cars and trucks do." Although it's true that plants emit hydrocarbons, and hydrocarbons are a component of smog, they also produce oxygen, whereas motor vehicles emit gases that combine with hydrocarbons to form smog. Vehicles pollute the air; trees provide the air that vehicles' emissions pollute.

- *Faulty causality,* also known as *post hoc, ergo propter hoc* (Latin for "after this, therefore because of this"), assumes that because one event followed another, the first event caused the second — for example, "Legalizing same-sex marriage in Sweden led to a decline in the marriage rate of opposite-sex couples." The statement contains no evidence to show that the first event caused the second.

- *Straw man* arguments misrepresent an opposing position to make it ridiculous or extreme and thus easy to refute, rather than dealing with the actual position. For example, if someone argues that funding for food stamps should be cut, a straw man response would be, "You want the poor to starve," transforming a proposal to cut a specific program into an exaggerated argument that the proposer hasn't made.

- *Hasty generalizations* are conclusions based on insufficient or inappropriately qualified evidence. This summary of a research study is a good example: "Twenty randomly chosen residents of Brooklyn, New York, were asked whether they found graffiti tags offensive; fourteen said yes, five said no, and one had no opinion. Therefore, 70 percent of Brooklyn residents find tagging offensive." In Brooklyn, a part of New York City with a population of over two million, twenty residents is far too small a group from which to draw meaningful conclusions. To be able to generalize, the researcher would have had to survey a much greater percentage of Brooklyn's population.

- *Slippery slope* arguments assert that one event will inevitably lead to another, often cataclysmic event without presenting evidence that such a chain of causes and effects will in fact take place. Here's an example: "If the state legislature passes this 2 percent tax increase, it won't be long before all the corporations in the state move to other states and leave thousands unemployed." According to this argument, if taxes are raised, the state's economy will be ruined—not a likely scenario, given the size of the proposed increase.

Considering the Rhetorical Situation

To argue effectively, you need to think about the message that you want to articulate, the audience you want to persuade, the effect of your stance, and the larger context you are writing in.

3–4

PURPOSE   What do you want your audience to do? To think a certain way? To take a certain action? To change their minds? To consider alternative views to their current ones? To accept your position as plausible? To see that you have thought carefully about an issue and researched it appropriately?

AUDIENCE   Who is your intended audience? What do they likely know   5–8
and believe about your topic? How personal is it for them?
To what extent are they likely to agree or disagree with
you? Why? What common ground can you find with them?
How should you incorporate other viewpoints they have?
What kind of evidence are they likely to accept?

GENRE   What genre will help you achieve your purpose? A posi-   9–11
tion paper? An evaluation? A review? A proposal? An
analysis?

STANCE   What's your attitude toward your topic, and why? What   12–15
strategies will help you to convey that stance? How do you
want your audience to perceive you? As an authority on
your topic? As someone much like them? As calm? reasonable? impassioned or angry? something else?

MEDIA / DESIGN   What media will you use, and how do your media affect   16–18
your argument? If you're writing on paper, does your argu-
ment call for photos or charts? If you're giving an oral
presentation, should you put your reasons and support on
slides? If you're writing online, should you add links to
sites representing other positions or containing evidence
that supports your position?

34 Classifying and Dividing

Classification and division are ways of organizing information: various items may be classified according to their similarities, or a single topic may be divided into parts. We might classify different kinds of flowers as annuals or perennials, for example, and classify the perennials further as dahlias, daisies, roses, and peonies. We might also divide a flower garden into distinct areas: for herbs, flowers, and vegetables.

Writers often use classification and division as ways of developing and organizing material. This book, for instance, classifies comparison, definition, description, and several other common ways of thinking and writing as strategies. It divides the information it provides about writing into seven parts: "Rhetorical Situations," "Genres," "Processes," and so on. Each part further divides its material into various chapters. Even if you never write a book, you will have occasion to classify and divide material in ANNOTATED BIBLIOGRAPHIES and essays ANALYZING TEXTS and other kinds of writing. This chapter offers advice for classifying and dividing information for various writing purposes—and in a way that suits your own rhetorical situation.

155–63
52–86

Classifying

When we classify something, we group it with similar things. A linguist would classify French and Spanish and Italian as Romance languages, for example—and Russian, Polish, and Bulgarian as Slavic languages. In a hilarious (if totally phony) news story from the *Onion* about a church bake

rhetorical situations

genres

processes

strategies

research MLA / APA

media / design

handbook

sale, the writer classifies the activities observed there as examples of the seven deadly sins:

> GADSDEN, AL—The seven deadly sins—avarice, sloth, envy, lust, glut-tony, pride, and wrath—were all committed Sunday during the twice-annual bake sale at St. Mary's of the Immaculate Conception Church.
>
> —"All Seven Deadly Sins Committed at Church Bake Sale," *The Onion*

The article goes on to categorize the participants' behavior in terms of the sins, describing one parishioner who commits the sin of pride by bragging about her cookies and others who commit the sin of envy by envying the popularity of the prideful parishioner's baked goods (the consumption of which leads to the sin of gluttony). In all, the article notes, "347 individual acts of sin were committed at the bake sale," and every one of them can be classified as one of the seven deadly sins.

Dividing

As a writing strategy, division is a way of breaking something into parts—and a way of making the information easy for readers to follow and understand. See how this example about children's ways of nagging divides their tactics into seven categories:

> James U. McNeal, a professor of marketing at Texas A&M University, is considered America's leading authority on marketing to children. In his book *Kids as Customers* (1992), McNeal provides marketers with a thorough analysis of "children's requesting styles and appeals." He [divides] juvenile nagging tactics into seven major categories. A *pleading* nag is one accompanied by repetitions of words like "please" or "mom, mom, mom." A *persistent* nag involves constant requests for the coveted product and may include the phrase "I'm gonna ask just one more time." *Forceful* nags are extremely pushy and may include subtle threats, like "Well, then, I'll go and ask Dad." *Demonstrative* nags are the most high risk, often characterized by full-blown tantrums in public places, breath holding, tears, a refusal to leave the store. *Sugar-coated* nags promise affection in

return for a purchase and may rely on seemingly heartfelt declarations, like "You're the best dad in the world." *Threatening* nags are youthful forms of blackmail, vows of eternal hatred and of running away if something isn't bought. *Pity* nags claim the child will be heartbroken, teased, or socially stunted if the parent refuses to buy a certain item. "All of these appeals and styles may be used in combination," McNeal's research has discovered, "but kids tend to stick to one or two of each that prove most effective . . . for their own parents."

—Eric Schlosser, *Fast Food Nation:*
The Dark Side of the All-American Meal

Here the writer announces the division scheme of "seven major categories." Then he names each tactic and describes how it works. And notice the italics: each nagging tactic is italicized, making it easy to recognize and follow. Take away the italics, and the divisions would be less visible.

Creating Clear and Distinct Categories

When you classify or divide, you need to create clear and distinct categories. If you're writing about music, you might divide it on the basis of the genre (hip-hop, rock, classical, gospel), artist (male or female, group or solo), or instruments (violins, trumpets, bongos, guitars). These categories must be distinct, so that no information overlaps or fits into more than one category, and they must include every member of the group you're discussing. The simpler the criteria for selecting the categories, the better. The nagging categories in the example from *Fast Food Nation* are based on only one criterion: a child's verbal behavior.

Sometimes you may want to highlight your categories visually to make them easier to follow. Eric Schlosser does that by italicizing each category: the *pleading* nag, the *persistent* nag, the *forceful* nag, and so on. Other **DESIGN** elements—bulleted lists, pie charts, tables, images—might also prove useful.

581–90 ☐

See, for instance, how *The World of Caffeine* authors Bennett Alan Weinberg and Bonnie K. Bealer use a two-column list to show what they say are the differing cultural connotations of coffee and tea:

Coffee Aspect	Tea Aspect
Male	Female
Boisterous	Decorous
Indulgence	Temperance
Hardheaded	Romantic
Topology	Geometry
Heidegger	Carnap
Beethoven	Mozart
Libertarian	Statist
Promiscuous	Pure

—Bennett Alan Weinberg and Bonnie K. Bealer,
The World of Caffeine

Sometimes you might show categories visually, as in this website promoting Michigan apples. Each of the sixteen varieties grown in Michigan is pictured and its taste, uses, and texture described.

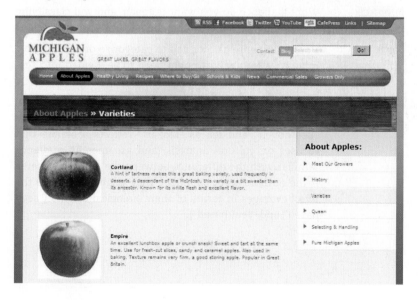

The photographs allow us to see the differences among the varieties at a glance. The varieties are arranged alphabetically, but could have been arranged by color, flavor (sweet or tart), or whether they are best for baking or eating raw.

Considering the Rhetorical Situation

As a writer or speaker, you need to think about the message that you want to articulate, the audience you want to reach, and the larger context you are writing in.

| 3–4 | **PURPOSE** | Your purpose for writing will affect how you classify or divide information. Weinberg and Bealer classify coffee as "boisterous" and tea as "decorous" to help readers understand the cultural styles the two beverages represent, whereas J. Crew might divide sweaters into cashmere, wool, and cotton to help shoppers find and buy things from their website. |

| 5–8 | **AUDIENCE** | What audience do you want to reach, and will classifying or dividing your material help them follow your discussion? |

| 9–11 | **GENRE** | Does your genre call for you to categorize or divide information? A long report might need to be divided into sections, for instance. |

| 12–15 | **STANCE** | Your stance may affect the way you classify information. Weinberg and Bealer's classification of coffee as "Beethoven" and tea as "Mozart" reflects a stance that focuses on cultural analysis (and assumes an audience familiar with the difference between the two composers). If the authors were botanists, they might categorize the two beverages in terms of their biological origins ("seed based" and "leaf based"). |

MEDIA / DESIGN   You can classify or divide in paragraph form, but sometimes a pie chart or list will show the categories better.

16–18

IF YOU NEED MORE HELP

See also **CLUSTERING, CUBING,** and **LOOPING,** three methods of generating ideas
that can be especially helpful for classifying material. And see all the **PROCESSES**
chapters for guidelines on drafting, revising, and so on if you need to write a classification essay.

260–62

249

35 Comparing and Contrasting

Comparing things looks at their similarities; contrasting them focuses on their differences. It's a kind of thinking that comes naturally and that we do constantly—for example, comparing Houston with Dallas, iPhones with Androids, or three paintings by Renoir. And once we start comparing, we generally find ourselves contrasting—Houston and Dallas have differences as well as similarities.

As a student, you'll often be asked to compare and contrast paintings or poems or other things. As a writer, you'll have cause to compare and contrast in most kinds of writing. In a **PROPOSAL,** for instance, you will need to compare your solution with other possible solutions; or in an **EVALUATION,** such as a movie review, you might contrast the film you're reviewing with some other film. This chapter offers advice on ways of comparing and contrasting things for various writing purposes and for your own rhetorical situations.

205–13
164–72

Most of the time, we compare obviously similar things: cars we might purchase, three competing political candidates, two versions of a film. Occasionally, however, we might compare things that are less obviously similar. See how John McMurtry, an ex–football player, compares football with war in an essay arguing that the attraction football holds for spectators is based in part on its potential for violence and injury:

> The family resemblance between football and war is, indeed, striking. Their languages are similar: "field general," "long bomb," "blitz," "take a shot," "front line," "pursuit," "good hit," "the draft," and so on. Their principles and practices are alike: mass hysteria, the art of intimidation, absolute command and total obedience, territorial aggression, censorship, inflated insignia and propaganda, blackboard maneuvers and strategies, drills, uniforms, marching bands, and training

rhetorical situations genres processes strategies research MLA / APA media / design handbook

camps. And the virtues they celebrate are almost identical: hyper-aggressiveness, coolness under fire, and suicidal bravery.

—John McMurtry, "Kill 'Em! Crush 'Em! Eat 'Em Raw!"

McMurtry's comparison helps focus readers' attention on what he's arguing about football in part because it's somewhat unexpected. But the more unlikely the comparison, the more you might be accused of comparing apples and oranges. It's important, therefore, that the things we compare be legitimately compared—as is the case in the following comparison of the health of the world's richest and poorest people:

> World Health Organization (WHO) data indicate that roughly 1.2 billion people are undernourished, underweight, and often hungry. At the same time, roughly 1.2 billion people are overnourished and over-weight, most of them suffering from excessive caloric intake and exercise deprivation. So while 1 billion people worry whether they will eat, another billion should worry about eating too much.
>
> Disease patterns also reflect the widening gap. The billion poorest suffer mostly from infectious diseases—malaria, tuberculosis, dysentery, and AIDS. Malnutrition leaves infants and small children even more vulnerable to such infectious diseases. Unsafe drinking water takes a heavier toll on those with hunger-weakened immune systems, resulting in millions of fatalities each year. In contrast, among the billion at the top of the global economic scale, it is diseases related to aging and lifestyle excesses, including obesity, smoking, diets rich in fat and sugar, and exercise deprivation, that cause most deaths.

> —Lester R. Brown, *Plan B 2.0: Rescuing a Planet under Stress and a Civilization in Trouble*

While the two groups of roughly a billion people each undoubtedly have similarities, this selection from a book arguing for global action on the environment focuses on the stark contrasts.

Two Ways of Comparing and Contrasting

Comparisons and contrasts may be organized in two basic ways: block and point by point.

The block method.   One way is to discuss separately each item you're comparing, giving all the information about one item and then all the information about the next item. A report on Seattle and Vancouver, for example, compares the firearm regulations in each city using a paragraph about Seattle and then a paragraph about Vancouver:

> Although similar in many ways, Seattle and Vancouver differ markedly in their approaches to the regulation of firearms. In Seattle, handguns may be purchased legally for self-defense in the street or at home. After a thirty-day waiting period, a permit can be obtained to carry a handgun as a concealed weapon. The recreational use of handguns is minimally restricted.
>
> In Vancouver, self-defense is not considered a valid or legal reason to purchase a handgun. Concealed weapons are not permitted. Recreational uses of handguns (such as target shooting and collecting) are regulated by the province, and the purchase of a handgun requires a restricted-weapons permit. A permit to carry a weapon must also be obtained in order to transport a handgun, and these weapons can be discharged only at a licensed shooting club. Handguns can be transported by car, but only if they are stored in the trunk in a locked box.
>
> —John Henry Sloan et al., "Handgun Regulations, Crime, Assaults, and Homicide: A Tale of Two Cities"

The point-by-point method.   The other way to compare things is to focus on specific points of comparison. In this paragraph, humorist David Sedaris compares his childhood with his partner's, discussing corresponding aspects of the childhoods one at a time:

> Certain events are parallel, but compared with Hugh's, my childhood was unspeakably dull. When I was seven years old, my family moved to North Carolina. When he was seven years old, Hugh's family moved to the Congo. We had a collie and a house cat. They had a monkey and two horses named Charlie Brown and Satan. I threw stones at stop signs. Hugh threw stones at crocodiles. The verbs are the same, but he definitely wins the prize when it comes to nouns and objects. An eventful day for my mother might have involved a trip to the dry cleaner or a conversation with the potato-chip deliveryman. Asked one ordinary

Congo afternoon what she'd done with her day, Hugh's mother answered that she and a fellow member of the Ladies' Club had visited a leper colony on the outskirts of Kinshasa.

—David Sedaris, "Remembering My Childhood
on the Continent of Africa"

Using Graphs and Images to Present Comparisons

Some comparisons can be easier to understand if they're presented visually, as a **CHART**, **GRAPH**, or **ILLUSTRATION**. For example, this excerpt from a chart from the *Huffington Post* shows the results of various opinion polls about Americans' identification with a political party in April and May 2012; it allows readers to compare not only percentages of Republicans, Democrats, and Independents but also differences in results among the polls. (In the third column, pop-up links explain that "Pop." means "Population," "A" means "adults," "RV" means "registered voters," and "LV" means "likely voters.")

591–99

Pollster	Dates	Pop.	Democrat	Independent	Republican	Undecided
AP-GfK	5/3–5/7	1,004 A	31	46	22	1
DailyKos/SEIU/ PPP (D)	5/3–5/6	1,000 RV	38	26	35	—
NBC/WSJ	4/13–4/17	800 A	30	42	24	4
CBS/Times	4/13–4/17	957 A	34	36	30	—
Ipsos/Reuters	4/12–4/15	1,044 A	29	49	22	—

—The Huffington Post

The following bar graph, from an economics textbook, compares the incomes of various professions in the United States, both with one another and with the average U.S. income (defined as 100 percent). Again, it would be possible to write out this information in a paragraph—but it is much easier to understand it this way:

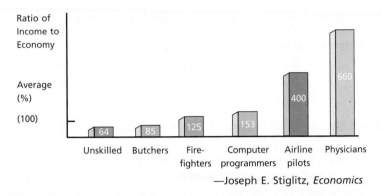

—Joseph E. Stiglitz, *Economics*

Sometimes photographs can make a comparison. The two photos below show areas of Japan before and after the 2011 tsunami.

Ishinomaki Prefecture before the 2011 tsunami (top) and after the storm (bottom).

Using Figurative Language to Make Comparisons

Another way we make comparisons is with figurative language: words and phrases used in a nonliteral way to help readers see a point. Three kinds of figurative language that make comparisons are similes, metaphors, and analogies. When Robert Burns wrote that his love was "like a red, red rose," he was comparing his love with a rose and evoking an image — in this case, a simile — that helps us understand his feelings for her. A simile makes a comparison using *like* or *as*. In the following example, from an article in the food section of the *New York Times*, a restaurant critic uses several similes (underlined) to help us visualize an unusual food dish:

> Once upon a time, possibly at a lodge in Wyoming, possibly at a butcher shop in Maurice, Louisiana, or maybe even at a plantation in South Carolina, an enterprising cook decided to take a boned chicken, a boned duck, and a boned turkey, stuff them one inside the other <u>like Russian dolls</u>, and roast them. He called his masterpiece turducken. . . .
>
> A well-prepared turducken is a marvelous treat, a free-form poultry terrine layered with flavorful stuffing and moistened with duck fat. When it's assembled, it looks <u>like a turkey</u> and it roasts <u>like a turkey</u>, but when you go to carve it, you can slice through it <u>like a loaf of bread</u>. In each slice you get a little bit of everything: white meat from the breast; dark meat from the legs, duck, carrots, bits of sausage, bread, herbs, juices, and chicken, too.
>
> — Amanda Hesser, "Turkey Finds Its Inner Duck (and Chicken)"

Metaphors make comparisons without such connecting words as *like* or *as*. See how desert ecologist Craig Childs uses a metaphor to help us understand the nature of water during a flood in the Grand Canyon:

> Water splashed off the desert and ran all over the surface, looking for the quickest way down. It was too swift for the ground to absorb. When water flows like this, it will not be clean tap water. It will be <u>a gravy of debris</u>, snatching everything it finds.
>
> — Craig Childs, *The Secret Knowledge of Water*

Calling the water "a gravy of debris" allows us to see the murky liquid as it streams through the canyon.

Analogies are extended similes or metaphors that compare something unfamiliar with something more familiar. Arguing that corporations should not patent parts of DNA whose function isn't yet clear, a genetics professor uses the familiar image of a library to explain an unfamiliar concept:

> It's like having a library of books and randomly tearing pages out. You may know which books the pages came from but that doesn't tell you much about them.
>
> —Peter Goodfellow, quoted in John Vidal and
> John Carvel, "Lambs to the Gene Market"

Sometimes analogies are used for humorous effect as well as to make a point, as in this passage from a critique of history textbooks:

> Another history text—this one for fifth grade—begins with the story of how Henry B. Gonzalez, who is a member of Congress from Texas, learned about his own nationality. When he was ten years old, his teacher told him he was an American because he was born in the United States. His grandmother, however, said, "The cat was born in the oven. Does that make him bread?"
>
> —Frances FitzGerald, *America Revised:*
> *History Schoolbooks in the Twentieth Century*

The grandmother's question shows how an intentionally ridiculous analogy can be a source of humor—and can make a point memorably.

Considering the Rhetorical Situation

As a writer or speaker, you need to think about the message that you want to articulate, the audience you want to reach, and the larger context you are writing in.

3–4 ■   **PURPOSE**   Sometimes your main purpose for writing will be to compare two or more things. Other times, you may want to compare several things for some other purpose—to compare your views with those of others in an argument essay or to compare one text with another as you analyze them.

AUDIENCE Who is your audience, and will comparing your topic with a more familiar one help them to follow your discussion? 5–8

GENRE Does your genre require you to compare something? Evaluations often include comparisons—one book to another in a review, or ten different cell phones in *Consumer Reports*. 9–11

STANCE Your stance may affect any comparisons you make. How you compare two things—evenhandedly, or clearly favoring one over the other, for example—will reflect your stance. 12–15

MEDIA / DESIGN Some things you will want to compare with words alone (lines from two poems, for instance), but sometimes you may wish to make comparisons visually (two images juxtaposed on a page, or several numbers plotted on a line graph). 16–18

IF YOU NEED MORE HELP

See **LOOPING** and **CUBING**, two methods of generating ideas that can be especially helpful for comparing and contrasting. If you're writing an essay whose purpose is to compare two or more things, see also the **PROCESSES** chapters for help drafting, revising, and so on. 260–62
249

36 Defining

Defining something says what it is — and what it is not. A terrier, for example, is a kind of dog. A fox terrier is a small dog now generally kept as a pet but once used by hunters to dig for foxes. Happiness is a jelly doughnut, at least according to Homer Simpson. All of those are definitions. As writers, we need to define any terms our readers may not know. And sometimes you'll want to stipulate your own definition of a word in order to set the terms of an **ARGUMENT** — as Homer Simpson does with a definition that's not found in any dictionary. This chapter details strategies for using definitions in your writing to suit your own rhetorical situations.

323–41

Formal Definitions

Sometimes to make sure readers understand you, you will need to provide a formal definition. If you are using a technical term that readers are unlikely to know or if you are using a term in a specific way, you need to say then and there what the word means. The word *mutual*, for example, has several dictionary meanings:

> **mu•tu•al** . . .
>
> **1a:** directed by each toward the other or the others <*mutual* affection> **b:** having the same feelings one for the other <they had long been *mutual* enemies> **c:** shared in common <enjoying their *mutual* hobby> **d:** joint
> **2:** characterized by intimacy
> **3:** of or relating to a plan whereby the members of an organization share in the profits and expenses; *specifically*: of, relating to, or taking the form of an insurance method in which the policyholders constitute the members of the insuring company
>
> — *Merriam-Webster.com*

356

rhetorical situations

genres

processes

strategies

research MLA / APA

media / design

handbook

The first two meanings are commonly understood and probably require no definition. But if you were to use *mutual* in the third sense, it might — depending on your audience. A general audience would probably need the definition; an audience from the insurance industry would not. A website that gives basic financial advice to an audience of non-specialists, for instance, offers a specific definition of the term *mutual fund*:

> *Mutual funds* are financial intermediaries. They are companies set up to receive your money and then, having received it, to make investments with the money.
>
> — Bill Barker, "A Grand, Comprehensive Overview to Mutual Funds Investing"

But even writers in specialized fields routinely provide formal definitions to make sure their readers understand the way they are using certain words. See how two writers define the word *stock* as it pertains to their respective (and very different) fields:

> Stocks are the basis for sauces and soups and important flavoring agents for braises. Admittedly, stock making is time consuming, but the extra effort yields great dividends.
>
> — Tom Colicchio, *Think Like a Chef*

> Want to own part of a business without having to show up at its office every day? Or ever? Stock is the vehicle of choice for those who do. Dating back to the Dutch mutual stock corporations of the sixteenth century, the modern stock market exists as a way for entrepreneurs to finance businesses using money collected from investors. In return for ponying up the dough to finance the company, the investor becomes a part owner of the company. That ownership is represented by stock — specialized financial "securities," or financial instruments, that are "secured" by a claim on the assets and profits of a company.
>
> — "Investing Basics: Stocks," *The Motley Fool*

To write a formal definition

- Use words that readers are likely to be familiar with.
- Don't use the word being defined in the definition.

- Begin with the word being defined; include the general category to which the term belongs and the attributes that make it different from the others in that category.

For example:

Term	General Category	Distinguishing Attributes
Stock is	a specialized financial "security"	that is "secured" by a claim.
Photosynthesis is	a process	by which plants use sunlight to create energy.
Astronomers are	scientists	who study celestial objects and phenomena.
Sacha Baron Cohen,	a comedian,	has acted in several films, including *Brüno* and *The Dictator*.

Note that the category and distinguishing attributes cannot be stated too broadly; if they were, the definition would be too vague to be useful. It wouldn't be helpful in most circumstances, for example, to say, "Sacha Baron Cohen is a man who has acted" or "Photosynthesis is something having to do with plants."

Extended Definitions

Sometimes you need to provide a more detailed definition. Extended definitions may be several sentences long or several paragraphs long and may include pictures or diagrams. Sometimes an entire essay is devoted to defining a difficult or important concept. Here is one writer's extended definition of *meme*:

> Richard Dawkins first came up with the idea of a meme in his 1976 book *The Selfish Gene*. Essentially, memes are ideas that evolve according to the same principles that govern biological evolution. Think about all the ideas that you have in your head right now. They are all memes, and they all came from somewhere. Some of them will have come from friends and some will have come from the internet or television.

Examples of memes are musical tunes, jokes, trends, fashions, catch phrases, and car designs. Now, the memes that inhabit your mind are in competition with all the other memes in the *memepool* (the collection of all existing memes). This means that they are all competing to get themselves copied into other people's minds. Some of these memes do quite well. Every time you whistle your favorite tune or utter a useful catch phrase, you are facilitating the spread of those memes. Every time you wear something that is "in fashion" you are helping the idea of that fashion enter other people's minds. Consider the first four notes of Beethoven's 5th symphony, or the "Happy Birthday" song. These are ideas that inhabit our minds and have been very successful at replicating. Not only have these memes found their way into literally millions of minds, they have also managed to leave copies of themselves on paper, in books, on audiotape, on compact disks, and in computer hard-drives.

There is a limited amount of memetic storage space on this planet, so only the best memes manage to implant themselves. Memes that are good at replicating tend to leave more copies of themselves in minds and in other mediums such as books. Memes that are not so good at replicating tend to die out. We can imagine what sorts of memes have become extinct. Ancient songs that were once sung and never written down are one example. Another example is the many stories that were once told but have since slipped into oblivion.

—Brent Silby, "What Is a Meme?"

That definition includes a description of the basic features and behavior of memes, examples of them, and the origin of the term. We can assume that it's written for a general audience, one that doesn't know anything about memes.

Abstract concepts often require extended definitions because by nature they are more complicated to define. There are many ways of writing an extended definition, depending in part on the term being defined and on your audience and purpose. The following examples show some of the methods that can be used for composing extended definitions of *democracy*.

Explore the word's origins. Where did the word come from? When did it first come into use? In the following example, from an essay considering what democracy means in the twenty-first century, the writer started by looking at the word's first known use in English. Though it's from an essay written for a first-year writing course and thus for a fairly general audience, it's a definition that might pique any audience's interest:

> According to the *Oxford English Dictionary*, the term *democracy* first appeared in English in a thirteenth-century translation of Aristotle's works — specifically, in his *Politics*, where he stated that the "underlying principle of democracy is freedom" and that "it is customary to say that only in democracies do men have a share in freedom, for that is what every democracy makes its aim." By the sixteenth century, the word was used much as it is now. One writer in 1586, for instance, defined it in this way: "where free and poore men being the greater number, are lords of the estate."
>
> —Susanna Mejía, "What Does Democracy Mean Now?"

Here's another example, this one written for a scholarly audience, from an essay about women, participation, democracy, and the information age:

> The very word *citizenship* carries with it a connotation of place, a "citizen" being, literally, the inhabitant of a city. Over the years the word has, of course, accumulated a number of associated meanings . . . and the word has come to stand in for such concepts as participation, equality, and democracy. The fact that the concept of locality is deeply embedded in the word *citizen* suggests that it is also fundamental to our current understanding of these other, more apparently abstract words.
>
> In Western thought, the concepts of citizenship, equality, and democracy are closely interlinked and can be traced back to a common source, in Athens in the fifth century B.C. Perhaps it is no accident that it was the same culture which also gave us, in its theater, the concept of the unity of time and space. The Greek city-state has been represented for centuries as the ideal model of democracy, with free and equal access for all citizens to decision making. Leaving aside, for the moment, the question of who was included, and who excluded from this notion of citizenship, we can see that the sense of place is fundamental to this model. Entitlement to participate in the democratic process is circumscribed by geography; it is the inhabitants of the geographical entity of the city-state, precisely defined and bounded, who have the rights to citizenship. Those who are not defined as inhabitants

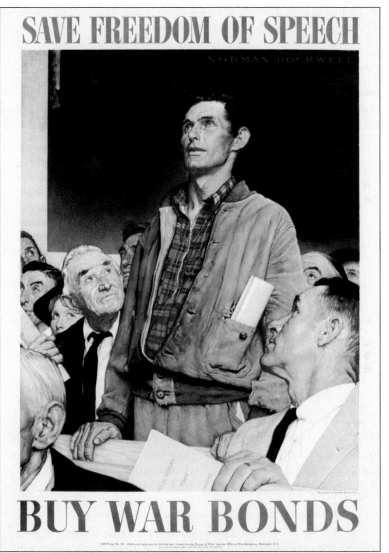

Norman Rockwell's 1943 painting Freedom of Speech presents a visual definition of democracy: a citizen stands to speak at a public meeting while his fellow citizens listen attentively.

of that specific city-state are explicitly excluded, although, of course, they may have the right to citizenship elsewhere.

—Ursula Huws, "Women, Participation, and
Democracy in the Information Society"

Provide details. What are its characteristics? What is it made of? See how a historian explores the basic characteristics of democracy in a book written for an audience of historians:

> As a historian I am naturally disposed to be satisfied with the meaning which, in the history of politics, men have commonly attributed to the word—a meaning, needless to say, which derives partly from the experience and partly from the aspirations of mankind. So regarded, the term *democracy* refers primarily to a form of government, and it has always meant government by the many as opposed to government by the one—government by the people as opposed to government by a tyrant, a dictator, or an absolute monarch. . . . Since the Greeks first used the term, the essential test of democratic government has always been this: the source of political authority must be and remain in the people and not in the ruler. A democratic government has always meant one in which the citizens, or a sufficient number of them to represent more or less effectively the common will, freely act from time to time, and according to established forms, to appoint or recall the magistrates and to enact or revoke the laws by which the community is governed.

—Carl Becker, *Modern Democracy*

Compare it with other words. How is this concept like other similar things? How does it differ? What is it *not* like? **COMPARE AND CONTRAST** it.

348–55

See how a political science textbook defines a *majoritarian democracy* by comparing its characteristics with those of a *consensual democracy*:

> A majoritarian democracy is one
>
> 1. having only two major political parties, not many
> 2. having an electoral system that requires a bare majority to elect one clear winner in an election, as opposed to a proportional

electoral system that distributes seats to political parties according to the rough share of votes received in the election

3. a strong executive (president or prime minister) and cabinet that
together are largely independent of the legislature when it comes
to exercising the executive's constitutional duties, in contrast to
an executive and cabinet that are politically controlled by the parties in the legislature and therefore unable to exercise much influence when proposing policy initiatives.

—Benjamin Ginsberg, Theodore J. Lowi, and Margaret Weir,
We the People: An Introduction to American Politics

And here's an example in which democracy is contrasted with various other forms of governments of the past:

Caesar's power derived from a popular mandate, conveyed through
established republican forms, but that did not make his government
any the less a dictatorship. Napoleon called his government a democratic republic, but no one, least of all Napoleon himself, doubted that
he had destroyed the last vestiges of the democratic republic.

—Carl Becker, *Modern Democracy*

Give examples. See how the essayist E. B. White defines democracy by
giving some everyday examples of considerate behavior, humility, and
civic participation — all things he suggests constitute democracy:

It is the line that forms on the right. It is the don't in "don't shove."
It is the hole in the stuffed shirt through which the sawdust slowly
trickles; it is the dent in the high hat. Democracy is the recurrent suspicion that more than half of the people are right more than half of
the time. . . . Democracy is a letter to the editor.

—E. B. White, "Democracy"

White's definition is elegant because he uses examples that his readers
will know. His characteristics — metaphors, really — define democracy
not as a conceptual way of governing but as an everyday part of
American life.

342–47 ◆

Classify it.   Often it is useful to divide or **CLASSIFY** a term. The ways in which democracy unfolds are complex enough to warrant entire textbooks, of course, but the following definition, from a political science textbook, divides democracy into two kinds, representative and direct:

> A system of government that gives citizens a regular opportunity to elect the top government officials is usually called a representative democracy or republic. A system that permits citizens to vote directly on laws and policies is often called a direct democracy. At the national level, America is a representative democracy in which citizens select government officials but do not vote on legislation. Some states, however, have provisions for direct legislation through popular referendum. For example, California voters in 1995 decided to bar undocumented immigrants from receiving some state services.
>
> —Benjamin Ginsberg, Theodore J. Lowi, and Margaret Weir,
> *We the People: An Introduction to American Politics*

Stipulative Definitions

Sometimes a writer will stipulate a certain definition, essentially saying, "This is how I'm defining x." Such definitions are not usually found in a dictionary—and at the same time are central to the argument the writer is making. Here is one example, from an essay by Toni Morrison. Describing a scene from a film in which a newly arrived Greek immigrant, working as a shoe shiner in Grand Central Terminal, chases away an African American competitor, Morrison calls the scene an example of "race talk," a concept she then goes on to define:

> This is race talk, the explicit insertion into everyday life of racial signs and symbols that have no meaning other than pressing African Americans to the lowest level of the racial hierarchy. Popular culture, shaped by film, theater, advertising, the press, television, and literature, is heavily engaged in race talk. It participates freely in this most enduring and efficient rite of passage into American culture: negative appraisals of the native-born black population. Only when the lesson of racial estrangement is learned is assimilation complete. Whatever

the lived experience of immigrants with African Americans — pleasant, beneficial, or bruising — the rhetorical experience renders blacks as noncitizens, already discredited outlaws.

All immigrants fight for jobs and space, and who is there to fight but those who have both? As in the fishing ground struggle between Texas and Vietnamese shrimpers, they displace what and whom they can. Although U.S. history is awash in labor battles, political fights and property wars among all religious and ethnic groups, their struggles are persistently framed as struggles between recent arrivals and blacks. In race talk the move into mainstream America always means buying into the notion of American blacks as the real aliens. Whatever the ethnicity or nationality of the immigrant, his nemesis is understood to be African American.

—Toni Morrison, "On the Backs of Blacks"

The following example is from a book review of Nancy L. Rosenblum's *Membership and Morals: The Personal Uses of Pluralism in America*, published in the *American Prospect*, a magazine for readers interested in political analysis. In it a Stanford law professor outlines a definition of "the democracy of everyday life":

Democracy, in this understanding of it, means simply treating people as equals, disregarding social standing, avoiding attitudes of either deference or superiority, making allowances for others' weaknesses, and resisting the temptation to respond to perceived slights. It also means protesting everyday instances of arbitrariness and unfairness — from the rudeness of the bakery clerk to the sexism of the car dealer or the racism of those who vandalize the home of the first black neighbors on the block.

—Kathleen M. Sullivan, "Defining Democracy Down"

Considering the Rhetorical Situation

As a writer or speaker, you need to think about the message that you want to articulate, the audience you want to reach, and the larger context you are writing in.

3–4 ▪
PURPOSE   Your purpose for writing will affect any definitions you include. Would writing an extended definition help you explain something? Would stipulating definitions of key terms help you shape an argument? Could an offbeat definition help you entertain your readers?

5–8 ▪
AUDIENCE   What audience do you want to reach, and are there any terms your readers are unlikely to know (and therefore need to be defined)? Are there terms they might understand differently from the way you're defining them?

9–11 ▪
GENRE   Does your genre require you to define terms? Chances are that if you're reporting information you'll need to define some terms, and some arguments rest on the way you define key terms.

12–15 ▪
STANCE   What is your stance, and do you need to define key terms to show that stance clearly? How you define *fetus,* for example, is likely to reveal your stance on abortion.

16–18 ▪
MEDIA / DESIGN   Your medium will affect the form your definitions take. In a print text, you will need to define terms in your text; if you're giving a speech or presentation, you might also provide images of important terms and their definitions. In an electronic text, you may be able to define terms by linking to an online dictionary definition.

IF YOU NEED MORE HELP

See also the **PROCESSES** chapters for help generating ideas, drafting, revising, and so on if you are writing a whole essay dedicated to defining a term or concept.

249 ○

Describing 37

When we describe something, we indicate what it looks like—and sometimes how it sounds, feels, smells, and tastes. Descriptive details are a way of showing rather than telling, of helping readers see (or hear, smell, and so on) what we're writing about—that the sky is blue, that Miss Havisham is wearing an old yellowed wedding gown, that the chemicals in the beaker have reacted and smell like rotten eggs. You'll have occasion to describe things in most of the writing you do—from describing a favorite hat in a MEMOIR to detailing a chemical reaction in a LAB REPORT. This chapter will help you work with description—and, in particular, help you think about the use of *detail*, about *objectivity and subjectivity*, about *vantage point*, about creating a clear *dominant impression*, and about using description to fit your rhetorical situation.

183–90
173–82

Detail

The goal of using details is to be as specific as possible, providing information that will help your audience imagine the subject or make sense of it. See, for example, how Nancy Mairs, an author with multiple sclerosis, describes the disease in clear, specific terms:

> During its course, which is unpredictable and uncontrollable, one may lose vision, hearing, speech, the ability to walk, control of bladder and/or bowels, strength in any or all extremities, sensitivity to touch, vibration, and/or pain, potency, coordination of movements—the list of possibilities is lengthy and, yes, horrifying. One may also lose one's sense of humor. That's the easiest to lose and the hardest to survive without.
>
> In the past ten years, I have sustained some of these losses. Characteristic of MS are sudden attacks, called exacerbations, followed by remissions, and these I have not had. Instead, my disease has been

slowly progressive. My left leg is now so weak that I walk with the aid of a brace and a cane, and for distances I use an Amigo, a variation on the electric wheelchair that looks rather like an electrified kiddie car. I no longer have much use of my left hand. Now my right side is weakening as well. I still have the blurred spot in my right eye. Overall, though, I've been lucky so far.

—Nancy Mairs, "On Being a Cripple"

Mairs's gruesome list demonstrates, through *specific details*, how the disease affects sufferers generally and her in particular. We know far more after reading this text than we do from the following more general description, from a National Multiple Sclerosis Society brochure:

Multiple sclerosis is a chronic, unpredictable disease of the central nervous system (the brain, optic nerves, and spinal cord). It is thought to be an autoimmune disorder. This means the immune system incorrectly attacks the person's healthy tissue.

MS can cause blurred vision, loss of balance, poor coordination, slurred speech, tremors, numbness, extreme fatigue, problems with memory and concentration, paralysis, and blindness. These problems may be permanent, or they may come and go.

—National Multiple Sclerosis Society, *Just the Facts*

Specific details are also more effective than labels, which give little meaningful information. Instead of saying that someone is a "moron" or "really smart," it's better to give details so that readers can understand the reasons behind the label: what does this person *do* or *say* that makes him or her deserve this label? See, for example, how the writer of a news story about shopping on the day after Thanksgiving opens with a description of a happy shopper:

Last Friday afternoon, the day ritualized consumerism is traditionally at its most frenetic, Alexx Balcuns twirled in front of a full-length mirror at the Ritz Thrift Shop on West Fifty-seventh Street as if inhabited by the soul of Eva Gabor in *Green Acres*. Ms. Balcuns was languishing in a $795 dyed-mink parka her grandmother had just bought her. Ms. Balcuns is six.

—Ginia Bellafante, "Staying Warm and Fuzzy during Uncertain Times"

rhetorical situations   genres   processes   strategies   research MLA / APA   media / design   handbook

The writer might simply have said, "A spoiled child admired herself in the mirror." Instead, she shows her subject twirling and "languishing" in a "$795 dyed-mink parka" and seemingly possessed by the soul of the actress Eva Gabor—all details that create a far more vivid description.

Sensory details help readers imagine sounds, odors, tastes, and physical sensations in addition to sights. In the following example, writer Scott Russell Sanders recalls sawing wood as a child. Note how visual details, odors, and even the physical sense of being picked up by his father mingle to form a vivid scene:

> As the saw teeth bit down, the wood released its smell, each kind with its own fragrance, oak or walnut or cherry or pine—usually pine because it was the softest, easiest for a child to work. No matter how weathered and gray the board, no matter how warped and cracked, inside there was this smell waiting, as of something freshly baked. I gathered every smidgen of sawdust and stored it away in coffee cans, which I kept in a drawer of the workbench. When I did not feel like hammering nails I would dump my sawdust on the concrete floor of the garage and landscape it into highways and farms and towns, running miniature cars and trucks along miniature roads. Looming as huge as a colossus, my father worked over and around me, now and again bending down to inspect my work, careful not to trample my creations. It was a landscape that smelled dizzyingly of wood. Even after a bath my skin would carry the smell, and so would my father's hair, when he lifted me for a bedtime hug.
>
> —Scott Russell Sanders, *The Paradise of Bombs*

Whenever you describe something, you'll select from many possible details you might use. Simply put, to exhaust all the details available to describe something is impossible—and would exhaust your readers as well. To focus your description, you'll need to determine the kinds of details appropriate for your subject. They will vary, depending on your **PURPOSE**. See, for example, how the details might differ in three different genres:

3–4

• *For a* **MEMOIR** *about an event,* you might choose details that are significant for you, that evoke the sights, sounds, and other sensations that give meaning to your event.

183–90

191–204 ▲

- *For a* **PROFILE,** you're likely to select details that will reinforce the dominant impression you want to give, that portray the event from the perspective you want readers to see.

173–82 ▲

- *For a* **LAB REPORT,** you need to give certain specifics — what equipment was used, what procedures were followed, what exactly were the results.

Deciding on a focus for your description can help you see it better, as you'll look for details that contribute to that focus.

Objectivity and Subjectivity

Descriptions can be written with objectivity, with subjectivity, or with a mixture of both. Objective descriptions attempt to be uncolored by personal opinion or emotion. Police reports and much news writing aim to describe events objectively; scientific writing strives for objectivity in describing laboratory procedures and results. See, for example, the following objective account of what happened at the World Trade Center on September 11, 2001:

> **World Trade Center Disaster — Tuesday, September 11, 2001**
>
> On Tuesday, September 11, 2001, at 8:45 a.m. New York local time, One World Trade Center, the north tower, was hit by a hijacked 767 commercial jet airplane loaded with fuel for a transcontinental flight. Two World Trade Center, the south tower, was hit by a similar hijacked jet eighteen minutes later, at 9:03 a.m. (In separate but related attacks, the Pentagon building near Washington, D.C., was hit by a hijacked 757 at 9:43 a.m., and at 10:10 a.m. a fourth hijacked jetliner crashed in Pennsylvania.) The south tower, WTC 2, which had been hit second, was the first to suffer a complete structural collapse, at 10:05 a.m., 62 minutes after being hit itself, 80 minutes after the first impact. The north tower, WTC 1, then also collapsed, at 10:29 a.m., 104 minutes after being hit. WTC 7, a substantial forty-seven-story office building in its own right, built in 1987, was damaged by the collapsing towers, caught fire, and later in the afternoon also totally collapsed.
>
> — "World Trade Center," *GreatBuildings.com*

rhetorical situations ■
genres ▲
processes ○
strategies ◆
research MLA / APA ●
media / design □
handbook ⬈

Subjective descriptions, on the other hand, allow the writer's opinions and emotions to come through. A house can be described as comfortable, with a lived-in look, or as rundown and in need of a paint job and a new roof. Here's a subjective description of the planes striking the World Trade Center, as told by a woman watching from a nearby building:

> Incredulously, while looking out [the] window at the damage and carnage the first plane had inflicted, I saw the second plane abruptly come into my right field of vision and deliberately, with shimmering intention, thunder full-force into the south tower. It was so close, so low, so huge and fast, so intent on its target that I swear to you, I swear to you, I felt the vengeance and rage emanating from the plane.
>
> —Debra Fontaine, "Witnessing"

Vantage Point

Sometimes you'll want or need to describe something from a certain vantage point. Where you locate yourself in relation to what you're describing will determine what you can perceive (and so describe) and what you can't. You may describe your subject from a *stationary vantage point*, from which you (and your readers) see your subject from one angle only, as if you were a camera. This description of one of three photographs that captured a woman's death records only what the camera saw from one angle at one particular moment:

> The first showed some people on a fire escape—a fireman, a woman and a child. The fireman had a nice strong jaw and looked very brave. The woman was holding the child. Smoke was pouring from the building behind them. A rescue ladder was approaching, just a few feet away, and the fireman had one arm around the woman and one arm reaching out toward the ladder.
>
> —Nora Ephron, "The Boston Photographs"

By contrast, this description of a drive to an Italian villa uses a *moving vantage point*; the writer recounts what he saw as he passed through a gate in a city wall, moving from city to country:

La Pietra—"the stone"—is situated one mile from the Porta San Gallo, an entry to the Old City of Florence. You drive there along the Via Bolognese, twisting past modern apartment blocks, until you come to a gate, which swings open—and there you are, at the upper end of a long lane of cypresses facing a great ocher palazzo; with olive groves spreading out on both sides over an expanse of fifty-seven acres. There's something almost comically wonderful about the effect: here, the city, with its winding avenue; there, on the other side of a wall, the country, fertile and gray green.

—James Traub, "Italian Hours"

The description of quarries in the following section uses *multiple vantage points* to capture the quarries from many perspectives.

This ad for Adidas uses a stationary vantage point (looking down on the basketball court or grassy court from above the backboard) to make a point about the universality of the game — and hence the need for Adidas.

■ rhetorical situations
▲ genres
○ processes
◆ strategies
● research MLA / APA
□ media / design
▨ handbook

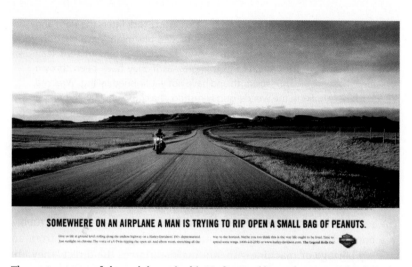

SOMEWHERE ON AN AIRPLANE A MAN IS TRYING TO RIP OPEN A SMALL BAG OF PEANUTS.

The vast expanse of sky and desert in this Harley-Davidson ad creates a dominant impression of spaciousness and freedom that's underscored by the image the text evokes — one of cramped confinement.

Dominant Impression

With any description, your aim is to create some dominant impression — the overall feeling that the individual details add up to. The dominant impression may be implied, growing out of the details themselves. For example, Scott Russell Sanders's memory of the smell of sawdust creates a dominant impression of warmth and comfort: the "fragrance . . . as of something freshly baked," sawdust "stored . . . away in coffee cans," a young boy "lifted . . . for a bedtime hug." Sometimes, though, a writer will state the dominant impression directly, in addition to creating it with details. In an essay about Indiana limestone quarries, Sanders makes the dominant impression clear from the start: "they are battlefields."

> The quarries will not be domesticated. They are not backyard pools; they are battlefields. Each quarry is an arena where violent struggles have taken place between machines and planet, between human ingenuity and brute

resisting stone, between mind and matter. Waste rock litters the floor and brim like rubble in a bombed city. The ragged pits might have been the basements of vanished skyscrapers. Stones weighing tens of tons lean against one another at precarious angles, as if they have been thrown there by some gigantic strength and have not yet finished falling. Wrecked machinery hulks in the weeds, grimly rusting, the cogs and wheels, twisted rails, battered engine housings, trackless bulldozers and burst boilers like junk from an armored regiment. Everywhere the ledges are scarred from drills, as if from an artillery barrage or machine-gun strafing. Stumbling onto one of these abandoned quarries and gazing at the ruins, you might be left wondering who had won the battle, men or stone.

—Scott Russell Sanders, *The Paradise of Bombs*

The rest of his description, full of more figurative language ("like rubble in a bombed city," "like junk from an armored regiment," "as if from an artillery barrage or machine-gun strafing") reinforces the direct "they are battlefields" statement.

Organizing Descriptions

You can organize descriptions in many ways. When your description is primarily visual, you will probably organize it spatially: from left to right, top to bottom, outside to inside. One variation on this approach is to begin with the most significant or noteworthy feature and move outward from that center, as Ephron does. Or you may create a chronological description of objects as you move past or through them in space, as Traub does in his description of his drive. You might even pile up details to create a dominant impression, as Sanders and Mairs do, especially if your description draws on senses besides vision.

Considering the Rhetorical Situation

As a writer or speaker, you need to think about the message that you want to articulate, the audience you want to reach, and the larger context you are writing in.

PURPOSE   Your purpose may affect the way you use description. If you're arguing that a government should intervene in another country's civil war, for example, describing the anguish of refugees from that war could make your argument more persuasive. If you're analyzing a painting, you will likely need to describe it.   ■ 3–4

AUDIENCE   Who is your audience, and will they need detailed description to understand the points you wish to make?   ■ 5–8

GENRE   Does your genre require description? A lab report generally calls for you to describe materials and results; a memoir about grandma should probably describe her — her smile, her dress, her apple pie.   ■ 9–11

STANCE   The way you describe things can help you convey your stance. For example, the details you choose can show you to be objective (or not), careful or casual.   ■ 12–15

MEDIA / DESIGN   Your medium will affect the form your description can take. In a print or spoken text, you will likely rely on words, though you may also include visuals. In an electronic text, you can easily provide links to visuals as well as audio clips and so may need fewer words of your own.   ■ 16–18

IF YOU NEED MORE HELP

See also **FREEWRITING, CUBING,** and **LISTING,** three methods of generating ideas that can be especially helpful for developing detailed descriptions. Sometimes you may be assigned to write a whole essay describing something: see the **PROCESSES** chapters for help drafting, revising, and so on.

● 259–62
249

38 Dialogue

183–90 ▲
191–204
81–86
119–49

Dialogue is a way of including people's own words in a text, letting readers hear those people's voices—not just what you say about them. **MEMOIRS** and **PROFILES** often include dialogue, and many other genres do as well: **LITERARY ANALYSES** often quote dialogue from the texts they analyze, and essays **ARGUING A POSITION** might quote an authoritative source as support for a claim. This chapter provides brief guidelines for the conventions of paragraphing and punctuating dialogue and offers some good examples of how you can use dialogue most effectively to suit your own rhetorical situations.

Why Add Dialogue?

Dialogue is a way of bringing in voices other than your own, of showing people and scenes rather than just telling about them. It can add color and texture to your writing, making it memorable. Most important, however, dialogue should be more than just colorful or interesting. It needs to contribute to your rhetorical purpose, to support the point you're making. See how dialogue is used in the following excerpt from a magazine profile of the Mall of America, how it gives us a sense of the place that the journalist's own words could not provide:

> Two pubescent girls in retainers and braces sat beside me sipping coffees topped with whipped cream and chocolate sprinkles, their shopping bags gathered tightly around their legs, their eyes fixed on the passing crowds. They came, they said, from Shakopee—"It's nowhere," one of them explained. The megamall, she added, was "a buzz at first, but now it seems pretty normal. 'Cept my parents are like Twenty Questions every time I want to come here. 'Specially since the shooting."

rhetorical situations

genres

processes

strategies

research
MLA / APA

media / design

handbook

On a Sunday night, she elaborated, three people had been wounded when shots were fired in a dispute over a San Jose Sharks jacket. "In the *mall*," her friend reminded me. "Right here at megamall. A shooting." "It's like nowhere's safe," the first added.

> —David Guterson, "Enclosed. Encyclopedic. Endured.
> One Week at the Mall of America"

Of course it was the writer who decided whom and what to quote, and Guterson deliberately chose words that capture the young shoppers' speech patterns, quoting fragments ("In the *mall*. . . . Right here at megamall. A shooting"), slang ("a buzz at first," "my parents are like Twenty Questions"), even contractions ("'cept," "'specially").

Integrating Dialogue into Your Writing

There are certain conventions for punctuating and paragraphing dialogue:

- *Punctuating.* Enclose each speaker's words in quotation marks, and put any end punctuation—periods, question marks, and exclamation marks—inside the closing quotation mark. Whether you're transcribing words you heard or making them up, you will sometimes need to add punctuation to reflect the rhythm and sound of the speech. In the last sentence of the example below, see how Chang-Rae Lee adds a comma after *well* and italicizes *practice* to show intonation—and attitude.

- *Paragraphing.* When you're writing dialogue that includes more than one speaker, start a new paragraph each time the speaker changes.

- *Signal phrases.* Sometimes you'll need to introduce dialogue with SIGNAL PHRASES — "I said," "she asked," and so on—to make clear who is speaking. At times, however, the speaker will be clear enough, and you won't need any signal phrases.

471–74

Here is a conversation between a mother and her son that illustrates each of the conventions for punctuating and paragraphing dialogue:

> "Whom do I talk to?" she said. She would mostly speak to me in Korean, and I would answer back in English.

"The bank manager, who else?"

"What do I say?"

"Whatever you want to say."

"Don't speak to me like that!" she cried.

"It's just that you should be able to do it yourself," I said.

"You know how I feel about this!"

"Well, maybe then you should consider it *practice*," I answered lightly, using the Korean word to make sure she understood.

— Chang-Rae Lee, "Coming Home Again"

Interviews

Interviews are a kind of dialogue, with different conventions for punctuation. When you're transcribing an interview, give each speaker's name each time he or she speaks, starting a new line but not indenting, and do not use quotation marks. Here is an excerpt from a National Public Radio interview that Audie Cornish conducted with writer Susan Cain:

Audie Cornish: In the 1940s and '50s, the message to most Americans was, don't be shy. And in the era of reality television, Twitter and relentless self-promotion, it seems that cultural mandate is in overdrive.

A new book tells the story of how things came to be this way, and it's called *Quiet: The Power of Introverts in a World that Can't Stop Talking*. The author is Susan Cain, and she joins us from the NPR studios in New York to talk more about it. Welcome, Susan.

Susan Cain: Thank you. It's such a pleasure to be here, Audie.

Cornish: Well, we're happy to have you. And to start out — I think we should get this on the record — do you consider yourself an introvert or an extrovert?

Cain: Oh, I definitely consider myself an introvert, and that was part of the fuel for me to write the book.

Cornish: And what's the difference between being an introvert versus being shy? I mean, what's your definition?

Cain: So introversion is really about having a preference for lower-stimulation environments — so just a preference for quiet, for less noise, for less action — whereas extroverts really crave more stimulation in

rhetorical situations

genres

processes

strategies

research MLA / APA

media / design

handbook

order to feel at their best. And what's important to understand about this is that many people believe that introversion is about being anti-social. And that's really a misperception because actually, it's just that introverts are differently social. So they would prefer to have, you know, a glass of wine with a close friend as opposed to going to a loud party full of strangers.

Now shyness, on the other hand, is about a fear of negative social judgment. So you can be introverted without having that particular fear at all, and you can be shy but also be an extrovert.

Cornish: And in the book, you say that there's a spectrum. So if some people are listening and they think, well, I, too, like a glass of wine and a party. It's like we all have these tendencies.

Cain: Yeah, yeah. That's an important thing. And, in fact, Carl Jung, the psychologist who first popularized these terms all the way back in the 1920s — even he said there's no such thing as a pure introvert or a pure extrovert, and he said such a man would be in a lunatic asylum.

Cornish: That makes me worry because I took your test in the book and I'm like, 90 percent extroverted, basically.

[*soundbite of laughter*]

Cornish: Now, you mentioned going back into the history. And I want to talk more about that because I was really fascinated by how you showed how this extrovert ideal — you call it — came to be. When did being introverted move from being a character trait to being looked at as a problem?

Cain: Yeah. What I found is, to some extent, we've always had an admiration for extroversion in our culture. But the extrovert ideal really came to play at the turn of the 20th century, when we had the rise of big business. And so suddenly, people were flocking to the cities, and they were needing to prove themselves in big corporations — at job interviews and on sales calls.

And so at that moment in time, we moved from what cultural historians call a culture of character to a culture of personality. So during the culture of character, what was important was the good deeds that you performed when nobody was looking. You know, Abraham Lincoln is the embodiment of the culture of character, and people celebrated him back then for being a man who did not offend by superiority.

But at the turn of the century, when we moved into this culture of personality, suddenly, what was admired was to be magnetic and charismatic. And then at the same time, we suddenly had the rise of movies and movie stars. And movie stars, of course, were the embodiment of what it meant to be a charismatic figure. And so part of people's fascination with these movie stars was for what they could learn from them, and bring with them to their own jobs.

—"Quiet, Please: Unleashing 'The Power of Introverts' "

In preparing the interview transcript for publication, NPR had to add punctuation, which of course was not part of the oral conversation, and probably deleted pauses and verbal expressions such as *um* and *uh*. At the same time, the editor kept informal constructions, such as incomplete sentences, which are typical answers to questions ("Yeah.") to maintain the oral flavor of the interview and to reflect Cain's voice.

Considering the Rhetorical Situation

As a writer or speaker, you need to think about the message that you want to articulate, the audience you want to reach, and the larger context of your writing.

PURPOSE Your purpose will affect any use of dialogue. Dialogue can help bring a profile to life and make it memorable. Interviews with experts or firsthand witnesses can add credibility to a report or argument.

AUDIENCE Whom do you want to reach, and will dialogue help? Sometimes actual dialogue can help readers hear human voices behind facts or reason.

GENRE Does your genre require dialogue? If you're evaluating or analyzing a literary work, for instance, you may wish to include dialogue from that work. If you're writing a profile of a person or event, dialogue can help you bring your subject to life. Similarly, an interview with an expert can add credibility to a report or argument.

3–4

5–8

9–11

STANCE What is your stance, and can dialogue help you communicate that stance? For example, excerpts of an interview may allow you to challenge someone's views and make your own views clear.

12–15

MEDIA / DESIGN Your medium will affect the way you present dialogue. In a print text, you will present dialogue through written words. In an oral or electronic text, you might include actual recorded dialogue.

16–18

IF YOU NEED MORE HELP

See also the guidelines on **INTERVIEWING EXPERTS** for advice on setting up and recording interviews and those on **QUOTING, PARAPHRASING,** and **SUMMARIZING** for help deciding how to integrate dialogue into your text.

448–49
462–74

the process of making French fries. She starts by listing the ingredients and then describes the steps:

4 medium baking potatoes
2 tablespoons olive oil
$1^1/_2$ teaspoons salt
$^1/_4$ teaspoon freshly ground pepper
malt vinegar (optional)

1. Heat oven to 400 degrees. Place a heavy baking sheet in the oven. Scrub and rinse the potatoes well, and then cut them lengthwise into $^1/_2$-inch-wide batons. Place the potato batons in a medium bowl, and toss them with the olive oil, salt, and pepper.

2. When baking sheet is hot, about 15 minutes, remove from the oven. Place prepared potatoes on the baking sheet in a single layer. Return to oven, and bake until potatoes are golden on the bottom, about 30 minutes. Turn potatoes over, and continue cooking until golden all over, about 15 minutes more. Serve immediately.

—Martha Stewart, *Favorite Comfort Food*

Coming from Martha Stewart, the explanation leaves out no details, giving a clear sequence of steps and descriptive verbs that tell us exactly what to do: "heat," "place," "scrub and rinse," and so on. After she gives the recipe, she even goes on to explain the process of *serving* the fries—"Serve these French fries with a bowl of malt vinegar"—and reminds us that "they are also delicious dipped in spicy mustard, mayonnaise, and, of course, ketchup."

Explaining a Process Visually

591–99

Some processes are best explained **VISUALLY**, with diagrams or photographs. See, for example, how a blogger explains one process of shaping dough into a bagel—giving the details in words and then showing us in photos how to do it:

rhetorical situations

genres

processes

strategies

research MLA / APA

media / design

handbook

Roll each portion into a ball and place on prepared baking sheet. Cover with a damp towel and let rest for 20 minutes.

Wrap the dough around your palm and the back of your hand, overlapping the ends by an inch or two.

Roll balls into 6- to 7-inch ropes. If the dough resists, just let it rest for a few minutes and try rolling it again.

Press the overlapping edges against the countertop, rolling the bagel back and forth to seal the seam.

Place bagels back on baking sheet and cover with plastic wrap that has been coated with cooking spray.

—Maggie Lauer, *The Other Side of Fifty*

Considering the Rhetorical Situation

As always, you need to think about the message that you want to articulate, the audience you want to reach, and the larger context you are writing in.

<table>
<tr><td>3–4</td><td>PURPOSE</td><td>Your purpose for writing will affect the way you explain a process. If you're arguing that we should avoid eating fast food, you might explain the process by which chicken nuggets are made. But to give information about how to fry chicken, you would explain the process quite differently.</td></tr>
<tr><td>5–8</td><td>AUDIENCE</td><td>Whom are you trying to reach, and will you need to provide any special background information or to interest them in the process before you explain it?</td></tr>
<tr><td>9–11</td><td>GENRE</td><td>Does your genre require you to explain a process? In a lab report, for example, you'll need to explain processes used in the experiment. You might want to explain a process in a profile of an activity or a proposal for a solution.</td></tr>
<tr><td>12–15</td><td>STANCE</td><td>If you're giving practical directions for doing something, you'll want to take a straightforward "do this, then do that" perspective. If you're writing to entertain, you need to take a clever or amusing stance.</td></tr>
<tr><td>16–18</td><td>MEDIA / DESIGN</td><td>Your medium will affect the way you explain a process. In a print text, you can use both words and images. On the web, you may have the option of showing an animation of the process as well.</td></tr>
</table>

IF YOU NEED MORE HELP

See also **LAB REPORTS** if you need to explain the process by which an experiment is carried out; and **PROFILES** if you are writing about an activity that needs to be explained. See **NARRATING** for more advice on organizing an explanation chronologically. Sometimes you may be assigned to write a whole essay or report that explains a process; see **PROCESSES** for help drafting, revising, and so on.

173–82
191–204
387–95
249

rhetorical situations   genres   processes   strategies   research MLA / APA   media / design   handbook

Narrating **40**

Narratives are stories. As a writing strategy, a good narrative can lend support to most kinds of writing—in a **POSITION PAPER** arguing for Title IX compliance, for example, you might include a brief narrative about an Olympic sprinter who might never have learned to run without Title IX. Or you can bring a **PROFILE** of a favorite coach to life with an anecdote about a pep talk he or she once gave before a championship track meet. Whatever your larger writing purpose, you need to make sure that any narratives you add support that purpose—they should not be inserted simply to tell an interesting story. You'll also need to compose them carefully—to put them in a clear *sequence*, include *pertinent detail*, and make sure they are appropriate to your particular rhetorical situation.

▲ 119–49

▲ 191–204

Sequencing

When we write a narrative, we arrange events in a particular sequence. Writers typically sequence narratives in chronological order, reverse chronological order, or as a flashback.

Use chronological order.   Often you may tell the story chronologically, starting at the beginning of an event and working through to the end, as Maya Angelou does in this brief narrative from an essay about her high school graduation:

> The school band struck up a march and all classes filed in as had been rehearsed. We stood in front of our seats, as assigned, and on a signal from the choir director, we sat. No sooner had this been accomplished than the band started to play the national anthem. We rose again and sang the song, after which we recited the pledge of allegiance. We

387

remained standing for a brief minute before the choir director and the principal signaled to us, rather desperately I thought, to take our seats.

—Maya Angelou, "Graduation"

Use reverse chronological order. You may also begin with the final action and work back to the first, as Aldo Leopold does in this narrative about cutting down a tree:

> Now our saw bites into the 1890s, called gay by those whose eyes turn cityward rather than landward. We cut 1899, when the last passenger pigeon collided with a charge of shot near Babcock, two counties to the north; we cut 1898, when a dry fall, followed by a snowless winter, froze the soil seven feet deep and killed the apple trees; 1897, another drouth year, when another forestry commission came into being; 1896, when 25,000 prairie chickens were shipped to market from the village of Spooner alone; 1895, another year of fires; 1894, another drouth year; and 1893, the year of "the Bluebird Storm," when a March blizzard reduced the migrating bluebirds to near zero.

—Aldo Leopold, *A Sand County Almanac*

222–29 ▲

RÉSUMÉS are one genre where we generally use reverse chronological order, listing the most recent jobs or degrees first and then working backward. Notice, too, that we usually write these as narratives — telling what we have done rather than just naming positions we have held:

Sept. 2011–present	*Student worker*, Department of Information Management, Central State University, Wilberforce, OH. Compile data and format reports using Excel, Word, and university database programs.
June–Sept. 2011	*Intern*, QuestPro Corporation, West Louisville, KY. Assisted in development of software programs.
Sept. 2010–June 2011	*Bagger*, Ace Groceries, Elba, KY. Bagged customers' purchases.

Use a flashback.   You can sometimes put a flashback in the middle of a narrative, to tell about an incident that illuminates the larger narrative. Terry Tempest Williams does this in an essay about the startling incidence of breast cancer in her family: she recalls a dinnertime conversation with her father right after her mother's death from cancer, when she learned for the first time what caused all of the cancer in her family:

> Over dessert, I shared a recurring dream of mine. I told my father that for years, as long as I could remember, I saw this flash of light in the night in the desert. That this image had so permeated my being, I could not venture south without seeing it again, on the horizon, illuminating buttes and mesas.
>
> "You did see it," he said.
>
> "Saw what?" I asked, a bit tentative.
>
> "The bomb. The cloud. We were driving home from Riverside, California. You were sitting on your mother's lap. She was pregnant. In fact, I remember the date, September 7, 1957. We had just gotten out of the Service. We were driving north, past Las Vegas. It was an hour or so before dawn, when this explosion went off. We not only heard it, but felt it. I thought the oil tanker in front of us had blown up. We pulled over and suddenly, rising from the desert floor, we saw it, clearly, this golden-stemmed cloud, the mushroom. The sky seemed to vibrate with an eerie pink glow. Within a few minutes, a light ash was raining on the car."
>
> I stared at my father. This was new information to me.
>
> —Terry Tempest Williams, "The Clan of the One-Breasted Women"

Williams could have simply announced this information as a fact—but see how much more powerful it is when told in narrative form.

Use time markers.   Time markers help readers follow a sequence of events. The most obvious time markers are those that simply label the time, as the narrative entries in a diary, journal, or log might. For example, here is the final part of the narrative kept in a diary by a doomed Antarctic explorer:

> WEDNESDAY, MARCH 21: Got within eleven miles of depot. Monday night; had to lay up all yesterday in severe blizzard. Today forlorn hope, Wilson and Bowers going to depot for fuel.

MARCH 22 and 23: Blizzard bad as ever — Wilson and Bowers unable to start — tomorrow last chance — no fuel and only one or two [days] of food left — must be near the end. Have decided it shall be natural — we shall march for the depot with or without our effects and die in our tracks.

THURSDAY, MARCH 29: Since the 21st we have had a continuous gale from W.S.W. and S.W. We had fuel to make two cups of tea apiece and bare food for two days on the 20th. Every day we have been ready to start for our depot eleven miles away, but outside the door of the tent it remains a scene of whirling drift. I do not think we can hope for any better things now. We shall stick it out to the end, but we are getting weaker, of course, and the end cannot be far. It seems a pity, but I do not think I can write more. . . .

Last Entry: For God's sake look after our people.

—Robert F. Scott, *Scott's Last Expedition: The Journals*

More often you will integrate time markers into the prose itself, as is done in this narrative about a woman preparing and delivering meals to workers at a cotton gin:

She made her plans meticulously and in secret. <u>One early evening</u> to see if she was ready, she placed stones in two five-gallon pails and carried them three miles to the cotton gin. She rested a little, and then, discarding some rocks, she walked in the darkness to the sawmill five miles farther along the dirt road. <u>On her way back</u> to her little house and her babies, she dumped the remaining rocks along the path.

<u>That same night</u> she worked into the early hours boiling chicken and frying ham. She made dough and filled the rolled-out pastry with meat. At last she went to sleep.

<u>The next morning</u> she left her house carrying the meat pies, lard, an iron brazier, and coals for a fire. <u>Just before lunch</u> she appeared in an empty lot behind the cotton gin. <u>As the dinner noon bell rang</u>, she dropped the savors into boiling fat, and the aroma rose and floated over to the workers who spilled out of the gin, covered with white lint, looking like specters.

—Maya Angelou, *Wouldn't Take Nothing for My Journey Now*

rhetorical situations

genres

processes

strategies

research MLA / APA

media / design

handbook

Use transitions. Another way to help readers follow a narrative is with TRANSITIONS, words like *first, then, meanwhile, at last,* and so on. See how the following paragraphs from Langston Hughes's classic essay about meeting Jesus use transitions (and time markers) to advance the action:

◆ 317

> <u>Suddenly</u> the whole room broke into a sea of shouting, <u>as</u> they saw me rise. Waves of rejoicing swept the place. Women leaped in the air. My aunt threw her arms around me. The minister took me by the hand and led me to the platform.
>
> <u>When</u> things quieted down, in a hushed silence, punctuated by a few ecstatic "Amens," all the new young lambs were blessed in the name of God. <u>Then</u> joyous singing filled the room. <u>That night</u>, for the last time in my life but one—for I was a big boy twelve years old—I cried.
>
> —Langston Hughes, "Salvation"

Including Pertinent Detail

When you include a narrative in your writing, you must decide which details you need—and which ones you don't need. For example, you don't want to include so much detail that the narrative distracts the reader from the larger text. You must also decide whether you need to include any background, to set the stage for the narrative. The amount of detail you include depends on your audience and purpose: How much detail does your audience need? How much detail do you need to make your meaning clear? In an essay on the suspicion African American men often face when walking at night, a journalist deliberately presents a story without setting the stage at all:

> My first victim was a woman—white, well dressed, probably in her late twenties. I came upon her late one evening on a deserted street in Hyde Park, a relatively affluent neighborhood in an otherwise mean, impoverished section of Chicago. As I swung onto the avenue behind her, there seemed to be a discreet, uninflammatory distance between us. Not so. She cast back a worried glance. To her, the youngish black

man—a broad six feet two inches with a beard and billowing hair, both hands shoved into the pockets of a bulky military jacket—seemed menacingly close. After a few more quick glimpses, she picked up her pace and was soon running in earnest. Within seconds she disappeared into a cross street.

—Brent Staples, "Black Men and Public Space"

Words like *victim* and phrases like "came upon her" lead us to assume the narrator is scary and perhaps dangerous. We don't know why he is walking on the deserted street because he hasn't told us: he simply begins with the moment he and the woman encounter each other. For his purposes, that's all the audience needs to know at first, and details of his physical appearance that explain the woman's response come later, after he tells us about the encounter. Had he given us those details at the outset, the narrative would not have been nearly so effective. In a way, Staples lets the story sneak up on us, as the woman apparently felt he had on her.

Other times you'll need to provide more background information, as an MIT professor does when she uses an anecdote to introduce an essay about young children's experiences with electronic toys. First the writer tells us a little about Merlin, the computer tic-tac-toe game that the children in her anecdote play with. As you'll see, the anecdote would be hard to follow without the introduction:

Among the first generation of computational objects was Merlin, which challenged children to games of tic-tac-toe. For children who had only played games with human opponents, reaction to this object was intense. For example, while Merlin followed an optimal strategy for winning tic-tac-toe most of the time, it was programmed to make a slip every once in a while. So when children discovered strategies that allowed them to win and then tried these strategies a second time, they usually would not work. The machine gave the impression of not being "dumb enough" to let down its defenses twice. Robert, seven, playing with his friends on the beach, watched his friend Craig perform the "winning trick," but when he tried it, Merlin did not slip up and the game ended in a draw. Robert, confused and frustrated, threw Merlin into the sand and said, "Cheater. I hope your brains break." He was overheard by Craig and Greg, aged six and eight, who salvaged the by-now very sandy toy and took it upon themselves to set Robert straight. "Merlin doesn't know if it cheats," says Craig. "It doesn't know if you break it, Robert. It's not alive." Greg adds, "It's smart enough to make the right kinds of noises. But it doesn't really know if it loses. And when it cheats, it don't even know it's cheating." Jenny, six, interrupts with disdain: "Greg, to cheat you have to know you are cheating. Knowing is part of cheating."

— Sherry Turkle, "Cuddling Up to Cyborg Babies"

Opening and Closing with Narratives

Narratives are often useful as **BEGINNINGS** to essays and other kinds of writing. Everyone likes a good story, so an interesting or pithy narrative can be a good way to get your audience's attention. In the following introductory paragraph, a historian tells a gruesome but gripping story to attract our attention to a subject that might not otherwise merit our interest, bubonic plague:

299–306

> In October 1347, two months after the fall of Calais, Genoese trading ships put into the harbor of Messina in Sicily with dead and dying men at the oars. The ships had come from the Black Sea port of Caffa (now Feodosiya) in the Crimea, where the Genoese maintained a trading post. The diseased sailors showed strange black swellings about the size of an egg or an apple in the armpits and groin. The swellings oozed blood and pus and were followed by spreading boils and black blotches on the skin from internal bleeding. The sick suffered severe pain and died quickly, within five days of the first symptoms. As the disease spread, other symptoms of continuous fever and spitting of blood appeared instead of the swellings or buboes. These victims coughed and sweated heavily and died even more quickly, within three days or less, sometimes in twenty-four hours. In both types everything that issued from the body — breath, sweat, blood from the buboes and lungs, bloody urine, and blood-blackened excrement — smelled foul. Depression and despair accompanied the physical symptoms, and before the end "death is seen seated on the face."
>
> — Barbara Tuchman, "This Is the End of the World: The Black Death"

Imagine how different the preceding paragraph would be if it weren't in the form of a narrative. Imagine, for example, that Tuchman began by defining bubonic plague. Would that have gotten your interest? The piece was written for a general audience; how might it have been different if it had been written for scientists? Would they need (or appreciate) the story told here?

306–10 Narrative can be a good way of ENDING a text, too, by winding up a discussion with an illustration of the main point. Here, for instance, is a concluding paragraph from an essay on American values and Las Vegas weddings.

> I sat next to one . . . wedding party in a Strip restaurant the last time I was in Las Vegas. The marriage had just taken place; the bride still wore her dress, the mother her corsage. A bored waiter poured out a few swallows of pink champagne ("on the house") for everyone but the bride, who was too young to be served. "You'll need something with more kick than that," the bride's father said with heavy jocularity to his new son-in-law; the ritual jokes about the wedding night had a certain Panglossian character, since the bride was clearly several months pregnant. Another round of pink champagne, this time not on the house, and the bride began to cry. "It was just as nice," she sobbed, "as I hoped and dreamed it would be."
>
> —Joan Didion, "Marrying Absurd"

No doubt Didion makes her points about American values clearly and cogently in the essay. But concluding with this story lets us *see* (and hear) what she is saying about Las Vegas wedding chapels, which sell " 'niceness,' the facsimile of proper ritual, to children who do not know how else to find it, how to make the arrangements, how to do it 'right.' "

Considering the Rhetorical Situation

As a writer or speaker, you need to think about the message that you want to articulate, the audience you want to reach, and the larger context you are writing in.

PURPOSE   Your purpose will affect the way you use narrative. For example, in an essay about seat belt laws, you might tell about the painful rehabilitation of a teenager who was not wearing a seat belt and was injured in an accident in order to persuade readers that seat belt use should be mandatory.

3–4

AUDIENCE   Whom do you want to reach, and do you have an anecdote or other narrative that will help them understand your topic or persuade them that your argument has merit?

5–8

GENRE   Does your genre require you to include narrative? A memoir about an important event might be primarily narrative, whereas a reflection about an event might focus more on the significance of the event than on what happened.

9–11

STANCE   What is your stance, and do you have any stories that would help you convey that stance? A funny story, for example, can help create a humorous stance.

12–15

MEDIA / DESIGN   In a print or spoken text, you will likely be limited to brief narratives, perhaps illustrated with photos or other images. In an electronic text, you might have the option of linking to full-length narratives or visuals available on the web.

16–18

IF YOU NEED MORE HELP

See also the **PROCESSES** chapters if you are assigned to write a narrative essay and need help drafting, revising, and so on. Two special kinds of narratives are **LAB REPORTS** (which use narrative to describe the steps in an experiment from beginning to end) and **RÉSUMÉS** (which essentially tell the story of the work we've done, at school and on the job).

249
173–82

222–29

41 Reading Strategies

We read newspapers and websites to learn about the events of the day. We read cookbooks to find out how to make brownies and textbooks to learn about history, chemistry, and other academic topics. We read short stories for pleasure — and, in literature classes, to analyze plot, setting, character, and theme. And as writers, we read our own drafts to make sure they say what we mean and to make sure they're correct. In other words, we read in various ways for many different purposes. But almost all of us could benefit from learning to read more effectively.

Taking Stock of Your Reading

One way to become a better reader is to understand your reading process; if you know what you do when you read, you're in a better position to decide what you need to change or improve. Consider the answers to the following questions:

- What do you read — for pleasure? for work? for school? for something else? Consider all the sorts of reading you do: books, magazines, newspapers, websites, *Facebook*, texting, blogs, instructions.

- When you're facing a reading assignment, what do you do? Do you do certain things to get comfortable? Do you play music or seek quiet? Do you plan your reading time or set reading goals for yourself? Do you flip through or skim the text before settling down to read it or just start at the beginning and work through it?

- When you begin to read something for an assignment, do you make sure you understand the purpose of the assignment — why you must read this text? Do you ever ask your instructor (or whoever else assigned the reading) what its purpose is?

- How do you motivate yourself to read material you don't have any interest in? How do you deal with boredom while reading?

- Does your mind wander? If you realize that you haven't been paying attention and don't know what you just read, what do you do?

- Do you ever highlight, underline, or annotate text as you read? Do you take notes? If so, what do you mark or write down? Why?

- When you read text you don't understand, what do you do?

- As you anticipate and read an assigned text, what attitudes or feelings do you typically have? If they differ from reading to reading, why do they?

- What do you do when you've finished reading an assigned text? Write out notes? Think about what you've just read? Move on to the next task? Something else?

- How well do your reading processes work for you, both in school and otherwise? What would you like to change?

The rest of this chapter offers advice and strategies that you may find helpful as you work to improve your reading skills.

Reading Strategically

Academic reading is challenging because it makes several demands on you at once. Textbooks present new vocabulary and concepts, and picking out the main ideas can be difficult. Scholarly articles present content and arguments you need to understand, but they often assume readers already know key concepts and vocabulary and so don't generally provide background information. As you read more texts in an academic field and participate in its conversations, the reading will become easier, but in the meantime you can develop strategies that will help you to read carefully and critically.

Different texts require different kinds of effort. Some texts can be read fairly quickly, if you're reading to get a general overview. Most of the time, though, you need to read carefully, matching the pace of your reading to the difficulty of the text. To read with a critical eye, you can't be in too much of a hurry. You'll likely need to skim the text for an overview of the basic ideas and then go back to read carefully. And then you may read the text again. That is true for visual as well as verbal texts — you'll often need to get an overview of a text and then reread to pay close attention to its details.

Preparing to Read

To learn, we need to place new information into a context of what we already know. For example, to understand photosynthesis, we need to already know something about plants, energy, and air, among other things. To learn a new language, we draw on similarities and differences between it and any other languages we know. A method of bringing to conscious attention our current knowledge on a topic and of helping us articulate our purposes for reading is a list-making process called KWL+. To use it, create a table with three columns:

K: What I Know	W: What I Want to Know	L: What I Learned

Before you begin reading a text, list in the "K" column what you already know about the topic. Brainstorm ideas, and list terms or phrases that come to mind. Then group them into categories. Also before reading, or after reading the first few paragraphs, list in the "W" column questions you have that you expect, want, or hope to be answered as you read. Number or reorder the questions by their importance to you.

Then read the text. As you read or afterward, list in the "L" column what you learned from the text. Compare your "L" list with your "W" list to see what you still want or need to know — and what you learned that you didn't expect.

Previewing a Text

It's usually a good idea to start by skimming a text: read the title and sub-title, any headings, the first and last paragraphs, the first sentences of all the other paragraphs. Study any illustrations and other visuals. Your goal is to get a sense of where the text is heading. At this point, don't stop to look up unfamiliar words; just mark them somehow (such as with underlining, highlighting, or electronic annotations), and look them up later.

Considering the Rhetorical Situation

As a reader, you need to think about the message that the writer wants to articulate, the intended audience, and the larger context in which the text was created.

PURPOSE   What is the writer's purpose? To entertain? inform? persuade readers to think something or take some action? What is *your* purpose for reading this text? ▌ 3–4

AUDIENCE   Who is the intended audience? Are you a member of that group? If not, should you expect that you'll need to look up unfamiliar terms or concepts or that you'll run into assumptions you don't necessarily share? ▌ 5–8

GENRE   What is the genre? Is it a report? an argument? an analysis? something else? Knowing the genre can help you anticipate certain key features. ▌ 9–11

STANCE   Who is the writer, and what is his or her stance? Critical? Curious? Opinionated? Objective? Passionate? Indifferent? Something else? Knowing the stance affects the way you understand a text, whether you're inclined to agree or disagree, to take it seriously, and so on. ▌ 12–14

MEDIA / DESIGN   What is the medium, and how does it affect the way you read? If it's a print text, what do you know about the publisher? If it's on the web, who sponsors the site, and when was it last updated? Are there any headings, summaries, color, or boxes that highlight key parts of the text? ▌ 15–18

Thinking about Your Initial Response

It's usually good to read a text first just to get a sense of it. Some readers find it helps to make brief notes about their first response to a text, noting their reaction and thinking a little about why they reacted as they did:

- *What are your initial reactions?* Describe both your intellectual reaction and any emotional reaction. Identify places in the text that caused you to react as you did. If you had no particular reaction, note that.

- *What accounts for your reaction?* Do you agree or disagree with the writer or have a different perspective? Why? Are your reactions rooted in personal experiences? positions you hold? As much as possible, you want to keep your opinions from coloring your analysis, so it's important to try to identify those opinions up front.

Annotating

Many readers find it helps to annotate as they read: highlighting key words, phrases, sentences; connecting ideas with lines or symbols; writing comments or questions in the margin or on sticky notes; circling new words so you can look up the definitions later; noting anything that seems noteworthy or questionable. Annotating forces you to read for more than just the surface meaning. Especially when you are going to be writing about or responding to a text, annotating creates a record of things you may want to refer to.

Annotate as if you're having a conversation with the author, someone you take seriously but whose words you do not accept without question. Put your part of the conversation in the margin, asking questions, talking back: "What's this mean?" "So what?" "Says who?" "Where's evidence?" "Yes!" "Whoa!" or even ☺ or ☹ or texting shorthand like LOL or INTRSTN. If you're using online sources, you may be able to copy them and annotate them electronically. If so, make your annotations a different color from the text itself.

What you annotate depends on your **PURPOSE** or what you're most interested in. If you're analyzing an argument, you would probably underline any **THESIS STATEMENT** and then the **REASONS AND EVIDENCE** that support the statement. It might help to restate those ideas in your own words, in the margins—in order to put them in your own words, you need to understand them! If you are trying to **IDENTIFY PATTERNS**, you might highlight each pattern in a different color or mark it with a sticky note and write any questions or notes about it in that color.

3–4

313–15
326–34

408–9

There are some texts that you cannot annotate, of course: library books, some materials you read on the web, and so on. Then you will need to use sticky notes or make notes elsewhere, and you might find it useful to keep a reading log for that purpose.

Coding

You may also find it useful to record your responses to your reading as you go through a text by using a coding system — for example, using "X" or "?" to indicate passages that contradict your assumptions or puzzle you. You can make up your own coding system, of course, but you could start with this one*:

- ✔ Confirms what you thought
- X Contradicts what you thought
- ? Puzzles you
- ?? Confuses you
- ☆ Strikes you as important
- → Is new or interesting to you

You might also circle new words that you'll want to look up later and highlight or underline key phrases.

---

*Adapted from *Subjects Matter: Every Teacher's Guide to Content-Area Reading* by Harvey Daniels and Steven Zemelman.

A Sample Annotated Text

Here is an annotated passage from Lawrence Lessig's essay "Some Like It Hot." These annotations rephrase key definitions, identify the essay's thesis and main ideas, ask questions, and comment on issues raised in the essay. Annotating the entire essay, which appears on pages 127–31, would provide a look at Lessig's ideas and a record of the experience of reading the essay—useful for both understanding it and analyzing it.

Piracy— unauthorized use of the artistic work of others.

"Content industry"—new term. Film, music, and so on? Doesn't include books and magazines?

Thesis: "Big media" are all based on piracy.

Hollywood film industry started in order to avoid Edison's patents. What were they for? Cameras and projectors? Is this true?

Record-industry piracy.

Player pianos?

If <u>piracy</u> means using the creative property of others without their permission, then the history of the <u>content industry</u> is a history of piracy. <u>Every important sector of big media today—film, music, radio, and cable TV—was born of a kind of piracy</u>. The consistent story is how each generation welcomes the pirates from the last. Each generation—until now.

<u>The Hollywood film industry was built by fleeing pirates.</u> Creators and directors migrated from the East Coast to California in the early twentieth century in part to escape controls that film patents granted the inventor Thomas Edison. These controls were exercised through the Motion Pictures Patents Company, a monopoly "trust" based on Edison's creative property and formed to vigorously protect his patent rights.

California was remote enough from Edison's reach that filmmakers like Fox and Paramount could move there and, without fear of the law, pirate his inventions. Hollywood grew quickly, and enforcement of federal law eventually spread west. But because patents granted their holders a truly "limited" monopoly of just seventeen years (at that time), the patents had expired by the time enough federal marshals appeared. A new industry had been founded, in part from the piracy of Edison's creative property.

<u>Meanwhile, the record industry grew out of another kind of piracy.</u> At the time that Edison and Henri Fourneaux invented machines for reproducing music (Edison the phonograph; Fourneaux the <u>player piano</u>), the law gave composers the exclusive right to

control copies and public performances of their music. Thus, in 1900, if I wanted a copy of Phil Russel's 1899 hit, "Happy Mose," the law said I would have to pay for the right to get a copy of the score, and I would also have to pay for the right to perform it publicly.

But what if I wanted to record "Happy Mose" using Edison's phonograph or Fourneaux's player piano? Here the law stumbled. If I simply sang the piece into a recording device in my home, it wasn't clear that I owed the composer anything. And more important, it wasn't clear whether I owed the composer anything if I then made copies of those recordings. Because of this gap in the law, I could effectively use someone else's song without paying the composer anything. The composers (and publishers) were none too happy about this capacity to pirate.

In 1909, Congress closed the gap in favor of the composer and the recording artist, amending <u>copyright law</u> to make sure that composers would be paid for "mechanical reproductions" of their music. But rather than simply granting the composer complete control over the right to make such reproductions, Congress gave recording artists a right to record the music, at a price set by Congress, after the composer allowed it to be recorded once. This is the part of copyright law that makes cover songs possible. Once a composer authorizes a recording of his song, others are free to record the same song, so long as they pay the original composer a fee set by the law. So, by limiting musicians' rights — by <u>partially pirating</u> their creative work — record producers and the public benefit.

—Lawrence Lessig, "Some Like It Hot"

Is copyright law different for books and other printed matter?

Partial piracy? Not sure about this — when artists use a song, they pay a fee but don't need permission. The composer doesn't have complete control. So it's piracy, but not completely?

Playing the Believing and Doubting Game

259–61 ○

One way to think about your response to a text is to **LIST** or **FREEWRITE** as many reasons as you can think of for believing what the writer says and then as many as you can for doubting it. First, write as if you agree with everything in the writer's argument; look at the world from his or her perspective, trying to understand the writer's premises and reasons for arguing as he or she does even if you strongly disagree. Then, write as if you doubt everything in the text: try to find every flaw in the argument, every possible way it can be refuted—even if you totally agree with it. Developed by writing theorist Peter Elbow, the believing and doubting game helps you consider new ideas and question ideas you already have—and at the same time see where you stand in relation to the ideas in the text you're reading.

Reflecting, Rereading, Persisting

Let's face it: Some texts are difficult. You may have no interest in the subject matter, or understanding the text requires knowledge you don't have, or you don't have a clear sense of why you have to read the text at all. Whatever the reason, reading such texts can be a challenge. Here are some tips for dealing with them:

Look for something familiar.   Difficult texts are often difficult and seem boring because we don't know what we need to know in order to read them effectively. By skimming the headings, the abstract or introduction, and the conclusion, you may find something that relates to knowledge you already have — and being aware of that prior knowledge can help you see how this new material relates to it.

Reread.   Reading a text the first time through is like driving to an unfamiliar destination on roads you've never traveled: you don't know where you're headed, you don't recognize anything along the way, and you're not sure how long getting there will take. As you drive the route again, though, you see landmarks along the way; you know where you're going. When you must read a difficult text, sometimes you need to get through it once just to understand what it is saying. On the second reading, look for parts of the text that relate to other parts, to other texts or course information, or to other knowledge you have.

Be persistent.   Studies reveal that students who do not do well in school attempt to read a difficult text and respond, "I don't understand this text. I'm too dumb to get it." And they quit reading. Successful students, on the other hand, see difficult texts as challenges: "I'm going to keep working on this text until I make sense of it." Remember that reading is an active process, and the more you work to control your reading processes, the more successful you will be.

Thinking about How the Text Works: What It Says, What It Does

Sometimes you'll need to think about how a text works, how its parts fit together. You may be assigned to analyze a text, or you may just need to make sense of a difficult text, to think about how the ideas all relate to one another. Whatever your purpose, a good way to think about a text's structure is by OUTLINING it, paragraph by paragraph. If you're interested in analyzing its ideas, look at what each paragraph *says*; if, on the other hand, you're concerned with how the ideas are presented, pay attention to what each paragraph *does*.

263–64

What it says.   Write a sentence that identifies what each paragraph says. Once you've done that for the whole text, look for patterns in the topics the writer addresses. Pay attention to the order in which the topics are presented. Also look for gaps, ideas the writer has left unsaid. Such paragraph-by-paragraph outlining of the content can help you see how the writer has arranged ideas and how that arrangement builds an argument or develops a topic. Here, for example, is such an outline of Lawrence

Lessig's essay (the left column refers to paragraph numbering noted in the full version of the essay on pages 127–31):

1	Every major type of media bases its development on piracy, the unauthorized use of artists' work.
2–3	To escape patents that restricted the copying of innovations in filmmaking, the movie industry moved from the East Coast to California.
4–5	Copyright law gave composers control over the performance of their music—but because it didn't cover the recording of music and the sale of copies of the recordings, it allowed piracy in the record industry.
6	Congress eventually changed the law, allowing musicians to record a song without the composer's permission if they paid the composer a fee.
7–11	When a radio station plays a song, it pays the composer but not the recording artist, thus pirating the artist's work.
12, 13	Cable TV has pirated works, too, by paying networks nothing for their broadcasts—despite protests by broadcasters and copyright owners.
14	Congress eventually extended the copyright law to cable TV, forcing the cable companies to pay for their broadcasts at a price controlled by Congress in order to protect the innovations of the cable industry.
15	The history of the major media industries suggests that piracy is not necessarily "plainly wrong."
16, 17	Peer-to-peer file sharing, like the earlier media-industry innovations, is being used to share artistic content and avoid industry controls, but it differs from the early cable industry in that it is not selling any content.
18	P2P file sharing provides access to music that can no longer be purchased, music that copyright holders want to share, and music that is no longer copyrighted.
19	P2P file sharing, like the earlier innovations, is the result of new technology, and it raises a similar question: how can it best be used without penalizing the artists whose works are "pirated"?
20	Copyright law must balance the protection of artists' works with the innovation in technologies, a process that takes time.

What it does.   Identify the function of each paragraph. Starting with the first paragraph, ask, What does this paragraph do? Does it introduce a topic? provide background for a topic to come? describe something? define something? entice me to read further? something else? What does the second paragraph do? the third? As you go through the text, you may identify groups of paragraphs that have a single purpose. For an example, look at this functional outline of Lessig's essay (again, the numbers on the left refer to the paragraphs):

1	Defines the key term, *piracy*, and illustrates the thesis using the history of four media industries in the United States.
2–3	Tells the history of the first medium, film, by focusing on piracy as a major factor in its development.
4–6	Tells the history of the second medium, the recording industry, again by focusing on the role of piracy in its development.
7–11	Tells the history of the third medium, radio, focusing on the role of piracy in its development.
12–14	Tells the history of the fourth medium, cable TV, focusing on the role of piracy in its development.
15	Offers conclusions about piracy based on the similar roles played by piracy in the histories of the four media.
16–17	Compares the current controversy over piracy in peer-to-peer file sharing on the internet with the role of piracy in the earlier media.
18	Describes the benefits of P2P file sharing.
19–20	Compares those benefits with those of the other media and offers a conclusion in the form of a problem to be solved.

Summarizing

Summarizing a text can help you both to see the relationships among its ideas and to understand what it's saying. When you **SUMMARIZE**, you restate a text's main ideas in your own words, leaving out most examples and other details. Here's a summary of Lawrence Lessig's essay:

470–71

> In his essay "Some Like It Hot," Lawrence Lessig argues that the development of every major media industry is based on piracy, the unauthorized

use of artists' or inventors' work. First, the film industry flourished by evading restrictions on the copying of innovations in filmmaking. Then, the recording industry benefited from copyright laws that gave composers control over the performance of their music but not over the recording of it or the sale of the recordings. A law passed in 1909 in effect allows musicians to record a song without the composer's permission if they pay the composer a fee. According to Lessig, radio broadcasters benefit from piracy, too, every time they play a song recorded by someone other than the composer: they pay the composer a fee but not the recording artist. Finally, when it first started operating, cable TV benefited from piracy — by paying the networks nothing for their broadcasts. Congress eventually extended the copyright law, forcing cable companies to pay for the content they broadcast — but at a price controlled by Congress so that the networks wouldn't be able to drive the cable companies out of business. Peer-to-peer file sharing, like the early media industries, is being used to share artistic content and avoid industry controls on that sharing. It benefits the public by allowing access to music that is out of print, that copyright holders want to share, and that is no longer copyrighted. Therefore, Lessig argues, the public needs to figure out how to make file-sharing work without penalizing musicians by pirating their songs. Copyright law must balance the protection of artists' work with the encouragement of technological innovation.

Identifying Patterns

Look for notable patterns in the text: recurring words and their synonyms, as well as repeated phrases, metaphors and other images, and types of sentences. Some readers find it helps to highlight patterns in various colors. Does the author repeatedly rely on any particular writing strategies: **NARRATION? COMPARISON?** Something else?

387–95

348–55

It might be important to consider the kind of evidence offered: Is it more opinion than fact? Nothing but statistics? If many sources are cited, is the information presented in any predominant patterns: as **QUOTATIONS?** **PARAPHRASES? SUMMARIES?** Are there repeated references to certain experts or sources?

462–74

In visual texts, look for patterns of color, shape, and line. What's in the foreground, and what's in the background? What's completely visible, partly visible, or invisible? In both verbal and visual texts, look for omissions and anomalies. What isn't there that you would expect to find? Is there anything that doesn't really fit in?

If you discover patterns, then you need to consider what, if anything, they mean in terms of what the writer is saying. What do they reveal about the writer's underlying premises and beliefs? What do they tell you about the writer's strategies for persuading readers to accept the truth of what he or she is saying?

See how color coding William Safire's essay on the Gettysburg Address reveals several patterns in the language Safire uses. In this excerpt from the essay, which appears in full in Chapter 8, religious references are colored yellow; references to a "national spirit," green; references to life, death, and rebirth, blue; and places where he directly addresses the reader, gray.

> But the selection of this poetic political sermon as the oratorical centerpiece of our observance need not be only an exercise. . . . now, as then, a national spirit rose from the ashes of destruction.
>
> Here is how to listen to Lincoln's all-too-familiar speech with new ears.
>
> In those 266 words, you will hear the word *dedicate* five times. . . .
>
> Those five pillars of dedication rested on a fundament of religious metaphor. From a president not known for his piety — indeed, often criticized for his supposed lack of faith — came a speech rooted in the theme of national resurrection. The speech is grounded in conception, birth, death, and rebirth.
>
> Consider the barrage of images of birth in the opening sentence. . . .
>
> Finally, the nation's spirit rises from this scene of death: "that this nation, under God, shall have a new birth of freedom." Conception, birth, death, rebirth. The nation, purified in this fiery trial of war, is resurrected. Through the sacrifice of its sons, the sundered nation would be reborn as one. . . .
>
> Do not listen on Sept. 11 only to Lincoln's famous words and comforting cadences. Think about how Lincoln's message encompasses but

goes beyond paying "fitting and proper" respect to the dead and the bereaved. His sermon at Gettysburg reminds "us the living" of our "unfinished work" and "the great task remaining before us"—to resolve that this generation's response to the deaths of thousands of our people leads to "a new birth of freedom."

The color coding helps us to see patterns in Safire's language, just as Safire reveals patterns in Lincoln's words. He offers an interpretation of Lincoln's address as a "poetic political sermon," and the words he uses throughout support that interpretation. At the end, he repeats the assertion that Lincoln's address is a sermon, inviting us to consider it differently. Safire's repeated commands ("Consider," "Do not listen," "Think about") offer additional insight into how he wishes to position himself in relation to his readers.

Count up the parts.   This is a two-step process. First, you count things: how many of this, how many of that. After you count, see what you can conclude about the writing. You may want to work with others, dividing up the counting.

- *Count words.* Count one-, two-, three-syllable words, repeated words, active and passive verbs, prepositions, jargon or specialized terms.

- *Count sentences.* Count the number of words in each sentence and the average number of words per sentence. Count the number of sentences in each paragraph. Count the number of simple sentences, compound sentences, complex sentences, and fragments. Count repeated phrases.

- *Count paragraphs.* Count the number of paragraphs, the average number of words and sentences per paragraph, the shortest and longest paragraphs. Consider the position of the longest and shortest paragraphs. Find parallel paragraph structures.

- *Count images.* List or mark images, similes, metaphors, and other figures of speech. Categorize them by meaning as well as type.

What do your findings tell you about the text? What generalizations can you make about it? Why did the author choose the words or images he or

rhetorical situations

genres

processes

strategies

research
MLA / APA

media / design

handbook

she used and in those combinations? What do those words tell you about the writer—or about his or her stance? Do your findings suggest a strategy, a plan for your analysis? For instance, Safire counts the number of times Lincoln uses *dedicate* and images of birth, death, and rebirth to argue something about Lincoln's speech and what it should mean to Safire's audience on the anniversary of 9/11.

Analyzing the Argument

All texts make some kind of argument, claiming something and then offering reasons and evidence as support for the claim. As a critical reader, you need to look closely at the argument a text makes—to recognize all the claims it makes, consider the support it offers for those claims, and decide how you want to respond. What do you think, and why? Here are some questions to consider when analyzing the argument:

- *What claim is the text making?* What is the writer's main point? Is it stated as a **THESIS** or only implied? Is it qualified somehow? If not, should it have been?

  313–15

- *How is the claim supported?* What **REASONS** does the writer provide for the claim, and what **EVIDENCE** is given for the reasons? What kind of evidence is it: facts? statistics? examples? expert opinion? images? How convincing do you find the reasons and evidence? Is there enough evidence?

  326–27
  327–34

- *What appeals besides* **LOGICAL** *ones are used?* Does the writer appeal to readers' **EMOTIONS?** Try to establish **COMMON GROUND?** Demonstrate his or her **CREDIBILITY** as trustworthy and knowledgeable? How successful are these appeals?

  324–34
  338
  334–35
  334–37

- *Are any* **COUNTERARGUMENTS** *acknowledged?* If so, are they presented accurately and respectfully? Does the writer accommodate them or try to refute them? How successfully does he or she deal with them?

  336–37

- *What outside sources of information does the writer cite?* What kinds of sources are they, and how credible do they seem? Are they current and authoritative? How well do they support the argument?

12–14 ■
- **What STANCE does the writer take toward readers?** What attitudes does it assume they hold? Do you feel that you are part of the intended audience? How can you tell?

338–40 ◆
Check for fallacies. FALLACIES are arguments that involve faulty reasoning. Because they often seem plausible, they can be persuasive. It is important, therefore, that you question the legitimacy of such reasoning when you run across it.

Considering the Larger Context

All texts are part of ongoing conversations with other texts that have dealt with the same topic. An essay arguing for handgun trigger locks is part of an ongoing conversation about gun control, which is itself part of a conversation on individual rights and responsibilities. Academic texts document their sources in part to show their relationship to the ongoing scholarly conversations on a particular topic. Academic reading usually challenges you to become aware of those conversations. And, in fact, any time you're reading to learn, you're probably reading for some larger context. Whatever your reading goals, being aware of that larger context can help you better understand what you're reading. Here are some specific aspects of the text to pay attention to:

- *Who else cares about this topic?* Especially when you're reading in order to learn about a topic, the texts you read will often reveal which people or groups are part of the conversation—and might be sources of further reading. For example, an essay describing the formation of Mammoth Cave could be of interest to geologists, spelunkers, travel writers, or tourists. If you're reading such an essay while doing research on the cave, you should consider how the audience addressed determines the nature of the information provided—and its suitability as a source for your research.

- *Ideas.* Does the text refer to any concepts or ideas that give you some sense that it's part of a larger conversation? An argument on airport security measures, for example, is part of larger conversations about government response to terrorism, the limits of freedom in a democracy, and the possibilities of using technology to detect weapons and explosives, among others.

- *Terms.* Is there any terminology or specialized language that reflects the writer's allegiance to a particular group or academic discipline? If you run across words like *false consciousness, ideology,* and *hegemony,* for example, you might guess the text was written by a Marxist scholar.

- *Citations.* Whom does the writer cite? Do the other writers have a particular academic specialty, belong to an identifiable intellectual school, share similar political leanings? If an article on politics cites Paul Krugman and Barbara Ehrenreich in support of its argument, you might assume the writer holds liberal opinions; if it cites Michelle Malkin and Sean Hannity, the writer is likely a conservative.

IF YOU NEED MORE HELP

See also the chapter on **EVALUATING SOURCES** for help analyzing the reliability of a text, and see the chapters on **ASSESSING YOUR OWN WRITING, GETTING RESPONSE AND REVISING,** and **EDITING AND PROOFREADING** for advice on reading your own writing.

453–56
269–74
275–81
282–86

Taking Essay Exams

Essay exams present writers with special challenges. You must write quickly, on a topic presented to you on the spot, to show your instructor what you know about a specific body of information. This chapter offers advice on how to take essay exams.

Considering the Rhetorical Situation

3–4 **PURPOSE**   In an essay exam, your purpose is to show that you have mastered certain material and that you can analyze and apply it in an essay. You may need to make an argument or simply to convey information on a topic.

5–8 **AUDIENCE**   Will your course instructor be reading your exam, or a TA? Sometimes standardized tests are read by groups of trained readers. What specific criteria will your audience use to evaluate your writing?

9–11 **GENRE**   Does the essay question specify or suggest a certain genre? In a literature course, you may need to write a compelling literary analysis of a passage. In a history course, you may need to write an argument for the significance of a key historical event. In an economics course, you may need to contrast the economies of the North and South before the Civil War. If the essay question doesn't specify a genre, look for key words such as *argue*, *evaluate*, or *explain*, which point to a certain genre.

12–15 **STANCE**   In an essay exam, your stance is usually unemotional, thoughtful, and critical.

rhetorical situations

genres

processes

strategies

research MLA / APA

media / design

handbook

MEDIA / DESIGN   Since essay exams are usually handwritten on lined paper or in an exam booklet, legible handwriting is a must.

16–18

Analyzing Essay Questions

Essay questions usually include key verbs that specify the kind of writing you'll need to do—argue a position, compare two texts, and so on. Following are some of the most common kinds of writing you'll be asked to do on an essay exam.

- *Analyze:* Break an idea, theory, text, or event into its parts and examine them. For example, a world history exam might ask you to **ANALYZE** European imperialism's effect on Africa in the late nineteenth century, and discuss how Africans responded.

52–86

- *Apply:* Consider how an idea or concept might work out in practice. For instance, a film studies exam might ask you to apply the concept of auteurism—a theory of film that sees the director as the primary creator, whose body of work reflects a distinct personal style—to two films by Clint Eastwood. An economics exam might ask you to apply the concept of opportunity costs to a certain supplied scenario.

- *Argue/prove/justify:* Offer reasons and evidence to support a position. A philosophy exam, for example, might ask you to **ARGUE** whether or not all stereotypes contain a "kernel of truth" and whether believing a stereotype is ever justified.

323–41

- *Classify:* Group something into categories. For example, a marketing exam might ask you to **CLASSIFY** shoppers in categories based on their purchasing behavior, motives, attitudes, or lifestyle patterns.

342–47

- *Compare/contrast:* Explore the similarities and/or differences between two or more things. An economics exam, for example, might ask you to **COMPARE** the effectiveness of patents and tax incentives in encouraging technological advances.

348–55

52–86
164–72

- *Critique:* **ANALYZE** and **EVALUATE** a text or argument, considering its strengths and weaknesses. For instance, an evolutionary biology exam might ask you to critique John Maynard Smith's assertion that "scientific theories say nothing about what is right but only about what is possible" in the context of the theory of evolution.

356–66

- *Define:* Explain what a word or phrase means. An art history exam, for example, might ask you to **DEFINE** negative space and discuss the way various artists use it in their work.

367–75

- *Describe:* Tell about the important characteristics or features of something. For example, a sociology exam might ask you to **DESCRIBE** Erving Goffman's theory of the presentation of self in ordinary life, focusing on roles, props, and setting.

164–72

- *Evaluate:* Determine something's significance or value. A drama exam, for example, might ask you to **EVALUATE** the setting, lighting, and costumes in a filmed production of *Macbeth*.

- *Explain:* Provide reasons and examples to clarify an idea, argument, or event. For instance, a rhetoric exam might ask you to explain the structure of the African American sermon and discuss its use in writings of Frederick Douglass and Martin Luther King Jr.

270–71

- *Summarize/review:* Give the major points of a text or idea. A political science exam, for example, might ask you to **SUMMARIZE** John Stuart Mill's concept of utilitarianism and its relation to freedom of speech.

- *Trace:* Explain a sequence of ideas or order of events. For instance, a geography exam might ask you to trace the patterns of international migration since 1970 and discuss how these patterns differ from those of the period between 1870 and World War I.

Some Guidelines for Taking Essay Exams

Before the exam

400–403

- *Read* over your class notes and course texts strategically, **ANNOTATING** them to keep track of details you'll want to remember.

rhetorical situations
genres
processes
strategies
research MLA / APA
media / design
handbook

- *Collaborate* by forming a **STUDY GROUP** to help one another master the course content.
○ 255–56

- *Review* key ideas, events, terms, and themes. Look for common themes and **CONNECTIONS** in lecture notes, class discussions, and any readings — they'll lead you to important ideas.
● 457–59

- **Ask** your instructor about the form the exam will take: how long it will be, what kind of questions will be on it, how it will be evaluated, and so on. Working with a study group, write questions you think your instructor might ask, and then answer the questions together.

- *Warm up* just before the exam by **FREEWRITING** for ten minutes or so to gather your thoughts.
○ 259–60

During the exam

- *Scan the questions* to determine how much each part of the test counts and how much time you should spend on it. For example, if one essay is worth 50 points and two others are worth 25 points each, you'll want to spend half your time on the 50-point question.

- *Read over* the entire test before answering any questions. Start with the question you feel most confident answering, which may or may not be the first question on the test.

- *Don't panic.* Sometimes when students first read an essay question, their minds go blank, but after a few moments they start to recall the information they need.

- *Plan.* Although you won't have much time for revising or editing, you still need to plan and allow yourself time to make some last-minute changes before you turn in the exam. So apportion your time. For a three-question essay test in a two-hour test period, you might divide your time like this:

Total Exam Time — 120 minutes
Generating ideas — 20 minutes (6–7 minutes per question)
Drafting — 85 minutes (45 for the 50-point question,
                    20 for each 25-point question)
Revising, editing, proofreading — 15 minutes

Knowing that you have built in time at the end of the exam period can help you remain calm as you write, as you can use that time to fill in gaps or reconsider answers you feel unsure about.

- **Jot down the main ideas** you need to cover in answering the question on scratch paper or on the cover of your exam book, number those ideas in the order you think makes sense — and you have an outline for your essay. If you're worried about time, plan to write the most important parts of your answers early on. If you don't complete your answer, refer your instructor to your outline to show where you were headed.

- **Turn the essay question into your introduction,** like this:

  Question: How did the outcomes of World War II differ from those of World War I?

  Introduction: The outcomes of World War II differed from those of World War I in three major ways: World War II affected more of the world and its people than World War I, distinctions between citizens and soldiers were eroded, and the war's brutality made it impossible for Europe to continue to claim cultural superiority over other cultures.

326–34 ◆

- **State your thesis explicitly,** provide REASONS and EVIDENCE to support your thesis, and use transitions to move logically from one idea to the next. Restate your main point in your conclusion. You don't want to give what one professor calls a "garbage truck answer," dumping everything you know into a blue book and expecting the instructor to sort it all out.

- **Write on every other line** and only on one side of each page so that you'll have room to make additions or corrections. If you're typing on a computer, double space.

- **If you have time left, go over your exam,** looking for ideas that need elaboration as well as for grammatical and punctuation errors.

After the exam.   If your instructor doesn't return your exam, consider asking for a conference to go over your work so you can learn what you did well and where you need to improve — important knowledge to take with you into your next exam.

part 5

Doing Research

We do research all the time, for many different reasons. We search the web for information about a new computer, ask friends about the best place to get coffee, try on several pairs of jeans before deciding which ones to buy. You have no doubt done your share of library research before now, and you probably have visited a number of schools' websites before deciding which college you wanted to attend. Research, in other words, is something you do every day. The following chapters offer advice on the kind of research you'll need to do for your academic work and, in particular, for research projects.

Doing Research

Developing a Research Plan **43**

When you need to do research, it's sometimes tempting to jump in and start looking for information right away. To do research well, however — to find appropriate sources and use them wisely — you need to work systematically. You need a research plan. This chapter will help you establish such a plan and then get started.

Establishing a Schedule

Doing research is complex and time-consuming, so it's good to establish a schedule for yourself. Research-based writing projects usually require you to come up with a topic (or to analyze the requirements of an assigned topic) and then come up with a research question to guide your research efforts. Once you do some serious, focused research to find the information you need, you'll be ready to turn your research question into a tentative thesis and sketch out a rough outline. After doing whatever additional research you need to fill in your outline, you'll write a draft — and get some response to that draft. Perhaps you'll need to do additional research before revising. Finally, you'll need to edit and proofread. And so you'll want to start by creating a timeline for getting all this work done, perhaps using the form on the next page.

Getting Started

Once you have a schedule, you can get started. The sections that follow offer advice on considering your rhetorical situation, coming up with a

rhetorical situations

genres

processes

strategies

research
MLA / APA

media / design

handbook

Scheduling a Research Project

Complete by:

Analyze your rhetorical situation. _____

Choose a possible topic or analyze the assignment. _____

Plan a research strategy and do _____
 preliminary research.

Come up with a research question. _____

Schedule interviews and other field research. _____

Find sources. _____

Read sources and take notes. _____

Do any field research. _____

Come up with a tentative thesis and outline. _____

Write a draft. _____

Get response. _____

Do any additional research. _____

Revise. _____

Prepare a list of works cited. _____

Edit. _____

Proofread the final draft. _____

Submit the final draft. _____

topic, and doing preliminary research; developing a research question, a tentative thesis, and a rough outline; and creating a working bibliography and keeping track of your sources. The chapters that follow offer guide-lines for **FINDING SOURCES**, **EVALUATING SOURCES**, and **SYNTHESIZING IDEAS**.

432–52
453–56
457–61

Considering the Rhetorical Situation

As with any writing task, you need to start by considering your purpose, your audience, and the rest of your rhetorical situation:

PURPOSE   Is this project part of an assignment—and if so, does it specify any one purpose? If not, what is your broad purpose? <u>To inform?</u> argue? entertain? a combination?

3–4

AUDIENCE   To whom are you writing? What does your audience likely know about your topic, and is there any background information you'll need to provide? What opinions or attitudes do your readers likely hold? What kinds of evidence will they find persuasive? How do you want them to respond to your writing?

5–8

GENRE   Are you writing to report on something? To compose a profile? To make a proposal? An argument? What are the requirements of your genre in terms of the number and kind of sources you must use?

9–11

STANCE   What is your attitude toward your topic? What accounts for your attitude? How do you want to come across? Curious? Critical? Positive? Something else?

12–15

MEDIA / DESIGN   What medium or media will you use? Print? Spoken? Electronic? Will you need to create any charts, photographs, video, presentation software slides, or other visuals?

16–18

Coming Up with a Topic

If you need to choose a topic, consider your interests as they relate to the course for which you're writing. What do you want to learn about? What do you have questions about? What topics from the course have you found intriguing? What community, national, or global issues do you care about?

    If your topic is assigned, you need to make sure you understand exactly what it asks you to do. Read the assignment carefully, looking for keywords: does it ask you to **ANALYZE, COMPARE, EVALUATE, SUMMARIZE,** or **ARGUE?** If the assignment offers broad guidelines but allows you to choose within them, identify the requirements and the range of possible topics and define your topic within those constraints.

52–86
348–55
164–72
470–71
323–41

For example, in an American history course, your instructor might ask you to "discuss social effects of the Civil War." Potential but broad topics might include poverty among Confederate soldiers or former slave-holders, the migration of members of those groups to Mexico or Northern cities, the establishment of independent African American churches, or the spread of the Ku Klux Klan — to name only a few of the possibilities.

Narrow the topic. As you consider possible topics, look for ways to narrow your topic's focus to make it specific enough to discuss in depths. For example:

> **Too general:** fracking
>
> **Still too general:** fracking and the environment
>
> **Better:** the potential environmental effects of extracting natural gas from under ground by hydraulic fracturing, or fracking

If you limit your topic, you can address it with specific information that you'll be more easily able to find and manage. In addition, a limited topic will be more likely to interest your audience than a broad topic that forces you to use abstract, general statements. For example, it's much harder to write well about "the environment" than it is to address a topic that covers a single environmental issue.

Think about what you know about your topic. Chances are you already know something about your topic, and articulating that knowledge can help you see possible ways to focus your topic or come up with potential sources of information. 259–62 ○ FREEWRITING, LISTING, CLUSTERING, and LOOPING are all good ways of tapping your knowledge of your topic. Consider where you might find information about it: Have you read about it in a textbook? Heard stories about it on the news? Visited websites focused on it? Do you know anyone who knows about this topic?

Consulting with Librarians and Doing Preliminary Research

Consulting with a reference librarian at your school and doing some preliminary research in the library can save you time in the long run. Reference librarians can direct you to the best scholarly sources for your topic and help you focus your topic by determining appropriate search terms and keywords. They can also help you choose the most appropriate reference works, sources that provide general overviews of the scholarship in a field. General internet searches can be time-consuming, as they often result in thousands of possible sites — too many to weed out efficiently, either by revising your search terms or by going through the sites themselves, many of which are unreliable. Library databases, on the other hand, include only sources that already have been selected by experts, and searches in them usually present manageable numbers of results.

Wikipedia can often serve as a jumping-off point for preliminary research, but since its entries are written and edited by people who may not have expertise in the subject, it is not considered a reliable academic source. Specialized encyclopedias, however, usually present subjects in much greater depth and provide more scholarly references that might suggest starting points for your research. Even if you know a lot about a subject, doing preliminary research can open you to new ways of seeing and approaching it, increasing your options for developing and narrowing your topic.

At this stage, pay close attention to the terms used to discuss your topic. These terms could be keywords that you can use to search for information on your topic in library catalogs, in databases, and on the web.

Find Keywords Using Word Clouds

One way to find keywords to help you narrow and focus your topic is to create a word cloud, a visual representation of words used in a text; the more often a word is used, the larger it looks in the word cloud. Several websites, including *Tagxedo*, *Wordle*, and *TagCrowd*, let you create word clouds. Examining a word cloud created from an article in a reference work may help you see what terms are used to discuss your topic — and may help you see new possible ways to narrow it. Here, for example, is a word cloud derived from an article in *Scientific American* discussing fracking. Many of the terms — *fracking, water, gas, wells, drilling* — are just what you'd expect. However, some terms—*Ingraffea, Marcellus, cementing*—may be unfamiliar and lead to additional possibilities for research. For instance,

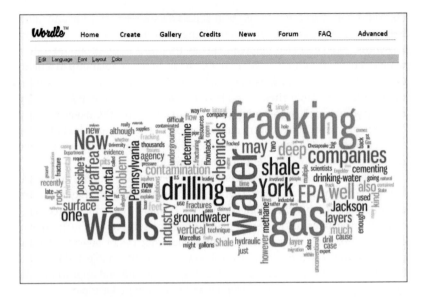

Ingraffea refers to an expert on fracking whose publications might be worth examining, while *cementing* refers to an important and controversial aspect of the hydraulic fracturing process.

Coming Up with a Research Question

Once you've surveyed the territory of your topic, you'll likely find that your understanding of your topic has become broader and deeper. You may find that your interests have changed and your research has led to surprises and additional research. That's okay: as a result of exploring avenues you hadn't anticipated, you may well come up with a better topic than the one you'd started with. At some point, though, you need to come up with a research question—a specific question that you will then work to answer through your research.

To write a research question, review your analysis of the **RHETORICAL SITUATION,** to remind yourself of any time constraints or length considerations. Generate a list of questions beginning with *What? When? Where? Who?*

How? Why? Would? Could? and *Should?* Here, for example, are some questions about the tentative topic "the potential environmental effects of extracting natural gas through the process of hydraulic fracturing, or fracking":

> *What* are the environmental effects of fracking?
>
> *When* was fracking introduced as a way to produce natural gas?
>
> *Where* is fracking done, and how does this affect the surrounding people and environment?
>
> *Who* will benefit from increased fracking?
>
> *How* much energy does fracking use?
>
> *Why* do some environmental groups oppose fracking?
>
> *Would* other methods of extracting natural gas be safer?
>
> *Could* fracking cause earthquakes?
>
> *Should* fracking be increased?

Select one question from your list that you find interesting and that suits your rhetorical situation. Use the question to guide your research.

Drafting a Tentative Thesis

Once your research has led you to a possible answer to your research question, try formulating that answer as a tentative **THESIS**. You need not be committed to the thesis; in fact, you should not be. The object of your research should be to learn about your topic, not to find information that simply supports what you already think you believe. Your tentative thesis may (and probably will) change as you learn more about your subject, consider the many points of view on it, and reconsider your topic and, perhaps, your goal: what you originally planned to be an argument for considering other points of view may become a call to action. However tentative, a thesis allows you to move forward by clarifying your purpose for doing research. Here are some tentative thesis statements on the topic of fracking:

313–15

> Fracking is a likely cause of earthquakes in otherwise seismically stable regions of the country.
>
> The federal government should strictly regulate the production of natural gas by fracking.

Fracking can greatly increase our supplies of natural gas, but other methods of producing energy should still be pursued.

As with a research question, a tentative thesis should guide your research efforts—but be ready to revise it as you learn still more about your topic. Research should be a process of **INQUIRY** in which you approach your topic with an open mind, ready to learn and possibly change. If you hold too tightly to a tentative thesis, you risk focusing only on evidence that supports your view, making your writing biased and unconvincing.

251–54 ○

Creating a Rough Outline

263–64 ○

After you've created a tentative thesis, write out a rough **OUTLINE** for your research project. Your outline can be a simple list of topics you want to explore, something that will help you structure your research efforts and organize your notes and other materials. As you read your sources, you can use your outline to keep track of what you need to find and where the information you do find fits into your argument. Then you'll be able to see if you've covered all the ideas you intended to explore—or whether you need to rethink the categories on your outline.

Keeping a Working Bibliography

A working bibliography is a record of all the sources you consult. You should keep such a record so that you can find sources easily when you need them and then cite any that you use. Your library likely offers tools to store source information you find in its databases and catalog, and software such as *Zotero* can also help you save, manage, and cite your sources. You may find it useful to print out bibliographical data you find useful or to keep your working bibliography on index cards or in a notebook. However you decide to compile your working bibliography, include all the information you'll need later to document any sources you use; follow the **DOCUMENTATION** style you'll use when you write so that you won't need to

480–83 ●

rhetorical situations

genres

processes

strategies

research MLA / APA

media / design

handbook

Information for a Working Bibliography

FOR A BOOK

Library call number
Author(s) or editor(s)
Title and subtitle
Publication information: city, publisher, year of publication
Other information: edition, volume number, translator, and so on
If your source is an essay in a collection, include its author, title, and page numbers.

FOR A SOURCE FROM A DATABASE

Publication information for the source, as listed above
Name of database
DOI (digital object identifier) or URL of original source, such as the periodical in which an article was published. (for APA style)
Stable URL or permalink for database
Date you accessed source

FOR AN ARTICLE IN A PRINT PERIODICAL

Author(s)
Title and subtitle
Name of periodical
Volume number, issue number, date
Page numbers

FOR A WEB SOURCE

URL
Author(s) or editor(s) if available
Name of site
Sponsor of site
Date site was first posted or last updated
Date you accessed site
If the source is an article or book reprinted on the web, include its title, the title and publication information of the periodical or book where it was first published, and any page numbers.

go back to your sources to find the information. Some databases make this step easy by preparing citations in several styles that you can copy and paste.

On the previous page is most of the basic information you'll want to include for each source in your working bibliography. Go to wwnorton.com/write/fieldguide for templates you can use to keep track of this information.

Keeping Track of Your Sources

- *Staple together photocopies and printouts.* It's easy for individual pages to get shuffled or lost on a desk or in a backpack. Keep a stapler handy, and fasten pages together as soon as you copy them or print them out.

- *Bookmark web sources* or save them using a free bookmark management tool. For database sources, use the DOI or stable URL, permalink, or document URL (the terms used by databases vary) — not the URL in the "Address" or "Location" box in your browser, which will expire after you end your online session.

- *Label everything.* Label your copies with the source's author and title.

- *Highlight sections you plan to use.* When you sit down to draft, your goal will be to find what you need quickly, so as soon as you decide you might use a source, highlight the paragraphs or sentences that you think you'll use. If your instructor wants copies of your sources to see how you used them, you've got them ready.

- *Use your rough outline to keep track of what you've got.* In the margin of each highlighted section, write the number or letter of the outline division to which the section corresponds. (It's a good idea to write it in the same place consistently so you can flip through a stack of copies and easily see what you've got.) Alternatively, attach sticky notes to each copy, using a different color for each main heading in your outline.

rhetorical situations

genres

processes

strategies

research
MLA / APA

media / design

handbook

- *Keep everything in an online folder, file folder, or box.* That way, even though your research material may not look organized, it will all be in one place—and if you highlight, number, and use sticky notes, your material will be organized and you'll be better prepared to write a draft. This folder or box will also serve you well if you are required to create a portfolio that includes your research notes, copies of sources, and drafts.

- *Use a reference management system.* Web-based reference or citation management systems allow you to create and organize a personal database of resources. You can import references from databases to a personal account, organize them, and draft citations in various formats. *RefWorks, EndNote, Mendeley, CiteULike,* and *Zotero* are five such systems; check with your librarian to see what system your library supports, or search online, as several of them are available for free.

IF YOU NEED MORE HELP

See the guidelines on **FINDING SOURCES** once you're ready to move on to in-depth research and those on **EVALUATING SOURCES** for help thinking critically about the sources you find.

432–52
453–56

44 Finding Sources

To analyze media coverage of the 2012 Democratic National Convention, you examine news stories and blogs published at the time. To write an essay interpreting a poem by Maya Angelou, you study the poem and read several critical interpretations in literary journals. To write a report on career opportunities in psychology, you interview a graduate of your university who is working in a psychology clinic. In each of these cases, you go beyond your own knowledge to consult additional sources of information.

This chapter offers guidelines for locating a range of sources—print and online, general and specialized, published and firsthand. Keep in mind that as you do research, finding and **EVALUATING SOURCES** are two activities that usually take place simultaneously. So this chapter and the next one go hand in hand.

453–56

Kinds of Sources

Primary and secondary sources.   Your research will likely lead you to both primary and secondary sources. *Primary sources* include historical documents, literary works, eyewitness accounts, field reports, diaries, letters, and lab studies, as well as any original research you do through interviews, observation, experiments, or surveys. *Secondary sources* include scholarly books and articles, reviews, biographies, textbooks, and other works that interpret or discuss primary sources. Novels and films are primary sources; articles interpreting them are secondary sources. The Declaration of Independence is a

rhetorical situations

genres

processes

strategies

research MLA / APA

media / design

handbook

primary historical document; a historian's description of the events surrounding the Declaration's writing is secondary. A published report of scientific findings is primary; a critique of that report is secondary.

Whether a work is considered primary or secondary sometimes depends on your topic and purpose: if you're analyzing a poem, a critic's article interpreting the poem is a secondary source — but if you're investigating that critic's work, the article would be a primary source for your own study and interpretation.

Primary sources are useful because they offer subjects for firsthand study, whereas secondary sources can help you understand and evaluate primary source material.

Scholarly and popular sources.   Scholarly sources are written by academic experts or scholars in a particular discipline and are *peer-reviewed* — evaluated by other experts in the same discipline for their factual accuracy and lack of bias. They are also written largely *for* experts in a discipline, as a means of sharing research, insights, and in-depth analysis with one another; that's why they must meet high standards of accuracy and objectivity and adhere to the discipline's accepted research methods, including its style for documenting sources. Scholarly articles are usually published in academic journals; scholarly books may be published by university presses or by other academically focused publishers.

Popular sources include just about all other online and print publications, from websites to magazines to books written for nonspecialists. These sources generally explain or provide opinion on current events or topics of general interest; when they discuss scholarly research, they tend to simplify the concepts and facts, providing definitions, narratives, and examples to make them understandable to nonspecialist audiences. They are often written by journalists or other professional writers who may specialize in a particular area but who report or comment on the scholarship of others rather than doing any themselves. Their most important difference from scholarly sources is that popular sources are not reviewed by other experts in the field being discussed, although editors or fact-checkers review the writing before it's published.

In most of your college courses, you'll be expected to rely primarily on scholarly sources rather than popular ones. However, if you're writing about a very current topic or need to provide background information on a topic, a mix of scholarly and popular sources may be appropriate. Here's a guide to determining whether or not a potential source is scholarly.

IDENTIFYING SCHOLARLY SOURCES: WHAT TO LOOK FOR

- *Author.* Look for the author's scholarly credentials, including his or her affiliations with academic or other research-oriented institutions.

- *Peer review.* Look for a list of reviewers at the front of the journal or on the journal's or publisher's website. If you don't find one, the source is probably not peer-reviewed.

- *Source citations.* Look for a detailed list of works cited or references at the end of the source and citations either parenthetically within the text or in footnotes or endnotes. (Popular sources may include a reference list but seldom cite sources within the text, except in signal phrases.)

- *Publisher.* Look for publishers that are professional scholarly organizations, such as the Modern Language Association or the Organization of American Historians, that are affiliated with universities or colleges, or that have a stated academic mission.

- *Language and content.* Look for abstracts (one-paragraph summaries of the contents) at the beginning of articles and for technical or specialized language and concepts that readers are assumed to be familiar with.

- *Other clues.* Look for little or no advertising on websites or within the journal; for a plain design with few or no illustrations, especially in print sources; and for listing in academic databases when you limit your search to *academic, peer-reviewed,* or *scholarly sources.*

To see how scholarly and popular sources differ in appearance, look at the Documentation Maps for scholarly journals (pp. 504 and 554) and popular magazines (pp. 505 and 549) and at the illustrations on the next page.

Identifying Scholarly and Popular Periodicals

Scholarly journal

KITAE SOHN

The Social Class Origins of U.S. Teachers, 1860–1920

1. Introduction

U.S. teachers have long been neglected in the history of education in spite of their important roles in education. Clifford calls this neglect a "virtual invisibility of teachers."[1] Hence, it is not surprising to encounter immense difficulty in tracing the social class origins of teachers in the late nineteenth and early twentieth centuries. This task is of great importance, however, because it allows one to understand the circumstances surrounding the individuals that entered the profession, to speculate on the quality of teaching, and to form an idea about class bias, intentional or not, inculcated by teachers in classrooms.

Research on the social class origins has been done for a century, as discussed in the next section. However, most of the research missed the broad picture of the profession. Some attention was paid to students in one college or normal school in one state even if few teachers attained such a high level of education at the time. In fact, a serious attempt was made to collect nationally representative data of teachers, but the data are severely biased. Of course, anecdotal evidence for the origins is scattered in qualitative historical materials such as diaries, letters, memoirs, and vacancy advertisements, but this evidence is highly selective. No one, to the best of my knowledge, has investigated the social class origins of U.S. teachers from 1860 to 1920 with nationally representative data, which would make one's understanding of the issue more comprehensive in terms of space and time.

This paper leads this line of study. In particular, this paper directly responds to the question raised by Perlmann and Margo, "Was teaching an engine of upward mobility into the middle class for relatively well-educated daughters of skilled workers and of low manual workers?" They propose using census data to answer this question because the data allow for a much wider perspective in terms of space and time. This paper closely follows their proposition and tries to answer the above question. Reaching further, OLS analyses are performed to

Author's note: This work was supported in part by the new faculty research program 2011 of Kookmin University in Korea. Address correspondence to Kitae Sohn, Department of Economics, Kookmin University, 861-1 Jeongneung-dong Seongbuk-gu Seoul 136-702, South Korea.

Journal of Social History vol. 45 no. 4 (2012), pp. 908–935
doi:10.1093/jsh/shr121

Plain cover and design suggest intellectual seriousness

Author's institutional affiliation

Formal documentation with endnotes

Paginated by volume, not issue

Popular magazine

GROWTH

"The first and simplest emotion which we discover in the human mind is, Curiosity." *Edmund Burke*

A leading researcher in the field of cognitive development says when children pretend, they're not just being silly—they're doing science

WHY PLAY IS SERIOUS

Walk into any preschool and you'll find toddling superheroes battling imaginary monsters. We take it for granted that young children play, especially, pretend. Why do they spend so much time in fantasy worlds?

People have suspected that play helps children learn, but until recently there was little research that showed this or explained why it might be true. In my lab at the University of California at Berkeley, we've been trying to explain how very young children can learn so much so quickly, and we've developed a new scientific approach to children's learning.

Where does pretending come in? It relates to what philosophers call "counterfactual" thinking, like Einstein wondering what would happen if a train went at the speed of light.

In one study, my student Daphna Buchsbaum introduced 3- and 4-year-olds to a stuffed monkey and a musical toy and told them, "It's Monkey's birthday, and this is a birthday machine we can use to sing to Monkey. It plays 'Happy Birthday' when you put a zando" (a funny-looking object) "on it like this." Then she held up a different object and explained that it wasn't a zando and therefore wouldn't make the music play. Then she asked some tricky counterfactual questions: "If this zando wasn't a zando, would the machine play

music or not?" What if the non-zando was a zando? About half the 3-year-olds answered correctly.

Then a confederate took away the toys and Daphna said, "We could just pretend that this box is the machine and that this block is a zando and this other one isn't. Let's put the blocks on the machine. What will happen next?" About half said the pretend zando made pretend music, while the pretend non-zando did nothing (well, pretend nothing, which is quite a concept even if you're older than 3).

We found children who were better at pretending could reason better about counterfactuals—they were better at thinking about different possibilities. And pretending play plays a crucial role in the latest understanding about how children learn. The idea is that children at play are like pint-sized scientists testing out their theories. They imagine ways the world could work and predict the pattern of data that would follow if their theories were true, and then compare that pattern with the pattern they actually see. Even toddlers turn out to be smarter than we would have thought if we ask them the right questions in the right way.

Play is under pressure right now, as parents and policymakers try to make preschools more like schools. But pretend play is not only important for kids; it's a crucial part of what makes all humans so smart.

What keeps Alison Gopnik up at night? Watch a conversation with her at Smithsonian.com/gopnik.

BY ALISON GOPNIK

Eye-catching cover and design intended to attract readers

Documentation with signal phrases only

Page numbers begin at 1 for each issue

Print and online sources.   Some sources are available only in print; some are available only online. But many print sources are also available on the web. You'll find print sources in your school's library, but chances are that many reference books in your library will also be available online. And when it comes to finding sources, it's likely that you'll search for most sources online. In general, for academic writing it's best to try to find most of your sources through the library's website rather than commercial search sites, which may lead you to unreliable sources and cause you to spend much more time sorting and narrowing search results. This chapter discusses four paths to finding sources you'll want to consult:

439–40 ●   **GENERAL REFERENCE WORKS,** for encyclopedias, dictionaries, and the like

441–42   **THE LIBRARY CATALOG,** for books

443–45   **INDEXES AND DATABASES,** for periodicals

445–46   **SEARCH SITES AND SUBJECT DIRECTORIES,** for material on the web

Take a look at a sample search page from the catalog of one university library. This page offers several options for searching. The buttons on the left allow searches by type of publication and medium ("Books & more," "Articles & more," "eJournals & eBooks"), while additional buttons provide information about requesting material from Interlibrary Loan (for materials your library doesn't have); accessing library resources when you're off campus, and accessing various media, digital, and government document collections, among other options. The "Ask us" button can be very useful, as it permits email, texting, or phone conversations with reference librarians when you need help but aren't working in the library.

Typing a search term into "Research starting point" leads to a list of possible sources, as you'll see in the list of sources that came up when we searched for "fracking." As with most databases, the left-hand column allows searches to be further limited to sources whose full text is available online, to those in scholarly or other types of publications, and so on; this search result also offers related search terms that might help in refining your topic.

■ rhetorical situations   ▲ genres   ○ processes   ◆ strategies   ● research MLA / APA   ▢ media / design   ◣ handbook

A library catalog homepage that allows searches by type of publication and medium.

Results of a refined search for "fracking."

Searching Effectively

Whether you're searching for books, articles in periodicals, or material available on the web, chances are you'll conduct most of your search online. Most materials produced since the 1980s and most library catalogs are online, and most periodical articles can be found by searching electronic indexes and databases. In each case, you can search for authors, titles, or subjects.

When you're looking for books, articles, or web sources, you'll need to come up with *keywords*. Usually if you start with only one keyword, you'll end up with far too many results—tens of thousands of references when you're searching the web—so the key to searching efficiently is to come up with keywords and combinations of them that will focus your searches on the information you need. Be more general (*education Japan* instead of *secondary education Japan*) when you get too few sources; be more specific (*homeopathy* instead of *medicine*) when you get far too many sources. If you don't get results with one set of keywords, substitute synonyms (if *folk medicine* doesn't generate much information, try *home remedy*). Or look through the sources that turn up in response to other terms to see what keywords you might use in subsequent searches. Searching requires flexibility, in the words you use and the methods you try.

Most search sites have "advanced search" options that will help you focus your research. Many offer these options in preprogrammed forms, and some even allow you to ask questions in conversational language: *What did Thomas Jefferson write about slavery?* Others require that you enter certain commands to activate options. Specific commands will vary among search sites and within databases, but here are some of the most common ones:

- Type quotation marks around words to search for an exact phrase— "Thomas Jefferson."
- Type AND to specify that more than one keyword must appear in sources: Jefferson AND Adams. Some search engines require a plus sign instead: +Jefferson +Adams.

rhetorical situations

genres

processes

strategies

research MLA / APA

media / design

handbook

- Type OR if you're looking for sources that include any of several terms: Jefferson OR Adams OR Madison.

- Type NOT to find sources *without* a certain word: Jefferson NOT Adams. Some search engines call for a minus sign (actually, a hyphen) instead: +Jefferson –Adams.

- Type an asterisk to search for words in different form. For example, teach* will yield sources containing *teacher* and *teaching*.

Reference Works

The reference section of your school's library is the place to find encyclopedias, dictionaries, atlases, almanacs, bibliographies, and other reference works in print. Many of these sources are also online and can be accessed from any computer that is connected to the Internet. Others are available only in the library. Remember, though, that whether in print or online, reference works are only a starting point, a place where you can get an overview of your topic.

General reference works. Consult encyclopedias for general background information on a subject, dictionaries for definitions of words, atlases for maps and geographic data, and almanacs for statistics and other data on current events. These are some works you might consult:

The New Encyclopaedia Britannica

The Columbia Encyclopedia

Webster's Third New International Dictionary

Oxford English Dictionary

National Geographic Atlas of the World

Statistical Abstract of the United States

The World Almanac and Book of Facts

Caution: *Wikipedia* is a popular online research tool, but since anyone can edit its entries, you can't be certain of its accuracy. Use it for general overviews, but look elsewhere — including *Wikipedia's* own references and citations — for authoritative sources.

Specialized reference works. You can also go to specialized reference works, which provide in-depth information on a single field or topic. These may also include authoritative bibliographies, leading you to more specific works. A reference librarian can refer you to specialized encyclopedias in particular fields, but good places to start are online collections of many topic-specific reference works that offer overviews of a topic, place it in a larger context, and sometimes provide links to potential academic sources. Collections that are available through libraries include the following:

CQ Researcher offers in-depth reports on topics in education, health, the environment, criminal justice, international affairs, technology, the economy, and social trends. Each report gives an overview of a particular topic, outlines of the differing positions on it, and a bibliography of resources on it.

Credo Reference provides access to more than 550 reference works, including several general reference encyclopedias and dictionaries, as well as subject-specific works. Users may search for specific topics, and *Credo* provides concept maps that show relationships among topics visually and offer immediate access to entries discussing those topics.

Gale Virtual Reference Library offers thousands of full-text specialized encyclopedias, almanacs, articles, and ebooks.

Oxford Reference Online contains almost 200 dictionaries, encyclopedias, and other reference works on a wide variety of subjects, as well as timelines with links to each item mentioned on each timeline.

SAGE Reference Online includes over 250 encyclopedias and handbooks on topics in the social sciences.

Bibliographies. Bibliographies provide an overview of what has been published on a topic, listing published works along with the information you'll need to find each work. Some are annotated with brief summaries of each work's contents. You'll find bibliographies at the end of scholarly articles and books, and you can also find book-length bibliographies, both in the reference section of your library and online. Check with a reference librarian for bibliographies on your research topic.

Books / Searching the Library Catalog

The library catalog is your primary source for finding books. Almost all library catalogs are computerized and can be accessed through the library's website. You can search by author, title, subject, or keyword. The image below shows the result of a keyword search for material on art in Nazi Germany. This search of the library's catalog revealed forty items — print books, ebooks, and video recordings — on the topic; to access information on each one, the researcher must simply click on the title or thumbnail image. The image on the next page shows detailed information for one source: bibliographic data about author, title, and publication; related subject headings (which may lead to other useful materials in the library) — and more. Library catalogs also supply a call number, which identifies the book's location on the library's shelves.

Results of a keyword search for material on art in Nazi Germany.

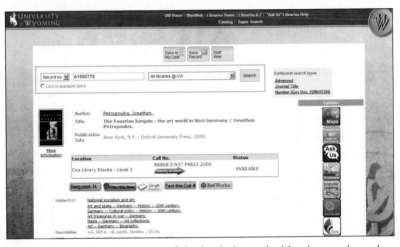

Detailed information about one of the books located with a keyword search.

Ebooks / Finding Books Online

Many books in the library catalog are available online. Some may be down-loaded to a tablet or mobile device. In addition, thousands of classic works that are in the public domain — no longer protected by copyright — may be read online. *Bartleby, Google Books, Open Library,* and *Project Gutenberg* are four collections of public-domain works. Here are some other sources of ebooks:

Hathi Trust Digital Library offers access to over 5 million ebooks, about half still under copyright protection, contributed by over sixty university libraries.

Internet Archive includes over 3 million ebooks, as well as audio, moving images, a live music archive, and the Way Back Machine, which archives historical webpages.

The *Gale Virtual Reference Library, Oxford Scholarship Online,* and *SAGE Reference Online* all contain large ebook collections.

Periodicals / Searching Indexes and Databases

To find journal, magazine, and newspaper articles, you will need to search periodical indexes and databases. Indexes provide listings of articles organized by topics; many databases provide the full texts. Some indexes are in print and can be found in the reference section of the library; most are online. Some databases are available for free; most of the more authoritative ones, however, are available only by subscription and so must be accessed through a library.

Many databases now include not only scholarly articles but also dissertations, theses, book chapters, book reviews, and conference proceedings. Dissertations and theses are formal works of scholarship done as requirements for graduate degrees; book reviews offer critical evaluations of scholarly and popular books; and conference proceedings are papers presented, usually orally, at scholarly meetings.

When you access a source through a database, the URL or link address is different each time you log in, so if you want to return to a source, look for a *stable URL, permalink,* or *document URL* option and choose it to copy and paste into your list of sources.

General indexes and databases. A reference librarian can help you determine which databases will be most helpful to you, but here are some useful ones:

> *Academic Search Complete* is a multidisciplinary index and database containing the full text of articles in nearly 9,000 journals and indexing of almost 13,000 journals, with abstracts of their articles.
>
> *EBSCOhost* provides interlinked databases of abstracts and full-text articles from a variety of periodicals.
>
> *FirstSearch* offers access to millions of full-text, full-image articles in dozens of databases covering many disciplines.
>
> *InfoTrac* offers over 20 million full-text articles in a broad spectrum of disciplines and on a wide variety of topics from nearly 6,000 scholarly and popular periodicals, including the *New York Times.*

JSTOR archives scanned copies of entire publication runs of scholarly journals in many disciplines, but it does not include current issues of the journals.

LexisNexis contains full-text publications and articles from a large number of sources—newspapers, business and legal resources, medical texts, and reference sources such as *The World Almanac* and the Roper public opinion polls.

ProQuest Central provides access to full-text articles from thousands of periodicals and newspapers from 1971 to the present, with many entries updated daily, and a large collection of dissertations and theses.

SIRS Issues Researcher contains records of articles from selected domestic and international newspapers, magazines, journals, and government publications.

Single-subject indexes and databases. The following are just a sample of what's available; check with a reference librarian for indexes and databases in the subject you're researching.

America: History and Life indexes scholarly literature on the history of the United States and Canada.

BIOSIS Previews provides abstracts and indexes for more than 5,500 sources on biology, botany, zoology, environmental studies, and agriculture.

ERIC is the U.S. Department of Education's Educational Resource Information Center database.

Historical Abstracts includes abstracts of articles on the history of the world, excluding the United States and Canada, since 1450.

Humanities International Index contains bibliographic references to more than 2,300 journals dealing with the humanities.

MLA International Bibliography indexes scholarly articles on modern languages, literature, folklore, and linguistics.

PsycINFO indexes scholarly literature in a number of disciplines relating to psychology.

PubMed includes millions of citations for biomedical literature.

Print indexes.   You many need to consult print indexes to find articles published before the 1980s. Here are six useful ones:

> *The Readers' Guide to Periodical Literature* (print, 1900–; online, 1983–)
>
> *Magazine Index* (print, 1988–; online via InfoTrac, 1973–)
>
> *The New York Times Index* (print and online, 1851–)
>
> *Humanities Index* (print, 1974–; online, 1984–)
>
> *Social Sciences Index* (print, 1974–; online, 1983–)
>
> *General Science Index* (print, 1978–; online, 1984–)

Images, Sound, and More

Your library likely subscribes to various databases that allow you to find and download video, audio, and image files. Here is a sampling:

> *AP Images* provides access to photographs taken for the Associated Press, the cooperative agency of more than 6.700 newspapers and radio and television stations worldwide.
>
> *ArtStor* provides images in the arts, architecture, humanities, and sciences.
>
> *Dance in Video* offers more than 600 videos of dance productions and documentaries on dance.
>
> *Education in Video* includes more than 3,000 videos of teaching demonstrations, lectures, documentaries, and footage of students and teachers in their classrooms.
>
> *Naxos Music Library* contains more than 60,000 classical, jazz, and world music recordings, as well as libretti and synopses of more and 700 operas and other background information.
>
> *Theatre in Video* provides videos of more than 250 performances of plays and more than 100 film documentaries.

The following indexes and databases are freely available on the internet:

> *Infomine* contains "useful Internet resources such as databases, electronic journals, electronic books, bulletin boards, mailing lists, online library card catalogs, articles, directories of researchers, and many other types of information."

ipl2 is a searchable, annotated subject directory of thousands of websites selected and evaluated by librarians for their usefulness to users of public libraries.

The WWW Virtual Library is a catalog of websites on a wide range of subjects, compiled by volunteers with expertise in particular subject areas.

CSA Discovery Guides provide comprehensive information on current issues in the arts and humanities, natural sciences, social sciences, and technology, with an overview of each subject, key citations with abstracts, and links to websites.

The Voice of the Shuttle: Web Site for Humanities Research offers information on subjects in the humanities, organized to mirror "the way the humanities are organized for research and teaching as well as the way they are adapting to social, cultural, and technological changes."

The Library of Congress offers online access to information on a wide range of subjects, including academic subjects, as well as prints, photographs, and government documents.

JURIST is a university-based online gateway to authoritative legal instruction, information, scholarship, and news.

Searching the Web

The web provides access to countless sites containing information posted by governments, educational institutions, organizations, businesses, and individuals. Such websites are different from other sources — including the kinds of online sources you access through indexes and databases — in two key ways: (1) their content varies greatly in its reliability and (2) they are not stable: what you see on a site today may be different (or gone) tomorrow. Anyone who wants to can post material on the web, so you need to evaluate carefully what you find there to eliminate sources that are not current, lack credibility, or are primarily advertisements or promotional in nature.

Because it is so vast and dynamic, finding what you want on the web can be a challenge. The primary way of finding information on the web is with a search site. There are several ways of searching the web:

- *Keyword searches.* *Google, Yahoo!, Bing* and most other search sites all scan the web looking for keywords that you specify.

- *Subject directories.* *Google, Yahoo!,* and some other search sites offer directories that arrange information by topics, much like a library cataloging system. Such directories allow you to broaden or narrow your search if you need to — for example, a search for "birds" can be broadened to "animals" or narrowed to "blue-footed booby."

- *Metasearches.* *Yippy, Dogpile, Copernic Agent,* and *SurfWax* are metasearch sites that allow you to use several search engines simultaneously. They are best for searching broadly; use a single search site for the most precise results.

- *Academic searches.* You may find more suitable results for academic writing at *Google Scholar,* a search site that finds scholarly literature, including peer-reviewed papers, technical reports, and abstracts, or at *Scirus,* which finds peer-reviewed documents on scientific, technical, and medical topics. In general, though, use academic databases whenever possible.

- *Blog searches.* Several search sites can help you find blog posts, including *Google Blog Search, Technorati,* and *Icerocket.*

- **Twitter searches.** In addition to *Twitter* Search, you can find *Twitter* content through search sites such as *Twazzup, Collecta,* and *Scoopler.*

Each search site and metasearch site has its own protocols for searching; most have an "advanced search" option that will help you search more productively. Remember, though, that you need to be careful about EVALUATING SOURCES that you find on the web because the web is unregulated and no one independently verifies the information posted on its sites.

453–56

Doing Field Research

Sometimes you'll need to do your own research, to go beyond the information you find in published sources and gather data by doing field research. Three kinds of field research you might want to consider are interviews, observations, and questionnaires.

Interviewing experts. Some kinds of writing—a profile of a living person, for instance—almost require that you conduct an interview. And sometimes you may just need to find information that you haven't been able to find in published sources. To get firsthand information on the experience of serving as a soldier in Afghanistan, you might interview your cousin who served a tour of duty there; to find current research on pesticide residues in food, you might need to interview a toxicologist. Whatever your goal, you can conduct interviews in person, using video-calling software, by telephone, through email, or by mail. In general, you will want to use interviews to find information you can't find elsewhere. Below is some advice on planning and conducting an interview.

Before the interview

3–4

1. Once you identify someone you want to interview, email or phone to ask the person, stating your **PURPOSE** for the interview and what you hope to learn.
2. Once you've set up an appointment, send a note or email confirming the time and place. If you wish to record the interview, be sure to ask for permission to do so. If you plan to conduct the interview by mail or email, state when you will send your questions.
3. Write out questions. Plan questions that invite extended response and supporting details: "What accounts for the recent spike in gasoline prices?" forces an explanation, whereas "Is the recent spike in gas prices a direct result of global politics?" is likely to elicit only a yes or a no.

At the interview

4. Record the full name of the person you interview, along with the date, time, and place of the interview; you'll need this information to cite and document the interview accurately.

5. Take notes, even if you are recording the interview.
6. Keep track of time: don't take more than you agreed to beforehand unless both of you agree to keep talking. End by saying "thank you" and offering to provide a copy of your final product.

After the interview

7. Flesh out your notes with details as soon as possible after the interview, while you still remember them. What did you learn? What surprised you? Summarize both the interviewee's words and your impressions.
8. Make sure you've reproduced quotations from the interview accurately and fairly. Avoid editing quotations in ways that distort the speaker's intended meaning.
9. Be sure to send a thank you note or email.

Observation.   Some writing projects are based on information you get by observing something. For a sociology report, you may observe how students behave in large lectures. For an education course, you may observe one child's progress as a writer over a period of time. The following advice can help you conduct observations.

Before observing

1. Think about your research PURPOSE: What are you looking for? What do you expect to find? How will your presence as an observer affect what you observe? What do you plan to do with what you find?

3–4

2. If necessary, set up an appointment. You may need to ask permission of the people you wish to observe and of your school as well. (Check with your instructor about your school's policy in this area.) Be honest and open about your goals and intentions; college students doing research assignments are often welcomed where others may not be.

While observing

3. If you're taking notes on paper, you may want to divide each page down the middle vertically and write only on the left side of the page, reserving the right side for information you will fill in later. If you're using a laptop, you can set up two columns or a split screen.

4. Note descriptive details about the setting. What do you see? What do you hear? Do you smell anything? Get down details about color, shape, size, sound, and so on. Consider photographing or making a sketch of what you see.

367–75
5. Who is there, and what are they doing? **DESCRIBE** what they look like, and make notes about what they say. Note any significant demographic details — about gender, race, occupation, age, dress, and so on.

6. What is happening? Who's doing what? What's being said? Make note

387–95
of these kinds of **NARRATIVE** details.

After observing

7. As soon as possible after you complete your observations, use the right side of your notes to fill in gaps and include additional details.

52–86
8. **ANALYZE** your notes, looking for patterns. Did some things appear or happen more than once? Did anything stand out? surprise or puzzle you? What did you learn?

Questionnaires and surveys.   Various kinds of questionnaires and surveys can provide information or opinions from a large number of people. For a political science course, you might conduct a survey to ask students who they plan to vote for. Or, for a marketing course, you might distribute a questionnaire asking what they think about an advertising campaign. The advice in this section will help you create useful questionnaires and surveys.

Define your goal.   The goal of a questionnaire or survey should be limited and focused, so that every question will contribute to your research question. Also, people are more likely to respond to a brief, focused survey.

Define your sample.   A survey gets responses from a representative sample of the whole group. The answers to these questions will help you define that sample:

1. Who should answer the questions? The people you contact should represent the whole population. For example, if you want to survey undergraduate students at your school, your sample should reflect

your school's enrollment in terms of gender, year, major, age, ethnicity, and so forth as closely as possible.

2. How many people make up a representative sample? In general, the larger your sample, the more the answers will reflect those of the whole group. But if your population is small—200 students in a history course, for example—your sample must include a large percentage of that group.

Decide on a medium.   Will you ask the questions face-to-face? over the phone? on a website such as *SurveyMonkey*? by mail? by email? Face-to-face questions work best for simple surveys or for gathering impersonal information. You're more likely to get responses to more personal questions with printed or online questionnaires, which should be neat and easy to read. Phone interviews may require well-thought-out scripts that anticipate possible answers and make it easy to record these answers.

Design good questions.   The way you ask questions will determine the usefulness of the answers you get, so take care to write questions that are clear and unambiguous. Here are some typical question types:

- *Multiple-choice*

  What is your current age?

  _____ 15–20   _____ 21–25   _____ 26–30   _____ 31–35   _____ Other

- *Rating scale*

  How would you rate the service at the campus bookstore?

  _____ Excellent   _____ Good   _____ Fair   _____ Poor

- *Agreement scale*

  How much do you agree with the following statements?

	Strongly Agree	Agree	Disagree	Strongly Disagree
The bookstore has sufficient numbers of textbooks available.	❐	❐	❐	❐

	Strongly Agree	Agree	Disagree	Strongly Disagree
Staff at the bookstore are knowledgeable.	❐	❐	❐	❐
Staff at the bookstore are courteous.	❐	❐	❐	❐

- *Open-ended*

  How often do you visit the campus bookstore?

  How can the campus bookstore improve its service?

Include all potential alternatives when phrasing questions to avoid biasing the answers. And make sure each question addresses only one issue — for example, "bookstore staff are knowledgeable and courteous" could lead to the response "knowledgeable, agree; courteous, disagree."

When arranging questions, place easier ones at the beginning and harder ones near the end (but if the questions seem to fall into a different natural order, follow it). Make sure each question asks for information you will need — if a question isn't absolutely necessary, omit it.

Include an introduction.   Start by stating your survey's purpose and how the results will be used. It's also a good idea to offer an estimate of the time needed to complete the questions. Remind participants of your deadline.

Test the survey or questionnaire.   Make sure your questions elicit the kinds of answers you need by asking three or four people who are part of your target population to answer them. They can help you find unclear instructions, questions that aren't clear or that lack sufficient alternatives, or other problems that you should correct to make sure your results are useful. But if you change the questionnaire as a result of their responses, don't include their answers in your total.

IF YOU NEED MORE HELP

See **EVALUATING SOURCES** for help determining their usefulness. See also Chapter 47 for help **TAKING NOTES** on your sources.

453–56 ●
462–63

Evaluating Sources **45**

Searching the *Health Source* database for information on the incidence of meningitis among college students, you find seventeen articles. A *Google* search on the same topic produces over 10,000 hits. How do you decide which sources to read? This chapter presents advice on evaluating sources—first to determine whether a source might be useful for your purposes and is worth looking at more closely and then to read with a critical eye the ones you choose.

Considering Whether a Source Might Be Useful

Think about your PURPOSE.   Are you trying to persuade readers to believe or do something? to inform them about something? If the former, it will be especially important to find sources representing various stances; if the latter, you may need sources that are more factual or informative. Reconsider your AUDIENCE. What kinds of sources will they find persuasive? If you're writing for readers in a particular field, what counts as evidence in that field? Following are some questions that can help you judge whether a possible source you've found deserves your time and attention:

3–4

5–8

- *Is it reliable?* Is it SCHOLARLY? peer-reviewed? published in a reputable journal or magazine, or by a reputable publisher? Did you find it in a library database? on the web? Evaluating web-based texts may require more work and scrutiny than results from library databases. But whatever kind of search you do, the results need to be scanned to quickly evaluate their reliability.

433–35

- *Is it relevant?* How does the source relate to your purpose? What will it add to your work? Look at the title and at any introductory material— a preface, abstract, or introduction—to see what it covers.

- *What are the author's credentials?* What are the author's qualifications to write on the subject? Is he or she associated with a particular position on the issue? See whether the source mentions other works this author has written. In any case, you might do a web search to see what else you can learn about him or her.

12–15 ▪

- *What is the* STANCE? Consider whether a source covers various points of view or advocates one particular point of view. Does its title suggest a certain slant? If it's online, you might check to see whether it includes links to other sites and if so, what their perspectives are. You'll want to consult sources with a variety of viewpoints.

- *Who is the publisher or sponsor?* If it's a book, what kind of company published it; if an article, what kind of periodical did it appear in? Books published by university presses and articles in scholarly journals are reviewed by experts before they are published. Books and articles written for the general public typically do not undergo rigorous review—and they may lack the kind of in-depth discussion that is useful for research. If it's online, is the site maintained by an organization? an interest group? a government agency? an individual? Look for clues in the URL: *edu* is used mostly by colleges and universities, *gov* by government agencies, *org* by nonprofit organizations, *mil* by the military, and *com* by commercial organizations. Evaluate the publisher's or sponsor's motives: to present information evenhandedly? To promote a certain point of view, belief, or position? To sell something?

- *What is the level?* Can you understand the material? Texts written for a general audience might be easier to understand but not authoritative enough for academic work. Texts written for scholars will be more authoritative but may be hard to comprehend.

- *When was it published?* See when books and articles were published. Check to see when online sources were created and last updated. (If the site lists no date, see if links to other sites still work.) Recent does not necessarily mean better — some topics may require very current information whereas others may call for older sources.

- **Is it available?** Is it a source you can get hold of? If it's a book and your school's library doesn't have it, can you get it through interlibrary loan?

- **Does it include other useful information?** Is there a bibliography that might lead you to other sources? How current are the sources it cites?

Once you've decided that a source should be examined more closely, use the following questions to give it critical scrutiny.

Reading Sources with a Critical Eye

- **What ARGUMENTS does the author make?** Does the author present a number of different positions, or does he or she argue for a particular position? Do you need to **ANALYZE THE ARGUMENT?**

  ▲ 83–110

  ◆ 411–12

- **How persuasive do you find the argument?** What reasons and evidence does the author provide in support of any position(s)? Are there citations or links — and if so, are they credible? Is any evidence presented without citations? Do you find any of the author's assumptions questionable? How thoroughly does he or she consider opposing arguments?

- **What is the author's STANCE?** Does the author strive for objectivity, or does the content or language reveal a particular bias? Does the author consider opposing views and treat them fairly?

  ■ 12–15

- **Do you recognize ideas you've run across in other sources?** Does the source leave out any information or perspective that other sources include — or include any that other sources leave out?

- **Does this source support or challenge your own position—or does it do both?** Does it support your thesis? Offer a different argument altogether? Does it represent a position you may need to **ACKNOWLEDGE** or **REFUTE?** Don't reject a source just because it challenges your views; your sources should reflect a variety of views on your topic, showing that you've considered the subject thoroughly.

  ▲ 104

  ▲ 105

- **What can you tell about the intended AUDIENCE and PURPOSE?** Are you a member of the audience addressed — and if not, does that affect the

  ■ 5–8

  3–4

way you interpret what you read? Is the main purpose to inform readers about a topic or to argue a certain point?

462–74
475–79

IF YOU NEED MORE HELP

See **QUOTING, PARAPHRASING, AND SUMMARIZING** for help in taking notes on your sources and deciding how to use them in your writing. See also **ACKNOWLEDGING SOURCES, AVOIDING PLAGIARISM** for advice on giving credit to the sources you use.

rhetorical situations

genres

processes

strategies

research MLA / APA

media / design

handbook

Synthesizing Ideas **46**

To **ANALYZE** the works of a poet, you show how she uses similar images
in three different poems to explore a recurring concept. To solve a crime,
a detective studies several eyewitness accounts to figure out who did it.
To trace the history of photojournalism, a professor **COMPARES** the uses of
photography during the Civil War and during the Vietnam War. These are
all cases where someone *synthesizes* — brings together material from two
or more sources in order to generate new information or to support a new
perspective. When you do research, you need to go beyond what your
sources say; you need to use what they say to inspire and support *what
you want to say.* This chapter focuses on how to synthesize ideas you find
in other sources as the basis for your own ideas.

52–86

348–55

Reading for Patterns and Connections

Your task as a writer is to find as much information as you can on your
topic — and then to sift through all that you have found to determine and
support what you yourself will write. In other words, you'll need to synthesize ideas and information from the sources you've consulted to figure
out first what arguments *you* want to make and then to provide support
for those arguments.

When you synthesize, you group similar bits of information together,
looking for patterns or themes or trends and trying to identify the key
points. For example, researching the effectiveness of the SAT writing
exam you find several sources showing that scores correlate directly

with length and that a majority of U.S. colleges and universities have decided not to count the results of the test in their admission decisions. You can infer that the test is not yet seen as an effective measure of writing ability. Here are some tips for reading to identify patterns and connections:

- Read all your sources with an open mind. Withhold judgment, even of sources that seem wrong-headed or implausible. Don't jump to conclusions.

470–71
- Take notes and write a brief **SUMMARY** of each source to help you see relationships, patterns, and connections among your sources. Take notes on your own thoughts, too.

259–62
263–64
- Pay attention to your first reactions. You'll likely have many ideas to work with, but your first thoughts can often lead somewhere that you will find interesting. Try **FREEWRITING, CLUSTERING,** or **LISTING** to see where they lead. How do these thoughts and ideas relate to your topic? Where might they fit into your rough **OUTLINE?**

- Try to think creatively, and pay attention to thoughts that flicker at the edge of your consciousness, as they may well be productive.

- Be playful. Good ideas sometimes come when we let our guard down or take ideas to extremes just to see where they lead.

Ask yourself these questions about your sources:

- What sources make the strongest arguments? What makes them so strong?

- Do some arguments recur in several sources?

336
- Which arguments do you agree with? disagree with? Of those you disagree with, which ones seem strong enough that you need to **ACKNOWLEDGE** them in your text?

- Are there any disagreements among your sources?

- Are there any themes you see in more than one source?

- Are any data — facts, statistics, examples — or experts cited in more than one source?

rhetorical situations   genres   processes   strategies   research MLA / APA   media / design   handbook

- Do several of your sources use the same terms? Do they use the terms similarly, or do they use them in different ways?

- What have you learned about your topic? How have your sources affected your thinking on your topic? Do you need to adjust your THESIS? If so, how?

313–15

- Have you discovered new questions you need to investigate?

- Keep in mind your RHETORICAL SITUATION — have you found the information you need that will achieve your purpose, appeal to your audience, and suit your genre and medium?

1

What is likely to emerge from this questioning is a combination of big ideas, including new ways of understanding your topic and insights into recent scholarship about it, and smaller ones, such as how two sources agree with each other but not completely and how the information in one source supports or undercuts the argument of another. These ideas and insights will become the basis for your own ideas and for what *you* have to say about the topic.

Synthesizing Ideas Using Notes

You may find that identifying connections among your sources is easier if you examine them together rather than reading them one by one. For example, taking notes on note cards and then laying the cards out on a desk or table (or on the floor) lets you see passages that seem related. Doing the same with photocopies or printouts of your sources can help you identify similarities as well.

In doing research for an essay arguing that the sale of assault weapons should be banned, you might find several sources that address the scope of U.S. citizens' right to bear arms. Here are notes taken on three such sources: Joe Klein, a journalist writing in *Time.com*; Antonin Scalia, a U.S. Supreme Court justice, quoted in an online news article; and Drew Westen, a professor of psychology writing in a blog sponsored by *The New York Times*. Though the writers hold very different views, juxtaposing these

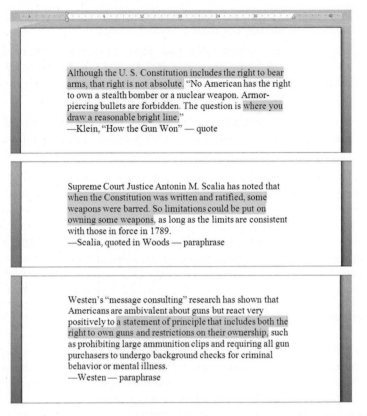

Although the U. S. Constitution includes the right to bear arms, that right is not absolute. "No American has the right to own a stealth bomber or a nuclear weapon. Armor-piercing bullets are forbidden. The question is where you draw a reasonable bright line."
—Klein, "How the Gun Won" — quote

Supreme Court Justice Antonin M. Scalia has noted that when the Constitution was written and ratified, some weapons were barred. So limitations could be put on owning some weapons, as long as the limits are consistent with those in force in 1789.
—Scalia, quoted in Woods — paraphrase

Westen's "message consulting" research has shown that Americans are ambivalent about guns but react very positively to a statement of principle that includes both the right to own guns and restrictions on their ownership, such as prohibiting large ammunition clips and requiring all gun purchasers to undergo background checks for criminal behavior or mental illness.
—Westen — paraphrase

notes and highlighting certain passages shows a common thread running through the sources. In this example, all three sources might be used to support the thesis that restrictions on the owning of weapons — but not an outright ban — are both constitutional and necessary.

Synthesizing Information to Support Your Own Ideas

87–118 If you're doing research to write a **REPORT,** your own ideas will be communicated primarily through which information you decide to include from the sources you cite and how you organize that information. If you're

rhetorical situations

genres

processes

strategies

research MLA / APA

media / design

handbook

writing a **TEXTUAL ANALYSIS,** your synthesis may focus on the themes, techniques, or other patterns you find. If you're writing a research-based **ARGUMENT,** on the other hand, your synthesis of sources must support the position you take in that argument. No matter what your genre, the challenge is to synthesize information from your research to develop ideas about your topic and then to support those ideas.

▲ 52–86

▲ 119–49

Entering the Conversation

As you read and think about your topic, you will come to an understanding of the concepts, interpretations, and controversies relating to your topic—and you'll become aware that there's a larger conversation going on. When you begin to find connections among your sources, you will begin to see your own place in that conversation, to discover your own ideas, your own stance on your topic. This is the exciting part of a research project, for when you write out your own ideas on the topic, you will find yourself entering that conversation. Remember that your **STANCE** as an author needs to be clear: simply stringing together the words and ideas of others isn't enough. You need to show readers *how* your source materials relate to one another and to your thesis.

▮ 12–15

IF YOU NEED MORE HELP

See Chapter 47, **QUOTING, PARAPHRASING, AND SUMMARIZING,** for help in integrating source materials into your own text. See also Chapter 48 on **ACKNOWLEDGING SOURCES, AVOIDING PLAGIARISM** for advice on giving credit to the sources you cite.

● 462–74

475–79

47 Quoting, Paraphrasing, and Summarizing

In an oral presentation about the rhetoric of Abraham Lincoln, you quote a memorable line from the Gettysburg Address. For an essay on the Tet Offensive in the Vietnam War, you paraphrase arguments made by several commentators and summarize some key debates about that war. Like all writers, when you work with the ideas and words of others, you need to clearly distinguish those ideas and words from your own and give credit to their authors. This chapter will help you with the specifics of quoting, paraphrasing, and summarizing source materials that you wish to use in your writing.

Taking Notes

When you find material you think will be useful, take careful notes. How do you determine how much or how little to record? You need to write down enough information so that when you refer to it later, you will be reminded of the main points and have a precise record of where the information comes from.

- *Use a computer file, note cards, or a notebook,* labeling each entry with the information that will allow you to keep track of where it comes from—author, title, and the pages or the URL (or DOI [digital object identifier]). You needn't write down full bibliographic information (you can abbreviate the author's name and title) since you'll include that information in your WORKING BIBLIOGRAPHY.

428–30

rhetorical situations

genres

processes

strategies

research MLA / APA

media / design

handbook

- *Take notes in your own words, and use your own sentence patterns.* If you make a note that is a detailed **PARAPHRASE,** label it as such so that you'll know to provide appropriate **DOCUMENTATION** if you use it.

467–70
480–83

- *If you find wording that you'd like to quote,* be sure to enclose it in quotation marks to distinguish your source's words from your own. Double-check your notes to be sure any quoted material is accurately quoted—and that you haven't accidentally **PLAGIARIZED** your sources.

475–79

- *Label each note with a subject heading* to relate it to a subject, supporting point, or other element in your essay. This will help you to sort your sources and match them up with your rough outline. Restrict each note to a single subject, and briefly cite your source in each one.

Here are a few examples of one writer's notes on a source discussing synthetic dyes, bladder cancer, and the use of animals to determine what causes cancers. Each note includes a subject heading and brief source information and identifies whether the source is quoted or paraphrased.

Synthetic dyes

The first synthetic dye was mauve, invented in 1854 and derived from coal. Like other coal-derived dyes, it contained aromatic amines.
Steingraber, "Pesticides," 976 —paraphrase

Synthetic dyes & cancer

Bladder cancer was common among textile workers who used dyes. Steingraber: "By the beginning of the twentieth century, bladder cancer rates among this group of workers had skyrocketed."
Steingraber, "Pesticides," 976 — paraphrase and quote

Synthetic dyes & cancer

In 1938, Wilhelm Hueper exposed dogs to aromatic amines and showed that the chemical caused bladder cancer.
Steingraber, "Pesticides," 976 —paraphrase

Deciding Whether to Quote, Paraphrase, or Summarize

266–68 ○

463–67 ●

When it comes time to **DRAFT,** you'll need to decide *how* to use the sources you've found—in other words, whether to quote, paraphrase, or summarize. You might follow this rule of thumb: **QUOTE** texts when the wording is worth repeating or makes a point so well that no rewording will do it justice, when you want to cite the exact words of a known authority on your topic, when an authority's opinions challenge or disagree with those of others, or when the source is one you want to emphasize. **PARAPHRASE**

467–70 ●

470–71 ●

sources that are not worth quoting but contain details you need to include. **SUMMARIZE** longer passages whose main points are important but whose details are not.

Quoting

Quoting a source is a way of weaving someone else's exact words into your text. You need to reproduce the source exactly, though you can modify it to omit unnecessary details (with ellipses) or to make it fit smoothly into your text (with brackets). You also need to distinguish quoted material from your own by enclosing short quotations in quotation marks, setting off longer quotes as a block, and using appropriate **SIGNAL PHRASES.**

471–74 ●

Incorporate short quotations into your text, enclosed in quotation marks. If you are following **MLA STYLE,** this rule holds for four typed lines or fewer; if using **APA STYLE,** as below, short means fewer than forty words.

484–532 ●

533–74

> Gerald Graff (2003) has argued that colleges make the intellectual life seem more opaque than it needs to be, leaving many students with "the misconception that the life of the mind is a secret society for which only an elite few qualify" (p. 1).

If you are quoting three lines or fewer of poetry, run them in with your text, enclosed in quotation marks. Separate lines with slashes, leaving one space on each side of the slashes.

Emma Lazarus almost speaks for the Statue of Liberty with the words inscribed on its pedestal: "Give me your tired, your poor, / Your huddled masses yearning to breathe free, / The wretched refuse of your teeming shore" (58).

Set off long quotations block style.   If you are using MLA style, set off quotations of five or more typed lines by indenting the quote one inch (or ten spaces) from the left margin. If you are using APA style, indent quotes of forty or more words one-half inch (or five-to-seven spaces) from the left margin. In either case, do not use quotation marks, and put any parenthetical citation *after* any end punctuation.

> Nonprofit organizations such as Oxfam and Habitat for Humanity rely on visual representations of the poor. What better way to get our attention, asks rhetorician Diana George:
>
>> In a culture saturated by the image, how else do we convince Americans that—despite the prosperity they see all around them—there is real need out there? The solution for most nonprofits has been to show the despair. To do that they must represent poverty as something that can be seen and easily recognized: fallen down shacks and trashed out public housing, broken windows, dilapidated porches, barefoot kids with stringy hair, emaciated old women and men staring out at the camera with empty eyes. (210)

If you are quoting four or more lines of poetry, they need to be set off block style in the same way.

Indicate any omissions with ellipses.   You may sometimes delete words from a quotation that are unnecessary for your point. Insert three ellipsis marks (leaving a space before the first and after the last one) to indicate the deletion. If you omit a sentence or more in the middle of a quotation, put a period before the three ellipsis dots. Be careful not to distort the source's meaning, however.

Faigley points out that Gore's "Information Superhighway" metaphor "associated the economic prosperity of the 1950s and . . . 1960s facilitated by new highways with the potential for vast . . . commerce to be conducted over the Internet" (253).

According to Welch, "Television is more acoustic than visual. . . . One can turn one's gaze away from the television, but one cannot turn one's ears from it without leaving the area where the monitor leaks its aural signals into every corner" (102).

Indicate additions or changes with brackets.   Sometimes you'll need to change or add words in a quote—to make the quote fit grammatically within your sentence, for example, or to add a comment. In the following example, the writer changes the passage "one of our goals" to fit the grammar of her sentences:

Writing about the dwindling attention among some composition scholars to the actual teaching of writing, Susan Miller notes that "few discussions of writing pedagogy take it for granted that one of [their] goals is to teach how to write" (480).

Here's an example of brackets used to add explanatory words to a quotation:

Barbosa observes that even Buarque's lyrics have long included "many a metaphor of *saudades* [yearning] so characteristic of *fado* music" (207).

Use punctuation correctly with quotations.   When you incorporate a quotation into your text, you have to think about the end punctuation in the quoted material and also about any punctuation you need to add when you insert the quote into your own sentence.

Periods and commas. With brief quotations, put periods or commas *inside* the quotation marks, except when you have a parenthetical citation at the end, in which case you put the period after the parentheses.

"Country music," Tichi says, "is a crucial and vital part of the American identity" (23).

With long quotes set off block style, however, there are no quotation marks, so the period goes *before* the citation, as shown in the example on page 465.

Question marks and exclamation points. These go *inside* closing quotation marks if they are part of the quoted material but *outside* when they are not. If there's a parenthetical citation at the end, it follows the closing quotation mark, and any punctuation that's part of your sentence comes after.

> Speaking at a Fourth of July celebration in 1852, Frederick Douglass asked, "What have I, or those I represent, to do with your national independence?" (35).

> Who can argue with W. Charisse Goodman's observation that media images persuade women that "thinness equals happiness and fulfillment" (53)?

Colons and semicolons. These always go *outside* closing quotation marks.

> It's hard to argue with W. Charisse Goodman's observation that media images persuade women that "thinness equals happiness and fulfillment"; nevertheless, American women today are more overweight than ever (53).

Paraphrasing

When you paraphrase, you restate information from a source in your own words, using your own sentence structures. Paraphrase when the source material is important but the original wording is not. Because it includes all the main points of the source, a paraphrase is usually about the same length as the original.

Here is a paragraph about synthetic dyes and cancer, followed by three example paraphrases. The first two demonstrate some of the challenges of paraphrasing:

ORIGINAL SOURCE

In 1938, in a series of now-classic experiments, exposure to synthetic dyes derived from coal and belonging to a class of chemicals called aromatic amines was shown to cause bladder cancer in dogs. These results helped explain why bladder cancers had become so prevalent among dyestuffs workers. With the invention of mauve in 1854, synthetic dyes began replacing natural plant-based dyes in the coloring of cloth and leather. By the beginning of the twentieth century, bladder cancer rates among this group of workers had skyrocketed, and the dog experiments helped unravel this mystery. The International Labor Organization did not wait for the results of these animal tests, however, and in 1921 declared certain aromatic amines to be human carcinogens. Decades later, these dogs provided a lead in understanding why tire-industry workers, as well as machinists and metalworkers, also began falling victim to bladder cancer: aromatic amines had been added to rubbers and cutting oils to serve as accelerants and antirust agents.

—Sandra Steingraber, "Pesticides, Animals, and Humans"

This paraphrase borrows too much of the language of the original or changes it only slightly, as the underlined words and phrases show.

UNACCEPTABLE PARAPHRASE: WORDING TOO CLOSE

<u>Now-classic experiments</u> in 1938 showed that when dogs were exposed to aromatic amines, chemicals used in <u>synthetic dyes derived from coal</u>, they developed bladder cancer. Similar cancers were <u>prevalent among dyestuffs workers</u>, and <u>these</u> experiments <u>helped</u> to <u>explain why</u>. Mauve, a synthetic dye, was invented in 1854, after which <u>cloth and leather</u> manufacturers replaced most of the natural plant-based dyes with synthetic dyes. <u>By the</u> early <u>twentieth century</u>, <u>this group of workers had skyrocketing</u> rates of bladder cancer, a <u>mystery</u> <u>the dog experiments helped to unravel</u>. As early as 1921, though, before the test results proved the connection, the International Labor Organization had labeled <u>certain aromatic amines</u> carcinogenic. Even so, <u>decades later</u> many metalworkers, machinists, and tire-industry workers began developing bladder cancer. The animal tests helped researchers understand that <u>rubbers and cutting oils</u> contained aromatic amines <u>as accelerants and antirust agents</u> (Steingraber 976).

This paraphrase uses original language but follows the sentence structure of Steingraber's text too closely.

UNACCEPTABLE PARAPHRASE: SENTENCE STRUCTURE TOO CLOSE

In 1938, several pathbreaking experiments showed that being exposed to synthetic dyes that are made from coal and belong to a type of chemicals called aromatic amines caused dogs to get bladder cancer.

These results helped researchers identify why cancers of the bladder had become so common among textile workers who worked with dyes. With the development of mauve in 1854, synthetic dyes began to be used instead of dyes based on plants in the dyeing of leather and cloth. By the end of the nineteenth century, rates of bladder cancer among these workers had increased dramatically, and the experiments using dogs helped clear up this oddity. The International Labor Organization anticipated the results of these tests on animals, though, and in 1921 labeled some aromatic amines carcinogenic. Years later these experiments with dogs helped researchers explain why workers in the tire industry, as well as metalworkers and machinists, also started dying of bladder cancer: aromatic amines had been put into rubbers and cutting oils as rust inhibitors and accelerants (Steingraber 976).

Patchwriting, a third form of unacceptable paraphrase, combines the other two. Composition researcher Rebecca Moore Howard defines it as "copying from a source text and then deleting some words, altering grammatical structures, or plugging in one-for-one synonym-substitutes." Even though the student in the example below cites the source, most of the language and structure are taken directly from the source without being identified through the use of quotation marks. (The source's exact words are shaded in yellow; paraphrases are in blue).

ORIGINAL SOURCE

In 1938, in a series of now-classic experiments, exposure to synthetic dyes derived from coal and belonging to a class of chemicals called aromatic amines was shown to cause bladder cancer in dogs. These results explain why bladder cancers had become so prevalent among dyestuffs workers.

PATCHWRITE

Scientists have known for a long time that chemicals in the environment can cause cancer. For example, in 1938, in a series of important experiments, being exposed to synthetic dyes made out of coal and belonging to a kind of chemicals called aromatic amines was shown to cause dogs to develop bladder cancer. These experiments explain why this type of cancer had become so common among workers who handled dyes.

Here is an acceptable paraphrase of the entire passage.

ACCEPTABLE PARAPHRASE

Biologist Sandra Steingraber explains that pathbreaking experiments in 1938 demonstrated that dogs exposed to aromatic amines (chemicals used in coal-derived synthetic dyes) developed cancers of the bladder that were similar to cancers common among dyers in the textile industry. After mauve, the first synthetic dye, was invented in 1854, leather and cloth manufacturers replaced most natural dyes made from plants with synthetic dyes, and by the early 1900s textile workers had very high rates of bladder cancer. The experiments with dogs proved the connection, but years before, in 1921, the International Labor Organization had labeled some aromatic amines carcinogenic. Even so, years later many metal-workers, machinists, and workers in the tire industry started to develop unusually high rates of bladder cancer. The experiments with dogs helped researchers understand that the cancers were caused by aromatic amines used in cutting oils to inhibit rust and in rubbers as accelerants (976).

Some guidelines for paraphrasing

- *Use your own words and sentence structure.* It is acceptable to use some words from the original, but as much as possible, the phrasing and sentence structures should be your own.

- *Put in quotation marks any of the source's original phrasing that you use.*

- *Indicate the source of your paraphrase.* Although the wording may be yours, the ideas and information come from another source; be sure to name the author and include an **IN-TEXT CITATION** to avoid the possibility of **PLAGIARISM.**

488–93 MLA
536–40 APA
475–79

Summarizing

A summary states the main ideas in a source concisely and in your own words. Unlike a paraphrase, a summary does *not* present all the details, and it is generally as brief as possible. Summaries may boil down an entire book or essay into a single sentence, or they may take a paragraph or more to present the main ideas. Here, for example, is a summary of the Steingraber paragraph:

> Steingraber explains that experiments with dogs demonstrated that aromatic amines, chemicals used in synthetic dyes, cutting oils, and rubber, cause bladder cancer (976).

In the context of an essay, the summary might take this form:

> Medical researchers have long relied on experiments using animals to expand understanding of the causes of disease. For example, biologist and ecologist Sandra Steingraber notes that in the second half of the nineteenth century, the rate of bladder cancer soared among textile workers. According to Steingraber, experiments with dogs demonstrated that synthetic chemicals in dyes used to color the textiles caused the cancer (976).

Some guidelines for summarizing

- *Include only the main ideas; leave out the details.* A summary should include just enough information to give the reader the gist of the original. It is always much shorter than the original, sometimes even as brief as one sentence.

- *Use your own words.* If you quote phrasing from the original, enclose the phrase in quotation marks.

- *Indicate the source.* Although the wording may be yours, the ideas and information come from another source. Name the author, either in a signal phrase or parentheses, and include an appropriate **IN-TEXT CITATION** to avoid the possibility of **PLAGIARISM**.

488–93 MLA
536–40 APA
475–79

Introducing Source Materials Using Signal Phrases

You need to introduce quotations, paraphrases, and summaries clearly, usually letting readers know who the author is—and, if need be, something about his or her credentials. Consider this sentence:

> Professor and textbook author Elaine Tyler May argues that many high school history books are too bland to interest young readers (531).

The beginning ("Professor and textbook author Elaine Tyler May argues") functions as a *signal phrase*, telling readers who is making the assertion and why she has the authority to speak on the topic—and making clear that everything between the signal phrase and the parenthetical citation comes from that source. Since the signal phrase names the author, the parenthetical citation includes only the page number; had the author not been identified in the signal phrase, she would have been named in the parentheses:

> Even some textbook authors believe that many high school history books are too bland to interest young readers (May 531).

MLA and APA have different conventions for constructing signal phrases. In MLA, the language you use in a signal phrase can be neutral — like X *says* or Y *thinks* or *according to* Z. Or it can suggest something about the **STANCE** — the source's or your own. The example above referring to the textbook author uses the verb *argues*, suggesting that what she says is open to dispute (or that the writer believes it is). How would it change your understanding if the signal verb were *observes* or *suggests*?

12–15 ■

In addition to the names of sources' authors, signal phrases often give readers information about institutional affiliations and positions authors have, their academic or professional specialties, and any other information that lets readers judge the credibility of the sources. You should craft each signal phrase you use so as to highlight the credentials of the author. Here are some examples:

> A study done by Anthony M. Armocida, professor of psychology at Duke University, showed that . . .

The signal phrase identifies the source's author, his professional position, and his university affiliation, emphasizing his title.

> Science writer Isaac McDougal argues that . . .

This phrase acknowledges that the source's author may not have scholarly credentials but is a published writer; it's a useful construction if the source doesn't provide much information about the writer.

> Writing in *Psychology Today*, Amanda Chao-Fitz notes that . . .

This is the sort of signal phrase you use if you have no information on the author; you establish credibility on the basis of the publication in which the source appears.

■ ▲ ○ ◆ ● □ ▨

rhetorical situations

genres

processes

strategies

research MLA / APA

media / design

handbook

If you're writing using APA style, signal phrases are typically briefer, giving only the author's last name and the date of publication:

According to Benzinger (2010), . . .

Quartucci (2011) observed that . . .

SOME COMMON SIGNAL VERBS

acknowledges	claims	disagrees	observes
admits	comments	disputes	points out
advises	concludes	emphasizes	reasons
agrees	concurs	grants	rejects
argues	confirms	illustrates	reports
asserts	contends	implies	responds
believes	declares	insists	suggests
charges	denies	notes	thinks

Verb tenses.   MLA and APA also have different conventions regarding the tenses of verbs in signal phrases. MLA requires present-tense verbs (*writes, asserts, notes*) in signal phrases to introduce a work you are quoting, paraphrasing, or summarizing.

In *Poor Richard's Almanack*, Benjamin Franklin notes, "He that cannot obey, cannot command" (739).

If, however, you are referring to the act of writing or saying something rather than simply quoting someone's words, you might not use the present tense. The writer of the following sentence focuses on the year in which the source was written—therefore, the verb is necessarily in the past tense:

Back in 1941, Kenneth Burke wrote that "the ethical values of work are in its application of the competitive equipment to cooperative ends" (316).

If you are following APA style, use the past tense or present-perfect tense to introduce sources composed in the past.

Dowdall, Crawford, and Wechsler (1998) <u>observed</u> that women attending women's colleges are less likely to engage in binge drinking than are women who attend coeducational colleges (p. 713).

APA requires the present tense, however, to discuss the results of an experiment or to explain conclusions that are generally agreed on.

The findings of this study <u>suggest</u> that excessive drinking has serious consequences for college students and their institutions.

The authors of numerous studies <u>agree</u> that smoking and drinking among adolescents are associated with lower academic achievement.

475–79
522–32 MLA
563–74 APA

IF YOU NEED MORE HELP

See **ACKNOWLEDGING SOURCES, AVOIDING PLAGIARISM** for help in giving credit to the sources you use. See also the **SAMPLE RESEARCH PAPERS** to see how sources are cited in MLA and APA styles.

rhetorical situations   genres   processes   strategies   research MLA / APA   media / design   handbook

Acknowledging Sources, **48**
Avoiding Plagiarism

Whenever you do research-based writing, you find yourself entering a conversation—reading what many others have had to say about your topic, figuring out what you yourself think, and then putting what you think in writing—"putting in your oar," as the rhetorician Kenneth Burke once wrote. As a writer, you need to *acknowledge* any words and ideas that come from others—to give credit where credit is due, to recognize the various authorities and many perspectives you have considered, to show readers where they can find your sources, and to situate your own arguments in the ongoing conversation. Using other people's words and ideas without acknowledgment is *plagiarism,* a serious academic and ethical offense. This chapter will show you how to acknowledge the materials you use and avoid plagiarism.

Acknowledging Sources

When you insert in your text information that you've obtained from others, your reader needs to know where your source's words or ideas begin and end. Therefore, you should introduce a source by naming the author in a **SIGNAL PHRASE,** and follow it with a brief parenthetical **IN-TEXT CITATION** or by naming the source in a parenthetical citation. (You need only a brief citation here, since your readers will find full bibliographic information in your list of **WORKS CITED** or **REFERENCES.)**

471–74
488–93 MLA
536–40 APA
494–521 MLA
541–61 APA

Sources that need acknowledgment. You almost always need to acknowledge any information that you get from a specific source. Material you should acknowledge includes the following:

- *Direct quotations.* Unless they are well known (see p. 478 for some examples), any quotations from another source must be enclosed in quotation marks, cited with brief bibliographic information in parentheses, and usually introduced with a signal phrase that tells who wrote or said it and provides necessary contextual information, as in the following sentence:

  > In a dissenting opinion on the issue of racial preferences in college admissions, Supreme Court justice Ruth Bader Ginsburg argues, "The stain of generations of racial oppression is still visible in our society, and the determination to hasten its removal remains vital" (*Gratz v. Bollinger*).

- *Arguable statements and information that may not be common knowledge.* If you state something about which there is disagreement or for which arguments can be made, cite the source of your statement. If in doubt about whether you need to give the source of an assertion, provide it. As part of an essay on "fake news" programs like *The Daily Show*, for example, you might make the following assertion:

  > The satire of *The Daily Show* complements the conservative bias of FOX News, since both have abandoned the stance of objectivity maintained by mainstream news sources, contends Michael Hoyt, executive editor of the *Columbia Journalism Review* (43).

  Others might argue with the contention that the FOX News Channel offers biased reports of the news, so the source of this assertion needs to be acknowledged. In the same essay, you might present information that should be cited because it's not widely known, as in this example:

  > According to a report by the Pew Research Center, 21 percent of Americans under thirty got information about the 2004 presidential campaign primarily from "fake news" and comedy shows like *The Daily Show* and *Saturday Night Live* (2).

- *The opinions and assertions of others.* When you present the ideas, opinions, and assertions of others, cite the source. You may have rewritten the concept in your own words, but the ideas were generated by someone else and must be acknowledged, as they are here:

> David Boonin, writing in the *Journal of Social Philosophy,* asserts that, logically, laws banning marriage between people of different races are not discriminatory since everyone of each race is affected equally by them. Laws banning same-sex unions are discriminatory, however, since they apply only to people with a certain sexual orientation (256).

- *Any information that you didn't generate yourself.* If you did not do the research or compile the data yourself, cite your source. This goes for interviews, statistics, graphs, charts, visuals, photographs—anything you use that you did not create. If you create a chart using data from another source, you need to cite that source.

- *Collaboration with and help from others.* In many of your courses and in work situations, you'll be called on to work with others. You may get help with your writing at your school's writing center or from fellow students in your writing courses. Acknowledging such collaboration or assistance, in a brief informational note, is a way of giving credit—and saying thank you. See guidelines for writing notes in the **MLA** and **APA** sections of this book.

494
541

Sources that don't need acknowledgment.   Widely available information and common knowledge do not require acknowledgment. What constitutes common knowledge may not be clear, however. When in doubt, provide a citation, or ask your instructor whether the information needs to be cited. You generally do not need to cite the following:

- *Information that most readers are likely to know.* You don't need to acknowledge information that is widely known or commonly accepted as fact. For example, in a literary analysis, you wouldn't cite a source saying that Harriet Beecher Stowe wrote *Uncle Tom's Cabin;* you can assume your readers already know that. On the other hand, you should cite the source from which you got the information that the book was first published in installments in a magazine and then, with revisions, in book form, because that information isn't common knowledge. As you do research in areas you're not familiar with, be aware that what constitutes common knowledge isn't always clear; the history of the novel's publication would be known to Stowe scholars and would likely need no acknowledgment in an essay written for them. In this case, too, if you aren't sure whether to acknowledge information, do so.

- *Information and documents that are widely available.* If a piece of information appears in several sources or reference works or if a document has been published widely, you needn't cite a source for it. For example, the date when astronauts Neil Armstrong and Buzz Aldrin landed a spacecraft on the moon can be found in any number of reference works. Similarly, the Declaration of Independence and the Gettysburg Address are reprinted in thousands of sources, so the ones where you found them need no citation.

- *Well-known quotations.* These include such famous quotations as Lady Macbeth's "Out, damned spot!" and John F. Kennedy's "Ask not what your country can do for you; ask what you can do for your country." Be sure, however, that the quotation is correct; Winston Churchill is said to have told a class of schoolchildren, "Never, ever, ever, ever, ever, ever, ever give up. Never give up. Never give up. Never give up." His actual words, however, taken from a longer speech, are much different and begin "Never give in."

- *Material that you created or gathered yourself.* You need not cite photographs that you took, graphs that you composed based on your own findings, or data from an experiment or survey that you conducted — though you should make sure readers know that the work is yours.

A good rule of thumb: *when in doubt, cite your source.* You're unlikely to be criticized for citing too much — but you may invite charges of plagiarism by citing too little.

Avoiding Plagiarism

When you use the words or ideas of others, you need to acknowledge who and where the material came from; if you don't credit those sources, you are guilty of plagiarism. Plagiarism is often committed unintentionally—as when a writer paraphrases someone else's ideas in language that is close to the original. It is essential, therefore, to know what constitutes plagiarism: (1) using another writer's words or ideas without in-text citation and documentation, (2) using another writer's exact words without quotation marks, and (3) paraphrasing or summarizing someone else's ideas using language or sentence structures that are too close to theirs.

To avoid plagiarizing, take careful **NOTES** as you do your research, clearly labeling as quotations any words you quote directly and being careful to use your own phrasing and sentence structures in paraphrases and summaries. Be sure you know what source material you must **DOCUMENT**, and give credit to your sources, both in the text and in a list of **REFERENCES** or **WORKS CITED**.

459–60

480–83
541–61 APA
494–521 MLA

Be aware that it's easy to inadvertently plagiarize when you're working with online sources, such as full-text articles, that you've downloaded or cut and pasted into your notes. Keep careful track of these materials, since saving copies of your sources is so easy. Later, be sure to check your draft against the original sources to make sure your quotations are accurately worded — and take care, too, to include quotation marks and cite the source correctly. Copying online material right into a document you are writing and forgetting to put quotation marks around it or to cite it (or both) is all too easy to do. You must acknowledge information you find on the web just as you must acknowledge all other source materials.

And you must recognize that plagiarism has consequences. Scholars' work will be discredited if it too closely resembles another's. Journalists found to have plagiarized lose their jobs, and students routinely fail courses or are dismissed from their school when they are caught cheating—all too often by submitting as their own essays that they have purchased from online "research" sites. If you're having trouble completing an assignment, seek assistance. Talk with your instructor, or if your school has a writing center, go there for advice on all aspects of your writing, including acknowledging sources and avoiding plagiarism.

49 Documentation

In everyday life, we are generally aware of our sources: "I read it on Andrew Sullivan's blog." "Amber told me it's your birthday." "If you don't believe me, ask Mom." Saying how we know what we know and where we got our information is part of establishing our credibility and persuading others to take what we say seriously.

The goal of a research project is to study a topic, combining what we learn from sources with our own thinking and then composing a written text. When we write up the results of a research project, we cite the sources we use, usually by quoting, paraphrasing, or summarizing, and we acknowledge those sources, telling readers where the ideas came from. The information we give about sources is called documentation, and we provide it not only to establish our credibility as researchers and writers but also so that our readers, if they wish to, can find the sources themselves.

Understanding Documentation Styles

The Norton Field Guide covers the documentation styles of the Modern Language Association (MLA) and the American Psychological Association (APA). MLA style is used chiefly in the humanities; APA is used mainly in the social sciences. Both are two-part systems, consisting of (1) brief in-text parenthetical documentation for quotations, paraphrases, or summaries and (2) more-detailed documentation in a list of sources at the end of the text. MLA and APA require that the end-of-text documentation provide the following basic information about each source you cite:

- author, editor, or creator of the source
- title of source (and of publication or site where it appears)
- place of publication
- name of publisher
- date of publication
- medium of publication (MLA only)
- retrieval information (for online sources; APA only)

MLA and APA are by no means the only documentation styles. Many other publishers and organizations have their own style, among them the University of Chicago Press and the Council of Science Editors. We focus on MLA and APA here because those are styles that college students are often required to use. On the following page are examples of how the two parts — the brief parenthetical documentation in your text and the more detailed information at the end — correspond in each of these systems.

The examples here and throughout this book are color-coded to help you see the crucial parts of each citation: tan for author and editor, yellow for title, and gray for publication information: place of publication, name of publisher, date of publication, page number(s), medium of publication, and so on.

As the examples of in-text documentation show, in either MLA or APA style you should name the author either in a signal phrase or in parentheses following the source information. But there are several differences between the two styles in the details of the citation. In MLA, the author's full name is used in a signal phrase; in APA, only the last name is used. In APA, the abbreviation *p.* is used with the page number, which is provided only for a direct quotation; in MLA, a page number (if there is one) is always given, but with no abbreviation before it. Finally, in APA the date of publication always appears just after the author's name. Comparing the MLA and APA styles of listing works cited or references also reveals some differences: MLA includes an author's first name while APA gives only initials; MLA puts the date near the end while APA places it right after the author's name; MLA requires the medium of publication while APA usually does not; MLA capitalizes most of the words in a book's title and subtitle while APA capitalizes only the first words and proper nouns and proper adjectives in each.

Some of these differences are related to the nature of the academic fields in which the two styles are used. In humanities disciplines, the authorship of a text is emphasized, so both first and last names are included in MLA citations. Scholarship in those fields may be several years old but still current, so the publication date doesn't appear in the in-text citation. In APA style, as in many citation styles used in the sciences, education, and engineering, emphasis is placed on the date of publication because in these fields, more recent research is usually preferred over older studies. However, although the elements are arranged differently, both MLA and APA — and other documentation styles as well — require similar information about author, title, and publication.

MLA Style

IN-TEXT DOCUMENTATION

As Lester Faigley puts it, "The world has become a bazaar from which to shop for an individual 'lifestyle' " (12).

As one observer suggests, "The world has become a bazaar from which to shop for an individual 'lifestyle' " (Faigley 12).

WORKS-CITED DOCUMENTATION

Faigley, Lester. *Fragments of Rationality: Postmodernity and the Subject of Composition.* Pittsburgh: U of Pittsburgh P, 1992. Print.

author   title   publication

APA Style

IN-TEXT DOCUMENTATION

As Faigley (1992) suggested, "The world has become a bazaar from which to shop for an individual 'lifestyle'" (p. 12).

As one observer has noted, "The world has become a bazaar from which to shop for an individual 'lifestyle'" (Faigley, 1992, p. 12).

REFERENCE-LIST DOCUMENTATION

Faigley, L. (1992). *Fragments of rationality: Postmodernity and the subject of composition.* Pittsburgh, PA: University of Pittsburgh Press.

50 MLA Style

Modern Language Association style calls for (1) brief in-text documentation and (2) complete documentation in a list of works cited at the end of your text. The models in this chapter draw on the *MLA Handbook for Writers of Research Papers*, 7th edition (2009). Additional information is available at www.mla.org.

A DIRECTORY TO MLA STYLE

Throughout this chapter, you'll find models and examples that are color-coded to help you see how writers include source information in their texts and list of works cited: tan for author or editor, yellow for title, gray for publication information: place of publication, publisher, date of publication, page number(s), and so on.

IN-TEXT DOCUMENTATION

Brief documentation in your text makes clear to your reader what you took from a source and where in the source you found the information.

462–74

In your text, you have three options for citing a source: **QUOTING, PARAPHRASING,** and **SUMMARIZING.** As you cite each source, you will need to decide whether or not to name the author in a signal phrase—"as Toni Morrison writes"—or in parentheses—"(Morrison 24)."

The first examples in this chapter show basic in-text citations of a work by one author. Variations on those examples follow. The examples illustrate the MLA style of using quotation marks around titles of short works and italicizing titles of long works.

1. AUTHOR NAMED IN A SIGNAL PHRASE

If you mention the author in a signal phrase, put only the page number(s) in parentheses. Do not write *page* or *p.*

> McCullough describes John Adams's hands as those of someone used to manual labor (18).

2. AUTHOR NAMED IN PARENTHESES

If you do not mention the author in a signal phrase, put his or her last name in parentheses along with the page number(s). Do not use punctuation between the name and the page number(s).

> Adams is said to have had "the hands of a man accustomed to pruning his own trees, cutting his own hay, and splitting his own firewood" (McCullough 18).

Whether you use a signal phrase and parentheses or parentheses only, try to put the parenthetical citation at the end of the sentence or as close as possible to the material you've cited without awkwardly interrupting the sentence. Notice that in the example above, the parenthetical reference comes after the closing quotation marks but before the period at the end of the sentence.

author   title   publication

3. TWO OR MORE WORKS BY THE SAME AUTHOR

If you cite multiple works by one author, include the title of the work you are citing either in the signal phrase or in parentheses. Give the full title if it's brief; otherwise, give a short version.

> Kaplan insists that understanding power in the Near East requires "Western leaders who know when to intervene, and do so without illusions" (*Eastward* 330).

Include a comma between author and title if you include both in the parentheses.

> Understanding power in the Near East requires "Western leaders who know when to intervene, and do so without illusions" (Kaplan, *Eastward* 330).

4. AUTHORS WITH THE SAME LAST NAME

Give the author's first name in any signal phrase or the author's first initial in the parenthetical reference.

> *Imaginative* applies not only to modern literature (E. Wilson) but also to writing of all periods, whereas *magical* is often used in writing about Arthurian romances (A. Wilson).

5. TWO OR MORE AUTHORS

For a work by two or three authors, name all the authors, either in a signal phrase or in the parentheses.

> Carlson and Ventura's stated goal is to introduce Julio Cortázar, Marjorie Agosín, and other Latin American writers to an audience of English-speaking adolescents (v).

For a work with four or more authors, either mention all their names or include just the name of the first author followed by *et al.*, Latin for "and others."

One popular survey of American literature breaks the contents into sixteen thematic groupings (Anderson et al. A19–24).

6. ORGANIZATION OR GOVERNMENT AS AUTHOR

Cite the organization either in a signal phrase or in parentheses. It's acceptable to shorten long names.

> The U.S. government can be direct when it wants to be. For example, it sternly warns, "If you are overpaid, we will recover any payments not due you" (Social Security Administration 12).

7. AUTHOR UNKNOWN

If you don't know the author, use the work's title or a shortened version of the title in the parentheses.

> A powerful editorial in last week's paper asserts that healthy liver donor Mike Hurewitz died because of "frightening" faulty postoperative care ("Every Patient's Nightmare").

8. LITERARY WORKS

When referring to literary works that are available in many different editions, cite the page numbers from the edition you are using, followed by information that will let readers of any edition locate the text you are citing.

NOVELS. Give the page and chapter number.

> In *Pride and Prejudice,* Mrs. Bennett shows no warmth toward Jane and Elizabeth when they return from Netherfield (105; ch. 12).

VERSE PLAYS. Give the act, scene, and line numbers; separate them with periods.

> Macbeth continues the vision theme when he addresses the Ghost with "Thou hast no speculation in those eyes / Which thou dost glare with" (3.3.96–97).

author   title   publication

POEMS. Give the part and the line numbers (separated by periods). If a poem has only line numbers, use the word *line(s)* in the first reference.

> Whitman sets up not only opposing adjectives but also opposing nouns in "Song of Myself" when he says, "I am of old and young, of the foolish as much as the wise, / . . . a child as well as a man" (16.330–32).

> One description of the mere in *Beowulf* is "not a pleasant place!" (line 1372). Later, the label is "the awful place" (1378).

9. WORK IN AN ANTHOLOGY

Name the author(s) of the work, not the editor of the anthology—either in a signal phrase or in parentheses.

> "It is the teapots that truly shock," according to Cynthia Ozick in her essay on teapots as metaphor (70).

> In *In Short: A Collection of Creative Nonfiction*, readers will find both an essay on Scottish tea (Hiestand) and a piece on teapots as metaphors (Ozick).

10. ENCYCLOPEDIA OR DICTIONARY

Cite an entry in an encyclopedia or dictionary using the author's name, if available. For an entry in a reference work without an author, give the entry's title in parentheses. If entries are arranged alphabetically, no page number is needed.

> According to *Funk & Wagnall's New World Encyclopedia*, early in his career, Kubrick's main source of income came from "hustling chess games in Washington Square Park" ("Kubrick, Stanley").

11. LEGAL AND HISTORICAL DOCUMENTS

For legal cases and acts of law, name the case or act in a signal phrase or in parentheses. Italicize the name of a legal case.

> In 2005, the Supreme Court confirmed in *MGM Studios, Inc. v. Grokster, Ltd.* that peer-to-peer file sharing is illegal copyright infringement.

Do not italicize the titles of laws, acts, or well-known historical documents such as the Declaration of Independence. Give the title and any relevant articles and sections in parentheses. It's okay to use common abbreviations such as *art.* or *sec.* and to abbreviate well-known titles.

> The president is also granted the right to make recess appointments (US Const., art. 2, sec. 2).

12. SACRED TEXT

When citing sacred texts such as the Bible or the Qur'an, give the title of the edition used, and in parentheses give the book, chapter, and verse (or their equivalent), separated by periods. MLA style recommends that you abbreviate the names of the books of the Bible in parenthetical references.

> The wording from *The New English Bible* follows: "In the beginning of creation, when God made heaven and earth, the earth was without form and void, with darkness over the face of the abyss, and a mighty wind that swept over the surface of the waters" (Gen. 1.1–2).

13. MULTIVOLUME WORK

If you cite more than one volume of a multivolume work, each time you cite one of the volumes, give the volume *and* the page number(s) in parentheses, separated by a colon.

> Sandburg concludes with the following sentence about those paying last respects to Lincoln: "All day long and through the night the unbroken line moved, the home town having its farewell" (4: 413).

If your works-cited list includes only a single volume of a multivolume work, give just the page number in parentheses.

14. TWO OR MORE WORKS CITED TOGETHER

If you're citing two or more works closely together, you will sometimes need to provide a parenthetical citation for each one.

author   title   publication

Tanner (7) and Smith (viii) have looked at works from a cultural perspective.

If you include both in the same parentheses, separate the references with a semicolon.

Critics have looked at both *Pride and Prejudice* and *Frankenstein* from a cultural perspective (Tanner 7; Smith viii).

15. SOURCE QUOTED IN ANOTHER SOURCE

When you are quoting text that you found quoted in another source, use the abbreviation *qtd. in* in the parenthetical reference.

Charlotte Brontë wrote to G. H. Lewes: "Why do you like Miss Austen so very much? I am puzzled on that point" (qtd. in Tanner 7).

16. WORK WITHOUT PAGE NUMBERS

For works without page numbers, including many online sources, identify the source using the author or other information either in a signal phrase or in parentheses.

Studies reported in *Scientific American* and elsewhere show that music training helps children to be better at multitasking later in life ("Hearing the Music").

If the source has paragraph or section numbers, use them with the abbreviation *par.* or *sec.*: ("Hearing the Music," par. 2). If an online work is available as a PDF with page numbers, cite the number(s) in parentheses.

17. AN ENTIRE WORK OR ONE-PAGE ARTICLE

If you cite an entire work rather than a part of it, or if you cite a single-page article, identify the author in a signal phrase or in parentheses. There's no need to include page numbers.

At least one observer considers Turkey and Central Asia explosive (Kaplan).

NOTES

Sometimes you may need to give information that doesn't fit into the text itself—to thank people who helped you, to provide additional details, to refer readers to other sources, or to add comments about sources. Such information can be given in a *footnote* (at the bottom of the page) or an *endnote* (on a separate page with the heading *Notes* just before your works-cited list). Put a superscript number at the appropriate point in your text, signaling to readers to look for the note with the corresponding number. If you have multiple notes, number them consecutively throughout your paper.

TEXT

This essay will argue that small liberal arts colleges should not recruit athletes and, more specifically, that giving student athletes preferential treatment undermines the larger educational goals.[1]

NOTE

[1] I want to thank all those who have contributed to my thinking on this topic, especially my classmates and my teachers Marian Johnson and Diane O'Connor.

LIST OF WORKS CITED

A works-cited list provides full bibliographic information for every source cited in your text. See page 523 for guidelines on preparing this list; for a sample work-cited list, see page 531.

Print Books

For most books, you'll need to provide information about the author; the title and any subtitle; and the place of publication, publisher, and date. At the end of the citation provide the medium—Print.

author   title   publication

IMPORTANT DETAILS FOR CITING PRINT BOOKS

- **AUTHORS**: Include the author's middle name or initials, if any.
- **TITLES**: Capitalize all principal words in titles and subtitles. Do not capitalize *a*, *an*, *the*, *to*, or any prepositions or coordinating conjunctions unless they are the first or last word of a title or subtitle.
- **PUBLICATION PLACE**: If there's more than one city, use the first.
- **PUBLISHER**: Use a short form of the publisher's name (Norton for W. W. Norton & Company, Yale UP for Yale University Press).
- **DATES**: If more than one year is given, use the most recent one.

1. ONE AUTHOR

Author's Last Name, First Name. *Title*. Publication City: Publisher, Year of publication. Medium.

Anderson, Curtis. *The Long Tail: Why the Future of Business Is Selling Less of More*. New York: Hyperion, 2006. Print.

2. TWO OR MORE WORKS BY THE SAME AUTHOR(S)

Give the author's name in the first entry, and then use three hyphens in the author slot for each of the subsequent works, listing them alphabetically by the first important word of each title.

Author's Last Name, First Name. *Title That Comes First Alphabetically*. Publication City: Publisher, Year of publication. Medium.

—. *Title That Comes Next Alphabetically*. Publication City: Publisher, Year of publication. Medium.

Kaplan, Robert D. *The Coming Anarchy: Shattering the Dreams of the Post Cold War*. New York: Random, 2000. Print.

—. *Eastward to Tartary: Travels in the Balkans, the Middle East, and the Caucasus*. New York: Random, 2000. Print.

Documentation Map (MLA)
Print Book

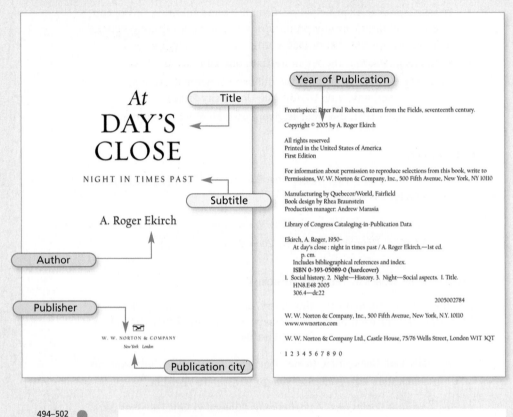

Title

At
DAY'S
CLOSE

NIGHT IN TIMES PAST

Subtitle

A. Roger Ekirch

Author

Publisher

W. W. NORTON & COMPANY
New York London

Publication city

Year of Publication

Frontispiece: Peter Paul Rubens, Return from the Fields, seventeenth century.

Copyright © 2005 by A. Roger Ekirch

All rights reserved
Printed in the United States of America
First Edition

For information about permission to reproduce selections from this book, write to Permissions, W. W. Norton & Company, Inc., 500 Fifth Avenue, New York, NY 10110

Manufacturing by Quebecor/World, Fairfield
Book design by Rhea Braunstein
Production manager: Andrew Marasia

Library of Congress Cataloging-in-Publication Data

Ekirch, A. Roger, 1950–
     At day's close : night in times past / A. Roger Ekirch.—1st ed.
        p. cm.
     Includes bibliographical references and index.
     ISBN 0-393-05089-0 (hardcover)
1. Social history. 2. Night—History. 3. Night—Social aspects. I. Title.
     HN8.E48 2005
     306.4—dc22
                                                    2005002784

W. W. Norton & Company, Inc., 500 Fifth Avenue, New York, N.Y. 10110
www.wwnorton.com

W. W. Norton & Company Ltd., Castle House, 75/76 Wells Street, London W1T 3QT

1 2 3 4 5 6 7 8 9 0

494–502
for more on
citing books
MLA style

Ekirch, A. Roger. *At Day's Close: Night in Times Past*. New York: Norton, 2005. Print.

author   title   publication

3. TWO OR THREE AUTHORS

> First Author's Last Name, First Name, Second Author's First and Last
> Names, and Third Author's First and Last Names. *Title*. Publication
> City: Publisher, Year of publication. Medium.

Malless, Stanley, and Jeffrey McQuain. *Coined by God: Words and
Phrases That First Appear in the English Translations of the Bible*.
New York: Norton, 2003. Print.

Sebranek, Patrick, Verne Meyer, and Dave Kemper. *Writers INC: A Guide
to Writing, Thinking, and Learning*. Burlington: Write Source,
1990. Print.

4. FOUR OR MORE AUTHORS

You may give each author's name or the name of the first author only,
followed by *et al.*, Latin for "and others."

> First Author's Last Name, First Name, Second Author's First and Last
> Names, Third Author's First and Last Names, and Final Author's First
> and Last Names. *Title*. Publication City: Publisher, Year of publication.
> Medium.

Anderson, Robert, John Malcolm Brinnin, John Leggett, Gary Q. Arpin,
and Susan Allen Toth. *Elements of Literature: Literature of the
United States*. Austin: Holt, 1993. Print.

Anderson, Robert, et al. *Elements of Literature: Literature of the United
States*. Austin: Holt, 1993. Print.

5. ORGANIZATION OR GOVERNMENT AS AUTHOR

> Organization Name. *Title*. Publication City: Publisher, Year of
> publication. Medium.

Diagram Group. *The Macmillan Visual Desk Reference*. New York:
Macmillan, 1993. Print.

For a government publication, give the name of the government first, followed by the names of any department and agency.

> United States. Dept. of Health and Human Services. Natl. Inst. of Mental
> Health. *Autism Spectrum Disorders*. Washington: GPO, 2004. Print.

6. ANTHOLOGY

> Editor's Last Name, First Name, ed. *Title*. Publication City: Publisher, Year
> of publication. Medium.

> Hall, Donald, ed. *The Oxford Book of Children's Verse in America*. New
> York: Oxford UP, 1985. Print.

If there is more than one editor, list the first editor last-name-first and the others first-name-first.

> Kitchen, Judith, and Mary Paumier Jones, eds. *In Short: A Collection of
> Brief Creative Nonfiction*. New York: Norton, 1996. Print.

7. WORK(S) IN AN ANTHOLOGY

> Author's Last Name, First Name. "Title of Work." *Title of Anthology*.
> Ed. Editor's First and Last Names. Publication City: Publisher, Year of
> publication. Pages. Medium.

> Achebe, Chinua. "Uncle Ben's Choice." *The Seagull Reader: Literature*.
> Ed. Joseph Kelly. New York: Norton, 2005. 23–27. Print.

To document two or more selections from one anthology, list each selection by author and title, followed by the names of the anthology editor(s) and the pages of the selection. Then include an entry for the anthology itself (see no. 6).

> Author's Last Name, First Name. "Title of Work." Anthology Editor's Last
> Name Pages.

> Hiestand, Emily. "Afternoon Tea." Kitchen and Jones 65–67.

> Ozick, Cynthia. "The Shock of Teapots." Kitchen and Jones 68–71.

Do not list the anthology separately if you're citing only one selection.

8. AUTHOR AND EDITOR

Start with the author if you've cited the text itself.

> Author's Last Name, First Name. *Title*. Ed. Editor's First and Last Names. Publication City: Publisher, Year of publication. Medium.

> Austen, Jane. *Emma*. Ed. Stephen M. Parrish. New York: Norton, 2000. Print.

Start with the editor to cite his or her contribution rather than the author's.

> Editor's Last Name, First Name, ed. *Title*. By Author's First and Last Names. Publication City: Publisher, Year of publication. Medium.

> Parrish, Stephen M., ed. *Emma*. By Jane Austen. New York: Norton, 2000. Print.

9. NO AUTHOR OR EDITOR

> *Title*. Publication City: Publisher, Year of publication. Medium.

> *2008 New York City Restaurants*. New York: Zagat, 2008. Print.

10. TRANSLATION

Start with the author to emphasize the work itself.

> Author's Last Name, First Name. *Title*. Trans. Translator's First and Last Names. Publication City: Publisher, Year of publication. Medium.

> Dostoevsky, Fyodor. *Crime and Punishment*. Trans. Richard Pevear and Larissa Volokhonsky. New York: Vintage, 1993. Print.

Start with the translator to emphasize the translation.

> Pevear, Richard, and Larissa Volokhonsky, trans. *Crime and Punishment*. By Fyodor Dostoevsky. New York: Vintage, 1993. Print.

11. GRAPHIC NARRATIVE

Start with the name of the person whose work is most relevant to your research, and include labels to indicate each collaborator's role.

> Pekar, Harvey, writer. *American Splendor*. Illus. R. Crumb. New York: Four Walls, 1996. Print.

Crumb, R., illus. *American Splendor*. By Harvey Pekar. New York: Four
Walls, 1996. Print.

If the work was written and illustrated by the same person, format the
entry like that of any other book.

12. FOREWORD, INTRODUCTION, PREFACE, OR AFTERWORD

Part Author's Last Name, First Name. Name of Part. *Title of Book*.
By Author's First and Last Names. Publication City: Publisher, Year
of publication. Pages. Medium.

Tanner, Tony. Introduction. *Pride and Prejudice*. By Jane Austen.
London: Penguin, 1972. 7–46. Print.

13. MULTIVOLUME WORK

If you cite more than one volume of a multivolume work, give the total
number of volumes after the title.

Author's Last Name, First Name. *Title of Complete Work*. Number of vols.
Publication City: Publisher, Year of publication. Medium.

Sandburg, Carl. *Abraham Lincoln: The War Years*. 4 vols. New York:
Harcourt, 1939. Print.

If you cite only one volume, give the volume number after the title.

Sandburg, Carl. *Abraham Lincoln: The War Years*. Vol. 2. New York:
Harcourt, 1939. Print.

14. ARTICLE IN A REFERENCE BOOK

Provide the author's name if the article is signed. If the reference work is
well known, give only the edition and year of publication.

Author's Last Name, First Name. "Title of Article." *Title of Reference
Book*. Edition number. Year of publication. Medium.

"Kiwi." *Merriam-Webster's Collegiate Dictionary*. 11th ed. 2003. Print.

If the reference work is less familiar or more specialized, give full publication information. If it has only one volume or is in its first edition, omit that information.

> Author's Last Name, First Name. "Title of Article." *Title of Reference*
> *Book*. Ed. Editor's First and Last Name. Edition number. Number of
> vols. Publication City: Publisher, Year of publication. Medium.

> Campbell, James. "The Harlem Renaissance." *The Oxford Companion to*
> *Twentieth-Century Poetry*. Ed. Ian Hamilton. Oxford: Oxford UP,
> 1994. Print.

15. BOOK IN A SERIES

> Editor's Last Name, First Name, ed. *Title of Book*. By Author's First and
> Last Names. Publication City: Publisher, Year of publication. Medium.
> Series Title abbreviated.

> Wall, Cynthia, ed. *The Pilgrim's Progress*. By John Bunyan. New York:
> Norton, 2007. Print. Norton Critical Ed.

16. SACRED TEXT

If you have cited a specific edition of a religious text, you need to include it in your works-cited list.

> *The New English Bible with the Apocrypha*. New York: Oxford UP, 1971.
> Print.

> *The Torah: A Modern Commentary*. Ed. W. Gunther Plaut. New York:
> Union of Amer. Hebrew Congregations, 1981. Print.

17. BOOK WITH TITLE WITHIN THE TITLE

When the title of a book contains the title of another long work, do not italicize that title. (See next page for examples.)

Walker, Roy. *Time Is Free: A Study of* Macbeth. London: Dakers, 1949.
Print.

When the book title contains the title of a short work, put the short work in quotation marks, and italicize the entire title.

Thompson, Lawrance Roger. *"Fire and Ice": The Art and Thought of Robert Frost.* New York: Holt, 1942. Print.

18. EDITION OTHER THAN THE FIRST

Author's Last Name, First Name. *Title.* Name or number of ed. Publication City: Publisher, Year of publication. Medium.

Hirsch, E. D., Jr., ed. *What Your Second Grader Needs to Know: Fundamentals of a Good Second-Grade Education.* Rev. ed. New York: Doubleday, 1998. Print.

19. REPUBLISHED WORK

Give the original publication date after the title, followed by the publication information of the republished edition.

Author's Last Name, First Name. *Title.* Year of original edition. Publication City: Current Publisher, Year of republication. Medium.

Bierce, Ambrose. *Civil War Stories.* 1909. New York: Dover, 1994. Print.

20. PUBLISHER AND IMPRINT

Some sources may provide both a publisher's name and an imprint on the title page; if so, include both, with a hyphen between the imprint and the publisher.

Author's Last Name, First Name. *Title.* Publication City: Imprint-Publisher, Year of publication. Medium.

Maguire, Gregory. Wicked: *The Life and Times of the Wicked Witch of the West.* New York: ReganBooks-HarperCollins, 1995. Print.

Print Periodicals

For most articles, you'll need to provide information about the author, the article title and any subtitle, the periodical title, any volume or issue number, the date, inclusive page numbers, and the medium—Print.

IMPORTANT DETAILS FOR CITING PRINT PERIODICALS

- **AUTHORS**: If there is more than one author, list the first author last-name-first and the others first-name-first.
- **TITLES**: Capitalize titles and subtitles as you would for a book. For periodical titles, omit any initial *A*, *An*, or *The*.
- **DATES**: Abbreviate the names of months except for May, June, or July: Jan., Feb., Mar., Apr., Aug., Sept., Oct., Nov., Dec. Journals paginated by volume or issue need only the year (in parentheses).
- **PAGES**: If an article does not fall on consecutive pages, give the first page with a plus sign (55+).

21. ARTICLE IN A JOURNAL

Author's Last Name, First Name. "Title of Article." *Title of Journal*
    Volume.Issue (Year): Pages. Medium.

Cooney, Brian C. "Considering *Robinson Crusoe*'s 'Liberty of Conscience'
    in an Age of Terror." *College English* 69.3 (2007): 197–215. Print.

22. ARTICLE IN A JOURNAL NUMBERED BY ISSUE

Author's Last Name, First Name. "Title of Article." *Title of Journal*
    Issue (Year): Pages. Medium.

Flynn, Kevin. "The Railway in Canadian Poetry." *Canadian Literature* 174
    (2002): 70–95. Print.

23. ARTICLE IN A MAGAZINE

Author's Last Name, First Name. "Title of Article." *Title of Magazine*
    Day Month Year: Pages. Medium.

Walsh, Bryan. "Not a Watt to Be Wasted." *Time* 17 Mar. 2008: 46–47. Print.

Documentation Map (MLA)
Article in a Print Journal

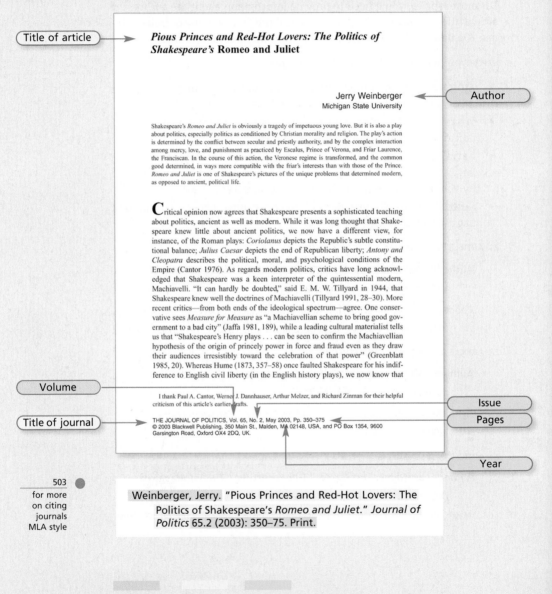

Title of article →

Pious Princes and Red-Hot Lovers: The Politics of Shakespeare's Romeo and Juliet

Jerry Weinberger
Michigan State University

← Author

Shakespeare's *Romeo and Juliet* is obviously a tragedy of impetuous young love. But it is also a play about politics, especially politics as conditioned by Christian morality and religion. The play's action is determined by the conflict between secular and priestly authority, and by the complex interaction among mercy, love, and punishment as practiced by Escalus, Prince of Verona, and Friar Laurence, the Franciscan. In the course of this action, the Veronese regime is transformed, and the common good determined, in ways more compatible with the friar's interests than with those of the Prince. *Romeo and Juliet* is one of Shakespeare's pictures of the unique problems that determined modern, as opposed to ancient, political life.

Critical opinion now agrees that Shakespeare presents a sophisticated teaching about politics, ancient as well as modern. While it was long thought that Shakespeare knew little about ancient politics, we now have a different view, for instance, of the Roman plays: *Coriolanus* depicts the Republic's subtle constitutional balance; *Julius Caesar* depicts the end of Republican liberty; *Antony and Cleopatra* describes the political, moral, and psychological conditions of the Empire (Cantor 1976). As regards modern politics, critics have long acknowledged that Shakespeare was a keen interpreter of the quintessential modern, Machiavelli. "It can hardly be doubted," said E. M. W. Tillyard in 1944, that Shakespeare knew well the doctrines of Machiavelli (Tillyard 1991, 28–30). More recent critics—from both ends of the ideological spectrum—agree. One conservative sees *Measure for Measure* as "a Machiavellian scheme to bring good government to a bad city" (Jaffa 1981, 189), while a leading cultural materialist tells us that "Shakespeare's Henry plays . . . can be seen to confirm the Machiavellian hypothesis of the origin of princely power in force and fraud even as they draw their audiences irresistibly toward the celebration of that power" (Greenblatt 1985, 20). Whereas Hume (1873, 357–58) once faulted Shakespeare for his indifference to English civil liberty (in the English history plays), we now know that

I thank Paul A. Cantor, Werner J. Dannhauser, Arthur Melzer, and Richard Zinman for their helpful criticism of this article's earlier drafts.

THE JOURNAL OF POLITICS, Vol. 65, No. 2, May 2003, Pp. 350–375
© 2003 Blackwell Publishing, 350 Main St., Malden, MA 02148, USA, and PO Box 1354, 9600 Garsington Road, Oxford OX4 2DQ, UK.

Volume →

Title of journal →

Issue ←

Pages ←

Year ←

503
for more
on citing
journals
MLA style

Weinberger, Jerry. "Pious Princes and Red-Hot Lovers: The Politics of Shakespeare's *Romeo and Juliet.*" *Journal of Politics* 65.2 (2003): 350–75. Print.

author   title   publication

Documentation Map (MLA)
Article in a Print Magazine

Title of article →

Author →

10 YEARS
PERSPECTIVES
Essays by leading thinkers
in celebration of the dog

The Wolf
in Your Dog
By Michael W. Fox, DVM, PhD

*Though in their deep heart's core,
there is a commonality of origin,
spirit, emotional intelligence and
empathetic sensibility, the wild wolf
looks through us, while the dog
looks to us.*

OF ALL THE MYRIAD MEMBERS OF THE ANIMAL KINGDOM, the domesticated dog (*Canis lupus familiaris*) is closest to us. With individual exceptions in other species, this canine species is the most understanding, if not also the most observant, of human behavior—of our actions and intentions. This is why dogs are so responsive to us, even mirroring or mimicking our behavior. And it is why dogs are so trainable.

Fear in unsocialized and abused dogs interferes with their attentiveness to and interpretation of human behavior and intentions. This is one reason wild species like the coyote and wolf, even when born and raised in captivity, are difficult to train. The wolf "Tiny," whom I bottle-raised and intensely socialized during her formative early days, never really lost her fear and distrust of strangers.

Tiny did not start mirroring human behavior until she was close to nine years old. At this point, she began to mimic the human-to-human greeting grin, revealing her front teeth as she curled her lips into a snarly smile. In my experience, dogs

who can do this do so at a much earlier age, even as early as four to six months.

In comparing socialized (human-bonded) wolves and dogs in terms of how they have related to me as well as to my family members, friends and strangers, I would say that the main difference between the two species is the fear factor. Differences in trainability hinge on this; as I theorize in my new book (*Dog Body, Dog Mind*), domestication has altered the tuning of the dog's adrenal and autonomic nervous systems. This tuning (which dampens adrenal fright, flight and fight reactions and possibly alters brain serotonin levels), is accomplished through selective breeding for docility, and by gentle handling during the critical period for socialization. According to the earlier research of my mentors—Drs. John Paul Scott and John L. Fuller of the Jackson Laboratory in Bar Harbor, Maine—pups with no human contact during this critical socialization period (which ends around 12 to 16 weeks of age) are wild and unapproachable.

Title of magazine →

Page →

Month and year → Mar/Apr 2008 | **Bark** 85

503, 506
for more
on citing
magazines
MLA style

Fox, Michael W. "The Wolf in Your Dog." *Bark* Mar.–Apr.
2008: 85–87. Print.

For a monthly magazine, include only the month and year.

> Fellman, Bruce. "Leading the Libraries." *Yale Alumni Magazine* Feb.
> 2002: 26–31. Print.

24. ARTICLE IN A DAILY NEWSPAPER

> Author's Last Name, First Name. "Title of Article." *Name of Newspaper*
> Day Month Year: Pages. Medium.

> Springer, Shira. "Celtics Reserves Are Whizzes vs. Wizards." *Boston Globe*
> 14 Mar. 2005: D4+. Print.

If you are citing a particular edition of a newspaper, list the edition (late ed., natl. ed., etc.) after the date. If a section is not identified by a letter or number, put the name of the section after the edition information.

> Burns, John F., and Miguel Helft. "Under Pressure, YouTube Withdraws
> Muslim Cleric's Videos." *New York Times* 4 Nov. 2010, late ed., sec.
> 1: 13. Print.

25. UNSIGNED ARTICLE

> "Title of Article." *Name of Publication* Day Month Year: Pages Medium.

> "Being Invisible Closer to Reality." *Atlanta Journal-Constitution* 11 Aug.
> 2008: A3. Print.

26. EDITORIAL

> "Title." Editorial. *Name of Publication* Day Month Year: Page. Medium.

> "Gas, Cigarettes Are Safe to Tax." Editorial. *Lakeville Journal* 17 Feb.
> 2005: A10. Print.

27. LETTER TO THE EDITOR

> Author's Last Name, First Name. "Title (if any)." Letter. *Name of
> Publication* Day Month Year: Page. Medium.

> Festa, Roger. "Social Security: Another Phony Crisis." Letter. *Lakeville
> Journal* 17 Feb. 2005: A10. Print.

author   title   publication

28. REVIEW

> Reviewer's Last Name, First Name. "Title (if any) of Review." Rev. of *Title of Work*, by Author's First and Last Names. *Title of Periodical* Day Month Year: Pages. Medium.
>
> Frank, Jeffrey. "Body Count." Rev. of *The Exception*, by Christian Jungersen. *New Yorker* 30 July 2007: 86–87. Print.

Online Sources

Not every online source gives you all the data that MLA would like to see in a works-cited entry. Ideally, you will be able to list the author's name, the title, information about any print publication, information about electronic publication (title of site, editor, date of first electronic publication and/or most recent revision, name of the publisher or sponsoring institution), the publication medium, the date of access, and, if necessary, a URL.

IMPORTANT DETAILS FOR CITING ONLINE SOURCES

- **AUTHORS OR EDITORS AND TITLES**: Format authors and titles as you would for a print book or periodical.

- **PUBLISHER**: If the name of the publisher or sponsoring institution is unavailable, use N.p.

- **DATES**: Abbreviate the months as you would for a print periodical. Although MLA asks for the date when materials were first posted or most recently updated, you won't always be able to find that information; if it's unavailable, use *n.d.* Be sure to include the date on which you accessed the source.

- **PAGES**: If the citation calls for page numbers but the source is unpaginated, use *n. pag.* in place of page numbers.

- **MEDIUM**: Indicate the medium—Web, Email, Tweet, and so on.

- **URL:** MLA assumes that readers can locate most sources on the Web by searching for the author, title, or other identifying information, so they don't require a URL for most online sources. When users can't locate the source without a URL, give the address of the website in angle brackets. When a URL won't fit on one line, break it only after a slash (and do not add a hyphen). If a URL is very long, consider giving the URL of the site's home or search page instead.

29. ENTIRE WEBSITE

For websites with an editor, compiler, director, narrator, or translator, follow the name with the appropriate abbreviation (*ed., comp.*).

> Author's Last Name, First Name. *Title of Site*. Publisher or Sponsoring Institution, Date posted or last updated. Medium. Day Month Year of access.

> Zalta, Edward N., ed. *Stanford Encyclopedia of Philosophy*. Metaphysics Research Lab, Center for the Study of Language and Information, Stanford U, 2007. Web. 14 Nov. 2012.

PERSONAL WEBSITE

> Author's Last Name, First Name. Home page. Sponsor, Date posted or last updated. Medium. Day Month Year of access.

> Nunberg, Geoffrey. Home page. School of Information, U of California, Berkeley, 2009. Web. 13 Apr. 2012.

30. WORK FROM A WEBSITE

> Author's Last Name, First Name. "Title of Work." *Title of Site*. Ed. Editor's First and Last Names. Sponsor, Date posted or last updated. Medium. Day Month Year of access.

> Buff, Rachel Ida. "Becoming American." *Immigration History Research Center*. U of Minnesota, 24 Mar. 2008. Web. 4 Apr. 2012.

Documentation Map (MLA)
Work from a Website

Title of site → Forum on Religion and Ecology

Title of article → Environmental Ethics: An Overview

Author → J. Baird Callicott

Date posted or last updated

Sponsoring institution

507–8
for more
on citing
websites
MLA style

Callicott, J. Baird. "Environmental Ethics: An Overview." *Forum on Religion and Ecology.* Yale School of Forestry & Environmental Studies, 2000. Web. 17 Sept. 2012.

31. ONLINE BOOK OR PART OF A BOOK

Cite a book you access online as you would a print book, adding the name of the site or database, the medium, and the date of access.

> Anderson, Sherwood. *Winesburg, Ohio*. New York: B. W. Huebsch, 1919.
> *Bartleby.com*. Web. 7 Apr. 2012.

If you are citing a part of a book, put the part in quotation marks before the book title. If the online book is paginated, give the pages; if not, use N. *pag.*

> Anderson, Sherwood. "The Strength of God." *Winesburg, Ohio*. New
> York: B. W. Huebsch, 1919. N. pag. *Bartleby.com*. Web. 7 Apr. 2012.

To cite a book you've downloaded onto a Kindle, Nook, or other digital device, follow the setup for a print book, but indicate the ebook format at the end of your citation.

> Larson, Erik. *The Devil in the White City: Murder, Mayhem, and Madness
> at the Fair That Changed America*. New York: Vintage, 2004. Kindle.

32. ARTICLE IN AN ONLINE SCHOLARLY JOURNAL

If a journal does not number pages or if it numbers each article separately, use *n. pag.* in place of page numbers.

> Author's Last Name, First Name. "Title of Article." *Title of Journal*
> Volume.Issue (Year): Pages. Medium. Day Month Year of access.

> Gleckman, Jason. "Shakespeare as Poet or Playwright? The Player's
> Speech in *Hamlet*." *Early Modern Literary Studies* 11.3 (2006):
> n. pag. Web. 24 June 2012.

33. ARTICLE IN AN ONLINE NEWSPAPER

> Author's Last Name, First Name. "Title of Article." *Title of Newspaper*.
> Publisher, Day Month Year. Medium. Day Month Year of access.

> Banerjee, Neela. "Proposed Religion-Based Program for Federal Inmates
> Is Canceled." *New York Times*. New York Times, 28 Oct. 2006. Web.
> 24 June 2012.

author   title   publication

34. ARTICLE IN AN ONLINE MAGAZINE

> Author's Last Name, First Name. "Title of Article." *Title of Magazine.*
> Publisher, Date of publication. Medium. Day Month Year of access.

Lithwick, Dahlia. "Privacy Rights Inc." *Slate.* Washington Post–Newsweek
Interactive, 14 Oct. 2010. Web. 25 Oct. 2012.

35. BLOG ENTRY

> Author's Last Name, First Name. "Title of Entry." *Title of Blog.* Sponsor,
> Day Month Year posted. Medium. Day Month Year of access.

Gladwell, Malcolm. "Enron and Newspapers." *Gladwell.com.* N.p., 4 Jan.
2007. Web. 26 Aug. 2012.

If the entry has no title, use "Blog entry" without quotation marks. Cite a
whole blog as you would an entire website (see no. 29). If the publisher or
sponsor is unavailable, use *N.p.*

36. ARTICLE ACCESSED THROUGH A DATABASE

For articles accessed through a library's subscription services, such as Info-
Trac and EBSCOhost, cite the publication information for the source, followed by the name of the database.

> Author's Last Name, First Name. "Title of Article." *Title of Periodical* Date
> or Volume.Issue (Year): Pages. *Database.* Medium. Day Month Year
> of access.

Stalter, Sunny. "Subway Ride and Subway System in Hart Crane's
'The Tunnel.'" *Journal of Modern Literature* 33.2 (2010): 70–91.
Academic Search Complete. Web. 28 May 2012.

37. ONLINE EDITORIAL

> "Title of Editorial." Editorial. *Title of Site.* Publisher, Day Month Year of
> publication. Medium. Day Month Year of access.

"Keep Drinking Age at 21." Editorial. *ChicagoTribune.com.* Chicago
Tribune, 26 Aug. 2008. Web. 28 Aug. 2012.

Documentation Map (MLA)
Article Accessed through a Database

Title of article → Title: "I'm Bart Simpson, who the hell are you?" A Study in Postmodern Identity (Re)Construction.

Year

Author → Authors: Ott, Brian L.[1]

Volume and issue

Source: Journal of Popular Culture; Summer2003, Vol. 37 Issue 1, p56-82, 27p

Title of periodical → Document Type: Article

Pages

Subject Terms: *SIMPSON, Bart (Fictitious character)
*SIMPSON, Homer (Fictitious character)
*SIMPSONS (Fictitious characters)
*ANIMATED television programs
SIMPSONS, The (TV program)

Reviews & Products: SIMPSONS, The (TV program)

People: GROENING, Matt

Author Affiliations: [1]Assistant Professor of Media Studies, Colorado State University

ISSN: 00223840

DOI: 10.1111/1540-5931.00054

Accession Number: 10130896

Persistent link to this record: http://search.ebscohost.com/login.aspx?direct=true&db=a9h&AN=10130896&site=ehost-live

Database: Academic Search Complete → Database

View Links: Find It! Find It!

Publisher Logo: Blackwell Publishing

511
for more
on citing an
article in a
database
MLA style

Ott, Brian L. "'I'm Bart Simpson, Who the Hell Are You?' A Study in
Postmodern Identity (Re)Construction." *Journal of Popular Culture*
37.1 (2003): 56–82. *Academic Search Complete*. Web. 24 Mar. 2012.

author   title   publication

38. ONLINE FILM REVIEW

> Reviewer's Last Name, First Name. "Title of Review." Rev. of *Title of*
> *Work*, dir. First and Last Names. *Title of Site*. Publisher, Day Month
> Year posted. Medium. Day Month Year of access.

Edelstein, David. "Best Served Cold." Rev. of *The Social Network*, dir.
David Fincher. *New York Magazine*. New York Media, 1 Oct. 2010.
Web. 3 Nov. 2012.

39. EMAIL

> Writer's Last Name, First Name. "Subject Line." Message to the author.
> Day Month Year of message. Medium.

Smith, William. "Teaching Grammar—Some Thoughts." Message to the
author. 19 Nov. 2012. Email.

40. POSTING TO AN ONLINE FORUM

> Writer's Last Name, First Name. "Title of Posting." *Name of Forum*.
> Sponsor, Day Month Year of posting. Medium. Day Month Year of
> access.

Mintz, Stephen H. "Manumission During the Revolution." *H-Net List on*
Slavery. Michigan State U, 14 Sept. 2006. Web. 18 Apr. 2012.

41. ARTICLE IN AN ONLINE REFERENCE WORK

> "Title of Article." *Title of Reference Work*. Sponsor, Date of work.
> Medium. Day Month Year of access.

"Dubai." *MSN Encarta*. Microsoft Corporation, 2008. Web. 20 June 2012.

42. WIKI ENTRY

> "Title of Entry." *Title of Wiki*. Sponsor, Day Month Year updated.
> Medium. Day Month Year of access.

"Pi." *Wikipedia*. Wikimedia Foundation, 28 Aug. 2008. Web. 2 Sept. 2012.

43. PODCAST

> Performer or Host's Last Name, First Name. "Title of Podcast." Host Host's First and Last Name. *Title of Program*. Sponsor, Day Month Year posted. Medium. Day Month Year of access.

> Blumberg, Alex, and Adam Davidson. "The Giant Pool of Money." Host Ira Glass. *This American Life*. Chicago Public Radio, 9 May 2008. Web. 18 Sept. 2012.

44. TWEET

> Author's Last Name, First Name (User Name). "Full text of tweet." Day Month Year, Time. Medium.

> Stern, Michael (Roadfood123). "Ice creamorama: Dr. Mike's is now open weekdays." 21 Mar. 2012, 5:21 p.m. Tweet.

Other Kinds of Sources

Many of the sources in this section can be found online, and you'll find examples here for how to cite them. If there is no Web model here, start with the guidelines most appropriate for the source you need to cite, omit the original medium, and end your citation with the title of the website, italicized; the medium (Web); and the day, month, and year of access.

45. ADVERTISEMENT

> Product or Company. Advertisement. *Title of Periodical* Date or Volume.Issue (Year): Page. Medium.

> Empire BlueCross BlueShield. Advertisement. *Fortune* 8 Dec. 2012: 208. Print.

ADVERTISEMENT ON THE WEB

Rolex. Advertisement. *Time*. Time, n.d. Web. 1 Apr. 2012.

46. ART

Artist's Last Name, First Name. *Title of Art*. Medium. Year. Institution, City.

Van Gogh, Vincent. *The Potato Eaters*. Oil on canvas. 1885. Van Gogh
     Museum, Amsterdam.

ART ON THE WEB

Warhol, Andy. *Self-Portrait*. 1979. J. Paul Getty Museum, Los Angeles.
     The Getty. Web. 29 Mar. 2012.

Cite photographs you find online by giving the photographer, title, and date of the image, if available. If the date is unavailable, use *n.d.* For photographs you take yourself, see no. 65.

Donnell, Ryan. At a *Pre-Civil War Railroad Construction Site Outside of*
     Philadelphia. 2010. Smithsonian Institution. Smithsonian.com. Web.
     3 Nov. 2012.

47. CARTOON

Artist's Last Name, First Name. "Title of Cartoon (if titled)." Cartoon. *Title
of Periodical* Date or Volume.Issue (Year): Page. Medium.

Chast, Roz. "The Three Wise Men of Thanksgiving." Cartoon. *New Yorker*
     1 Dec. 2003: 174. Print.

CARTOON ON THE WEB

Horsey, David. Cartoon. *Seattle Post-Intelligencer*. Seattle Post-Intelligencer,
     20 Apr. 2012. Web. 21 Apr. 2012.

48. DISSERTATION

Treat a published dissertation as you would a book, but after its title, add the abbreviation Diss., the institution, and the date of the dissertation.

Author's Last Name, First Name. *Title*. Diss. Institution, Year.
     Publication City: Publisher, Year. Medium.

> Goggin, Peter N. *A New Literacy Map of Research and Scholarship in Computers and Writing*. Diss. Indiana U of Pennsylvania, 2000. Ann Arbor: UMI, 2001. Print.

For unpublished dissertations, put the title in quotation marks and end with the degree-granting institution and the year.

> Kim, Loel. "Students Respond to Teacher Comments: A Comparison of Online Written and Voice Modalities." Diss. Carnegie Mellon U, 1998. Print.

49. CD-ROM OR DVD-ROM

> *Title*. Any pertinent information about the edition, release, or version. Publication City: Publisher, Year of publication. Medium.

> *Othello*. Princeton: Films for the Humanities and Sciences, 1998. CD-ROM.

If you are citing only part of the CD-ROM or DVD-ROM, name the part as you would a part of a book.

> "Snow Leopard." *Encarta Encyclopedia 2007*. Seattle: Microsoft, 2007. CD-ROM.

50. FILM, DVD, OR VIDEO CLIP

> *Title*. Dir. Director's First and Last Names. Perf. Lead Actors' First and Last Names. Distributor, Year of release. Medium.

> *Casablanca*. Dir. Michael Curtiz. Perf. Humphrey Bogart, Ingrid Bergman, and Claude Rains. Warner, 1942. Film.

To cite a particular person's work, start with that name.

> Cody, Diablo, scr. *Juno*. Dir. Jason Reitman. Perf. Ellen Page, Michael Cera, Jennifer Garner, and Jason Bateman. Fox Searchlight, 2007. DVD.

author   title   publication

Cite a video clip as you would a short work from a website.

> Director's Last Name, First Name, dir. "Title of Video." *Title of Site*.
>   Sponsor, Day Month Year of release. Medium. Day Month
>   Year of access.

> PivotMasterDX, dir. "Bounce!" *YouTube*. YouTube, 14 June 2008. Web.
>   21 June 2012.

51. BROADCAST INTERVIEW

> Subject's Last Name, First Name. Interview. *Title of Program*. Network.
>   Station, City. Day Month Year. Medium.

> Gates, Henry Louis, Jr. Interview. *Fresh Air*. NPR. WNYC, New York.
>   9 Apr. 2002. Radio.

52. PUBLISHED INTERVIEW

> Subject's Last Name, First Name. Interview, or "Title of Interview." *Title
>   of Periodical* Date or Volume.Issue (Year): Pages. Medium.

> Stone, Oliver. Interview. *Esquire* Nov. 2004: 170. Print.

53. PERSONAL INTERVIEW

> Subject's Last Name, First Name. Personal interview. Day Month Year.

> Roddick, Andy. Personal interview. 17 Aug. 2012.

54. UNPUBLISHED LETTER

For medium, use MS for a hand-written letter and TS for a typed one.

> Author's Last Name, First Name. Letter to the author. Day Month Year.
>   Medium.

> Quindlen, Anna. Letter to the author. 11 Apr. 2012. MS.

55. PUBLISHED LETTER

Letter Writer's Last Name, First Name. Letter to First and Last Names. Day Month Year of letter. *Title of Book*. Ed. Editor's First and Last Names. City: Publisher, Year of publication. Pages. Medium.

White, E. B. Letter to Carol Angell. 28 May 1970. *Letters of E. B. White*. Ed. Dorothy Lobarno Guth. New York: Harper, 1976. 600. Print.

56. MAP OR CHART

Title of Map. Map. City: Publisher, Year of publication. Medium.

Toscana. Map. Milan: Touring Club Italiano, 1987. Print.

MAP ON THE WEB

"Portland, Oregon." Map. *Google Maps*. Google, 25 Apr. 2012. Web. 25 Apr. 2012.

57. MUSICAL SCORE

Composer's Last Name, First Name. *Title of Composition*. Year of composition. Publication City: Publisher, Year of publication. Medium. Series Information (if any).

Beethoven, Ludwig van. *String Quartet No. 13 in B Flat, Op. 130*. 1825. New York: Dover, 1970. Print.

58. SOUND RECORDING

Artist's Last Name, First Name. *Title of Long Work*. Other pertinent details about the artists. Manufacturer, Year of release. Medium.

Beethoven, Ludwig van. *Missa Solemnis*. Perf. Westminster Choir and New York Philharmonic. Cond. Leonard Bernstein. Sony, 1992. CD.

author   title   publication

Whether you list the composer, conductor, or performer first depends on where you want to place the emphasis. If you are citing a specific song, put it in quotation marks before the name of the recording.

> Brown, Greg. "Canned Goods." *The Live One*. Red House, 1995. MP3 file.

For a spoken-word recording, you may begin with the writer, speaker, or producer, depending on your emphasis.

> Dale, Jim, narr. *Harry Potter and the Deathly Hallows*. By J. K. Rowling.
> Random House Audio, 2007. CD.

59. ORAL PRESENTATION

> Speaker's Last Name, First Name. "Title of Presentation." Sponsoring
> Institution. Site, City. Day Month Year. Medium.

> Cassin, Michael. "Nature in the Raw—The Art of Landscape Painting."
> Berkshire Institute for Lifetime Learning. Clark Art Institute,
> Williamstown. 24 Mar. 2005. Lecture.

60. PAPER FROM PROCEEDINGS OF A CONFERENCE

> Author's Last Name, First Name. "Title of Paper." *Title of Conference
> Proceedings*. Date, City. Ed. Editor's First and Last Names.
> Publication City: Publisher, Year. Pages. Medium.

> Zolotow, Charlotte. "Passion in Publishing." *A Sea of Upturned Faces:
> Proceedings of the Third Pacific Rim Conference on Children's
> Literature*. 1986, Los Angeles. Ed. Winifred Ragsdale. Metuchen:
> Scarecrow P, 1989. 236–49. Print.

61. PERFORMANCE

> *Title*. By Author's First and Last Names. Other appropriate details about
> the performance. Site, City. Day Month Year. Medium.

Take Me Out. By Richard Greenberg. Dir. Scott Plate. Perf. Caleb Sekeres. Dobama Theatre, Cleveland. 17 Aug. 2007. Performance.

62. TELEVISION OR RADIO PROGRAM

"Title of Episode." *Title of Program.* Other appropriate information about the writer, director, actors, etc. Network. Station, City, Day Month Year of broadcast. Medium.

"The Silencer." *Criminal Minds.* Writ. Erica Messer. Dir. Glenn Kershaw. NBC. WCNC, Charlotte, 26 Sept. 2012. Television.

TELEVISION OR RADIO ON THE WEB

"Bush's War." *Frontline.* Writ. and Dir. Michael Kirk. PBS, 24 Mar. 2008. *PBS.org.* Web. 10 May 2012.

63. PAMPHLET, BROCHURE, OR PRESS RELEASE

Author's Last Name, First Name. *Title of Publication.* Publication City: Publisher, Year. Medium.

Bowers, Catherine. *Can We Find a Home Here? Answering Questions of Interfaith Couples.* Boston: UUA Publications, n.d. Print.

To cite a press release, include the day and month before the year.

64. LEGAL SOURCE

The name of a court case is not italicized in a works-cited entry.

Names of the First Plaintiff v. First Defendant. Volume Name Page numbers of law report. Name of Court. Year of decision. Source information for medium consulted.

District of Columbia v. Heller. 540 US 290. Supreme Court of the US. 2008. *Supreme Court Collection.* Legal Information Inst., Cornell U Law School, n.d. Web. 18 Mar. 2012.

For acts of law, include both the Public Law number and the Statutes at Large volume and page numbers.

> Name of Law. Public law number. Statutes at Large Volume Stat. Pages. Day Month Year enacted. Medium.

> Military Commissions Act. Pub. L. 109-366. 120 Stat. 2083–2521. 17 Oct. 2006. Print.

65. MP3, JPEG, PDF, OR OTHER DIGITAL FILE

For downloaded songs, photographs, PDFs, and other documents stored on your computer or another digital device, follow the guidelines for the type of work you are citing (art, journal article, and so on) and give the file type as the medium.

> Talking Heads. "Burning Down the House." *Speaking in Tongues*. Sire, 1983. Digital file.

> Taylor, Aaron. "Twilight of the Idols: Performance, Melodramatic Villainy, and *Sunset Boulevard.*" *Journal of Film and Video* 59 (2007): 13–31. PDF file.

Citing Sources Not Covered by MLA

To cite a source for which MLA does not provide guidelines, look for models similar to the source you are citing. Give any information readers will need in order to find your source themselves—author; title, subtitle; publisher and/or sponsor; medium; dates; and any other pertinent information. You might want to try out your citation yourself, to be sure it will lead others to your source.

FORMATTING A PAPER

Name, course, title. MLA does not require a separate title page. In the upper left-hand corner of your first page, include your name, your professor's name, the name of the course, and the date. Center the title of your paper on the line after the date; capitalize it as you would a book title.

Page numbers.   In the upper right-hand corner of each page, one-half inch below the top of the page, include your last name and the page number. Number pages consecutively throughout your paper.

Font, spacing, margins, and indents.   Choose a font that is easy to read (such as Times New Roman) and provides a clear contrast between regular and italic text. Double-space the entire paper, including your works-cited list. Set one-inch margins at the top, bottom, and sides of your text; do not justify your text. The first line of each paragraph should be indented one-half inch from the left margin.

Long quotations.   When quoting more than three lines of poetry, more than four lines of prose, or dialogue between characters in a drama, set off the quotation in the rest of your text, indenting it one inch (or ten spaces) from the left margin. Do not use quotation marks, and put any parenthetical documentation *after* the final punctuation.

> In *Eastward to Tartary*, Kaplan captures ancient and contemporary Antioch for us:
>> At the height of its glory in the Roman-Byzantine age, when it had an amphitheater, public baths, aqueducts, and sewage pipes, half a million people lived in Antioch. Today the population is only 125,000. With sour relations between Turkey and Syria, and unstable politics throughout the Middle East, Antioch is now a backwater—seedy and tumbledown, with relatively few tourists. I found it altogether charming. (123)

> In the first stanza of Arnold's "Dover Beach," the exclamations make clear that the speaker is addressing someone who is also present in the scene:
>> Come to the window, sweet is the night air!
>> Only, from the long line of spray
>> Where the sea meets the moon-blanched land,
>> Listen! You hear the grating roar
>> Of pebbles which the waves draw back, and fling. (6–10)

Illustrations.   Insert illustrations in your paper close to the text that discusses them. For tables, provide a number (Table 1) and a title on separate lines above the table. Below the table, include a caption and provide information about the source. For figures (graphs, charts, photos, and so on), provide a figure number (Fig. 1), caption, and source information below the figure. If you give only brief information about the source (such as a parenthetical citation), or if the source is cited elsewhere in your text, include it in your list of works cited. Be sure to discuss any illustrations, and make it clear how they relate to the rest of your text.

List of Works Cited.   Start your list on a new page, following any notes. Center the title and double-space the entire list. Each entry should begin at the left margin, and subsequent lines should be indented one-half inch (or five spaces). Alphabetize the list by authors' last names (or by editors' or translators' names, if appropriate). Alphabetize works that have no identifiable author or editor by title, disregarding A, An, and The. If you cite more than one work by a single author, list them all alphabetically by title, and use three hyphens in place of the author's name after the first entry (see no. 2 on p. 495).

SAMPLE RESEARCH PAPER

Dylan Borchers wrote the following report for a first-year writing course. It is formatted according to the guidelines of the *MLA Handbook for Writers of Research Papers*, 7th edition (2009). While the MLA guidelines are used widely in literature and other disciplines in the humanities, exact documentation requirements may vary across disciplines and courses. If you're unsure about what your instructor wants, ask for clarification.

Dylan Borchers

Professor Bullock

English 102, Section 4

31 March 2012

Against the Odds:

Harry S. Truman and the Election of 1948

"Thomas E. Dewey's Election as President Is a Foregone

Conclusion," read a headline in the *New York Times* during the

presidential election race between incumbent Democrat Harry S.

Truman and his Republican challenger, Thomas E. Dewey. Earlier,

Life magazine had put Dewey on its cover with the caption "The

Next President of the United States" (qtd. in "1948 Truman-Dewey

Election"). In a *Newsweek* survey of fifty prominent political writers,

each one predicted Truman's defeat, and *Time* correspondents

declared that Dewey would carry 39 of the 48 states (Donaldson

210). Nearly every major media outlet across the United States

endorsed Dewey and lambasted Truman. As historian Robert H.

Ferrell observes, even Truman's wife, Bess, thought he would be

beaten (270).

   The results of an election are not so easily predicted, as the

famous photograph in fig. 1 shows. Not only did Truman win the

election, but he won by a significant margin, with 303 electoral

votes and 24,179,259 popular votes, compared to Dewey's 189

electoral votes and 21,991,291 popular votes (Donaldson 204-7). In

fact, many historians and political analysts argue that Truman

Borchers   2

Fig. 1. President Harry S. Truman holds up an Election Day edition of the *Chicago Daily Tribune*, which mistakenly announced "Dewey Defeats Truman." St. Louis, 4 Nov. 1948 (Rollins).

Illustration close to the text to which it relates. Figure number, caption, and parenthetical source citation included.

would have won by an even greater margin had third-party Progressive candidate Henry A. Wallace not split the Democratic vote in New York State and Dixiecrat Strom Thurmond not won four states in the South (McCullough 711). Although Truman's defeat was heavily predicted, those predictions themselves, Dewey's passiveness as a campaigner, and Truman's zeal turned the tide for a Truman victory.

In the months preceding the election, public opinion polls predicted that Dewey would win by a large margin. Pollster Elmo Roper stopped polling in September, believing there was no reason to continue, given a seemingly inevitable Dewey landslide. Although the margin narrowed as the election drew near, the other

Paragraphs indent $\frac{1}{2}$ inch or 5 spaces.

No signal phrase; author and page number in parentheses.

pollsters predicted a Dewey win by at least 5 percent (Donaldson 209). Many historians believe that these predictions aided the president in the long run. First, surveys showing Dewey in the lead may have prompted some of Dewey's supporters to feel overconfident about their candidate's chances and therefore to stay home from the polls on Election Day. Second, these same surveys may have energized Democrats to mount late get-out-the-vote efforts ("1948 Truman-Dewey Election"). Other analysts believe that the overwhelming predictions of a Truman loss also kept at home some Democrats who approved of Truman's policies but saw a Truman loss as inevitable. According to political analyst Samuel Lubell, those Democrats may have saved Dewey from an even greater

Text quoted in another source.

defeat (qtd. in Hamby, *Man of the People* 465). Whatever the impact on the voters, the polling numbers had a decided effect on Dewey.

Historians and political analysts alike cite Dewey's overly cautious campaign as one of the main reasons Truman was able to achieve victory. Dewey firmly believed in public opinion polls. With all indications pointing to an easy victory, Dewey and his staff believed that all he had to do was bide his time and make no foolish mistakes. Dewey himself said, "When you're leading, don't talk" (qtd. in McCullough 672). Each of Dewey's speeches was well-crafted and well-rehearsed. As the leader in the race, he kept his remarks faultlessly positive, with the result that he failed to deliver a solid message or even mention Truman or any of Truman's policies. Eventually, Dewey began to be perceived as aloof and stuffy. One observer compared him to the plastic groom on top of a wedding cake (Hamby, "Harry S. Truman"), and others noted his stiff, cold demeanor (McCullough 671–74).

Two or more works cited closely together.

As his campaign continued, observers noted that Dewey seemed uncomfortable in crowds, unable to connect with ordinary people. And he made a number of blunders. One took place at a train stop when the candidate, commenting on the number of children in the crowd, said he was glad they had been let out of school for his arrival. Unfortunately for Dewey, it was a Saturday ("1948: The Great Truman Surprise"). Such gaffes gave voters the feeling that Dewey was out of touch with the public.

Again and again through the autumn of 1948, Dewey's campaign speeches failed to address the issues, with the candidate declaring that he did not want to "get down in the gutter" (qtd. in McCullough 701). When told by fellow Republicans that he was losing ground, Dewey insisted that his campaign not alter its course. Even *Time* magazine, though it endorsed and praised him, conceded that his speeches were dull (McCullough 696). According to historian Zachary Karabell, they were "notable only for taking place, not for any specific message" (244). Dewey's numbers in the polls slipped in the weeks before the election, but he still held a comfortable lead over Truman. It would take Truman's famous whistle-stop campaign to make the difference.

Few candidates in U.S. history have campaigned for the presidency with more passion and faith than Harry Truman. In the

autumn of 1948, he wrote to his sister, "It will be the greatest
campaign any President ever made. Win, lose, or draw, people will
know where I stand" (91). For thirty-three days, Truman traveled
the nation, giving hundreds of speeches from the back of the
Ferdinand Magellan railroad car. In the same letter, he described the
pace: "We made about 140 stops and I spoke over 147 times, shook
hands with at least 30,000 and am in good condition to start out
again tomorrow for Wilmington, Philadelphia, Jersey City, Newark,
Albany and Buffalo" (91). McCullough writes of Truman's
campaign:

> No President in history had ever gone so far in quest of
> support from the people, or with less cause for the effort,
> to judge by informed opinion. . . . As a test of his skills and
> judgment as a professional politician, not to say his
> stamina and disposition at age sixty-four, it would be like
> no other experience in his long, often difficult career, as
> he himself understood perfectly. More than any other
> event in his public life, or in his presidency thus far, it
> would reveal the kind of man he was. (655)

Quotations of 4 or more lines indented 1 inch (10 spaces).

Parenthetical reference after final punctuation.

He spoke in large cities and small towns, defending his
policies and attacking Republicans. As a former farmer and
relatively late bloomer, Truman was able to connect with the public.
He developed an energetic style, usually speaking from notes rather
than from a prepared speech, and often mingled with the crowds
that met his train. These crowds grew larger as the campaign

progressed. In Chicago, over half a million people lined the streets as he passed, and in St. Paul the crowd numbered over 25,000. When Dewey entered St. Paul two days later, he was greeted by only 7,000 supporters ("1948 Truman-Dewey Election"). Reporters brushed off the large crowds as mere curiosity seekers wanting to see a president (McCullough 682). Yet Truman persisted, even if he often seemed to be the only one who thought he could win. By going directly to the American people and connecting with them, Truman built the momentum needed to surpass Dewey and win the election.

Use the title if no author is given.

The legacy and lessons of Truman's whistle-stop campaign continue to be studied by political analysts, and politicians today often mimic his campaign methods by scheduling multiple visits to key states, as Truman did. He visited California, Illinois, and Ohio 48 times, compared with 6 visits to those states by Dewey. Political scientist Thomas M. Holbrook concludes that his strategic campaigning in those states and others gave Truman the electoral votes he needed to win (61, 65).

The 1948 election also had an effect on pollsters, who, as Elmo Roper admitted, "couldn't have been more wrong" (qtd. in Karabell 255). *Life* magazine's editors concluded that pollsters as well as reporters and commentators were too convinced of a Dewey victory to analyze the polls seriously, especially the opinions of undecided voters (Karabell 256). Pollsters assumed that undecided voters would vote in the same proportion as decided voters—and that turned out to be a false assumption (Karabell 258). In fact, the lopsidedness of the polls might have led voters who supported Truman to call themselves undecided out of an unwillingness to associate themselves with the losing side, further skewing the polls' results (McDonald, Glynn, Kim, and Ostman 152). Such errors led pollsters to change their methods significantly after the 1948 election.

Work by 4 authors.

After the election, many political analysts, journalists, and historians concluded that the Truman upset was in fact a victory for the American people, who, the *New Republic* noted, "couldn't be ticketed by the polls, knew its own mind and had picked the rather unlikely but courageous figure of Truman to carry its banner" (qtd. in McCullough 715). How "unlikely" is unclear, however; Truman biographer Alonzo Hamby notes that "polls of scholars consistently rank Truman among the top eight presidents in American history" (*Man of the People* 641). But despite Truman's high standing, and despite the fact that the whistle-stop campaign is now part of our political landscape, politicians have increasingly imitated the style of the Dewey campaign, with its "packaged candidate who ran so as not to lose, who steered clear of controversy, and who made a good show of appearing presidential" (Karabell 266). The election of 1948 shows that voters are not necessarily swayed by polls, but it may have presaged the packaging of candidates by public relations experts, to the detriment of public debate on the issues in future presidential elections.

Borchers 8

Works Cited

Donaldson, Gary A. *Truman Defeats Dewey*. Lexington: UP of Kentucky, 1999. Print.

Ferrell, Robert H. *Harry S. Truman: A Life*. Columbia: U of Missouri P, 1994. Print.

Hamby, Alonzo L., ed. "Harry S. Truman (1945–1953)." *American President: A Reference Resource*. Miller Center, U of Virginia, 11 Jan. 2012. Web. 17 Mar. 2012.

—. *Man of the People: A Life of Harry S. Truman*. New York: Oxford UP, 1995. Print.

Holbrook, Thomas M. "Did the Whistle-Stop Campaign Matter?" PS: *Political Science and Politics* 35.1 (2002): 59–66. Print.

Karabell, Zachary. *The Last Campaign: How Harry Truman Won the 1948 Election*. New York: Knopf, 2000. Print.

McCullough, David. *Truman*. New York: Simon, 1992. Print.

McDonald, Daniel G., Carroll J. Glynn, Sei-Hill Kim, and Ronald E. Ostman. "The Spiral of Silence in the 1948 Presidential Election." *Communication Research* 28.2 (2001): 139–55. Print.

"1948: The Great Truman Surprise." *The Press and the Presidency*. Dept. of Political Science and International Affairs, Kennesaw State U, 29 Oct. 2003. Web. 20 Mar. 2012.

"1948 Truman-Dewey Election." *American Political History*. Eagleton Inst. of Politics, Rutgers, State U of New Jersey, 2012. Web. 19 Mar. 2012.

1"

Heading centered.

Double-spaced.

Alphabetized by authors' last names.

Each entry begins at the left margin; subsequent lines are indented.

Multiple works by a single author listed alphabetically by title.

Rollins, Byron. Untitled photograph. "The First 150 Years: 1948." *AP History*. Associated Press, n.d. Web. 23 Mar. 2009.

Truman, Harry S. "Campaigning, Letter, October 5, 1948." *Harry S. Truman*. Ed. Robert H. Ferrell. Washington: CQ P, 2003. 91. Print.

Every source used is in the list of works cited.

American Psychological Association (APA) style calls for (1) brief documentation in parentheses near each in-text citation and (2) complete documentation in a list of references at the end of your text. The models in this chapter draw on the *Publication Manual of the American Psychological Association*, 6th edition (2009). Additional information is available at www.apastyle.org.

A DIRECTORY TO APA STYLE

In-Text Documentation   536

author   title   publication

Throughout this chapter, you'll find models and examples that are color-coded to help you see how writers include source information in their texts and reference lists: tan for author or editor, yellow for title, gray for publication information: place of publication, publisher, date of publication, page number(s), and so on.

IN-TEXT DOCUMENTATION

Brief documentation in your text makes clear to your reader precisely what you took from a source and, in the case of a quotation, precisely where (usually, on which page) in the source you found the text you are quoting.

462–74

PARAPHRASES and **SUMMARIES** are more common than **QUOTATIONS** in APA-style projects. As you cite each source, you will need to decide whether to name the author in a signal phrase—"as McCullough (2001) wrote"— or in parentheses—"(McCullough, 2001)." Note that APA requires you to use the past tense or present perfect tense for verbs in **SIGNAL PHRASES**: "Moss (2003) argued," "Moss (2003) has argued."

471–74

1. AUTHOR NAMED IN A SIGNAL PHRASE

If you are quoting, you must give the page number(s). You are not required to give the page number(s) with a paraphrase or a summary, but APA encourages you to do so, especially if you are citing a long or complex work; most of the models in this chapter do include page numbers.

AUTHOR QUOTED

Put the date in parentheses right after the author's name; put the page in parentheses as close to the quotation as possible.

> McCullough (2001) described John Adams as having "the hands of a man accustomed to pruning his own trees, cutting his own hay, and splitting his own firewood" (p. 18).

Notice that in this example, the parenthetical reference with the page number comes *after* the closing quotation marks but *before* the period at the end of the sentence.

AUTHOR PARAPHRASED OR SUMMARIZED

Put the date in parentheses right after the author's name; follow the date with the page.

author   title   publication

John Adams's hands were those of a laborer, according to McCullough (2001, p. 18).

2. AUTHOR NAMED IN PARENTHESES

If you do not mention an author in a signal phrase, put his or her name, a comma, and the year of publication in parentheses as close as possible to the quotation, paraphrase, or summary.

AUTHOR QUOTED

Give the author, date, and page in one parenthesis, or split the information between two parentheses.

> One biographer (McCullough, 2001) has said John Adams had "the hands of a man accustomed to pruning his own trees, cutting his own hay, and splitting his own firewood" (p. 18).

AUTHOR PARAPHRASED OR SUMMARIZED

Give the author, date, and page in one parenthesis toward the beginning or the end of the paraphrase or summary.

> John Adams's hands were those of a laborer (McCullough, 2001, p. 18).

3. AUTHORS WITH THE SAME LAST NAME

If your reference list includes more than one person with the same last name, include initials in all documentation to distinguish the authors from one another.

> Eclecticism is common in contemporary criticism (J. M. Smith, 1992, p. vii).

4. TWO AUTHORS

Always mention both authors. Use *and* in a signal phrase, but use an ampersand (&) in parentheses. (See next page for examples.)

Carlson and Ventura (1990, p. v) wanted to introduce Julio Cortázar, Marjorie Agosín, and other Latin American writers to an audience of English-speaking adolescents.

According to the Peter Principle, "In a hierarchy, every employee tends to rise to his level of incompetence" (Peter & Hull, 1969, p. 26).

5. THREE OR MORE AUTHORS

In the first reference to a work by three to five persons, name all contributors. In subsequent references, name the first author followed by *et al.*, Latin for "and others." Whenever you refer to a work by six or more contributors, name only the first author, followed by *et al.* Use *and* in a signal phrase, but use an ampersand (&) in parentheses.

Faigley, George, Palchik, and Selfe (2004, p. xii) have argued that where there used to be a concept called *literacy*, today's multitude of new kinds of texts has given us *literacies*.

Peilen et al. (1990, p. 75) supported their claims about corporate corruption with startling anecdotal evidence.

6. ORGANIZATION OR GOVERNMENT AS AUTHOR

If an organization has a long name that is recognizable by its abbreviation, give the full name and the abbreviation the first time you cite the source. In subsequent citations, use only the abbreviation. If the organization does not have a familiar abbreviation, always use its full name.

FIRST CITATION

(American Psychological Association [APA], 2008)

SUBSEQUENT CITATIONS

(APA, 2008)

author   title   publication

7. AUTHOR UNKNOWN

Use the complete title if it is short; if it is long, use the first few words of the title under which the work appears in the reference list.

> *Webster's New Biographical Dictionary* (1988) identifies William James as "American psychologist and philosopher" (p. 520).

> A powerful editorial asserted that healthy liver donor Mike Hurewitz died because of "frightening" faulty postoperative care ("Every Patient's Nightmare," 2007).

8. TWO OR MORE WORKS CITED TOGETHER

If you cite multiple works in the same parenthesis, place them in the order that they appear in your reference list, separated by semicolons.

> Many researchers have argued that what counts as "literacy" is not necessarily learned at school (Heath, 1983; Moss, 2003).

9. TWO OR MORE WORKS BY AN AUTHOR IN THE SAME YEAR

If your list of references includes more than one work by the same author published in the same year, order them alphabetically by title, adding lowercase letters ("a," "b," and so on) to the year.

> Kaplan (2000a) described orderly shantytowns in Turkey that did not resemble the other slums he visited.

10. SOURCE QUOTED IN ANOTHER SOURCE

When you cite a source that was quoted in another source, let the reader know that you used a secondary source by adding the words *as cited in*.

> During the meeting with the psychologist, the patient stated repeatedly that he "didn't want to be too paranoid" (as cited in Oberfield & Yasik, 2004, p. 294).

11. WORK WITHOUT PAGE NUMBERS

Instead of page numbers, some electronic works have paragraph numbers, which you should include (preceded by the abbreviation *para.*) if you are referring to a specific part of such a source. In sources with neither page nor paragraph numbers, refer readers to a particular part of the source if possible, perhaps indicating a heading and the paragraph under the heading.

> Russell's dismissals from Trinity College at Cambridge and from City
> College in New York City have been seen as examples of the controversy
> that marked his life (Irvine, 2006, para. 2).

12. AN ENTIRE WORK

You do not need to give a page number if you are directing readers' attention to an entire work.

> Kaplan (2000) considered Turkey and Central Asia explosive.

When you are citing an entire website, give the URL in the text. You do not need to include the website in your reference list. To cite part of a website, see no. 20 on page 000.

> Beyond providing diagnostic information, the website for the Alzheimer's
> Association includes a variety of resources for family and community
> support of patients suffering from Alzheimer's (http://www.alz.org).

13. PERSONAL COMMUNICATION

Cite email, telephone conversations, interviews, personal letters, messages from nonarchived discussion sources, and other personal texts as *personal communication*, along with the person's initial(s), last name, and the date. You do not need to include such personal communications in your reference list.

> L. Strauss (personal communication, December 6, 2012) told about
> visiting Yogi Berra when they both lived in Montclair, New Jersey.

NOTES

You may need to use content notes to give an explanation or information that doesn't fit into your text. To signal a content note, place a superscript numeral at the appropriate point in your text. Put the notes on a separate page with the heading *Notes*, after your text but before the reference list. If you have multiple notes, number them consecutively throughout your text. Here is an example from *In Search of Solutions: A New Direction in Psychotherapy* (2003).

TEXT WITH SUPERSCRIPT

An important part of working with teams and one-way mirrors is taking the consultation break, as at Milan, BFTC, and MRI.[1]

CONTENT NOTE

[1]It is crucial to note here that, while working within a team is fun, stimulating, and revitalizing, it is not necessary for successful outcomes. Solution-oriented therapy works equally well when working solo.

REFERENCE LIST

A reference list provides full bibliographic information for every source cited in your text with the exception of entire websites and personal communications. See page 563 for guidelines on preparing such a list; for a sample reference list see pages 573–74.

Print Books

For most books, you'll need to provide the author, the publication date, the title and any subtitle, and the place of publication and publisher.

IMPORTANT DETAILS FOR CITING PRINT BOOKS

- **AUTHORS**: Use the author's last name but replace the first and middle names with initials (D. Kinder for Donald Kinder).

- **DATES**: If more than one year is given, use the most recent one.

- **TITLES**: Capitalize only the first word and proper nouns and proper adjectives in titles and subtitles.

- **PUBLICATION PLACE**: Give city followed by state (abbreviated) or country, if outside the United States (for example, Boston, MA; London, England; Toronto, Ontario, Canada). If more than one city is given, use the first. Do not include the state or country if the publisher is a university whose name includes that information.

- **PUBLISHER**: Use a shortened form of the publisher's name (Little, Brown for Little, Brown and Company), but retain *Association*, *Books*, and *Press* (American Psychological Association, Princeton University Press).

1. ONE AUTHOR

Author's Last Name, Initials. (Year of publication). *Title*. Publication City, State or Country: Publisher.

Louis, M. (2003). *Moneyball: The art of winning an unfair game*. New York, NY: Norton.

2. TWO OR MORE WORKS BY THE SAME AUTHOR

If the works were published in different years, list them chronologically.

Lewis, B. (1995). *The Middle East: A brief history of the last 2,000 years*. New York, NY: Scribner.

Lewis, B. (2003). *The crisis of Islam: Holy war and unholy terror*. New York, NY: Modern Library.

If the works were published in the same year, list them alphabetically by title, adding "a," "b," and so on to the year (see p. 544).

author　　　　title　　　publication

Documentation Map (APA)
Print Book

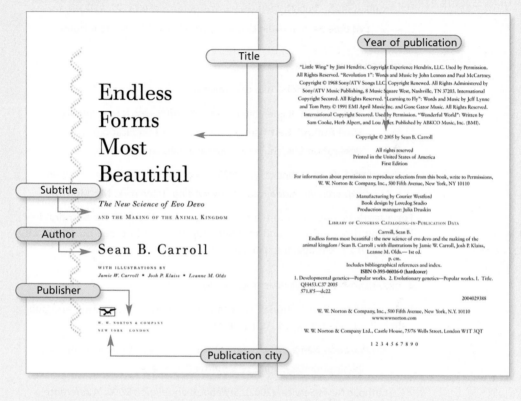

541–47
for more on
citing books
APA style

Carroll, S. B. (2005). *Endless forms most beautiful: The new science of evo devo and the making of the animal kingdom.* New York, NY: Norton.

Kaplan, R. D. (2000a). *The coming anarchy: Shattering the dreams of the post cold war.* New York, NY: Random House.

Kaplan, R. D. (2000b). *Eastward to Tartary: Travels in the Balkans, the Middle East, and the Caucasus.* New York, NY: Random House.

3. TWO OR MORE AUTHORS

For two to seven authors, use this format.

First Author's Last Name, Initials, Next Author's Last Name, Initials, & Final Author's Last Name, Initials. (Year of publication). *Title.* Publication City, State or Country: Publisher.

Leavitt, S. D., & Dubner, S. J. (2005). *Freakonomics: A rogue economist explores the hidden side of everything.* New York, NY: Morrow.

For a work by eight or more authors, name just the first six authors, followed by three ellipses, and end with the final author (see no. 21 for an example from a magazine article).

4. ORGANIZATION OR GOVERNMENT AS AUTHOR

Sometimes an organization or government agency is both author and publisher. If so, use the word *Author* as the publisher.

Organization Name or Government Agency. (Year of publication). *Title.* Publication City, State or Country: Publisher.

Catholic News Service. (2002). *Stylebook on religion 2000: A reference guide and usage manual.* Washington, DC: Author.

5. AUTHOR AND EDITOR

Author's Last Name, Initials. (Year of edited edition). *Title.* (Editor's Initials Last Name, Ed.). Publication City, State or Country: Publisher. (Original work[s] published year[s])

author   title   publication

Dick, P. F. (2008). *Five novels of the 1960s and 70s.* (J. Lethem, Ed.). New York, NY: Library of America. (Original works published 1964–1977)

6. EDITED COLLECTION

First Editor's Last Name, Initials, Next Editor's Last Name, Initials, & Final Editor's Last Name, Initials. (Eds.). (Year of edited edition). *Title.* Publication City, State or Country: Publisher.

Raviv, A., Oppenheimer, L., & Bar-Tal, D. (Eds.). (1999). *How children understand war and peace: A call for international peace education.* San Francisco, CA: Jossey-Bass.

7. WORK IN AN EDITED COLLECTION

Author's Last Name, Initials. (Year of publication). Title of article or chapter. In Initials Last Name (Ed.), *Title* (pp. pages). Publication City, State or Country: Publisher.

Harris, I. M. (1999). Types of peace education. In A. Raviv, L. Oppenheimer, & D. Bar-Tal (Eds.), *How children understand war and peace: A call for international peace education* (pp. 46–70). San Francisco, CA: Jossey-Bass.

8. UNKNOWN AUTHOR

Title. (Year of publication). Publication City, State or Country: Publisher.

Webster's new biographical dictionary. (1988). Springfield, MA: Merriam-Webster.

If the title page of a work lists the author as *Anonymous*, treat the reference-list entry as if the author's name were Anonymous, and alphabetize it accordingly.

9. EDITION OTHER THAN THE FIRST

Author's Last Name, Initials. (Year). *Title* (name or number ed.). Publication City, State or Country: Publisher.

Burch, D. (2008). *Emergency navigation: Find your position and shape your course at sea even if your instruments fail* (2nd ed.). Camden, ME: International Marine/McGraw-Hill.

10. TRANSLATION

Author's Last Name, Initials. (Year of publication). *Title* (Translator's Initials Last Name, Trans.). Publication City, State or Country: Publisher. (Original work published Year)

Hugo, V. (2008). *Les misérables* (J. Rose, Trans.). New York, NY: Modern Library. (Original work published 1862)

11. MULTIVOLUME WORK

Author's Last Name, Initials. (Year). *Title* (Vols. numbers). Publication City, State or Country: Publisher.

Nastali, D. P., & Boardman, P. C. (2004). *The Arthurian annals: The tradition in English from 1250 to 2000* (Vols. 1–2). New York, NY: Oxford University Press USA.

ONE VOLUME OF A MULTIVOLUME WORK

Author's Last Name, Initials. (Year). *Title of whole work (Vol. number).* Publication City, State or Country: Publisher.

Spiegelman, A. (1986). *Maus (Vol. 1).* New York, NY: Random House.

12. ARTICLE IN A REFERENCE BOOK

UNSIGNED

Title of entry. (Year). In *Title of reference book* (Name or number ed., Vol. number, pp. pages). Publication City, State or Country: Publisher.

Macrophage. (2003). In *Merriam-Webster's collegiate dictionary* (10th ed., p. 698). Springfield, MA: Merriam-Webster.

author　　　title　　　publication

SIGNED

Author's Last Name, Initials. (Year). Title of entry. In *Title of reference book* (Vol. number, pp. pages). Publication City, State or Country: Publisher.

Wasserman, D. E. (2006). Human exposure to vibration. In *International encyclopedia of ergonomics and human factors* (Vol. 2, pp. 1800–1801). Boca Raton, FL: CRC.

Print Periodicals

For most articles, you'll need to provide information about the author; the date; the article title and any subtitle; the periodical title; and any volume or issue number and inclusive page numbers.

IMPORTANT DETAILS FOR CITING PRINT PERIODICALS

- **AUTHORS**: List authors as you would for a book.

- **DATES**: For journals, give year only. For magazines and newspapers, give year followed by a comma and then month or month and day.

- **TITLES**: Capitalize article titles as you would for a book. Capitalize the first and last words and all principal words of periodical titles. Do not capitalize *a, an, the,* or any prepositions or coordinating conjunctions unless they begin the title of the periodical.

- **VOLUME AND ISSUE**: For journals and magazines, give volume or volume and issue, depending on the journal's pagination method. For newspapers, do not give volume or issue.

- **PAGES**: Use *p.* or *pp.* for a newspaper article but not for a journal or magazine article. If an article does not fall on consecutive pages, give all the page numbers (for example, 45, 75–77 for a journal or magazine; pp. C1, C3, C5–C7 for a newspaper).

13. ARTICLE IN A JOURNAL PAGINATED BY VOLUME

Author's Last Name, Initials. (Year). Title of article. *Title of Journal, volume*, pages.

Gremer, J. R., Sala, A., & Crone, E. E. (2010). Disappearing plants: Why they hide and how they return. *Ecology, 91*, 3407–3413.

14. ARTICLE IN A JOURNAL PAGINATED BY ISSUE

Author's Last Name, Initials. (Year). Title of article. *Title of Journal, volume*(issue), pages.

Weaver, C., McNally, C., & Moerman, S. (2001). To grammar or not to grammar: That is *not* the question! *Voices from the Middle, 8*(3), 17–33.

15. ARTICLE IN A MAGAZINE

If a magazine is published weekly, include the day and the month. If there are a volume number and an issue number, include them after the magazine title.

Author's Last Name, Initials. (Year, Month Day). Title of article. *Title of Magazine, volume*(issue), page(s).

Gregory, S. (2008, June 30). Crash course: Why golf carts are more hazardous than they look. *Time, 171*(26), 53.

If a magazine is published monthly, include the month(s) only.

16. ARTICLE IN A NEWSPAPER

If page numbers are consecutive, separate them with a dash. If not, separate them with a comma.

Author's Last Name, Initials. (Year, Month Day). Title of article. *Title of Newspaper*, p(p). page(s).

Schneider, G. (2005, March 13). Fashion sense on wheels. *The Washington Post*, pp. F1, F6.

Documentation Map (APA)
Article in a Print Magazine

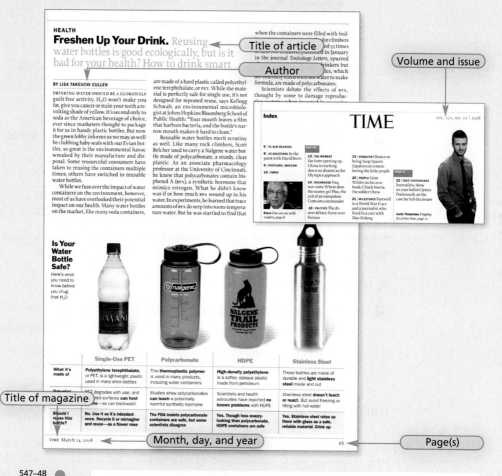

Title of article

Author

Volume and issue

Title of magazine

Month, day, and year

Page(s)

547–48 for more on citing magazines APA style

Cullen, L. T. (2008, March 24). Freshen up your drink: Reusing water bottles is good ecologically, but is it bad for your health? How to drink smart. *Time, 171*(12), 65.

17. ARTICLE BY AN UNKNOWN AUTHOR

Title of article. (Year, Month Day). *Title of Periodical, volume*(issue), page(s) or p(p). page(s).

Hot property: From carriage house to family compound. (2004, December). *Berkshire Living, 1*(1), 99.

Clues in salmonella outbreak. (2008, June 21). *New York Times*, p. A13.

18. BOOK REVIEW

Reviewer's Last Name, Initials. (Date of publication). Title of review [Review of by the book *Title of Work*, by Author's Initials Last Name]. *Title of Periodical, volume*(issue), page(s).

Brandt, A. (2003, October). Animal planet [Review of the book *Intelligence of apes and other rational beings*, by D. R. Rumb & D. A. Washburn]. *National Geographic Adventure, 5*(10), 47.

If the review does not have a title, include the bracketed information about the work being reviewed, immediately after the date of publication.

19. LETTER TO THE EDITOR

Author's Last Name, Initials. (Date of publication). Title of letter [Letter to the editor]. *Title of Periodical, volume*(issue), page(s) or p(p). page(s).

Hitchcock, G. (2008, August 3). Save our species [Letter to the editor]. *San Francisco Chronicle*, p. P-3.

Online Sources

Not every online source gives you all the data that APA would like to see in a reference entry. Ideally, you will be able to list author's or editor's name; date of first electronic publication or most recent revision; title of document; information about print publication if any; and retrieval information: DOI (Digital Object Identifier, a string of letters and numbers that

author   title   publication

identifies an online document) or URL. In some cases, additional information about electronic publication may be required (title of site, retrieval date, name of sponsoring institution).

IMPORTANT DETAILS FOR CITING ONLINE SOURCES

- **AUTHORS**: List authors as you would for a print book or periodical.
- **TITLES**: For websites and electronic documents, articles, or books, capitalize titles and subtitles as you would for a book; capitalize periodical titles as you would for a print periodical.
- **DATES**: After the author, give the year of the document's original publication on the Web or of its most recent revision. If neither of those years is clear, use *n.d.* to mean "no date." For undated content or content that may change (for example, a wiki entry), include the month, day, and year that you retrieved the document. You don't need to include the retrieval date for content that's unlikely to change.
- **DOI OR URL**: Include the DOI instead of the URL in the reference whenever one is available. If no DOI is available, provide the URL of the home page or menu page. If you do not identify the sponsoring institution, you do not need a colon before the URL or DOI. Don't include any punctuation at the end of the URL or DOI. When a URL won't fit on the line, break the URL before most punctuation, but do not break *http://*.

20. WORK FROM A NONPERIODICAL WEBSITE

> Author's Last Name, Initials. (Date of publication). Title of work. *Title of site*. DOI or Retrieved Month Day, Year [if necessary], from URL

Cruikshank, D. (2009, June 15). Unlocking the secrets and powers of the brain. *National Science Foundation*. Retrieved from http://www.nsf.gov /discoveries/disc_summ.jsp?cntn_id=114979&org=NSF

To cite an entire website, include the URL in parentheses in an in-text citation. Do not list the website in your list of references.

Documentation Map (APA)

Work from a Website

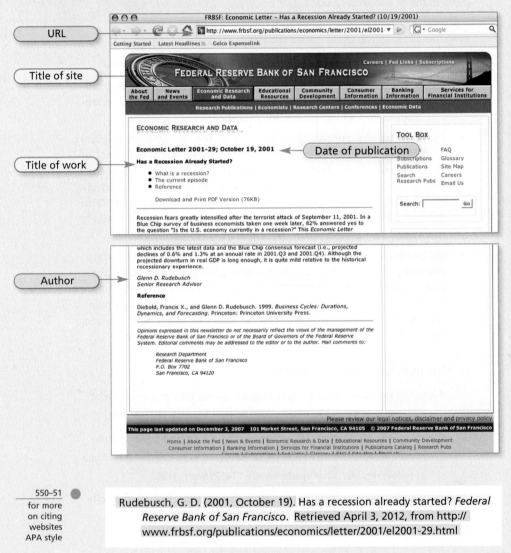

URL → `http://www.frbsf.org/publications/economics/letter/2001/el2001 ▼`

Title of site → FEDERAL RESERVE BANK OF SAN FRANCISCO

Title of work → Has a Recession Already Started?

Date of publication → Economic Letter 2001-29; October 19, 2001

Author → Glenn D. Rudebusch / Senior Research Advisor

550–51 ●
for more
on citing
websites
APA style

Rudebusch, G. D. (2001, October 19). Has a recession already started? *Federal Reserve Bank of San Francisco*. Retrieved April 3, 2012, from http://www.frbsf.org/publications/economics/letter/2001/el2001-29.html

author   title   publication

21. ARTICLE IN AN ONLINE PERIODICAL

When available, include the volume number and issue number as you would for a print source. If no DOI has been assigned, provide the URL of the home page or menu page of the journal or magazine, even for articles that you access through a database.

ARTICLE IN AN ONLINE JOURNAL

Author's Last Name, Initials. (Year). Title of article. *Title of Journal,*
volume(issue), pages. DOI or Retrieved from URL

Corbett, C. (2007). Vehicle-related crime and the gender gap. *Psychology,*
Crime & Law, 13, 245–263. doi:10.1080/10683160600822022

ARTICLE IN AN ONLINE MAGAZINE

Author's Last Name, Initials. (Year, Month Day). Title of article. *Title of*
Magazine, volume(issue). DOI or Retrieved from URL

Barreda, V. D., Palazzesi, L., Tellería, M. C., Katinas, L., Crisci, J. N.,
Bromer, K., . . . Bechis, F. (2010, September 24). Eocene Patagonia
fossils of the daisy family. *Science, 329,* 1621. doi:10.1126/science
.1193108

ARTICLE IN AN ONLINE NEWSPAPER

If the article can be found by searching the site, give the URL of the home page or menu page.

Author's Last Name, Initials. (Year, Month Day). Title of article. *Title of*
Newspaper. Retrieved from URL

Collins, G. (2012, September 12). Game time. *The New York Times.*
Retrieved from http://www.nytimes.com

22. ARTICLE AVAILABLE ONLY THROUGH A DATABASE

Some sources, such as an out-of-print journal or rare book, can be accessed only through a database. When no DOI is provided, give either the name of the database or its URL. (See p. 556 for a template and example.)

Documentation Map (APA)
Article in a Journal with DOI

Title of journal

Year

DOI

Volume

Pages

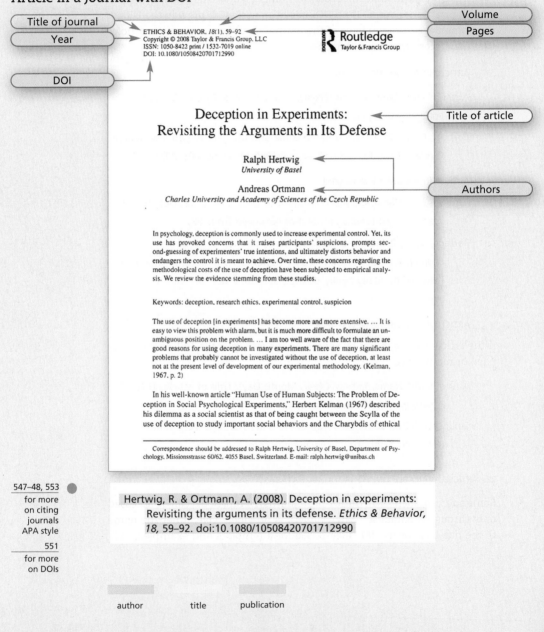

ETHICS & BEHAVIOR, *18*(1), 59–92
Copyright © 2008 Taylor & Francis Group, LLC
ISSN: 1050-8422 print / 1532-7019 online
DOI: 10.1080/10508420701712990

R Routledge
Taylor & Francis Group

Title of article

Deception in Experiments:
Revisiting the Arguments in Its Defense

Ralph Hertwig
University of Basel

Andreas Ortmann
Charles University and Academy of Sciences of the Czech Republic

Authors

In psychology, deception is commonly used to increase experimental control. Yet, its use has provoked concerns that it raises participants' suspicions, prompts second-guessing of experimenters' true intentions, and ultimately distorts behavior and endangers the control it is meant to achieve. Over time, these concerns regarding the methodological costs of the use of deception have been subjected to empirical analysis. We review the evidence stemming from these studies.

Keywords: deception, research ethics, experimental control, suspicion

The use of deception [in experiments] has become more and more extensive. ... It is easy to view this problem with alarm, but it is much more difficult to formulate an unambiguous position on the problem. ... I am too well aware of the fact that there are good reasons for using deception in many experiments. There are many significant problems that probably cannot be investigated without the use of deception, at least not at the present level of development of our experimental methodology. (Kelman, 1967, p. 2)

In his well-known article "Human Use of Human Subjects: The Problem of Deception in Social Psychological Experiments," Herbert Kelman (1967) described his dilemma as a social scientist as that of being caught between the Scylla of the use of deception to study important social behaviors and the Charybdis of ethical

Correspondence should be addressed to Ralph Hertwig, University of Basel, Department of Psychology, Missionsstrasse 60/62, 4055 Basel, Switzerland. E-mail: ralph.hertwig@unibas.ch

547–48, 553
for more
on citing
journals
APA style

551
for more
on DOIs

Hertwig, R. & Ortmann, A. (2008). Deception in experiments: Revisiting the arguments in its defense. *Ethics & Behavior*, *18*, 59–92. doi:10.1080/10508420701712990

author   title   publication

Documentation Map (APA)
Article Accessed through a Database with DOI

Title of article → **Title:** *Exploring Dream Work* at End of Life.

Author → **Authors:** Goelitz, Ann[1] agoelitz@yahoo.com

Pages

Title of journal → **Source:** Dreaming; Sep2007, Vol. 17 Issue 3, p159-171, 13p

Document Type: Article

Volume and issue

Year

Subject Terms: *DREAMS
*TERMINALLY ill
*SLEEP -- Physiological aspects
*SUBCONSCIOUSNESS
*PSYCHOLOGY

the copyright holder's express written permission. However, users may print, download, or email articles for individual use. This abstract may be abridged. No warranty is given about the accuracy of the copy. Users should refer to the original published version of the material for the full abstract. (Copyright applies to all Abstracts)

Author Affiliations: [1]Hunter College School of Social *Work*

ISSN: 10530797

DOI: 10.1037/1053-079717.3.159 ← DOI

Accession Number: 27089888

Persistent link to this record (Permalink): http://search.ebscohost.com/login.aspx?direct=true&db=a9h ▣ BOOKMARK

Database: Academic Search Complete

View Links: Find It! Find It!

553, 556
for more
on citing an
article in a
database
APA style

Goerlitz, A. (2007). Exploring dream work at end of life. *Dreaming, 17*(3), 159–171. doi:10.1037/1053-0797.17.3.159

> Author's Last Name, Initials. (Year). Title of article. *Title of Journal,*
> *volume*(issue), pages. DOI or Retrieved from Name of database
> or URL

Simpson, M. (1972). Authoritarianism and education: A comparative
approach. *Sociometry, 35*(2), 223–234. Retrieved from
http://www.jstor.org/stable/2786619

23. ARTICLE OR CHAPTER IN A WEB DOCUMENT OR ONLINE REFERENCE WORK

Give the URL of the chapter or article if no DOI is provided.

> Author's Last Name, Initials. (Year). Title of entry. In Initials Last Name
> (Ed.), *Title of reference work.* DOI or Retrieved from URL

Korfmacher, C. (2006). Personal identity. In J. Fieser & B. Dowden (Eds.),
Internet encyclopedia of philosophy. Retrieved from
http://www.iep.utm.edu/person-i/

24. ELECTRONIC BOOK

> Author's Last Name, Initials. (Year). *Title of book.* DOI or Retrieved from URL

TenDam, H. (n.d.). *Politics, civilization & humanity.* Retrieved from
http://onlineoriginals.com/showitem.asp?itemID=46&page=2

For an ebook based on a print version, include a description of the digital
format in brackets after the book title.

Blain, M. (2009). *The sociology of terror: Studies in power, subjection,*
and victimage ritual [Adobe Digital Editions version]. Retrieved
from http://www.powells.com/sub/AdobeDigitalEditionsPolitics
.html?sec_big_link=1

25. WIKI ENTRY

Give the entry title and the date of posting, or *n.d.* if there is no date. Then
include the retrieval date, the name of the wiki, and the URL for the entry.

author   title   publication

Title of entry. (Year, Month Day). Retrieved Month Day, Year, from Title
of wiki: URL

Discourse. (n.d.). Retrieved November 8, 2012, from Psychology Wiki:
http://psychology.wikia.com/wiki/Discourse

26. ONLINE DISCUSSION SOURCE

If the name of the list to which to the message was posted is not part of
the URL, include it after *Retrieved from*. The URL you provide should be for
the archived version of the message or post.

Author's Last Name, Initials. (Year, Month Day). Subject line of message
[Descriptive label]. Retrieved from URL

Baker, J. (2005, February 15). Re: Huffing and puffing [Electronic
mailing list message]. Retrieved from American Dialect Society
electronic mailing list: http://listserv.linguistlist.org/cgi-bin
/wa?A2=ind0502C&L=ADS-L&P=R44

Do not include email or other nonarchived discussions in your list of
references. Simply cite the sender's name in your text. See no. 13 on
page 540 for guidelines on identifying such sources in your text.

27. BLOG ENTRY

Author's Last Name, Initials. (Year, Month Day). Title of post [Blog post].
Retrieved from URL

Collins, C. (2009, August 19). Butterfly benefits from warmer springs?
[Blog post]. Retrieved from http://www.intute.ac.uk/blog
/2009/08/19/butterfly-benefits-from-warmer-springs/

28. ONLINE VIDEO

Last Name, Initials (Writer), & Last Name, Initials (Producer). (Year, Month
Day posted). *Title* [Descriptive label]. Retrieved from URL

Coulter, J. (Songwriter & Performer), & Booth, M. S. (Producer). (2006, September 23). *Code Monkey* [Video file]. Retrieved from http://www.youtube.com/watch?v=v4Wy7gRGgeA

29. PODCAST

Writer's Last Name, Initials. (Writer), & Producer's Last Name, Initials. (Producer). (Year, Month Day). Title of podcast. *Title of site or program* [Audio podcast]. Retrieved from URL

Britt, M. A. (Writer & Producer). (2009, June 7). Episode 97: Stanley Milgram study finally replicated. *The Psych Files Podcast* [Audio podcast]. Retrieved from http://www.thepsychfiles.com/

Other Kinds of Sources

30. FILM, VIDEO, OR DVD

Last Name, Initials (Producer), & Last Name, Initials (Director). (Year). *Title* [Motion picture]. Country: Studio.

Wallis, H. B. (Producer), & Curtiz, M. (Director). (1942). *Casablanca* [Motion picture]. United States: Warner.

31. MUSIC RECORDING

Composer's Last Name, Initials. (Year of copyright). Title of song. On *Title of album* [Medium]. City, State or Country: Label.

Veloso, C. (1997). Na baixado sapateiro. On *Livros* [CD]. Los Angeles, CA: Nonesuch.

32. PROCEEDINGS OF A CONFERENCE

Author's Last Name, Initials. (Year of publication). Title of paper. In *Proceedings Title* (pp. pages). Publication City, State or Country: Publisher.

Heath, S. B. (1997). Talking work: Language among teens. In *Symposium about Language and Society–Austin* (pp. 27–45). Austin: Department of Linguistics at the University of Texas.

33. TELEVISION PROGRAM

Last Name, Initials (Writer), & Last Name, Initials (Director). (Year). Title of episode [Descriptive label]. In Initials Last Name (Producer), *Series title*. City, State or Country: Network.

Dunkle, R. (Writer), & Lange, M. (Director). (2012). Hit [Television series episode]. In E. A. Bernero (Executive Producer), *Criminal minds.* New York, NY: NBC.

34. SOFTWARE OR COMPUTER PROGRAM

Title and version number [Computer software]. (Year). Publication City, State or Country: Publisher.

Elder Scrolls V: Skyrim [Computer software]. (2011). Rockwood, MD: Bethesda.

35. GOVERNMENT DOCUMENT

Government Agency. (Year of publication). *Title*. Publication City, State or Country: Publisher.

U.S Department of Health and Human Services, Centers for Disease Control and Prevention. (2009). *Fourth national report on human exposure to environmental chemicals.* Washington, DC: Government Printing Office.

ONLINE GOVERNMENT DOCUMENT

Government Agency. (Year of publication). *Title* (Publication No. [if any]). Retrieved from URL

U.S Department of Health and Human Services, National Institutes of
　　Health, National Institute of Mental Health. (2006). *Bipolar disorder*
　　(NIH Publication No. 06-3679). Retrieved from http://www.nimh.nih
　　.gov/health/publications/bipolar-disorder/nimh-bipolar-adults.pdf

36. DISSERTATION

Include the database name and accession number for dissertations that
you retrieve from a database.

Author's Last Name, Initials. (Year). *Title of dissertation* (Doctoral
　　dissertation). Retrieved from Name of database. (accession number)

Knapik, M. (2008). *Adolescent online trouble-talk: Help-seeking in
　　cyberspace* (Doctoral dissertation). Retrieved from ProQuest
　　Dissertation and Theses database. (AAT NR38024)

For a dissertation that you access on the Web, include the name of institution after *Doctoral dissertation*. For example: (Doctoral dissertation, University of North Carolina). End your citation with *Retrieved from* and the URL.

37. TECHNICAL OR RESEARCH REPORT

Author's Last Name, Initials. (Year). *Title of report* (Report number).
　　Publication City, State or Country: Publisher.

Elsayed, T., Namata, G., Getoor, L., & Oard., D. W. (2008). *Personal name
　　resolution in email: A heuristic approach* (Report No. LAMP-TR-150).
　　College Park: University of Maryland.

Citing Sources Not Covered by APA

To cite a source for which APA does not provide guidelines, look at models similar to the source you are citing. Give any information readers will
need in order to find it themselves — author; date of publication; title;
publisher; information about electronic retrieval (DOI or URL); and any other
pertinent information. You might want to try your citation yourself, to be
sure it will lead others to your source.

author　　　　title　　　publication

FORMATTING A PAPER

Title page.   APA generally requires a title page. At the upper left-hand corner of the page, include "Running head:" and a shortened version of your title in uppercase letters. The page number (1) should go in the upper right-hand corner. Center the full title of the paper, your name, and the name of your school on separate lines about halfway down the page. You may add an "Author Note" at the bottom of the page to provide course information, acknowledgments, or contact information.

Page numbers.   Use a shortened title in uppercase letters in the upper left-hand corner of each page; place the page number in the upper right-hand corner. Number pages consecutively throughout your paper.

Fonts, spacing, margins, and indents.   Use a serif font (such as Times New Roman or Cambria) for the text, and a sans serif font (such as Calibri or Arial) for figure labels. Double-space the entire paper, including any notes and your list of references. Leave one-inch margins at the top, bottom, and sides of your text; do not justify the text. Paragraphs should be indented one-half inch (or five-to-seven spaces) from the left margin. APA recommends using two spaces after end-of-sentence punctuation.

Headings.   Though they are not required in APA style, headings can help readers follow your organization. The first level of heading should be bold, centered, and capitalized as you would any other title; the second level of heading should be bold and flush with the left margin; the third level should be bold and indented, with only the first letter and proper nouns capitalized and with a period at the end of the heading, with the text following on the same line.

First Level Heading

Second Level Heading

   Third level heading.

Abstract.　An abstract is a concise summary of your paper that briefly introduces readers to your topic and main points. Most scholarly journals require an abstract; check with your instructor about his or her preference. Put your abstract on the second page, with the word Abstract centered at the top. Unless your instructor specifies a length, limit your abstract to 250 words or fewer.

Long quotations.　Indent quotations of more than forty words to one-half inch (or five-to-seven spaces) from the left margin. Do not use quotation marks, and place page number(s) in parentheses after the end punctuation.

> Kaplan (2000) captured ancient and contemporary Antioch for us:
>> At the height of its glory in the Roman-Byzantine age, when it had an amphitheater, public baths, aqueducts, and sewage pipes, half a million people lived in Antioch. Today the population is only 125,000. With sour relations between Turkey and Syria, and unstable politics throughout the Middle East, Antioch is now a backwater—seedy and tumbledown, with relatively few tourists. (p. 123)
>
> Antioch's decline serves as a reminder that the fortunes of cities can change drastically over time.

Illustrations.　For each table, provide a number (*Table* 1) and a descriptive title on separate lines above the table; below the table, include a note with information about the source. For figures — charts, diagrams, graphs, photos, and so on — include a figure number (*Figure* 1) and information about the source in a note below the figure. Number tables and figures separately, and be sure to refer to any illustrations in your text and clarify how they relate to the rest of your text.

author　　　　title　　　publication

Table 1

Hours of Instruction Delivered per Week

	American classrooms	Japanese classrooms	Chinese classrooms
First Grade			
Language Arts	10.5	8.7	10.4
Mathematics	2.7	5.8	4.0
Fifth Grade			
Language Arts	7.9	8.0	11.1
Mathematics	3.4	7.8	11.7

Note. Adapted from "Peeking Out from Under the Blinders: Some Factors We Shouldn't Forget in Studying Writing," by J. R. Hayes, 1991, National Center for the Study of Writing and Literacy (Occasional Paper No. 25). Retrieved from National Writing Project website: http://www.nwp.org/

List of references. Start your list on a new page after any notes. Center the title and double-space the entire list. Each entry should begin at the left margin, and subsequent lines should be indented one-half inch (or five-to-seven spaces). Alphabetize the list by authors' last names (or by editors' names, if appropriate). Alphabetize works that have no author or editor by title, disregarding *A*, *An*, and *The*. Be sure every source listed is cited in the text; don't include sources that you consulted but didn't cite.

SAMPLE RESEARCH PAPER

Carolyn Stonehill wrote the following paper for a first-year writing course. It is formatted according to the guidelines of the *Publication Manual of the American Psychological Association,* 6th edition (2009). While APA guidelines are used widely in linguistics and the social sciences, exact requirements may vary from discipline to discipline and course to course. If you're unsure about what your instructor wants, ask for clarification.

"Running head:" and shortened title.

Running head: IT'S IN OUR GENES

1

Page number.

It's in Our Genes:

Title, name, and school name.

The Biological Basis of Human Mating Behavior

Carolyn Stonehill

Wright State University

IT'S IN OUR GENES   2

Abstract

While cultural values and messages certainly play a part in the
process of mate selection, the genetic and psychological
predispositions developed by our ancestors play the biggest role in
determining to whom we are attracted. Women are attracted to
strong, capable men with access to resources to help rear children.
Men find women attractive based on visual signs of youth, health,
and, by implication, fertility. While perceptions of attractiveness
are influenced by cultural norms and reinforced by advertisements
and popular media, the persistence of mating behaviors that have
no relationship to societal realities suggests that they are part of our
biological heritage.

Heading centered.

Limited to 120 words or fewer.

Two spaces after end punctuation.

IT'S IN OUR GENES   3

Title centered.

It's in Our Genes:

Double-spaced throughout.

The Biological Basis of Human Mating Behavior

Consider the following scenario: It's a sunny afternoon on campus, and Jenny is walking to her next class. Out of the corner of her eye, she catches sight of her lab partner, Joey, parking his car. She stops to admire how tall, muscular, and stylishly dressed he is, and she does not take her eyes off him as he walks away from his shiny new BMW. As he flashes her a pearly white smile, Jenny melts, then quickly adjusts her skirt and smooths her hair.

Paragraphs indent 5 to 7 spaces ($\frac{1}{2}$ inch).

This scenario, while generalized, is familiar: Our attraction to people—or lack of it—often depends on their physical traits. But why this attraction? Why does Jenny respond the way she does to her handsome lab partner? Why does she deem him handsome at

1"

all? Certainly Joey embodies the stereotypes of physical attractiveness prevalent in contemporary American society. Advertisements, television shows, and magazine articles all provide Jenny with signals telling her what constitutes the ideal American man. Yet she is also attracted to Joey's new sports car even though she has a new car herself. Does Jenny find this man striking because of the influence of her culture, or does her attraction lie in a more fundamental part of her constitution? Evolutionary psychologists, who apply principles of evolutionary biology to research on the human mind, would say that Jenny's responses in this situation are due largely to mating strategies developed by her prehistoric ancestors. Driven by the need to reproduce and

1"

1"

IT'S IN OUR GENES   4

propagate the species, these ancestors of ours formed patterns of
mate selection so effective in providing for their needs and those of
their offspring that they are mimicked even in today's society.
While cultural values and messages clearly play a part in the
process of mate selection, the genetic and psychological
predispositions developed by our ancestors play the biggest role in
determining to whom we are attracted.

Women's Need to Find a Capable Mate

Pioneering evolutionary psychologist Trivers (as cited in Allman,
1993) observed that having and rearing children requires women to
invest far more resources than men because of the length of
pregnancy, the dangers of childbirth, and the duration of infants'
dependence on their mothers (p. 56). According to Fisher (as cited in
Frank, 2001), one of the leading advocates of this theory, finding a
capable mate was a huge preoccupation of all prehistoric reproductive
women, and for good reason: "A female couldn't carry a baby in one
arm and sticks and stones in the other arm and still feed and protect
herself on the very dangerous open grasslands, so she began to need a
mate to help her rear her young" (p. 85). So because of this it became
advantageous for the woman to find a strong, capable man with
access to resources, and it became suitable for the man to find a
healthy, reproductively sound woman to bear and care for his
offspring. According to evolutionary psychologists, these are the
bases upon which modern mate selection is founded, and there are
many examples of this phenomenon to be found in our own society.

First-level headings boldface, centered.

Authors referred to by last name.

Source quoted in another source; secondary source and date in first parentheses, page number in second parentheses.

IT'S IN OUR GENES   5

One can see now why Jenny might be attracted by Joey's display of resources—his BMW. In our society, men with good job prospects, a respected social position, friends in high places, or any combination thereof have generally been viewed as more desirable mates than those without these things because they signal to women that the men have resources (Buss & Schmitt, 1993, p. 226). Compared with males, females invest more energy in bearing and raising children, so it is most advantageous for females to choose mates with easy access to resources, the better to provide for their children.

Author names in parentheses when no signal phrase is used.

Men's Need to Find a Healthy Mate

For men, reproductive success depends mainly on the reproductive fitness of their female counterpart: No amount of available resources can save a baby miscarried in the first month of gestation. Because of this need for a healthy mate, men have evolved a particular attraction "radar" that focuses on signs of a woman's health and youth, markers that are primarily visual (Weiten, 2001, p. 399). Present-day attractiveness ratings are based significantly on this primitive standard: "Some researchers have suggested that cross-cultural standards of beauty reflect an evolved preference for physical traits that are generally associated with youth, such as smooth skin, good muscle tone, and shiny hair" (Boyd & Silk, 2000, p. 625). This observation would explain why women of our time are preoccupied with plastic surgery, makeup, and—in Jenny's case—a quick hair check as a potential date

Ampersands used in parenthetical references, and used in signal phrases.

IT'S IN OUR GENES   6

approaches. As Cunningham, Roberts, Barbee, Druen, and Wu (1995) •·······

Author named in a signal phrase, publication date in parentheses after the name.

noted, "A focus on outer beauty may have stemmed from a need for desirable inner qualities," such as health, strength, and fertility, and "culture may build on evolutionary dynamics by specifying grooming attributes that signal successful adaptation" (pp. 262–263).

The Influence of the Media on Mate Selection

There is, however, a good deal of opposition to evolutionary theory. Some critics say that the messages fed to us by the media are a larger influence on the criteria of present-day mate selection than any sort of ancestral behavior. Advertisements and popular media have long shown Americans what constitutes a physically ideal mate: In general, youthful, well-toned, symmetrical features are considered more attractive than aging, flabby, or lopsided ones. Evolutionary psychologists argue that research has not determined what is cause and what is effect. Cosmides and Tooby (1997) offered the following analogy to show the danger of assigning culture too powerful a causal role:

For example, people think that if they can show that there is •·······

Quotations of 40+ words indented 5 to 7 spaces.

information in the culture that mirrors how people behave, then *that* is the cause of their behavior. So if they see that men on TV have trouble crying, they assume that their example is *causing* boys to be afraid to cry. But which is cause and which effect? Does the fact that men don't cry much on TV *teach* boys to not cry, or does it merely *reflect* the way boys normally develop? In the absence of research on the particular topic,

Major heading and paragraph number cited for quote from unpaginated work from a website.

there is no way of knowing. ("Nature and Nurture: An Adaptationist Perspective," para. 16)

We can hypothesize, then, that rather than media messages determining our mating habits, our mating habits determine the media messages. Advertisers rely on classical conditioning to interest consumers in their products. For instance, by showing an image of a beautiful woman while advertising a beauty product, advertisers hope that consumers will associate attractiveness with the use of that particular product (Weiten, 2001). In order for this method to be effective, however, the images depicted in conjunction with the beauty product must be ones the general public already finds attractive, and an image of a youthful, clear-skinned woman would, according to evolutionary psychologists, be attractive for reasons of reproductive fitness. In short, what some call media influence is not an influence at all but merely a mirror in which we see evidence of our ancestral predispositions.

If Not Media, Then What?

Tattersall (2001), a paleoanthropologist at the American Museum of Natural History, offered another counterargument to the evolutionary theory of mate selection. First, he argued that the behavior of organisms is influenced not only by genetics, but also by economics and ecology working together (p. 663). Second, he argued that no comparisons can be made between modern human behavior and that of our evolutionary predecessors because the appearance of *Homo sapiens* presented a sudden, qualitative change

IT'S IN OUR GENES   8

from the Neanderthals — not a gradual evolution of behavioral traits:

> As a cognitive and behavioral entity, our species is truly
> unprecedented. Our consciousness is an emergent quality,
> not the result of eons of fine-tuning of a single instrument.
> And, if so, it is to this recently acquired quality of uniqueness,
> not to the hypothetical "ancestral environments," that we
> must look in the effort to understand our often unfathomable
> behaviors. (p. 665)

End punctuation before parentheses in block quotations.

The key to Tattersall's argument is this "emergent quality" of symbolic thought; according to his theories, the ability to think symbolically is what separates modern humans from their ancestors and shows the impossibility of sexual selection behaviors having been passed down over millions of years. Our sexual preferences, Tattersall said, are a result of our own recent and species-specific development and have nothing whatsoever to do with our ancestors.

Opponents of the evolutionary theory, though, fail to explain how "unfathomable" mating behaviors can exist in our present society for no apparent or logical reason. Though medicine has advanced to the point where fertility can be medically enhanced, Singh (1993) observed that curvy women are still viewed as especially attractive because they are perceived to possess greater fertility — a perception that is borne out by several studies of female fertility, hormone levels, and waist-to-hip ratio (p. 304). Though more and more women are attending college and achieving high-paying positions, women are still "more likely than men to consider economic prospects a high priority in a mate" (Sapolsky, 2001–2002, p. 18). While cultural norms and economic conditions influence our taste in mates, as Singh (1993) showed in observing that "the degree of affluence of a society or of an ethnic group within a society may, to a large extent, determine the prevalence and admiration of fatness [of women]" (pp. 304–305), we still react to potential mates in ways determined in Paleolithic times. The key to understanding our mating behavior does not lie only in an emergent modern quality, nor does it lie solely in the messages relayed to us by society; rather, it involves as well the complex mating strategies developed by our ancestors.

IT'S IN OUR GENES   10

References

Allman, W. F. (1993, July 19). The mating game. *U.S. News & World Report, 115*(3), 56–63.

Boyd, R., & Silk, J. B. (2000). *How humans evolved* (2nd ed.). New York, NY: Norton.

Buss, D. M., & Schmitt, D. P. (1993). Sexual strategies theory: An evolutionary perspective on human mating. *Psychological Review, 100*(2), 204–232.

Cosmides, L., & Tooby, J. (1997). *Evolutionary psychology: A primer.* Retrieved February 2, 2012, from http://www.psych.ucsb.edu/research/cep/primer.html

Cunningham, M. R., Roberts, A. R., Barbee, A. P., Druen, P. B., & Wu, C.-H. (1995). "Their ideas of beauty are, on the whole, the same as ours": Consistency and variability in the cross-cultural perception of female physical attractiveness. *Journal of Personality and Social Psychology, 68,* 261–279.

Frank, C. (2001, February). Why do we fall in — and out of — love? Dr. Helen Fisher unravels the mystery. *Biography,* 85–87, 112.

Sapolsky, R. M. (2001–2002, December–January). What do females want? *Natural History,* 18–21.

Singh, D. (1993). Adaptive significance of female physical attractiveness: Role of waist-to-hip ratio. *Journal of Personality and Social Behavior, 65,* 293–307.

Heading centered.

Alphabetized by authors' last names.

All lines after the first line of each entry indented.

IT'S IN OUR GENES   11

Tattersall, I. (2001). Evolution, genes, and behavior. *Zygon: Journal of Religion & Science, 36,* 657–666. Retrieved from the Psychology and Behavioral Sciences Collection database.

Weiten, W. (2001). *Psychology: Themes & variations* (5th ed.). San Bernardino, CA: Wadsworth.

All sources cited in the text are listed.

part 6

Media / Design

Consciously or not, we design all the texts we write, choosing typefaces, setting up text as lists or charts, deciding whether to add headings — and then whether to center them or align them on the left. Sometimes our genre calls for certain design elements — essays begin with titles, letters begin with salutations ("Dear Auntie Em"). Other times we design texts to meet the demands of particular audiences, formatting documentation in MLA or APA or some other style, setting type larger for young children, and so on. And our designs always depend upon our medium. A memoir might take the form of an essay in a book, be turned into a bulleted list for a slide presentation, or include links to images or other pages if presented on a website. The chapters in this part offer advice for CHOOSING MEDIA; working with DESIGN, IMAGES, and SOUND; WRITING ONLINE; and GIVING PRESENTATIONS.

Media / Design

Choosing Media **52**

USA Today reports on contract negotiations between automakers and autoworkers with an article that includes a large photo and a colorful graph; the article on the same story on *nytimes.com* includes a video of striking workers. In your economics class, you give a presentation about the issue that includes *Prezi* slides.

These examples show how information about the same events can be delivered using three different media: print (*USA Today*), electronic (*nytimes.com*), and spoken (the main medium for your class presentation). They also show how different media offer writers different modes of expressing meaning, ranging from words to images to sounds and hyperlinks. A print text can include written words and still visuals; online, the same text can also incorporate links to moving images and sound as well as to other written materials. A presentation with slides can include both spoken and written words, can incorporate video and audio elements — and can also include print handouts.

In college writing, the choice of medium often isn't up to you: your instructor may require a printed essay or a classroom talk, a website, or some combination of media. Sometimes, though, you'll be the one deciding. Because your medium will play a big part in the way your audience receives and reacts to your message, you'll need to think hard about what media best suits your audience, purpose, and message. This chapter will help you choose media when the choice is yours.

rhetorical situations

genres

processes

strategies

research MLA / APA

media / design

handbook

Print

When you have a choice of medium, print has certain advantages over spoken and electronic text in that it's more permanent and doesn't depend on audience access to technology. Depending on your own access to technology, you can usually insert photos or other visuals and can present data and other information as graphs or charts. Obviously, though, print documents are more work than electronic ones to update or change, and they don't allow for sound, moving images, or hyperlinks to other materials.

Electronic

Online writing is everywhere: on course learning platforms and class websites; in virtual discussion groups and wikis; in emails, text messages, tweets, and social media. And when you're taking an online course, you are, by definition, always using an electronic medium. Remember that this medium has advantages as well as limitations and potential pitfalls. You can add audio, video, and hyperlinks — but your audience may not have the same access to technology that you do. These are just some of the things you'll need to keep in mind when deciding, say, whether to include or to link to videos or a site that has restricted access.

Spoken

If you deliver your text orally, as a speech or presentation, you have the opportunity to use your tone of voice, gestures, and physical bearing to establish credibility. But you must write your text so that it's easy to understand when it is heard rather than read. The spoken medium can be used alone with a live, face-to-face audience, but it's often combined with print, in the form of handouts, or with electronics, in the form of presentation software like *PowerPoint* or *Prezi*, or designed for remote audiences in formats like webcasts, webinars, podcasts, or video-calling services such as *Skype*.

Multimedia

It's increasingly likely that you'll be assigned to create a multimedia text, one that includes some combination of print, oral, and electronic elements. It's also possible that you'll have occasion to write a multimodal text, one that uses more than one mode of expression: words, images, audio, video, hyperlinks, and so on. The words *multimedia* and *multimodal* are often used interchangeably, but *multimodal* is the term that's used most often in composition classes, whereas *multimedia* is the one used in other disciplines and in industry. In composition classes, the word generally refers to writing that includes more than just words.

For example, let's say that in a U.S. history class you're assigned to do a project about the effects of the Vietnam War on American society. You might write an essay using words alone to discuss such effects as increased hostility toward the military and government, generational conflict within families and society at large, and increased use of recreational drugs. But you could in addition weave such a text together with many other materials to create a multimodal composition.

If you're using print, for example, you could include famous photographs from the Vietnam era, such as of antiwar protests or military funerals. Another possibility might be a time line that puts developments in the war in the context of events going on simultaneously elsewhere in American life, such as in fashion and entertainment or in the feminist and civil rights movements. If you're posting your project online, you might also incorporate video clips of TV news coverage of the war and clips from films focusing on it or its social effects, such as *Apocalypse Now* or *Easy Rider*. Audio elements could include recorded interviews with veterans who fought in the war, people who protested against it, or government officials who were involved in planning or overseeing it. Many of these elements could be inserted into your document as hyperlinks.

If your assignment specifies that you give an oral presentation, you could play some of the music of the Vietnam era, show videos of government officials defending the war and demonstrators protesting it, maybe hang some psychedelic posters from the era.

Considering the Rhetorical Situation

3–4 ■ **PURPOSE**
What's your purpose, and what media will best suit that purpose? A text or email may be appropriate for inviting a friend to lunch, but neither would be ideal for demonstrating to a professor that you understand a complex historical event; for that, you'd likely write a report, either in print or online — and you might include photos or maps or other such texts to provide visual context.

5–8 ■ **AUDIENCE**
What media are your audience likely to expect — and be able to access? A blog may be a good way to reach people who share your interest in basketball or cupcakes, but to reach your grandparents, you may want to put a handwritten note in the mail. Some employers require applicants to submit résumés and applications online, while others prefer to receive them in print form.

9–11 ■ **GENRE**
Does your genre require a particular medium? If you're giving an oral presentation, you'll often be expected to include slides. Academic essays are usually formatted to be printed out, even if they are submitted electronically. An online essay based on field research might include audio files of those you've interviewed, but if your essay were in print, you'd need to quote (or paraphrase or summarize) what they said.

12–15 ■ **STANCE**
If you have a choice of media, think about whether a particular medium will help you convey your stance. A print document in MLA format, for instance, will make you seem scholarly and serious. Tweeting or blogging, however, might work better for a more informal stance. Presenting data in charts will sometimes help you establish your credibility as a knowledgeable researcher.

Once you decide on the media and modes of expression you're using, you'll need to design your text to take advantage of their possibilities and to deal with their limitations. The next chapters will help you do that.

Designing Text 53

You're trying to figure out why a magazine ad you're looking at is so funny, and you realize that the font used for the text is deliberately intended to make you laugh. In giving an assignment for a research paper, your psychology professor specifies that you are to follow APA format. Your classmates complain that the *PowerPoint* slides you use for a presentation are hard to read, and one of them suggests that it's because there's not enough contrast between the colors of the words and the background. Whether you're putting together your résumé, creating a website for your intramural soccer league, or writing a research essay for a class, you need to think about how you design what you write.

Sometimes you can rely on established conventions: in academic writing using MLA and APA style, for example, there are specific guidelines for margins, headings, and the use of single-, double-, or triple-spaced lines of text. But often you'll have to make design decisions on your own — and not just about words and spacing. If what you're writing includes photos, charts, tables, graphs, or other visuals, you'll need to figure out how to integrate these with your written text in the most attractive and effective way; online, you may also need to decide where and how to include video clips and hyperlinks. You might even use scissors, glue, and staples to attach objects to a poster or create pop-ups in a brochure.

No matter what your text includes, its design will influence how your audience responds to it and therefore how well it achieves your purpose. This chapter offers general advice on designing print and online texts to suit your purpose, audience, genre, and stance.

Considering the Rhetorical Situation

As with all writing tasks, your rhetorical situation should affect the way you design a text. Here are some points to consider.

3–4 **PURPOSE** How can you design your text to help achieve your purpose? If you're reporting information, for instance, you may want to present statistical data in a chart or table rather than in the main text to help readers grasp it more quickly. If you're trying to get readers to care about an issue, a photo or pull quote—a brief selection of text "pulled out" and reprinted in a larger font—might help you do so.

5–8 **AUDIENCE** How can you make your design appeal to your intended audience? By using a certain font style or size to make your text look hip, serious, or easy to read? What kind of headings — big and bold, simple and restrained? — would your readers expect or find helpful? What colors would appeal to them?

9–11 **GENRE** Are you writing in a genre that has design conventions, such as an annotated bibliography, a lab report, or a résumé? Do you need to follow a format such as those prescribed in MLA or APA style?

12–15 **STANCE** How can your design reflect your attitude toward your audience and subject? Do you need a businesslike font or a playful one? Would tables and graphs help you establish your credibility? How can illustrations help you convey a certain tone?

Some Basic Principles of Design

Be consistent.   To keep readers oriented while reading documents or browsing multiple webpages, any design elements should be used consistently. In a print academic essay, that task may be as simple as using the same font throughout for your main text and using boldface or italics for headings. If you're writing for the web, navigation buttons and other major elements should be in the same place on every page. In a presentation, each slide should use the same background and the same font unless there's a good reason to introduce differences.

Keep it simple.   One of your main design goals should be to help readers see quickly — even intuitively — what's in your text and how to find specific information. Adding headings to help readers see the parts, using consistent colors and fonts to help them recognize key elements, setting off steps in lists, using white space to set off blocks of text or to call attention to certain elements, and (especially) resisting the temptation to fill pages with fancy graphics or unnecessary animations: these are all ways of making your text simple to read.

Look, for example, at a furniture store's simple, easy-to-understand webpage design on page 584. This webpage contains considerable information: a row of links across the top, directing readers to various products; a search option; a column down the right side that provides details about the chair shown in the wide left-hand column; thumbnail photos below the chair, showing its various options; and suggestions across the bottom for furniture to go with it. Despite the wealth of content, the site's design is both easy to figure out and, with the generous amount of white space, easy on the eyes.

Aim for balance.   On the webpage on page 584, the photo takes up about a quarter of the screen and is balanced by a narrower column of text, and the "Matching Products" and "More POÄNG series" sections across the page bottom balance the company logo and links bar across the top. For a page without images, balance can be created through the use of margins, headings, and spacing. MLA and APA styles have specific design guidelines for academic research papers that cover these elements. A magazine page might create a sense of balance by using pull quotes and illustrations to break up dense vertical columns of text. In the magazine page shown on

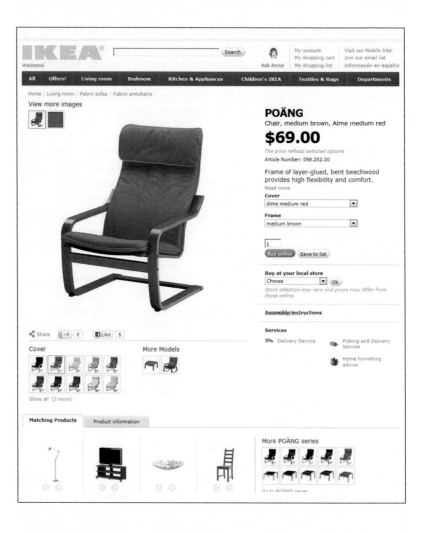

page 505, for example, the large title at the top left is broken into two short lines, leaving a large blank space on the right. Below, two photos in the left column and a brief summary of the article in large italic type on the right, surrounded by more blank space, provide additional visual relief from the two columns of solid text at the bottom.

Use color and contrast carefully.   Academic readers usually expect black text on a white background, with perhaps one other color for headings. Presentation slides and webpages are most readable with a plain, light-colored background and dark text that provides contrast. Remember that not everyone can see all colors and that an online text that includes several colors might be printed out and read in black and white; make sure your audience will be able to distinguish any color variations well enough to grasp your meaning. Colored lines on a graph, for example, should be distinguishable even if readers cannot see the colors. Red-green contrasts are especially hard to see and should be avoided.

Use available templates.   Good design takes time, and most of us do not have training as designers. If you're pressed for time or don't feel up to the challenge of designing your own text, take advantage of the many templates available. In *Microsoft Word*, for example, you can customize "styles" to specify the font, including its size and color; single- or double-spacing; paragraph indentations; and several other features that will then automatically apply to your document. Websites that host personal webpages and blogs offer dozens of templates that you can use or modify to suit your needs. And presentation software offers many templates that can simplify creating slides.

Some Elements of Design

Fonts.   You can usually choose from among many fonts, and the one you choose will affect how well the audience can read your text and how they will perceive your TONE. Times Roman will make a text look businesslike or academic; *Comic Sans* will make it look playful. For most academic writing,

13

you'll want to use a font size between 10 and 12 points and a serif font (such as Times Roman or Bookman) rather than a sans serif font (such as Arial, Verdana, or Century Gothic) because serif fonts are generally easier to read. Reserve sans serif for headings and parts of the text that you want to highlight. Decorative fonts (such as *Magneto*, *Amaze*, *Chiller*, and *Jokerman*) should be used sparingly and only when they're appropriate for your audience, purpose, and the rest of your RHETORICAL SITUATION. If you use more than one font in a text, use each one consistently: one for HEADINGS, one for captions, one for the main body of your text. And don't go overboard—you won't often have reason to use more than two or, at most, three fonts in any one text.

1 ▣
588–89 ▢

Every font has regular, **bold**, and *italic* forms. In general, choose regular for the main text and lower-level headings, bold for major headings, and italic within the main text to indicate titles of books and other long works and, occasionally, to emphasize words or brief phrases. Avoid italicizing or boldfacing entire sentences or paragraphs, especially in academic writing. If you are following MLA, APA, or some other style format, be sure your use of fonts conforms to its requirements.

484–532 ●
533–74

Finally, consider the line spacing of your text. Generally, academic writing is double-spaced, whereas JOB LETTERS and RÉSUMÉS are usually single-spaced. Some kinds of REPORTS may call for single-spacing; check with your instructor if you're not sure. You'll often need to add extra space to set off parts of a text—items in a list, for instance, or headings.

222–34 ▲
87–118

Layout.   Layout is the way text is arranged on a page. An academic essay, for example, will usually have a title centered at the top, one-inch margins all around, and double-spacing. A text can be presented in paragraphs—or in the form of LISTS, TABLES, CHARTS, GRAPHS, and so on. Sometimes you'll need to include other elements as well: headings, images and other graphics, captions, lists of works cited.

593–95 ▢

Paragraphs.   Dividing text into paragraphs focuses information for readers and helps them process the information by dividing it into manageable chunks. If you're writing a story for a print newspaper with narrow columns, for example, you'll divide your text into shorter paragraphs

■ rhetorical situations

▲ genres

○ processes

◆ strategies

● research MLA / APA

▢ media / design

▨ handbook

than you would if you were writing an academic essay. In general, indent paragraphs five to seven spaces (one-half inch) when your text is double-spaced; either indent or skip a line between paragraphs that are single-spaced.

Lists.   Put information into list form that you want to set off and make easily accessible. Number the items in a list when the sequence matters (in instructions, for example); use bullets when the order is not important. Set off lists with an extra line of space above and below, and add extra space between the items on a list if necessary for legibility. Here's an example:

> Darwin's theory of how species change through time derives from three postulates, each of which builds on the previous one:
>
> 1. The ability of a population to expand is infinite, but the ability of any environment to support populations is always finite.
> 2. Organisms within populations vary, and this variation affects the ability of individuals to survive and reproduce.
> 3. The variations are transmitted from parents to offspring.
>
> —Robert Boyd and Joan B. Silk, *How Humans Evolved*

Do not set off text as a list unless there's a good reason to do so, however. Some lists are more appropriately presented in paragraph form, especially when they give information that is not meant to be referred to more than once. In the following example, there is no reason to highlight the information by setting it off in a list—and bad news is softened by putting it in paragraph form:

> I regret to inform you that the Scholarship Review Committee did not approve your application for a Board of Rectors scholarship for the following reasons: your grade-point average did not meet the minimum requirements; your major is not among those eligible for consideration; and the required letter of recommendation was not received before the deadline.

Presented as a list, that information would be needlessly emphatic.

150–54 ▲
523 ●
87–118 ▲

Headings.   Headings make the structure of a text easier to follow and help readers find specific information. Some genres require standard headings — announcing an **ABSTRACT**, for example, or a list of **WORKS CITED**. Other times you will want to use headings to provide an overview of a section of text. You may not need any headings in brief texts, but when you do, you'll probably want to use one level at most, just to announce major topics. Longer texts, information-rich genres such as brochures or detailed **REPORTS**, and websites may require several levels of headings. If you decide to include headings, you will need to decide how to phrase them, what fonts to use, and where to position them.

Phrase headings concisely.   Make your headings succinct and parallel in structure. You might make all the headings nouns (**Mushrooms**), noun phrases (**Kinds of Mushrooms**), gerund phrases (**Recognizing Kinds of Mushrooms**), or questions (**How Do I Identify Mushrooms?**). Whatever form you decide on, use it consistently for each heading. Sometimes your phrasing will depend on your purpose. If you're simply helping readers find information, use brief phrases:

HEAD	**Forms of Social Groups among Primates**
SUBHEAD	*Solitary Social Groups*
SUBHEAD	*Monogamous Social Groups*

If you want to address your readers directly with the information in your text, consider writing your headings as questions:

How can you identify morels?
Where can you find morels?
How can you cook morels?

Make headings visible.   Headings need to be visible, so if you aren't following an academic style like MLA or APA, consider making them larger than the regular text, putting them in **bold** or *italics*, or using underlining — or a different font. For example, you could make your main text a serif font like Times Roman and your headings in a sans serif font like Arial. On the web, consider making headings a different color from the body text.

When you have several levels of headings, use capitalization, bold, and italics to distinguish among the various levels:

First-Level Head
Second-Level Head
Third-level head

APA format requires that each level of heading appear in a specific style: centered bold uppercase and lowercase for the first level, flush-left bold uppercase and lowercase for the second level, and so on.

Position headings appropriately.   If you're following APA format, center first-level headings. If you're following MLA format, first-level headings should be typed to align with the left-hand margin. If you are not following a prescribed format, you get to decide where to position your headings: centered, flush with the left margin, or even alongside the text in a wide left-hand margin. Position each level of head consistently throughout your text. Generally, online headings are positioned flush left.

561–63
522–23

White space.   Use white space to separate the various parts of a text. In general, use one-inch margins for the text of an essay or report. Unless you're following MLA or APA format, include space above headings, above and below lists, and around photos, graphs, and other visuals. See the two SAMPLE RESEARCH PAPERS in this book for examples of the formats required by MLA and APA.

MLA 523–32
APA 563–74

Evaluating a Design

Does the design suit your PURPOSE?   Does the overall look of the design help convey the text's message, support its argument, or present information?

3–4

How well does the design meet the needs of your AUDIENCE?   Will the overall appearance of the text appeal to the intended readers? Is the font large enough for them to read? Are there headings to help them find their

5–8

way through the text? Does the design help readers find the information they need?

9–11 **How well does the text meet any GENRE requirements?** Can you tell by looking at the text that it is an academic essay, a lab report, a résumé, a blog? Do its fonts, margins, headings, and page layout meet the require- 484–532
533–74 ments of **MLA**, **APA**, or whatever style is being followed?

12–15 **How well does the design reflect your STANCE?** Do the page layout and fonts convey the appropriate tone—serious, playful, adventuresome, con- servative, or whatever other tone you intended?

rhetorical
situations

genres

processes

strategies

research
MLA / APA

media /
design

handbook

Using Visuals, Incorporating Sound 54

For an art history class, you write an essay comparing two paintings by Willem de Kooning. For an engineering class project, you design a model of a bridge and give an in-class presentation explaining the structures and forces involved, which you illustrate with slides. For a psychology assignment, you interview several people who've suffered foreclosures on their homes in recent years about how the experience affected them and how they've tried to cope with the resulting stress — and then create an online text weaving together a slideshow of photos of the people outside their former homes, a graph of foreclosure rates, video and audio clips from the interviews, and your own insights.

All of these writing tasks require you to incorporate and sometimes to create visuals and sound. Many kinds of visuals can be included in print documents: photos, diagrams, graphs, charts, and more. And with writing that's delivered online or as a spoken presentation, your choices expand to include audio and video, voice-over narration, and links to other materials.

Visuals and sound aren't always appropriate, however, or even possible—so think carefully before you set out to include them. But they can help you make a point in ways that words alone cannot. Election polling results are easier to see in a bar graph than the same information would be in a paragraph; an audio clip can make a written analysis of an opera easier to understand. This chapter provides some tips for using visuals and incorporating sound in your writing.

Considering the Rhetorical Situation

Use visuals that are appropriate for your audience, purpose, and the rest of your RHETORICAL SITUATION. If you're trying to persuade voters in your

1

591

town to back a proposal on an issue they don't know or care much about, for example, you might use dramatic pictures just to get their attention. But when it's important to come across as thoughtful and objective, maybe you need a more subdued look — or to make your points with written words alone. A newspaper article on housing prices might include a bar graph or line graph and also some photos. A report on the same topic for an economics class would probably have graphs with no photos; a community website might have graphs, links to related sites, and a video interview with a homeowner.

In your academic writing, especially, be careful that any visuals you use support your main point — and don't just serve to decorate the text. (Therefore, avoid clip art, which is primarily intended as decoration.) Images should support what you say elsewhere with written words and add information that words alone can't provide as clearly or easily.

Using Visuals

Photos, videos, tables, pie charts, bar graphs: these are many kinds of visuals you could use.

An essay discussing the work of Willem de Kooning might contrast one of his more representational works (such as the one on the left) with one that's more abstract (right).

rhetorical situations

genres

processes

strategies

research MLA / APA

media / design

handbook

Photographs can support an **ARGUMENT,** illustrate **NARRATIVES** and **PROCESSES,** present other points of view, and help readers "place" your information in time and space. You may use photos you take yourself, or you can download photos and other images from the internet — within limits. Most downloadable photos are copyrighted, meaning that you can use them without obtaining permission from the copyright owner only if you are doing so for academic purposes, to fulfill an assignment. If you are going to publish your text, either in print or on the web, you must have permission. Consider, too, the file size of digital images; large files can clog readers' email in-boxes, take a long time to display on their screens, or be hard for you to upload in the first place, so you may have to compress an image or reduce its resolution (which can diminish its sharpness).

323–41
387–95
382–86

Videos If you're writing online, you can include video clips for readers to play. If you're using a video already available online, such as on *YouTube*, you can show the opening image with an arrow for readers to click on to start the video, or you can simply copy the video's URL and paste it into your text as a **LINK.** In either case, you need to introduce the video in your text with a **SIGNAL PHRASE.** As with any other source, you need to provide an in-text citation and full documentation.

597
471–73

If you want to include a video you made yourself, you can edit it using such programs as *iMovie* or *Windows Movie Maker*. Once you're ready to insert it into your document, the easiest way is to first upload it to *YouTube*, choosing the Private setting so only those you authorize may view it, and then create a link in your document.

Graphs, charts, and tables are excellent ways to present statistical and other numerical information. If you can't find the right one for your purpose, you can create your own, as long as it's based on sound data from reliable sources. To do so, you can use various spreadsheet programs or online chart and graph generators.

In any case, remember to follow basic design principles: be **CONSISTENT,** label all parts clearly, and **KEEP THE DESIGN SIMPLE,** so readers can focus on the information and, not be a distracted by a needlessly complex design. In particular, use color and contrast wisely to emphasize what's

582–83

Line graphs are a good way of showing changes in data over time. Each line here represents a different social networking site. Plotting the lines together allows readers to compare the data at different points in time. Be sure to label the x and y axes and limit the number of lines to four at the most.

Bar graphs are useful for comparing quantitative data, measurements of how much or how many. The bars can be horizontal or vertical. This graph shows IKEA's earnings between 2000 and 2011. Some software offers 3-D and other special effects, but simple graphs are often easier to read.

Pie charts can be used to show how a whole is divided into parts or how parts of a whole relate to one another. The segments in a pie should always add up to 100 percent, and each segment should be clearly labeled.

Tables are useful for displaying numerical information concisely, especially when several items are being compared. Presenting information in columns and rows permits readers to find data and identify relationships among them.

Diagrams and flowcharts are ways of showing relationships and processes. This diagram shows how carbon moves between the Earth and its atmosphere. Flowcharts can be made using widely available templates; diagrams, on the other hand, can range from simple drawings to works of art. Some simple flowcharts may be found in the Genre chapters (for example, p. 221).

rhetorical situations

genres

processes

strategies

research MLA / APA

media / design

handbook

most significant. Choose **COLORS** that are easy to distinguish from one — and that remain so if the graph or chart is printed out in black and white. (Using gradations of color from light to dark will show in black and white.) Some common kinds of graphs, charts, and tables are shown on the facing page.

◻ 585

SOME TIPS FOR USING VISUALS

- Position images as close as possible to the discussion to which they relate. In *Microsoft Word*, simply position your cursor where you want to insert an image; click Picture on the Insert tab; choose the appropriate image from your files; and click Insert. You may then need to adjust the way the text flows or wraps around the image: in the Page Layout tab, choose the appropriate option in Wrap Text.

- In academic writing, number all images, using separate sequences of numbers for figures (photos, graphs, diagrams, video clips, and drawings) and tables: Fig. 1, Fig. 2; Table 1, Table 2.

- Explain in your written text whatever information you present in an image — don't expect it to speak for itself. Refer to the image before it appears, identifying it and summarizing its point. For example: "As Table 1 shows, Italy's economic growth rate has been declining for thirty years."

- Provide a title or caption for each image to identify it and explain its significance for your text. For example: "Table 1: Italy's Economic Growth Rate, 1980–2010."

- Label the parts of visuals clearly to ensure that your audience will understand what they show. For example, label each section of a pie chart to show what it represents.

- Cite the source of any images you don't create yourself. You need not document visuals you create, based on data from your own experimental or field research, but if you use data from a source to create a graph or chart, **CITE THE SOURCE** of the data.

● 475–78

- In general, you may use visuals created by someone else in your academic writing as long as you include full **DOCUMENTATION**. If you post your writing online, however, you must first obtain permission from the copyright owner.

● 480–83

Incorporating Sound

Audio clips, podcasts, and other sound files can serve various useful purposes in online writing. Music, for example, can create a mood for your text,
giving your audience hints about how to interpret the meaning of your words
and images or what emotional response you're evoking. Other types of sound
effects — such as background conversations, passing traffic, birdsongs, crowd
noise at sports events — can provide a sense of immediacy, of being part of
the scene or event you're describing. Spoken words can serve as the primary
way you present an online text or as an enhancement of or even a counter-
point to a written text. (And if your audience includes visually impaired people,
an audio track can allow or help them to follow the text.)

The Library of Congress >> Researchers

🔊 **Recorded Sound Reference Center** MOTION PICTURE, BROADCASTING & RECORDED SOUND DIVISION

Home >> online collections   Find [   ] in [Recorded Sound Web Pages ▼] **go**

Online Audio Collections and Presentations

The Library provides access to a portion of its audio collections through the Recorded Sound Reference Center's web page,
the <u>American Memory</u> site, <u>The Performing Arts Encyclopedia</u> and the <u>American Folklife Center</u> pages. These collections are
described below. To listen to recordings that are unavailable online, contact the <u>Recorded Sound Reference Center</u>.

Recorded Sound Section Online Collections

<u>National Jukebox</u>
The Library of Congress presents the National Jukebox, which makes historical sound recordings available to
the public free of charge. The Jukebox includes recordings from the extraordinary collections of the Library of
Congress Packard Campus for Audio Visual Conservation and other contributing libraries and archives.
Recordings in the Jukebox were issued on record labels now owned by Sony Music Entertainment, which has
granted the Library of Congress a gratis license to stream acoustical recordings.

At launch, the Jukebox includes more than 10,000 recordings made by the Victor Talking Machine Company between 1901
and 1925. Jukebox content will be increased regularly, with additional Victor recordings and acoustically recorded titles made
by other Sony-owned U.S. labels, including Columbia, OKeh, and others.

<u>Tony Schwartz Collection</u>
These recordings are a sampling from the Library's Tony Schwartz collection. Considered a master of the
electronic media, Tony Schwartz changed the face of radio and television advertising by creating socially
conscientious campaigns such as the nation's first anti-smoking ad. Throughout his career Schwartz was a
pioneer in the field of soundscape recording, capturing the people, sounds and events of his native New York
City. Click "selected recordings" to listen to some of Schwartz's historic radio broadcasts.

*The Library of Congress is a good source for online recordings of music, speeches,
and radio broadcasts.*

You can download or link to various spoken texts online, or you can record voice and music as podcasts using programs such as *GarageBand* and *Audacity*. Remember to provide an **IN-TEXT CITATION** and full **DOCUMENTATION** of any sound material you obtain from another source.

● 480–83

Adding Links

If you're writing an online text in which you want to include images, video, or sound material available on the web, it's often easier and more effective to create links to them within the text than to embed them by copying and pasting. Such links allow readers to see the materials' original context and to explore it if they wish.

The example below shows a blog post from the Archives of American Art with links to additional detail and documentation.

John Singer Sargent

This lively caricature from the Francis Davis Millet and Millet family papers features an artist fervently painting his subject, just in the background. Most likely it is John Singer Sargent at work on his painting *Carnation, Lily, Lily, Rose*. His posture and the expression on his face suggest an exuberance that matches the action of the paint dripping and splashing as it prepares to meet the canvas with energetic strokes.

Caricature of an artist painting vigorously, ca. 1885-1886, Francis Davis Millet and Millet family papers, Archives of American Art, Smithsonian Institution.

SOME TIPS FOR CREATING LINKS

471–73 ●

- Indicate links with underlining and color (most often blue), and introduce them with a SIGNAL PHRASE.

- Don't include your own punctuation in a link. In the example on page 597, the period is not part of the link.

- Try to avoid having a link open in a new browser window. Readers expect links to open in the same window.

Editing Carefully — and Ethically

You may want to edit a photograph, cropping to show only part of it or using *Photoshop* or similar programs to enhance the colors or otherwise alter it. Similarly, you may want to edit a video, podcast, or other audio file to shorten it or remove irrelevant parts. If you are considering making a change of this kind, however, be sure not to do so in a way that misrepresents the content. If you alter a photo, be sure the image still represents the subject accurately; if you alter a recording of a speech or interview, be sure the edited version maintains the speaker's intent. Whenever you alter an image, a video, or a sound recording, tell your readers how you have changed it.

The same goes of editing charts and graphs. Changing the scale on a bar graph, for example, can change the effect of the comparison, making the quantities being compared seem very similar or very different, as shown in the two bar graphs of identical data in figures 1 and 2.

Because of the different fund-raising goals implied by the graphs ($800 or $5,000) and the different increments of the dollars raised ($200 or $1,000), the graphs send very different messages, though the dollars raised by each fund-raiser remain the same. Just as you shouldn't edit a quotation or a photograph in a way that might misrepresent its meaning, you should not present statistical data in a way that could mislead readers.

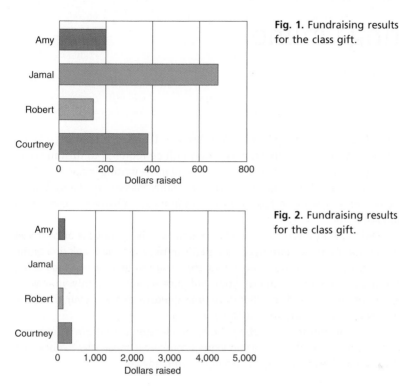

Fig. 1. Fundraising results for the class gift.

Fig. 2. Fundraising results for the class gift.

55 Writing Online

Email. *Facebook*. Texts. Tweets. It may seem as if almost all writing is done online now. In college courses, you may still be required to turn in some writing assignments on paper, but more and more writing is not only done online but submitted that way too. And many classes are being taught online, with little or no face-to-face communication between instructors and students.

Online, your instructor and classmates usually cannot see or hear you — and that matters more than you might think. A puzzled look or a smile of recognition can start an important conversation in a face-to-face class, but in an online environment, your audience usually has only your written words to respond to. Therefore, you need to express your thoughts and feelings as clearly as you can *in writing*.

So it's useful to think about how the electronic medium affects the way we write — and how we can express ourselves most effectively when we write online. This chapter provides some advice.

Online Genres

For most of us, email, texting, and social networking sites like *Facebook* are already parts of everyday life. But using them for academic purposes may require some careful attention. Following are some guidelines.

Email.   When emailing faculty members and school administrators, you are writing in an academic context, so your messages should reflect it: use an appropriate salutation ("Dear Professor Hagzanian"); write clearly and concisely in complete sentences; use standard capitalization and punctuation; proofread; and sign your full name. If you're writing about a specific

rhetorical situations

genres

processes

strategies

research MLA / APA

media / design

handbook

course or group work, identify the course or group explicitly. Also, craft a specific subject line; instead of writing "Question about paper," be specific: "Profile organization question." If you change topics, change your subject line as well rather than simply replying to an old email. And be careful before you hit Send — you want to be good and sure that your email neither says something you'll regret later (don't send an email when you're angry!) nor includes anything you don't want the whole world reading (don't put confidential or sensitive information in email).

Texting   is a way of sending and receiving brief text messages on a phone. Texting is inherently informal and often serves as an alternative to a phone call. Since texting often takes place as a conversation in real time (and phone keyboards can be hard to use), those who write texts often use acronyms, shorthand, and emoticons — ROTFL (rolling on the floor laughing), OST (on second thought), 2nite (tonight), 10Q (thank you), :) (happy) — to get their meaning across quickly and efficiently. If you use these abbreviations, though, be sure your readers will understand them!

Social media.   You may take a course that involves using *Facebook* or another social media site as a way for class members to communicate or as part of a **LEARNING MANAGEMENT SYSTEM.** If so, you need to consider your rhetorical situation to make sure your course postings represent you as a respectful (and respectable) member of the class. Also, remember that many employers routinely check job applicants' social media pages, so don't post writing or photos that you wouldn't want a potential employer to see.

□ 606–8

Websites   are groups of webpages organized around a homepage and connected to one another (and to other websites) through hyperlinks, which take users automatically from one page to another. While it's possible to create your own websites from scratch, free website builders such as *Weebly, Google Sites,* or *Wix* make it easy to create a site by providing templates for homepages, page designs, and navigation systems.

One key element in a website is the use of links to bring material from other sources into your text. You can link to the definition of a key term,

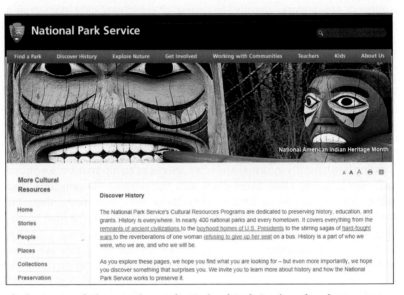

The homepage of Discover History, the National Park Service cultural resource program, provides a navigation menu on the left that leads to various sections of the site. Links embedded within the introductory text connect to Park Service pages outside the program.

for instance, rather than defining it yourself, or you can summarize a source and link to the full text rather than quoting or paraphrasing it. Providing links lets readers decide whether they need or want to see more detailed information — or not.

Blogs   are websites that generally focus on a single topic — politics, celebrities, gaming, baseball, you name it. They're maintained and updated regularly by individuals or groups who post opinions, reflections, information, and more — with writing, photos, video and audio files, and links to other sites. Blogs are an easy way to share your writing with others — and to invite response. Free blog hosting sites such as *WordPress* or *Blogger* offer templates that let you create a blog and post to it easily, and some learning management systems include blogging capability as well.

This blog, hosted by the Smithsonian Institution, focuses on marine biology and includes video, audio, slideshows and written narratives. Readers can interact with and respond to the text by clicking on icons for Facebook, Twitter, *and other social networking sites.*

If your blog is public, anyone can read it, including potential employers, so just as with *Facebook* and other social media, you'll want to be careful about how you present yourself and avoid posting anything that others could see as offensive. (Think twice before posting when you're angry or upset.) You may want to activate privacy settings that let you restrict access to some of the content or that make your blog unsearchable by *Google* and other search tools. Also, assume that what you post in a blog is permanent: your friends, family, employer — anyone — may read a posting years in the future, even if the blog is no longer active.

Wikis are websites that allow a group to work collaboratively, with all users free to add, edit, and delete content. *Wikipedia,* the online encyclopedia, is one of the most famous wikis: its content is posted and edited by people all over the world. You may be asked to contribute to a class wiki, such as the one below from a writing course at Sinclair Community College. Students post their work to the wiki, and everyone in the class has access to everyone else's writing and can comment on or revise it. When contributing to a wiki, you should be careful to write precisely, edit carefully, and make sure your research is accurate and appropriately cited — others may be quick to question and rewrite your work if it's sloppy or inaccurate.

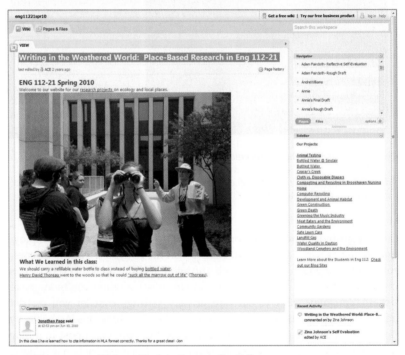

A writing-course wiki from Sinclair Community College.

Managing Online Course Work

Because so much of your college work will be done online — at the very least, you'll do most of your writing on a computer and submit some assignments via email — it's important to set up some procedures for yourself. In a single writing course, for example, you may write three or four drafts of four essays — that's twelve to sixteen documents. To keep track of your files, you'll need to create folders, establish consistent file names, and back up your work.

Creating folders.   Create a folder for each course, and name it with the course title or number and the academic term: ENG 101 Fall 2013. Within each course folder, create a folder for each major assignment. Save your work in the appropriate folder, so you can always find it.

Saving files.   Your word processor likely saves documents to a specific format identified by a three- or four-letter ending automatically added to the file name: .doc, .docx, .txt, and so on. However, this default format may not be compatible with other programs. If you're not sure what format you'll need, use the Save As command to save each document in Rich Text Format, or .rtf, which most word processors can read.

Naming files.   If you are expected to submit files electronically, your instructor may ask you to name them in a certain way. If not, devise a system that will let you easily find the files, including multiple drafts of your writing. For example, you might name your files using *Your last name + Assignment + Draft number + Date:* Jones Evaluation Draft 2 10-5-2013.docx. You'll then be able to find a particular file by looking for the assignment, the draft number, or the date. Saving all your drafts as separate files will make it easy to include them in a portfolio; also, if you lose a draft, you'll be able to use the previous one to reconstruct it.

Backing up your work.   Hard drives fail, laptops get dropped, flash drives are left in public computers. Because files stored in computers can be damaged or lost, you should save your work in several places: on your computer, on a flash drive or portable hard drive, in space supplied by your school, or online. You can also ensure that an extra copy of your work exists by emailing a copy to yourself.

Finding Basic Course Information

You'll need to learn some essential information about any online courses you take:

606–8

- *The phone number for the campus help desk* or technology center. Check the hours of operation, and keep the number handy.

- *The syllabus,* list of assignments, and calendar with deadlines.

- *Where to find tutorials* for your school's LEARNING MANAGEMENT SYSTEM and other programs you may need help with.

- *How and when you can contact your instructor* — in person during office hours? by phone or email? — and how soon you can expect a response.

- *What file format you should use* to submit assignments — .doc, .docx, .rtf, .pdf, something else? — and how to submit them.

- *How to use the spellcheck function* on your word processor or learning management system.

- *How to participate in online discussions* — will you use a discussion board? a chat function in a learning management system? a blog? a social network? something else?

Using Learning Management Systems

Whether you're in a face-to-face, hybrid, or online class, you may be asked to do some or all of your classwork online using a learning management system (LMS) such as *Blackboard* or *Desire2Learn*. An LMS is a web-based educational tool that brings together all the course information your

A *course homepage from Wright State's Pilot LMS.*

instructor wants you to have, along with features that allow you to participate in the class in various ways. Your school's LMS likely includes the following features that you'll be expected to use:

A course homepage   contains posts from your instructor; a calendar with due dates for assignments; and links to the course syllabus, other course content, and additional features available on the site.

A discussion board   allows you to communicate with classmates even if everyone isn't logged in to the board at the same time. These conversations may be organized in "threads" so that posts on a particular topic appear together and may be read in order. When you contribute to a threaded discussion, treat it as an ongoing conversation: you need not introduce the topic but can simply add your comments.

A chat tool　allows you to engage in written conversations in real time, with all participants logged in simultaneously. In a classroom, doing this may be like texting with many others at once, so the rules for class discussion apply: be patient while waiting for a response; focus on the topic being discussed; avoid sarcasm or personal attacks.

A dropbox　is a place where you submit assignments online. If your course dropbox has folders for each assignment, be sure to upload your assignment into the correct folder. Keep in mind that systems go down, so don't wait until the last minute to submit a file. It's a good idea to double-check that the file you've submitted has been uploaded; often you can simply exit the dropbox and then return to it to see that your file is where it should be.

Online portfolios.　Many LMSs allow you to create an online portfolio where you may post your coursework as well as photos, personal information, and links to other websites.

Additional features.　An LMS may also include email; a space to keep a journal; a whiteboard for posting images, graphics, and presentations; a gradebook; a social network (sometimes called a Ning) for class members only; and other features that can help you keep track of your work in a class.

Giving Presentations **56**

In a marketing class, you give a formal presentation that includes slides and handouts as part of a research project on developing brand loyalty to clothing labels among college students. As a candidate for student government, you deliver several speeches to various campus groups that are simultaneously broadcast over the web. At a good friend's wedding, after you make a toast to the married couple, another friend who couldn't attend in person toasts them remotely using *Skype*; a third guest records both toasts on his cell phone and uploads them to *Facebook*. Whether or not you include electronic and print media, whenever you are called on to give a spoken presentation, you need to make your points clear and memorable. This chapter offers guidelines to help you prepare and deliver effective presentations. We'll start with two good examples.

ABRAHAM LINCOLN
Gettysburg Address

Given by the sixteenth president of the United States, at the dedication of the Gettysburg battlefield as a memorial to those who died in the Civil War, this is one of the most famous speeches ever delivered in the United States.

> Four score and seven years ago our fathers brought forth on this continent, a new nation, conceived in Liberty, and dedicated to the proposition that all men are created equal.
>   Now we are engaged in a great civil war, testing whether that nation, or any nation so conceived and so dedicated, can long endure.

We are met on a great battle-field of that war. We have come to dedicate a portion of that field, as a final resting place for those who here gave their lives that that nation might live. It is altogether fitting and proper that we should do this.

But, in a larger sense, we can not dedicate — we can not consecrate — we can not hallow — this ground. The brave men, living and dead, who struggled here, have consecrated it, far above our poor power to add or detract. The world will little note, nor long remember what we say here, but it can never forget what they did here. It is for us the living, rather, to be dedicated here to the unfinished work which they who fought here have thus far so nobly advanced. It is rather for us to be here dedicated to the great task remaining before us — that from these honored dead we take increased devotion to that cause for which they gave the last full measure of devotion — that we here highly resolve that these dead shall not have died in vain — that this nation, under God, shall have a new birth of freedom — and that government of the people, by the people, for the people, shall not perish from the earth.

You won't likely be called on to deliver such an address, but the techniques Lincoln used — brevity, rhythm, recurring themes — are ones you can use in your own spoken texts. The next example represents the type of spoken text we are sometimes called on to deliver at important occasions in the lives of our families.

JUDY DAVIS

Ours Was a Dad . . .

This short eulogy was given at the funeral of the writer's father, Walter Boock. Judy Davis lives in Davis, California, where she was for many years the principal of North Davis Elementary School.

Elsa, Peggy, David, and I were lucky to have such a dad. Ours was a dad who created the childhood for us that he did not have for himself.

The dad who sent us airborne on the soles of his feet, squealing with delight. The dad who built a platform in the peach tree so we could eat ourselves comfortably into peachy oblivion. The dad who assigned us chores and then did them with us. The dad who felt our pain when we skinned our knees.

Ours was the dad who took us camping, all over the U.S. and Canada, but most of all in our beloved Yosemite. The one who awed us with his ability to swing around a full pail of water without spilling a drop and let us hold sticks in the fire and draw designs in the night air with hot orange coals.

Our dad wanted us to feel safe and secure. On Elsa's eighth birthday, we acquired a small camping trailer. One very blustery night in Minnesota, Mom and Dad asleep in the main bed, David suspended in the hammock over them, Peggy and Elsa snuggled in the little dinette bed, and me on an air mattress on the floor, I remember the most incredible sense of well-being: our family all together, so snug, in that little trailer as the storm rocked us back and forth. It was only in the morning that I learned about the tornado warnings. Mom and Dad weren't sleeping: they were praying that when morning came we wouldn't find ourselves in the next state.

Ours was the dad who helped us with homework at the round oak table. He listened to our oral reports, taught us to add by looking for combinations of 10, quizzed us on spelling words, and when our written reports sounded a little too much like the *World Book* encyclopedia, he told us so.

Ours was a dad who believed our round oak table that seated twelve when fully extended should be full at Thanksgiving. Dad called the chaplain at the airbase, asked about homesick boys, and invited them to join our family. Or he'd call International House in Berkeley to see if someone from another country would like to experience an American Thanksgiving. We're still friends with the Swedish couple who came for turkey forty-five years ago. Many people became a part of our extended family around that table. And if twelve around the table was good, then certainly fourteen would be better. Just last fall, Dad commissioned our neighbor Randy to make yet another leaf for the table. There were fourteen around the table for Dad's last Thanksgiving.

Ours was a dad who had a lifelong desire to serve. He delivered Meals on Wheels until he was eighty-three. He delighted in picking up the day-old doughnuts from Mr. Rollen's shop to give those on his route an extra treat. We teased him that he should be receiving those meals himself! Even after walking became difficult for him, he continued to drive and took along an able friend to carry the meals to the door.

Our family, like most, had its ups and downs. But ours was a dad who forgave us our human failings as we forgave him his. He died in peace, surrounded by love. Elsa, Peggy, David, and I were so lucky to have such a dad.

This eulogy, in honor of the writer's father, provides concrete and memorable details that give the audience a clear image of the kind of man he was. The repetition of the phrase "ours was a dad" provides a rhythm and unity that moves the text forward, and the use of short, conventional sentences makes the text easy to understand — and deliver.

Key Features / Spoken Presentations

A clear structure.   Spoken texts need to be clearly organized so that your audience can follow what you're saying. The **BEGINNING** needs to engage their interest, make clear what you will be talking about, and perhaps forecast the central parts of your talk. The main part of the text should focus on a few main points — only as many as your listeners can be expected to absorb and retain. (Remember, they can't go back to reread!) The **ENDING** is especially important: it should leave your audience with something, to remember, think about, or do. Davis ends as she begins, saying that she and her sisters and brother "were so lucky to have such a dad." Lincoln ends with a dramatic resolution: "that government of the people, by the people, for the people, shall not perish from the earth."

Signpost language to keep your audience on track.   You may need to provide cues to help your listeners follow your text, especially **TRANSITIONS** that lead them from one point to the next. Sometimes you'll also want to stop and **SUMMARIZE** a complex point to help your audience keep track of your ideas and follow your development of them.

299–306

306–10

317

470–71

rhetorical situations   genres   processes   strategies   research MLA / APA   media / design   handbook

A tone to suit the occasion.   Lincoln spoke at a serious, formal event, the dedication of a national cemetery, and his address is formal and even solemn. Davis's eulogy is more informal in TONE, as befits a speech given for friends and loved ones. In a presentation to a panel of professors, you probably would want to take an academic tone, avoiding too much slang and speaking in complete sentences. If you had occasion to speak on the very same topic to a neighborhood group, however, you would likely want to speak more casually.

■ 13

Repetition and parallel structure.   Even if you're never called on to deliver a Gettysburg Address, you will find that repetition and parallel structure can lend power to a presentation, making it easier to follow — and more likely to be remembered. "We can not dedicate — we can not consecrate — we can not hallow": the repetition of "we can not" and the parallel forms of the three verbs are one reason these words stay with us more than 150 years after they were written and delivered. These are structures any writer can use. See how the repetition of "ours was a dad" in Davis's eulogy creates a rhythm that engages listeners and at the same time unifies the text.

Slides and other media.   Depending on the way you deliver your presentation, you will often want or need to use other media — *PowerPoint* or other presentation slides, video and audio clips, handouts, flip charts, whiteboards, and so on — to present certain information and to highlight key points.

Considering the Rhetorical Situation

As with any writing, you need to consider your rhetorical situation when preparing a presentation:

PURPOSE   Consider what your primary purpose is. To inform? persuade? entertain? evoke another kind of emotional response?

■ 3–4

5-8 ■ **AUDIENCE** Think about whom you'll be addressing and how well you know them. Will they be interested, or will you need to get them interested? Are they likely to be friendly? How can you get and maintain their attention, and how can you establish common ground with them? How much will they know about your subject — will you need to provide background or define any terms?

9-11 ■ **GENRE** The genre of your text will affect the way you structure and present it. If you're making an argument, for instance, you'll need to consider counterarguments — and, depending on the way you're giving the presentation, perhaps to allow for questions and comments from members of the audience who hold other opinions. If you're giving a report, you may have reasons to prepare handouts with detailed information you don't have time to cover in your spoken text, or links to online documents or websites.

12-15 ■ **STANCE** Consider the attitude you want to express. Is it serious? thoughtful? passionate? well-informed? humorous? something else? Choose your words and any other elements of your presentation accordingly. Whatever your attitude, your presentation will be received better by your listeners if they perceive you as comfortable and sincere.

A Brief Guide to Writing Presentations

Whether you're giving a poster presentation at a conference or an oral report in class, what you say will differ in important ways from what you might write for others to read. Here are some tips for composing an effective presentation.

Budget your time. A five-minute presentation calls for about two and a half pages of writing, and ten minutes means only four or five pages. Your introduction and conclusion should each take about one-tenth of the total time available; time for questions (if the format allows for them) should take about one-fifth; and the body of the talk, the rest. In a ten-minute presentation, then, allot one minute for your introduction, one minute for your conclusion, and two minutes for questions, leaving six minutes for the body of your talk.

Organize and draft your presentation. Readers can go back and reread if they don't understand or remember something the first time through a text. Listeners can't. Therefore, it's important that you structure your presentation so that your audience can follow your text — and remember what you say.

- *Craft an introduction* that engages your audience's interest and tells them what to expect. Depending on your rhetorical situation, you may want to **BEGIN** with humor, with an anecdote, or with something that reminds them of the occasion for your talk or helps them see the reason for it. In any case, you always need to summarize your main points, provide any needed background information, and outline how you'll proceed.

299–306

- *In the body of your presentation,* present your main points in more detail and support them with **REASONS** and **EVIDENCE.** As you draft, you may well find that you have more material than you can present in the time available, so you'll need to choose the most important points to focus on and leave out the rest.

326–35

- *Let your readers know you're concluding* (but try to avoid saying "in conclusion"), and then use your remaining time to restate your main points and to explain why they're important. End by saying "thank you" and offering to answer questions or take comments if the format allows for them.

Consider whether to use visuals.   You may want or need to include some visuals to help listeners follow what you're saying. Especially when you're presenting complex information, it helps to let them see it as well as hear it. Remember, though, that visuals should be a means of conveying information, not mere decoration.

DECIDING ON THE APPROPRIATE VISUALS

- *Slides* are useful for listing main points and for projecting illustrations, tables, and graphs.

- *Videos, animations, and sounds* can add additional information to your presentations.

- *Flip charts, whiteboards, or chalkboards* allow you to create visuals as you speak or to keep track of comments from your audience.

- *Posters* sometimes serve as the main part of a presentation, providing a summary of your points. You then offer only a brief introduction and answer any questions.

- *Handouts* can provide additional information, lists of works cited, or copies of any slides you show.

What visual tools (if any) you decide to use is partly determined by how your presentation will be delivered. Will you be speaking to a crowd or a class, delivering your presentation through a podcast, or creating an interactive presentation for a web conference? Make sure that any necessary equipment and programs are available — and that they work. If at all possible, check out any equipment in the place where you'll deliver your presentation before you go live. If you bring your own equipment for a live presentation, make sure you can connect to the internet if you need to and that electrical outlets are in reach of your power cords. Also, make sure that your visuals can be seen. You may have to rearrange the furniture or the screen to make sure everyone can see.

And finally, have a backup plan. Computers fail; projector bulbs burn out; marking pens run dry. Whatever your plan is, have an alternative in case any problems occur.

Presentation software.   *PowerPoint, Keynote,* and other presentation software can include images, video, and sound in addition to displaying written text. They are most useful for linear presentations that move audiences along one slide at a time. Cloud-based programs like *Prezi* also allow you to arrange words or slides in various designs, group related content together, and zoom in and out. Here are some tips for writing and designing slides:

- *Use* LISTS *or images, not paragraphs.* Use slides to emphasize your main points, not to reproduce your talk onscreen: keep your audience's attention focused on what you're saying. A list of brief points, presented one by one, reinforces your words. An image can provide additional information that your audience can take in quickly.

- *Make your text easy for your audience to read.* FONTS should be at least 18 points, and larger than that for headings. Projected slides are easier to read in sans serif fonts like Arial, Helvetica, and Tahoma than in serif fonts like Times New Roman. And avoid using all capital letters, which can be hard to read.

- *Choose colors carefully.* Your text and any illustrations must contrast with the background. Dark content on a light background is easier to read than the reverse. And remember that not everyone sees all colors; be sure your audience doesn't need to be able to see particular colors or contrasts in order to get your meaning. Red-green and blue-yellow contrasts are especially hard for some people to see and should be avoided.

- *Use bells and whistles sparingly, if at all.* Presentation software offers lots of decorative backgrounds, letters that fade in and out or dance across the screen, and sound effects. These features can be more distracting than helpful; use them only if they help to make your point.

- *Mark your text.* In your notes or prepared text, mark each place where you need to click a mouse to call up the next slide.

587

585–86

This Prezi presentation rotates, includes audio and video, and zooms in and out to let viewers take closer look.

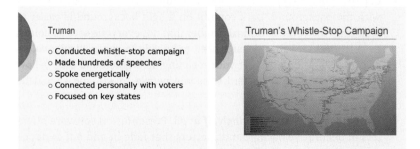

Two PowerPoint slides on the U.S. presidential election of 1948. The slide on the left outlines the main points; the one on the right shows a map of Truman's whistle-stop campaign, providing a graphic illustration of the miles he traveled as he campaigned to be president.

Handouts.   When you want to give your audience information they can refer to later — reproductions of your visuals, bibliographic information about your sources, printouts of your slides — do so in the form of handouts. Refer to the handouts in your presentation, but unless they include material your audience needs to consult before or as you talk, wait until you are finished to distribute them so as not to distract listeners. Clearly label everything you give out, including your name and the date and title of the presentation.

Delivering a Presentation

The success of a presentation often hinges on how you deliver it. As you work on your spoken texts, bear in mind the following points:

Practice.   Practice, practice, and then practice some more. The better you know your talk, the more confident you will be, and your audience will respond positively to that confidence. If you're reading a prepared text, try to write it as if you were talking. Then practice by recording it as you read it; listen for spots that sound as if you're reading, and work on your delivery to sound more relaxed. As you practice, pay attention to keeping within your time limit. If possible, rehearse your talk with a small group of friends to test their response and to get used to speaking in front of an audience.

Speak clearly.   When you're giving a spoken presentation, your first goal is to be understood by your audience. If listeners miss important words or phrases because you don't pronounce them distinctly, your talk will not succeed. Make sure, too, that your pace matches your audience's needs. Often you'll need to make yourself speak more slowly than usual to explain complex material (or to compensate for nerves); sometimes you may need to speed up to keep your audience's attention. In general, though, strive for a consistent pace throughout, one that ensures you don't have to rush at the end.

Pause for emphasis.   In writing, you have white space and punctuation to show readers where an idea or discussion ends. When speaking, you need to pause to signal the end of a thought, to give listeners a moment to consider something you've said, or to get them ready for a surprising or amusing statement.

Stand up (or sit up) straight and look at your audience.   If you're in the same physical space as your audience, try to maintain some eye contact with them. If that's uncomfortable, fake it: pick a spot on the wall just above the head of a person in the back of the room, and focus on it. You'll appear as if you're looking at your audience even if you're not looking them in the eye. And if you stand or sit up straight, you'll project the sense that you have confidence in what you're saying. If you appear to believe in your words, others will, too. If you're speaking via an online forum like *Skype,* look at the computer's camera — not at the screen. Also, make sure the camera is positioned at your eye level, so you aren't looking down at it (and showing your viewers the ceiling behind you!).

Use gestures for emphasis.   If you're not used to speaking in front of a group, you may let your nervousness show by holding yourself stiffly, elbows tucked in. To overcome some of that nervousness, take some deep breaths, try to relax, and move your arms and the rest of your body as you would if you were talking to a friend. Use your hands for emphasis: most public speakers use one hand to emphasize specific points and both hands to make larger gestures. Watch politicians on C-SPAN to see how people who speak on a regular basis use gestures as part of their overall delivery.

part 7

Handbook

"Pfft, English, who needs that? I'm never going to England." So says the illustrious Homer Simpson on an early episode called "The Way We Was." Maybe Homer can ignore the conventions of English grammar and usage, but that's not the case for the rest of us. If we want the world to take seriously what we think and say, we need to pay attention to our grammar and language. We need to edit our SENTENCES so they're clear, choose our LANGUAGE carefully, and use PUNCTUATION purposefully. This handbook provides guidelines to help you edit what you write.

Handbook

Sentences   **S**

S-1 Complete Sentences

In casual situations, we often use a kind of shorthand, because we know our audience will fill in the gaps. When we say to a dinner guest, "Coffee?" he knows we mean, "Would you like some coffee?" When we email a friend, "7:00 at Starbucks?" our friend will understand that we are asking, "Should we meet at 7:00 at Starbucks?" In more formal writing or speaking situations, though, our audience may not share the same context, so to be sure we're understood we usually need to present our ideas in complete sentences. This section reviews the parts of a sentence.

S-1a Elements of a Sentence

Subjects and predicates

Glossary

HB-25–31

HB-11–25

A sentence contains a subject and a predicate. The subject, usually a **NOUN** or **PRONOUN,** names the topic of the sentence; the predicate, which always includes a **VERB,** says what the subject is or does.

>   s   p
> ▶ Birds fly.
>   s   p
> ▶ Birds are feathered vertebrates.

The subject and the predicate each may contain only one word. Usually, however, both the subject and the predicate contain more than one word.

>   s   p
> ▶ Birds of many kinds fly south in the fall.

A sentence may contain more than one subject or verb.

>   s   s   v
> ▶ Birds and butterflies fly south in the fall.
>   s   v   v
> ▶ Birds fly south in the fall and return north in the spring.

At times, the subject comes after the verb.

▶ Here comes the sun.

Expressing subjects explicitly

English requires an explicit subject in every **CLAUSE**, even if all of the clauses in a sentence are about the same subject.

HB-6

▶ Although the dinner cost too much, *it* impressed my guests.

The only exception is commands, in which the subject is understood to be *you*.

▶ Eat smaller portions at each meal.

Sentences beginning with *there* or *it*.   In some cases the subject comes after the verb and an **EXPLETIVE**—*there* or *it*—comes before the verb.

Glossary

▶ *There is* ~~Is~~ no place like home.

▶ *It is* ~~Is~~ both instructive and rewarding to work with young children.

You can also rephrase the sentence to avoid using the expletive.

▶ *Working with young children is* ~~Is~~ both instructive and rewarding. ~~to work with young children~~.

If English is not your first language, be aware that English does not emphasize a subject by repeating it in the same clause.

▶ My friend Jing Jing ~~she~~ changed her name to Jane.

▶ The students who visited ~~they~~ were detained at the airport.

Clauses

A clause is a group of words containing a subject and predicate. An independent clause can function alone as a sentence: *Birds fly.* A subordinate clause begins with a **SUBORDINATING WORD** such as *as*, *because*, or *which* and cannot stand alone as a sentence: *because birds fly.*

HB-8

INDEPENDENT CLAUSE   SUBORDINATE CLAUSE

▶ My yard is now quiet because most of the birds flew south.

Phrases

A phrase is a word group that lacks a subject, a verb, or both and thus cannot stand alone as a sentence. Some common ones are prepositional, appositive, participial, gerund, and infinitive phrases.

HB-42–43

A prepositional phrase starts with a **PREPOSITION** such as *at*, *from*, *of*, or *in* and usually ends with a noun: *at school*, *from home*, *in bed.*

▶ The day *after the World Series* San Francisco celebrated.

An appositive phrase follows and gives further information about a noun or pronoun. Appositives function as nouns.

▶ I knew I was in the right house because my daddy's only real possessions, *a velvet-covered board pinned with medals*, sat inside a glass cabinet on a table.   —Rick Bragg, "All Over But the Shoutin' "

A participial phrase contains the present or past participle of a verb plus any **OBJECTS**, **MODIFIERS**, and **COMPLEMENTS**.

Glossary

▶ *Brimming with optimism*, I headed over to the neighborhood watering hole and waited.   —Hal Niedzviecki, "Facebook in a Crowd"

▶ A study from Princeton *issued at the same time as the Duke study* showed that women in the sciences reported less satisfaction in their jobs and less of a sense of belonging than their male counterparts.
—Anna Quindlen, "Still Needing the F Word"

A gerund phrase includes the -*ing* form of a verb plus any objects, modifiers, and complements. It functions as a noun.

▶ For roller coasters, *being the star of summer amusement park rides* certainly has its ups and downs.　　　—Cathi Eastman and Becky Burrell,
　　　"The Science of Screams: Laws of Physics Instill Thrills in Roller Coasters"

An infinitive phrase includes an infinitive (*to* plus the base form of a verb: *to read*, *to write*) and any objects, modifiers, and complements.

▶ *To commit more troops* seemed crazy when we couldn't win the war.

▶ The point of ribbon decals is *to show support for the troops*.

S-2 Sentence Fragments

Sentence fragments show up often in advertising: "Got milk?" "Good to the last drop." "Not bad for something that tastes good too." We use them in informal speech and text messages as well. But some readers consider fragments too informal, and in many academic writing situations it's best to avoid them altogether. This section helps you identify and edit out fragments.

S-2a Identifying Fragments

A sentence fragment is a group of words that is capitalized and punctuated as a sentence but is not a sentence. A sentence needs at least one INDEPENDENT CLAUSE, which contains a SUBJECT and VERB and does not start with a SUBORDINATING WORD.

HB-6

HB-4–5

HB-11–25

HB-8

NO SUBJECT　　The catcher batted fifth. Fouled out, ending the inning.
　　　　　　　　Who fouled out?

NO VERB	The first two batters walked. Manny Ramirez again.
	What did Ramirez do again?
SUBORDINATE CLAUSE	Although the Yankees loaded the bases.
	There is a subject (Yankees) and a verb (loaded), but although makes this a subordinate clause. What happened after the Yankees loaded the bases?

SOME SUBORDINATING WORDS

after	because	so that	until	while
although	before	that	when	who
as	if	though	where	which
as if	since	unless	whether	why

Writers often use sentence fragments for emphasis or to be informal.

FOR EMPHASIS	Throughout my elementary and middle school years, I was a strong student, always on the honor roll. I never had a GPA below 3.0. I was smart, and I knew it. *That is, until I got the results of the proficiency test.*
	—Shannon Nichols, " 'Proficiency' "
TO BE INFORMAL	The SAT writing test predicts how successful a student will be in college. *Since when?*

S-2b Editing Fragments

Since some readers regard fragments as errors, it's generally better to write complete sentences. Here are four ways to make fragments into sentences.

Remove the subordinating word

▶ I'm thinking about moving to a large city. ~~Because~~ I dislike the lack of privacy in my country town of three thousand.

Add a subject

> ▶ The catcher batted fifth. ~~Fouled~~ *He fouled* out, ending the inning.

Add a verb

> ▶ The first two batters walked. Manny Ramirez *walked* again.

Sometimes a fragment contains a verb form, such as a present or past participle, that cannot function as the main verb of a sentence. In these cases, you can either substitute an appropriate verb form or add a **HELPING VERB**.

HB-16–17

> ▶ As the game progressed, the fans' excitement diminished. The pitcher's arm ~~weakening,~~ *weakened,* and the fielders ~~making~~ *made* a number of errors.
> ▶ The media influence the election process. Political commercials *are* appearing on television more frequently than in years past.

Attach the fragment to a nearby sentence

> ▶ Some candidates spread nasty stories*/* ~~About~~ *about* their opponents.
> ▶ These negative stories can deal with many topics*/* ~~Such~~ *, such* as marital infidelity, sources of campaign funds, and drug use.
> ▶ Put off by negative campaigning*/* ~~Some~~ *, some* people decide not to vote at all.

S-3 Comma Splices, Fused Sentences

When you join two independent clauses using only a comma, you've created a comma splice: "He dropped the bucket, the paint spilled on his feet." Without the comma—"He dropped the bucket the paint spilled on his feet"—it's a fused sentence. You'll sometimes see comma splices and fused sentences in ads or literary works, but they're generally regarded as errors in academic writing. This section shows how to recognize comma splices and fused sentences and edit them out of your writing.

S-3a Identifying Comma Splices and Fused Sentences

HB-6

A comma splice occurs when an **INDEPENDENT CLAUSE** follows another independent clause with only a comma between them.

> **COMMA SPLICE**   T. S. Eliot is best known for his poetry, he also wrote and produced several plays.

A fused sentence occurs when one independent clause follows another with no punctuation in between.

> **FUSED SENTENCE**   The school board debated the issue for three days they were unable to reach an agreement.

S-3b Editing Comma Splices and Fused Sentences

There are several ways to edit comma splices or fused sentences.

Make the clauses two sentences

▶ T. S. Eliot is best known for his poetry. He also wrote several plays.

HB-3–4

Add a comma and a **COORDINATING CONJUNCTION**

▶ The school board debated the issue for three days, but they were unable to reach an agreement.

Add a semicolon

If the relationship between the two clauses is clear without a coordinating conjunction, you can simply join them with a semicolon.

▶ Psychologists study individuals' behavior; sociologists focus on group-level dynamics.

When clauses are linked by a **TRANSITION** such as *therefore* or *as a result*, the transition needs to be preceded by a semicolon and followed by a comma.

317

▶ The hill towns experienced heavy spring and summer rain/; therefore, the fall foliage fell far short of expectations.

Recast one clause as a **SUBORDINATE CLAUSE**

HB-6

Add a **SUBORDINATING WORD** to clarify the relationship between the two clauses.

HB-8

Although initial
▶ ~~Initial~~ critical responses to *The Waste Land* were mixed, the poem has been extensively anthologized, read, and written about.

S-4 Verbs

Verbs are the engines of sentences, giving energy, action, and life to writing. "I Googled it" is much more vivid than "I found it on the internet"—and the difference is the verb. Sometimes our use of verbs can obscure meaning, however, as when a politician avoids taking responsibility by saying, "Mistakes were made." Our choice of verbs shapes our writing in important ways, and this section reviews ways of using verbs appropriately and effectively.

S-4a Verb Tenses

To express time, English verbs have three simple tenses—present, past, and future. In addition, each of these verb tenses has perfect and progressive forms that indicate more complex time frames. The present perfect, for example, indicates an action that began in the past but is continuing into the present. The lists that follow show each of these tenses for the regular verb *talk* and the irregular verb *write*.

Simple tenses

PRESENT	PAST	FUTURE
I talk	I talked	I will talk
I write	I wrote	I will write

Use the simple present to indicate actions that take place in the present or that occur habitually. Use the simple past to indicate actions that were completed in the past. Use the simple future to indicate actions that will take place in the future.

▶ Every few years the Republicans *propose* a tax cut.
—David Brooks, "The Triumph of Hope over Self-Interest"

▶ One day my mother *came* home from Coffee Dan's with an awful story.
—Mike Rose, "Potato Chips and Stars"

▶ Prohibiting English *will do* for the language what Prohibition *did* for liquor.
—Dennis Baron, "Don't Make English Official—Ban It Instead"

Use the present tense to express scientific or general facts even when the rest of the sentence is in the past tense.

▶ Agatston showed that South Beach dieters ~~lost~~ *lose* about ten pounds in the first two weeks.

In general, use the present tense to write about literature.

▶ In *The Bluest Eye*, Pecole *evokes* the theme of vision when she *says* that she *wishes* for blue eyes that will be seen as beautiful and *earn* her the respect of the cruel people in her life.

▶ As in many fantasy novels and fairy tales, the central character *is* on a quest; however, the narrative of Harry's quest *unfolds* more like a classic mystery.
—Philip Nel, "Fantasy, Mystery, and Ambiguity"

In **APA STYLE,** use the past tense or the present perfect to report results of an experiment and the present tense to give your own insights into or conclusions about the results.

533–74

▶ The bulk of the data collected in this study *validated* the research of Neal Miller; the subjects *appeared* to undergo operant conditioning of their smooth muscles in order to relax their frontalis muscles and increase their skin temperatures. Subjects 3 and 6 each *failed* to do this in one session; subject 7 *failed* to do this several times. This finding *is* difficult to explain precisely.   —Sarah Thomas, "The Effect of Biofeedback Training on Muscle Tension and Skin Temperature"

Perfect tenses

PRESENT PERFECT	PAST PERFECT	FUTURE PERFECT
I have talked	I had talked	I will have talked
I have written	I had written	I will have written

Use the present perfect to indicate actions that took place at no specific time in the past or that began in the past and continue into the present.

▶ As a middle-class black I *have* often *felt* myself contriving to be "black."
                 —Shelby Steele, "On Being Black and Middle Class"

Use the past perfect for an action that was completed before another past action began.

▶ By the time I was born, the Vietnam War ^had^ already ended.

The war ended before the writer was born.

Use the future perfect to indicate actions that will be completed at a specific time in the future.

▶ By this time next year, you *will have graduated*.

Progressive tenses

PRESENT PROGRESSIVE	PAST PROGRESSIVE	FUTURE PROGRESSIVE
I am talking	I was talking	I will be talking
I am writing	I was writing	I will be writing

PRESENT PERFECT PROGRESSIVE	PAST PERFECT PROGRESSIVE	FUTURE PERFECT PROGRESSIVE
I have been talking	I had been talking	I will have been talking
I have been writing	I had been writing	I will have been writing

Use progressive tenses to indicate continuing action.

▶ Congress *is considering*, and may soon pass, legislation making English the official language of the United States.
>—Dennis Baron, "Don't Make English Official—Ban It Instead"

▶ The night after Halloween, we *were watching* TV when the doorbell rang.
>—David Sedaris, "Us and Them"

▶ As they do every year on the Friday before exams, the Kenyon Kokosingers *will be singing* next Friday evening in Rosse Hall.

▶ Willie joined the Grace Church Boys Choir when he was ten, and he *has been singing* ever since.

S-4b Verb Forms

There are four forms of a verb: the base form, the past, the past participle, and the present participle. Samples of each appear in the lists below. All of the various tenses are generated with these four forms.

The past tense and past participle of all regular verbs are formed by adding *-ed* or *-d* to the base form (*talked*, *lived*). Irregular verbs are not as predictable; see the list of some common ones below. The present participle consists of the base form plus -ing (*talking, living*).

BASE FORM	On Thursdays, we *visit* a museum.
PAST TENSE	Last week, we *visited* the Museum of Modern Art.
PAST PARTICIPLE	I have also *visited* the Metropolitan Museum, but I've not yet *been* to the Cloisters.
PRESENT PARTICIPLE	We will be *visiting* the Cooper-Hewitt Museum tomorrow to see the cutlery exhibit.

Some common irregular verbs

BASE FORM	PAST TENSE	PAST PARTICIPLE	PRESENT PARTICIPLE
be	was/were	been	being
choose	chose	chosen	choosing
do	did	done	doing
eat	ate	eaten	eating
fall	fell	fallen	falling
give	gave	given	giving
go	went	gone	going
hang (suspend)	hung	hung	hanging
have	had	had	having
know	knew	known	knowing
lay	laid	laid	laying
lie (recline)	lay	lain	lying
make	made	made	making
prove	proved	proved, proven	proving
rise	rose	risen	rising
set	set	set	setting
sit	sat	sat	sitting
teach	taught	taught	teaching
write	wrote	written	writing

It's easy to get confused about when to use the past tense and when to use a past participle. One simple guideline is to use the past tense if there is no helping verb and to use a past participle if there is one.

> *went*
> ▶ For vacation last spring, my family ~~gone~~ to Turkey.
>   ^

> *eaten*
> ▶ After two weeks in Istanbul, we had ~~ate~~ a lot of Turkish delight.
>   ^

Helping verbs

Glossary

HB-11–14

HB-19–20

Do, have, be, and **MODALS** such as *can* and *may* all function as helping verbs that work with main verbs to express certain verb **TENSES** and **MOODS**. *Do, have,* and *be* change form to indicate tenses; modals do not. The appropriate forms of main verbs and helping verbs are discussed in this section.

FORMS OF *DO*	do, does, did
FORMS OF *HAVE*	have, has, had
FORMS OF *BE*	be, am, is, are, was, were, been
MODALS	can, could, may, might, must, shall, should, will, would, ought to

Do, does, and *did* require the base form of the main verb.

> ▶ That professor *did take* class participation into account when calculating grades.

> ▶ Sometimes even the smartest students *do* not *like* to answer questions out loud in class.

Have, has, and *had* require the past participle of the main verb.

> ▶ I *have written* to my senator to express my views on global warming.

> ▶ When all of the visitors *had gone*, the security guards locked the building for the night.

HB-18–19

Forms of *be* are used with a present participle to express a continuing action or with a past participle to express the **PASSIVE VOICE.**

CONTINUING ACTION

▶ The university *is considering* a change in its policy on cell phone use.

▶ I *was studying* my notes from last week as I walked to class.

PASSIVE VOICE

▶ Six classes per semester *is considered* a heavy course load.

▶ Ancient Greek *was studied* by many university students in the early twentieth century, but it is not a popular major today.

Modals are used with the base form of the main verb.

▶ After each class, small groups of students *will meet* for focused discussion.

▶ Each student *should participate* in every group session.

Gerunds and infinitives

A gerund is a verb form ending in -*ing* that functions as a noun: *hopping, skipping, jumping.*

▶ Although many people like *driving*, some prefer *walking*.

An infinitive is *to* plus the base form of a verb: *to hop, to skip, to jump.*

▶ Although many people like *to drive*, some prefer *to walk*.

In general, use infinitives to express intentions or desires, and use gerunds to express plain facts.

▶ I planned *to learn* Spanish, Japanese, and Arabic.

▶ I also really wanted *to know* Russian.

▶ Unfortunately, I ended up *studying* only Spanish and Arabic—and *speaking* only Spanish.

▶ Just in time for Thanksgiving, the painters finished ~~to put~~ *putting* up the wallpaper.

With several verbs—*forget, remember, stop,* and a few others—the choice of an infinitive or gerund changes the meaning.

▶ I stopped *to eat* lunch.

In other words, I took a break so that I could eat lunch.

▶ I stopped *eating* lunch.

In other words, I no longer ate lunch.

HB-42–43

Always use a gerund after a **PREPOSITION.**

▶ The water is too cold for ~~to swim.~~ *swimming.*

S-4c Active and Passive Voice

Verbs can be active or passive. When a verb is in the active voice, the subject performs the action (*she threw the ball*). When a verb is in the passive voice, the subject receives the action (*the ball was thrown to her*).

ACTIVE The wealthiest 1 percent of the American population *holds* 38 percent of the total national wealth.

—Gregory Mantsios, "Class in America—2003"

PASSIVE By the 1970s, Leslie had developed a distinctive figural style in which subjects *are shown* in frontal, confrontational poses, at close range. —David S. Rubin, "It's the Same Old Song"

Active verbs tend to be more direct and easier to understand, but the passive voice can be useful when you specifically want to emphasize the recipient of the action.

rhetorical situations

genres

processes

strategies

research MLA / APA

media / design

handbook

▶ In a sense, little girls *are urged* to please adults with a kind of
coquettishness, while boys *are enjoined* to behave like monkeys toward
each other.   —Paul Theroux, "Being a Man"

The passive voice is also appropriate in scientific writing when you wish
to emphasize the research itself, not the researchers.

▶ The treatment order was random for each subject, and it *was reversed* for
his or her second treatment.
                                    —Sarah Thomas, "The Effect of Biofeedback Training
                                             on Muscle Tension and Skin Temperature"

S-4d Mood

There are three moods in English: indicative, imperative, and subjunctive.
The indicative is used to state facts or opinions and to ask questions.

▶ Thanks to its many volunteers, Habitat for Humanity *has built* twelve
houses in the region this year.

▶ What other volunteer opportunities *does* Habitat *offer*?

The imperative is used to give commands or directions.

▶ *Sit* up straight and *do* your work.

The subjunctive is used to indicate hypothetical or unlikely conditions
or to express wishes or requests.

Conditional Sentences

The subjunctive is used most often in conditional sentences, ones that
include a clause beginning with *if* or another word that states a condition. Use the indicative to show you are confident the condition can be
met and the subjunctive to show it's doubtful or possible.

If it's a fact.   When there's no doubt that the information in the *if* clause
is true or possible, use the same tense in both clauses.

▶ If an earthquake *strikes* that region, forecasters *expect* a tsunami.

▶ One hundred years ago, if a hurricane *hit*, residents *had* very little warning.

If it's a possibility. When the information in the *if* clause is probably possible, use the present tense in the *if* clause and a modal such as *will* or *might* + the base form of the verb in the other clause.

▶ If you faithfully *follow* the South Beach Diet for two weeks, you *will lose* about ten pounds.

If it's hypothetical or unlikely. When the information in the *if* clause is not likely to be possible, use the past form in the *if* clause and *would* (or *could* or *might*) + the base form of the verb in the other clause. For *be*, use *were* in the *if* clause, not *was*.

▶ If doctors *discovered* a cure for cancer, they *could save* millions of lives.

▶ If Martin Luther King Jr. *were* alive, he *would acknowledge* progress in race relations, but he *would* also *ask* significant questions.

When the *if* clause is about an event in the past that never happened, use the past perfect in the *if* clause and *would have* (or *could have* or *might have*) + a past participle in the other clause.

▶ If the police officer *had separated* the witnesses, their evidence *would have been* admissible in court.

Requests and demands

Use the subjunctive in *that* clauses following verbs such as *ask, insist,* or *suggest* in order to express a request, a demand, or a recommendation. Use the base form of the verb in the *that* clause.

▶ I recommend that Hannah *study* French as an undergraduate.

▶ The CEO will insist that you *be* at your desk before nine each morning.

S-5 Subject-Verb Agreement

Subjects and verbs should agree: if the subject is in the third-person singular, the verb should be in the third-person singular—"Dinner is on the table." Yet sometimes context affects subject-verb agreement, as when we say that "macaroni and cheese *are* available in most grocery stores" but that "macaroni and cheese *is* our family's favorite comfort food." This section focuses on subject-verb agreement.

S-5a Agreement in Number and Person

Subjects and verbs should agree with each other in number (singular or plural) and person (first, second, or third). To make a present-tense verb agree with a third-person singular subject, add -s or -es to the base form.

▶ A 1922 *ad* for Resinol soap *urges* women to "make that dream come true" by using Resinol.
> —Doug Lantry, " 'Stay Sweet As You Are' "

To make a present-tense verb agree with any other subject, simply use the base form without any ending.

▶ *I listen* to NPR every morning while I brush my teeth.

▶ Drunk *drivers cause* thousands of preventable deaths each year.

Be and *have* have **IRREGULAR** forms and so do not follow the -s/-es rule.   △ HB-15

▶ The test of all knowledge *is* experiment.
> —Richard Feynman, "Atoms in Motion"

▶ The scientist *has* a lot of experience with ignorance and doubt and uncertainty, and this experience *is* of great importance.
> —Richard Feynman, "The Value of Science"

S-5b Subjects and Verbs Separated

A verb should agree with its subject, not with another word that falls in between.

▶ In the backyard, the *leaves* of the apple tree *rattle* across the lawn.
—Gary Soto, "The Guardian Angel"

fluctuates
▶ The price of soybeans ~~fluctuate~~ according to demand.
                        ^

S-5c Compound Subjects

Two or more subjects joined by *and* are generally plural.

▶ Obviously, safety and security *are* important issues in American life.
—Andie McDonie, "Airport Security"

However, if the parts of the subject form a single unit, they take a singular verb.

is
▶ Forty acres and a mule ~~are~~ what General William T. Sherman promised
                         ^
each freed slave.

If the subjects are joined by *or* or *nor*, the verb should agree with the closer subject.

is
▶ Either you or she ~~are~~ mistaken.
                    ^

were
▶ Neither the teacher nor his students ~~was~~ able to solve the equation.
                                       ^

S-5d Subjects That Follow the Verb

English verbs usually follow their subjects. Be sure the verb agrees with the subject even when the subject follows the verb, such as when the sentence begins with *there is* or *there are*.

▶ There *are* too many *unresolved problems* for the project to begin.

▶ In the middle of the baby pool *is* a *hot tub,* just for little kids.
—Michael Lewis, *Home Game*

S-5e Collective Nouns

Collective nouns such as *group, team, audience,* or *family* can take singular or plural verbs, depending on whether the noun refers to the group as a single unit or to the multiple members that make up the group.

▶ The choir *sings* The Messiah every Christmas.

▶ Gregor's family *keep* reassuring themselves that things will be just fine again.   —Scott Russell Sanders, "Under the Influence"

The individual members of the family reassure one another.

S-5f *Everyone* and Other Indefinite Pronouns

Most **INDEFINITE PRONOUNS,** such as *anyone, anything, each, either, everybody, everything, neither, nobody, no one, one, somebody, someone,* and *something,* take a singular verb.

Glossary

▶ But . . . no one *is* selling the content that gets shared on P2P services.
—Lawrence Lessig, "Some Like It Hot"

▶ Each of the candidates *agrees* with the president.

Both, few, many, others, and *several* are always plural.

▶ Already, few *know* how to read a serious book.
—Paul West, "Borrowed Time"

All, any, enough, more, most, none, and *some* are singular when they refer to a singular noun, but they are plural whenever they refer to a plural noun.

> ▶ Don't assume that all of the members of a family ~~votes~~ the same way.
> _{vote}

> ▶ None of the music we heard last night ~~come~~ from the baroque period.
> _{comes}

S-5g *Who, That,* or *Which*

Glossary

The **RELATIVE PRONOUNS** *who, that,* and *which* take a singular verb when they come after a singular noun and a plural verb when they come after a plural noun.

> ▶ I find it refreshing to have *work* that *rewards* initiative and effort.
> —Lars Eighner, "On Dumpster Diving"

> ▶ We fell in with some other *hippie-groupie types* who *were* obsessed with Hendrix, the Doors, Janis Joplin, and Zeppelin as well as the Stones.
> —Susan Jane Gilman, "Mick Jagger Wants Me"

One of the is always followed by a plural noun, and the verb should be plural.

> ▶ Jaime is one of the speakers who ~~asks~~ provocative questions.
> _{ask}
>
> *Several speakers ask provocative questions. Jaime is one. Who refers to speakers, so the verb is plural.*

The only one, however, takes a singular verb.

> ▶ Jaime is the only one of the speakers who ~~ask~~ provocative questions.
> _{asks}
>
> *Only one speaker asks provocative questions: Jaime. Who thus refers to one, so the verb is singular.*

S-5h Singular Words Such as *News* and *Physics*

Words like *news*, *athletics*, and *physics* seem plural but are in fact singular in meaning and take singular verb forms.

▶ The *news* of widespread dismissals *alarms* everyone in the company.

Some words such as *economics*, *mathematics*, *politics*, and *statistics* are usually singular but have plural meanings in some contexts.

▶ For my roommate, mathematics *is* an endlessly stimulating field.

▶ The complex mathematics involved in this proof *are* beyond the scope of this lecture.

S-5i Titles and Words Used as Words

Titles and words that you discuss as words are singular.

▶ *The Royal Tenenbaums* ~~depict~~ *depicts* three talented siblings who are loosely based on characters created by J. D. Salinger.

▶ *Man-caused disasters* ~~are~~ *is* a term favored by some political analysts as a substitute for the term *terrorist attacks*.

S-6 Pronouns

We use pronouns to take the place of nouns so we don't have to write or say the same word or name over and over. Imagine how repetitive our writing would be without pronouns: *Little Miss Muffet sat on Little Miss Muffet's tuffet eating Little Miss Muffet's curds and whey.* Luckily, we have pronouns, and this section demonstrates how to use them clearly.

S-6a Pronoun-Antecedent Agreement

A pronoun must agree with its antecedent in gender and in number.

IN GENDER   *Grandma* took *her* pie out of the oven.

IN NUMBER   *My grandparents* spent weekends at *their* cabin on White Bear Lake.

Generic nouns

A noun that is used as a typical example of the members of a group can be either singular or plural; make sure that your pronoun agrees with the noun antecedent.

▶ A lab technician should always wear goggles to protect ~~their~~ *his or her* eyes while working with chemicals.

▶ ~~A lab technician~~ *Lab technicians* should always wear goggles to protect their eyes while working with chemicals.

Indefinite pronouns

Glossary

INDEFINITE PRONOUNS such as *anyone, each, either, everyone, neither, no one, someone,* and *something* take a singular pronoun.

▶ Everyone in the class did ~~their~~ *his or her* best.

If you find *his or her* awkward, you can rewrite the sentence.

▶ ~~Everyone~~ *All of the students* in the class did their best.

Collective nouns

Collective nouns such as *audience, committee,* or *team* take a singular pronoun when they refer to the group as a whole and a plural pronoun when they refer to members of the group as individuals.

▶ The winning team drew ~~their~~ *its* inspiration from the manager.

▶ The winning team threw ~~its~~ *their* gloves in the air.

He, his, *and other masculine pronouns*

To avoid **SEXIST LANGUAGE,** use *he*, *him*, *his*, or *himself* only when you know that the antecedent is male.

HB-58–59

▶ Before meeting a new doctor, many people worry about not liking him/ *or her.*

S-6b Pronoun Reference

A pronoun needs to have a clear antecedent, a specific word to which the pronoun points.

▶ My grandmother spent a lot of time reading to me. She mostly read the standards, like *The Little Engine That Could.*

    —Richard Bullock, "How I Learned about the Power of Writing"

Ambiguous reference

A pronoun is ambiguous if it could refer to more than one antecedent.

▶ After I plugged the printer into the computer, ~~it~~ *the printer* sputtered and died.

What sputtered and died—the computer or the printer? The edit makes the reference clear.

Implied reference

If a pronoun does not refer clearly to a specific word, rewrite the sentence to omit the pronoun or insert an antecedent.

Unclear reference of *this, that,* and *which*. These three pronouns must refer to specific antecedents.

▶ Ultimately, the Justice Department did not insist on the breakup of
  an oversight that
  Microsoft, ~~which~~ set the tone for a liberal merger policy.
              ^

Indefinite use of *they, it,* and *you*. *They* and *it* should be used only to refer to people or things that have been specifically mentioned. *You* should be used only to address your reader.

  Many
▶ ~~In many~~ European countries, ~~they~~ don't allow civilians to carry handguns.
  ^

  The
▶ ~~On the~~ weather station, ~~it~~ said that storms would hit Key West today.
  ^

▶ Many doctors argue that age should not be an impediment to
            for people who
  physical exercise ~~if you~~ have always been active.
                    ^

S-6c Pronoun Case

The pronouns in the list below change case according to how they function in a sentence. There are three cases: subjective, objective, and possessive. Pronouns functioning as subjects or subject complements are in the subjective case; those functioning as objects are in the objective case; those functioning as possessives are in the possessive case.

SUBJECTIVE   *We* lived in a rented house three blocks from the school.

OBJECTIVE   I went to my room and shut the door behind *me*.

POSSESSIVE   All *my* life chocolate has made me ill.

—David Sedaris, "Us and Them"

rhetorical situations
genres
processes
strategies
research MLA / APA
media / design
handbook

SUBJECTIVE	OBJECTIVE	POSSESSIVE
I	me	my / mine
we	us	our / ours
you	you	your / yours
he / she / it	him / her / it	his / her / hers / its
they	them	their / theirs
who / whoever	whom / whomever	whose

In subject complements

Use the subjective case for pronouns that follow **LINKING VERBS** such as *be*, *seem*, *become*, and *feel*.

Glossary

▶ In fact, Li was not the one who broke the code; it was ~~me.~~ *I.*

If It was I *sounds awkward, revise the sentence further:* I broke it.

In compound structures

When a pronoun is part of a compound subject, it should be in the subjective case. When it's part of a compound object, it should be in the objective case.

▶ On our vacations, my grandfather and ~~me~~ *I* went fishing together.

▶ There were never any secrets between ~~he~~ *him* and ~~I.~~ *me.*

After *than* or *as*

Often comparisons with *than* or *as* leave some words out. When such comparisons include pronouns, your intended meaning determines the case of the pronoun.

▶ You trust John more than *me.*

This sentence means You trust John more than you trust me.

▶ You trust John more than *I.*

This sentence means You trust John more than I trust him.

Before or after infinitives

Glossary

Pronouns that come before or after an **INFINITIVE** are usually in the objective case.

> ▶ The professor asked Scott and ~~I~~ to act the scene for ~~she~~ and the class.
>
> *me* ... *her*

Before gerunds

HB-17–18

Pronouns that come before a **GERUND** are usually in the possessive.

> ▶ Savion's fans loved ~~him~~ tap dancing to classical music.
>
> *his*

With who and whom

Use *who* (and *whoever*) where you would use *he* or *she,* and use *whom* (and *whomever*) where you would use *him* or *her.* These words appear

Glossary

more often in questions and in **SUBORDINATE CLAUSES.**

In subordinate clauses.   To figure out whether to use *who* or *whom* in a subordinate clause, you need to determine how it functions in the clause. If it functions as a subject, use *who;* if it functions as an object, use *whom.*

> ▶ You may invite ~~whoever~~ you like.
>
> *whomever*

Whomever is the object of you like.

> ▶ I will invite Josh, ~~whom~~ likes dancing.
>
> *who*

Who is the subject of likes dancing.

> ▶ ~~Who~~ do the critics admire most?
>
> *Whom*

They admire her, *so change* who *to* whom.

> ▶ ~~Whom~~ will begin the discussion on this thorny topic?
>
> *Who*

She will begin the discussion, so change whom *to* who.

When **we** *or* **us** *precedes a noun*

If you don't know whether to use *we* or *us* before a noun, choose the pronoun that you would use if the noun were omitted.

▶ *We* students object to the recent tuition increases.

   Without students, *you would say* We object, *not* Us object.

▶ The state is trying to solve its budget shortfall by unfairly charging
   us students.

   Without students, *you would say* unfairly charging us, *not* unfairly charging we.

S-7 Parallelism

Been there, done that. Eat, drink, and be merry. For better or for worse. Out of sight, out of mind. All of these common sayings are parallel in structure, putting parallel words in the same grammatical form. Parallel structure emphasizes the connection between the elements and can make your writing rhythmic and easy to read. This section offers guidelines for maintaining parallelism in your writing.

S-7a In a Series or List

Use the same grammatical form for all items in a series or list—all nouns, all gerunds, all prepositional phrases, and so on.

▶ The seven deadly sins—*avarice, sloth, envy, lust, gluttony, pride,* and
   wrath—were all committed Sunday during the twice-annual bake sale at
   St. Mary's of the Immaculate Conception Church.   —*The Onion*

▶ After fifty years of running, biking, swimming, weight lifting, and
   playing squash
   ~~on the squash court~~ to stay in shape, Aunt Dorothy was unhappy to learn
   ^

   she had a knee problem requiring arthroscopic surgery.

S-7b With Paired Ideas

One way to emphasize the connection between two ideas is to put them in identical grammatical forms. When you connect ideas with *and*, *but*, or another COORDINATING CONJUNCTION, make the ideas parallel in structure, and when you link ideas with *either . . . or* or another CORRELATIVE CONJUNCTION, use the same grammatical structure after each part.

HB-34

HB-35

▶ Many rural residents are voting on conservation issues and ~~agree~~ *agreeing* to pay higher property taxes in order to keep community land undeveloped.

▶ General Electric paid millions of dollars to dredge the river and ~~for removing~~ *to remove* carcinogens from backyards.

▶ Sweet potatoes are highly nutritious, providing both dietary fiber and ~~as a good source of~~ vitamins A and C.

▶ Information on local cleanup efforts can be obtained not only from the town government but also ~~by going to~~ *at* the public library.

S-7c On Presentation Slides

PowerPoint and other presentation slides present most information in lists. Entries on these lists should be in parallel grammatical form.

During the 1946 presidential race, Truman
• Conducted a whistle-stop campaign
• Made hundreds of speeches
• Spoke energetically
• Connected personally with voters

S-7d On a Résumé

Entries on a résumé should be grammatically and typographically parallel. Each entry in the example below has the date on the left; the job title in bold followed by the company on the first line; the city and state on the second line; and the duties performed on the remaining lines, each starting with a verb.

2010–present	**INTERN,** Benedetto, Gartland, and Co. New York, NY Assist in analyzing data for key accounts. Design PowerPoint slides and presentations.
2009, summer	**SALES REPRESENTATIVE,** Vector Marketing Corporation New York, NY Sold high-quality cutlery, developing my own client base.
2008, summer	**TUTOR,** Grace Church Opportunity Project New York, NY Tutored low-income children in math and reading.

S-7e In Headings

When you add headings to a piece of writing, put them in parallel forms—all nouns, all prepositional phrases, and so on. Consider, for example, the following three headings in the chapter on developing a research plan.

Establishing a Schedule
Getting Started
Considering the Rhetorical Situation

S-7f With All the Necessary Words

Be sure to include all the words necessary to make your meaning clear and your grammar parallel.

>   *in*
> ▶ Voting gained urgency in cities, ‸ suburbs, and on farms.

>   *she loved*
> ▶ She loved her son more than ‸ her husband.

> *The original sentence was ambiguous; it could also mean that she loved her son more than her husband did.*

S-8 Coordination and Subordination

When we combine two or more ideas in one sentence, we can use coordination to give equal weight to each idea or subordination to give emphasis to one of the ideas. Assume, for example, that you're writing about your Aunt Irene. Aunt Irene made great strawberry jam. She did not win a blue ribbon at the Iowa State Fair.

COORDINATION	Aunt Irene made great strawberry jam, but she did not win the blue ribbon at the Iowa State Fair.
SUBORDINATION	Though Aunt Irene made great strawberry jam, she did not win the blue ribbon at the Iowa State Fair.

S-8a Linking Equal Ideas

To link ideas that you consider equal in importance, use a coordinating conjunction, a pair of correlative conjunctions, or a semicolon.

COORDINATING CONJUNCTIONS

and	or	so	yet
but	nor	for	

▶ The line in front of Preservation Hall was very long, *but* a good tenor sax player was wandering up and down the street, *so* I took my place at the end of the line.   —Fred Setterberg, "The Usual Story"

▶ Now models of coursework may need to be developed, *and* instructors may need to be hired.   —Megan Hopkins, "Training the Next Teachers for America"

Be careful not to overuse *and*. Try to use the coordinating conjunction that best expresses your meaning.

▶ Mosquitoes survived the high-tech zapping devices, ~~and~~ *but* bites were a small price for otherwise pleasant evenings in the country.

CORRELATIVE CONJUNCTIONS

either . . . or	not only . . . but also	whether . . . or
neither . . . nor	just as . . . so	

▶ *Not only* are the majority of students turning to student loans, *but* debt levels are *also* escalating.
—Tracey King and Ellynne Bannon, "The Burden of Borrowing"

While a semicolon alone can signal equal importance, you might use a **TRANSITION** such as *therefore* or *however* to make the relationship between the ideas especially clear.

◆ 317

▶ Second, reading and spelling require much more than just phonics; spelling strategies and word-analysis skills are equally important.
—Debra Johnson, "Balanced Reading Instruction: A Review of the Literature"

▶ As in many fantasy novels and fairy tales, the central character is on a quest; *however*, the narrative of Harry's quest unfolds more like a classic mystery. —Philip Nel, "Fantasy, Mystery, and Ambiguity"

S-8b Emphasizing One Idea over Others

To emphasize one idea over others, put the most important one in an **INDEPENDENT CLAUSE** and the less important ones in **SUBORDINATE CLAUSES** or **PHRASES**.

△ HB-6–7

▶ Because storytelling lies at the heart of Pueblo culture, it is absurd to attempt to fix the stories in time.

—Leslie Marmon Silko, "Language and Literature from a Pueblo Perspective"

▶ Even ignoring the extreme poles of the economic spectrum, we find enormous class differences in the life-styles among the haves, the have-nots, and the have-littles.   —Gregory Mantsios, "Class in America—2003"

S-9 Shifts

You're watching the news when your brother grabs the remote and changes the channel to a cartoon. The road you're driving on suddenly changes from asphalt to gravel. These shifts are jarring and sometimes disorienting. Similarly, shifts in writing—from one tense to another, for example—can confuse your readers. This section explains how to keep your writing consistent in verb tense and point of view.

S-9a Shifts in Tense

Only when you want to emphasize that actions took place at different times should you shift VERB TENSE.

HB-11–14

▶ My plane *will arrive* in Albuquerque two hours after it *leaves* Portland.

Otherwise, keep tenses consistent.

▶ As the concert ended, several people ~~are~~ *were* already on their way up the aisle, causing a distraction.

In writing about literary works, use the present tense. Be careful not to shift to the past.

▶ The two fugitives start down the river together, Huck fleeing his abusive father and Jim running away from his owner. As they ~~traveled,~~ *travel,* they ~~met~~ *meet* with many colorful characters, including the Duke and King, two actors and con artists who involve Huck and Jim in their schemes.

rhetorical situations
genres
processes
strategies
research MLA / APA
media / design
handbook

S-9b Shifts in Point of View

Do not shift between first person (*I, we*), second person (*you*), and third person (*he, she, it, they, one*).

▶ When ~~one has~~ *you have* a cold, you should stay home rather than risk exposing others.

S-9c Shifts in Number

Unnecessary shifts between singular and plural subjects can confuse readers.

▶ Because of late frosts, oranges have risen dramatically in price. But since ~~the orange is~~ *oranges are* such a staple, they continue to sell.

L Language

rhetorical situations   genres   processes   strategies   research MLA / APA   media / design   handbook

L-1 Appropriate Words

Cool. Sweet. Excellent. These three words can mean the same thing, but each has a different level of formality. We usually use informal language when we're talking with friends, and we use slang and abbreviations when we send text messages, but we choose words that are more formal for most of our academic and professional writing. Just as we wouldn't wear an old T-shirt to most job interviews, we wouldn't write in a college essay that *Beloved* is "an awesome book." This section offers you help in choosing words that are appropriate for different audiences and purposes.

L-1a Formal and Informal Words

Whether you use formal or informal language depends on your **PURPOSE** and **AUDIENCE**.

3–4
5–8

> **FORMAL**   Four score and seven years ago our fathers brought forth on this continent, a new nation, conceived in Liberty, and dedicated to the proposition that all men are created equal.
> —Abraham Lincoln, Gettysburg Address
>
> **INFORMAL**   Our family, like most, had its ups and downs.
> —Judy Davis, "Ours Was a Dad"

Abraham Lincoln delivered the first, more formal sentence in 1863 to 20,000 people, including officials and celebrities. The second, less formal sentence was spoken in 2004 by a woman to a small gathering of family and friends at her father's funeral.

Colloquial language (What's up? No clue) and slang (A-list, S'up?) are not appropriate for formal speech and may be too informal for most academic and professional writing.

▶ ~~A lot of~~ ^Many^ drivers are ~~hot~~ ^excited^ about the fuel efficiency of the new hybrid cars.

▶ We ~~wolfed down~~ ^ate^ our lunches and then ~~hit the books.~~ ^went to the library.^

L-1b Pretentious Language

Long or complicated words might seem to lend authority to your writing, but often they make it sound pretentious and stuffy. Use such words sparingly and only when they best capture your meaning and suit your RHETORICAL SITUATION.

▶ ~~Subsequent to~~ ^After^ adopting the new system, managers ~~averred~~ ^claimed^ that their staff worked ~~synergistically~~ ^together^ ~~in a way that exceeded parameters.~~ ^better than expected.^

L-1c Jargon

Jargon is a specialized vocabulary used in a profession, trade, or field and should be used only when you know your audience will understand what you are saying. The following paragraph might be easily understandable to a computer enthusiast, but most readers would not be familiar with terms like *HDMI*, *DVI*, and *1080p*.

> ▶ HDMI is the easiest and most convenient way to go about high-def. Why? Because you get audio and sound in a single, USB-like cable, instead of a nest of component cables or the soundless garden hose of DVI. Also, unless you're trying to run 1080p over 100 feet or somesuch, stay away from premium brands. Any on-spec cheapie HDMI cable will be perfect for standard living room setups.
> —Rob Beschizza, "Which Is Better, HDMI or Component?"

When you are writing for an audience of nonspecialists, resist the temptation to use overly technical language.

■ rhetorical situations
▲ genres
○ processes
◆ strategies
● research MLA / APA
□ media / design
⬈ handbook

▶ The ~~mini-sternotomy~~ at the lower end of the ~~sternum~~
 small incision *breastbone*
 preserved her appearance.
 ~~resulted in satisfactory cosmesis.~~

L-1d Clichés

Steer clear of clichés, expressions that are so familiar as to have become trite (*white as snow*, *the grass is always greener*).

▶ The company needs a recruiter who thinks ~~outside the box.~~
 unconventionally.

▶ After canoeing all day, we all slept ~~like logs.~~
 soundly.

▶ Nita ~~is a team player,~~ so we hope she will be assigned to the project.
 collaborates well,

L-2 Precise Words

Serena Overpowers Zvonareva. Nadal Triumphs over Berdych. In each case, the writer could have simply used the word *defeats*. But at least to tennis fans, these newspaper headlines are a bit more precise and informative as a result of the words chosen. This section offers guidelines for editing your own writing to make it as precise as it needs to be.

L-2a *Be* and *do*

Try not to rely too much on *be* or *do*. Check your writing to see if you can replace forms of these words with more precise verbs.

▶ David Sedaris's essay "Us and Them" ~~is about~~ his love/hate relationship with his family.
 focuses on

▶ Some doctors believe that ~~doing~~ *solving* crossword puzzles can delay the onset of senility and even Alzheimer's disease.

Sometimes using a form of *be* or *do* is unavoidable, such as when you are describing someone or something.

▶ Barnes *is* a legend among southern California Met lovers—an icon, a beacon, and a font of useful knowledge and freely offered opinions.
—Bob Merlis, "Foster Cars"

L-2b Balancing General and Specific Words

Abstract words refer to general qualities or ideas (*truth, beauty*), whereas concrete words refer to specific things we can perceive with our senses (*books, lipstick*). You'll often need to use words that are general or abstract, but remember that specific, concrete words can make your writing more precise and more vivid—and can make the abstract easier to understand.

▶ In Joan Didion's work, there has always been a fascination with what she once called "the unspeakable peril of the everyday"—the coyotes by the interstate, the snakes in the playpen, the fires and Santa Ana winds of California.
—Michiko Kakutani, "The End of Life as She Knew It"

The concrete coyotes, snakes, fires, *and* winds *help explain the abstract* peril of the everyday.

L-2c Prepositions

Prepositions are words like *at, in,* and *on* that express relationships between words. Do you live *in* a city, *on* an island, or *at* the beach? In each case, you need to use a certain preposition. You'll often need to check a dictionary to decide which preposition to use. Here are some guidelines for using *in, on,* and *at* to indicate place and time.

Prepositions of place

IN

a container, room, or area: in the mailbox, *in* my office, *in* the woods
a geographic location: in San Diego, *in* the Midwest
a printed work: in the newspaper, *in* chapter 3

ON

a surface: on the floor, *on* the grass
a street: on Ninth Street, *on* Western Avenue
an electronic medium: on DVD, *on* the radio
public transportation: on the bus, *on* an airplane

AT

a specific address or business: at 33 Parkwood Street, *at* McDonald's
a public building or unnamed business: at the courthouse, *at* the bakery
a general place: at home, *at* work

Prepositions of time

IN

a defined time period: in an hour, *in* three years
a month, season, or year: in June, *in* the fall, *in* 2007
a part of the day: in the morning, *in* the evening

ON

a day of the week: on Friday
an exact date: on September 12
a holiday: on Thanksgiving, *on* Veteran's Day

AT

a specific time: at 4:30 p.m., *at* sunset, *at* lunchtime, *at* night

L-2d Figurative Language

Figures of speech such as **SIMILES** and **METAPHORS** are words used imaginatively rather than literally. They can help readers understand an

Glossary

abstract point by comparing it to something they are familiar with or can easily imagine.

SIMILE   His body is in almost constant motion—rolling those cigarettes, rubbing an elbow, reaching for a glass—but the
rhythm is tranquil and fluid, *like a cat licking its paw.*
—Sean Smith, "Johnny Depp: Unlikely Superstar"

METAPHOR   And so, before the professor had even finished his little
story, *I had become a furnace of rage.*
—Shelby Steele, "On Being Black and Middle Class"

L-3 Commonly Confused Words

When you're tired, do you *lay* down or *lie* down? After dinner, do you eat *desert* or *dessert*? This section's purpose is to alert you to everyday words that can trip you up and to help you understand the differences between certain words people tend to confuse.

accept, except   *Accept* means "to receive willingly": *accept an award.* *Except* as a preposition means "excluding": *all Western languages except English.*

adapt, adopt   *Adapt* means "to adjust": *adapt the recipe to be dairy free.* *Adopt* means "to take as one's own": *adopt a pet from a shelter.*

advice, advise   *Advice* means "recommendation": *a lawyer's advice.* *Advise* means "to give advice": *We advise you to learn your rights.*

affect, effect   *Affect* as a verb means "to produce a change in": *Stress can affect people's physical health. Effect* as a noun means "result": *cause and effect.*

all right, alright   *All right* is the preferred spelling.

allusion, illusion   *Allusion* means "indirect reference": *an allusion to Alice in Wonderland. Illusion* means "false appearance": *an optical illusion.*

a lot   Always two words, *a lot* means "a large number or amount" or "to a great extent": *a lot of voters; he misses her a lot.* The phrase is too informal for most academic writing.

among, between   Use *among* for three or more items: *among the fifty states.* Use *between* for two items: *between you and me.*

amount, number   Use *amount* for items you can measure but not count: *a large amount of water.* Use *number* for things you can count: *a number of books.*

as, as if, like   *Like* introduces a noun or noun phrase: *It feels like silk.* To begin a subordinate clause, use *as* or *as if*: *Do as I say, not as I do; It seemed as if he had not prepared at all for the briefing.*

bad, badly   Use *bad* as an adjective following a linking verb: *I feel bad.* Use *badly* as an adverb following an action verb: *I play piano badly.*

capital, capitol   A *capital* is a city where the government of a state, province, or country is located: *Kingston was the first state capital of New York.* A *capitol* is a government building: *the dome of the capitol.*

cite, sight, site   *Cite* means to quote: *Cite your sources. Sight* is the act of seeing or something that is seen: *an appalling sight.* A *site* is a place: *the site of a famous battle.*

compose, comprise   The parts *compose* the whole: *Fifty states compose the Union.* The whole *comprises* the parts: *The Union comprises fifty states.*

could of   In writing, use *could have* (*could've*).

council, counsel   *Council* refers to a body of people: *the council's vote. Counsel* means "advice" or "to advise": *her wise counsel; she counseled victims of domestic abuse.*

criteria, criterion   *Criteria* is the plural of *criterion* and takes a plural verb: *certain criteria have been established.*

data   *Data*, the plural of *datum*, technically should take a plural verb (*The data arrive from many sources*), but some writers treat it as singular (*The data is persuasive*).

desert, dessert   *Desert* as a noun means "arid region": *Mojave Desert.* As a verb it means "to abandon": *he deserted his post. Dessert* is a sweet served toward the end of a meal.

disinterested, uninterested   *Disinterested* means "fair; unbiased": *disinterested jury.* *Uninterested* means "bored" or "indifferent": *uninterested in election results.*

emigrate (from), immigrate (to)   *Emigrate* means "to leave one's country": *emigrate from Slovakia. Immigrate* means "to move to another country": *immigrate to Canada.*

etc.   The abbreviation *etc.* is short for the Latin *et cetera*, "and other things." Avoid using *etc.* in your writing, substituting *and so on* if necessary.

everyday, every day   *Everyday* is an adjective meaning "ordinary": *After the holidays, we go back to our everyday routine. Every day* means "on a daily basis": *Eat five or more servings of fruits and vegetables every day.*

fewer, less   Use *fewer* when you refer to things that can be counted: *fewer calories.* Use *less* when you refer to an amount of something that cannot be counted: *less fat.*

good, well   *Good* is an adjective indicating emotional health, appearance, or general quality: *She looks good in that color; a good book. Well* is used as an adjective indicating physical health after a linking verb: *She looks well despite her recent surgery. Well* as an adverb follows an action verb: *He speaks Spanish well.*

hopefully   In academic writing, avoid *hopefully* to mean "it is hoped that"; use it only to mean "with hope": *to make a wish hopefully.*

imply, infer   *Imply* means "to suggest": *What do you mean to imply? Infer* means "to conclude": *We infer that you did not enjoy the trip.*

its, it's   *Its* is a possessive pronoun: *The movie is rated PG-13 because of its language. It's* is a contraction of "it is" or "it has": *It's an exciting action film.*

lay, lie   *Lay,* meaning "to put" or "to place," always takes a direct object: *She lays the blanket down. Lie,* meaning "to recline" or "to be positioned," never takes a direct object: *She lies on the blanket.*

lead, led   The verb *lead* (rhymes with *heed*) is the present tense and base form: *I will lead the way. Led* is the past tense and past participle of *lead*: *Yesterday I led the way.* The noun *lead* (rhymes with *head*) is a type of metal: *Use copper pipes instead of lead.*

literally   Use *literally* only when you want to stress that you don't mean figuratively: *While sitting in the grass, he realized that he literally had ants in his pants.*

loose, lose   *Loose* means "not fastened securely" or "not fitting tightly": *a pair of loose pants. Lose* means "to misplace" or "to not win": *lose an earring; lose the race.*

man, mankind   Use *people, human,* or *humankind* instead.

may of, might of, must of   In writing, use *may have, might have,* or *must have* (*may've, might've, must've*).

media   *Media,* a plural noun, takes a plural verb: *The media report another shooting.* The singular form is *medium: Television is a popular medium for advertising.*

percent, percentage   Use *percent* after a number: *eighty percent.* Use *percentage* after an adjective or article: *an impressive percentage, the percentage was impressive.*

principal, principle   As a noun, *principal* means "a chief official" or "a sum of money": *in the principal's office; raising the principal for a down payment.* As an adjective, it means "most important": *the principal cause of death. Principle* means "a rule by which one lives" or "a basic truth or doctrine": *Lying is against her principles; the principles of life, liberty, and the pursuit of happiness.*

raise, rise   Meaning "to grow" or "to cause to move upward," *raise* always takes a direct object: *He raised his hand.* Meaning "to get up," *rise* never takes a direct object: *The sun rises at dawn.*

the reason . . . is because   Use *because* or *the reason . . . is (that),* but not both: *The reason for the price increase was a poor growing season* or *Prices increased because of a poor growing season.*

reason why   Instead of this redundant phrase, use *the reason* or *the reason that: Psychologists debate the reasons that some people develop depression and others do not.*

respectfully, respectively *Respectfully* means "full of respect": *Speak to your elders respectfully.* *Respectively* means "in the order given": *George H. W. Bush and George W. Bush were the forty-first president and the forty-third president, respectively.*

sensual, sensuous *Sensual* suggests sexuality: *a sensual caress.* *Sensuous* involves pleasing the senses through art, music, and nature: *the violin's sensuous solo.*

set, sit *Set*, meaning "to put" or "to place," takes a direct object: *Please set the table.* *Sit*, meaning "to take a seat," does not take a direct object: *She sits on the bench.*

should of In writing, use *should have* (*should've*).

stationary, stationery *Stationary* means "staying put": *a stationary lab table.* *Stationery* means "paper to write on": *the college's official stationery.*

than, then *Than* is a conjunction used for comparing: *She is taller than her mother.* *Then* is an adverb used to indicate a sequence: *Finish your work and then reward yourself.*

that, which Use *that* to add information that is essential for identifying something: *The horses that live on this island are endangered.* Use *which* to give additional but nonessential information: *Abaco Barb horses, which live on an island in the Bahamas, are endangered.*

their, there, they're *Their* signifies possession: *their canoe.* *There* tells where: *Put it there.* *They're* is the contraction of *they are*: *They're too busy to come.*

to, too, two *To* is either a preposition that tells direction (*Give it to me*) or part of an infinitive (*To err is human*). *Too* means "also" or "excessively": *The younger children wanted to help, too; too wonderful for words.* *Two* is a number: *tea for two.*

unique Because *unique* suggests that an item or person is the only one of its kind, avoid using comparative or superlative adjectives (*more, most, less, least*), intensifiers (such as *very*), or hedges (such as *somewhat*) to modify it.

weather, whether   *Weather* refers to atmospheric conditions: *dreary weather. Whether* refers to a choice between options: *whether to stay home or go out.*

who's, whose   *Who's* is a contraction for *who is* or *who has: Who's the most experienced candidate for the job? Whose* asks or tells who owns something: *Whose keys are these? Jenna, whose keys were lying on the table, had left.*

would of   In writing, use *would have (would've).*

your, you're   *Your* signifies possession: *your diploma. You're* is a contraction for *you are: You're welcome.*

L-4 Unnecessary Words

At this point in time. Really unique. In a manner of speaking. Each of these phrases includes words that are unnecessary or says something that could be said more concisely. This section shows you how to edit your own writing to make every word count.

L-4a *Quite, very,* and Other Empty Words

Intensifiers such as *quite* and *very* are used to strengthen what we say. Hedges such as *apparently, possibly,* and *tend* are a way to qualify what we say. It's fine to use words of this kind when they are necessary. Sometimes, however, they are not. You shouldn't say something is "very unique," because things either are unique or they're not; there's no need to add the intensifier. And why say someone is "really smart" when you could say that he or she is "brilliant"?

▶ Accepted by five Ivy League schools, Jackson ~~seems to be facing an~~ *is facing a* ~~apparently very~~ difficult decision.

Glossary

L-4b *There is, it is*

The **EXPLETIVE** constructions *there is* and *it is* are useful ways to introduce and emphasize an idea, but often they add unnecessary words and can be replaced with stronger, more precise verbs.

▶ ~~It is necessary for~~ Americans today ~~to~~ ^must^ learn to speak more than one language.

▶ ~~There are four~~ ^Four^ large moons and more than thirty small ones ~~that~~ orbit Jupiter.

In certain contexts, *there is* and *it is* can be the best choices. Imagine the ending of *The Wizard of Oz* if Dorothy were to say *No place is like home* instead of the more emphatic (and sentimental) *There's no place like home.*

L-4c Wordy Phrases

Many common phrases use several words when a single word will do. Editing out such wordy phrases will make your writing more concise and easier to read.

WORDY	CONCISE
as far as . . . is concerned	concerning
at the time that	when
at this point in time	now
in spite of the fact that	although, though
in the event that	if
in view of the fact that	because, since

▶ ~~Due to the fact that~~ ^Because^ Professor Lee retired, the animal sciences department now lacks a neurology specialist.

L-4d Redundancies

Eliminate words and phrases that are unnecessary for your meaning.

▶ Painting the house purple ~~in color~~ will make it stand out from the many white houses in town.

▶ Dashing ~~quickly~~ into the street to retrieve the ball, the young girl was almost hit by a car.

▶ How much wood is ~~sufficient~~ enough for the fire to burn all night?

L-5 Adjectives and Adverbs

Adjectives and adverbs are words that describe other words, adding important information and detail. When Dave Barry writes that the Beatles "were the *coolest* thing you had ever seen" and that "they were *smart*; they were *funny*; they didn't take themselves *seriously*," the adjectives and adverbs (italicized here) make clear why he "wanted *desperately* to be a Beatle." This section will help you use adjectives and adverbs in your own writing.

L-5a When to Use Adjectives and Adverbs

Adjectives are words used to modify **NOUNS** and **PRONOUNS.** They usually answer one of these questions: which? what kind? how many?

Glossary
HB-25–31

▶ *Parallel* rows of *ancient oak* trees lined the *narrow* driveway.

▶ Years of testing will be needed to prove whether geneticists' theories are *correct*.

▶ If you are craving something *sweet*, have a piece of fruit.

Adverbs are words used to modify **VERBS**, adjectives, and other adverbs. They usually answer one of these questions: how? when? where? why?

Glossary

under what conditions? to what degree? Although many adverbs end in -ly (*tentatively, immediately*), many do not (*now, so, soon, then, very*).

▶ Emergency personnel must respond *quickly* when an ambulance arrives.

▶ Environmentalists are *increasingly* worried about Americans' consumption of fossil fuels.

▶ If the senator had known that the news cameras were on, she would not have responded *so angrily*.

***Well* and *good*.**   Use *well* as an adjective to describe physical health; use *good* to describe emotional health or appearance.

▶ Some herbs can keep you feeling ~~good~~ *well* when everyone else has the flu.

▶ Staying healthy can make you feel *good* about yourself.

Good should not be used as an adverb; use *well*.

▶ Because both Williams sisters play tennis so ~~good,~~ *well,* they frequently compete against each other in major tournaments.

Glossary

***Bad* and *badly*.**   Use the adjective *bad* after a **LINKING VERB** to describe an emotional state or feeling. In such cases, the adjective describes the subject.

▶ Arguing with your parents can make *you* feel *bad*.

Glossary

Use the adverb *badly* to describe an **ACTION VERB**.

▶ Arguing with your parents late at night can make you *sleep badly*.

L-5b Comparatives and Superlatives

Most adjectives and adverbs have three forms: the positive, the comparative, and the superlative. The comparative is used to compare two things, and the superlative is used to compare three or more things.

COMPARATIVE	Who's the *better* quarterback, Eli Manning or his brother?
SUPERLATIVE	Many Broncos fans consider Peyton Manning to be the *greatest* quarterback ever.

The comparative and superlative of most adjectives are formed by adding the endings *-er* and *-est*: *slow, slower, slowest.* Longer adjectives and most adverbs use *more* and *most* (or *less* and *least*): *helpful, more helpful, most helpful.* If you add *-er* or *-est* to an adjective or adverb, do not use *more, most, less,* or *least.*

▶ The ~~most~~ lowest point in the United States is Death Valley.

L-5c Modifier Placement

Place adjectives, adverbs, and other **MODIFIERS** close to the words they describe.

Glossary

    at the seminar
▶ The doctor˄explained advances in cancer treatment to the families of patients.˄ ~~at the seminar.~~

The doctor, not the patients, is at the seminar.

    Before the anesthesiologist arrived, the
▶ ~~The~~ doctors˄assured the patient that they intended to make only two small incisions.˄ ~~before the anesthesiologist arrived.~~

The original sentence suggests that the incisions will be made without anesthesia, surely not the case.

To avoid ambiguity, position limiting modifiers such as *almost, even, just, merely,* and *only* next to the word or phrase they modify — and be careful that your meaning is clear. See how the placement of *only* results in two completely different meanings.

▶ A triple-threat athlete, Martha ~~only~~ *only* played soccer in college.

▶ A triple-threat athlete, Martha ~~only~~ *only* played soccer in college.

Be careful that your placement of ~~not~~ doesn't result in a meaning you don't intend.

▶ When I attended college, every student was ~~not~~ *not* using a laptop.

Dangling modifiers

Modifiers are said to be dangling when they do not clearly modify any particular word in the sentence. You can fix a dangling modifier by adding the **SUBJECT** that the modifier is intended to describe to the main clause or by adding a subject to the modifier itself.

▶ Speaking simply and respectfully, many people *the doctor comforted* ~~felt comforted by the~~ *with his* ~~doctor's~~ presentation.

The doctor was speaking, not the other people.

▶ While *I was* running to catch the bus, the shoulder strap on my fake Balenciaga bag broke.

Split infinitives

When a modifier comes between *to* and the verb in an **INFINITIVE,** you create a split infinitive: *to deliberately avoid.* When a split infinitive is awkward or makes a sentence difficult to follow, put the modifier elsewhere in the sentence.

▶ Professional soccer players are expected to ~~rigorously~~ train every day. *rigorously*

Glossary

Glossary

Sometimes, however, a split infinitive is easier to follow:

▶ One famous split infinitive appears in the opening sequence of *Star Trek:* "to boldly go where no man has gone before."

L-6 Articles

A, an, and *the* are articles, which tell whether something is indefinite or definite. Use *a* or *an* with nouns whose specific identity is not known to your audience — for example, when you haven't mentioned them before: *I'm reading a great book.* Use *the* with nouns whose specific identity is known to your audience — for instance, a noun that describes something specific, as in *the book on the table,* or something that you've mentioned before, as in *Francesca finally finished writing her book. The book will be published next year.*

L-6a When to Use *a* or *an*

Use *a* or *an* with singular count nouns whose identity is not known to your audience. Count nouns refer to things that can be counted: *one book, two books.* Use *a* before a consonant sound: *a tangerine;* use *an* before a vowel sound: *an orange.*

▶ Do you want to see *a movie* this afternoon?

▶ Yesterday we went to see *a fascinating* documentary about World War II.

▶ There was *an article* about the film in last Saturday's newspaper.

▶ I'd like to watch *an amusing* movie today rather than a serious one.

Do not use *a* or *an* before a noncount noun. Noncount nouns refer to abstractions or masses that can be quantified only with certain modifiers or units: *too much information, two cups of coffee.*

▶ These students could use *some encouragement* from their teacher.

▶ The last thing Portland needs this week is *more rain.*

L-6b When to Use *the*

Use *the* before nouns whose identity is clear to your audience and before superlatives.

▶ Our teacher warned us that *the poem she had assigned* had multiple levels of meaning.

▶ *The Secretary-General of the United Nations* will speak later this morning about *the military crackdown in Myanmar.*

▶ Some of *the fastest runners in the country* compete at *the Penn Relays.*

Glossary

Do not use *the* with most singular PROPER NOUNS (*Judge Judy*, *Lake Titicaca*), but do use it with most plural proper nouns (*the Adirondack Mountains*, *the Philippines*).

Do use *the* before singular proper nouns in the following categories.

LARGER BODIES OF WATER   the Arctic Ocean, the Mississippi River

GOVERNMENT BODIES   the U.S. Congress, the Canadian Parliament

HISTORICAL PERIODS   the Renaissance, the Tang Dynasty

LANDMARKS   the Empire State Building, the Taj Mahal

REGIONS   the East Coast, the Middle East, the Mojave Desert

RELIGIOUS ENTITIES, TEXTS, AND LEADERS   the Roman Catholic Church, the Qur'an, the Dalai Lama

L-7 Words That Build Common Ground

A secretary objects to being called one of "the girls." The head of the English department finds the title "chairman" offensive. Why? The secretary is male, the department head is a woman, and those terms don't include them. We can build common ground—or not—by the words we choose, by including others or leaving them out. This section offers tips for using language that is positive and inclusive and that will build common ground with those we wish to reach.

L-7a Avoiding Stereotypes

Stereotypes are generalizations about groups of people and as such can offend because they presume that all members of a group are the same. The writer Geeta Kothari explains how she reacts to a seemingly neutral assumption about Indians: "Indians eat lentils. I understand this as an absolute, a decree from an unidentifiable authority that watches and judges me."

We're all familiar with stereotypes based on sex or race, but stereotypes exist about other characteristics: age, body type, education, income, occupation, physical ability, political affiliation, region, religion, sexual orientation, and more. Be careful not to make any broad generalizations about any group — even neutral or positive ones (that Asian students work hard, for example, or that Republicans are patriotic).

Also, be careful not to call attention to a person's group affiliation if that information is not relevant.

▶ The ~~gay~~ physical therapist who worked the morning shift knew when to let patients rest and when to push them.

L-7b Using Preferred Terms

When you are writing about a group of people, try to use terms that members of that group use themselves. This advice is sometimes easier said than done, because language changes—and words that were commonly used ten years ago may not be in wide use today. Americans of African ancestry, for example, were referred to many years ago as "colored" or "Negro" and then as "black"; today the preferred terminology is "African American."

When you are referring to ethnicities, it's usually best to be as specific as possible. Instead of saying someone is Latin or Hispanic, for instance, it's better to say he or she is Puerto Rican or Dominican or Cuban, as appropriate. The same is true of religions; it's better to specify a religion when you can (Sunni Muslims, Episcopalians, Orthodox Jews). And while "Native American" and "American Indian" are both acceptable general terms, the only truly accurate method is to refer to particular tribal nations (Dakota, Chippewa).

L-7c Editing Out Sexist Language

Sexist language is language that stereotypes or ignores women or men—or that gratuitously calls attention to someone's gender. Try to eliminate such language from your writing.

Default he

Writers once used *he, him,* and other masculine pronouns as a default to refer to people whose sex is unknown. Today such usage is not widely accepted—and is no way to build common ground. Here are some alternatives.

Use both masculine and feminine pronouns joined by or. (Note, however, that using this option repeatedly may become awkward.)

▶ Before anyone can leave the country, he *or she* must have a passport or other documentation.

Replace a singular noun or pronoun with a plural noun.

▶ Before ~~anyone~~ *travelers* can leave the country, ~~he~~ *they* must have a passport or other documentation.

Eliminate the pronoun altogether.

▶ Before ~~anyone can leave~~ *leaving* the country, ~~he~~ *a traveler* must have a passport or other documentation.

You should also avoid nouns that include *man* when you're referring to people who may be either men or women.

INSTEAD OF	USE
man, mankind	humankind, humanity, humans
salesman	salesperson
fireman	firefighter
congressman	representative, member of congress
male nurse	nurse
female truck driver	truck driver

P Punctuation / Mechanics

rhetorical situations

genres

processes

strategies

research MLA / APA

media / design

handbook

P-1 Commas

Commas matter. Consider the title of the best-selling book *Eats, Shoots & Leaves*. The cover shows two pandas, one with a gun in its paw, one whitewashing the comma. Is the book about a panda that dines then fires a gun and exits? Or about the panda's customary diet? In fact, it's a book about punctuation; the ambiguity of its title illustrates how commas affect meaning. This section shows when and where to use commas in your writing.

P-1a To Join Independent Clauses with *and, but,* and Other Coordinating Conjunctions

Put a comma before the **COORDINATING CONJUNCTIONS** *and, but, for, nor, or, so,* and *yet* when they connect two **INDEPENDENT CLAUSES**. The comma signals that one idea is ending and another is beginning.

HB-34

HB-6

▶ I do not love Shakespeare, but I still have those books.
                                        —Rick Bragg, "All Over But the Shoutin' "

▶ Most people think the avocado is a vegetable, yet it is actually a fruit.

▶ They awarded the blue ribbon to Susanna, and Sarah got the red ribbon.

   Without the comma, readers might first think that both girls got the blue ribbon.

Although some writers omit the comma, especially with short independent clauses, you'll never be wrong to include it.

▶ I was smart, and I knew it.   —Shannon Nichols, " 'Proficiency' "

No comma is needed between the verbs when a single subject performs two actions—but you need commas when a third verb is added.

▶ Many fast-food restaurants now give calorie counts on menus and offer a variety of healthy meal options.

▶ Augustine wrote extensively about his mother/but mentioned his father only briefly.

▶ Kim bought the sod, delivered it, and rolled it out for us.

P-1b To Set Off Introductory Words

HB-6–7 ☒

Use a comma after an introductory word, **PHRASE**, or **CLAUSE** to mark the end of the introduction and the start of the main part of the sentence.

▶ Consequently, our celebration of Howard Stern, Don Imus, and other heroes of "shock radio" might be evidence of a certain loss of moral focus.
—Stephen L. Carter, "Just Be Nice"

▶ On the other hand, opponents of official English remind us that without legislation we have managed to get over ninety-seven percent of the residents of this country to speak the national language.
—Dennis Baron, "Don't Make English Official—Ban It Instead"

▶ Even ignoring the extreme poles of the economic spectrum, we find enormous class differences in the life-styles among the haves, the have-nots, and the have-littles.   —Gregory Mantsios, "Class in America—2003"

▶ When Miss Emily Grierson died, our whole town went to her funeral.
—William Faulkner, "A Rose for Emily"

Some writers don't use a comma after a short introductory word, phrase, or clause, but it's never wrong to include one.

P-1c To Separate Items in a Series

Use a comma to separate the items in a series.

▶ I spend a great deal of time thinking about the power of language—the way it can evoke an emotion, a visual image, a complex idea, or a simple truth.   —Amy Tan, "Mother Tongue"

Though some writers leave out the comma between the final two items in a series, this omission can confuse readers. It's never wrong to include the final comma.

▶ Nadia held a large platter of sandwiches—egg salad, peanut butter, ham, and cheese.

Without the last comma, it's not clear whether there are three or four kinds of sandwiches on the platter.

P-1d To Set Off Nonessential Elements

A nonessential (or nonrestrictive) element is one that could be deleted without changing the basic meaning of the sentence; it should be set off with commas. An essential (or restrictive) element is one that is needed to understand the sentence and therefore should not be set off with commas.

NONESSENTIAL

▶ Spanish, which is a Romance language, is one of six official languages at the United Nations.

The detail about being a Romance language adds information, but it is not essential to the meaning of the sentence and so is set off with a comma.

ESSENTIAL

▶ Navajo is the Athabaskan language that is spoken in the Southwest by the Navajo people.

The detail about where Navajo is spoken is essential: Navajo is not the only Athabaskan language; it is the Athabaskan language that is spoken in the Southwest.

Essential and nonessential elements can be clauses, phrases, or words.

CLAUSES

▶ He always drove Chryslers, which are made in America.

▶ He always drove cars that were made in America.

PHRASES

▶ I fumble in the dark, trying to open the mosquito netting around my bed.
—Chanrithy Him, "When Broken Glass Floats"

▶ I see my mother clutching my baby sister.
—Chanrithy Him, "When Broken Glass Floats"

WORDS

▶ At 8:59, Flight 175 passenger Brian David Sweeney tried to call his wife,
Julie. —The 9/11 Commission, "The Hijacking of United 175"

▶ At 9:00, Lee Hanson received a second call from his son Peter.
—The 9/11 Commission, "The Hijacking of United 175"

*Sweeney had only one wife, so her name provides extra but nonessential
information. Hanson presumably had more than one son, so it is essential to
specify which son called.*

P-1e To Set Off Parenthetical Information

Information that interrupts the flow of a sentence needs to be set off
with commas.

▶ Bob's conduct, most of us will immediately respond, was gravely wrong.
—Peter Singer, "The Singer Solution to World Poverty"

▶ With as little as two servings of vegetables a day, it seems to me,
you can improve your eating habits.

P-1f To Set Off Transitional Expressions

TRANSITIONS such as *thus, nevertheless, for example,* and *in fact* help connect sentences or parts of sentences. They are usually set off with commas. When a transition connects two **INDEPENDENT CLAUSES** in the same
sentence, it is preceded by a semicolon and is followed by a comma.

■ ▲ ○ ◆ ● □ ◪
rhetorical   genres   processes   strategies   research   media /   handbook
situations   MLA / APA   design

▶ [S]torytelling always includes the audience, the listeners. *In fact,* a great deal of the story is believed to be inside the listener; the storyteller's role is to draw the story out of the listeners.

—Leslie Marmon Silko, "Language and Literature from a Pueblo Indian Perspective"

▶ There are few among the poor who speak of themselves as lower class; *instead,* they refer to their race, ethnic group, or geographic location.

—Gregory Mantsios, "Class in America—2003"

P-1g To Set Off Direct Quotations

Use commas to set off quoted words from the speaker or the source.

▶ Pa shouts back, "I just want to know where the gunfire is coming from."

—Chanrithy Him, "When Broken Glass Floats"

▶ "You put a slick and a con man together," she said, "and you have predatory lenders."

—Peter Boyer, "Eviction: The Day They Came for Addie Polk's House"

▶ "Death and life are in the power of the tongue," says the proverb.

P-1h To Set Off Direct Address, *Yes* or *No*, Interjections, and Tag Questions

DIRECT ADDRESS	"Yes, Virginia, there really is a Santa Claus."
YES* OR *NO	No, you cannot replace the battery on your iPhone.
INTERJECTION	Oh, a Prius. How long did you have to wait to get it?
TAG QUESTION	That wasn't so hard, was it?

P-1i With Addresses, Place Names, and Dates

▶ Send contributions to Human Rights Campaign, 1640 Rhode Island Ave., Washington, DC 20036.

▶ Athens, Georgia, has been famous since the 1970s for its thriving music scene.

▶ On July 2, 1937, the aviator Amelia Earhart disappeared over the Pacific Ocean while trying to make the first round-the-world flight at the equator.

Omit the commas, however, if you invert the date (on 2 July 1937) or if you give only the month and year (in July 1937).

P-1j Checking for Unnecessary Commas

Commas have so many uses that it's easy to add them unnecessarily. Here are some situations when you should not use a comma.

Between subject and verb

▶ What the organizers of the 1969 Woodstock concert did not anticipate/ was the turnout.

▶ The event's promoters/turned down John Lennon's offer to play with his Plastic Ono Band.

Between verb and object

▶ Pollsters wondered/how they had so poorly predicted the winner of the 1948 presidential election.

▶ Virtually every prediction indicated/that Thomas Dewey would defeat Harry Truman.

After a coordinating conjunction

▶ The College Board reported a decline in SAT scores and/attributed the decline to changes in "student test-taking patterns."

▶ The SAT was created to provide an objective measure of academic potential, but/studies in the 1980s found racial and socioeconomic biases in some test questions.

After like *or* such as

▶ Many American-born authors, such as/Henry James, Ezra Pound, and F. Scott Fitzgerald, lived as expatriates in Europe.

With a question mark or an exclamation point

▶ Why would any nation have a monarch in an era of democracy?/you might ask yourself.

▶ "O, be some other name!/" exclaims Juliet.

P-2 Semicolons

Semicolons offer one way to connect two closely related thoughts. Look, for example, at Martha Stewart's advice about how to tell if fruit is ripe: "A perfectly ripened fruit exudes a subtle but sweet fragrance from the stem end, appears plump, and has deeply colored skin; avoid those that have wrinkles, bruises, or tan spots." Stewart could have used a period, but the semicolon shows the connection between what to look for and what to avoid when buying peaches or plums.

P-2a Between Independent Clauses

Closely related independent clauses are most often joined with a **COMMA** plus *and* or another **COORDINATING CONJUNCTION**. If the two clauses are closely related and don't need a conjunction to signal the relationship, they may be linked with a semicolon.

HB-61–67
HB-34

▶ The silence deepened; the room chilled.
—Wayson Choy, "The Ten Thousand Things"

▶ The life had not flowed out of her; it had been seized.
—Valerie Steiker, "Our Mother's Face"

A period would work in either of the examples above, but the semicolon suggests a stronger connection between the two independent clauses.

317 ◆ Another option is to use a semicolon with a **TRANSITION** that clarifies the relationship between the two independent clauses. Put a comma after the transition.

▶ There are few among the poor who speak of themselves as lower class; instead, they refer to their race, ethnic group, or geographic location.
—Gregory Mantsios, "Class in America—2003"

P-2b In a Series with Commas

Use semicolons to separate items in a series when one or more of the items contain commas.

▶ There are images of a few students: Erwin Petschaur, a muscular German boy with a strong accent; Dave Sanchez, who was good at math; and Sheila Wilkes, everyone's curly-haired heartthrob.
—Mike Rose, "Potato Chips and Stars"

P-2c Checking for Mistakes with Semicolons

Use a comma, not a semicolon, to set off an introductory clause.

▶ When the sun finally sets/, everyone gathers at the lake to watch the fireworks.
                        ^

HB-78–79 Use a **COLON,** not a semicolon, to introduce a list.

▶ Every American high school student should know that the U.S. Constitution contains three sections/: preamble, articles, and amendments.
                                              ^

rhetorical situations · genres · processes · strategies · research MLA / APA · media / design · handbook

P-3 End Punctuation

She married him. She married him? She married him! In each of these three sentences, the words are the same, but the end punctuation completely changes the meaning, from a simple statement to a bemused question to an emphatic exclamation. This section will help you use periods, question marks, and exclamation points in your writing.

P-3a Periods

Use a period to end a sentence that makes a statement.

▶ Rose Emily Meraglio came to the United States from southern Italy as a little girl in the early 1920s and settled with her family in Altoona, Pennsylvania.   —Mike Rose, "The Working Life of a Waitress"

An indirect question, which reports something someone else has asked, ends with a period, not a question mark.

▶ Presidential candidates are often asked how they will address the ballooning national debt?.

When a sentence ends with an **ABBREVIATION** that has its own period, do not add another period.

HB-89

▶ The Rat Pack included Frank Sinatra and Sammy Davis Jr./

P-3b Question Marks

Use a question mark to end a direct question.

▶ Did I think that because I was a minority student jobs would just come looking for me? What was I thinking?
                    —Richard Rodriguez, "None of This Is Fair"

Use a period rather than a question mark to end an indirect question.

▶ Aunt Vivian often asked what Jesus would do?.

P-3c Exclamation Points

Use an exclamation point to express strong emotion or add emphasis to a statement or command. Exclamation points should be used sparingly, however, or they may undercut your credibility.

▶ "Keith," we shrieked as the car drove away, "Keith, we love you!"
—Susan Jane Gilman, "Mick Jagger Wants Me"

When the words themselves are emotional, an exclamation point is often unnecessary and a period is sufficient.

▶ It was so close, so low, so huge and fast, so intent on its target that I swear to you, I swear to you, I felt the vengeance and rage emanating from the plane.
—Debra Fontaine, "Witnessing"

P-4 Quotation Marks

"Girls Just Want to Have Fun," "Two thumbs up!" "Frankly, my dear, I don't give a damn." These are just some of the ways that quotation marks are used—to indicate a song title, to cite praise for a movie, to set off dialogue. In college writing, you will use quotation marks frequently to acknowledge when you've taken from others. This section will show you how to use quotation marks correctly and appropriately.

P-4a Direct Quotations

Use quotation marks to enclose words spoken or written by others.

▶ "Nothing against Tom, but Johnny may be the bigger star now," says director John Waters.   —Sean Smith, "Johnny Depp: Unlikely Superstar"

▶ Newt Gingrich and Jesse Jackson have both pounded nails and raised funds for Habitat for Humanity. This is what Millard Fuller calls the "theology of the hammer."

—Diana George, "Changing the Face of Poverty"

When you introduce quoted words with *he said*, *she claimed*, or the like, use a comma between the verb and the quote. When you follow a quote with such an expression, use a comma before the closing quotation mark (unless the quote is a question or an exclamation).

▶ When my mother reported that Mr. Tomkey did not believe in television, my father said, "Well, good for him. I don't know that I believe in it either."
"That's exactly how I feel," my mother said, and then my parents watched the news, and whatever came on after the news.

—David Sedaris, "Us and Them"

You do not need any punctuation between *that* and a quotation.

▶ We were assigned to write one essay agreeing or disagreeing with George Orwell's statement that / "the slovenliness of our language makes it easier for us to have foolish thoughts."

In dialogue, insert a new pair of quotation marks to signal each change of speaker.

▶ "What's this?" the hospital janitor said to me as he stumbled over my right shoe.
"My shoes," I said.
"That's not a shoe, brother," he replied, holding it to the light. "That's a brick."

P-4b Long Quotations

Long quotations should be set off without quotation marks as **BLOCK QUOTATIONS**. If you are following **MLA STYLE**, set off quotations of five or more typed lines of prose by indenting them ten spaces (or one inch) from the left margin. Note that in the following example, the period precedes the parenthetical citation.

465

522–23

Biographer David McCullough describes Truman's railroad campaign as follows:

> No president in history had ever gone so far in quest of support from the people, or with less cause for the effort, to judge by informed opinion. . . . As a test of his skills and judgment as a professional politician, not to say his stamina and disposition at age sixty-four, it would be like no other experience in his long, often difficult career, as he himself understood perfectly. (655)

562 ● If you are following **APA STYLE**, set off quotations of forty words or more by indenting them five spaces (or one-half inch) from the left.

> In an article in *The Nation*, Maggie Cutler questions the common assumption that media violence causes some children's violent behavior:
> > Do temperamentally violent kids seek out shows that express feelings they already have, or are they in it for the adrenaline boost? Do the sort of parents who let kids pig out on gore tend to do more than their share of other hurtful things that encourage violent behavior?

P-4c Titles of Short Works

HB-86–88 △

Use quotation marks to enclose the titles of articles, chapters, essays, short stories, poems, songs, and episodes of television series. Titles of books, films, newspapers, and other longer works should be in **ITALICS** rather than enclosed in quotation marks.

▶ In "Unfriendly Skies Are No Match for El Al," Vivienne Walt, a writer for *USA Today,* describes her experience flying with this airline.
            —Andy McDonie, "Airport Security"

Note that the title of the newspaper is italicized, whereas the newspaper article title takes quotation marks.

▶ With every page of Edgar Allan Poe's story "The Tell-Tale Heart," my own heart beat faster.

▶ Rita Dove's poem "Dawn Revisited" contains vivid images that appeal to the senses of sight, sound, smell, and taste.

P-4d Single Quotation Marks

When you quote a passage that already contains quotation marks, whether they enclose a quotation or a title, change the inner ones to single quotation marks.

▶ Debra Johnson notes that according to Marilyn J. Adams, "effective reading instruction is based on 'direct instruction in phonics, focusing on the orthographic regularities of English.'"

▶ Certain essays and stories are so good (or so popular) that they are included in almost every anthology. *The Norton Reader* notes, for example, "Some essays—Martin Luther King Jr.'s 'Letter from Birmingham Jail' and Jonathan Swift's 'Modest Proposal,' for example—are constant favorites" (xxiii).

P-4e With Other Punctuation

The following examples show how to use other punctuation marks inside or outside quotation marks.

Commas and periods

Put commas and periods inside closing quotation marks.

▶ "On the newsstand, the cover is acting as a poster, an ad for what's inside," she said. "The loyal reader is looking for what makes the magazine exceptional."   —Katharine Q. Seelye, "Lurid Numbers on Glossy Pages!"

When there is parenthetical DOCUMENTATION after an end quotation mark, the period goes after the parentheses.

480–82

▶ Dewey himself said, "When you're leading, don't talk" (qtd. in McCullough 672).   —Dylan Borchers, "Against the Odds"

Semicolons and colons

Put semicolons and colons outside closing quotation marks.

▶ No elder stands behind our young to say, "Folks have fought and died for your right to pierce your face, so do it right"; no community exists that can model for a young person the responsible use of the "right"; for the right, even if called self-expression, comes from no source other than desire.

—Stephen L. Carter, "Just Be Nice"

▶ According to James Garbarino, author of *Lost Boys: Why Our Sons Turn Violent and How We Can Save Them*, it makes no sense to talk about violent media as a direct cause of youth violence. Rather, he says, "it depends": Media violence is a risk factor that, working in concert with others, can exacerbate bad behavior.

—Maggie Cutler, "Whodunit—The Media?"

Question marks and exclamation points

Put question marks and exclamation points inside closing quotation marks if they are part of the quotation but outside if they apply to the whole sentence.

▶ Then she began to talk more loudly. "What he want, I come to New York tell him front of his boss, you cheating me?"

—Amy Tan, "Mother Tongue"

▶ How many people know the words to "Louie, Louie"?

If there's a parenthetical citation at the end, it immediately follows the closing quotation mark, and any punctuation that's part of your sentence comes after it.

▶ An avid baseball fan, Tallulah Bankhead once said, "There have been only two geniuses in the world: Willie Mays and Willie Shakespeare" (183)!

P-4f Checking for Mistakes with Quotation Marks

HB-39–40

Avoid using quotation marks to identify SLANG, to indicate irony, or to emphasize a word. Remove the quotation marks or substitute a better word.

SLANG	Appearing /hip/ is important to many parents in New York.
IRONY	Natalie was more interested in ~~"facilitating"~~ *delegating tasks* than in doing work herself.
EMPHASIS	The woman explained that she is /only/ a masseuse, not the owner of the health club.

Do not enclose indirect quotations in quotation marks.

▶ Even before winning her fourth Wimbledon singles title, Venus Williams said that /she expected to play well./

P-5 Apostrophes

McDonald's: "I'm lovin' it" proclaims a recent advertisement, demonstrating two common uses of the apostrophe: to show ownership (*McDonald's*) and to mark missing letters (*I'm, lovin'*). This section offers guidelines on these and other common uses for apostrophes.

P-5a Possessives

Use an apostrophe to make a word possessive: *Daniel Craig's eye, someone else's problem, the children's playground.*

Singular nouns

To make most singular nouns possessive, add an apostrophe and -s.

▶ Some bloggers are getting press credentials for this summer**'s** Republican Convention.
—Lev Grossman, "Meet Joe Blog"

▶ The magical thinking of denial became Ms. Didion**'s** companion.
—Michiko Kakutani, "The End of Life As She Knew It"

▶ Bill Gates**'s** philanthropic efforts focus on health care and education.

If adding -'s makes a word hard to pronounce, use only an apostrophe.

▶ Euripides' plays are more realistic than those of Aeschylus and Sophocles.

Plural nouns

To form the possessive of a plural noun not ending in -s, add an apostrophe and -s. For plural nouns that end in -s, add only an apostrophe.

▶ Are women's minds different from men's minds?
—Evelyn Fox Keller, "Women in Science"

▶ The surrounding neighbors' complaints about noise led the club owner to install soundproof insulation.

▶ Did you hear that Laurence Strauss is getting married? The reception will be at the Strausses' home.

Something, everyone, *and other indefinite pronouns*

HB-23–24

To form the possessive of an **INDEFINITE PRONOUN,** add an apostrophe and -s.

▶ Clarabelle was everyone's favorite clown.

Joint possession

To show that two or more individuals possess something together, use the possessive form for the last noun only.

▶ Carlson and Ventura's book is an introduction to Latino writers for English-speaking adolescents.

To show individual possession, make each noun possessive.

▶ Jan's and Stuart's heart transplants inspired me to become an organ donor.

Compound nouns

For compound nouns, make the last word possessive.

▶ The surgeon general's report persuaded many people to stop smoking.

P-5b Contractions

An apostrophe in a contraction indicates where letters have been omitted.

▶ "Let's do it, Susie," she said. "We're really going to do it."
　　　　　　　　　　　　　—Susan Jane Gilman, "Mick Jagger Wants Me"

　　Let's *is a contraction of* let us; we're *is a contraction of* we are.

P-5c Plurals

Most writers add an apostrophe and -s to pluralize numbers, letters, and words discussed as words, but usage is changing and some writers now leave out the apostrophe. Either way is acceptable, as long as you are consistent. Notice that you need to italicize the number, letter, or word but not the plural ending.

▶ The resolution passed when there were more *aye*'s than *nay*'s.

▶ The winning hand had three *7*'s.

▶ The admissions officers at Brown spoke enthusiastically about their no-grades option—and then told us we needed mostly *A*'s to get in.

Most writers omit the apostrophe when pluralizing decades.

▶ During the 1950s, the civil rights movement and environmentalism began to develop in the United States.

To make an abbreviation plural, add only an -s.

▶ How many computers and TVs does the average American family have in its home?

▶ The United States has been seeking comprehensive free trade agreements (FTAs) with the Middle Eastern nations most firmly on the path to reform.
　　　　　　　　　　　　　—The 9/11 Commission, "Prevent the Continued
　　　　　　　　　　　　　　　　　Growth of Islamist Terrorism"

P-5d Checking for Mistakes with Apostrophes

Do not use an apostrophe in the following situations.

With plural nouns that are not possessive

> ▶ Both ~~cellist's~~ played encores.
>   *cellists*

With his, hers, ours, yours, and theirs

> ▶ Look at all the lettuce. ~~Our's~~ is organic. Is ~~your's?~~
>   *Ours*   *yours?*

With the possessive its

> ▶ It's an unusual building; ~~it's~~ style has been described as postmodern, but it
>   *its*
>   fits beautifully with the gothic buildings on our campus.

> It's *is a contraction meaning it is;* its *is the possessive form of it.*

P-6 Other Punctuation Marks

Some carpenters can do their jobs using only a hammer and a saw, but most rely on additional tools. The same is true of writers: you can get along with just a few punctuation marks, but having some others in your toolbox—colons, dashes, parentheses, brackets, ellipses, and slashes—can help you say what you want to say in your writing and can help readers follow what you write. This section can help you use these other punctuation marks effectively.

P-6a Colons

Colons are used to direct attention to words that follow the colon: an explanation or elaboration, a list, a quotation, and so on.

▶ What I remember best, strangely enough, are the two things I couldn't understand and over the years grew to hate: grammar lessons and mathematics. —Mike Rose, "Potato Chips and Stars"

▶ I sized him up as fast as possible: tight black velvet pants pulled over his boots, black jacket, a red-green-yellow scarf slashed around his neck. —Susan Jane Gilman, "Mick Jagger Wants Me"

▶ She also voices some common concerns: "The product should be safe, it should be easily accessible, and it should be low-priced." —Dara Mayers, "Our Bodies, Our Lives"

▶ Fifteen years after the release of the Carnegie report, College Board surveys reveal data are no different: test scores still correlate strongly with family income. —Gregory Mantsios, "Class in America—2003"

Colons are also used after the salutation in a business letter, in ratios, between titles and subtitles, between city and publisher in bibliographies, between chapter and verse in biblical references, and between numbers that indicate hours, minutes, and seconds.

▶ Dear President Michaels:

▶ For best results, add water to the powder in a 3:1 ratio.

▶ *The Last Campaign: How Harry Truman Won the 1948 Election*

▶ New York: Norton, 2008.

▶ "Death and life are in the power of the tongue" (Proverbs 18:21).

▶ The morning shuttle departs at 6:52 a.m.

P-6b Dashes

You can create a dash by typing two hyphens (--) with no spaces before or after or by selecting the em dash from the symbol menu of your word-processing program.

Use dashes to set off material you want to emphasize. Unlike colons, dashes can appear not only after an independent clause but also at other points in a sentence. To set off material at the end of a sentence, place a dash before it; to set off material in the middle of the sentence, place a dash before and after the words you want to emphasize.

▶ After that, the roller coaster rises and falls, slowing down and speeding up—all on its own.

—Cathi Eastman and Becky Burrell, "The Science of Screams"

▶ It did not occur to me—possibly because I am an American—that there could be people anywhere who had never seen a Negro.

—James Baldwin, "Stranger in the Village"

Dashes are often used to signal a shift in tone or thought.

▶ The best way to keep children home is to make the home atmosphere pleasant—and let the air out of the tires.   —Dorothy Parker

Keep in mind that dashes are most effective if they are used only when material needs particular emphasis. Too many dashes can interfere with the flow and clarity of your writing.

P-6c Parentheses

Use parentheses to enclose supplemental details and digressions.

▶ When I was a child, attending grade school in Washington, D.C., we took classroom time to study manners. Not only the magic words "please" and "thank you" but more complicated etiquette questions, like how to answer the telephone ("Carter residence, Stephen speaking") and how to set the table (we were quizzed on whether knife blades point in or out).   —Stephen L. Carter, "Just Be Nice"

▶ In their apartments they have the material possessions that indicate success (a VCR, a color television), even if it means that they do without necessities and plunge into debt to buy these items.

—Diana George, "Changing the Face of Poverty"

▶ Before participating in the trials, Seeta and Ratna (not their real names) knew nothing about H.I.V.   —Dara Mayers, "Our Bodies, Our Lives"

P-6d Brackets

Put brackets around words that you insert or change in a QUOTATION.

466

▶ As Senator Reid explained, "She [Nancy Pelosi] realizes that you cannot make everyone happy."

If you are quoting a source that contains an error, put the Latin word *sic* in brackets after the error to indicate that the mistake is in the original source.

▶ Warehouse has been around for 30 years and has 263 stores, suggesting a large fan base. The chain sums up its appeal thus: "styley [*sic*], confident, sexy, glamorous, edgy, clean and individual, with it's [*sic*] finger on the fashion pulse."   —Anne Ashworth, "Chain Reaction: Warehouse"

P-6e Ellipses

Ellipses are three spaced dots that indicate an omission or a pause. Use ellipses to show that you have omitted words within a QUOTATION. If you omit a complete sentence or more in the middle of a quoted passage, put a period before the three dots.

465–66

ORIGINAL

▶ The Lux ad's visual content, like Resinol's, supports its verbal message. Several demure views of Irene Dunne emphasize her "pearly-smooth skin," the top one framed by a large heart shape. In all the photos, Dunne wears a feathery, feminine collar, giving her a birdlike appearance: she is a bird of paradise or an ornament. At the bottom of the ad, we see a happy Dunne being cuddled and admired by a man.

WITH OMISSIONS

▶ The Lux ad's visual content, . . . supports its verbal message. Several demure views of Irene Dunne emphasize her "pearly-smooth skin," the top one framed by a large heart shape. . . . At the bottom of the ad, we see a happy Dunne being cuddled and admired by a man.
                    —Doug Lantry, " 'Stay Sweet As You Are': An Analysis of Change and Continuity in Advertising Aimed at Women"

P-6f Slashes

When you quote two or three lines of poetry and run them into the rest of your text, use slashes to show where one line ends and the next begins. Put a space before and after each slash.

▶ In the opening lines of the poem, he warns the reader to "Lift not the painted veil which those who live / Call Life" (1–2).

   —Stephanie Huff, "Metaphor and Society in Shelley's 'Sonnet'"

522–23

When you quote more than three lines of poetry, set them up as a **BLOCK QUOTATION, MLA STYLE**.

> The chorus warns Oedipus,
> > We look at this man's words and yours, my king,
> > and we find both have spoken them in anger.
> > We need no angry words but only thought
> > how we may best hit the God's meaning for us. (446–449)

P-7 Hyphens

If your mother gives you much needed advice, has she given you a great deal of advice that you needed, or advice that you needed badly? What about a psychiatry experiment that used thirty five year old subjects: were there thirty-five subjects who were a year old? Thirty subjects who were five years old? Or an unspecified number of thirty-five-year-old subjects? Hyphens could clear up the confusion. This section provides tips for when to use hyphens and when to omit them.

P-7a Compound Words

Compound words can be two words (*ground zero*), hyphenated (*self-esteem*), or one word (*outsource*). Check a dictionary, and if a compound word is not there, assume that it is two words.

rhetorical situations

genres

processes

strategies

research MLA / APA

media / design

handbook

Compound adjectives

A compound adjective is made up of two or more words. Most compound adjectives take a hyphen before a noun.

▶ a well-known trombonist

▶ a foul-smelling river

Do not use a hyphen to connect an -ly adverb and an adjective.

▶ a carefully executed plan

A compound adjective after a noun is usually easy to read without a hyphen; insert a hyphen only if the compound is unclear without it.

▶ The river has become foul smelling in recent years.

Prefixes and suffixes

A hyphen usually isn't needed after a prefix or before a suffix (*preschool, antislavery, counterattack, catlike, citywide*). However, hyphens are necessary in the following situations.

WITH *GREAT-*, *SELF-*, *-ELECT* great-aunt, self-hate, president-elect

WITH CAPITAL LETTERS anti-American, post-Soviet literature

WITH NUMBERS post-9/11, the mid-1960s

TO AVOID DOUBLE AND TRIPLE LETTERS anti-intellectualism, ball-like

FOR CLARITY re-cover (cover again) *but* recover (get well)

Numbers

Hyphenate fractions and compound numbers from twenty-one to ninety-nine.

▶ three-quarters of their income

▶ thirty-five-year-old subjects

P-7b At the End of a Line

Use a hyphen to divide a multisyllabic word that does not fit on one line. (A one-syllable word is never hyphenated.) Divide words between syllables as given in a dictionary, after a prefix, or before a suffix. Divide compound words between the parts of the compound if possible. Do not leave only one letter at the end or the beginning of a line.

op-er-a-tion   knot-ty   main-stream

Dividing Internet addresses

Do not insert a hyphen in a URL that you break at the end of a line. **MLA STYLE** suggests that you divide an Internet address only after a slash. **APA STYLE** allows breaks before most punctuation (except *http://*).

508 ●

551 ●

P-8 Capitalization

Capital letters are an important signal, either that a new sentence is beginning or that a specific person, place, or brand is being discussed. Capitalize *Carol* and it's clear that you're referring to a person; write *carol*, and readers will know you're writing about a song sung at Christmas. This section offers guidelines to help you know what to capitalize and when.

P-8a Proper Nouns and Common Nouns

Capitalize proper nouns, those naming specific people, places, and things. All other nouns are common nouns and should not be capitalized.

PROPER NOUNS	COMMON NOUNS
Sanjay Gupta	a doctor
Senator Schumer	a U.S. senator
Uncle Daniel	my uncle

PROPER NOUNS	COMMON NOUNS
France	a republic
Mississippi River	a river
the West Coast	a coast
Christianity	a religion
Allah	a god
the Torah	a sacred text
Central Intelligence Agency	an agency
U.S. Congress	the U.S. government
Ohio University	a university
Composition 101	a writing course
World War II	a war
July	summer
the Middle Ages	the fourteenth century
Kleenex	tissues

Adjectives derived from proper nouns, especially the names of people and places, are usually capitalized: *Shakespearean, Swedish, Chicagoan*. There are exceptions to this rule, however, such as *french fries, roman numeral*, and *congressional*. Consult your dictionary if you are unsure whether an adjective should be capitalized.

Many dictionaries capitalize the terms *Internet, Net*, and *World Wide Web*, but you'll see variations such as *Website* and *website*. Whether you capitalize or not, be consistent throughout a paper.

P-8b Titles before a Person's Name

A professional title is capitalized when it appears before a person's name but not when it appears after a proper noun or alone.

Senator Dianne Feinstein   Dianne Feinstein, the California senator

P-8c The First Word of a Sentence

Capitalize the first word of a sentence. The first word of a quoted sentence should be capitalized but not the first word of a quoted phrase.

▶ Speaking about acting, Clint Eastwood notes, "You can show a lot with a look. . . . It's punctuation."

▶ Sherry Turkle argues that we're living in "techno-enthusiastic times" and that we're inclined "to celebrate our gadgets."

Interrupted quotations

Capitalize the second part of an interrupted quotation only if it begins a new sentence.

▶ "It was just as nice," she sobbed, "as I hoped and dreamed it would be."
—Joan Didion, "Marrying Absurd"

▶ "On the newsstand, the cover is acting as a poster, an ad for what's inside," she said. "The loyal reader is looking for what makes the magazine exceptional."   —Katharine Q. Seelye, "Lurid Numbers on Glossy Pages!"

P-8d Titles and Subtitles

Capitalize the first and last words and all other important words of a title and subtitle. Do not capitalize less important words such as ARTICLES, COORDINATING CONJUNCTIONS, and PREPOSITIONS.

HB-55–56
HB-34
HB-42–43

"Give Peace a Chance"

Pride and Prejudice

The Shallows: What the Internet Is Doing to Our Brains

P-9 Italics

Italic type tells us to read words a certain way. Think of the difference between the office and *The Office*, or between time and *Time*. In each case, the italicized version tells us it's a specific television show or magazine. This section provides guidelines on using italics in your writing.

■ rhetorical situations
▲ genres
○ processes
◆ strategies
● research MLA / APA
□ media / design
⬠ handbook

P-9a   Titles of Long Works

Titles and subtitles of long works should appear in italics (or under-lined). A notable exception is sacred writing such as the Qur'an or the Old Testament.

BOOKS   *The Norton Field Guide to Writing, War and Peace*
PERIODICALS   *Newsweek, Teen Vogue, College English*
NEWSPAPERS   *Los Angeles Times*
PLAYS   *Medea, Six Degrees of Separation*
LONG POEMS   *The Odyssey, Paradise Lost*
FILMS AND VIDEOS   *Up in the Air, Baseball*
MUSICAL WORKS OR ALBUMS   *The Four Seasons, Rubber Soul*
RADIO AND TV SERIES   *Fresh Air, Glee*
PAINTINGS, SCULPTURES   the *Mona Lisa*, Michelangelo's *David*
DANCES BY A CHOREOGRAPHER   Mark Morris's *Gloria*
SOFTWARE   *Adobe Acrobat 9 Standard*
SHIPS, SPACESHIPS   *Queen Mary, Challenger*

A short work, such as a short story, an article, an episode of a series, or a song, takes **QUOTATION MARKS**.

HB-72

P-9b   Words as Words

Italicize a word you are discussing as a word. The same practice applies to numbers as numbers, letters as letters, and symbols as symbols.

▶ In those 236 words, you will hear the word *dedicate* five times.
        —William Safire, "A Spirit Reborn"

▶ Most American dictionaries call for one *t* in the word *benefited*.

▶ All computer codes consist of some combination of *0*'s and *1*'s.

Some writers use quotation marks rather than italics to signal words discussed as words.

▶ I would learn, when I asked some people who didn't show up the next day, that "definitely attending" on Facebook means "maybe" and "maybe attending" means "likely not."

—Hal Niedzviecki, "Facebook in a Crowd"

P-9c Non-English Words

Use italics for an unfamiliar word or phrase in a language other than English. Do not italicize proper nouns.

▶ *Verstehen*, a concept often associated with Max Weber, is the sociologist's attempt to understand human actions from the actor's point of view.

If the word or phrase has become part of everyday English or has an entry in English-language dictionaries, it does not need italics.

▶ An ad hoc committee should be formed to assess the university's use of fossil fuels and ways to incorporate alternative energy sources.

▶ The plot of *Jane Eyre* follows the conventions of a bildungsroman, or a coming-of-age story.

P-9d For Emphasis

You can use italics occasionally to lend emphasis to a word or phrase, but do not overuse them.

▶ It is, perhaps, as much what Shakespeare did *not* write as what he did that seems to indicate something seriously wrong with his marriage.

—Stephen Greenblatt, "Shakespeare on Marriage"

▶ Despite a physical beauty that had . . . hordes of teenage girls (and a few boys) dreaming of touching his hair *just once*, Depp escaped from the Hollywood star machine.

—Sean Smith, "Johnny Depp"

P-10 Abbreviations

MTV. USA. OC. DNA. fwiw. D.I.Y. These are some common abbrevia-tions, shortcuts to longer words and phrases. This section will help you use abbreviations appropriately in academic writing.

You can use common abbreviations if you are sure your readers will recognize them. If your readers might not be familiar with an abbrevia-tion, include the full version the first time with the abbreviation in parentheses immediately after. Throughout the rest of the paper, you can use the abbreviation alone.

▶ In a recent press release, officials from the international organization
   Médicins Sans Frontières (MSF) stressed the need for more effective
   tuberculosis drugs.

Periods are generally used in personal titles that precede a name and in Latin abbreviations such as *e.g.* or *etc.* They are not needed for state abbreviations such as *CA, NY,* or *TX,* or for organizations that use ini-tials, like *AP* or *YMCA.* In some cases, periods are optional (*BCE* or *B.C.E.*). Be sure to use them or omit them consistently. If you're not sure about a particular abbreviation, check a dictionary.

P-10a With Names

Most titles are abbreviated when they're used before or after a name.

Mr. Ed Stanford	Ed Stanford, Jr.
Dr. Ralph Lopez	Ralph Lopez, MD
Prof. Susan Miller	Susan Miller, PhD

Do not abbreviate job titles that are not attached to a name.

▶ The ~~RN~~ nurse who worked with trauma victims specialized in cardiac care.

P-10b With Numbers

The following abbreviations can be used when attached to a number.

> 632 BC ("before Christ")
>
> 344 BCE ("before the common era")
>
> AD 800 ("*anno Domini*")
>
> 800 CE ("common era")
>
> 10:30 AM (*or* a.m.)
>
> 7:00 PM (*or* p.m.)

Notice that *BC*, *BCE*, and *CE* follow the date, while *AD* precedes the date. Remember that the above abbreviations cannot be used without a date or time.

> ▶ By early ~~p.m.~~ *afternoon,* all prospective subjects for the experiment had checked in.

P-10c In Notes and Documentation

Abbreviations such as *etc.*, *i.e.*, and *et al.* are not acceptable in the body of a paper but are acceptable in footnotes or endnotes, in-text documentation, and bibliographies.

P-11 Numbers

Numbers may be written with numerals (97) or words (ninety-seven). This section presents general guidelines for when to use numerals and when to spell numbers out.

Spell out numbers and fractions that you can write in one or two words (*thirteen, thirty-seven, thirty thousand, two-thirds*). Any number at the beginning of a sentence should be spelled out as well.

▶ Yohji Yamamoto designed ~~75~~ *seventy-five* pieces for his first Paris collection.

▶ The number of reporters there approached ten thousand.

▶ *A collection of* 110 pieces ~~for a collection~~ struck the fashion editors as excessive.

Use numerals if you cannot express a number in one or two words.

▶ He designed ~~one hundred ten~~ *110* pieces for his first Paris collection.

For very large numbers that include a fraction or decimal, use a combination of numerals and words.

▶ One of the larger retailers had sold more than 4.5 million of its basic T-shirts the previous year.

In addition, always use numerals in the following situations.

ADDRESSES   500 Broadway, 107 175th Street

DATES   December 26, 2012; 632 BCE; the 1990s

DECIMALS AND FRACTIONS   59.5, $59^1/_2$

PARTS OF WRITTEN WORKS   volume 2; chapter 5; page 82; act 3, scene 3

PERCENTAGES   66 percent (*or* 66%)

RATIOS   16:1 (*or* 16 to 1)

STATISTICS   a median age of 32

TIMES OF DAY   6:20 AM (*or* a.m.)

Acknowledgments

IMAGE ACKNOWLEDGMENTS

27 Courtesy of Emily Vallowe; 37, 39 Courtesy of Sofia Gomez; 52 Courtesy of Hannah Berry; 54 Courtesy of The Clarks Companies; 56 Courtesy of Sorel; 57 Courtesy of Emily Nussbaum; 58 Aby Baker/Getty Images; 62 © The New York Times/Redux; 64 Seth Wenig/AP; 79 Jeff Darcy/The Plain Dealer; 82 The Granger Collection, New York/The Granger Collection; 87 Courtesy of Michaela Cullington; 95 © Colin McPherson/Corbis; 100 © 2010 Larry D. Moore/ Wikimedia Commons; 101 (left) Charles Bennett/AP; 101 (right) Mark Duncan/AP; 105 Courtesy of The Atlantic; 106 The Advertising Archives; 124 Courtesy of Heather Douglas; 125 Photo Researchers/Getty Images; 127 Wikimedia Commons; 129 Bettmann/Corbis; 131 Courtesy of Andrew Leonard; 132–34 YouTube; 157 Courtesy of Jessica Ann Olson; 164 ConsumerReports.org; 165 Courtesy of Ali Heinekamp; 166 The Kobal Collection; 183 John Amis/AP; 191 Courtesy of Christian Danielsen; 193 John Burgess © The Press Democrat, Santa Rosa, CA; 202 Courtesy of Dan Meyer; 205 Courtesy of Michael Granof; 209 Heather Ainsworth/The New York Times/ Redux; 214 Wikimedia Commons; 235 Steye Raviez/Hollandse Hoogte/Redux; 303 Jim Mone/AP; 333 © Reagan Louie; 334 RecycleManiacs.org; 345 Courtesy of Michiganapples.com; 352 (top) From Stiglitz, Joseph, *Economics*. New York: Norton; 352 (middle and bottom) © GOOGLE; 361 © Swim Ink 2, LLC/CORBIS; 372–73 The Advertising Archives; 385 Courtesy of The Other Side of Fifty — otherside offifty.com; 426 www.wordle.net/create; 435 (top) The Journal of Social History; 435 (bottom) The Smithsonian Magazine; 437, 441–42 The University of Wyoming Library; 496 From *At Day's Close: Night in Times Past* by A. Roger Ekirch. Copyright © 2005 by A. Roger Ekirch. Used by permission of W. W. Norton & Company. This selection may not be reproduced, stored in a retrieval system, or transmitted in any form or by any means without the prior written permission of the publisher; 504 Jerry Weinberger, "Pious Princes and Red-Hot Lovers: The Politics of Shakespeare's *Romeo and Juliet*," *The Journal of Politics* 65 (2003), p. 350. Copyright © 2003, Southern Political Science Association. Reprinted with the permission of Cambridge University Press; 505 (left) Jim Krueger; 505 (right) D1ILL/Corbis; 509 Courtesy of Forum on Religion and Ecology, Yale University and J. Baird Callicott; 512 Reprinted with permission of EBSCO Publishing, 2008; 525 Bettmann/CORBIS; 543 From *Endless Forms Most Beautiful: The New Science of Evo Devo and the Making of the Animal Kingdom* by Sean B. Carroll. Copyright © 2005 by Sean B. Carroll. Used by permission of W. W. Norton & Company. This selection may not be reproduced, stored in a retrieval system, or

TEXT ACKNOWLEDGMENTS

Sarah McGlone Thomas: "Effect of Biofeedback Training on Muscle Tension and Skin Temperature." Reprinted by permission of the author.

Emily Vallowe: "Write or Wrong Identity." Reprinted by permission of the author.

Every effort has been made to gain permission for images and selections used in this book. Unless otherwise noted, all images not cited in this section have been provided by the editors and authors of this publication. Rightsholders of any images or selections not properly credited should contact Permissions Department, W. W. Norton & Company, Inc., 500 Fifth Avenue, New York, NY 10110, in order for a correction to be made in the next reprinting of our work.

Glossary / Index

Note: This glossary/index defines key terms and concepts and directs you to pages in the book where you can find specific information on these and other topics. Please note the words set in SMALL CAPITAL LETTERS are themselves defined in the glossary/index. *Page numbers in italics indicate visuals.*

analysis, 253   A writing GENRE that methodically examines something by breaking it into its parts and noting how they work in relation to one another.

anecdote, 329–31   A brief NARRATIVE used to illustrate a point.

annotated bibliography, 155–63, 244   A writing GENRE that gives an overview of published research and scholarship on a topic. Each entry includes complete publication information and a SUMMARY or an ABSTRACT. A *descriptive annotation* summarizes the content of a source without commenting on its value; an *evaluative annotation* gives an opinion about the source along with a description of it. Key Features: statement of the scope • complete bibliographic information • relevant commentary • consistent presentation

antecedent, 284, HB-26–28   The NOUN or PRONOUN to which a pronoun refers. In <u>Maya</u> lost <u>her</u> wallet, Maya is the antecedent of *her*.

APA style, 22, 480–83, 533–74   A system of DOCUMENTATION used in the social sciences. APA stands for the American Psychological Association. *See also detailed directory at back of book*

appendix, 180   A section at the end of a written work for supplementary material that would be distracting in the main part of the text.

application letters, 229–34   Letters written to apply for a job or other position. Key Features: succinct indication of qualifications • reasonable and pleasing tone • conventional, businesslike form

arguing, 323–41   A STRATEGY that can be used in any kind of writing to support a claim with REASONS and EVIDENCE.

arguing a position, **119–49, 244, 247**   A writing GENRE that uses REASONS and EVIDENCE to support a CLAIM or POSITION and, sometimes, to persuade an AUDIENCE to accept that position. Key Features: clear and arguable position • necessary background • good reasons • convincing support for each reason • appeal to readers' values • trustworthy TONE • careful consideration of other positions

article, **HB-55–56**   The word *a, an,* or *the,* used to indicate that a NOUN is indefinite (*a writer, an author*) or definite (*the author*).

cliché, 284–85, HB-41   An expression used so frequently that it is no longer fresh: *busy as a bee.*

clustering, 44, 112, 202, 259, 261–62, 261, 268   A PROCESS for GENERATING IDEAS AND TEXT, in which a writer visually connects thoughts by jotting them down and drawing lines between related items.

coherence   The quality that allows an AUDIENCE to follow a text and to the connections among ideas, sentences, and paragraphs. Elements that can help to achieve coherence include the title, a clearly stated or implied THESIS, TOPIC SENTENCES, an easy-to-follow organization with clear TRANSITIONS, and PARALLELISM among comparable ideas.

collaboration, 477, 255–58   The PROCESS of working with others.

collective noun, HB-23, HB-26–27   A NOUN — such as *committee, crowd, family, herd,* or *team* — that refers to a group.

comma splice, HB-9–11   Two or more INDEPENDENT CLAUSES joined with only a comma: *I came, I saw, I conquered.*

common ground, 334–35, 411   Shared values. Writers build common ground with AUDIENCES by acknowledging others' POINTS OF VIEW, seeking areas of compromise, and using language that includes, rather than excludes, those they aim to reach.

comparing and contrasting, 252, 348–55   A STRATEGY that highlights the similarities and differences between items. Using the *block method* of comparison-contrast, a writer discusses all the points about one item and then all the same points about the other item; using the *point-by-point method,* a writer discusses one point for both items

dialogue, 279, 376–81   A STRATEGY for adding people's own words to a text.

discovery drafting, 259, 265   A PROCESS of DRAFTING something quickly, mostly for the purpose of discovering what one wants to say.

documentation, 22, 480–574   Publication information about the sources cited in a text. The documentation usually appears in an abbreviated form in parentheses at the point of CITATION or in an endnote or a footnote. Complete documentation usually appears as a list of WORKS CITED or REFERENCES at the end of the text. Documentation styles vary by discipline. For example, Modern Language Association (MLA) style requires an author's complete first name if it appears in a source, whereas American Psychological Association (APA) style requires only the initial of an author's first name.

dominant impression, 373–74   The overall effect created through specific details when a writer DESCRIBES something.

drafting, 266–68   The PROCESS of putting words on paper or screen. Writers often write several drafts, REVISING until they achieve their goal or reach a deadline. At that point, they submit a finished final draft.

E

editing, 282–86   The PROCESS of fine-tuning a text by examining each word, PHRASE, sentence, and paragraph to be sure that the text is correct and precise and says exactly what the writer intends.

evidence, 21, 136–37, 327–33　In ARGUMENT, the data you present to support your REASONS. Such data may include statistics, calculations, examples, ANECDOTES, QUOTATIONS, case studies, or anything else that will convince your reader that your reasons are compelling. Evidence should be sufficient (enough to show that the reasons have merit) and relevant (appropriate to the argument you're making).

explaining a process, 252, 382–86　A STRATEGY for telling how something is done or how to do something. An explanation of a process can serve as the ORGANIZING principle for a whole text.

• vivid detail • indication of the narrative's significance

   beginnings, 48, 49

   choosing a topic, 43–44

   describing and, 45–46

   design and, 49

   detail and, 42–43

   dialogue and, 46, 51

   drafting, 47–49

   endings, 48, 50

   examples of, 27–43

   generating ideas and text for, 45–46

   indicating significance of, 43

   interviewing and, 45–46

   key features of, 42–43

   key people in, 45–46

   literacy portfolios and, 295–96

   organizing, 46–47

   outlining, 46–47

   proofreading, 51

   responses to, 49–50

   revising, 49–50

   rhetorical situation and, 44–45

   significance of, 46

   summary and, 46

   taking stock of, 51

   title of, 49

   transitions in, 50

   verb tense in, 50–51

   writing, 27–51

literacy portfolio, 43, 295–96 An organized collection of materials showing examples of one writer's progress as a reader and/or writer.

literally, HB-47

literary analysis, 81–86 A writing GENRE that examines a literary text (most often fiction, poetry, or drama) and argues for a particular INTERPRETATION of the text. Key Features: arguable THESIS • careful

attention to the language of the text • attention to patterns or themes • clear interpretation • MLA style *See also* analysis; textual analysis

   argument and, 323

   attention to language, 85

   dialogue and, 376

   documentation style and, 86

   examples of, 82–84

   interpretation and, 85

   key features of, 85–86

   MLA style and, 86

   patterns and, 85

   of poetry, 82–84

   rhetorical situation and, 86

   themes and, 85

   thesis and, 85

literature Literary works — including fiction, poetry, drama, and some nonfiction; also, the body of written work produced in given field.

"Little Things Can Mean a Lot" (Petroski), 307–8

logical appeal, 323–33 ARGUMENT, appeal to readers on use of reasoning and of EVIDENCE such as facts, statistics, authorities on the subject, and so on.

logos. *See* logical appeal

long quotations, 465, 522, 562, HB-71–72

looping, 44, 203, 259, 260, 268, 424 A PROCESS for GENERATING IDEAS AND TEXT in which a writer writes about a topic quickly for several minutes and then reads the results and writes a one-sentence summary of the most important or interesting idea, which becomes the beginning of another round of writing and summarizing, and so on, until the writer finds a tentative focus for writing.

loose, HB-47

lose, HB-47

M

metaphor, 352, 354, HB-43–44   A figure of speech that makes a comparison without using the word *like* or *as*: "All the world's a stage / And all the men and women merely players" (Shakespeare, *As You Like It* 2.7.138–39). *See also* simile

MLA style, 482, 484–532   A system of DOCUMEN-TATION used in the humanities. MLA stands for the Modern Language Association. *See also detailed directory at back of book*

modal, HB-16   A helping VERB — such as *can, could, may, might, must, ought to, should, will,* or *would* — that

organizing   Arranging parts of a text so that the text as a whole has COHERENCE. The text may use one STRATEGY throughout or may combine several strategies to create a suitable organization.

outlining, 259, 263–64   A PROCESS for GENERATING IDEAS AND TEXT or for organizing or examining a text. An *informal outline* simply lists ideas and then numbers them in the order that they will appear; a *working outline* distinguishes supporting from main ideas by indenting the former; a *formal outline* is arranged as a series of headings and indented subheadings, each on a separate line, with letters and numerals indicating relative levels of importance.

Q

questioning, 251–54, 259, 262–63 A PROCESS of GENERATING IDEAS AND TEXT about a topic — asking, for example, *What? Who? When? Where? How?* and *Why?* or other questions.

quotation, 21, 462–74 The use of someone else's words exactly as they were spoken or written. Quoting is most effective when wording is worth repeating or makes a point so well that no rewording will do it justice. Quotations need to be acknowledged with DOCUMENTATION.

relative pronoun, HB-24   A PRONOUN such as *that,
which, who, whoever, whom,* or *whomever* that introduces a SUBORDINATE CLAUSE: *The professor <u>who</u> gave
the lecture is my adviser.*

reporting, 87–118, 235, 239, 244, 247   A writing
GENRE that presents information to readers on a subject. Key Features: tightly focused TOPIC • accurate,
well-researched information • various writing
STRATEGIES • clear DEFINITIONS • appropriate DESIGN

written to submit to potential employers. DESIGN and word choice depend on whether a résumé is submitted as a print document or in an electronic or scannable form. Key Features: organization that suits goals and experience • succinctness • design that highlights key information (for print) or that uses only one typeface (for scannable).

revision, 276–79   The PROCESS of making substantive changes, including additions and cuts, to a draft so that it contains all the necessary content and presents it in an appropriate organization. During revision, writers generally move from whole-text issues to details with the goals of sharpening their focus and strengthening their position. *See also specific genres and strategies*

rewriting, 279–81   A PROCESS of composing a new draft from another perspective — with a different POINT OF VIEW, AUDIENCE, STANCE, GENRE, or MEDIUM, for example.

rhetorical situation, 1–24   The context in which writing or other communication takes place, including PURPOSE, AUDIENCE, GENRE, STANCE, and MEDIA/DESIGN. *See also specific genres and strategies*

S

secondary source, 432–33   An ANALYSIS or INTERPRETATION of a PRIMARY SOURCE. In writing about the Revolutionary War, a researcher would

stance, 12–15, 22, 271   A writer's or speaker's attitude toward his or her subject — for example, reasonable, neutral, angry, curious. Stance is conveyed through TONE.

style   In writing, the arrangement of sentences, CLAUSES, PHRASES, words, and punctuation to achieve a desired effect; also, the rules of capitalization, punctuation, and so on recommended for DOCUMENTATION of a source.

subject, HB-4–5   A word or word group, usually including at least one NOUN or PRONOUN plus its MODIFIERS, that tells who or what a sentence or CLAUSE is about. In the sentence A *frustrated group of commuters waited for the late bus,* the subject is A *frustrated group of commuters.*

subordinate clause, HB-30, HB-35–36   A clause that begins with a SUBORDINATING WORD and therefore cannot stand alone as a sentence: *She feels good*

Revision Symbols

abbr	abbreviation **HB-89**		*ital*	italics **HB-86**
adj	adjective **HB-51**		*jarg*	jargon **HB-40**
adv	adverb **HB-51**		*lc*	lowercase letter **HB-84**
agr	agreement **HB-21, HB-26**		*mm*	misplaced modifier **HB-53**
art	article **HB-55**		*num*	number **HB-90**
awk	awkward		¶	new paragraph
cap	capitalization **HB-84**		//	parallelism **HB-31**
case	pronoun case **HB-28**		*pass*	passive voice **HB-18**
cliché	cliché **HB-41**		*ref*	pronoun reference **HB-27**
⌣	close up space		*run-on*	comma splice or fused sentence **HB-9**
cs	comma splice **HB-9**		*sexist*	sexist language **HB-58**
def	define **356–66**		*shift*	confusing shift **HB-36**
⌒	delete		*sl*	slang **HB-39**
dm	dangling modifier **HB-54**		#	insert space
doc	documentation **480–574**		*sp*	spelling
emph	emphasis **HB-35**		*trans*	transition **317**
frag	sentence fragment **HB-7**		⌣	transpose
fs	fused sentence **HB-9**		*vb*	verb **HB-11**
hyph	hyphen **HB-82**		*wrdy*	wordy **HB-49**
^	insert		*ww*	wrong word **HB-44**

Submitting Papers for Publication by W. W. Norton & Company

We are interested in receiving writing from college students to consider including in our textbooks as examples of student writing. Please send this form with the work that you would like us to consider to Marilyn Moller, Student Writing, W. W. Norton & Company, 500 Fifth Avenue, New York NY 10110.

Text Submission Form

Student's name _____

School _____

Address _____

Department _____

Course _____

Writing assignment the text responds to _____

_____

_____

_____

_____

Instructor's name _____

(continued next page)

Please write a few sentences about what your primary purposes were for writing this text. Also, if you wish, tell us what you think you learned about writing from the experience writing it.

_____

_____

_____

_____

_____

_____

_____

Contact Information

Please provide the information below so that we can contact you if your work is selected for publication.

Name _____

Permanent address _____

Email _____

Phone _____

A Directory to MLA Style

A Directory to APA Style

Handbook Menu